SYMBOLIC INTERACTION:
AN INTRODUCTION TO SOCIAL PSYCHOLOGY

THE REYNOLDS SERIES IN SOCIOLOGY

Larry T. Reynolds, *Editor*

by **GENERAL HALL, INC.**

SYMBOLIC INTERACTION:
AN INTRODUCTION TO SOCIAL PSYCHOLOGY

Nancy J. Herman and Larry T. Reynolds
Central Michigan University

GENERAL HALL, INC.
Publishers
5 Talon Way
Dix Hills, New York 11746

SYMBOLIC INTERACTION:
AN INTRODUCTION TO SOCIAL PSYCHOLOGY

GENERAL HALL, INC.
5 Talon Way
Dix Hills, New York 11746

Copyright © 1994 by General Hall, Inc.

All rights reserved. No part of this publication may be
reproduced, stored in a retrieval system or transmitted
in any form or by any means, except for the inclusion of
brief quotations in a review, without the prior permission
of the publisher.

Publisher: Ravi Mehra
Composition: *Graphics Division,* General Hall, Inc.

LIBRARY OF CONGRESS CATALOG CARD NUMBER: **93–79473**

ISBN:1–882289–21–8 [paper]
    1–882289–22–6 [cloth]

Manufactured in the United States of America

In memory of

Emma Herman

Penni Fetters

Edward McKenna

Contents

I. Introduction   1

PART I
INTELLECTUAL ANTECEDENTS OF SYMBOLIC INTERACTIONISM

1. Intellectual Antecedents *Larry T. Reynolds*   6

PART II
VARIETIES OF SYMBOLIC INTERACTIONISM AND LEADING EARLY REPRESENTATIVES

2. The Early Interactionists: Cooley and Thomas *Larry T. Reynolds*   30

3. Mead's Social Psychology *Bernard N. Meltzer*   38

4. Theoretical and Ideological Variations in Contemporary Interactionism *John W. Petras* and *Bernard N. Meltzer*   55

5. Herbert Blumer: Sociologist Par Excellence *Lewis M. Killian*   64

6. Kuhn's Formulation of the Self *Stephan Spitzer, Carl Couch,* and *John Stratton*   70

7. Erving Goffman *Don Martindale*   76

8. Harold Garfinkel: The Founder of Ethnomethodology *Ruth A. Wallace* and *Alison Wolf*   80

PART III
METHODOLOGICAL STANCES

9. Interactionist Research Methods: An Overview *Nancy J. Herman*   90

10. Sociological Analysis and the "Variable" *Herbert Blumer*   112

11. Beyond Blumer and Kuhn: Researching and Studying Across-time Data Through the Use of Point-in-space Laboratory Procedures *Carl Couch, Michael A. Katovich,* and *Steven L. Buban*   121

12. Walking a Tightrope: Dilemmas of Participant Observation of Groups in Conflict *Anson D. Shupe Jr.* and *David G. Bromley* — 139

PART IV
MINDED BEHAVIOR

13. Mind, Experience, and Behavior *John Dewey* — 153

14. The Regulation of the Wishes *W.I. Thomas* — 156

15. Rapists' Vocabulary of Motives *Diana Scully* and *Joseph Marolla* — 162

16. Emergence and Human Conduct *Bernard N. Meltzer* and *Jerome Manis* — 180

17. Baseball Magic *George M. Gmelch* — 188

PART V
THE SELF

18. The Looking-Glass Self *Charles H. Cooley* — 196

19. The Presentation of Self in Everyday Life *Erving Goffman* — 199

20. Generic Processes of Impression Management: Two Case Studies of Physical and Mental Disability *Charlene Miall* and *Nancy J. Herman* — 208

21. Negotiating a Religious Identity: The Case of the Gay Evangelical *Scott Thumma* — 224

22. The Problem of Identity Construction Among the Homeless *David A. Snow* and *Leon Anderson* — 239

PART VI
SOCIAL STRUCTURE

23. Society as Symbolic Interaction *Herbert Blumer* — 263

24. Reference Groups as Perspectives *Tamotsu Shibutani* — 267

25. In Search of Mesostructure: Studies in the Negotiated Order *David R. Maines* — 277

26. Interactionism and the Study of Social Organization *Peter M. Hall* — 286

27. Unobtrusive Power: Interaction Between Health Providers and Consumers at Council Meetings *Warren R. Paap* and *Bill Hanson*   309

PART VII
RESEARCH APPLICATIONS

28. Becoming Observant and Falling from Faith: Variations of Jewish Conversion Experiences *William Shaffir*   326

29. Family Caregivers of the Mentally Ill: Negative and Positive Adaptive Responses *Nancy J. Herman* and *Larry T. Reynolds*   342

30. The Social Construction of Hypnosis *Dan E. Miller*   351

31. The Emergence and Maintenance of a Deviant Sub-culture: The Case of Hunting/Poaching Sub-culture *Richard A. Brymer*   363

32. He's a Lumberjack and He's Not Okay: The Fall of the Urban Treeman *Mary Lorenz Dietz*   377

PART VIII
SOME NEW DIRECTIONS: GENERIC PRINCIPLES, GENDER, EMOTIONS, POSTMODERNISM, DISCURSIVE ACTS

33. Everyday Life Sociology *Patricia A. Adler, Peter Adler,* and *Andrea Fontana*   407

34. Human Emotions: An Expanding Sociological Frontier *C. Eddie Palmer*   424

35. Generic Social Processes and the Study of Human Lived Experiences: Achieving Transcontextuality in Ethnographic Research *Robert Prus*   436

36. And a Child Shall Lead Us? Children, Gender, and Perspectives by Incongruity *Spencer Cahill*   459

37. Forms of Discourse *Robert S. Perinbanayagam*   470

38. The Collective Story: Postmodernism and the Writing of Sociology *Laurel Richardson*   477

Index   487

ACKNOWLEDGEMENTS

The editors and publisher wish to thank the following who have kindly given permission for use of copyright materials.

"Intellectual Antecedents," Larry T. Reynolds. Pp.5–31 In *Interactionism: Exposition and Critique*. Dix Hills, New York: General Hall, 1993. Reprinted with permission.

"Theoretical and Ideological Variations in Contemporary Interactionism," John W. Petras and Bernard N. Meltzer. *Catalyst* No. 7: 1–8, 1973. Reprinted with permission.

"The Early Interactionists," Larry T. Reynolds. Pp. 32–42 In *Interactionism: Exposition and Critique*. Dix Hills, New York: General Hall, 1993. Reprinted with permission.

"Mead's Social Psychology," Bernard N. Meltzer. Center for Sociological Research, Western Michigan University, 1957. Reprinted with permission of author.

"Herbert Blumer: Sociologist Par Excellence, Lewis Killian, original contribution.

"Kuhn's Formulation of the Self," Stephan Spitzer, Carl Couch and John Stratton. Reprinted with permission of the authors.

"Erving Goffman," Don Martindale. Pp. 362–363 In *The Nature and Types of Sociological Theory*, second edition. Boston: Houghton Mifflin, 1981.

"Harold Garfinkel: The Founder of Ethnomethodology," Ruth A. Wallace and Alison Wolf. Pp. 267–279 In *Contemporary Sociological Theory*. Englewood Cliffs, New Jersey: Prentice-Hall, 1980. Reprinted with permission.

"Interactionist Research Methods: An Overview," Nancy J. Herman, original contribution.

"Sociological Analysis and the 'Variable,'" Herbert Blumer.*American Sociological Review* 21 (December, 1956): 683–90. Reprinted with permission of the American Sociological Association.

"Walking a Tightrope: Dilemmas of Participant Observation of Groups in Conflict, Anson D. Shupe, Jr. and David G. Bromley. *Qualitative Sociology* 2: 3–21, 1980. Reprinted with permission of Human Sciences Press.

"Beyond Blumer and Kuhn: Researching and Studying Across-Time Data Through the Use of Point-in-Space Laboratory Procedures," Carl Couch, Michael A. Katovich and Steven Buban, original contribution.

"Mind, Experience, and Behavior," John Dewey. From *Reconstruction in Philosophy*, pp. 84–87, copyright 1920 by Henry Holt and Company, 1942 by John Dewey. Reprinted with permission of Holt, Rinehart and Winston, Inc.

"The Regulation of the Wishes."W.I. Thomas. From *The Unadjusted Girl*. Copyright 1923 by Little, Brown and Company (Inc.). Reprinted with permission of Little, Brown and Inc.

"Rapists' Vocabulary of Motives," Diana Scully and Joseph Marolla. *Social Problems* 31(5): 530–544, 1982. Reprinted with permission.

"Emergence and Human Conduct," Bernard N. Meltzer and Jerome G. Manis, *Journal of Psychology* 126(4):333–342, 1982. Reprinted with permission of Heldref Publications.

"Baseball Magic," George J. Gmelch. *Transaction* 8, no. 8, 1971. Reprinted with permission.

"The Looking-Glass Self," Charles Horton Cooley. Pp. 183–84, 196–99 In *Human Nature and the Social Order*, 1922. New York: MacMillan Publishing Company. Reprinted with permission.

"Generic Processes of Impression Management: Two Case Studies of Physical and Mental Disability," Charlene E. Miall and Nancy J. Herman, original contribution.

"Negotiating a Religious Identity: The Case of the Gay Evangelical," Scott Thumma, *Sociological Analysis* 52(4): 333–347, 1991.

"Identity Work Among the Homeless: The Verbal Construction and Avowal of Personal Identities," David Snow and Leon Anderson, *American Journal of Sociology* 92 (6): 1336–1371, 1987. Reprinted with permission of the University of Chicago Press.

"Society as Symbolic Interaction," Herbert Blumer. SOURCE: Arnold Rose (editor), *Human Behavior and Social Processes*. Copyright 1962 by Houghton-Mifflin. Used with permission. It is a violation of the law to reproduce this selection by any means whatsoever without written permission of the copyright holder.

"In Search of Mesostructure: Studies in the Negotiated Order," David R. Maines. *Urban Life* 11: 267–79, 1983.

"Reference Groups as Perspectives," Tamotsu Shibutani, *American Journal of Sociology* 60: 562–569, 1955. Reprinted with permission.

"Interactionism and the Study of Social Organization," Peter Hall, *Sociological Quarterly* 28: 1–22, 1987. Reprinted with permission of JAI Press.

"Unobtrusive Power: Interaction Between Health Providers and Consumers at Council Meetings," Warren R. Paap and Bill Hanson, *Urban Life* 10:409–13, 1982.

"Becoming Observant and Falling From the Faith: Variations of Jewish Conversion Experiences," William Shaffir, original contribution.

"Family Caregivers of the Mentally Ill: Negative and Positive Adaptive Responses," Nancy J. Herman and Larry T. Reynolds, *Michigan Sociological Review* No. 6, (Fall):28–41, 1992. Reprinted with permission.

"The Social Construction of Hypnosis," Dan E. Miller, original contribution.

"The Emergence and Maintenance of a Deviant Sub-Culture: The Case of Hunting/Poaching Sub-Culture," Richard A. Brymer, *Anthropologica* XXXIII, No. 1–2: 177–94, 1991. Reprinted with permission.

"He's a Lumberjack and He's *Not* Okay: The Fall of the Urban Tree Man," Mary Lorenz Dietz, original contribution.

"Everyday Life Sociology," Patricia A. Adler, Peter Adler and Andrea Fontana, *Annual Review of Sociology* 13: 217–35, 1987. Reprinted with permission.

"Human Emotions: An Expanding Sociological Frontier," C. Eddie Palmer, *Sociological Spectrum* 11: 213–29. Reprinted with permission.

"Generic Social Processes and the Study of Human Lived Experiences: Achieving Transcontextuality in Ethnographic Research," Robert Prus, original contribution.

"And a Child Shall Lead Us? Children, Gender and Perspective by Incongruity," Spencer E. Cahill, original contribution.

"Forms of Discourse," R. S. Perinbanayagam. Pp. 113–20 In *Discursive Acts*, New YorK: Aldine de Gruyter, 1992. Reprinted with permission.

"The Collective Story: Postmodernism and the Writing of Sociology," Laurel Richardson, *Sociological Focus* 22 no. 3: 199–208. Reprinted with permission.

INTRODUCTION

Symbolic interactionism, as a distinctive perspective in social psychology, focuses on the nature of human social interaction. Humans are portrayed as "acting" as opposed to being "acted upon." As such, interactionists present an active image of human beings, and they reject any view of humans as passive, robot-like entities. People interact with one another; society is comprised of people interacting. Individuals are constantly changing as a result of social interaction. Society too changes due to interaction.

A number of symbolic interactionists (Blumer, 1969; Manis and Meltzer, 1978; Rose, 1962) have enumerated the basic assumptions of this theory. These elements are listed below:

(1) Humans live in a symbolic world of learned meanings.

(2) Symbols arise in the social process and are shared;

(3) Symbols have motivational significance; meanings and symbols allow individuals to carry out distinctively human action and interaction;

(4) The mind is a functional, volitional, teleological entity serving the interests of the individual. Humans, unlike the lower animals, are endowed with the capacity for thought; The capacity for thought is shaped by social interaction;

(5) The self is a social construct; just as individuals are born mindless, so too, are they born selfless; our selves arise in social interaction with others;

(6) Society is a linguistic or symbolic construct arising out of the social process; it consists of individuals interacting

(7) Sympathetic introspection is a mandatory mode of inquiry.

In the following paragraphs, we shall briefly explicate each of these propositions.

A basic proposition of symbolic interactionism is that humans live in a world of meanings. The objective world has no reality for humans, only subjectively-defined objects have meaning. Individuals respond to objects and events on the basis of the subjective meanings that these things have for them. Meanings, according to interactionists, are neither static entities, nor are they entities that are merely bestowed on humans and learned by habituation. The meanings of objects and events can be altered through the creative capabilities of humans, and individuals may influence the many meanings that form their society, as well as being influenced by these meanings themselves. Meanings then, are conceived as social products arising through the defining acts of individuals as they engage in social interaction—social products that may, in turn, exert influences upon them.

These socially-created and socially-shared meanings function in determining the behavior of individuals. The meanings that humans give to objects, events, and other people have motivational significance.

According to symbolic interactionists, humans are self-conscious beings; individuals possess selves and minds, which although absent at birth, originate as a consequence of their participation in society. Turning to the nature of mind, interactionists contend that, in contrast to the lower animals (who respond to their environment but are neither able to understand factors affecting their behavior nor are they able to conceive of alternative behaviors) humans are able to *select out* and indicate to themselves and to others the meanings of certain environmental stimuli to which they are responding. Through the concept of mind, individuals are able to acquire control over meanings. For interactionists, the mind is a functional, volitional, teleological process serving the interests of individuals.

Just as the mind is conceived of as a social product, so too, do interactionists conceive of the self in a similar manner. The self is not present at birth. The self develops within the social process, and it undergoes continual development and modification throughout the lifespan of the individual. The distinctive aspect of the self is its duality: that is, it has the capacity to be both subject and object unto itself. As that which can be an object to itself, the self is basically a social structure, arising in the social context. In this sense, the self can be said to exist in the act of viewing oneself in a reflexive manner. Such activity is made possible through the use of language, a group of significant symbols which allows one to employ the standpoints of others in order to view oneself as an object — to see oneself as others do.

For interactionists, human society, like mind and self is a social product. Emphasizing its processual nature, society is conceived as consisting of individuals involved in symbolic interaction. A society is comprised of social actors who act back and forth, and form their acts in relation to one another. Such "joint action" (Blumer, 1969) may involve as few as two individuals, or involve the actions of large institutions. It involves interpretation and communication on the part of actors. Society is made possible when individuals act with one another in mind, alter their behaviors as they go along, symbolically communicate behaviors to others, and interpret the behaviors of others.

A final proposition of this theory centers on its methodological orientation. If humans act toward things on the basis of their symbolic meanings, then it logically follows that understanding human behavior requires the researcher to "get at" the actors' meanings. Understanding requires "*sympathetic introspection*" (Cooley, 1909) or "*verstehen*" (Weber, 1946). The researcher must immerse herself or himself in the world of her or his subjects, place herself or himself in their shoes. The researcher must be socialized into the groups she or he wishes to understand. Only in this manner will the researcher be able to learn the symbols and referents of the group—only in this manner will she or he learn their "definitions of the situation" (Thomas, 1928) and "constructions of reality" (Berger and Luckmann, 1967).

REFERENCES

Berger, Peter and Luckmann, Thomas. 1967. *The Social Construction of Reality*. Garden City, NY: Doubleday.

Blumer, Herbert. 1969. *Symbolic Interaction*. Englewood Cliffs, NJ: Prentice Hall.

Cooley, Charles H. 1909. *Social Organization*. New York: Scribner's.

Manis, Jerome G. and Bernard N. Meltzer. 1978. *Symbolic Interaction: A Reader in Social Psychology.* Third edition. Boston: Allyn and Bacon.

Rose, Arnold M. 1962. *Human Behavior and Social Processes.* Boston: Houghton Mifflin.

Weber, Max. 1946. *From Max Weber: Essays in Sociology.* (Hans Gerth and C. Wright Mills, eds.) New York: Oxford University Press.

PART I
INTELLECTUAL ANTECEDENTS

Symbolic interactionism emerged as a distinctive theoretical perspective in American sociology around the turn of the century. No theory develops in a vacuum, and symbolic interactionism is by no means an exception. It was inspired by certain intellectual movements of the time, as well as influenced by the intellectual works of those historically prior. Although often assumed to be, symbolic interactionism is by no means a unitary theoretical perspective. Depending on which author one reads, there are between 2 and 15 varieties or *flavors* of symbolic interactionism (Dreitzel, 1970; Kuhn, 1964; Manis and Meltzer, 1972; Meltzer and Petras, 1970; Petras and Meltzer, 1970; Reynolds and Meltzer, 1973; Vaughan and Reynolds, 1968; Warshay, 1971, 1975).[1] We shall discuss these major variants in Section II.

Given that there are several styles of symbolic interactionism, compiling a list of intellectual precursors is not a simple task. Others have attempted to trace the roots of this theory (Manis and Meltzer, 1978; Rock, 1979; Meltzer et al., 1975; Lewis, 1976; Shott, 1976), and they point to a number of sources: Phenomenology, Existentialism, German Idealism, Formalism, Evolutionary theory, Functional psychological theory, American Pragmatism, and the philosophy of the Scottish Moralists.

The following selection, by Larry T. Reynolds, provides an overview of some of the major intellectual antecedents of Meadian symbolic interactionism: the German Idealists, Evolutionism, the Scottish Moralists, the American pragmatists, and the Functional psychologists.

Notes

1. For a detailed discussion of intellectual influences on symbolic interactionism, ranging from classic to contemporary influences, see Blumer (1969); Denzin(1992); Fine (1990); Fisher and Strauss (1978); and Plummer (1991).

REFERENCES

Blumer, Herbert. 1969. *Symbolic Interaction.* Englewood Cliffs, N.J.: Prentice Hall.
Denzin, Norman K. 1992. *Symbolic Interactionism and Cultural Studies: The Politics of Interpretation.* Oxford: Blackwell.
Dreitzel, Hans P. 1970. *Recent Sociology* No. 2. London: MacMillan.
Fine, Gary A. 1990. "Symbolic Interaction in the Post-Blumerian Age." Pp.117–157. In *Frontiers of Social Theory: The New Synthesis*, George Ritzer (ed.) New York: Columbia University Press.
Fisher, Bernice and Anslem Strauss. 1978. "The Chicago Tradition and Social Change: Thomas, Parke, and Their Successors." *Symbolic Interaction* 1(2):5–23.

Kuhn, Manford H. 1964. "Major Trends on Symbolic Interaction Theory in the Past Twenty-five Years." *Sociological Quarterly* 5:61–84.
Lewis, J. David. 1976. "The Classic American Pragmatists as Forerunners to Symbolic Interactionism." *Sociological Quarterly* 17:347–359.
Manis, Jerome G. and Bernard N. Meltzer. 1972. *Symbolic Interaction: A Reader in Social Psychology* Second Edition. Boston: Allyn and Bacon.
———. 1978. *Symbolic Interaction: A Reader in Social Psychology* Third Edition. Boston: Allyn and Bacon.
Meltzer, Bernard M. and John W. Petras. 1970. "The Chicago and Iowa Schools of Symbolic Interactionism." Pp. 3–17 in Tomatsu Shibutani, (ed.), *Human Nature and Collective Behavior*. Englewood Cliffs, NJ: Prentice-Hall.
Meltzer, Bernard N., John W. Petras, and Larry T. Reynolds. 1975. *Symbolic Interactionism: Genesis, Varieties, and Criticism*. London: Routledge and Kegan Paul.
Plummer, Kenneth. 1991. "Introduction: The Future of Interactionist Sociologies." Pp.ix-xix. In *Symbolic Interactionism: Volume I: Foundations and History*. Kenneth Plummer(ed.) Hantz, England: Edward Elgar Publishing.
Reynolds, Larry T. and Bernard N. Meltzer. 1973. "The Origins of Divergent Methodological Stances in Symbolic Interactionism." *Sociological Quarterly* 14:189–199.
Rock, Paul. 1979. *The Making of Symbolic Interactionism*. Totowa, N.J.: Rowman and Littlefield.
Shott, Susan. 1976. "Society, Self and Mind in Moral Philosophy: The Scottish Moralists as Precursors of Symbolic Interactionism." *Journal of the History of the Behavioral Sciences*. 12:39–46.
Vaughan, Ted R. and Larry T. Reynolds. 1968. "The Sociology of Symbolic Interactionism." *American Sociologist* 3:208–214.
Warshay, Leon H. 1971. "The Current State of Sociological Theory: Diversity, Polarity, and Small Theories." *Sociological Quarterly* 12:23–45.
———. 1975. *The Current State of Sociological Theory*. New York: McKay.

SUGGESTED READINGS

Farberman, Harvey A. 1985. "The Foundations of Symbolic Interaction: James, Cooley and Mead. Pp. 13–27, supplement 1 In Norman K. Denzin (ed.),*Foundations of Interpretive Sociology: Original Essays in Symbolic Interaction*. Studies in Symbolic Interaction. An overview of three major influences upon interactionist theory.
Mead, George Herbert. 1929. "Cooley's Contribution to American Social Thought." *American Journal of Sociology* 35(5):693–706. An early interactionist who contributed ideas on the development of self, "looking-glass self" theory, socialization, and sympathetic introspection is appraised by interactionism's leading representative.
Mead, George Herbert. 1934. *Mind, Self and Society*. The single most influential book on symbolic interactionism.
Petras, John. 1968. "Psychological Antecedents of Sociological Theory in America: William James and James Mark Baldwin." *Journal of the History of the Behavioral Sciences* 2 (April): 132–42. The author illustrates the psychological roots of this theory.
———. 1968. "John Dewey and the Rise of Interactionism in American Social Theory." *Journal of the History of the Behavioral Sciences* 4:18–27. Points to the influence of American pragmatism on interactionism.
Rock, Paul. 1979. *The Making of Symbolic Interactionism*. London: MacMillan. Documents the history of the Movement.
Shott, Sue. 1976. "Society, Self and Mind in Moral Philosophy: The Scottish Moralists as Precursors of Symbolic Interactionism." *Journal of the History of the Behavioral Sciences* 12:39–46. Illustrates that numerous symbolic interactionist concepts have their roots in eighteenth century philosophical thought.

Chapter 1   INTELLECTUAL ANTECEDENTS

Larry T. Reynolds

The intellectual precursors of symbolic interactionism are both numerous and diverse. Miller (1973:x), for one, has argued that the primary impetus for interactionism springs both from Darwinism and from that revolt agains introspection that he terms "objective psychology." Others have noted the impact of American pragmatic philosophy on the perspective's initial formulation. The influence of functional psychology during the early stages of symbolic interactionism's development also has been pointed out. Perhaps the best available listing of the philosophical antecedents of symbolic interactionism in general and of the thought of George Herbert Mead in particular is provided by Jerome G. Manis and Bernard N. Meltzer. These authors specify the following antecedents:

1. Evolutionism, 2. German idealism, 3. The Scottish Moralists 4. Pragmatism 5. Functional psychology (1978:1-3)

As they directly affected Mead's initial social-psychological interpretation of human behavior, Manis and Meltzer, and David L. Miller would add to the listing above the physiological psychology of Wilhelm Wundt (with its emphasis on the social implications of the gesture) and (2) the writings of those early sociologists who were contemporaries of Mead's and whose ideas also helped lay the foundations for symbolic interactionism (e.g., Cooley, Baldwin, and Thomas). Lastly, both the dramaturgical and ethnomethodological varieties of symbolic interactionism have additional philosophical roots in phenomenology and existentialism (Petras and Meltzer, 1973:1-8). Only the briefest discussion of the European precursors of symbolic interactionism: evolutionism, the Scottish Moralists, and German idealism are provided here because symbolic interactionism is, in large measure, a particularly American perspective. And because it is, the American intellectual roots: pragmatism, functional psychology, and the sociologies of Cooley and Thomas are discussed in somewhat greater detail.

Evolution

The nineteenth-century Darwinian doctrine of evolution was a major source of ideas for the American pragmatists in general and for George Herbert Mead in particular. It was, however, only to selected aspects of Darwin's theory that the founders of interactionism were to direct their attention. Mead, for example, was critical of Darwin's argument concerning emotions and their expression by animals; and Mead, along with most of the key figures in pragmatic philosophy, rejected the one notion deriving from Darwin that Spencer and Sumner had seized on and incorporated in their sociologies: the doctrine of the survival of the fittest. Mead and the pragmatists turned their backs on social Darwinism. In fact, as C. Wright Mills (1966:447) has noted, it was in the process of rejecting both instinctivist psychology and social Darwinism that American pragmatism began to move forward as an "influential variant of sociological reasoning." That strain of social Darwinism that had worked its way into sociology was rejected just as readily by Mead as it was by his pragmatic predecessors and colleagues. Leon Shaskolsky puts it this way: "not for Mead a Summerian jungle society favoring the fittest, but a society undergoing gradual change and held together by the emphatic understanding of interacting individuals" (1970:17). If Mead and the pragmatists flatly rejected social Darwinism, wherein lay the attraction of Darwin's thought for their respective social theories? Stone and Farberman (1970:17) provide the clue: "For Mead, the attraction was Darwin's emphasis upon process. Indeed, he ignored the *laissez-faire* implications of Darwinism and seized the basic theoretical import: *the same process gives rise to different forms.*" More specifically, Mead was attracted to Darwin's view that a particular relationship existed between the behavior of all living organisms and their environments—namely, that behavior, all behavior, is never accidental, mysterious, or random but is a form of adaptation to the environment. Behavior is performed by organisms, human and otherwise, in the attempt to cope with their environments. Furthermore, as John Dewey (in Mills, 1966:450) noted,". . . all conduct (behavior) is *interaction* between elements of human nature and the environment, natural and social." In this process of interaction, organisms and environments are mutually determinative; they are codeterminants. Manis and Meltzer present the case for codeterminism as follows:

> . . . evolutionary theory conveyed the idea that each organism and its environment fit together in a dialectical relationship, each influencing the nature and impact of the other. That is, the way the environment impinges on an organism is shaped, in part, by the nature of past experiences, and current activity of the organism itself. Environments differ for different organisms, and at times even for the same organism depending upon its activity. The converse of this relationship is also true: Organisms can affect their environment, thereby altering its influence upon them. (1978:2)

Applying the insights of evolutionism discussed above to human beings, one notes that interactionism was to argue that human social life is a *process* of interaction between the person and his or her natural and social environments. As this interaction unfolds, the person's behavior is performed in adaptation to the environment, and person and environment come mutually to influence each other.

The final key formulation drawn from the evolutionary perspective that was to exert a lasting influence on interactionist thought was Henri Bergson's conception of "the reality of qualitative change, emergence, and the coming into being of new forms" (Miller, 1973:28-29). Employing a notion of evolution as a creative and emergent process, Bergson argued that evolution is not solely composed of gradual developments unfolding in a fixed, step-by-step manner. If and when new combinations of behavioral or biological components occur, then radical, abrupt departures from earlier life forms emerge. Bergson's conception of evolution strongly influenced Mead. In fact, as Miller notes below, Mead is logically constrained to adopt Bergson's basic view:

> Being a process philosopher, Mead must by implication accept the theory of evolution and, more specifically, emergent evolution, which makes room for the emergence of novel events and new biological forms. Each new form requires a new environment, which is to say new environmental characteristics and objects emerge with new forms. In this sense there is a continuous restructuring of the world or part of it. (1973:101)

It is not just Mead who embraced the Bergsonian theory of emergence, "... many symbolic interactionists employ the concept of emergence in describing the presumed unpredictability of much human conduct" (Manis and Meltzer, 1978:3). The evolutionary doctrines of process and emergence were employed by Mead and other interactionists not only to deal with overt behavior but also to deal with the phenomena of mind and self. Discussing the impact of the doctrine of evolution with respect to the topic of "mind," Charles Morris put the matter as follows:

> ... the implication seemed to be that not only the human organism but the entire life of the mind as well had to be interpreted within the evolutionary development, sharing in the quality of change, and arising in the interactivity of organism and environment. Mind had to appear within, and presumably to stay within conduct. (Mead, 1934:ix)

Applying the same basic reasoning to the phenomenon of self, Stone and Farberman were to argue that "social psychology must focus its inquiries on *process,* specifically the *process* of comunication. Different selves (forms) *emerge* from differential participation in the general and universal *process* of communication" (1970:17). So the evolutionary conceptions of the processual, emergent character of life, the adaptative function of behavior, and the mutually determinative relationship between organisms and environments were to be a part of the intellectual heritage of symbolic interactionism.

The Scottish Moralists

If evolutionism first directed symbolic interactionism's founders' attention to the possibility that minds and selves, rather than "givens," were emergents, the Scottish Moralists directed the early interactionists toward an even more specific search of the social sources of self and mind. Selves and minds are social products.

The principal spokesmen of the Scottish Moralists' brand of eighteenth-century philosophy were Adam Ferguson, Henry Holmes, David Hume, Francis Hutcheson, John Millar, Thomas Reid, and Adam Smith. The principal significance of the Scottish Moralists for the symbolic interactionists is that the former anticipated many of the key or pivotal social-psychological concepts of the latter. As Manis and Meltzer have pointed out, the Scottish Moralists' concepts of "sympathy" and of the "impartial spectator" clearly foreshadow the interactionists' working concepts of "role-taking" and the "generalized other," and in the writings of Adam Smith are to be found views anticipating the interactionist conceptions of a spontaneous, or "I," component of self, as well as the selve's "me," or internalized view of others, component (Manis and Meltzer, *1978:2).* Of all the Scottish Moralists, perhaps Adam Smith was the most influential as far as symbolic interactionism is concerned. Smith not only foreshadowed the "I" and "me" concepts of Mead, but his ideas also shaped Charles Horton Cooley's views on the nature of self. One author summarized Smith's influence on Cooley, and through Cooley on Mead, in the following fashion:

Though Cooley is known as a sociologist, he was definitely influenced by Adam Smith's looking-glass theory of the self. Adam Smith stressed that, in the economic world, the seller must look at himself from the point of view of the buyer, and vice versa, each must take the attitude of the other. Or as Cooley put it, in social behavior we can, through "sympathetic imagination," look at things as others in different situations do, and have the feelings others have in circumstances actually different from our own. (Miller, 1973:xix)

Furthermore, still by way of stressing the importance of Smith's ideas for interactionism, Miller points out that "Cooley's sympathetic imagination" became, with modifications, Mead's "taking the role of the other" (Miller, 1973:xx). The Scottish Moralists, then, helped provide symbolic interactionism with some of its most indispensable concepts.

German Idealism

According to Manis and Meltzer (1978:2), the principal spokesmen of that variety of German idealism who exerted an influence on George Herbert Mead and symbolic interactionism were Johann Gottlief Fichte, Friedrick Von Schelling, and Immanuel Kant. Here one quickly concedes the correctness of Manis and Meltzer's assertion with respect to Fichte and Schelling. While Kant undoubtedly influenced the thinking of Mead and the interactionists, the nature of this influence and whether it was, on balance, positive or negative is not so easy to specify. On the positive side, one can, and should, note that Kant always defended the importance of the individual, clearly a characteristic to be found in the writings of most interactionists. From the Kantian perspective, the individual was never a passive recipient of, or a willing yielder to, pressure applied from a larger natural or social order. To the extent that symbolic interactionism rejected the human image contained in the social-deterministic arguments of the positivists and organicists, Kant's influence was both large and positive. One more point is worth mentioning. In speaking of Kant's theories of the social world, Don Martindale notes, ". . . he tried to reconcile the ideas of a free and simultaneously lawful world" (1960:230). This endeavor is indeed close to the very task that Mead, Dewey, and numerous interactionists were to set for themselves.

On the negative side, Kant assumed an unalterable structure of the mind, and because he did, he was forced to argue for the fixed nature of thought and perception. From Kant's vantage point, forms are logically prior to their objects. This conception Mead rejected. In fact, Mead's appreciation of Fichte and Schelling derived, in large part, from the fact that they too rejected Kant's views with respect to this matter. Fichte and Schelling did not believe, as Kant did, that forms are logically prior to the rational process. Just as evolutionism had argued that biological forms had origins, so too Fichte and Schelling argued that the forms of perception and thought had their origins, that they did not, in fact, exist prior to their objects. Furthermore, another German idealist, Hegel was making this self same argument. As Hegel profoundly influenced Josiah Royce and, to a lesser extent, John Dewey, and as both Royce and Dewey directly influenced Mead, one could make a case for the argument that Hegel's influence on symbolic interaction was at least as great as Kant's. In an earlier work, Meltzer (1964) mentioned Hegel's influence, and Mead's own words here are instructive: "What the Romantic idealists, and Hegel in particular, were saying was that the world evolves, that reality is in a process of evolution" (1936:154). The specific Romantic idealists Mead was referring to were Fichte and Schelling. Manis and Meltzer (1978:2) have shown that the influence of German idealism on symbolic interactionism lay in the fact that the idealists had argued that ". . . human beings construct their worlds, their realities.' Clearly, Fichte and Schelling believed that human beings inhabited a self-created world. It was Fichte's concept of the "ethical self" and Schelling's discussion of artistic creativity that led each to conclude that the world in which we live was, at least in part, created by ourselves. Lastly, Fichte may have anticipated a central concept of Mead's in that "Fichte's not-self is analogous to Mead's *other* and especially the generalized other" (Miller, 1 973 :xiv-xv).

Before proceeding to a discussion of the American intellectual antecedents of symbolic interactionism, it is perhaps best to take a quick look at Wilhelm Wundt. Wundt was himself an heir to the tradition of German idealism, and his work on language and gestures was an important source of ideas for the social psychology of George Herbert Mead.

In nineteenth century Germany, Wilhelm Wundt was one of the leading figures in the field of human psychology. Wundt's doctrines of apperception and psychophysical parallelism were gaining influence in the intellectual community, as were his ideas on folk psychology and on the conducting of laboratory experiments concerned with the workings of basic psychological processes. He established the Psychological Institute, and noted American psychologists came to study there. William James found several of Wundt's ideas especially worthwhile. But it was his reasoning and writing on language and the gesture that was to exert a lasting impact on the perspective of symbolic interactionism. George Herbert Mead would turn to Wundt's conception of the nature of language and especially to Wundt's concept of the gesture. Although Mead borrowed from Wundt, he was nevertheless critical of him. Particularly displeasing to Mead was Wundt's doctrine of psychophysical parallelism, especially his concepts of mind and society. Wundt's theory of society "was based upon the presupposition of the existence of individual minds" (Meltzer, Petras, and Reynolds, 1975:31). Wundt had failed to provide an understanding of the origins of minds in the individuals constituting a society. Mead proposed ongoing activity as the prior content out of which minds emerged; it is out of communicative and interactive processes that minds are formed. But here Mead did turn to Wundt and his concept of the gesture, for ". . . involved in the idea of the gesture is the concept of communication as a social process" (Miller, 1973:xvi). It was in the phenomenon of the gesture that Mead sought the mechanism for the initial rise of the self. Martindale puts the matter in the following terms:

Following Wundt, Mead took the gesture as the transitional link to language from action, and also as the phenomenon establishing the continuities of human and infrahuman social life. The gesture mediates the development of language as the basic mechanism permitting the rise of the self in the course of ongoing social activity. (1960:335)

From the larger camp of German idealism, then, symbolic interactionism was to draw upon the doctrine that dictated that what Mead termed "the World that is there" was, in fact, a self-created world. People were to be seen as responding to their own working conceptions and definitions of that self-created world and not to the world per se. And from Wundt would be taken the conception of the gesture as the initial phase of the social act, a phase that draws out a response made by the other party or parties in the act, a necessary response for the act's completion. A brief discussion of the American precursors of symbolic interactionism follows.

Pragmatism

If forced to single out the one philosophical school of thought that most influenced symbolic interationism, one would be on safe ground in concluding that pragmatism provides its primary intellectual underpinnings. It is not surprising that pragmatism, "the most influential philosophy in America [and] . . . the most distinctive and major contribution of America to the world of philosophy" should profoundly influence symbolic interactionism (Thayer, 1967:430-431). Symbolic interactionism is, after all, the most distinctively American variety of social psychology, and it is the major contribution of America to the world of sociological theory. Pragmatism is a philosophy intimately tied to its American social context. In fact, so closely is pragmatism linked to the "American way of life" that George Novak (1975:18) has argued that the methods of pragmatism "belong among such unquestionable values as individual enterprise, monogamy, the two party system, and big-league baseball." Ruggiero put the case still more directly: "Pragmatism was born in America, the country of 'business,' and is, *par excellence,* the philosophy of the business man" (in Martindale, 1960:297). In somewhat more sophisticated form, Ruggiero's basic argument can be seen again in the following statement:

> The quest for personal material gain was the most powerful and persistent stimulus to economic and social progress [in America]. And the urge to cut down overhead expenses in order to facilitate accumulation manifested itself in all branches of bourgeois activity. This extended to the height of Philosophical thought. Just as the bourgeoisie repudiated unproductive labor in material production, their thinkers turned away from theories which justified pursuits not immediately productive or gainful. They demanded that a philosophy prove its worth in practice. (Novak, 1975:21)

Pragmatism, of course, was the philosophy that strove to prove its worth in practice. The pragmatists were, however, always keenly aware of and sensitive to critics who alleged that their philosophy was an anti-intellectual national philosophy of the American business class. Perhaps no writer has as succinctly and eloquently summarized such criticisms as has George Herbert Mead himself:

> Pragmatism is regarded as a pseudo-philosophic formulation of that most obnoxious American trait, the worship of success; as the endowment of the four-flusher with a faked philosophic passport; the contemptuous swagger of a glib and restless upstart in the company of the mighty but reverent spirit worshipping at the shrine of subsistent entities and timeless truth; a blackleg pacemaker introduced into the leisurely workshop of the spirit to speed up the process of thinking *sub-specie aeternitatis;* a Ford efficiency engineer bent on the mass production of philosophical tin lizzies. (1938:97)

As more than one author points out, pragmatism "does not completely deserve the unfriendly estimate [that it is] . . . the philosophy of the business man" (Martindale, 1960:297). As William Skidmore argues:

> Some say it [pragmatism] was a peculiarly American philosophy because it took a disapproving view of pure abstraction for its own sake and because it put considerable emphasis on action, as opposed to thinking and logic, and in general, the mind. This is supposed to be an American philosophy because America was a place where there was considerable action, movement, building, and change, and where traditional philosophical concerns received little attention. But pragmatism, to its philosophical adherents, did not mean simply "If it works, it's good," as is sometimes said . . . pragmatism was a movement which used the traditional concerns of philosophy as a point of departure from which to defend a somewhat novel way of looking at these problems. (1975:201)

Lest one forget why Martindale qualified his defense of pragmatism by stating that it did not *completely* deserve unfriendly estimates, one can see in the two statements below that such "unfriendly estimates" are not totally misdirected:

> [truths] have only this quality in common, that they *pay.* William James

> A businessman proceeds by comparing today's liabilities and assets with yesterday's, and projects plans for tomorrow by a study of the movement thus indicated in conjunction with study of the conditions of the environment now existing. *It is not otherwise with the business of living.* John Dewey

It is most difficult to offer the reader a concise yet accurate definition of pragmatism, since pragmatism does not represent "a single unified body of philosophic ideas" (Martindale, 1960: 297). Furthermore, under the differing influences of Peirce, James, and Dewey, pragmatism exhibited some rather profound shifts in its basic formulations, as well as in the direction it was taking as a philosophical movement (Thayer,

1967:431). Pragmatism's critics have offered several short descriptions of pragmatism, such as the one presented here:

> What is pragmatism? First pragmatism is what pragmatism does. It is the habit of acting in disregard of solidly based scientific rules and tested principles. (Novak, 1975: 17)

As early as 1808, however, A. O. Lovejoy was able to distinguish between over a dozen possible forms of pragmatism, and, as H. S. Thayer points out, while pragmatism made its initial appearance in a paper titled "How to Make Our Ideas Clear," ". . . pragmatists continued to have so much trouble in doing so" (1967:431). Perhaps we should accept Thayer's (1967:431, 435) conclusions that pragmatism is "a way of investigating problems and clarifying communication rather than a fixed system of ultimate answers and great truths . . . [hence] a single definitive statement of a single thesis is not to be hoped for."

Thayer's advice aside, one can summarize several key characteristics of American pragmatism:

1. Humans are not passive recipients of stimuli; they are creative, active agents.
2. As people inhabit a world that they themselves have helped shape, even as this self-made world limits and places constraints on the activities of its creators, the world is once again subject to planned change.
3. Subjective experience flows from behavior and does not exist prior to it. From behavior, consciousness and meaning emerge, and an object's meaning resides in the behavior directed toward it and not in the object itself (Manis and Meltzer, 1978:3).
4. The same basic assumptions that shore up and guide empirical science should also guide philosophical analysis.
5. The solution of practical problems and the analysis of social issues should be the prime focus of philosophical concern (Lauer and Handel, 1977:10).
6. It is necessary and desirable to reconcile science with idealism.
7. Action is the means for checking the accuracy of a hypothesis and hence the focus of reality (Weinberg, 1962:403).
8. The best theory of value is the interest theory of value; that is good which satisfies an impulse or an interest.

With this summary of pragmatism's characteristics in mind, it may be best to turn to a discussion of their expression in the writings of a specific set of pragmatists in order to ascertain what relevance they have for symbolic interactionism.

The key founders of pragmatic philosophy in America were Josiah Royce, Charles Peirce, William James, and John Dewey. In terms of its impact on American sociology, the most influential variant of pragmatic philosophy was that emanating from the Chicago school of pragmatism, whose leader was John Dewey, and whose other members included J.H. Tufts, Edward Scribner Ames, James Rowland Angell, Addison Weber Moore, and George Herbert Mead. By stretching the point, the sociologists Albion Small and W. I. Thomas and the economist Thorstein Veblen could also be considered members of the school of Chicago pragmatists. Here one is restricted to dealing with C. S. Peirce, William James, and John Dewey. These three original founders of pragmatism held ideas that directly helped shape Mead's thought, and hence, through Mead, helped shape the structure of symbolic interaction theory. In passing one should note that Royce's ideas of the social source of self and of the affinity between the individual and society (one could not be understood save in reference to the other) were also to have a substantial impact on Mead's theories of self and society. Lastly, one feels constrained to point out, as others already have, that dealing with James and Dewey as representatives of pragmatism does not conclude a treatment of them. Their role as spokesmen of functional psychology is also discussed. Furthermore, one could just as readily treat James and Dewey as "early symbolic interactionists." They are not dealt with as early interactionists, but during the course of discussion of pragmatism and functional psychology, an attempt is made to present those of their ideas that have directly affected symbolic interactionism.

Charles S. Peirce

C. S. Peirce (in Thayer, 1967:431) once asked of William James: "who originated the term *pragmatism,* I or you?" James responded to Peirce's inquiry as follows: "You invented 'pragmatism' for which I gave you full credit...." Yet the label Peirce applied to his philosophy differed from the pragmatism of James, just as Dewey's pragmatism differed considerably from James's. In fact, Peirce became so disenchanted with the development of pragmatism at James's hands that he relabeled his own brand of philosophy *pragmaticism.* John Dewey briefly but accurately summarized the difference between Peirce's and James's varieties of pragmatism in the following terms: "Peirce wrote as a logician and James as a humanist" (Thayer, 1967:434). Peirce was indeed a logician; and much, much more. In his work one can see in rudimentary form a methodology that transcends the limits of the then-current methodologies by developing a self-reflecting philosophy of science (Habermas, 1970:36). Charles Morris said that "the philosophical task of pragmatism [was] to reinterpret the concept of mind and intelligence in the biological, psychological, and sociological terms which post-Darwinian currents of thought have made prominent . . ." (in Mead, 1934:x). In a very real sense, C. S. Peirce took on this task with the argument that ". . . the technically exploitable knowledge that is produced and tested in the research process of the natural sciences belongs to the same category as the pragmatic knowledge of everyday life acquired through trial and error in the realm of feedback controlled action" (Habermas, 1970:36).

Peirce began the formulation of the pragmatic criterion of truth: One searched for truth in practice. One could achieve a clear idea of any object only by subjecting that object to experimental treatment and then observing its reaction: "To say that an object is hard is to say that it will not be scratched by other substances" (Ezorsky, 1967:427). The meaning of an object adheres not in the object but in the use we would make of that object, in the practices we would engage in with respect to it, and the experimental handling to which we would subject it. From Peirce's perspective, truth was not an individual matter. Peirce was a realist, not a nominalist. Truth was something to be accepted by the community; therefore, individual judgement would not, and could not, be the real test of truth. Truth was sought in practice because, as Peirce noted, "... there is no distinction of meaning so fine as to consist in anything but a possible difference of practice" (in Ezorsky, 1967:427). This dictum was to be widely adopted in American philosophical circles, and its associated notion that the meaning of objects lies solely in the practice (behavior) we direct toward them became a core assumption of symbolic interactionism.

In addition to Peirce's conception of truth, certain other of his ideas were important for the soon-to-be-developed perspective of symbolic interactionism. In particular, Peirce's discussions of thought and language were relevant. Of greatest relevance is his assumption that thought is "a form of behavior initiated by the irritation of doubt and proceeding to some resolution in a state of belief" (Thayer, 1967:433). Peirce's "situation of doubt" as the phenomenon giving rise to thought became Dewey's "indeterminate situation" and Mead's "problematic situation" (Eames, 1973:139). These situations of doubt, indeterminate situations, and problematic situations as existential conditions become "the focal point(s) from which pragmatists developed their method of inquiry"(Eames, 1973:139). Just as Peirce said that truth is established with the arrest of doubt, so too Mead was to say that truth is "synonymous with the solution of the problem... judgment must be either true or false for the problem is either solved or it is not solved" (Eames, 1973:139). Of equal importance with Peirce's notion of doubt as the trigger for thought are his ideas on language, specifically on the nature of "signs." Just as Wundt's concept of the gesture is important for interactionist reasoning, so too is the concept of the sign. A sign is a standardized way in which something stands for something else. For Peirce, "... the main thing was that signs are socially standardized ways in which something (a thought, word, gesture, object) refers us (a community) to something else (the interpretant the significant effect or translation of the sign, being itself another sign)" (Thayer, 1967:431). As socially standardized items, signs assume the existence of minds in touch (communication) with one another; this in turn presupposes both the existence of a system of communicating and a human collectivity (society). Here the similarity of Peirce's reasoning to Mead's is obvious.

If it is true that Peirce's influence on symbolic interactionism has been recognized only belatedly, it is perhaps equally true that, apart from direct positive influence on Mead, his greatest influence is on that variety of symbolic interactionism known as the "Iowa school." Peirce's style of pragmatism is not half so much a theory of either truth or meaning as it is a schema, a method, a device for clarifying and unearthing the "empirically significant content of concepts by determining the roles they play in classes of empirically verifiable statements" (Thayer, 1967:433). Hence, Peirce's method clearly foreshadowed the coming of operationalism, verifiability theory, and the preferred methodological posture of Manford Kuhn and other representatives of the Iowa school of symbolic interactionism.

William James as Pragmatist

William James's conception of pragmatism is not only different from Peirce's view but it is so different that it seems almost senseless to classify them as proponents of the same philosophical school of thought. If it is true that pragmatism is more "a way of investigating problems and clarifying communication rather than a fixed system of ultimate answers," then the disparity between Peirce's "way" (or, for that matter, Dewey's) and James's "way" would appear to be even greater (Thayer, 1967:435). Dewey referred to Peirce as a logician and to James as a humanist. In contrasting James with Dewey, it could be said that "Dewey's outlook is scientific and his arguments are largely derived from an examination of scientific method [much like Peirce], but James is concerned primarily with religion and morals" (Martindale, 1960:298). James made pragmatism famous, however, and it was he who successfully proselytized for it as a new philosophy. In the world at large, it was the name of William James that first became synonymous with the word pragmatism.

Two of James's works served to popularize pragmatism in the intellectual community: "Philosophical Conceptions," a lecture delivered in 1898, and *Pragmatism: A New Name for Some Old Ways of Thinking,* a series of lectures delivered in 1906 and published as a book in 1907. It is useful to quickly relate Peirce's position and to contrast it with that of James. When C. S. Peirce spoke of the practical consequence of an idea, activity, or object, he meant results or consequences that the human community could openly, publicly, effectively, and experimentally ascertain. Peirce was a realist; his final court of last resort for the truth was not its being embraced by an individual but its being accepted by the collectivity. James is a nominalist: When he spoke of practical consequences, he meant consequences for the individual; and when he spoke of truth, he meant what was true for the individual. Peirce saw the function of thought as being the eradication of doubt through a clearer perception of reality. For James, thought was not primarily directed at grasping reality; rather, thought gave rise to beliefs and ideas that could satisfy the interests and wants of the individual regardless of whether or not these beliefs and ideas corresponded to any collectively defined "reality." Peirce's notion of "practical for the community" became in James's hands "practical for the individual"; James's term "practical" referred, and referred exclusively, to the specific impact a given brief or idea had on the life of a concrete individual. Peirce and Dewey were concerned with the generality of truth and meaning, James only with its direct importance for the individual. James is most emphatic on this point: "We cannot reject any hypothesis if consequences useful to [the] life [of the individual] flow from it" (in Martindale, 1960:298). James pushes his argument further: "If the hypothesis of God works satisfactorily [for the individual] in the widest sense of the word, it is true [for the individual]" (in Martindale, 1960:298). What satisfies the individual's need is not only good but true. Applying James's pragmatic rule of thumb to James himself, it led him to accept as true "anything that made him happy" (Martindale, 1960:301). What manifestly did not make him happy were the systems of deterministic, scientific explanation. In Don Martindale's words: "The materialistic determinism of nineteenth-century science overwhelmed James with a sense of psychic oppression, and he resolved to make the first act of free will the abandonment of all determinism" (1960:299).

Pragmatists made the attempt to reconcile science with idealism. James was a pragmatist, and so, in spite of his aversion to deterministic science, James too made the attempt. Employing his notion that the truth is that which satisfies needs or interests, he conceded that scientific, experimental methods led to truth because they produced verified ideas. Verified ideas are true, he reasoned, because they "serve our need to predict experience and cope with our environment, scientific truth fulfills our practical interests . . . [hence] the true and the verified are one" (Thayer, 1967:430). James's reconciliation of science and idealism severely restricted both the scope and purpose of science. Ultimately he came out much stronger for idealism and indeterminacy than he did for science and determinism, just as in his social psychology the "social" was forced to take the back seat.

In the pragmatism of William James were to be found all the planks necessary to erect a platform from which to launch a full-fledged assault on those theories perpetrating what Dennis Wrong (1961) would come to call the "Over-Socialized Conception of Man." James never lost sight of either the individual or of the role of creativity in shaping social affairs, and neither did George Herbert Mead. Furthermore, James argued that people "figure out" or give meaning to their surroundings in order to formulate successful "plans of action" for coping with them. The "plans of action" conception of James came to play an important role in Mead's social psychology. It was primarily James's image of people as active and not merely reactive agents that appealed to Mead; James clearly "provided the basis for an image of humans that was congruent with the developing interactionist perspective" (Meltzer, Petras, and Reynolds, 1975:8).

John Dewey as Pragmatist

John Dewey was the titular head of the Chicago school of pragmatism: "Central in the philosophy of this Chicago school was a concern for process, for seeing ideas as part of ongoing activity" (Schellenberg, 1978:42). For Dewey, mental activity was a process, and thought was not an entity but an instrument of response and behavior. Life is caught up with activity, activity and life are synonymous terms. Activity is naturally occurring; and its cause is set by *goals,* which emerge, reemerge, and are altered and modified as organisms constantly adjust and readjust to their environments. These goals or ends, Dewey informs us, are "foreseen consequences which arise in the course of activity and which are employed to give activity added meaning and to direct its future course. They are in no sense ends *of* action. In being ends of *deliberation* they are redirecting pivots *in* action" (in Stone and Farberman, 1970:52). Life is active; people are active. James said it, Dewey said it. It was, in fact, James who turned Dewey toward pragmatism and away from his Hegelian vantage point. Yet although Dewey was intellectually beholden to James, he also rejected many of his views. James had argued that truth is that which gives satisfaction to the individual. From his perspective, it was not necessary that others empirically confirm the individual's "truth." That which satisfied the individual was true; it needed no empirical validation. Dewey's brand of pragmatism dictated that one could not unearth meaning in any notion, idea, or "truth" that could never be empirically verified (Ezorsky, 1967:428). Truth to Dewey was what he termed a "warranted assertion."

Dewey maintained, as Peirce had, that the search for truth is triggered off by doubt, or, to use Dewey's own term, by an *indeterminate situation*. In fact, thought itself starts with an indeterminate situation, with an upset of a previously balanced situation. From Dewey's perspective, every thought, every act flows out of an indeterminate situation and is carried through until such time as the situation is no longer in doubt, no longer indeterminate, no longer unbalanced. When the settlement of doubt is brought about and warranted by inquiry, then the truth is known and we have a warranted assertion. The "warranted assertion" differs from James's "truth" in that it is subject to, and produced by, collective verification; warranted assertion as truth is not an individual matter.

The thought-action process that begins with the *indeterminate situation* and terminates with a *warranted assertion* is the same process for the scientific community as it is for the human community, for, as Morris points out, pragmatism "fails to see any sharp separation or any antagonism between the activities of science and philosophy" (in Mead, 1934:ix). As Mead (1934:ix) put it, "... the philosophy of a period is always an attempt to interpret its most secure knowledge." If the world of science is popularly conceived of as concerned with facts while the rest of the world (philosophy included) is supposedly concerned with values, it is Dewey who demonstrates that there is a tremendous continuity between values and facts. The continuity is so great, in fact, that it is nearly impossible to distinguish between "what is objectively real, apart from any human purposes (values) . . . the former [objective reality] is not factually perceived unless it relates to human values facilitating its perception, and the latter [values] require a physical reality of some sort in order to carry meaning" (Thayer, 1967:435).

It is the aim of all thought, all inquiry, to create solutions, goods, satisfactions, and so forth in what was initially a troubled, unbalanced, nonharmonious, and discordant situation. Hence, as Thayer (1967:435) notes, "In this respect all intelligence is evaluative, and no separation of moral, scientific, practical, or theoretical experience is to be made." If we are to comprehend a scientist's use of facts and ideas, we must first understand his or her purposes in beginning the process of inquiry. Similarly, if we are to understand any person's thought or activity, we must come to understand why that thought and activity arose in the first place. Human thought arises when the person sees his or her doubt (indeterminate situation) as a problem. An idea, a thought, is nothing more or less than a proposed solution to the problem. Ideas are plans of action; they are "proposals formed in the context of a problem as a possible solution" (Ezorsky, 1967:429). Ideas in either scientific or practical inquiries coincide with facts when they have "through action, worked out the state of things which [they] contemplated or intended" (Ezorsky, 1967:429). What this means is that Dewey does not see truth (or facts) as immutable; it is meaningless to contend that truth exists separate from or prior to the process of inquiry. From Dewey's perspective, "truth 'happens to an idea' when it becomes a verified or warranted assertion" (Ezorsky, 1967:429). Because of the interactional character of all experience in human society, there could be no fact, no thought, no truth which was antecedent to the person as a thinking being (Meltzer, Petras, and Reynolds, 1975:17). Dewey extended and refined James's conception of individuals as active agents; he went beyond James in elucidating the process by which both thought arises and minds develop in the context of human association. While Dewey's position remained nominalistic, he did go beyond James in demonstrating the relationship between thought, mind, and society. Mead, while drawing heavily on Dewey's work, would, as a realist, go beyond him in depicting the social origins of mind and self in society. But *pragmatism, as* it was *shaped* especially *by* John *Dewey,* would become the *primary* philosophical *foundation* for *symbolic interactionism.* John Dewey would launch the successful attack on those varieties of philosophy that the pragmatists thought little aided human beings in their practical dealings with an emerging, evolving social reality. Among the pragmatists, it was Dewey who argued that the questions posed by traditional philosophy were not worth raising in the first place. Dewey saw human beings, their thoughts, and their societies caught in a larger, interrelated whole; it was he who demonstrated the relativity of philosophical systems in showing their connection with particular kinds of social formations (Meltzer, Petras, and Reynolds, 1975:17). Dewey set a new task for philosophy, and it was Dewey who made of the philosophical underpinnings of symbolic interactionism the "national philosophy of America" (Novak, 1975:15).

Like Marx, the pragmatists sought to avoid, and often successfully did avoid the use of such artificial dualisms as mind and matter, theory and practice, and experience and nature (Mead, 1934:x). Just as Marx had successfully bridged the people-nature dichotomy, and in so doing proved it to be a false dichotomy, the pragmatists were laying the groundwork for the attempt to bridge the individual-society dichotomy. Pragmatism set a new standard for judging the worth of theory; theories were to be judged on the basis of the fruitfulness of the practical consequences that resulted from their adoption. Among the more significant contributions of pragmatism to the developing theory of symbolic interactionism were its arguments that it is senseless to draw hard distinctions between mind and matter or between society and the individual, as well as its theories of the existential basis of mind, intelligence, and self.

Functional Psychology

In addition to pragmatism, functional psychology was the American-style school of thought that provided intellectual pilings for symbolic interactionism. The principal spokesmen for functional psychology in America were James Rowland Angell, John Dewey, William James, and Charles Hubbard Judd. Of the four, John Dewey and William James had, by far, the largest impact on sociology in general and interactionism in particular; hence only Dewey and James will be singled out for treatment here. But before proceeding to Dewey and James, it may prove worthwhile to specify, in outline fashion, the basic assumptions of the American school of functional psychology. These assumptions are as follows:

1. The process that makes human association (society) possible is the process of linguistic communication.

2. Language not only makes human society possible but is the thing that distinguishes humans from other species; it is a species-specific characteristic of Homo sapiens.

3. Humans are active beings who do not simply respond to stimuli, but select out and pay attention to those stimuli that help to further an ongoing activity.

4. A stimulus embodies no fixed quality of its own; hence the nature of sensation is dependent on the ongoing activity taking place at the time.

5. The mind is not an organ or structure; it is a function that helps the person adapt to his or her environment. Thought is adaptive behavior.

6. Social learning both inhibits and modifies instincts and their expression.

7. Action follows the course of habit until encountering a blockage that, in turn, triggers an impulse that conflicts with the habit; intelligence arbitrates between habit and impulse, thereby securing the release of action.

8. In the formation and development of the individual self, other persons play a key role.

A quick glance at this list reveals that some assumptions of functional psychology overlap with certain basic assumptions of pragmatism. This is hardly surprising in view of the fact that both Dewey and James are widely regarded as being both pragmatists and functional psychologists. James Rowland Angell is also considered by some to be both functional psychologist and pragmatist. Neither should it come as a surprise if it turns out that interactionism shares many assumptions with functional psychology and pragmatism, not merely because they are its intellectual precursors, but because pragmatism is an American philosophy, functional psychology is an American psychology, and symbolic interactionism is either an American social psychology or an American sociology, depending on one's point of view (noninteractionists tend to regard interactionism as social psychological, while many interactionists are pleased to see their perspective as being sociological). I turn now to a brief discussion of the functional psychologies of James and Dewey.

James as Functional Psychologist

The functional psychology of William James is laid out in his 1890 publication, *Principles of Psychology*. In this two-volume work, James sets forth and details the interrelationships that exist between his three pivotal, indispensable concepts: instinct, habit, and self. Now James's treatment of the instinct concept stood in marked contrast to the way in which that concept was handled by the so-called instinct theorists. For the instinct theorists, the most important thing about instincts was that "they were there"; they were essentially fixed faculties of acting unmodified by experience and directed toward the production of certain ends. These instincts, if one concedes their existence in the first place, were of little concern to James. For James, the single most important feature of instincts is that they are inhibited and modified. And, most important, they are inhibited and modified by the action of another of James's key concepts: habits. Habits, in turn, are not part of one's initial biological equipment; they are socially acquired, they are learned. Instincts are socially modified in human beings because Homo sapiens possesses capabilities not characteristic of other species; most notable of these is the ability of the human brain to engage in high-level mental activities such as memory. Because of memory, repeating behavior that was at one time instinctual "can call to mind the performance of the act at that previous time" (Meltzer, Petras, and Reynolds, 1975:4). This kind of behavior, then, must "cease to be blind after being repeated, and must be accompanied with foresight of its end just so far as that end may have fallen under the animal's cognizance" (James, 1 890:390).

Therefore, the complexity of a species' behavior is not necessarily related to the number of instincts in its repertoire. A species may have a large number of instincts and yet exhibit a fairly simple system of behavior. Conversely, in the case of humans, instincts are few, but behavior is enormously complex. With respect to human beings, then, "... attention should be focused upon the number of *repeated* behavioral experiences that are traceable to a particular instinct" (Meltzer, Petras, and Reynolds, 1975:4). In James's view, "... as most instincts are implanted for the sake of giving rise to habits, then, when that purpose has been realized the instincts are destined to simply fade away" (1890:402).

Habits that modify and inhibit instincts are themselves products of the individual's previous experiences, and as such they act to further inhibit the original instinct's range of expression because, as James (1890:394) notes, "When objects of a certain class elicit a certain sort of reaction, ... [the person] ... becomes partial to the first specimen of the class on which [he or she] has reacted, and will not afterward react on any other specimen." Not only are humans born with fewer instincts and greater plasticity than other species, but many of the instincts humans do possess come to the fore during a certain developmental period in their lives and then disappear. It is worth noting that, from James's perspective, not only are instincts plastic, subject to inhibition, and prone to fade away, but those instincts we do possess frequently work at cross purposes, cancel each other's effect, or block each other out. Again, instincts are a part of the makeup of Homo sapiens; they are factors helping to determine behavior but their most important characteristic is that, due to the action of habit, they are modifiable and can be inhibited.

The last key concept of James, at least as far as its direct relevance for symbolic interactionism is concerned, is the concept of *self*. It is most interesting to note James's working conception of self because it is held to by a sizable number of present-day interactionists, and it is flatly rejected by an equally large number of the current practitioners of that perspective. James began by noting that humans had four distinct selves: the self of pure ego, a material self, a spiritual self, and a social self. This notion is, of course, rejected by all contemporary interactionists. Nevertheless, one of James's selves, the social self, became, and pretty much the way James defined it, a key concept for numerous interactionists. In speaking of the social self, he argued as follows:

> Properly speaking, a man has as many social selves as there are individuals who recognized him and carry an image of him in their mind ... but as the individuals who carry the images fall naturally into classes, we may practically say that he has as many different social selfs as there are distinct groups of persons about whose opinion he cares. (1890:294)

James's *social self* became, for many symbolic interactionists, *the self*. They dropped those "separate types of selves" that were not derived from interaction and were not products of participation in the social milieu, namely, the spiritual, material, and pure ego selves. James's conception of the social self is what has been termed "the multiple entity conception" (Reynolds et al., 1970). Numerous symbolic interactionists, but by no means all of them, would find themselves in basic agreement with James's contention that the individual has more than one self. Some would argue that it is more appropriate to state that the individual has as many selves as there are *groups to which he or she belongs,* rather than to say, as James did, that one has *as many selves as there are groups whose opinion one cares about.* Both definitions are "multiple entity conceptions" of self. Because many interactionists accept the "multiple self" notion, and because all of them agree that basic biological endowments are only seen as they have already been profoundly altered by social experience, James's functional psychology may be said to have exerted a significant impact on interactionism.

Dewey as Functional Psychologist

John Dewey's functional psychology employs a host of concepts, but three stand out as more important than the rest: impulse, habit, and intellect. Of these three, habit and intellect are central, with habit perhaps the most important. Dewey was not, of course, the first spokesman of functional psychology to employ the concept of habit as a central one. William James utilized the concept, but he did so solely for the purpose of dealing with repetitious individual behavior. Dewey was more concerned with the role of social variables in behavior, and as this concern developed on Dewey's part, his basic concepts, habit included, were redefined to reflect that concern. When Dewey (1922:42) eventually defined habit as an acquired predisposition to *"ways* or modes of response, not to particular acts," he was further led to argue that conditions that constitute habit lie in the social order, not in the individual, and because they do, one cannot change habits by merely changing individuals. Social conditions too must be altered.

Dewey's three concepts of habit, impulse, and intellect relate to one another in the following manner: Activity runs the path of habit until it is blocked by an obstacle. In the face of blocked activity, impulse emerges and seeks an outlet in activity. In seeking the outlet, the old (habit) and the new (impulse) collide, producing a problem. Intellect mediates between habit and impulse, "thus facilitating the release of action, which will be a projection of existent habits newly combined so as to satisfy the stymied impulse" (Mills, 1966:455). Thus Dewey (1922:30) argued that action, at least blocked action, precedes thought, or as he put it, "The act must come before the thought, and a habit before the ability to evoke the thought at will." It was through the concept of habit that Dewey came to his view on the relationship between the individual and the collectivity. He emphasized the role of social elements in shaping habits, indeed in shaping all behavior, and because he did he was led to conclude further that habits cannot be changed by merely changing individuals; social conditions must also be altered. The social conditions he most ardently sought to alter were those affecting the individual during his or her early years. Specifically, Dewey was concerned with educational institutions and educational processes. *Minds* must be shaped in such a way that they become receptive to the changes necessary if a decent society were to be wrought out of the existing social order. Dewey's conception of mind is crucial here: "Dewey proposed that the mind be viewed as function, with "minded activity" extrapolated from adaptive behavior in an ever-changing environment. This . . . view of the human mind is most congenial with attempts at intelligent social planning" (Meltzer, Petras, and Reynolds, 1975:19).

As Dewey (1971:273) saw it, any view of mind as a fixed and frozen phenomenon stood squarely in the path of social reform because ". . . the most powerful apologetics for any arrangement or institution is the conception that it is the inevitable result of fixed conditions of human nature." In conceptualizing the mind as function, Dewey was moved to argue that the mind's social development was facilitated only through the process of communication, specifically through the use of language. Language enabled individuals to incorporate into their own selves the beliefs, sentiments, and thoughts taken from their respective social environments.

Dewey's contribution to functional psychology in terms of reconceptualizing, reworking, and rethinking its basic concepts and their relationship to one another was enormous, especially with respect to such concepts as mind, impulse, habit, and language. Dewey's other major contribution to functional psychology derives from the classic statement on the reflex-arc concept in psychology. In this work he attacked the stimulus-response conception of human behavior. Interested as he was in the role of interaction in understanding human behavior, he objected to any dualistic notions of stimulus and response in the following words:

> Sensation as stimulus . . . means simply a function, and it will have its value shift according to the special work requiring to be done . . . what the sensation will be in particular at a given time, therefore, will depend entirely upon the way in which an activity is being used. It has no fixed quality of its own. The search for the stimulus is the search for the exact conditions of action; that is, for the state of things which decides how a beginning coordination should be completed. (Dewey, 1896:369)

The attack on the dualism of stimulus and response contained in the above statement paved the way for a view of the role of both individual and social elements in explaining distinctly human conduct. In the functional psychology of John Dewey, the discipline of psychology had stuck its foot in sociology's door.

REFERENCES

Baldwin, John D. 1985. *George Herbert Mead: A Unifying Theory for Sociology*. Newbury Park: Sage Publications.
Cooley, Charles Horton. 1918. *Social Process*. New York: Scribner's.
Dewey, John. 1896. "The Reflex Arc Concept in Psychology." *Psychological Review* 3:357-370.

———. 1922. *Human Nature and Conduct.* New York: Holt.
Eames, S. Morris. "Mead and the Pragmatic Conception of Truth." Pp. 135-152 in Walter R. Corti (Ed.), *The Philosophy of George Herbert Mead.* Winterhur, Switzerland: Amrisuiler Burcherei.
Ezorsky, Gertrude. 1967. "Pragmatic Theory of Truth." Pp. 427-429 in Paul Edwards (Ed.), *The Encyclopedia of Philosophy Vol. 5.* New York: MacMillan.
Habermas, Jurgen. 1970. *Toward a Rational Society.* Boston: Beacon Press.
James, William. 1890. *Principles of Psychology.* New York: Holt.
Lauer, Robert and Warren Handel. 1977. *Social Psychology: The Theory and Application of Symbolic Interactionism.* Boston: Houghton Mifflin.
Manis, Jerome G. and Bernard N. Meltzer. 1978. *Symbolic Interaction: A Reader in Social Psycholoqy.* Third Edition. Boston: Allyn and Bacon.
Martindale, Don. 1960. *The Nature and Types of Sociological Theory.* Boston: Houghton Mifflin.
Mead, George Herbert. 1934. *Mind, Self, and Society: From the Standpoint of a Social Behaviorist.* Chicago: University of Chicago Press. Edited by Charles W. Morris.
Meltzer, Bernard N. 1964. *The Social Psychology of George Herbert Mead.* Kalamazoo: Center for Sociological Research, Western Michigan University.
Meltzer, Bernard N., John W. Petras, and Larry T. Reynolds. 1975. *Symbolic Interactionism: Genesis. Varieties. and Criticism.* London: Routledge and Kegan Paul.
Miller, David L. 1973. *George Herbert Mead: Self, Language, and the World.* Austin: University of Texas Press.
Mills, C. Wright. 1966. *Sociology and Pragmatism.* New York: Oxford University Press.
Novak, George. 1975. *Pragmatism Versus Marxism: An Appraisal of John Dewey's Philosophy.* New York: Pathfinder Press.
Petras, John W. and Bernard N. Meltzer. 1973. "Theoretical and the Ideological Variations in Contemporary Interactionism." *Catalyst* 7:1-8.
Reynolds, Larry T., et al. 1970. "The Self in Symbolic Interaction Theory." Pp. 422-438 in Larry T. Reynolds and Janice M. Reynolds (Eds.), *The Sociology of Sociology.* New York: McKay.
Shaskosky, Leon. 1970. "The Development of Sociological Theory: A Sociology of Knowledge Interpretation." Pp. 6-30 in Janice M. Reynolds and Larry T. Reynolds (Eds.) *The* Sociology of Sociology. New York: McKay.
Skidmore, William. 1970. *Theoretical Thinking in Sociology.* Cambridge, England: Cambridge University Press.
Stone, Gregory P. and Harvey A. Farberman. 1970. *Social Psychology Through Symbolic Interaction.* Waltham, MA: Ginn-Blaisdell.
Thayer, H.S. 1967. "Pragmatism." Pp. 430-435 in Paul Edwards (Ed.) *The Encyclopedia of Philosophy Vol. 5.* New York: MacMillan.
Thomas, W.I. 1937. *Primitive Behavior.* New York: McGraw Hill.
Wrong, Dennis. 1961. "The Oversocialized Conception of Man in Modern Sociology." *American Socioloay Review,* 26:183-193.

PART II
VARIETIES OF SYMBOLIC INTERACTIONISM AND LEADING EARLY REPRESENTATIVES

The major intellectual influences on symbolic interactionism are not confined to those precursors discussed in the previous chapter. A number of other scholars have made significant contributions to the development of this theory. Our brief discussion and choice of the remaining readings for this section, does *not* cover every intellectual influence on the perspective.[1]

The first selection in this section by Reynolds deals with the contributions of two early symbolic interactionists, Charles Horton Cooley and W. I. Thomas. As the author rightly notes, Cooley not only introduced to interactionism the concepts of "looking-glass self" and the "primary group," but also developed a theory which conceived of human society as fundamentally mental in nature. In addition, he developed a theory of human nature, and he documented stages in the development of the self. Finally, in terms of methodological contributions, Reynolds points out that Cooley was responsible for coining the term, "sympathetic introspection"—the notion that individuals must place themselves in the shoes of those they wish to understand. W. I. Thomas may be credited for making important theoretical contributions to symbolic interactionism. Among Thomas' contributions are: his writings on self-society interrelationships, his methodological emphasis on "sympathetic introspection," his ideas on "adult socialization," and his formulation of the concept, the "definition of the situation." An important concept in symbolic interactionism, the "definition of the situation" refers to that moment of deliberation before humans act—when we assemble meanings, objects, etc. in space and time; subsequently, we act toward them in a meaningful fashion.

George Herbert Mead is considered to be the individual who laid the foundation of symbolic interactionist theory. In our next piece, Bernard N. Meltzer provides what the editors believe to be one of the very best summaries of Meadian social behaviorism.

As we noted in the previous section, depending upon which author one happens to read, there may be between two and fifteen varieties of symbolic interactionism. Meltzer and Petras (1970), for example, based upon methodological distinctions, have identified the "Chicago" and "Iowa" schools. Warshay (1971) identifies eight varieties of symbolic interactionism: (1) the Blumer school (2) the Iowa school (3) a role-theory view (4) an emphasis on interaction (5) the dramaturgical school (6) a field-theory version (7) an existential approach and (8) the ethnomethodological approach. Still others, such as Manford Kuhn (1964) have divided symbolic interactionism into fifteen different orientations: (1) reference group theory (2) role theory (3) Kuhnian self theory (4) social and person perception theory, (5) the Sapir-Whorf-Cassier language and culture approach, (6) phenomenology, (7) Sullivan's interpersonal theory, (8) self-actualizing theory, (9) self-consistency theory, (10) dramaturgy (11) development theory, (12) field theory, (13) cognitive theory, (14) identity theory, and (15) the self theory of Carl Rogers.

Following Petras and Meltzer (1973), we would argue that there exist four major varieties of symbolic interactionism. Their article deals with the Chicago school, the Iowa school, the dramaturgical approach, and ethnomethodology.

Herbert Blumer, a student of Mead's, became symbolic interactionism's chief spokesperson, after the death of his mentor. Although some conceive of Blumer as Mead's interpreter, it seems that since his death in 1987, Blumer has been redefined as an original thinker. Interactionists have produced a number of books and articles discussing Blumer's importance.[1] Blumer made a number of significant theoretical, methodological, and substantive contributions to this perspective. The piece by Lewis Killian, a student of Blumer's, deals with those major theoretical, methodological, and substantive contributions. In particular, Killian discusses Blumer's contributions in the areas of social organization and race relations.

While Mead, Blumer, Thomas, and Cooley are considered to have made significant contributions to the development of the Chicago approach to symbolic interactionism, our next selection deals with the contributions to the Iowa approach of another scholar. Spitzer et al. focus on Manford Kuhn's contribution to self theory.

The next selection by Martindale deals with the intellectual contributions of a third generation interactionist, Erving Goffman. Rooted in the dramaturgical approach, Goffman is credited for making significant contributions to interactionist theory, particularly through his ideas on the self, "presentation of self." the art of "impression management," the effects of institutional processing on the self, and frame analysis. Lastly, Ruth Wallace and Alison Wolf detail a leading ethnomethodologist's contributions to the perspective by discussing the work of Harold Garfinkel. Garfinkel, through his research and writing, seeks to interpret how people make sense—to uncover the *"taken-for-granted"* assumptions underlying everyday social interaction.

NOTES

1. The reader may consult: Becker (1988); Shubutani (1988) for examples.

REFERENCES

Becker, Howard S. 1988. "Herbert Blumer's Conceptual Impact." *Symbolic Interaction* 11(1):13–23.
Garfinkel, Harold. 1967. *Studies in Ethnomethodology*. Englewood Cliffs, N.J.: Prentice Hall.
Goffman, Erving. 1959. *The Presentation of Self in Everyday Life*. Garden City, N.Y.: Doubleday.
Kuhn, Manford. 1964. "Major Trends in Symbolic Interactionism in the Past Twenty-five Years." *Sociological Quarterly* 5:61–84.
Meltzer, Bernard N. and John W. Petras. 1970. "The Chicago and Iowa Schools of Symbolic Interaction," Pp. 3–17. In *Human Nature and Collective Behavior*, (ed.) Tomatsu Shibutani. Englewood, Cliffs, N.J.: Allyn and Bacon.
Petras, John W. and Bernard N. Meltzer. 1973. "Theoretical and Ideological Variations in Symbolic Interactionism," *Catalyst* 7:1–8.

Shibutani, Tomatsu. 1988. "Herbert Blumer's Contributions to Twentieth-Century Sociology." *Symbolic Interaction* 11(1):23–31.
Warshay, Leon H. 1971. "The Current State of Sociological Theory: Structuralism and Theoretical Breadth; Deductivism, Fictionalism, and Methodological Narrowness." *Sociological Quarterly* 5:141–147.

SUGGESTED READINGS

Blumer, Herbert. 1969. *Symbolic Interactionism.* Englewood Cliffs, New Jersey: Prentice-Hall. Blumer, who coined the term "Symbolic Interaction," addresses the major theoretical and methodological components of the theory.

Brittan, Arthur. 1973. *Meanings and Situations.* London: Routledge. An essay from the interactionist vantage point by a leading British practitioner of the perspective.

Bernice M. Fisher and Anselm L. Strauss. 1979. "George Herbert Mead and the Chicago Tradition of Sociology." parts 1 & 2. *Symbolic Interaction* 2(1): 9–25 & 2(2): 9–20. A summation of Mead's contributions to the Chicago school. The authors also suggest other equally significant influences on the development of symbolic interactionism.

Hickman, C. Addison and Manford Kuhn. *Individuals, Groups and Economic Behavior.* New York: Dryden Press. A detailed statement of the self theory, the Iowa approach; the latter is compared with field, learning, and Freudian theories.

Kuhn, Manford H. 1964. "Major Trends in Symbolic Interactionist Theory in the Past Twenty-five Years." *Sociological Quarterly* 5: 66–84. A comprehensive summation of trends by the leading early spokesperson for the "Iowa School".

Plummer, Ken. 1990. "Herbert Blumer and the Life History Tradition." *Symbolic Interaction* 13 (2):125–44. A student of Mead who made significant theoretical and methodological contributions is examined in the context of the life history tradition.

Thomas, W.I., and Florian Znaniecki. 1923. *The Polish Peasant.* New York: Alfred Knopf. A classic historical comparative, empirical study dealing with the constructions of reality and subjective definitions of Polish immigrants.

Warshay, Leon H. and Diana Warshay. 1986. "The Individualizing and Subjectivizing of George Herbert Mead." *Sociological Focus* 19(2):177–88. A statement on the position of the leading progenitor of symbolic interactionism.

READINGS BY OTHER LEADING REPRESENTATIVES NOT COVERED IN TEXT

Becker, Howard S. 1963. *Outsiders: Studies in the Sociology of Deviance.* New York: Free Press. Work details the "labelling" or "societal reaction" approach to the study of deviance — an approach clearly rooted within symbolic interactionism.

Burke, Kenneth. 1962. *A Grammar of Motives and a Rhetoric of Motives.* Cleveland: World. A general theoretical treatise by a major contributor to the dramaturgical perspective.

Cicourel, Aaron. 1964. *Method and Measurement in Sociology.* New York: Free Press. A statement on the nature of sociological inquiry by a major ethnomethodologist.

Deegan, Mary Jo and Michael R. Hill. 1987. *Women and Symbolic Interaction.* Boston: Allyn and Bacon. The role of leading women in both symbolic interaction history and in sociology is detailed.

Freidson, Eliot. 1970. *The Profession of Medicine.* New York: Dodd, Mead. A symbolic interactionist approach to the sociology of health and illness.

Glaser, Barney and Anselm Strauss. 1967. *The Discovery of Grounded Theory.* Chicago: Aldine. A classic piece detailing the analytic induction approach to social research.

Hughes, Everett C. 1956. *The Sociological Eye.* Chicago: Aldine.

The views of one of symbolic interactionism's important "early influences" in the fields of organization, education, and social processes.

——. 1958. *Men and Their Work*. New York: Free Press. Early Chicagoan sociologist who sought to connect concepts of status and role to the self, moral careers, work, and deviance.

Manis Jerome G. and Bernard N. Meltzer (eds.). 1967. *Symbolic Interaction*. Boston: Allyn and Bacon. One of the earliest and most comprehensive collections of representative selections in the interactionist tradition.

Rose, Arnold. 1962. (ed.). *Human Behavior and Social Processes*. Boston: Houghton Mifflin. Theoretical statements by many leading interactionists representing a broad-based approach to social reality.

Stone Gregory P. and Harvey D. Farberman (eds.). 1981. *Social Psychology through Symbolic Interaction*. 2nd edition New York: Wiley. Along with Manis and Meltzer, another early attempt to provide the reader with an introduction to the theory and methods of symbolic interactionism.

Stone, Gregory P. 1962. "Appearance and The Self." Pp. 86–118 In Arnold Rose (ed.),*Human Behavior and Social Processes*. Boston: Houghton Mifflin. The author reanalyzes the Meadian notions of "self" and the "social act," and emphasizes the importance of discourse, appearance and meaning in social interaction.

Strauss, Anselm. 1959. *Mirrors and Masks: The Search for Identity*. New York: Free Press. A symbolic interactionist analysis of the process of identity formation is presented by one of interactionism's key spokespersons.

Stryker, Sheldon. 1980. *Symbolic Interaction*. Menlo Park, Ca: Benjamin/Cummings. Summarizes the structural approach. Stryker advocates that symbolic interactionism bridge the individual and social structure gap through the use of role theory.

ALLIED PERSPECTIVES/SYMPATHETIC FRAMEWORKS/FELLOW TRAVELERS

Abel, Theodore. 1953. "The Operation Called Verstehen", Pp. 677–687 In Herbert Feigl and May Brodbeck (eds.) *Readings in the Philosophy of Science*. New York: Appleton-Century-Crofts, Inc. A discussion of a Weberian approach to the empirical world.

Adler, Patricia, Peter Adler, and Andrea Fontana. 1970. *Understanding Everyday Life*. London: Routledge and Kegan Paul. This volume presents detailed discussions of the normative and interpretive paradigms, ethnomethodology, and symbolic interactionism; the differences between the ethnomethodological and interactionist stances are addressed.

Attwell, Paul. 1974. "Ethnomethodology Since Garfinkel." *Theory and Society* 1:179–210. An accent on the developing diversity with the camp of the ethnomethodologists.

Berger, Peter and Thomas J. Luckmann. 1967. *The Social Construction of Reality*, pp. 47–128. Deals with such concepts as habitualization, institutionalization, legitimation, recipe knowledge, and the social distribution of knowledge.

Denzin, Norman K. 1969. "Symbolic Interactionism and Ethnomethodology: a Proposed Synthesis," *American Sociological Review*, 34 (December: 922–934). Good piece comparing the basic theoretical and methodological assumptions of symbolic interactionism and ethnomethodology, points of synthesis are proposed.

Douglas, Jack. 1967. *The Social Meaning of Suicide*. Princeton, New Jersey: Princeton University Press. An examination of the phenomenon of suicide utilizing the ethnomethodological approach. Douglas' work was conducted in reaction against Durkheim's functionalist theory on suicide rates.

Garfinkel, Harold. 1967. *Studies in Ethnomethodology* Englewood Cliffs, N.J: Prentice Hall. Collection of thought-provoking pieces, including the piece "What is Ethnomethodology", by the "founder" of ethnomethodology.

Goffman, Erving. 1969. *The Presentation of Self in Everyday Life*. Garden City, New Jersey: Doubleday Anchor. Classical piece illustrating the dramaturgical approach. Conceiving of life as a theater, Goffman speaks of backstage/front stage performances and of the symbolic devices we employ in an effort to manage impressions.

Heeren, John. 1972. "Alfred Schutz and the Sociology of Common-Sense Knowledge", Chapter 2, Pp. 45–56 In Jack Douglas (ed.) *Understanding Everyday Life*. An assessment of Schutz's contribution to the sociology of everyday life.

Hilbert, Richard A. 1992. *The Classical Roots of Ethnomethodology: Durkheim, Weber, and Garfinkel*. Chapel Hill: University of North Carolina Press. The piece examines the philosophical foundations of the ethnomethodological perspective.

Hill, Richard J. and Kathleen Stones Crittenden (eds.) 1981. *Proceedings of the Purdue Symposium on Ethnomethodology*. Presents the range of views on the ethnomethodological framework expressed during a major conference on the perspective.

Hindess, Barry. 1972. "The 'Phenomenological' Sociology of Alfred Schutz", *Economy and Society*, vol. 1, no. 1, February, 1–27. An extremely non-sympathetic analysis of Schutz's phenomenological approach.

Holzner, Burkart. 1971. *Reality Construction in Society* Boston, Massachusetts: Schenckman 2nd edition. This was written at the same time as Berger and Luckmann's, *The Social Construction of Reality* and draws similarity on Schutz; however, it pays more attention to the social distribution of knowledge.

Husserl, Edmund. 1936. *Phenomenology and the Crisis of Western Philosophy*. New York: Harper and Row. Summary of Husserl's basic ideas.

Light, Ivan. 1969. "The Social Construction of Uncertainty," *Berkeley Journal of Sociology* 14: 189–199. An excellent critical summary of the position of Berger and Luckmann.

Mehan, Hugh and Houston Wood. 1973. *The Reality of Ethnomethodology* New York: Wiley and Sons. This title is an excellent statement of the ethnomethodological perspective.

McNall, Scott and James C.M. Johnson. 1975. "The New Conservatives: Ethnomethodologists, Phenomenologists, and Symbolic Interactionists." *Insurgent Sociologist* 5 no. 4:49–65. The status quo supporting consequences of the "social definitional" frameworks are discussed.

Natanson, Maurice. 1970. "Phenomenology and Typification: A Study in the Philosophy of Alfred Schutz". *Social Research*, 37:1: (Spring) 1–22. Presents Schutz's philosophy in terms readily grasped by a sociological audience.

———. 1962. *The Journeying Self*, Introduction, chs. 1 and 2, pp. 1–46. A noted phenomenological philosopher's views on the nature of human nature are presented.

Psathas, George. 1973. *Phenomenological Sociology*. New York: John Wiley and Sons. A readable offering on phenomenology as a form of sociological reasoning.

Rogers, Mary E. 1983. *Sociology, Ethnomethodology, and Experience: A Phenomenological Critique*. New York: Cambridge. A phenomenonological assessment which encourages sociologists to employ a less narrow definition of what constitutes social reality.

Sacks, Harvey. 1963. "Sociological Description," *Berkeley Journal of Sociology* 8: 1–16. An account of the process of sociological descriptions by the late Harvey Sacks, a key spokesperson for ethnomethodology in the early days of its development.

Schutz, Alfred. 1967. "The Problem of Rationality in the Social World", Pp. 89–111 In P.Emmet and A. MacIntyre (eds.), *Sociological Theory and Philosophical Analysis* . A leading exponent of the phenomenological approach presents a detailed discussion of the role of rationality in social life.

———. 1962. "The Stranger", *Collected Papers 11*, 91–105; "The Homecomer" *Collected Papers 11*, 106–119; and the "The Well Informed Citizen," *C.P. 11*, 120–134. The Hague, Holland: Martinus Nijhoff. Three of Schutz' applications of his perspective to the understanding of particular concrete phenomenon.

VanGennep, Arnold. 1960. *The Rites of Passage*. Chicago: University of Chicago Press. Phenomenological Approach to the Study of Identity.

Chapter 2
THE EARLY INTERACTIONISTS: COOLEY AND THOMAS

Larry T. Reynolds

Charles Horton Cooley

The initial entry into American sociology of several key ideas springing from the functional psychologists, the pragmatist philosophers, and perhaps even the Scottish Moralists was gained through the writings of Charles Horton Cooley. Cooley was a student of John Dewey and was well acquainted with the writings of both William James and James Mark Baldwin. One would have to further agree with those who argue that the parallels between Cooley's views and those of Adam Ferguson, David Hume, and especially Adam Smith are both too strong and too striking not to suggest that Cooley was conversant with the social philosophy of the Scottish Moralists (Stryker, 1980:26). It would appear that the influence of the pragmatists on Cooley was great. Much of his work concerns itself with the *practical* problems people grapple with in a technologically complex society, and indeed it has been argued that:

> In fact, all of Cooley's writings impart the impression that his sociological theorizing on the structure and organization of society was guided by moral principles derived from the pragmatic tradition, and these, in turn were tempered by the reality of social life as interpreted in his sociological theories. (Meltzer, Petras, and Reynolds, 1975:9)

Much philosophy and psychology, then, make their way into early American sociology in the person of Charles Horton Cooley.

Cooley is perhaps best known for introducing sociologists to the concepts *primary group* and *looking-glass self;* yet, from Cooley's perspective, his major contribution was his particular theory of human society, a phenomenon he viewed as being essentially mental in nature (Meltzer, Petras, and Reynolds, 1975:8). Unlike many figures in early American sociology, Cooley did not approach the study of society from the vantage point of the concrete individual and then infer or build up general societal properties based on that individual-centered viewpoint(Bodenhafer, 1920-1921:425-474). Instead, he began with the collectivity or group, for it is from the group that the real basis of individual motivation and behavior comes. In fact, for those concerned with depicting social reality, Cooley warned that the "real person" exists only in what Cooley termed the "personal idea":

> So far as the study of immediate social relations is concerned the personal idea is the real person. That is to say, it is in this alone that one man exists

for another, and acts directly upon his mind. My association with you evidently consists in the relation between my idea of you and the rest of my mind. If there is something in you that is wholly beyond this and makes no impression on me it has no social reality.... (Cooley, 1902:84)

The individual as a real person thus has no existence independent of the views of others, of other members of the collectivity. One sees in this statement by Cooley evidence of one of the two unique characteristics he attributed to human society: its thoroughly "mental nature." From Cooley's perspective, "The imaginations which people have of one another are the solid facts of society" (1902:87). Society lives in the minds of the members constituting the social unit, and this is precisely what makes the unit something very real as far as that unit's members are concerned: "In actuality, there is no 'mind of society,' but many different minds that exist through a sharing of expectations and patterns of behavior, thereby providing the 'glue' which holds the larger organization together" (Meltzer, Petras, and Reynolds, 1975:9). Cooley put the matter as follows:

Not in agreement but in organization, in the fact of reciprocal influence of causation among its parts, by virtue of which everything that takes place in it is connected with everything else, and so is an outcome of the whole. This differentiated unity of mental or social life . . . is what I mean . . . by social organization. (1909:4)

While this quotation, by equating mental and social life, again clearly reveals Cooley's mentalistic conception of society, he also tells us that society manifests a further distinctive characteristic: its "organic nature." A society possesses a structure, and that structure, in turn, displays the characteristics or properties of a complex organism:

It is a complex of forms of processes each of which is living or growing by interaction with the others, the whole thing being so unified that what takes place in one part affects all the rest. It is a vast tissue of reciprocal activity, differentiated into innumerable systems, some of them quite distinct, others not readily traceable, and all interwoven to such a degree that you see different systems according to the point of view you take. (Cooley, 1918:28)

One sees in all these quotations from Cooley concerning his view of the nature of human society that he has pulled off a rather novel feat: He has forcefully attacked both the individualistic and classical organic conceptions of society while retaining key elements of both. He focuses not on individuals but on social organization, but only as the organization is maintained in the imaginations or minds of individuals. He has simultaneously avoided the overpowering social determinism of the classic European organicists and the instinct or propensity driven human model of the hyperindividualists. Given such a conception of the nature of human collectivities, it is not difficult to see how Cooley was led to conclude that the individual and society are but two sides of the same coin. While Cooley has, in his theory of human society, managed to avoid the dangers inherent in both classic organicism and classic liberalism, his image of society is not without its shortcomings. As Stryker points out, it is Cooley's

> way of thinking about social relationships that has been criticized as solipsistic. That is, if imaginations are the solid facts of society, it seems to follow that there are as many societies as there are individual imaginations. If our imaginations differ, how can we get beyond these differences and to what do we refer these differences in order to build general knowledge of society? (1980:27)

Such limitations noted, Cooley nevertheless did something many sociologists fail to do: He developed a methodology compatible with his theory. If "the imaginations which people have of one another are the solid facts of society," it follows that in order to understand best both the nature of society and its workings one must somehow gain access to the "imaginations" of society's members. Furthermore, the sociologist must be certain that it is the imaginations of others that he or she is tapping, not just his or her own imagination imposed on the data. As imaginations are not directly accessible through the mere observation of external behavior, and as these imaginations are, in a sense, only accessible to those who experience them, Cooley put forth a methodology he labeled "sympathetic introspection." One sympathetically comes into contact with others of society's members, one strives to imagine as they imagine, one seeks to uncover the interpretations of and meanings attached to events and objects experienced by members of the collectivity. In short, one places oneself in contact with society's members and sympathetically tries to imagine life as these others live it. One then seeks to detail, describe, and understand the imagination of others, because these imaginations are the solid facts of society. It is not that nonmental factors play no role in influencing human conduct. They do, but from Cooley's perspective, these "material facts" are not nearly as important as those human bonds whose existence depends on the *ideas* society's members have of one another. These are what Cooley called "the social facts." If one would understand society, one must first understand the social facts. One comes to understand social facts by employing the methodology of sympathetic introspection. Given Cooley's views on the nature of human society and how best to approach it, he went on to construct two major concepts that better facilitated his task. These concepts have been of lasting value to symbolic interactionists; they are the *primary group* and the *looking-glass self*. Not only do these two concepts tie directly to Cooley's image of society, but they also fit in closely with his conception of human nature.

In Cooley's writings, the concepts of self and group are dynamically intertwined. The self develops in a group context, and the group that Cooley called the primary group is the real seat of self-development. Primary groups are triply important: They are the true building blocks for larger and more complex social forms and relationships; they are the mechanisms through which the self evolves; and they are the linkage points between individuals and the larger social order.

Cooley provides the following definition of primary groups:

> By primary groups I mean those characterized by intimate face-to-face association and co-operation. They are primary in several senses, but chiefly in that they are fundamental in forming the social nature of the ideals of individuals. (1909:23)

It is within such groups that the feeling of social unity is first experienced by the child. In the primary group, the person for the first time comes to identify himself or herself as a vital and necessary part of a social unit. Here emerges the sense of belonging that Cooley termed the "we" feeling. Among the more important primary groups are the neighborhood and play groups, and especially the family. From such groups, one's basic motivations as well as one's feelings of self-worth are taken.

As John Petras has pointed out, in Cooley's early works he spoke of three different levels at which human nature can be said to exist (Meltzer, Petras and Reynolds, 1975:11). The first level was largely hereditary in character. At the second level, Cooley dealt with the role played in the motivation of behavior by biology. This second level of human nature was essentially stable, being modified only slowly in an evolutionary process. Lastly, there is a level of human nature that is fundamentally social, and this third level was the object of much of Cooley's attention in his later writings. In speaking of human nature's third level, Petras has remarked:

> This is the human nature that develops with primary groups, and it is here that a link is provided between the three concepts of primary group, human nature, and looking-glass self. This is the human nature that is characterized not only by the acquisition of ethical standards, but, more importantly, by the development of a sense of self that reflects the definitions *of* the society as interpreted by the primary groups. At this level human nature is most flexible and, consequently, most susceptible to social influences. It is here that human nature can be seen in its principal aspect, that of *plasticity,* or what Cooley calls "teachability." (Meltzer, Petras and Reynolds, 1975: 11-12)

James Mark Baldwin argued that the child goes through three basic stages in the course of self-development: the projective, subjective, and ejective stages. Baldwin's theory concerning how the self develops influenced both Cooley and Mead in the formulation of their respective theories of the "self," and his theory is one of the earliest and most fruitful expositions on the "social self," on the self as a social product. Although few contemporary sociologists give Baldwin's views the attention they merit, a brief synopsis of them may be helpful here, as Cooley's theory of the looking-glass self owes much to Baldwin's insights.

During the first, or projective, stage of self-development, the child becomes aware or develops a consciousness of others. These others are then classified by the child according to the previous experiences he or she has had with them. A set of regular and sustained contacts with a specific person in the past triggers off quite a different group of perceptions and expectations in the person's presence than those that are given rise to when a still different person confronts the child. In this manner the child comes to distinguish between mother, father, sister, brother, and so on. In the projective stage, then, the child not only becomes aware of others but also begins to categorize these others (Baldwin, 1895).

In the subjective, or second, stage, self-consciousness begins to emerge. It emerges by the child's imitating the behavior of other persons and by then learning of the feeling states that go along with this behavior. In the ejective, or third, stage, the child becomes aware of the fact that others too have feelings. The child "ejects" his or her interpretations and feelings on to other persons. Such ejecting "represents an elementary form of empathy, and it provides a foundation on which Cooley's methodology of sympathetic introspection and Mead's theory of role-taking rest" (Meltzer, Petras and Reynolds, 1975:13). Furthermore, "These processes occur within the context of the 'dialectic of personal growth' that Baldwin believed characterized a lifetime give-and-take relationship constituting the individual and society bond" (Meltzer et al., 1975:13). In Baldwin's writings, then, are to be found ideas that impact on the later theories of both Mead and Cooley: ideas such as the ejecting process, which help lay a base for Cooley's methodology of sympathetic introspection, and the notion of the self as a social product, which foreshadows Cooley's concept of the looking-glass self.

How are we to view the self? Not in isolation. In *Human Nature and the Social Order,* Cooley (1902:91-92) put it as follows: "... there is no view of the self, that will bear examination, which makes it altogether distinct in our minds from other persons." The self, then, is an outgrowth of social interaction; it is developed and defined in the course of our interaction with others, especially other members of the "primary group."

From Cooley's vantage point, then, the self is a social product, a product "produced" largely in the primary group. It is a product best labeled a "looking-glass self," in that a child obtains an identity only with the realization that his or her picture, idea, or image of himself or herself "reflects" other people's picture of him or her. In Cooley's terms, what is reflected is the imaginations of others concerning the individual. The self resides in the minds of the members of the collectivity, or society; it constitutes an imaginative fact.

> Persons and society must be studied primarily in imagination. It is true, *prima facie,* that the best way of observing things is that which is most direct; and I do not see how we can hold that we know persons directly except as imaginative ideas in the mind. (1902:86)

The specific social reference for the self, notes Cooley,

> takes the form of a somewhat definite imagination of how one's self that is, any idea he appropriates appears in a particular mind, and the kind of self-feeling one has is determined by the attitude toward this attributed to the other mind. A social self of this sort might be called the reflected or looking-glass self. (1902:151-152)

More succinctly, Cooley (1902:152-153) states, "We always imagine, and in imagining, share, the judgments of the other mind." The social self depicted by Cooley has three basic ingredients: (1) our imagination of how we *appear* to others; (2) our imagination of how others *judge* our appearance; and (3) our resultant self-feelings, which are products of such imaginings. The above conceptualization of the self and the way it is formed has important consequences: "... there is and can be no individuality outside of the social order; individual personality is a 'natural' development from existing social life and the state of communication among the persons sharing that life; and, the expectations of others are central to this development" (Stryker, 1980:29). In the writings of Charles Horton Cooley, especially in his theories of self, society, and human nature, was much food for future interactionist thought.

W.I. Thomas

While Charles Horton Cooley was largely concerned with the process of self-acquisition and self-formation during the childhood years, William Isaac Thomas concentrated on the latter years. His interest in social disorganization and social change led him to be "primarily concerned with the processes through which the adult self came to be redefined" (Stryker, 1980:30). Thomas, among other things, was concerned with developing a theory of human motivation, and especially with developing a motivational theory that dealt directly with the dynamic interaction between the social and individual sources of conduct (Meltzer, Petras and Reynolds, 1975:23).

Thomas began by looking at instincts—sex and food instincts specifically as the most basic motivational elements in humans. He was then led to look at organic differences between the sexes as basic explanatory factors in behavior. Next he used the concept of "wishes" as the prime explanatory basis for human motivation. Lastly, he turned back to his earlier "definition of the situation" concept as the prime theoretical construct in his theory of motivation. The definition-of-the-situation concept is widely regarded as being the one direct link between W. 1. Thomas and the large, growing tradition of symbolic interactionism. However, as Martindale (1960:349) has pointed out, "At every critical point Thomas' affinities are with the pragmatists and symbolic interactionists." Furthermore, as John Petras has noted, Thomas, through his work with Znaniecki, provided "the first large-scale test of many of the propositions that had been developed with respect to the social nature of the self and the role of society in determining individual behavior" (Meltzer, Petras and Reynolds, 1975:22). Thomas's writings on self-society interrelationships, his focus on sympathetic introspection as a methodological tool, his emphasis on self redefinition in adulthood, and his advocacy of the utilization of personal documents and life histories in sociological research all have exerted a lasting impact on contemporary symbolic interactionism. Such contributions aside, the definition of the situation concept is Thomas's best-known addition to the conceptual inventory of the symbolic interactionists, and it is fitting to conclude this very brief discussion of his work by focusing on this concept.

According to W. 1. Thomas, in the course of carrying out the practical activities of everyday life, human beings act in what he termed an "as if" fashion. People always act in an "as if" manner, which is to say that "... there is an effort to define each of the paths of contemplated behavior on the basis of what will result if a person follows one path and not another" (Meltzer, Petras and Reynolds, 1975:27). The effort to define, and subsequent deliberation about, paths of potential behavior before carrying out self-determined behavior is what Thomas termed "the definition of the situation." A definition of the situation is formed prior to all "self-determined" action: "An adjustive effort of any kind is preceded by a decision to act or not to act along a given line and the decision is itself preceded by a *definition of the situation* (Thomas, 1937:8).

Very much like the pluralistic behaviorists, Thomas argued that it was the job of the sociologist to study adjustive responses of both individuals and collectivities to other persons and groups. Such adjustments transpire in social situations, and coming between these situations and adjustive responses to them are actors' definitions of the situation. As the same objective situation may lead to different behavior on the part of different persons, and even on the part of the same person on different occasions, Thomas concluded that people do not react to situations or facts in and of themselves. In a sense there are no facts in and of themselves: "Facts do not have a uniform existence apart from the persons who observe them. Rather, the 'real' facts are the ways in which different people come to define situations" (Volkhart, 1951: 30).

If sociologists are to deal, then, with the real facts of social life, they must come to grips with "definitions of the situation." These definitions are themselves the real facts of social life; they are the real forces shaping behavior because, as Thomas argued, "... if men define situations as real, they are real in their consequences" (1928:572).

None of this is to say that the objective situation itself is unimportant. Both the situation and people's definitions of it, both the "objective" and "subjective" facts of human experience, have to be dealt with by any adequate theory of human behavior. Thomas puts it as follows: "The total situation will always contain more and less subjective factors, and the behavior reaction can be studied only in connection with the whole context, i.e., the situation as it exists in verifiable, objective terms, and as it has seemed to exist in terms of the interested persons" (1928: 572).

So, while objective situations cannot be ignored, neither can people's subjective definitions of them. Both the "lifepolicies" of individuals as well as their personalities spring from constructed definitions of the situation. Many of the definitions taken on by the individual are, in fact, initially provided by others. Stryker argues as follows:

> Children ... are always born into an ongoing group that has developed definitions of the kinds of situations faced and has formulated rules of conduct premised on these definitions: moral codes are the outcome of "successive definitions of the situation." Children cannot create their own definitions independently of society, or behave in those terms without societal interference. And individual spontaneous definitions and societal definitions will always conflict to some extent. (1980:32)

Furthermore, "... social as well as personal disorganization are resultants of there being rival social definitions of the situation, none of them fully constraining the person" (1980:32).

All social situations, then, require as key explanatory variables definitions of the situation. When actors' definitions are not amenable to direct asssessment, some method for inferring them must be found. Thomas found such a method in those objects he called "personal documents," letters, case studies, autobiographies, and life histories. These were the sources that could be expected to reveal the "point of view," the "perspective," the "definition of the situation" of their authors and participants. These personal documents would, from Thomas's vantage point, be a major source of fruitful sociological hypotheses.

William Isaac Thomas, then, would endeavor to (1) explain the proper methodological approach to social life; (2) develop a theory of human motivation; (3) spell out a working conception of adult socialization; and (4) provide the correct perspective on deviance and disorganization. And he would do it all in reference to the definition-of-the-situation idea. In this particular concept he thought he had found one of the real keys necessary to unlock the secrets of human behavior. Apparently, many symbolic interactionists agree with his assessment.

REFERENCES

Baldwin, John D. 1985. "Social Behaviorism on Emotions: Mead and Modern Behaviorism Compared." *Symbolic Interaction*, 8:263-289.
Bodenhafer, W.B. 1920. "The Comparative Role of the Group Concept in Ward's *Dynamic Sociology* and Contemporary American Sociology." *American Journal of Sociology*, 26:425-474.
Cooley, Charles H. 1902. *Human Nature and Social Order*. New York: Scribner's.
———. 1909. *Social Organization*. New York: Scribner's.
———. 1918. *Social Process*. New York: Scribner's.
Meltzer, Bernard N., John W. Petras, and Larry T. Reynolds. 1975. *Symbolic Interactionism: Genesis, Varieties, and Criticism*. London: Routledge & Kegan Paul.
Stryker, Sheldon. 1980. *Symbolic Interactionism*. Melno Park, CA: Benjamin Cummings.
Thomas, W.I. 1937. *Primitive Behavior*. New York: McGraw-Hill.
Thomas, W.I. and Dorothy S. Thomas. 1928. *The Child in America*. New York: Knopf.
Volkhart, Edmund H. 1951. *Social Behavior and Personality*. New York: Social Science Research Council.

Chapter 3: MEAD'S SOCIAL PSYCHOLOGY

Bernard N. Meltzer

A. Preliminary Remarks

While Mead's system of Social Psychology is given its fullest exposition in *Mind, Self and Society*, each of three other books (as well as a few articles) rounds out the complete picture. It should be pointed out at this juncture that Mead himself published no full-length systematic statement of his theory. All four of the books bearing his authorship are posthumously collected and edited works. They comprise a loose accumulation of his lecture notes, fragmentary manuscripts, and tentative drafts of unpublished essays. Since the chief aim of his editors has been completeness—rather than organization—the books consist, in considerable part, of alternative formulations, highly repetitive materials, and sketchily developed ideas.

Nevertheless, a brief description of these volumes is in order, since they constitute the major source-materials concerning Mead's social psychology. *Philosophy of the Present* (1932) contains the Paul Carus Foundation lectures delivered by Mead in 1930, a year before his death. These lectures present a philosophy of history from the pragmatist's point of view. Moreover, this volume presents his ideas on the analogous developments of social experience and of scientific hypotheses.

Mind, Self and Society (1943) is chiefly a collection of lectures delivered to his classes in Social Psychology at the University of Chicago.

Movements of Thought in the 19th Century (1936) is largely a collection of lectures delivered to his classes in the History of Ideas.

Philosophy of the Act (1938), according to Paul Schilpp, represents a fairly systematic statement of the philosophy of pragmatism. This "systematic" statement I found (as did G. S. Lee) to be made up of essays and miscellaneous fragments, which are technical and repetitious, obscure and difficult.

A final observation regarding the content of these books should be made: Mead's orientation is generally *philosophical*. Rather than marshalling his own empirical evidence, he uses the findings of various sciences and employs frequent apt and insightful illustrations from everyday life. These illustrations usually are not used to provide points, but rather to serve as data to be analyzed in terms of his scheme.

Before launching upon a presentation of Mead's social psychological theories, it might be wise to explain his designation of his viewpoint as that of "Social Behaviorism." By this term Mead means to refer to the description of behavior at the distinctively human level. Thus, for social behaviorism, the basic datum is the social act. As we shall later see, the study of social acts entails concern with the covert aspects of behavior. Further, the concept of the "social act" implies that human conduct and experience has a fundamental social dimension—that the social context is an inescapable element in distinctively human actions.

Like Watsonian radical behaviorism, Mead's social behaviorism starts with the observable actions of individuals; but, *unlike* the former, social behaviorism conceives behavior in broad enough terms to include *covert* activity. This inclusion is deemed necessary to understanding the distinctive character of human conduct, which Mead considers a qualitatively different emergent from infrahuman behavior. Watson's behaviorism, on the other hand, reduces human behavior to the very same mechanisms as are found on the infrahuman level. As a corollary, Watson sees the social dimension of human behavior as merely a sort of external influence upon the individual. Mead, by contrast, views generically human behavior as *social* behavior, human acts as *social* acts. For Mead, both the content and the very existence of distinctively human behavior are accountable only on a social basis. (These distinctions should become more clear in the course of this report).

It can readily be inferred from this brief explanation of Mead's usage of the term "social behaviorism" that, before we can explore the nature and function of mind—which Mead considers a uniquely human attribute—supporting theories of society, and of self—another uniquely human attribute—require elaboration. Hence, the natural, logical order of Mead's thinking seems to have been society, self, and mind—rather than "Mind, Self, and Society."

B. Content of Mead's Social Psychology

1. Society

According to Mead, all group life is essentially a matter of cooperative behavior. Mead makes a distinction, however, between infrahuman society and human society. Insects—whose society most closely approximates the complexity of human social life—act together in certain ways because of their biological make-up. Thus, their cooperative behavior is physiologically determined. This is shown by many facts, among which is the fact of the fixity, the stability, of the relationships of insect-society members to one another: Insects, according to the evidence, go on for countless generations without any difference in their patterns of association. This picture of infrahuman society remains essentially valid as one ascends the scale of animal life, until we arrive at the human level.

In the case of human association, the situation is fundamentally different. Human cooperation is not brought about by mere physiological factors. The very diversity of the patterns of human group life makes it quite clear that human cooperative life cannot be explained in the same terms as the cooperative life of insects and the lower animals. The fact that human patterns are not stabilized and cannot be explained in biological terms led Mead to seek another basis of explanation of human association. Such cooperation can only be brought about by some process wherein: (a) each acting individual ascertains the intention of the acts of others, and then (b) makes his own response on the basis of that intention. What this means is that, in order for human beings to cooperate, there must be present some sort of mechanism whereby each acting individual: (a) can come to understand the lines of action of others, and (b) can guide his own behavior to fit in with those lines of action. Human behavior is not a matter of responding directly to the activities of others. Rather, it involves responding to the *intentions* of others, i.e., to the future, intended behavior of others—not merely to their present actions.

We can better understand the character of this distinctively human mode of interaction between individuals by contrasting it with the infrahuman "conversation of gestures." For example, when a mother hen clucks, her chicks will respond by running to her. This does not imply however, that the hen clucks *in order* to guide the chicks, i.e., with the *intention* of guiding them. Clucking is a natural sign or signal—rather than a significant (meaningful) symbol—as it is not meaningful to the hen. That is, the hen (according to Mead) does not take the role, or viewpoint, of the chicks toward its own gesture and respond to it, in imagination, as they do. The hen does not envision the response of the chicks to her clucking. Thus, hen and chicks do not share the same experience.

Let us take another illustration by Mead: Two hostile dogs, in the pre-fight stage, may go through an elaborate conversation of gestures (snarling, growling, baring fangs, walking stiff-leggedly around one another, etc.). The dogs are adjusting themselves to one another by responding to one another's gestures. (A gesture is that portion of an act which represents the entire act; it is the initial, overt phase of the act, which epitomizes it, e.g., shaking one's fist at someone.) Now, in the case of the dogs the response to a gesture is dictated by preestablished tendencies to respond in certain ways. Each gesture leads to a direct, immediate, automatic, and unreflecting response by the recipient of the gesture (the other dog). Neither dog responds to the *intention* of the gestures. Further, each dog does not make his gestures with the intent of eliciting certain responses in the other dog. Thus, animal interaction is devoid of conscious, deliberate meaning.

To summarize: Gestures, at the non-human, or non-linguistic level, do not carry the connotation of conscious meaning or intent, but serve merely as cues for the appropriate responses of others. Gestural communication takes place immediately, without any interruption of the act, without the mediation of a definition or meaning. Each organism adjusts "instinctively" to the other; it does not stop and figure out which response it will give. Its behavior is, largely, a series of direct, automatic responses to stimuli.

Human beings, on the other hand, respond to one another on the basis of the intentions or meanings of gestures. This renders the gestures *symbolic*, i.e., the gesture becomes a symbol to be interpreted; it becomes something which, in the imaginations of the participants, stands for the entire act.

Thus, individual A begins to act, i.e., makes a gesture: for example, he draws back an arm. Individual B (who perceives the gesture) completes, or fills in, the act in his imagination; i.e., B imaginatively projects the gesture into the future: "He will strike me." In other words, B perceives what the gesture stands for, thus getting its meaning. In contrast to the direct responses of the chicks and the dogs, the human being inserts an interpretation between the gesture of another and his response to it. Human behavior involves responses to *interpreted* stimuli.[1]

We see, then, that people respond to one another on the basis of imaginative activity. In order to engage in concerted behavior, however, each participating individual must be able to attach the same meaning to the same gesture. Unless interacting individuals interpret gestures similarly, unless they fill out the imagined portion in the same way, there can be no cooperative action. This is another way of saying what has by now become a truism in sociology and social psychology: Human society rests upon a basis of *consensus*, i.e., the sharing of meanings in the form of common understandings and expectations.

In the case of the human being, each person has the ability to respond to his own gestures: and, thus,.it is possible to have the same meaning for the gestures as other persons. (For example: As I say "chair," I present to myself the same image as to my hearer; moreover, the same image as when someone else says "chair.") This ability to stimulate oneself as one stimulates another, and to respond to oneself as another does, Mead ascribes largely to man's vocal-auditory mechanism. (The ability to hear oneself implies at least the potentiality for responding to oneself). When a gesture has a shared, common meaning, when it is—in other words—a *linguistic* element, we can designate it as a significant symbol." (Take the words, "Open the window": The pattern of action symbolized by these words must be in the mind of the speaker as well as the listener. Each must respond, in imagination to the words in the same way. The speaker must have an image of the listener responding to his words by opening the window, and the listener must have an image of his opening the window).

The imaginative completion of an act—which Mead calls "meaning" and which represents mental activity—necessarily takes place through *role-taking*. To complete imaginatively the total act which a gesture stands for, the individual must put himself in the position of the other person, must identify with him. The earliest beginnings of role-taking occur when an already established act of another individual is stopped short of completion, thereby requiring the observing individual to fill in or complete, the activity imaginatively. (For example, a crying infant may have an image of its mother coming to stop its crying).

As Mead points out, then, the relation of human beings to one another arises from the developed ability of the human being to respond to his own gestures. This ability enables different human beings to respond in the same way to the same gesture, thereby sharing one another's experience.

This latter point is of great importance. Behavior is viewed as "social" not simply when it is a response to others, but rather when it has incorporated in it the behavior of others. The human being responds to himself as other persons respond to him, and in so doing he imaginatively shares the conduct of others. That is, in imagining their response he shares that response.[2]

1. The foregoing distinctions can also be expressed in terms of the differences between "signs," or "signals," and symbols. A sign stands for something else because of the fact that it is present at approximately the same time and place with that "something else." A symbol, on the other hand, stands for something else because its users have agreed to let it stand for that "something else." Thus, signs are directly and intrinsically linked with present or approximate situations; while symbols, having arbitrary and conventional rather than intrinsic, meanings, transcend the immediate situation. (We shall return to this important point in our discussion of "mind.") Only symbols, of course, involve interpretation, self-stimulation and shared meaning

2. To anyone who has taken even one course in Sociology it is probably superfluous to stress the importance of symbols, particularly language, in the acquisition of all other elements of culture. The process of socialization is essentially a process of symbolic interaction.

2. Self

To state that the human being can respond to his own gestures necessarily implies that he possesses a *self*. In referring to the human being as having a self, Mead simply means that such an individual may act socially toward himself, just as toward others. He may praise, blame, or encourage himself; he may become disgusted with himself, may seek to punish himself, and so forth. Thus, the human being may become the object of his own actions. The self is formed in the same way as other objects—through the "definitions" made by others.

The mechanism whereby the individual becomes able to view himself as an object is that of role-taking, involving the process of communication, especially by vocal gestures or speech. (Such communication necessarily involves role-taking.) It is only by taking the role of others that the individual can come to see himself as an object. The standpoint of others provides a platform for getting outside oneself and thus viewing oneself. The development of the self is concurrent with the development of the ability to take roles.

The crucial importance of language in this process must be underscored. It is through language (significant symbols) that the child acquires the meanings and definitions of those around him. By learning the symbols of his groups, he comes to internalize their definitions of events or things, including their definitions of his own conduct.

It is quite evident that, rather than assuming the existence of selves and explaining, society thereby, Mead starts out from the prior existence of society as the context within which selves arise. This view contrasts with the nominalistic position of the Social Contract theorists and of various individualistic psychologies.

Genesis of the Self

The relationship between role-playing and various stages in the development of the self is described below:

1) *Preparatory Stage* (not explicitly named by Mead, but inferable from various fragmentary essays). This stage is one of meaningless imitation by the infant (for example, "reading" the newspaper). The child does certain things that others near it do without any understanding of what he is doing. Such imitation, however, implies that the child is incipiently taking the roles of those around it, i.e., is on the verge of putting itself in the position of others and acting like them.

2) *Play Stage* In this stage the actual playing of roles occurs. The child plays mother, teacher, storekeeper, postman, streetcar conductor, Mr. Jones, etc. What is of central importance in such play-acting is that it places the child in the position where it is able to act back toward itself in such roles as "mother" or "teacher." In this stage, then, the child first begins to form a self, that is, to direct activity toward itself—and it does so by taking the roles of others. This is clearly indicated by use of the third person in referring to oneself instead of the first person: "John wants...", "John is a bad boy." However, in this stage the young child's configuration of roles is unstable; the child

passes from one role to another in unorganized, inconsistent fashion. He has, as yet, no unitary standpoint from which to view himself, and hence, he has no unified conception of himself. In other words, the child forms a number of separate and discrete objects of itself, depending on the roles in which it acts toward itself.

3) *Game Stage* This is the "completing" stage of the self. In time, the child finds himself in situations wherein he must take a number of roles simultaneously. That is, he must respond to the expectations of several people at the same time. This sort of situation is exemplified by the game of baseball—to use Mead's own illustration: Each player must visualize the intentions and expectations of several-other players. In such situations the child must take the roles of groups of individuals as over against particular roles. The child becomes enabled to do this by abstracting a "composite" role out of the concrete roles of particular persons. In the course of his association with others, then, he builds up a *generalized other*, a generalized role or standpoint from which he views himself and his behavior. This generalized other represents, then, the set of standpoints which are common to the group.

Having achieved this generalized standpoint, the individual can conduct himself in an organized, consistent manner. He can view himself from a consistent standpoint. This means, then, that the individual can transcend the local and present expectations and definitions with which he comes in contact. An illustration of this point would be the Englishman who "dresses for dinner" in the wilds of Africa. Thus, through having a generalized other, the individual becomes emancipated from the pressures of the peculiarities of the immediate situation. He can act with a certain amount of consistency in a variety of situations because he acts in accordance with a generalized set of expectations and definitions that he has internalized.

The "I" and the "Me"

The self is essentially a social process within the individual involving two analytically distinguishable phases: The "I" and the "Me."

The "I" is the impulsive tendency of the individual. It is the initial, spontaneous, unorganized aspect of human experience. Thus, it represents the undirected tendencies of the individual. The "Me" represents the incorporated other within the individual. Thus, it comprises the organized set of attitudes and definitions, understandings and expectations—or simply meanings—common to the group. In any given situation, the "Me" comprises the generalized other and, often, some particular other.

Every act begins in the form of an "I" and usually ends in the form of the "Me." For the "I" represents the initiation of the act prior to its coming under control of the definitions or expectations of others (the "Me"). The "I" thus gives *propulsion* while the "Me" gives *direction* to the act. Human behavior, then, can be viewed as a perpetual series of initiations of acts by the "I" and of acting-back upon the act (that is, guidance of the act) by the "Me." The act is a resultant of this interplay.

The "I," being spontaneous and propulsive, offers the potentiality for new, creating activity. The "Me," being regulatory, disposes the individual to both goal-directed activity and conformity. In the operation of these aspects of the self, we have the basis for, on the one hand, social control and, on the other, novelty and innovation. We are thus provided with a basis for understanding the mutuality of the relationship between the individual and society.[1]

Implications of Selfhood

Some of the major implications of selfhood in human behavior are as follows:

1) The possession of a self makes of the individual a society in miniature. That is, he may engage in interaction with himself just as two or more different individuals might. In the course of this interaction, he can come to view himself in a new way, thereby bringing about changes in himself.

2) The ability to act toward oneself makes possible an inner experience which need not reach overt expression. That is, the individual, by virtue of having a self, is thereby endowed with the possibility of having a mental life: He can make indications to himself—which constitutes *mind*.

3) The individual with a self is thereby enabled to direct and control his behavior. Instead of being subject to all impulses and stimuli directly playing upon him, the individual can check, guide, and organize his behavior. He is, then, *not* a mere passive agent. All three of these implications of selfhood may be summarized by the statement that the self and the mind (mental activity) are twin emergents in the social process.

3. Mind

Development of Mind

As in the instance of his consideration of the self, Mead rejects individualistic psychologies, in which the social process (society, social interaction) is viewed as presupposing and being a product of, mind. In direct contrast is his view that mind presupposes, and is a product of, the social process. Mind is seen by Mead as developing correlatively with the self, constituting (in a very important sense) the self in action.

1. At first glance, Mead's "I" and "Me" may appear to bear a close affinity with Freud's Concepts of Id, Ego, and Superego. The resemblance is, for the most part, more apparent than real. While the superego is held to be harshly frustrating and repressive of the instinctual, libidinous, and aggressive Id, the "Me" is held to provide necessary direction—often of a gratifying nature—to the otherwise undirected impulses constituting the "I." Putting the matter in figurative terms Freud views the Id and the Superego as locked in combat upon the battleground of the Ego, Mead sees the "I" and "Me" engaged in close collaboration. This difference in perspective may derive from different preoccupations: Freud was primarily concerned with tension, anxiety, and "abnormal" behavior; Mead was primarily concerned with behavior generically. It is true, on the other hand, that the Id, Ego, and Superego—particularly as modified by such neo-Freudians as Karen Horney, Erich Fromm, and H. S. Sullivan converge at a few points with the "I" and "Me." This is especially evident in the emphasis of both the Superego and "Me" concepts upon the internalization of the norms of significant others through the process of identification, or role-taking. Incidentally, it should be noted that both sets of concepts refer to processes of behavior, not to concrete entities or structures. See also, the discussion of "mind" which follows.

Mead's hypothesis regarding mind (as regarding the self) is that the mental emerges out of the organic life of man through communication. The mind is present only at certain points in human behavior, viz., when significant symbols are being used by the individual. This view dispenses with the substantive notion of mind as existing as a box-like container in the head, or as some kind of fixed, ever-present entity. Mind is seen as a *process*, which manifests itself whenever the individual is interacting with himself by using significant symbols.

Mead begins his discussion of the mind with a consideration of the relation of the organism to its environment. He points out that the central principle in all organic behavior is that of continuous adjustment, or adaptation, to an environing field. We cannot regard the environment as having a fixed character for all organisms, as being the same for all organisms. All behavior involves selective attention and perception. The organism accepts certain events in its field, or vicinity, as stimuli and rejects or overlooks certain others as irrelevant to its needs. (For example, an animal battling for life ignores food.) Bombarded constantly by stimuli, the organism selects those stimuli or aspects of its field which pertain to, are functional to, the acts in which the organism is engaged. Thus, the organism has a hand in determining the nature of its environment. What this means, then, is that Mead, along with Dewey, regards all life as ongoing activity, and views stimuli—not as initiators of activity—but as elements selected by the organism in the furtherance of that activity.

Perception is thus an activity that involves selective attention to certain aspects of a situation, rather than a mere matter of something coming into the individual's nervous system and leaving an impression. Visual perception, e.g., is more than a matter of just opening one's eyes and responding to what falls on the retina.

The determination of the environment by the biologic individual (infrahumans and the unsocialized infant) is not a cognitive relationship. It is selective, but does not involve consciousness, in the sense of reflective intelligence. At the distinctively human level, on the other hand, there is a hesitancy, an inhibition of overt conduct, which is not involved in the selective attention of animal behavior. In this period of inhibition, mind is present.

For, human behavior involves inhibiting an act and trying out the varying approaches in imagination. In contrast, as we have seen, the acts of the biologic individual are relatively immediate, direct, and made up of innate or habitual ways of reacting. In other words, the unsocialized organism lacks consciousness of meaning. This being the case, the organism has no means for the abstract analysis of its field when new situations are met, and hence no means for the reorganization of action-tendencies in the light of that analysis.[1]

Minded behavior (in Mead's sense) arises around problems. It represents, to repeat an important point, a temporary inhibition of action wherein the individual is attempt-

---

1. The reader should recognize here, in a new guise, our earlier distinction between signs and symbols. Signs have "intrinsic" meanings which induce direct reactions; symbols have arbitrary meanings which require interpretations by the actor prior to his response or action. The former, it will be recalled, are "tied to" the immediate situation, while the latter "transcend" the immediate situation. Thus, symbols may refer to past or future events, to hypothetical situations, to nonexistent or imaginary objects, and so forth.

ing to prevision the future. It consists of presenting to oneself, tentatively and in advance of overt behavior, the different possibilities or alternatives of future action with reference to a given situation. The future is thus, present in terms of images of prospective lines of action from which the individual can make a selection. The mental process is, then, one of delaying, organizing, and selecting a response to the stimuli of the environment. This implies that the individual *constructs* his act, rather than responding in predetermined ways. Mind makes it possible for the individual purposively to control and organize his responses. Needless to say, this view contradicts the stimulus-response conception of human behavior.

When the act of an animal is checked, it may engage in overt trial and error or random activity. In the case of blocked human acts, the trial and error may be carried on covertly, implicitly. Consequences can be imaginatively "tried out" in advance. This is what is primarily meant by "mind," "reflective thinking," or "abstract thinking."

What this involves is the ability to indicate elements of the field or situation, abstract them from the situation, and recombine them so that procedures can be considered in advance of their execution. Thus, to quote a well-known example, the intelligence of the detective as over against the intelligence of the bloodhound lies in the capacity of the former to isolate and indicate (to himself and to others) what the particular characters are which will call out the response of apprehending the fugitive criminal.

The mind is social in both origin and function. It arises in the social process of communication. Through association with the members of his groups, the individual comes to internalize the definitions transmitted to him through linguistic symbols, learns to assume the perspectives of others, and thereby acquires the ability to think. When the mind has risen in this process, it operates to maintain and adjust the individual in his society; and it enables the society to persist. The persistence of a human society depends, as we have seen, upon consensus; and consensus necessarily entails minded behavior.

The mind is social in function in the sense that the individual continually indicates to himself in the role of others and controls his activity with reference to the definitions provided by others. In order to carry on though, he must have some standpoint from which to converse with himself. He gets this standpoint by importing into himself the role of others.

By "taking the role of the other," as I earlier pointed out—we can see ourselves as others see us, and arouse in ourselves the responses that we call out in others. It is this conversation with ourselves, between the representation of the other (in the form of the "Me") and our impulses (in the form of the "I") that constitutes the mind. Thus, what the individual actually does in minded behavior is to carry on an internal conversation. By addressing himself from the standpoint of the generalized other, the individual has a universe of discourse, a system of common symbols and meanings, with which to address himself. These are presupposed as the context for minded behavior.

Mead holds, then, that mental activity is a peculiar type of activity that goes on in the experience of the person. The activity is that of the person responding to himself, of indicating things to himself.

To repeat, mind originates in the social process, in association with others. There is little doubt that human beings lived together in groups before mind ever evolved. But, there emerged, because of certain biological developments, the point where human beings were able to respond to their own acts and gestures. It was at this point that mind, or minded behavior, emerged. Similarly, mind comes into existence for the individual at the point where the individual is capable of responding to his own behavior, i.e., where he can designate things to himself.

Summarizing this brief treatment of mind, mental activity, or reflective thinking, we may say that it is a matter of making indications of meanings to oneself as to others. This is another way of saying that mind is the process of using significant symbols. For, thinking goes on when an individual uses a symbol to call out in himself the responses which others would make. Mind, then is symbolic behavior.[1] As such, mind is an emergent from non-symbolic behavior and is fundamentally irreducible to the stimulus-response mechanisms which characterize the latter form of behavior.

It should be evident that Mead avoids both the behavioristic fallacy of reduction and the individualistic fallacy of taking for granted the phenomenon that is to be explained.

Objects

Returning to Mead's discussion of the organism-in-environment, we can now give more explicit attention to his treatment of *objects*. As we have seen, we cannot regard the environment as having a fixed character for all organisms. The environment is a function of the animal's own character, being greatly determined by the make-up of the animal. Each animal largely selects its own environment. It selects out the stimuli toward which it acts, its make-up and on-going activity determining the kinds of stimuli it will select. Further, the qualities which are possessed by the objects toward which the animal acts arise from the kind of experiences that the animal has with the objects. (To illustrate, grass is not the same phenomenon for a cat and for a cow). The environment and its qualities, then, are always functional to the structure of the animal.

As one passes on to the human level, the relation of the individual to the world becomes markedly more complicated. This is so because the human being is capable of forming objects. Animals, lacking symbols, see stimuli, such as patches of color—not objects. An object has to be detached, pointed out, "imaged" to oneself. The human being's environment is constituted largely by objects.

---

1. The contrast between this view of learning and the neo-behavioristic "learning theory" of Clark Hull and other psychologists should be clearly evident. Basically, learning theorists attempt to reduce human learning to the mechanisms found in infrahuman learning. This is reflected in their tendency to ignore the role of linguistic symbols in human behavior, their conceptualization of human activity in terms of stimulus-response couplets, and their view of learning as equivalent with conditioning. (For an excellent critique of learning theory from the symbolic interactionist standpoint, see: Manford H. Kuhn, "Kinsey's View of Human Behavior," *Social Problems*, 1 (April 1954), pp. 119-125).

Now, let us look at the relation of the individual to objects. An object represents a plan of action. That is, an object doesn't exist for the individual in some pre-established form. Perception of any object has telescoped in it a series of experiences which one would have if he carried out the plan of action toward that object. The object has no qualities for the individual, aside from those which would result from his carrying out of a plan of action. In this respect, the object is constituted by one's activities with reference to it. (For example, chalk is the sum of qualities which are perceived as a result of one's actions: a hard, smooth, white, writing implement).

The objects which constitute the "effective environment," the individual's experienced environment, are established by the individual's activities. To the extent that his activity varies, his environment varies. In other words, objects change as activities toward them change. (Chalk, for instance, may become a missile).

Objects, which are constituted by the activities of the human individual, are largely *shared* objects. They stand for common patterns of activity of individuals. This is true, Mead points out, by virtue of the fact that objects arise, and are present in experience, only in the process of being indicated to oneself (and, hence, explicitly or implicitly, to others). In other words, the perspective from which one indicates an object implicates definitions by others. Needless to say, these definitions involve language, or significant symbols. The individual acquires a commonality of perspective with others by learning the symbols by which they designate aspects of the world.

4. The Act

All human activity other than reflex and habitual action is built up in the process of its execution; i.e., behavior is constructed as it goes along, for decisions must be made at several points. The significance of this fact is that people act—rather than merely reacting.

For Mead, the unit of study is "the act," which comprises both overt and covert aspects of human action. Within the act, all the separated categories of the traditional, orthodox psychologies find a place. Attention, perception, imagination, reasoning, emotion, and so forth, are seen as parts of the act—rather than as more or less extrinsic influences upon it. Human behavior presents itself in the form of acts, rather than of concatenations of minute responses.

The act, then, encompasses the total process involved in human activity. It is viewed as a complete span of action: its initial point is an impulse and its terminal point some objective which gives release to the impulse. In between, the individual is in the process of constructing, organizing his behavior. It is during this period that the act undergoes its most significant phase of development. In the case of human behavior, this period is marked by the play of images of possible goals or lines of action upon the impulse, thus directing the activity to its consummation.

In pointing out that the act begins with an impulse, Mead means that organisms experience disturbances of equilibrium. In the case of the lower animals, their biological make-up channelizes the impulse toward appropriate goals. In the case of the human being, the mere presence of an impulse leads to nothing but mere random, unorganized activity. This is most clearly—but definitely not exclusively—seen in the instance of the behavior of infants. Until the defining actions of others set up goals for it, the human infant's behavior is unchannelized. It is the function of images to direct, organize and construct this activity. The presence in behavior of images implies, of course, a process of indicating to oneself, or mind.

The act may have a short span (e.g., attending a particular class meeting, or starting a new page of notes) or may involve the major portion of a person's life (e.g., trying to achieve a successful career). Moreover, acts are parts of an interlacing of previous acts, and are built up, one upon another. This is in contradistinction to the view that behavior is a series of discrete stimulus-response bonds. Conceiving human behavior in terms of acts, we become aware of the necessity for viewing any particular act within its psychosocial context.[1] Using the concept of the act, Mead sets up classes of acts— the automatic act, the blocked act, the incomplete act, and the retrospective act—and analyzes them in terms of his frame of reference. Space does not permit presentation of these intriguing analyses.

C. Summary

At several points in this report the reader must have been aware of the extremely closely interwoven character of Mead's various concepts. In the discussions of society, of self, and of mind, certain ideas seemed to require frequent (and, perhaps, repetitious) statement. A brief summary of Mead's position may help to reveal more meaningfully the way in which his key concepts interlock and logically imply one another.

The human individual is born into a society characterized by *symbolic interaction*. The use of *significant symbols* by those around him enables him to pass from the conversation of gestures—which involves direct, unmeaningful response to the overt acts of others—to the occasional *taking of the roles* of others. This role-taking enables him to share the perspectives of others. Concurrent with role-taking, the *self* develops, i.e., the capacity to act toward oneself. Action toward oneself comes to take the form of viewing oneself from the standpoint, or perspective, of the *generalized* other (the composite representative of others, of society, within the individual), which implies defining one's behavior in terms of the expectations of others. In the process of such viewing of oneself, the individual must carry on symbolic interaction with himself, involving an internal conversation between his impulsive aspect (the "I") and the

---

1. The reader may have noted that this discussion makes no explicit reference to the problem of motivation. Mead had little to say regarding motives. Adherents to his general orientation have tended either to regard motives as implicit in the concept of object ("a plan of action") or to consider them "mere" verbal labels offered in supposed explanation of the actions of oneself or of others. In my judgment, a conception of motivation can be formulated that is both useful and consistent with Mead's theories. Motivation can refer to "a process of defining (symbolically, of course) the goal of an act." Thus, while both human and infrahuman behavior may be viewed as goal-directed, only human behavior would be considered "motivated." Just as "motive" would be restricted to the human level, "drive" might serve a comparable function on the infrahuman level. This would not imply that motives lie back of, or "cause," human acts Rather, human acts are in constant process of construction, and the goal definitions by individuals undergo constant reformulation. I mean to designate by "motive," however, the definition the individual makes, at any given time, of the objectives of his own specific acts. Such definitions, obviously would be socially derived.

incorporated perspectives of others (the "Me"). The *mind*, or mental activity, is present in behavior whenever such symbolic interaction goes on—whether the individual is merely "thinking" (in the everyday sense of the word) or is also interacting with another individual. (In both cases the individual must indicate things to himself.) Mental activity necessarily involves *meanings*, which usually attach to, and define, objects. The meaning of an object or event is simply an image of the pattern of action which defines the object or event. That is, the completion in one's imagination of an act, or the mental picture of the actions and experiences symbolized by an object, defines the act or the object. In the unit of study that Mead calls "the *act*," all of the foregoing processes are usually entailed. The concluding point to be made in this summary is the same as the point with which I began: Mead's concepts intertwine and mutually imply one another. To drive home this important point, I must emphasize that human society (characterized by symbolic interaction) both precedes the rise of individual selves and minds and is maintained by the rise of individual selves and minds. This means, then, that symbolic interaction is both the medium for the development of human beings and the process by which human beings associate as human beings.

Finally, it should be clearly evident by now that any distinctively human act necessarily involves: symbolic interaction, role-taking, meaning, mind, and self. Where one of these concepts is involved, the others are, also, necessarily involved. Here we see, unmistakably, the organic unity of Mead's position.

III. EVALUATION

A. Critique

In criticizing Mead's social psychology, it should be borne in mind that he gave his position no extended systematic write-up: that most of the published material which forms the basis of our knowledge of that position was not originally intended for publication, at least not in the form in which it has been printed and that the various alternative statements of that position that appear in his posthumous works sometimes carry conflicting particulars. Still, we can evaluate only on the basis of the available, published materials.

1. Many of Mead's major concepts are somewhat vague and "fuzzy," necessitating an "intuitive" grasp of their meaning. This vagueness stems, I believe, primarily from two sources: (1) the fragmentary and alternative formulations of his idea; and (2) his emergent view of human conduct, which inescapably entangles him in the necessity of striking a balance between the continuity of infrahuman and human behavior, on the one hand, and the novelty of human behavior, on the other.

(a) For example, the exact nature of "impulses" is not clearly specified. Whether impulses are biological in character, or can also be socially-derived, is not clear from Mead's exposition. However, the contexts in which the term sometimes appears suggest that the latter interpretation would be more valid and useful.

(b) Similarly, the intertwined concepts of "meaning" and of "mind" are not consistently employed. At times, these terms are used generically, applying to both infrahuman and human levels of behavior, and at times specifically, applying only at the level of self-conscious human conduct. Fortunately, the context of each usage usually provides a key to Mead's intended meanings.

(c) Coincident with Mead's varying referents of "mind" and of "meaning," we find his vacillation between a restriction of role-taking ability to the human level (in symbolic interaction) and his granting of that ability to infrahuman animals (in the conversation of gestures). Again, we are fortunate in having his distinction between self-conscious role-playing and unwitting role-playing. The reader of Mead must bear in mind that the latter type of "role-playing" is not what Mead usually has in mind when he employs the concept.

(d) The concept of the "I," as William Kolb indicates, represents a vaguely-defined residual category. Mead clearly specifies the nature of the "Me," but, in effect, labels the "I" as simply the not-Me aspect of the self. As in the case of the very closely related concept of "impulse," Mead does not indicate the limits of the "I." From his discussion, the "I" would seem, however—and this is an inference—to include everything from biological urges to the effects of individual variations in life-history patterns. Still, as Barnes and Becker point out, the "I" serves the very useful purpose of evading a complete collective, or sociological, determinism of human conduct.

The ambiguity of the concept of the "I" also reveals itself in the various discussions in the secondary literature on Mead's treatment of habitual behavior. For some writers, habitual acts represent manifestations of the operation of the "I" alone; for others, of the "Me" alone; and for still others, a fusion of the "I" and the "Me."

(e) The concept of "self" also lacks clear, unambiguous definition in Mead's work. A certain amount of confusion enters the picture when the self is defined in terms of "the individual's viewing himself as an object." This confusion is not at all dissipated by Mead's tendency to vary between, on the one hand, synonymous usages of "self" and "self-consciousness" and on the other hand, slightly different usages of these two terms.

(f) Mead's concept of the "generalized other" needs sharpening. He oversimplifies the concept by assuming, apparently, a single, universal generalized other for the members of each society—rather than a variety of generalized others (even for the same individuals), at different levels of generality.[1] The inadequacy of his concept is clearly shown in his characterization of the criminal as one who "has not taken on the attitude of the generalized other toward property, (and who therefore) lacks a completely developed self." Such a characterization overlooks, of course, the sociogenic elements in crime causation.

(g) A final case of vagueness of conceptualization that we shall consider relates to Mead's usages of "object" and "image." Both of these are described as "telescopedacts," and both are used at times interchangeably and at times slightly differently. It is probably safe to infer that images are the mental representations of objects, i.e., that

---

1. Current work on "reference groups" has served to remedy this deficiency. True, several competing definitions of this concept are extant. I have in mind, however, the conception of reference groups as collections of "significant others," that is, of persons with whom a given individual identifies and who, therefore, have a significant influence upon his personality.

images are the imaginative projections of the acts which define objects. Other sources of ambiguity lie in Mead's varying uses of the concepts of "attitude," "gesture," and "symbol;" his vacillation between, on the one hand, ascribing objects and images to the infrahuman level of behavior and, on the other hand, denying them to that level; etc. All of these ambiguities and inconsistencies reflect chiefly the confusion engendered by publication of all the alternative formulations of Mead's ideas—the early formulations along with the later. The thoughtful and assiduous reader of Mead, however, should be able to abstract out some single, fairly consistent statement of Mead's position.

2. A second series of adverse criticisms centers around certain broad substantive omissions in Mead's theory.

(a) Mead's position, as Blumer states, constitutes a purely analytical scheme, which lacks content. That is, he presents an analysis of human conduct in terms of the mechanisms of development of such conduct, but indicates few ingredients of that conduct. In concerning himself wholly with process, but not content, with the "how" but not the "why" of conduct, he provides no basis for explaining specific behaviors. For example, he gives no clues as to why one object rather than another will be formed by an individual or group. Thus, his scheme, as it stands, has no explanatory value with reference to such matters as the rise of particular popular heroes, or the high valuation of money, or the myth of Santa Claus.

(b) Related to this "error" of omission is Mead's virtual ignoring of the role of affective elements in the rise of the self and in social interaction generally. The importance of the sentiments and emotions manifested in personal relationships are given no recognition in Mead's position. This lack is supplied—perhaps, oversupplied—in Cooley's work.

(c) Nothing in Mead's theory enables a clear stand on the matter of the nature (or even existence) of the unconscious, or subconscious, and the related mechanisms of adjustment.

3. Mead's position can also be criticized from a third and final general standpoint, that of methodology.

(a) First of all, Mead's theory, for the most part, does not seem to be highly researchable. As yet, little truly significant research has been conducted chiefly in terms of his frame of reference. Recent efforts to measure self-conceptions may help to remedy this deficiency.

(b) Mead, himself, gives no explicit formulation as to how his analytical scheme can be used in research. He makes no specific recommendations as to the techniques appropriate to the study of human behavior.

(c) As I indicated earlier in this report, Mead presents no systematic evidence for his position. Nevertheless, many social psychologists find his theory highly congruent with the experiences of everyday life—something which cannot be as readily said for a number of competing positions.

B. Positive Contribution

The extent of Mead's contribution to social psychology can be only roughly gauged by reference to the work of other adherents of the Symbolic Interactionist approach. Among the more eminent sociologists and social psychologists influenced by his viewpoint are: Cooley, Thomas, Park, Burgess, E. Faris, and Blumer. Some of the textbooks which incorporate his position are: in sociology, those by Park and Burgess, Dawson and Gettys, Francis Merrill, Kingsley Davis; in social psychology, Lindesmith and Strauss, M. Sherif, T. Newcomb, Walter Coutu, and Hubert Bonner. In addition, the recent interests in "role theory," "reference-group theory," and "self-theory" represent, basically, derivatives of Symbolic Interactionism.

Mead's substantive contribution has converged with, or at least has found some parallels in, certain methodological positions in modern sociology and social psychology. Such positions are those in which study of the inner, subjective part of the act is deemed indispensable. Methodologies of this sort are indicated by (1) Thomas' concept of 'definition of the situation," (2) Cooley's "sympathetic introspection," (3) Weber's "*Verstehen*," (4) Znaniecki's "humanistic coefficient," (5) MacIver's "dynamic assessment," (6) Sorokin's "logico-meaningful analysis," and other references to the covert aspects of human conduct.

Mead's more specific contributions can be only briefly listed in this report:

1. He contributed to the increasing acceptance of the view that human conduct is carried on primarily by the defining of situations in which one acts; that is, the view that distinctively human behavior is behavior in terms of what situations *symbolize*. This is the essence of the Symbolic Interactionist viewpoint.

2. Adopting a distinctly sociological perspective, he helped direct attention to the fact that mind and self are not biologically given, but are social emergents.

3. He delineated the way in which language serves as a mechanism for the appearance of mind and self.

4. His concept of the "self" explains how the development, or socialization, of the human being both enmeshes the individual in society and frees him from society. For the individual with a self is not passive, but can employ his self in an interaction which may result in selections divergent from group definitions.

5. An extremely provocative conception of the nature of the human mind is provided by him: He views mind, or the mental as an importation within the individual of the social process, i.e., of the process of social interaction.

6. His concept of the "act" points out the tendency for individuals to construct their behavior in the course of activity and, thus, to "carve out" their objects, their environments. What this means is that human beings are not passive puppets who respond mechanically to stimuli. They are, rather, active participants in a highly organized society, and what they perceive is functional in their ongoing activity. This theoretical position implies the importance of acquired predispositions (interests, values, etc.) and of the social context of behavior. It points to the influential significance of the group settings in which perceptions occur, and also places the meaning of what is perceived in the context of the ongoing activities of persons. This leads directly into the next contribution by Mead.

7. He described how the members of a human group develop and form a common world, i.e., common objects, common understandings and expectations.

8. He illuminated the character of social interaction by showing that human beings *share* one another's behavior instead of merely responding to each other's overt, external behavior as do infrahuman organisms. As a concluding and over-all evaluation of Mead as a contributor to social psychology, I can do no better than to repeat Dewey's oft-quoted appraisal: "His was a seminal mind of the first order."

Chapter 4 THEORETICAL AND IDEOLOGICAL VARIATIONS IN CONTEMPORARY INTERACTIONISM

John W. Petras and *Bernard N. Meltzer*

During the past few years there has been growing evidence for the view that symbolic interactionism is not a homogenous or monolithic orientation as portrayed in the minds of many contemporary American sociologists.[1] Our purpose in this paper is to give a brief overview of the more significant theoretical and ideological varieties currently found within interactionism. We have identified four major varieties: the Chicago school, the Iowa school, The Dramaturgical Approach, and Ethnomethodology.

The Chicago and Iowa Schools[2]

During the past twenty-five years, the two leading exponents of the symbolic interaction perspective have been Herbert Blumer and the late Manford H. Kuhn. Blumer, through his writings and his students at Chicago and Berkeley, has developed the best known variety of interactionism—an approach that we have labelled the "Chicago school." This orientation is characterized primarily by its insistence upon following the theoretical framework laid down by George Herbert Mead, with a secondary emphasis upon methodological structures. The "Iowa school" developed through the works of Kuhn and his students at the State University of Iowa. This orientation represents a more eclectic form of interactionism, with primary emphasis placed upon the operationalization and empirical verification of interactionist concepts.

Those interactionists sharing the orientation of the Chicago school tend to define some form of sympathetic introspection as the only "true" method for understanding human behavior from the viewpoint of the actor. In this view, the image of man—a symbol-using organism—prescribes an approach to the study of human behavior quite different from that used in the natural sciences. This orientation, however, does not characterize the mainstream of American sociology. As Blumer notes:

> The overwhelming bulk of what passes today as methodology is made up of sophisticated research techniques, usually of an advanced statistical character; the construction of logical and mathematical models, all too frequently guided by a criterion of elegance; the elaboration of formal schemes on how to construct concepts and theories; valiant application of imported schemes as input-output analysis, systems analysis, and stochastic analysis; studious conformity to the canons of research design; and the promotion of a particular procedure, such as survey research, as *the* method of scientific study. I marvel at the supreme confidence with which these preoccupations are advanced as the stuff of methodology.[3]

On the other hand, Kuhn has written that the key contribution of the Iowa research has been the demonstration that, "the key ideas of symbolic interactionism could be operationalized and utilized successfully in empirical research."[4]

In his works and lectures, Kuhn reiterated a call for work that would meet the "usual scientific criteria."[5] While not denying the covert facets of human behavior, the Iowa school has always emphasized that objective and empirically verifiable indices can and should be taken as indicators of the subjective. For example, Kuhn defined the self as "answers which an individual gives to the question which he directs to himself, `Who am I?' or to the question another directs to him, 'What kind of person are you?', Who are you?, etc."[6]

By building explicitly upon the works of Mead, members of the Chicago school, and, in particular, Blumer, have developed an image of man that incorporates the idea of an impulsive, spontaneous component in behavior. This is most often conceptualized as the "I." Accordingly, it is believed to be essential that any attempt to understand human behavior include an awareness of this non-determinate phase of human behavior. In other words, the image of man arising from the Meadian tradition dictates a special type of data—human beings.

Members of the Iowa school, especially in conjunction with Kuhn's self-theory, tend to make no explicit mention of the human side of human behavior at either the biological or social level. Behavior, for Kuhn, is determined—as in conventional role theory—by one's definitions of himself and the definitions placed upon him by others. The self is defined solely in terms of the "Me." This is extended into another major distinction between these two varieties of interactionism, a distinction between process and structure.

Basically, the argument here is whether the self is a process that must be studied within a framework of emergence, or whether it can adequately be conceptualized as an organized set of self and other attitudes. The latter view provides the basis for Kuhn's use of the Twenty Statements Test as an indicator of the individual's self-concept. Kuhn writes:

> As self theory views the individual, he derives his plans of action from the roles he plays and the statuses he occupies in the groups with which he feels identified—his reference groups. His attitudes toward himself as an object are the best indexes to these plans of action, and hence to the action itself, in that they are the anchoring points from which self-evaluations and other evaluations are made.[7]

On the other hand, Blumer maintains a position that is characteristically Meadian and summarizes his view as follows:

> Instead of being merely an organism that responds to the play of factors on or through it, the human being...has to deal with what it notes by engaging in a process of self-indication in which it makes an object of what it notes, gives it a meaning, and uses the meaning as the basis for directing this action.[8]

Thus, while both Blumer and Kuhn label themselves as "interactionists," they choose to accentuate very different qualities of the self in theory and research. Blumer has always emphasized the deliberative element, out of which a "new" image emerges. Kuhn approaches the self as a structured set of attitudes and responses that tend to coincide with prescribed role patterns.

In summary, the members of the Chicago school, led by Herbert Blumer, have emphasized a strict adherence to the principal ideas of George Herbert Mead and his image of man. Members of this school tend to be more interested in the accuracy with which research reflects the picture of man portrayed by this image than they are with the development and refinement of research techniques that might provide empirical verification of basic interactionist concepts. The members of the Iowa school, led by the late Manford Kuhn, have emphasized an equally strict adherence to the principles of the natural-scientific method. The members of this school focus more upon the necessity of obtaining empirical verification of the concepts of interactionism than upon compatibility with an abstract philosophical description of man. In the former, man is portrayed as deliberative; the latter sees man as determined.

The Dramaturgical Approach

The major exponent of the dramaturgical approach has been Erving Goffman. At Chicago, he was exposed to Blumer, Hughes, and Warner (as well as other mentors) and, through them, to the influential ideas of Mead, Durkheim, and Simmel. From these latter, he appears to have derived the inspiration for his views on the reality-constructing behavior of humans, the pervasive significance of ceremony and ritual in human social life, and the value of a "formal" orientation that overlooks historical specificities in a quest for universal generalizations. Both methodologically and substantively, his approach shows greater affinity for the Chicago than for the Iowa school. Commenting upon a related fact, Lofland refers to Goffman's prolific invention of "mini-concepts" and credits (or blames) the "conceptually impoverished" symbolic interactionist tradition at the University of Chicago in the late 'forties and early 'fifties.[9]

Goffman's dramaturgical metaphor has as its point of departure the premise that when human beings interact each desires to "manage" the impressions the others receive of him. Each, in effect, must put on a "show" for the others. As Goffman puts it in the preface to his first monograph in the "life as theater" vein:

> The perspective employed in this report is that of the theatrical performance, the principles derived are dramaturgical ones. I shall consider the way in which the individual...presents himself and his activity to others, the ways in which he guides and controls the impression they form of him, and the kinds of things he may and may not do while sustaining his performance before them.[10]

Thus, interactionists give "performances," during which they enact "parts," or "routines," which make use of a "setting" and "props," as well as both the "front region" of the "scene" and the "backstage" (hidden from the "audience"). The result of each performance is the imputation by the audience of a particular kind of self to the performed character. Such imputation is as much, or more a product of the expressive, ritualistic, or ceremonial, elements in the actor's behavior as of the instrumental, or substantive, elements.

"Information about the individual," Goffman points out, "helps to define the situation, enabling others to know in advance what he will expect of them and what they may expect of him."[11] It is to the individual's advantage, of course, to present himself in ways that will serve his ends. In Goffman's analysis, then, the self becomes something about which we wish to foster an impression.

Goffman's scheme of imagery suggests, to many, a sordid view of man and society, one marked by both duplicity and despair. This view, it is contended, celebrates the subordination of reality to appearance, of *Gemeinschaft* to pseudo-*Gemeinschaft*, of morality to opportunism. Thus, commentators refer to Goffman's view of man as "an amoral merchant of morality," or as a "detached, rational impression-manager," and of "the self as pure commodity." This conception of Goffman's imagery is cleverly described by Lyman and Scott:

> Goffman's social actor, like Machiavelli's prince, lives externally. He engages in a daily round of impression management, presenting himself to advantage when he is able, rescuing what he can from a bad show. His everyday life consists of interaction rituals, employing defence and demeanor, saving his own and someone else's face, inhibiting actions that would spoil the fun in games, being intimate when occasion demands, maintaining his distance when proximity would be unwise, and in general being continuously alive to the requirements of behavior in public places.[12]

Goffman's predecessors in the symbolic interactionist perspective gave no extensive attention to insecurity, hypocrisy, or unauthentic self-presentations. In his analysis we find, in effect, a significant reconstruction of the image of man in symbolic interactionism. We shall essay a possible explanation of this reconstruction in later paragraphs.

Messinger, Sampson, and Towne, however, challenge the foregoing interpretation of Goffman's imagery, contending that the dramaturgic analyst does not consider the theatrical model as representing his subjects' view of the world. Rather, the dramaturgical frame of reference is a device used by the analyst to focus upon the effects of the actor's behavior upon the perceptions of him by others. Whatever the actor's beliefs about what he is doing, the dramaturgist attends to the impression the actor has upon others. The analyst's frame of reference, then, may or may not comport with the frame of reference used by the actor in viewing his own conduct. As a matter of fact, the strength of dramaturgical analysis may reside in the discrepancy between the two frames of reference. Such discrepancy may enable the analyst to elucidate matters of which his subjects are unaware. Specifically, he may then reveal the way in which interactionists construct through their own acts the "reality" that they "take for granted" is "out there."[13]

From another quarter, some critics have questioned Goffman's concept of the functional necessity of "performances" in the maintenance of social order.[14] The increasing informality of modern interpersonal relationships and the erosion of rank in contemporary America raise doubts about the degree to which such ceremonies are essential to social life. In any event, there appears to be good reason to doubt the ubiquity of cool, calculating impression-management.

How does Goffman come by his image of man in society? A good case can be made for linking the genesis and popular appeal of the dramaturgical approach to the changing character of American society. Mass society, with its mass production, mass marketing, and mass manipulation of tastes, directs sociological attention to social appearances. As Martindale puts it:

> Since the days of James, Cooley, and Mead, the full implications of mass society have gradually become clear....The old intimacy of small town image and incident disappears as the elaborate complexities of the mass society are presupposed. The analysis shifts to social appearances and takes place in terms of roles, acts, scenes, and incidents. Man as an opportunist rather than a mortal agent is visualized operating at the center of his web. Both the religious and the humanistic view of man are excluded from the new theory.[15]

In much the same manner, Gouldner elaborates upon several interrelated sources of the dramaturgical imagery.[16] He points to the fact that modern men tend to be functionaries or clients of large-scale bureaucratic organizations over which they have little influence. Hence, Goffman pays little attention to the efforts of men to alter the structure of such organizations. Further, in such organizations individuals tend to become readily interchangeable units whose sense of worth and power is, consequently, impaired. Lacking impact on the organizational structure and functioning, they bend their efforts to the management of impressions. These efforts, Gouldner asserts plausibly, are more likely to be made by individuals who retain individualistic and competitive orientations, but who are dependent upon large-scale organizations.

It is the newer, salaried middle classes who are most directly vulnerable to the foregoing conditions. Gouldner describes Goffman's dramaturgy as "a revealing symptom of the latest phase in the long-term tension between the middle class's orientation to morality and its concern with utility."[17] Constrained by the new exigencies, their faith in both utility and morality seriously undermined, the new middle class endeavors to "fix its perspective in aesthetic standards, in the appearance of things."[18]

One final impingement of the societal situation described above upon the dramaturgical view is found in a focus upon the episodic or situational, micro-analysis of brief encounters, without reference to historical circumstances or institutional framework.[19] This feature of Goffman's imagery is, of course, *common* to the varieties of contemporary symbolic interactionism.

While the dramaturgical analysis has its detractors, chiefly on the basis of its ideologically unpalatable imagery and its "soft" methodology, it also has equally ardent admirers. Among the latter, Collins and Makowsky are especially laudatory, perhaps extravagantly so. Hailing the dramaturgical perspective for making human social behavior "the central focus of attention, not in unrealistic laboratory situations, but in the real-life encounters that make up the substance of society," they claim that, "For the first time there opens up a real possibility of sociology's becoming a science—a precise and rigorous body of knowledge..."[20]

Ethnomethodology

The relationship between ethnomethodology and symbolic interaction theory has been discussed by several writers.[21] Our concern in this paper is not so much to detail similarities and differences between the two, but to look at ethnomethodology as a variation of the general interactionist perspective. We are agreeing with Wallace, who writes, "Insofar as ethnomethodology embraces a theoretic (rather than methodologic) viewpoint, it is clearly symbolic interactionist."[22]

Lindsey Churchill notes that, "the ethnomethodologist continually asks the technical question, 'How is that social activity done?'"[23] Ethnomethodology involves the study of human behavior on both the conscious and, more importantly, taken-for-granted levels of interaction. In his excellent summary of the content of ethnomethodology, Paul Filmer focuses upon the following ideas. Commonplace (everyday, taken-for-granted) activities are characterized by an implicit order that emerges during the course of interaction and the activity itself. This order functions to make our situations "accountable." For example, much of our daily activity assumes the existence of an "etcetera clause," whereby our expressions (verbal and nonverbal) imply a continued directive toward a certain type of social activity that is not explicitly stated. Filmer concludes:

> ...According to ethnomethodology, sociology is the study of all aspects of everyday social life, however trivial they may seem, just as much as it is the study of extraordinary events; and second, sociology is, in an important sense, itself an everyday activity.[24]

Ethnomethodologists, as well as their critics, have noted the debt owed to the earlier work of the phenomenologists, especially Alfred Schutz.[25] But, ethnomethodology involves an attempt to move beyond the understanding of human behavior in terms of the meanings that are constructed by each individual in social interaction, to a systematic search ("documentary interpretation") for the ways in which shared meanings ("indexical expressions") come to be taken for granted in human society.[26]

For our purposes here, we should like to point out two significant departures of ethnomethodology from the general interactionist tradition. One of these has been detailed by Drietzel, who notes that the ethnomethodologists, unlike the interactionists, claim that:

> The social order, including all its symbols and meanings, exists only precariously but has no existence at all independent of the members' accounting and describing practices.[27]

Secondly, ethnomethodology has established itself as an important force in the resurgence, during the past few years, of the sociology of sociology. Work of such individuals as Cicourel and Douglas[28] serves to indicate not only the flimsy nature of social reality in general society, but also the ways in which sociologists share with each other an equally flimsy social reality, often leading to the assumption of certain givens that hinder attempts to understand social behavior from the perspective of the actor.

Thus, to assume the existence of a social reality actually existing "out there" appears to be universal. Exactly *what* system of reality is defined as warranting our trust varies, as "social realities" emerge relative to our particular positions in social and cultural matrices. This assumed reality, in turn, defines the ways in which the relationships themselves are interpreted and carried out during interaction. Ethnomethodologists are interested in the "methods" used by the observed and the observer for dealing with their everyday life reality.[29]

It comes as no surprise, therefore, that ethnomethodologists closely approximate the Chicago school, with an emphasis upon sympathetic introspection and participant research. In many instances, however, the ethnomethodologists have shown a greater cognizance of the role of history in behavior, as well as traditional interactionist concerns such as time, place, and situation.[30] Generally speaking, interactionism has been notably ahistorical, and has not followed the kind of analysis contained in George Herbert Mead's *Movement of Thought in the Nineteenth Century*. We shall end this section of the paper by looking at the image of man that is reflected in the writings of ethnomethodology.

Most of the criticisms levelled at ethnomethodology are aimed at dealing with the perspective as a sociological theory that utilizes a particular methodological approach. For example, ethnomethodology has been criticized for ignoring relationships between individuals and larger social units, for giving no clear demonstration as to how taken-for-granted assumptions operate in interaction, and for a lack of precision in explicating the documentary method.[31] It seems to us that there is a much more serious criticism, of an ideological nature, that does nor involve traditional problems of theory and research; a criticism touched upon by Gouldner.

In *The Coming Crisis in Western Sociology*, Gouldner writes that, "Garfinkel's is a sociology more congenial to the activistic 1960's and particularly to the more politically rebellious campuses of the present period."[32] As Warshay points out, ethnomethodology is a sociology of involvement at all levels.[33] More than that, however, ethnomethodology is often a sociology of instigation. Whereas Goffman appears content to study the drama of coping with the depersonalization and alienation common in modern society, ethnomethodology often relies upon inflicting these conditions on others. The demonstrations of the acquisition of power by disrupting taken-for-granted assumptions, e.g., not accepting statements at their face value, bargaining for fixed-value items in a store and purporting to help individuals with personal problems, all position the investigator as a superordinate manipulator.[34] Goffman's opportunist becomes Garfinkel's blundering fool, trusting in something that isn't there, willfully destroyed by those pretending to share his trust.

Summary

In this paper, we have given a brief overview of several of the most prominent varieties of symbolic interactionism that appear in contemporary American sociology. These approaches differ not only in terms of what they consider to be the appropriate theoretical stance of the interactionist but also in terms of the image of man that results from, and interacts with, that particular stance.

The Chicago school constructed a view of man as playing an active role in creating the social environment that, in turn, influences his behavior. In a very real sense, methodology for understanding man remains an ideal, not yet attained in sociology, as present techniques are not adequate for in-depth analysis of this unique feature of human society. By insisting upon the necessity of following the scientific method, the Iowa school has focused upon a relatively passive "man the internalizer," studying the products of internalization as verbally expressed. The Dramaturgical approach has added a new dimension to the interactionist tradition—the manipulative nature of man. This concern drew attention to the taken-for-granted world that has provided the subject matter of Ethnomethodology.

It should be noted that, in ascribing the label "schools" to these varieties, we do not mean to infer that the individuals theorizing and carrying out research in accordance with the various perspectives define themselves as members of a particular school.[35] Indeed, it seems to us that members of the Iowa school share little in the form of "consciousness of kind." We would suggest that this is due primarily to the fact that the major thrust of this approach serves to incorporate, rather than differentiate, it from the mainstream of American sociological theory and research, where attention is directed toward the supposed universality of the canons of scientific investigation. Members of the Chicago school, on the other hand, appear much more cognizant of their distinctive theoretical and ideological position. Goffman and his disciples stand out as clearly identifiable, while self-identification is highest among the group that is self—and other—defined to be most at variance with the mainstream of American sociology—the ethnomethodologists.

NOTES

[1] See for example, Jerome Manis and Bernard Meltzer, eds., *Symbolic Interaction* (Boston; Allyn & Bacon, 1967); Michael Overington, "The image of man in symbolic interactionism: an essay in support of Pogo's contention 'we have met the enemy and he is us.'" (M.A. Thesis, University of Wisconsin, 1970); Larry T. Reynolds, "The sociology of symbolic interactionism" (Ph.D Dissertation, Ohio State University, 1969); Larry T. Reynolds and C. McCart, "The institutional basis of theoretical diversity" *Sociological Focus* vol. 5 (Spring 1972).

[2] A more complete statement of the differences and similarities between the Chicago and Iowa schools can be found in Bernard Meltzer and John Petras, "The Chicago and Iowa schools of symbolic interactionism," in *Human Nature and Collective Behavior*, ed., Tomatsu Shibutani (Englewood Cliffs, N.J.: Prentice-Hall, 1970).

[3] Herbert Blumer, *Symbolic Interactionism* (Englewood Cliffs, NJ: Prentice Hall, 1969), p.26-27.

[4] Manford Kuhn, "Major Trends in Symbolic Interaction Theory in the Past Twenty-five Years," *Sociological Quarterly*, 5(Winter 1972), p. 72.

⁵C. Addison Hickman and Manford H. Kuhn, *Individuals, Groups, and Social Behavior*, (New York: Dryden, 1956), Pp.21-27.
⁶ Manford H. Kuhn, "Lectures on the Self," Mimeographed. 1964.
⁷ Hickman and Kuhn, *op. cit.*, p.45.
⁸ Blumer, *op. cit.*, p.14.
⁹ John Lofland, "Interactionist Imagery and Analytic Interruptus," in Tamotsu Shibutani, *op. cit.*, p.38.
¹⁰ Erving Goffman, *The Presentation of Self in Everyday Life*, (Garden City: Doubleday, 1959), p. xi.
¹¹ *Ibid.*, p.1.
¹² Stanford M. Lyman and Marvin B. Scott, *A Sociology of the Absurd*, (New York: Appleton-Century-Crofts, 1970), p.20.
¹³ S.E. Messinger, H. Sampson, and R.D. Towne, "Life as Theater: Some Notes on the Dramaturgical Approach to Social Reality," *Sociometry*, vol. 25 (1962).
¹⁴ Randall Collins and Michael Makowsky, *The Discovery of Society*, (New York: Random House, 1972), p.212.
¹⁵ Don Martindale, *American Society*, (Princeton: Van Nostrand, 1960), p.79.
¹⁶ Alvin W. Gouldner, *The Coming Crisis in American Society* (New York: Basic Books, 1970), pp.378-390.
¹⁷ *Ibid.*, p.386.
¹⁸ *Ibid.*, p. 390.
¹⁹ *Ibid.*, p. 379.
²⁰ Collins and Makowsky, *op. cit.*, p.213.
²¹ N.K. Denzin, "Symbolic Interactionism and Ethnomethodology," *American Sociological Review*, vol. 34 (December 1969); Hans Peter Dreitzel, ed., *Recent Sociology* No. 2, (London: Macmillan, 1970); Walter L. Wallace, ed., *Sociological Theory* (Chicago: Aldine, 1969), L. Warshay, "The Current State of Sociological Theory: Diversity, Polarity, Empiricism, and Small Theories," *Sociological Quarterly*, vol. 12, (Winter 1971); T.P. Wilson, "Conceptions of Interaction and Forms of Sociological Explanation," *American Sociological Review*, vol.35 (August 1970).
²² Wallace, *op. cit.*, p.213.
²³ Lindsey Churchill, "Ethnomethodology and Measurement," *Social Forces*, vol.50 (December 1971), p.103.
²⁴ P. Filmer, "On Harold Garfinkel's Ethnomethodology," in *New Directions in Sociological Theory*, edited by Paul Filmer, et al. (London: Collier Macmillan, 1972) p.10.
²⁵ Aaron V. Cicourel, *The Social Organization of Juvenile Justice* (New York: Wiley, 1968), p. 6; Jack D. Douglas, *American Social Order* (New York: Free Press, 1971), p.175; Harold Garfinkel, *Studies in Ethnomethodology* (Englewood Cliffs: Prentice Hall, 1967), p.ix; Gouldner, *op. cit.*, p.390; Peter McHugh, *Defining the Situation* (Indianapolis: Bobbs-Merrill, 1968), pp.16-17.
²⁶ G. Psathas, "Ethnomethods and Phenomenology," *Social Research*, vol.35 (September 1968).
²⁷ Dreitzel, *op. cit.*, p.xv.
²⁸ Aaron V. Cicourel, *Method and Measurement in Sociology* (New York: Free Press, 1964); Jack D. Douglas, ed., *The Impact of Sociology* (New York: Appleton-Century-Crofts, 1970).
²⁹ Collins and Makowsky, *op. cit.*, p. 209.
³⁰ Warshay, *op. cit.*, p.25.
³¹ Denzin, *op. cit.*, p.929.
³² Gouldner, *op. cit.*, p.395.
³³ Warshay, *op. cit.*, p.25.
³⁴ Garfinkel, *op. cit.*, pp.62-71 and Chapter III.
³⁵ It should be clear that we are using the term "school" in the sense of an intellectual perspective, not a geographical location. Two "deviant cases" are especially notable — Arnold Rose who studied with Blumer at Chicago, and Norman Denzin who received his Ph.D. from the State University of Iowa.

Chapter 5 HERBERT BLUMER: SOCIOLOGIST PAR EXCELLENCE

Lewis M. Killian

When, as a student, I initially encountered Herbert Blumer I thought of him as first and foremost a social psychologist. Courses I took with him included social psychology, attitudes, and human nature, supplemented by collective behavior and social movements. The preliminary examination areas for which he wrote questions were social psychology and collective behavior. While my own perception has changed radically, I feel that, as Herbert Blumer has passed into history, most sociologists still think of him not as a mainstream sociologist but as the prophet of the Chicago school of symbolic interactionism, a branch of the hybrid field of social psychology. With other symbolic interactionists, he has been charged with espousing an approach that is astructural, not dealing adequately with social structure (particularly at the macro level), history, and power. In this view, he was not a real sociologist.

Before I sat at the big oval table in Blumer's seminar room, my conception of social psychology had been shaped by undergraduate courses embodying a naive social behaviorism symbolized by the concept "cultural conditioning." It was highly individualistic. Society and culture constituted an environment in which ego's personality was formed. Such an approach, even when taught under the rubric "sociology," did indeed separate the study of the psychology of the individual from the study of society. In his courses Blumer quickly forced me to revise my conception of the relationship between the individual and the group and of human nature itself. The kind of social psychology which he taught me was profoundly sociological. "Interaction" replaced "conditioning" in my vocabulary. I did not, however, go on to concentrate in social psychology but instead focused on ethnic relations in most of my research and writing. As my own ideas evolved, and as I followed Herbert Blumer's many writings in a variety of areas of sociology, including race relations, I came to realize how truly sociological his approach was. He began the study of human association with *the group*. The self, role-taking, incorporating the meaning of others' into one's own actions — all were products of the group and were to be studied as such rather than as ends in themselves. They were the keys to understanding the dynamics of social life on the micro and the macro level, not mere explanations of the nature of individual personality.

A statement in Blumer's essay entitled "The Psychological Import of the Human Group" (1953) might appear at first thought as a prescription for ethnomethodology. He declared, "Human association should be viewed in its most fundamental form, namely, that of two human beings interacting on each other. The larger instances of human association, such as we have in mind in talking about group life in its wider aspects, are still based on interaction between individuals" (1953:193). Despite the apparent emphasis on individuals, even just two persons interacting constitute a group, so Blumer was indeed proposing that the study of human association must begin with the group. In the same essay, he rejected instincts or drives, attitudes, and culture as preexisting variables which determined the course of human association. This, like many other of his articles, reflected one of his major tenets, one which may lead to the charge of astructuralism. This is his rejection of any form of determinism. In his writings on a wide variety of topics, he surely takes social structure into account as a variable influencing human interaction, but he never assigns it a determining role.

As he moved to macro levels of analysis, he never forgot that it was people who interacted, not organizations or groups as realities existing on the superorganic level. He was equally emphatic, however, that it was not isolated individuals or mere aggregates of discrete, unrelated individuals who interacted, but people who acted as they did partly because of their group memberships. He was particularly preoccupied with the importance of organizations in modern society.

This can be seen in his 1947 attack on public opinion polling as failing actually to deal with public opinion. He asserted, "Public opinion must obviously be recognized as having its setting in a society and as being a function of that society in operation. This means, patently, that public opinion gets its form from the social framework in which it moves and from the social processes in play in that framework; also that the function and role of public opinion is determined by the part it plays in the operation of the society" (1947, 1988: 150). He went on to criticize the sort of public opinion polling then and now so much in vogue for treating society as a mere aggregation of disparate individuals, labor unions, and lobbies and the individuals empowered by them to speak as really expressing public opinion, except in the social instance of elections and referenda. His comments of a quarter of a century ago remain relevant to the current political discussion of the importance of lobbies and to Ross Perot's idea of using polling techniques to go directly to the people for the determination of public policy.

During the same period his attack on sociological theory in industrial relations, particularly the fad of "human relations industry," stressed the importance of organized groups even more strongly. He declared, "...Labor relations become increasingly a matter of relationships between gigantic organizations of workers and management, each of which functions through central policy and executive groups" (1946, 1988: 300). He added the variable of power to his analysis, stating, "conflicts develop naturally between employers and employees as each group pursues its own interests" (1958:242). The principal characteristics of industrial relations in modern society had become, for him, mobility and guidance by organizations. He objected that attitude scales and sociograms fail to catch the "play of events in a dynamic moving situation." Forty years later Rick Fantasia, in a brilliant synthesis of symbolic interactionist and Marxist approaches, documented the mobile, dynamic emergent nature of class consciousness in his *Cultures of Solidarity* (1988). Blumer's influence, though indirect, was very real. Fantasia, challenging the dominant trend in research methods, said that he abandoned survey research as essentially inappropriate to a dynamic approach to working-class consciousness (1988:247). He reflected Blumer's emphasis on organizations but showed how organizations themselves were transformed in the course of industrial conflict.

Thus Blumer took into account social structure, organizations, and power in his analysis of human association at all levels. His overriding consideration was expressed in such terms as "dynamic," "flowing," and "mobile," all of which I interpret as reflecting his deep appreciation of the historic dimension. This dimension I found most clearly represented in his significant writings on race relations, including his essay "Industrialization and Race Relations" and his even better known articles "Race Prejudice as a Sense of Group Position" and "The Future of the Color Line." In the first of these essays, he was replying to the then-common prediction that industrialization, with its rational imperative of industrial efficiency, would lead race to vanish as a factor which structures social relations. Deeply committed to humanitarian ideals, he was still capable of describing in realistic, not wishful, terms the durability of a color line established through long, historic experience. His insight that a color line, where it arises, becomes part of the very warp and woof of the fabric of a society is reflected in his assertation that the theory of race relations must be "concerned with the *establishment and maintenance of a hierarchial racial order within a given society*" (1954:14). Not only did he predict that managers attempting the rational operation of enterprises introduced into a racially ordered society might seek to avoid trouble and maximize efficiency by deferring to the canons of the racial order, he also predicted that racial tension and conflict during the transition would arise not only between dominant and minority groups but would be more likely to arise between different subordinate racial groups. He would not have been surprised at attacks on Asian-American workers by unemployed white automobile workers in Detroit in the 1990s, nor at the rivalry and conflict between African-Americans, Chicanos, and Koreans in Los Angeles. He summed up his ideas on industrialization with the statement, "Industrialization will continue to be an incitant to change, without providing the definition of how the change is to be met" (1956:253). He argued that industrialization and racial alignment will act on each other, with neither being dominant. In reading his papers on industrialization and the racial order, one can barely recognize Blumer, the social psychologist, but can see him as the sociologist par excellence writing about racial orders, the structural imperatives of industrialization, and broad social forces sweeping through national and international arenas. His analysis is eminently on the macro level.

During an era when a highly individualistic, psychologistic mode of analysis held sway in the study of race relations, he maintained a consistently sociological approach. He never lost sight of the significance of the fact that race relations are essentially relations between *groups*, arising out of a collective process in which one racial group opposes another and, by opposition, defines itself. Racial identification and race prejudice arises within this framework; they do not precede it. He proposed, "It is the *sense of social position* emerging from this collective process of characterization which provides the basis of race prejudice" (1958:4). Reflecting his hypothesis that in the formation of public opinion not all attitudes are equal in importance, he also proposed that the collective process of definition "operates chiefly through the public media in which individuals who are accepted as the spokesmen of a racial group characterize publicly another racial group" (1958:3).

Blumer always attached great importance to the historical dimension as essential to the understanding of any given instance of racial prejudice. He stated that "...the content of collective experience of one group will determine what classifications they will make of other peoples and so what conceptualized objects they will build up" (1939:13), citing as an example the differences in the conceptions of "the Negro" formed in the southern United States and Brazil.

Like his mentor, Robert E. Park, Blumer saw race relations as one outcome of the competition for status between diverse people thrown together in a single, heterogenous society, usually as a result of migration or conquest. Variations in the intensity of prejudice are to be explained primarily in terms of changes in social conditions, not of variations in individual life experiences. He proposed that racial prejudice would be most pronounced and serious in a social situation with three features: (1) two groups live together as parts of a unitary society; (2) the acceptance of the subordinate group is limited, and it is assigned to an inferior status; and (3) the dominant group fears that the subordinate group is not keeping its place. Following this same line of theory, he characterized race prejudice as a "sense of group position" involving four basic feelings:

(1) a feeling of superiority;
(2) a feeling that the subordinate race is intrinsically different and alien;
(3) a feeling of propriety claim to certain areas of privilege;
(4) a fear and suspicion that the subordinate race harbors designs on the prerogative of the dominant race (1958:3).

He did not classify the feelings of antipathy and aversion arising from the first two groups as "prejudice." It was, to him, the fourth element, the sense of threatened status, which gives rise to race prejudice. "The dominant group," he wrote, "is concerned with its position vis-a-vis the subordinate group" (1958:4).

Consistent with this definition was the proposition that the analysis of prejudice must start with the empirical study of the historical process through which the sense of group position is formed, is threatened, and changes. The collective image and feelings which constitute race prejudice are forged in a long, complicated social process. This image is an abstract one, "a vast entity which spreads out far beyond individuals [of the minority group] and transcends experience with such individuals" (1958:6). The image building takes place primarily in the public arena, in the area of the remote and not of the immediate experiences between individual members of the two groups. During the current intensification of anti-black sentiment in the United States, the Willie Horton "sound bites" and Jesse Helm's image of the white worker denied a job because of affirmative action appear as timely examples of such image building. Major influence is, he said, "exercised by individuals and groups who have the public ear and who are felt to have standing, prestige, authority, and power" (1958:4). Their formulations are extended and perpetuated, however, through gossip, anecdotes, jokes, and the like. Strong interest groups have an opportunity to direct the lines of discussion in a way which works to their advantage. During the 1980s, political candidates at both local and national levels did not hesitate to "play the race card" to win elections.

Repeatedly rejecting individual experiences and consequent attitudes as the explanation of race prejudice and race relations, Blumer constantly emphasized the historical process and the process of public definition. An historical, collective product, the sense of group position is not therefore a reflection or summation of individual attitudes or personality traits but a matrix in which the individual himself or herself is shaped and organized. Moreover, it is not merely a reflection of individual predispositions but it is a powerful social norm. It is more than a feeling of hatred, contempt, or condescension — it involves "a fundamental kind of group affiliation for the members of the dominant racial group" (1958:5).

In view of Blumer's conception of race prejudice as a central feature of the identification of self within a firmly established racial order, it is not surprising that he viewed the prospects for rapid improvement of race relations in the United Sates with pessimism. He saw the struggle to transform the racial order following the Supreme Court's desegregation decision of 1954 as taking place chiefly in the public arena, not in the hearts and minds of men and women. In "The Future of the Color Line," written in 1965, he accurately predicted that the struggle of blacks in the public arena would prove to be only the prelude to a more intense struggle. To his oft-repeated propositions that the color line, or sense of group position, represents a definition of whites and blacks as abstract groups with normatively defined positions in the social order, and that this color line is a collective definition of a social position and not a mere expression of individual feelings, he added a third. This was that "the color line is not appropriately represented by a single, sharply drawn line but appears rather as a series of ramparts, of which outer portions may be given up while inner bastions are still steadfastly defended" (1965:323). The area of civil rights — free access to public accommodations and voting rights — constituted only the outer citadel. As he was writing his essay, the battle was shifting to what he characterized as the next defense of the color line — the area of economic subordination. This he described as an area which would be "exceedingly tough because it is highly complicated by private and quasi-private property rights, managerial rights, and organizational rights" (1965:323). The battle at this rampart goes on as African Americans still struggle to gain a condition even approximating economic equality.

Persuaded of the great tenacity of the color line, Blumer saw indications of the shift of African-Americans toward pluralism even before the emergence of the Black Power movement. He identified the formation of a large, urban, black proletariat as a new element in the positioning of the two races. He noted that certain conditions in the new urban black community, including increased bitterness toward whites and a stronger disposition to fight back, pointed to the probability that "the urban Negro proletariat, unlike Negroes at the bottom of the social and economic ladder in the past will not humbly accept this position but be poised to protest and rebel in some fashion" (1965:333).

Blumer was bold in his predictions of trends in race relations. His predictions were not based on survey research and opinion polls showing trends in racial attitudes. Instead they were based on painstaking review of historical and comparative studies focused on the sociological level. Consistently Blumer looked at racial groups as complex, highly structured, and differentiated entities, not as aggregates of discrete individuals possessed of attitudes and personality traits which added up to race prejudice. Prejudice, as a sense of group position, he defined as eminently a group product. In "The Future of the Color Line" he was one of the first sociologists to take serious account of the new spirit of bitterness, hostility to whites, and black self-consciousness and of what Michael Omi and Howard Winant would later call the "rearticulation of racial ideology" (1986:125). This has developed as many whites came to see themselves as the victims of racial discrimination as the battle over group position shifted to the rampart of entrenched economic privilege. Above all, Blumer consistently insisted that every outcome would emerge from a process of interaction between individuals within a social framework and would not be determined by preexisting variables, whether lodged in the psyches of individuals or in the social structure.

REFERENCES

Blumer, Herbert. 1939. "The Nature of Racial Prejudice." *Social Process in Hawaii* 511-21.

———. 1953. "The Psychological Import of the Human Group," pp. 185-202 in *Group Relations at the Crossroads*, edited by Muzafer Sherif and M.O. Wilson. New York: Harper.

———. 1955. "Reflections on Theory of Race Relations," pp. 3-21 in *Race Relations in World Perspective*, edited by Andrew S. Lind. Honolulu: University of Hawaii Press.

———. 1958"Race Prejudice as a Sense of Group Position." *Pacific Sociological Review* 1:3-7.

———. 1965. "Industrialization and Race Relations," pp. 220-253 in *Industrialization and Race*, edited by Guy Hunter. London: Oxford University Press.

———. 1988. (1946) "Sociological Theory in Industrial Relations," pp. 297-308 in *Social Order and the Public Philosophy*, edited by Stanford M. Lyman and Arthur J. Vidich. Fayetteville: The University of Arkansas Press.

———. 1988. (1947) "Public Opinion and Public Opinion Polling," pp. 147-160 in *Social Order and the Public Philosophy*, edited by Stanford M. Lyman and Arthur J. Vidich. Fayetteville: The University of Arkansas Press.

———. 1988. (1958) "The Rationale of Labor-Management Relations," pp. 234-269 in *Social Order and the Public Philosophy*, edited by Stanford M. Lyman and Arthur J. Vidich. Fayetteville: University of Arkansas Press.

Fantasia, Rick. 1988. *Cultures of Solidarity*. Berkeley: University of California Press.

Omi, Michael and Howard Winant. 1986. *Racial Formation in the United States*. New York: Routledge and Kegan Paul.

Chapter 6   KUHN'S FORMULATION OF THE SELF

Stephan Spitzer, Carl Couch and John Stratton

Manford H. Kuhn (1911-1963), the progenitor of the Iowa School, was born in 1911 in Kennard, Indiana. At the age of seventeen, he was stricken by polio, a disease which crippled him for life. A strong civil rights activist, Kuhn was a member of such organizations as the American Civil Liberties Union. He attended Earlham College where he earned an A. B. in Sociology and Economics in 1931. Subsequently, he began graduate work in Sociology at the University of Wisconsin. It is here, studying under Kimbal Young, that he earned an M.A. and Ph.D.

For the next six years, Kuhn taught at the University of Wisconsin, Whittier College and Mount Holyoke. In 1946, he went to the State University of Iowa, where he remained until his death.

According to Kuhn, of the current social psychological theories..."only symbolic interactionism is logically consistent with the basic propositions of social science" (Kuhn, 1964a, p. 79). Other social psychological and personality theories were regarded as inconsistent with one or more of the following established findings of social sciences: "...the extreme cultural variability of man; the creativity of man; the continual socializability and modifiability of man; the ability of man to feed back complex correctives to his behavior without engaging in trial and error, or conditioning learning" (Kuhn, 1964a, p.79).

Kuhn saw the symbolic interaction tradition as an orientation that specified some of the significant variables that had to be taken into account in the development of a theory of human behavior (Kuhn, 1964a; Hickman and Kuhn,1956). However, Kuhn was aware that Mead's notion of the self contained "...such a dynamically volatile process of self-indicators that...the whole matter is so evanescent in time to make usable or testable predictions" (Kuhn, 1964a, p.64). Accordingly, he maintained that if the central concepts of the symbolic interaction orientation were to be used to organize and interpret empirical studies, they needed to be translated and modified into a form making operationalization possible.

The self-concept as defined by Kuhn is an "...individual's attitudes (plans of action) toward his own mind and body viewed as an object," (Hickman and Kuhn, 1956, p. 46). In contrast to the emphasis on the process and the extremely fluid nature of the self posited by some representatives of the Chicago school, Kuhn conceptualized the self as having consistency derived from and maintained in social affiliations. "Central to an individual's conception of himself is his *identity*; that is, his generalized position in society deriving from his statuses in the groups of which he is a member, the roles which stem from these statuses, and the social categories which his group membership lead him to assign himself (sex, age, class, race, etc.)" (Kuhn, 1964b. p.630-631). The self forms "...the basis for (a) the organized character of personality as well as to be the requisite for (b) the integration of the person into the on-going group process of interaction." (Kuhn, 1964b, p. 631).

Postulates

The Twenty Statements Test was developed to measure the self in a manner consistent with symbolic interactionist theory. Symbolic interactionist theory specifies that the self-definitions of greatest significance are those made by the person himself. Thus, "A self attitude test,...must be constructed in such a manner that it will elicit the person's own conception of his identity." (Kuhn, 1960, p. 54) Moreover, to approach the self from the symbolic interactionist position, "...the assumptions made in investigating individual behavior must be consistent with those made in investigating behavior on the societal and cultural level" (Hickman and Kuhn, 1956, p. 22). Specifically, some of the assumptions upon which the TST is based are:

(1) The self is a set of statuses and identities, plans of action, values, and definitions.

(2) The self is acquired and maintained in symbolic interaction with others, and is a reflection of the   social system in which it is acquired and maintained.

(3) The self, as a phenomenological identity, is relevant to all human associations.

(4) The self is instrumental in the organization of social conduct.

(5) The self is not unique to a given social situation.

(6) The self can be articulated to others.

(7) Self-statements can be systematically coded.

Postulate 1: *The self is a set of statuses and identities, plans of action, values, and definitions.*

The self is a classification and identification system, plans about oneself as an object related to other objects, and a set of thoughts about what one does, and some judgement as to the quality of one's performance which are derived from the status-role systems of the groups of which an actor is a part. For example, a plumber when conversing with others will ordinarily define himself as a plumber. He need not go beyond this if he imagines that the others share definitions of what a plumber does. A significant part of this person's daily activity is devoted to a set of behaviors that constitute a category of phenomena which has high codability; that is, a category frequently used and widely shared in perception and thought. Thus, it can be talked about in shorthand fashion by using the label "plumber."

We may expect that the plumber will have some notion of the quality of his activities as a plumber; his self-concept will contain some evaluation of himself as a plumber.

A person thinks of himself in terms of what he does and how well he does it, and much of what a person does is conveniently and consensually codified in terms of statuses. If a person thinks of himself as a plumber, he will tend to conduct himself in accordance with the behaviors he believes are expected of a plumber.

Persons also identify themselves by their values (attractions-aversions) and by designating their attributes. These dimensions of self also locate the person in social situations and provide a basis for symbolically organized behavior. Self-esteem, self-evaluation, and similar dimensions of the self are significant aspects of the self. However, one can only have self-esteem in terms of an identity or set of identities. First, the person must be able to answer the question, "Who Am I?" before he can have thoughts (feelings) of esteem, pride, or satisfaction. Self-conceptions are composed of a variety of identities that include identifications such as personal name, family, occupation, skin color, or a complex combination of these.

Given the above, the task of acquiring measures of the self is to develop techniques that elicit the symbolic system that a person applies to himself. The number of statements an adult can make about himself is relatively large, so the further task is to elicit those dimensions of the self that are most instrumental in the organization of a person's behavior, i.e., the most significant and salient dimensions of the self.

Postulate 2: *The self is acquired and maintained in symbolic interaction with others, and is a reflection of the social system in which it is acquired and maintained.*

The self presumes others; it cannot develop or continue without others. A person "...becomes an object to himself only by taking the attitude of other individuals toward himself within a social environment or context of experience and behavior in which he and they are involved" (Mead, 1934, p. 38). However, the self is not simply a mirror reflection of the labels, evaluations, and definitions applied to a person by others. Not all people defined by others as stupid conceive of themselves as stupid.

The acceptance or rejection of an identity offered by others is a function of several factors, including the nature of the relationship between the person and others, the self-identifications already held, the personal evaluation of the identification offered, and the level of consensuality among those extending the identity.

The young child acquiring the rudiments of language can do little else but accept the statuses and identities offered. His language and social experiences are provided for him by others. The greater the extent to which a symbolic system has been acquired and applied to oneself, the more effectively one can direct his own social experiences and respond to the directions of others.

Postulate 3: *The self, as a phenomenological identity, is relevant to all human associations and actions.*

Humans can conduct coordinated behavior only by conceiving of self in relation to others. Consequently, to obtain a complete portrayal of a social act, some measure of self-identity is required. The self is the one object present in all social conduct.

The symbolic interaction position maintains that in every social situation the participants must identify themselves and others before they can organize their behavior. Unless a person can determine his identity, it is impossible for him to behave in an organized fashion. In situations where a person cannot establish his identity, or even when there is uncertainty about it, interaction tends to be held in abeyance until one's identity is established. In these situations, the interaction that does take place tends to be structured around attempts to establish situations where a person is a stranger without an identity within a group.

Social conduct is not always organized with a high level of self-awareness of one's identities and relations with others. Some social conduct is organized with little or no self-consciousness. For example, an experienced automobile driver may be incapable of recounting the number of cars he passed in traveling from one place to another. Yet, in making the trip, he engaged in an elaborate series of social acts. Social behavior that at one time had a high level of self-consciousness may become "habitual," where the person short circuits the elaborate processes of identifying self and relating self to others. However, when a person learns habitual social behavior, he also acquires an identity related to the behavior; and how the behavior is expressed is related to the identity acquired. The use of the TST to acquire measures of self-identification, then, assumes that significant dimensions of self that are associated with "habitual" behavior can be elicited.

Postulate 4: *The self is instrumental in the organization of social conduct.*

Symbolic interactionists view behavior as, in part, flowing from the identities that constitute the self in the social situation. Persons must first make self-identifications before they can organize and direct their own activity. There are occasions where the self is not instrumental in the organization of behavior. The year old child who gives no indication of commanding a symbol system does engage in "organized" behavior of a sort. He sucks his bottle, plays with buttons, and pulls his toes. It would be stretching the meaning of the concept to maintain that he had a self. A human organism on this level does not engage in any cooperative play, or any other form of coordinated behavior stemming from self. Superficially, a very young child may engage in coordinated behavior. This pseudo-coordinated behavior is enforced by the socializing agent. The bar of soap is placed in the child's hand, and he may hold it as the mother "instructs" him. But it is not until he acquires a symbol system that allows him to relate self to others that he can be said to engage in truly cooperative behavior. Similarly, a child cannot play at being a movie star until he has learned the behaviors and expectations associated with the position of movie star.

When an individual has acquired self-identification he is not simply a passive agent responding to external stimuli. Self-identifications determine, in part, which objects are given attention, the interpretations made of them, and the conduct taken toward them. People must know what kinds of objects they are before they can control and direct their own activity. The theory does not maintain that the self is the only relevant variable in organized conduct. It only maintains that the self is instrumental in social behavior in conjunction with other variables. The person's conception of others, of other objects, and claims made on the person by others are also significant in the organization of behavior in most social encounters.

Postulate 5: *The self is not unique to a given situation.*

Different dimensions of the self are implemented in different social settings. But the self developed in one situation also has consequences in other situations. If this is not the case, it is meaningless to acquire measurements of the self, for all that could be obtained is the self of that situation.

Different components of the self can have different levels of significance for different lines of conduct. The self-definitions of a person derived from his status as a student are assumed to be more relevant to his behavior as a student than to his behavior as a family member. Yet, unless the self-definitions a person makes when in the role of respondent to a researcher are relevant to his conduct in other relationships no meaningful measure of the self can be acquired.

Postulate 6: *The self can be articulated to others.*

If language ability is the human animal's distinguishing characteristic, then it is reasonable to suppose that we can better understand man's behavior by analyzing his activities with concepts derived from this uniqueness. Language provides a means for persons to present themselves to each other on a symbolic level. Persons routinely present themselves to others in terms of social identities. One means by which this is accomplished is by giving oneself titles and stating who we are in relationship to others. For example, the teaching assistant goes to the Examination Service and states not only his name and that he is a student, but that he is employed by a particular professor. In other encounters, these identities might be taken for granted.

The TST is a procedure which requires persons to articulate their identities and aims to elicit both (1) those identities which are commonly articulated and (2) those identities which are not commonly articulated but which constitute a part of the person's self-conception.

Postulate 7: *Self-statements can be systematically codified.*

The symbolic interaction orientation presupposes that the self exists by virtue of and in terms of a language community. Consequently, one task is to develop procedures to tap those symbols a person uses to locate himself. Only after this step has been taken is it meaningful to develop systems of codification that allow for the systematic analysis of the data.

In one sense, every self is unique. Each member of society has a unique combination of experiences. Consequently, there will be variation in the composition of each self. But by virtue of the fact that everyone belongs to social systems having a language, each person's self is composed of elements held in common with some others. To avoid empirical solipsism, procedures for the classification of similarities and variations of self-statements must be established. The coding systems must allow for inter-researcher manipulation of data and inter-researcher communication regarding the dimensions established and associations observed.

Summary

Self is one of the central variables of symbolic interaction theory. It has been commonly been employed by sociologists as a sensitizing concept. Kuhn conceptualized the TST as providing a means for the study of the self that was consistent with the symbolic interaction orientation. The TST translates the concept into a variable, or set of variables, that facilitates empirical studies of the self. Employment of the TST as a measurement device rests upon the assumptions that the self is symbolic and capable of being communicated.

Bibliography

Hickman, C. Addison & Manford H. Kuhn. 1956. *Individuals, Groups, & Economic Behavior.* New York. Dryden Press.
Kuhn, Manford H. 1964a. Major Trends in Symbolic Interaction Theory. *Sociological Quarterly,* 5, 61-84.
———. 1960. Self-Attitudes by Sex and Professional Training. *Sociological Quarterly,* 1, 39-55.

Chapter 7

ERVING GOFFMAN

Don Martindale

Erving Goffman was born in Manville, Alberta, Canada in 1922. He earned the A.B. at the University of Toronto in 1944, the M.A. at the University of Chicago in 1949, and the Ph.D. in 1953. He was a member of the Shetland field research at the University of Edinburgh (Scotland) from 1949 to 1951 and visiting scientist of the National Institute of Mental Health from 1954 to 1957. He joined the department of sociology at the University of California at Berkeley as assistant professor in 1958, rising to full professor by 1962. In 1968 he became Benjamin Franklin professor of anthropology and sociology at the University of Pennsylvania, Philadelphia.

Goffman completed his studies at a time when Blumer's version of Mead's social thought was most influential and when the work of Kenneth Burke was popular in interactionist circles. He shows the influence of both traditions. He brought to symbolic interactionism an unusually strong sense of embattled, anarchistic individualism.[1] In his first book, *The Presentation of Self in Everyday Life*, Goffman took over the dramatistic model of society suggested by Burke and Duncan, but carried the analogy a step further and worked it out in a manner Burke never intended. Social life is conceived as composed of performances in which various routines, or patterns of activity, are enacted. In any individual roles of the routine only a few formal, idealized elements are involved. A performance occurs in two regions: front and back stage. The front stage performance before the audience is possible in large measure because both actor and audience conspire to save the show. The impression management may, to be sure, fail because of accidents, self-consciousness, or lack of dramaturgical direction, in which case discrepancies between the real and the social self may be unexpectedly revealed. Seen from this point of view, social life is an affair of collective deceit and illusion. The real individual who sustains the pretense is rather pathetic.

> Whether the character that is being presented is sober or carefree, of high station or low, the individual who performs the character will be seen as for what he largely is, a solitary player involved in a harried concern for his production. Behind many masks and many characters, each performer tends to wear a single look, a naked unsocialized look, a look of concentration, a look of one who is privately engaged in a difficult, treacherous task.[2]

There is, in Goffman's view, a basic dialect of self-presentation in everyday life. As performers, individuals are busy maintaining impressions, seemingly living up to the standards in terms of which they are judged. In the process they are conveying the impression that they are living in a moral world. As performers individuals are "merchants of morality." However, the very act of merchandizing morality creates distance from its substance. The real concern is with merchandizing. "The very obligation and profitability of appearing always in a steady moral light, of being a socialized character, forces one to be the sort of person who is practiced in the ways of the stage."[3]

If one were to phrase in Meadian terms Goffman's transformation of symbolic interactionism in his version of the dramatistic tradition, he no longer locates the traditional problem of selfhood in an internal dialectic between the "I," the principle of action, and the "me," the internalized standards of the community or "conscience." The dialectic is between the private and public self in which the real self is a naked, unsocialized, and unsocializable expediency.

In a series of essays completed around 1960 and collected in *Asylums*, Goffman applied the same general type of analysis appearing in *Presentation of Self* to institutions and the inmates of mental hospitals. Total institutions were defined as places of residence and work of large numbers of similarly situated individuals who were cut off from the wider society and for a time led an enclosed, formally administered round of life. Denizens of total institutions include mental hospital patients, TB patients, cloistered monks and nuns, military recruits, and incarcerated prisoners of all types. *Total institution* was Goffman's term for a specialized kind of community; however, he carefully avoids the use of the term *community*— possibly because it had a positive connotation he wished to avoid. As Goffman sees it, total institutions, through a series of humiliations and degradation ceremonies, strip away the individual's (patient's, novice's, recruit's) sense of dignity and worth and reduce him or her to complete dependency on the hierarchical powers of the institution. In the moral career of the mental patient, he reviewed what he considered to be the contingencies that transform an individual into a mental patient. In Goffman's view, accident plays a major role in the making of a mental patient. Because of some offence, an individual no different from any others on the street finds himself or herself facing both family and public servants who operate like a "funnel of betrayal" to incarcerate him or her; once in the mental hospital, he or she experiences complete deracination. However, once again, suddenly and unexpectedly the mental patient may find him- or herself stripped down to real self, but with the unusual opportunity to reveal it publicly.

> In the usual cycle of adult socialization one expects to find alienation and mortification followed by a new set of beliefs about the world and a new way of conceiving of selves...The moral career of the mental patient has unique interest, however; it can illustrate the possibility that in casting off the raiments of the old self — or in having this cover torn away — the person need not seek a new robe and a new audience before which to cower. Instead he can learn, at least for a time, to practice before all groups the amoral arts of shamelessness.[4]

In "The Underlife of a Public Institution" Goffman describes multiple ways in which mental patients cope with the mental institution and work the system to their advantage. In *Stigma* Goffman considers at length the presentations of self by a variety of persons including the blind, members of minority groups, ex-mental patients, ex-convicts, women, obese persons, dwarfs, and even childless married couples who engage in impression management to deal with their "spoiled identities." In *Encounters* Goffman examines impression management in temporary or nonenduring face-to-face groups. He elaborates the concept of role distance, to characterize the potential separateness between individuals and their punitive roles, a separation essential to all of the more cynical forms of impression management. In *Behavior in Public Places* he examined contact in streets, parks, restaurants, theaters, shops, dance halls, and meeting halls to explore impression management in such transitory situations. However, over and again Goffman returns to his primary interest, the stigmatized, the alienated, and the disadvantaged.

Finally, in *Frame Analysis*, where he turns back to the analysis of fraud, deceit, con games, and shows of various kinds,[5] Goffman indicates that he was seeking a general theoretical statement of his position.

Goffman cited William James, W.I. Thomas, and Alfred Schutz as sources of his basic conceptualization of elementary intersubjective life. A *strip* is a slice from the stream of ongoing activity. Frame analysis is such a strip cut from the flow characterized by "definitions of a situation" and made according to "principles of organization which govern events...and our subjective involvement with them."[6] The basic idea here is that the flow of intersubjective experience is not undifferentiated but is organized, characterized, and identified by its participants in terms of shared definitions or, as Alfred Schutz argued, "typifications." They form a basic stock of experience in terms of which any given group does its business. They constitute its shared or common culture.[7]

A set of frames (Goffman's elementary forms of social life) established in everyday experience is viewed as basic — presumably they are the most shared intersubjective forms of the group — and supplying the building blocks of larger patterns of social life. They can, Goffman thinks, be used for fun, deception, experiment, rehearsal, dream, fantasy, ritual, demonstration, analysis, and charity.[8] The basic devices by which they are employed for other than their original function are *keying* (utilizing a set of conventions originating in one area of life to give meaning to activity in another) and *fabrication* (the deliberate use of basic frames for deceit). As a result of keying, complex frames may be viewed as operators and deceivers and those taken in as dupes, marks, pigeons, suckers, butts, victims, or gulls.[9] Fabrications, of course, are subject to discrediting. However, it must be remembered that fabrications may be benign as well as malignant[10] and sometimes we not only fabricate others but fabricate (that is, deceive) ourselves.[11]

In his frame analysis, Goffman no longer takes the drama as the sole basic model for social life. Theatrical frames are viewed as a special complex type which he differentiates into stage, movie, and novelistic types.[12] He also discusses what he calls structural issues in fabrications, out-of-frame analysis and, while defining mental illness as a special kind of out-of-frame behavior, indicates that a frame perspective permits all of us "to generate crazy behavior and to see that it is not all that crazy."[13]

While frames have been submitted for the theatrical role as the basic units of social life, Goffman restores in his analysis a parallel to his contrast between front and back stage — an idealized reality versus a more grubby real reality. What the individual does in everyday life while real enough in itself, often seems to be a laminated adumbration of a pattern or model that is a typification of quite uncertain status. ("A famous face who models a famous-name dress provides in her movements a keying, a mock-up, of an everyday person walking about in an everyday dress, something, in short, modeled *after* actual wearings; but obviously she is also a model *for* everyday appearance-while-dressed, which appearance is, as it were, always a bridesmaid but never a bride.)"[14] Ordinary life is "an imitation of the properties, a gesture at the exemplary forms, and the primal realization of these ideals belongs more to make-believe than to reality." And in all this the self "is not an entity half-concealed behind events, but a changeable formula for managing oneself during them."[15]

It is perhaps significant that Goffman has often been heralded as "one of the greatest writers alive." This can only mean that many share his view that our civilization is largely an ever changing panorama of fabrication in which the most basic stratification is between the deceivers and the deceived and the self in the end always remains, as Goffman phrased it in his first book, an amoral merchant of morality ever intent on the pillage of others or the avoidance of their pillage of him or her. Goffman transformed paranoia and schizophrenia into the norms of contemporary life.

NOTES

[1] Goffman's major works include: *The Presentation of Self in Everyday Life* (New York: Doubleday Anchor, 1959); *Asylums: Essays on the Social Situation of Mental Patients and Other Inmates* (New York: Doubleday Anchor, 1961); *Encounters: Two Studies on the Sociology of Interaction* (Indianapolis: Bobbs-Merrill, 1961); *Behavior in Public Places: Notes on the Social Organization of Gatherings* (Glencoe, Ill.: The Free Press, 1963); *Stigma: Notes on the Management of Spoiled Identity* (Englewood Cliffs, N.J.: Prentice-Hall, 1963); *Relations in Public* (New York: Harper Colophon Books, 1971); *Frame Analysis: An Essay on the Organization of Experience* (New York: Harper Colophon Books, 1974).
[2] Goffman, *The Presentation of Self in Everyday Life*, P. 235.
[3] *Ibid.*, p.251.
[4] Goffman, *Asylums*, p.169
[5] Goffman, *Frame Analysis*, p.14.
[6] *Ibid.*, p.10.
[7] *Ibid.*, p.26.
[8] *Ibid.*, p.560.
[9] *Ibid.*, p.83.
[10] *Ibid.*, p.14.
[11] *Ibid.*, p.116.
[12] *Ibid.*, pp.124ff.
[13] *Ibid.*, p.246.
[14] *Ibid.*, p.562.
[15] *Ibid.*, p.573.

Chapter 8   **HAROLD GARFINKEL: THE FOUNDER OF ETHNOMETHODOLOGY**

Ruth A. Wallace and Alison Wolf

Of the current phenomenological approaches in sociology, ethnomethodology is the most prominent and the most unified.[1] Harold Garfinkel is recognized as its leading figure...

BACKGROUND

Born in 1917, Garfinkel completed his Ph.D. at Harvard in 1952. Aside from two years of teaching at Ohio State and a brief interim on a research project at the University of Chicago (the jury deliberation project), Garfinkel has spent his entire career at the University of California at Los Angeles, where he has been since 1954. Because of Garfinkel's leadership, UCLA became a training center for ethnomethodologists. Both the University of California at Santa Barbara and the University of California at San Diego could be labeled its "branches" because of the presence of such ethnomethodologists as Aaron Cicourel, a very important early student of Garfinkel who was at UCSB from 1966 to 1971 and has been at UCSD since 1971. Wagner says that California also became a stronghold of ethnomethodology because the state was rapidly expanding its educational system about the time ethnomethodology surfaced; thus, there was less resistance than we would expect from the kind of rigidly established system we find in the East.[2] Garfinkel spent a year at the Center for Advanced Studies in the Behavioral Sciences at Stanford University, where, as he put it, he was engaged in putting together a manual of the "studies of naturally organized activities of an everyday nature" (ethnomethodological studies) that have been published since 1967, the date when his *Studies in Ethnomethodology* appeared.[3]

Garfinkel names four persons whose "writings have provided me with inexhaustible directives into the world of everyday activities."[4] They are Talcott Parsons, under whom he studied at Harvard; Alfred Schutz, whom he visited and studied under at the New School for Social Research; and the phenomenological philosophers Aron Gurwitsch and Edmund Husserl.[5] *Studies in Ethnomethodology* is replete with references to Schutz, and Garfinkel says that his own work is heavily indebted to him.[6] Parsons' influence is less obvious but relates to a point that is fundamental to both functionalism and ethnomethodology: an underlying trust as the basis of human behavior. As we will see in the following section, Garfinkel wants to break the taboo on questioning the social order and uncover the "taken-for-granted" assumptions" or "myths" that are operating in the interaction situation.[7]

ETHNOMETHODOLOGY DEFINED

Garfinkel disagrees with Durkheim's view that social facts, the subject matter of sociology for Durkheim, have objective reality, are *sui generis*, and are "out there somewhere." Instead, Garfinkel says, ethnomethodology sees the objective reality of social facts as an "ongoing accomplishment of the concerted activities of everyday life."[8] By this he means that in everyday situations the individual invokes or recognizes social facts, such as taken-for-granted norms or values, that interpret the meaning of the situation for that person. When he "makes sense" of the situation by recognizing implicit social norms, the individual is constructing the social reality. In other words, he is ordering his experiences so that they are in line with what we consider the everyday social world to be like. Garfinkel proclaims that ethnomethodological studies "analyze everyday activities as members' methods for making those same activities visibly-rational-and-reportable-for-all-practical-purposes, that is 'accountable' as organizations of commonplace everyday activities.[9]

Garfinkel's special language, like Parsons's, creates a great deal of consternation in the reader. Garfinkel's writing is reminiscent of Parsons's in that it takes much time and patience to understand what he is trying to communicate, a real impediment for nonethnomethodologists trying to read his work.

What Garfinkel is saying, essentially, is that ethnomethodology denies the functionalists' suggestion that social facts have a reality of their own that impinges on the individual.

... By contrast, ethnomethodologists do not treat order as "out there somewhere," created by society independently of the individual experiencing and living within it. Instead, ethnomethodology studies the process by which people invoke certain taken-for-granted rules about behavior with which they interpret an interaction situation and make it meaningful. To ethnomethodology, in fact, the interpretive process itself is a phenomenon for investigation. Thus, for functionalists, norms and values are explicit and "out there" acting on the individual; . . . for ethnomethodologists, the origin of norms and values is not of primary interest. Their interest is in the process by which human beings interact and prove to each other that they are following norms and values.

It should be clear by now that ethnomethodology does not aim to "explain" human behavior or to show why, for example, places and generations vary in their suicide and divorce rates, or why religion "really" exists. The emphasis in this perspective is on description, and the subject matter-people's methods of making sense of their social world-poses different questions from those asked by traditional sociology. Ethnomethodologists are interested in the interpretations people use to make sense of social settings. Hugh Mehan provides us with a graphic illustration of the incorrect assessments made about students by teachers who interpret test results without examining the children's own perceptions and understandings of the testing materials. As Mehan describes:

> The California Reading Test consists of a number of words, sentences and paragraphs along the left side of the page contained in an arrow which points to a series of three pictures arrayed along the right side of the page.

The child is told to "mark the picture that goes best with the words in the arrow."

One question had the word "fly" in the arrow pointing to pictures of an elephant, a bird, and a dog. The correct answer to this (obviously) is "the bird." The answer sheet of many of the first grade children showed that they had chosen the elephant alone or along with the bird as a response to that question. When Mehan asked them why they chose that answer, they replied: "That's Dumbo." Dumbo, of course, is Walt Disney's flying elephant, well known as an animal that flies, to children who watch television and read children's books.[10]

Mehan concludes that when children apply the word *fly* to an elephant, this many be "evidence to the tester that the child cannot abstract the similar features of objects and has 'impoverished' conceptual abilities. But this conclusion denies the actual complexity and richness of the child's day to day lived life." According to the way the tester views and interprets the test, the child has shown an inability to use some of the background skills of conceptual thought. But the children, who do not yet necessarily know the "right way" to answer the test, may have made sense of it-differently, yes, but on the basis of conceptual skills nonetheless. Incorrect answers, therefore, can result from a discrepancy between adult and student views of the world. Rather than take the question and the responses on the test sheet at their "face value," as the teachers did, Mehan probed for the way the student interpreted the question and the answer. The child's response told Mehan what meaning that particular student got out of the situation; in a real sense, the student was "accounting for" a previous action by showing how she or he had made sense of the task. This notion of "accounting" is one Garfinkel has devoted considerable attention to.

ACCOUNTS

Accounting is people's ability to announce to themselves and others the meaning they are getting out of a situation. Accounts involve both language and meaning; people are constantly giving linguistic or verbal accounts as they explain their actions. Garfinkel urges ethnomethodologists to call attention to reflexive practices: ". . . by his accounting practices the member makes familiar, commonplace activities of everyday life recognizable *as* familiar commonplace activities; . . . on each occasion that an account of human activities is used, . . . they (should) be recognized for 'another first time' . . ."[11]

For instance, when a child is asked to "tell about" his or her own creative production and then proceeds to do so and to interpret the figures, shapes, and colors in the drawing to another person, the child is giving an "account." If an art teacher is truly interested in the student's own interpretation of a drawing, that teacher will carefully phrase the request as something like, "tell me about it," so as to invite an interpretation from the student's own world of meaning; and from the "account" will emerge the student's meaning.

Much of the accounting that people "make" to each other about their behavior is done in an abbreviated form, because commonplace conversation assumes a "common understanding" of many things that are "left out" of the conversation. Terms that require mutual understanding and that are not explicated verbally Garfinkel calls "indexical expressions." One of the assignments Garfinkel gives to his students is to "report common conversations by writing on the left side of a sheet what the parties actually said and on the right side what they and their partners (in the conversation) understand that they were talking about."[12] The result is that much more is written on the right-hand side that the left-hand side. What is "left out" on the left-hand side is related (as Garfinkel puts it) to the "previous course of the conversation, or the particular relationship of actual or potential interaction that exists between user and auditor."[13] Garfinkel refers to this practice of "filling in" the meanings to talk as the "et cetera" principle; it is a "shorthand" way of talking.

Accounts and meanings in any situation are largely dependent on the nature of the situation they are a part of. Garfinkel points out that the meanings two people attach to any interaction are linked to its location and time, the persons present, the purpose or intention of the actors, their knowledge of each other's intentions-all of which are aspects of the indexicality. Garfinkel is saying that social interaction is explicable only in context, and contextual relevance is at the heart of ethnomethodology's concerns. He therefore places contextuality and indexicality at the center stage in his discussion of ethnomethodology.

Garfinkel mentions a related issue, the "sanctioned properties of common discourse."[14] This refers to people's expectation that there will be no interference with the conduct of everyday affairs in the form of questions about what is "really said." In other words, it is expected and required that people *will* understand plain, everyday talk so that common conversational affairs can be conducted without interference. To illustrate the "sanctioned character" of these properties, Garfinkel presents the following experiment: "Students were instructed to engage an acquaintance or a friend in an ordinary conversation and, without indicating that what the experimenter was asking was in any way unusual, to insist that the person clarify the sense of his commonplace remarks."[15]

Below is one student's account of this experiment:

> The subject was telling the experimenter, a member of the subject's car pool, about having had a flat tire while going to work the previous day.
> (S) I had a flat tire.
> (E) What do you mean, you had a flat tire?
> She appeared momentarily stunned. Then she answered in a hostile way. "What do you mean, 'What do you mean?' A flat tire is a flat tire. That is what I meant. Nothing special. What a crazy question."[16]

This account is a good illustration of "sanctioned character" because the subject actually became hostile. Also, she attempted to "make sense" of the situation by treating it as a "crazy question." Obviously, there are many occasions when the question "What do you mean?" is perfectly acceptable and, in fact, is expected for purposes of clarification. But there are other occasions, like the one just described, when the question becomes a "violation of the scene" for the subject. The student actually "made trouble" by questioning indexical expressions based on mutual understanding, and the questioning introduced a sense of distrust into the situation. The subject attempted to make order of a disorderly scene. Her announcement that it was a crazy question was her way of assembling an orderly scene.

Accounts, then, are the actors' announcements to one another of the situation as they see it. It is important to study how people build "accounts" of social actions while doing that action, because making sense of a situation is involved in giving linguistic accounts of social interaction. (As Garfinkel puts it, "To do interaction is to tell interaction"). It is not surprising, therefore, that many ethnomethodologists are engaged in linguistic analysis, for these endeavors are at the heart of ethnomethodology's concerns.

DOING ETHNOMETHODOLOGY

The ways of "doing" ethnomethodology, or the various methods that have been utilized by ethnomethodologists in gathering data for analysis, include open-ended, or depth interviews; participant observation; the documentary method of interpretation; and ethnomethodological "experiments."

The meaning that the individual imparts to everyday life situations is of prime importance to ethnomethodologists. Therefore, we can expect to see them conducting open-ended depth interviews with people, because this is an excellent way of gathering data that convey subjective meaning. Two projects employing this methodology were Garfinkel's jury deliberation study and Mehan's school testing study. Garfinkel had taped sessions of the actual jury deliberations, but the personal interviews with the jurors revealed the sources of the knowledge that they drew on in order to do the work of jurors. Thus, Garfinkel's interviews with jurors revealed the following about how the jurors knew what they were doing in doing the work of jurors:

> Jurors learned the official line from various places: from the juror's handbook; from the instructions they received from the court; from the procedure of the *voire dire* when jurors were invited by the court to disqualify themselves if they could find for themselves reasons why they could not act in this fashion. They learned it from court personnel; they learned it from what jurors told each other, from T.V., and from the movies. Several jurors got a quick tutoring by their high school children who had taken courses in civics.[17]

In like manner, Mehan used personal interviews with students who had been tested to get at their own interpretations of the test questions as well as their own personal meanings of their responses to the test questions. Another example is the case study of a transsexual reported by Garfinkel in "Passing and the Managed Achievement of Sex Status in an Intersexed Person."[18] Most of the data presented there were gleaned from thirty-five hours of tape-recorded conversations with Agnes, a nineteen-year-old girl raised as a boy, who was constantly experiencing the risks and uncertainties involved in learning to act and feel like a woman.

Depth interviewing combined with participant observation can highlight the problematic areas of an individual's everyday life, areas that might otherwise have been hidden and never brought to light. For instance, in his study, *Passing On*, David Sudnow says that his ethnomethodological perspective enabled him to spot the ambiguity of the bereaved status and thus to highlight the "essentially troublesome character of the normative elements in grief."[19] Sudnow notes:

> Bereaved persons apparently have considerable difficulty in their management of the properties of their own situation. They frequently don't know at what point they should undertake activities typically engaged in prior to death, and a large part of their difficulty derives from the sheer fact of their known status as a bereaved, which leaves them open to being treated sorrowfully no matter how they might conduct themselves. It is felt that only with time do they lose their status as bereaved in the eyes of others and cease to encounter treatments as a grievous person, and that time can often come long after they have ceased regarding themselves in that fashion.[20]

Functionalists like Parsons, for instance, maintain that grief is functional for the release and reduction of tension, and they assume that the role of the bereaved and those around the bereaved are societally clear cut. Ethnomethodologists like Sudnow may be revealing to us the limits of the culturally created role. There are wide gaps in the cultural prescription, and individuals experience the gaps very sharply. (For example, Sudnow's research shows that the bereaved person may be anxiously asking, "How am I supposed to act here?").

Another method used by sociologists who are "doing ethnomethodology" is called the "documentary method of interpretation." Garfinkel credits Mannheim with the label and quotes his definition as the search for "an identical homologous pattern underlying a vast variety of totally different realizations of meaning." Garfinkel says:

> The method consists of treating an actual appearance as "the document of," as "pointing to," as "standing on behalf of" a presupposed underlying pattern. Not only is the underlying pattern derived from its individual documentary evidences, but the individual documentary evidences, in their turn, are interpreted on the basis of "what is known" about the underlying pattern.[21]

To Garfinkel, the documentary method is something people are constantly using as they continually interpret and reinterpret each others' behavior and look for underlying patterns. One use of the documentary method by an ethnomethodologist is found in a study of the convict code by D. Lawrence Wieder.[22] As a participant observer at a halfway house, Wieder, after several months and many conversations with residents, detected a code that was operative. The code included prohibitions against snitching, copping out, taking advantage of other residents, messing with other residents, and trusting staff, as well as positive injunctions to share what you had and to help and show loyalty to other residents. "Telling the code," did not simply describe, analyze, and explain a situation in that environment. It was also the way residents actually guided conduct. For instance, when a resident terminated a conversation by saying, "You know I won't snitch," he was not only negatively sanctioning the prior conduct of the person with whom he was interacting and thereby terminating the conversation; he was also pointing out potential consequences if his associate persisted. Thus, "telling the code" was extremely persuasive.

A final method, or way of "doing ethnomethodology," is to engage in an ethnomethodological "experiment" in which researchers disrupt ordinary activity, or, as Garfinkel puts it, "violate the scene." When they do this, the researchers are interested in what the subjects do and what they look to in order to give the situation an appearance of order, or to "make sense" of the situation.[23]

However, although some ethnomethodologists, like Garfinkel, find ways to "make trouble" themselves so that they can study how people attempt to bring order out of chaos-and many of Garfinkel's own students assignments are this type of endeavor-we would like to enter a note of caution. We suggest that a rather acute sensitivity is required for researchers who decide to "violate the scene" and thus "create" ethnomethodological data. For example, when one of the authors gave Garfinkel's "boarder" assignment to her students, there were some disturbing results. To summarize briefly, in this assignment the students were to spend "from fifteen minutes to an hour in their homes imagining that they were boarders and acting out this assumption. They were instructed to conduct themselves in a circumspect and polite fashion. They were to avoid getting personal, to use formal address, to speak only when spoken to."[24]

The rather distressing result we found with our own students is related to the question of sensitivity and trust. One of the students who attempted to complete the boarder assignment was a recently divorced woman with two young children. The children were so threatened by the shattering of their world at home when the mother began to act out the boarder role that they simply could not handle it, even for fifteen minutes. Though the mother ended the experiment immediately, she said that it took her at least a month to reassure the children that their world was not, in fact, shattered; and she went to great lengths to prove herself with them after that incident, until they finally came to the point where they felt they could trust her again. She felt that it was too soon after their father's departure from the home; when the mother become a boarder, she was, in a sense, "leaving them" also.

Garfinkel's concept of trust explains how people comply with a certain order of events and is, as we have seen, close to Parsons' idea of shared normative expectations. How do people perceive and interpret their daily lives and how do objects and events and facts come to be seen as normal, as making sense? Garfinkel's answer is "trust." That is, rules are ambiguous, and they are perceived and interpreted differently; but the actor "trusts" the environment in the face of this uncertainty.[25]

The notion of trust is an important element in the incident with the divorced mother and her children. Their reaction to her taking on the role of boarder should underscore the complexities involved in the decision to "violate the scene." Our position is that certain ethical questions should be addressed in advance, well before the ethnomethodologists go out into the field to "make trouble."

NOTES

[1] Helmut R. Wagner, "Sociologists of Phenomenological Orientations: Their Place in American Sociology," *The American Sociologist* 10 (1975), p. 181.
[2] Helmut R. Wagner, "Sociologists of Phenomenological Orientations," p. 184.
[3] Personal interview, September 1975.
[4] Garfinkel, *Studies in Ethnomethodology*, (Englewood Cliffs, N.J.: Prentice-Hall, 1967), p. ix.
[5] Mullins, *Theories and Theory Groups*, New York: Harper & Row, 1973), p. 185.
[6] Garfinkel, *Studies in Ethnomethodology*, pp.31-37.
[7] See Randall Collins, *Conflict Sociology*, (New York: Academic Press, 1975).
[8] Garfinkel, *Studies in Ethnomethodology*, p. vii.
[9] Ibid.
[10] Hugh Mehan, "*Ethnomethodology and Education*." In D. O'Shea, ed., *Sociology of the School and Schooling* (Washington, D.C.: National Institute of Education, 1974), p. 20. See also Hugh Mehan, "*Structuring School Structure*," *Harvard Educational Review*, 48 (1978), pp. 50-51.
[11] Garfinkel, *Studies in Ethnomethodology*, p. 9.
[12] Ibid., p. 38.
[13] Ibid., p. 40.
[14] Ibid., p. 41.
[15] Ibid., p. 42.
[16] Ibid.
[17] Garfinkel, *Studies in Ethnomethodology*, p.110.
[18] Ibid., pp. 116-85.
[19] David Sudnow, *Passing On: The Social Organization of Dying* (Englewood Cliffs, N.J.: Prentice-Hall, Inc., 1967), p. 140.
[20] Ibid., p. 137.
[21] Garfinkel, *Studies in Ethnomethodology*, p. 78.
[22] See Turner, *Ethnomethodology: Selected Readings*. (Baltimore: Penguin, 1974), pp. 144-72.
[23] We have found, incidentally, that students tend to get a better grasp of what ethnomethodology is all about by completing some of the experiments and/or assignments mentioned by Garfinkel. (See especially the experiments on pp. 38, 42, 47, 79, and 85 in *Studies in Ethnomethodology*.)
[24] Garfinkel, *Studies in Ethnomethodology*, p. 47.
[25] Aaron V. Cicourel, *Method and Measurement in Sociology* (New York: The Free Press, 1964), p. 206.

PART III
METHODOLOGICAL STANCES

From our exposition of the major underlying assumptions, it should be evident that symbolic interactionism is both a theory in social psychology and a particular methodological approach. From underlying assumption #7, the necessity of sympathetic introspection, the emphasis is to gain a subjective understanding of human behavior. In order to discover the symbols and meanings that a group defines as important and real, their "definition of the situation" and "constructions of reality," the researcher must get as close as possible to the individuals. One must place herself or himself in their subject's shoes.

Two major, opposing theoretical approaches have dominated the field of social psychology: (a) logical positivism, and (b) phenomenology. The former approach, following the natural sciences, aims at "objective knowledge" by seeking to discover the causal factors underlying human behavior. Often termed the "behaviorist" approach, it is based on the premise that the behavior of humans can be analyzed in the same manner as that of the "lower animals"—using the same theories, concepts, and methods. These social psychologists contend that the results obtained from studies on animals can be utilized to explain human behavior. Another proposition upon which their approach is based is the notion that behavior, both animal and human, is unconscious, automatic, rooted in physiological processes, with no choice being involved. Behavior is viewed as "stimulus-response."

Over and against this approach, phenomenological social psychologists emphasize the unique nature of human relationships. Human behavior is conceived of as entirely different from the behavior of animals. A proposition of this approach centers on the voluntaristic, emergent, unpredictable nature of human behavior. For phenomenological social psychologists, humans are not robots operating mindlessly according to a stimulus-response model. Humans have the capacity to choose the stimuli to which they wish to respond. Positivists and phenomenologists are both found among interactionists.

The selections in this section deal with the methodological approaches used by symbolic interactionists. The readings illustrate the divergent views on how one should study human behavior, ranging from a phenomenological approach to one that comes close to the positivist stances, to all shades in between.

The first selection, by Herman, underscores the diversity in interactionist methodological approaches by contrasting the methodologies of Herbert Blumer, a Chicagoan, with Manford Kuhn, an Iowan. The author then presents an overview of the variety of methods used by symbolic interactionists to conduct their research. Such methods include: participant observation, interviewing, life histories, experiments, surveys, film, and photography.

The selection on "Sociological Analysis and the 'Variable'" presents Herbert Blumer's criticisms of conventional research methods. As Herman emphasized, Blumer mounted a consistent and persistent attack upon prevailing sociological theory and research. His criticisms question the validity and reliability of data collected through quantitative research methods. For Blumer, current "fads" of research protocol—that is, beginning with *apriori* theory, shifts analysis away from the direct examination of the empirical social world to preconceived notions about what is "real" and "true." Instead, he argues that the nature of the empirical world should dictate the types of methods used to study it. In short, Blumer advocates the more frequent use of exploratory methods, whereby the researcher is able to gain an understanding of the symbolic processes that shape social interaction.

Carl Couch, Michael Katovich and Steven Buban, in our next paper, further amplify the differences between the methodological agendas of the Chicago and the Iowa school proponents. Specifically, the authors critically compare the ontological and epistemological assumptions of the Iowa and Chicago schools of symbolic interactionism. Further, they demontrate how each school has contributed to the development and maintenance of a new Iowa school of thought that has synthezied the best elements from both traditions.

Our final selection by Anson Shupe and David Bromley deals with five methodological problems they faced in conducting participant observational research on two antagonistic groups: members of the Unification Church, and an organization that deprograms cult members. Such problems included: pressures to "go native," problems regarding their role definition, pressures to take a public stand, problems with gathering comparable data and problems related to evolving commitments—common dilemmas faced by most researchers at one time or another.

SUGGESTED READINGS

Blumer, Herbert. 1969. "The Methodological Position of Symbolic Interactionism." Pp. 1–69 In Herbert Blumer, *Symbolic Interaction*. New York: Prentice-Hall. A classic statement on the inductive approach espoused by Chicago interactionists.

Cooley, Charles H. 1926. "The Roots of Social Knowledge." *American Journal of Sociology* 32: 59–79. A classical statement of the "sympathetic introspective" methodological stance.

Couch, Carl. 1986. "Questionnaires, Naturalistic Observation and Recordings." Pp. 45–69 Supplement 2 In Norman K. Denzin (ed.), *Studies in Symbolic Interaction:The Iowa School Part (A)*. A discussion of the major methods utilized by the Iowa school to test hypotheses.

———. 1987. *Researching Social Processes in the Laboratory*. Greenwich, Connecticut: JAI Press. Comprehensive text dealing with how to carry out the deductive, confirmatory approach in the laboratory.

Denzin, Norman K. 1970. "The Methodologies of Symbolic Interaction: A Critical Review of Research Techniques." Pp. 447–465 In Gregory Stone and Harvey Farberman (eds.), *Social Psychology Through Symbolic Interaction*. Waltham, MA: Ginn-Blaisdell. An overview of the major research methods utilized by interactionists.

———. 1989. *The Research Act*. Chicago: Aldine. Comprehensive exposition on the methods of symbolic interaction.

Kuhn, Manford H., and Thomas McPartland. 1954. "An Empirical Investigation of Self-Attitudes." *American Sociological Review* 19:68–76. A classic example of the Iowa school methodological approach.

Manning, Peter K. 1982. "Analytic Induction."Pp. 273–302 In Robert Smith and Peter K. Manning (eds.), *Qualitative Methods*. Cambridge: Ballinger. Deals with the logic of the inductive, exploratory approach.

Chapter 9 INTERACTIONIST RESEARCH METHODS: AN OVERVIEW

Nancy J. Herman

In the broadest sense, the concept methodology refers to the processes, principles, and procedures by which we approach problems and seek answers. Within the discipline of sociology, the term refers to the manner by which one conducts research.

Two major philosophical approaches have dominated sociology: (1) logical positivism and (2) phenomenology. The former, stemming from the works of Comte (1896) and Durkheim (1950), among others, seeks to discover grand, external laws operating above and beyond the level of the individual case or to ascertain the social facts or the causal factors underlying human behavior. Society is studied from "outside to inside" with little regard for the subjective states of the individuals themselves.

By contrast, the phenomenological approach, stemming from the works of such scholars as Alfred Schutz (1921, 1964, 1970, 1971), Edmund Husserl (1913) (1936); Immanuel Kant,(1963), Wilhelm Dilthey,(in Buber 1955), Max Weber (1964) initially seeks to discover neither laws of nature nor the causal factors underlying human behavior. The primary concern of the phenomenologist is to "get back to the phenomena themselves", to obtain "Verstehen," or "subjective understanding," of human behavior from the actors' points of view. Society is studied from "inside to outside."

Given that the positivists and phenomenologists focus on different questions and seek different answers, their research undoubtedly requires different methods. The positivist, following the "Scientific Method," is interested in confirmatory research; that is, the aim is to statistically test a priori theories specified at the onset of the study. The positivist is interested in searching for correlations or associations between phenomena. Using deductive logic, in an effort to explain some class of empirical phenomena, broad, abstract statements are narrowed down to more concrete propositions. Specific hypotheses or sets of predictions based on the theory are constructed and lend themselves to testing. The aim of this research then, is to confirm or refute these hypotheses statistically.

The phenomenologist, on the other hand, begins with no a priori theory, no preconceptions or hypotheses; the aim is not to statistically test relationships between operationally-defined variables. The phenomenologist, rather, is interested in generating theory; the aim of the research is exploratory in nature. Through inductive logic, the researcher gathers descriptive data on the nature of social life. An analytic inductive approach is one in which the acquisition of knowledge works out from the actual data to the development of theoretical models. The end result is the discovery of "grounded theory" (Glaser and Strauss, 1967)—theory embedded in the real life experiences of the actors themselves. The phenomenologist rejects the canons of the scientific method and argues instead for "inter-subjective" (Welch, 1958) and "trans-subjective" (Tiryakian, 1965) understanding of the data. In short, phenomenologists advocate an approach to studying the empirical world wherein the researcher interprets the world from the subjective perspectives of the subjects under examination.

Within symbolic interactionism, there has arisen considerable controversy surrounding not only its ontological assumptions and concepts but also with respect to its methodological agenda. The poles around which such controversy rages, are termed the "Chicago" and "Iowa" schools of symbolic interactionism. The principal exponent of the Chicago school is Herbert Blumer, who trained students in this approach at the University of Chicago. Manford Kuhn is considered to be the leading spokesperson of the Iowa approach, a version of symbolic interactionism developed at the University of Iowa. The differences between the two have been discussed in detail elsewhere. (Meltzer and Petras, 1970; Reynolds, 1993). We shall briefly summarize the similarities and differences here.

In terms of points of convergence, both Chicago and Iowa symbolic interactionists agree that humans have the creative capacities to develop and employ symbols to denote aspects of the world around them. Moreover, what makes humans unique are their symbolic capacities. Humans are capable of symbolically denoting social objects which can be utilized to shape their definitions of situations and their interactions. Humans are able to engage in self-reflection and view themselves as objects. In terms of sociological methods, the Chicago and Iowa schools agree that methods must focus upon the social processes by which humans define their social situations and select particular courses of action. From this initial starting point however, Blumer and Kuhn and their respective followers diverge in terms of what each conceives to be the appropriate method for studying humans and society. Their methodological approaches follow from the thinkers' ontological assumptions about what they are capable of discovering.

The divergence between Blumer's and Kuhn's varying methodological approaches centers on their assumptions concerning the operation of symbolic processes. As Turner (1986) rightly notes, the issue is one of causality. Whether events are conceived as resulting deterministically from causes ultimately bears upon the methodologies adopted. In Blumer's (1969) indeterministic schema, social structure is conceived of as emergent phenomenon, the product of shared interpretations. It is the result of actors' internal symbolic processes in attempting to group together their behaviors into an organized, coherent pattern. "Rather than being the result of system forces, societal needs, and structured mechanisms, social organization is the result of mutual interpretations, evaluations, definitions, and mappings of individual actors" (Turner, 1986:342). For Blumer and the Chicagoans, the symbolic processes of humans cannot be conceived as a mechanism through which social forces operate; rather, they must be viewed as shaping the manner by which structures are created, maintained, and transformed. In this scheme, it is difficult to establish causality. Social structures, or organizations, do *not* cause human behavior, as they are merely one type of object affecting an individual's symbolic thinking. Humans thus insert a number of objects into situations. According to Blumer's conception of the social world then, human behavior does not have clear causes. The kinds of factors affecting a person's definition of the situation are of the person's own choosing and thus not subject to causal analysis.

By contrast, Kuhn argues for a deterministic model of social organization. Kuhn conceives of social situations as comprising relatively stable networks of positions with attendant norms and expectations. While symbolic interactions between individuals create and alter these situations and structures, once created, they operate to constrain individuals. In this view then, social structures are viewed as relatively stable, particularly when the person's core self is invested in these networks of positions. If one has knowledge of the nature of the core self, of the expectations that one has internalized, and also of the specific expectations of a given situation, it is possible, according to Kuhn to *predict* people's definitions of situations and their behavior. Methods should, therefore, he held, focus on the causes of human behavior.

The divergent assumptions about human interaction, social structure, and causality have led Chicagoans and Iowans to adopt widely different methodological approaches. Blumer long argued for a distinctive methodology in the social sciences. Criticizing current research protocols, based upon the canons of logical positivism, he writes:

> ...much of present-day methodology is inadequate and misguided. The overwhelming bulk of what passes today as methodology is made up of such preoccupation as the following: the devising and use of sophisticated research techniques ... the construction of logical and mathematical models ... and the promotion of a particular procedure, such as survey research, as the method of scientific study. I marvel at the supreme confidence with which these preoccupations are advanced as the stuff of methodology (Blumer, 1969:26–27).

Blumer, borrowing from the phenomenologists, espouses a distinctive methodology for the social sciences, a nongeneralizing, idiographic method. Blumer's aim was to simply make social life intelligible. He argues that the research act itself must be viewed as a process of discovery or exploration—a process of symbolic interaction in which researchers take the role of the subjects under examination. Researchers must employ a set of concepts that will "sensitize" them to the people they are studying. Blumer argues for a two-fold research agenda involving: (1) *exploration*, wherein the researcher observes specific situations; this is followed by (2) *inspection*, whereby researchers utilize their data to refine concepts and incorporate them into general statements about human behavior. As he (1969:188) argues, those espousing the positivist philosophical approach do a serious injustice to the character and nature of the empirical world by making assumptions without tapping into them, by imposing their own social reality on the world; refusing to tap into them on the grounds of "scientific objectivity" undoubtedly leads to biased research:

> To try and catch the interpretative process by remaining aloof as a so-called "objective" observer and refusing to take the role of the acting unit is to risk the worst kind of subjectivism—the objective observer is likely to fill in the process of interpretation with his own surmises in place of

catching the process as it occurs in the experience of the acting unit which uses it.

In short, Blumer and the Chicago symbolic interactionists advocate an inductive exploratory approach to studying the empirical world, wherein the researcher interprets the real world from the subjective perspectives of the subjects under examination. One needs, carefully and empathetically, to "feel one's way inside the experience of the actor." The guiding maxim of exploration involves using such methods as direct observation, interviewing, letters and diaries, autobiographies and the like.

By contrast, Kuhn and proponents of the Iowa school, with their deterministic emphasis, stress the commonality of the methods in all the sciences—following the canons of logical positivism. For these scholars, the aim of methodology is to specify operational definitions of concepts that can be tested in various cases. As Hickman and Kuhn (1956:224) point out, the Iowans conceive of sociology as a generalizing science, meeting the usual scientific criteria in its effort to search for "standardized, objective, and dependable process[es] of measurement." Kuhn and his followers have spent much of their time redefining interactionism's basic concepts so that there would be no conflicts between them and the orthodox requirement for quantification measurement. Much of their effort has been devoted to developing operational measures of such concepts as the self, social act, object and reference group. One measurement for which Kuhn is most noted is the "Twenty Statements Test(TST)—an empirical measurement of the core self (Kuhn and McPartland, 1954). Kuhn and his followers assume that human behavior is not only organized but also directed. Moreover, self-attitudes are assumed to be the sources of such organization and direction. Self-attitudes are rooted in certain prescribed role patterns. Their elucidation will allow the sociologist to predict social behavior. The TST was developed as a standardized attempt to measure self-attitudes operationally.

To summarize, the Kuhnians conceive of the world in a deterministic fashion. Human behavior is structured or constrained by the core self. It involves actions that conform to situational expectations as mediated by requirements of the core self. For the Iowans, a positivist research agenda is advocated, a more "rigorous," "scientific", deductive format for sociological theorizing than their Chicagoan counterparts employ. Sociological methods must seek to measure with reliable rigor the actors' symbolic processes. Research should focus upon the definition and measurement of those variables having a causal influence on behaviors. Thus, research should use such structured measuring instruments as questionnaires and experiments to measure key variables.

Symbolic interactionist social psychologists (whether they be of the Chicagoan or Iowan orientation), adopt a variety of techniques to gather data on aspects of human behavior. Such methods include: (1) fieldwork/participant observation; ethnography; (2) interviewing; (3) the life history method (personal documents/archival documents, autobiographies); (4) the social experiment; and (5) film, photography. We shall now turn to a brief discussion of each.

(1) FIELD METHODS/ETHNOGRAPHY/PARTICIPANT OBSERVATION

The Chicago sociologist, Robert Park is quoted as having said to his students:

> You have been told to go grubbing in the library, thereby accumulating a mass of notes and a liberal coating of grime. You have been told to choose problems wherever you can find musty stacks of routine records based on trivial schedules prepared by tired bureaucrats...This is called "getting your hands dirty in real research."....But one more thing is needed: firsthand observation. Go and sit in the lounges of the luxury hotels and on the doorsteps of the flophouses; sit on the Gold Coast settees and on the slum shakedowns. In short, go get the seats of your pants dirty in real research. (McKinney, 1966:71).

Park and others felt that, in order to understand human behavior and social processes, researchers must immerse themselves in the worlds of their subjects, must study individuals "in their own terms," must attempt to grasp the symbolic meanings that the people themselves define as important and real—their "definitions of situations" (Thomas, 1928) and "constructions of reality" (Berger and Luckmann, 1967). This method, known variously as "field research," "qualitative research," "observational field research," "ethnographic research," "Chicago school research," and "participant observation," "signifies the relation which the human enters in some fashion in the experience and action of those he observes" (Blumer, 1966: vi). For the purposes of this paper, this method will be hereafter referred to as participant observation and will be defined as: a field strategy that concomitantly combines active participation with subjects, intensive observation in natural settings, with open-ended informal interviewing and document analysis.

As Rosalie Wax (1971) points out, the history of fieldwork can be traced back to Greek and Roman times, when travellers, intrigued with cultural differences, documented their observations, albeit in an ethnocentric fashion. In the early twentieth century, professionals (namely, doctors, lawyers, and government officials), gathered firsthand information on segments of their own society. So, for example, British reformers Charles Booth (1902, in Wax, 1971) and Beatrice Potter utilized participant observation in combination with formal interviewing and statistical analysis to analyze the working class of London.

Ethnographic research has a long history of use among anthropologists.[1] Franz Boas, often considered the founder of modern cultural anthropology, did field work with the Inuit of Baffin Island and, subsequently, with the North American Indians. Boas argued for the importance of developing detailed accounts of the natives' experiences and interpreting their practices within the cultural contexts in which they were situated. Unfortunately, most of Boas's experiences in the field were rather short; he relied heavily on interpreters and native informers. By contrast Malinowski (1922) lived with a tribe in the Trobriand Islands for a "extended period of time, during which he participated in their activities and ceremonial customs, learned their language, ate their foods, and traced genealogies and kinship systems. Ethnography is the task of describing a culture from the native's point of view. As Malinowski (1922:25) put it, the goal of ethnography is "to grasp the native's point of view, his relation to life, to realize his vision of his world."

In the 1920's, at the University of Chicago, a group of sociologists, borrowing from their anthropological counterparts, began doing first-hand fieldwork, participant observation studies of various social groups not located in some far-off land but in their own society. In his now classic study, *Street Corner Society*, William Foote Whyte (1943) spent over three years studying Cornerville, a lower-class Italian neighborhood in Boston's North end. Whyte not only moved to Cornerville but also lived with an Italian family. All of the data he collected were based upon his first-hand encounters and experiences with the people in the neighborhood. The researcher hung out on the streets with the "corner boys," and the "college boys." He participated in a wide variety of activities of his subjects, including bowling, an important activity in their lives.

Another Chicagoan, Herbert Gans (1962), conducted a somewhat similar study, which he published as *The Urban Villagers*. Gans moved into Levittown, another Italian neighborhood in Boston, where he not only made detailed observations but also actively participated in the lives of his subjects. The picture Gans painted of the West End was broader than Whyte's study of Cornerville. The former included descriptions of the family, work experiences, medical care, social relationships with social workers, and the web of social relationships that gave meaning to their lives.

A third community study utilizing fieldwork as the primary method of data collection was Eliot Liebow's (1967) work, *Tally's Corner*, in which he described his observations and experiences with black street-corner men with whom he interacted for over a year.

The community studies discussed above constitute only one small arena in which participant observation or field observation has been utilized. Other such studies include Adler's (1987) work on drug dealers; Anderson's (1923) classic ethnographic work on the hobo; Cressey's (1932) hallmark study of the marginal institution known as the taxi-dance hall; Denzin's (1987) study on alcoholics; Fine's (1987) work on Little Leaguers; Goffman's (1961) in-depth study of the mental institution, and Haas and Shaffir's (1977, 1987) research on the professionalization of medical students. Still other examples using participant observational methods are Lofland's (1966) study of the "Doomsday" religious cult, Sutherland's (1949) investigation of the world of the professional thief, Trarder's (1989) study of the homosexuals and Weinberg's (1960) examination of the Nudest subculture.

In all of these instances, the researcher "penetrated beneath the veil" (Boas, 1923), immersed herself in the natural settings of her subjects, joked with them, empathized with them, shared their concerns and experiences. The central aim of the researcher is to place herself in the shoes of those she desires to understand, to achieve "subjective understanding" (Weber, in Shils and Finch, 1949) or "sympathetic introspection." (Blumer, 1969).

In my own research with ex-psychiatric clients, (Herman, 1986, 1987, 1989) for over a four-year period, I interacted with them on street-corners, played cards with ex-patients at drop-in centers, shot billiards with them, attended their medical appointments, ate countless donuts and drank cups of coffee with them at a local coffee shop, interacted with many at homeless shelters, boarding homes, and so forth. I was, thus intimately involved in the everyday lives of my subjects. I became friends not only with the patients but also with many of their family members.

The Major Features of Participant Observation[2]

The primary component of ethnographic, or participant observation, research is the ethnographic account. Detailed accounts of what goes on in the everyday lives of the subjects are derived from the fieldnotes taken by the researcher. Fieldnotes are the "meat" of any study; the study is only as good as the quality of the fieldnotes kept. Fieldnotes should be written immediately following every trip into the field, every setting in which the researcher interacts with the subjects. There are many different prescriptions on how to "take notes." Some ethnographers, for example, (Bogdan and Taylor, 1975; Shaffir et al. 1987) argue that researchers should wait until they have left the setting and then commence recording their observations and conversations. Others (Festinger et al., 1956) secretly record a number of observations while in the field, and later translate their notes into full-fledged fieldnotes. In my own research on the psychiatric ward, (Herman, 1981b) I did both. For the most part, I waited until I left the setting, went home and then wrote up my complete fieldnotes of what had transpired that day. Sometimes, however, while in the setting, a respondent said something particularly complex or thought-provoking, or made a statement that I thought was central to my study. In these instances, I excused myself, went to the rest room, and wrote down the entire conversation on pieces of toilet paper which I shoved into my pockets. (On some nights, I am sure the patients thought I had chronic diarrhea, as I excused myself a number of times.) Some researchers keep fieldnotes by taking a tape recorder into the setting. There are both pros and cons to using a tape recorder. Certainly, its use eliminates the researcher's need to try to remember every conversation *verbatim*, or in sequence. However, sometimes one's subjects feel inhibited by this mechanical device and will "hold back" on information, especially if you are dealing with highly sensitive information. In my own research on the psychiatric ward, at some point in my research I had become overwhelmed with the wealth of information being told to me during my sessions on the ward. So, on my next excursion into the field, I decided to take a tape recorder. I asked my subjects' permission to use it—to do otherwise, would have been unethical. When permission was granted, I chit chatted with them and, when I felt they were at ease, I turned the machine on. From that moment on, the patients "froze." They were very much inhibited by the tape recorder. Although it was placed inconspicuously, my subjects stared at it, bent over to talk directly into the machine. Their answers were short and robot-like in tone. Clearly, our interactions were constrained by the tape recorder. Hence, I didn't use it again. I relied on my memory, and taking notes on toilet paper. As soon as I left the setting, on my ride back to my house, I turned on the tape recorder in my car and began recounting, in temporal sequence—every conversation, verbatim, the facial grimaces, smirks, all sights, sounds, smells—everything that had occurred on the ward.

Gold (1958) has identified four major roles a researcher may take in order to collect data: (1) the complete participant; (2) the participant as observer; (3) the observer as participant; and (4) the complete observer. Let us briefly examine each.

Complete participant—In this role, the researcher enters a setting without disclosing any aspects of the project or the researcher's true identity. The researcher is a covert observer whose scientific or professional aims are unknown to the subjects. The subjects are led to believe that the researcher is "one of them." Wallis (1977), for example secretly studied a religious group, the Scientologists. Lofland and Lejeune (1960) conducted secret observations on several Alcoholics Anonymous groups; Dalton (1959) conducted secret research on several large corporations; Humphreys (1970) covertly observed men engaging in sex in public rest rooms.

Researchers justifying the covert researcher role, (Douglas, 1976) make the argument that entry might otherwise be denied if their true identities as sociologists were presented to the group prior to the study. Taking an ethical relativist stance, these sociologists feel that they have the "right" to study all groups whether they desire to be studied or not. Another justification made is that subjects alter their behavior if they know they are being studied; thus, covert data collection yields more valid data. The majority of social researchers vehemently oppose covert research on both ethical and pragmatic grounds (Davis, 1961; Erikson, 1965; Gold, 1958; Johnson, 1976; Shils, 1959). In response, these sociologists, taking an ethical absolutist stance, argue that social scientists have no right to invade the privacy of individuals; and deliberate disguising of the intentions of research can potentially cause harm to the subjects. Further, opponents of covert research, or taking on a complete participant role, argue that difficulties undoubtedly arise with researchers recording their observations. Obviously, note pads cannot be visible, nor could tape recorders be used. Resorting to using hidden tape recorders also raises certain ethical issues. A further problem centers on the researcher being constrained within certain social roles. That is, as a complete participant, the researcher is forced to act in a certain way—to play a part, to say certain things, to have a great deal of knowledge about the group, its structure, ideology, etc. The researcher is unable to ask the types of questions a non-member might ask for fear of being discovered and perhaps forced to leave the group. As Gold (1958) concludes, "While the complete observer role offers possibilities of learning about aspects of behavior that might otherwise escape a field observer, it places him in pretended roles which call for delicate balances of role and self."

Participant-as-Observer—A second role that a researcher may assume is that of participant-as-observer. In contrast to the complete observer, the participant observer role is one in which the researcher has received consent from the subjects to participate and observe them in their natural environments. All of the subjects are aware of the scientific study and the role of the researcher. The researcher negotiates a bargain— a set of mutual obligations and promises agreed upon at the outset of the research. In some cases, the researcher negotiates the bargain with the subjects themselves, in other cases, negotiation occurs with the gatekeepers (see Herman 1981a; Haas and Shaffir, 1980). The type of bargain that is struck is crucial to the research endeavor. Time, setting, or sample constraints imposed by the subjects or gatekeepers at the outset may seriously hamper the study or the quality of data collected. In my study on institutionalized psychiatric patients (Herman, 1981), the administrative gatekeepers tried to strike a bargain with me wherein I would visit the ward only once a week for a period of one month. Moreover, they would "select" the patients that I was to interview. If I had agreed to accept these conditions, my study would undoubtedly have been incomplete and biased in nature. The aim of the researcher is to negotiate for free rein within the setting, to stay for an extended period of time, to interact with whoever wishes to speak with her.

Once access has been granted, the researcher begins to participate in the natural setting(s) of the subjects. During the first days (perhaps even weeks) in the field, the researcher may feel uncomfortable, anxious, or afraid. As Geer (1964) points out, such feelings are completely normal. Researchers inevitably make mistakes at work, especially during the first days in the field—they may say or do something that proves embarrassing. Bogdan and Taylor (1975) and others suggest that it is best to remain fairly passive during this time. They advise that one do more observing than participating. As the researcher begins to acquaint herself with the setting and participants, she will become more comfortable interacting.

During the early stages of fieldwork, subjects are sometimes wary or even hostile. The aim of the researcher is to develop rapport and establish their trust. Such a relationship is not built over night. It may take several weeks or months to acquire a relationship wherein subjects will be open and honest. In my own research on hospitalized mental patients (Herman, 1981b) trust was established in about one month. The patients asked me countless questions—many of which were quite embarrassing and highly personal in nature. They were as interested in my life as I was in theirs. Failure to open up and share with them would have hampered our relationship. Moreover, as subjects will sometimes do in the early stages of fieldwork, I was given a series of "tests" to see "whose side" I was on—tests to evaluate my trustworthiness. At the outset, I had ensured my subjects confidentiality and anonymity with respect to anything they told me. However, during the first days, I was "fed" tidbits of information— information such as ways to escape from the institution and ways to secure sex, drugs, and other commodities. My subjects wanted to see if I would report such information to the staff. When I did not, I passed their test and they certified me trustworthy. A bond developed between they and me. Once rapport has been established, the researcher is accepted as a member of the group, the task now centers on "learning the ropes" (Shaffir et al., 1987; Geer et al., 1968; Lofland, 1971) —obtaining intimate familiarity with the group, acquiring their perspectives, learning the meanings and symbols that the group defines as important and real. While there are no magical formulas for learning the ropes, the researcher must participate actively in the social world of her subjects.

At some point, affected by time, financial, and other constraints, the researcher makes the decision to leave the field and begin analyzing the data and writing up the findings. At this stage, known as "the disengagement process," the investigator is often faced with several difficulties (Maines et al., 1987; Letkemann, 1987; Altheide, 1987). Although I had told my subjects on a number of occasions of my impending leave, when I no longer returned to the psychiatric ward my subjects felt abandoned and cheated. Over the two years, I had become a large part of their lives and I was missed.

I, too, felt a void in my life when I no longer visited them on a regular basis. In retrospect, it would have been better had I gradually phased myself out of their lives rather than leaving cold-turkey.

Observer-as-Participant—In this role, the researcher typically interacts with the subjects only one or, perhaps, two times. In contrast to the previously described role in which the researcher may interact in the setting for several months or even several years, the observer as participant has brief contact with the subject. The researcher may orally administer a formal questionnaire (Miall, 1984); there is no attempt to establish rapport or develop a relationship between the two parties. (We shall discuss this method more fully in the next section, on interviewing).

Complete Observer—A fourth role is that of complete observer, wherein the investigator is completely removed from interacting with the subjects. The reader studies individuals in a laboratory environment. All variables are strictly controlled by the investigator who will observe and record behavior behind a one-way mirror (Brehm and Weintrab, 1977; Couch, 1988; Couch et al., 1986a, 1986b). We shall turn to a detailed discussion of this researcher role in our section on the social experiment.

II INTERVIEWS

A second basic research tool utilized by social psychologists is the interview. In many cases, the interview is used in conjunction with other data-collection methods, such as participant observation {previously discussed in this article} and the experimental method (discussion to follow). Simply put, interviewing may be defined as a conversation between two or more parties with a specific purpose in mind—that is, the researcher attempts to secure information from her respondent(s). Interviews may be categorized as follows: (1) unstructured or unstandardized; (2) semi-structured or focused; and (3) structured or standardized. (Babbie, 1983; Denzin, 1987; Fitzgerald and Cox, 1987).

The Structured/Standardized Interview

The standardized interview utilizes a predetermined, structured set of questions that are orally administered to respondents in exactly the same wording and order. The underlying rationale is that investigators have specific hypotheses/ideas or information that they want to uncover during the interview. They make the assumption that the questions asked will be all-encompassing and comprehensive so as to elicit all relevant data. Moreover, researchers make the assumption that all interviewees will share the same meaning of the questions being asked.

The Unstructured/Unstandardized Interview

Unstandardized, or unstructured, interviews do not include pre-specified sets of questions. Researchers begin with the underlying assumption that they do not know in advance what pertinent questions they will ask. In an unstructured interview, the interviewers must *in situ* develop, alter, and generate questions during the interview.

In many cases, unstructured interviews will be used to supplement participant observation. Howard Becker (1953) employed this method in his study of marijuana smokers. Similarly, Shaffir (1974) employed this method in his study of Hassidic communities. In my own research on psychiatric clients, I supplemented participant observation with informal, unstructured interviewing. In an effort to gain a fuller understanding of the social worlds of psychiatric clients, I used this method to gather additional information about my subjects, and to clarify observations or statements that were unclear to me. Sometimes, the unstructured interview might be utilized for establishing rapport through what Douglas (1985) terms "chit chat." Often this method will be employed when the researcher has little or no knowledge about the group she is studying. Questions are generated in the setting as the researcher attempts to make sense of the situations in which she is participating.

The Semi-Standardized or Focused Interview

Placed somewhere between the two extremes discussed above is the semi-standardized, semi-structured, or focused, interview. This kind of interview typically involves asking a number of predetermined questions in a specified order. However, this method allows the interviewer considerable leeway and freedom to probe beyond the set list of questions. So, for example, McCaghy and Skipper (1969), in their study on strippers and their occupational predispositions to lesbianism, used semi-structured interviews as their primary means of data collection. The interviews were designed to elicit information on the background of the strippers, the processual dimensions of their entrance into the occupation, and various aspects of the occupational subculture. McCaghy and Skipper followed their list of prepared questions, but the use of each question was guided by the responses of the interviewee. That is, if the latter was particularly responsive to a question, the researcher probed more extensively by asking supplementary questions (devised in advance). Questions that evoked minimal response were reworded by the interviewer. In short, utilizing the semi-structured, or focused, interview allows the interviewer to "tailor" or "customize" the interview to the respondent. In another classic study, Becker and Geer (1957; 1958) used the semistructured method in their study of medical students. A semi-structured interview might look like the following example:

Group Interviews

As social groups create their subjective understandings and structures of meaning, it is often useful to interview subjects in a group setting. For example, sometimes subjects provide the researcher with contradictory information. Group interviews can function as a locus for clarification of various discrepancies. In my own research in the psychiatric institution, I was informed by one patient of an underground economy, that is, commodities such as illegal drugs, cigarettes, and sex could be purchased. Another respondent denied such information. A group interview functioned to clarify the situation.

III THE LIFE HISTORY/BIOGRAPHICAL
METHOD/DOCUMENT ANALYSIS

Termed variously as the "life history method," "biographical method," "personal history," "document analysis," or the "life story" (Bogdan and Taylor, 1975; Denzin, 1970, 1989; Kluckholn, 1971; Titon, 1980), this method presents the subjective experiences and definitions of situations held by one person, one group, or one institution or organization as they interpret such experiences. Such materials refer to an individual's descriptive, first-person account of her life, in whole or part. Life history materials include any written records or documents, case histories of social agencies, letters, personal autobiographies, diaries, newspaper accounts, court records, and the like.[3]

The life history method was popularized by such early Chicagoan sociologists as Ernest Burgess, Robert Park, W.I. Thomas and Florian Znaniecki, among others. Although its popularity has diminished, we have seen a resurgence of interest in the past decade (Denzin, 1986; Plummer, 1983).

A basic underlying assumption of the life history method (similar to that of participant observation) is that human behavior must be understood from the perspectives of the acting units involved. Concern is directed toward recording the unfolding history of the individual's, group's, or institution's experiences. This method documents, in sequence, the various events that have affected their lives as they see them. The aim of the researcher is to record the subjects' stories as they tell them—their "definition of the situation" (Thomas, 1928). Subsequently, the subjective perspectives of others are studied.

The life history method may be divided into three major types (Allport, 1942; Denzin, 1989): (1) the comprehensive life history, (2) the topical life history, and (3) the edited life history. Moreover, two basic types of data are utilized to construct life histories: public archival records (birth and death, marriage records; judicial reports; case studies of welfare agencies; crime statistics, hospitalization records; mass media accounts) and private archival records or personal documents (autobiographies, diaries, letters, verbatim reports).

The comprehensive life history spans the entire life of the subjects under investigation from earliest memories up to and including the time of writing of the piece. This form of life history attempts to cover all of subjects' life experiences, providing a rounded, complete description of their life experiences. A comprehensive life history will combine as many data sources as possible (both public and private), but will focus upon the subject's own documents. Shaw's (1966) study, using autobiographical material, represents a comprehensive, biographical picture of the life of a juvenile delinquent.

By contrast, the topical life history offers a more fragmented, or segmented, picture of the life of a subject. It represents a "slice of their life." Denzin (1989) points to, as an example of this type of method, Edwin Sutherland's (1937) presentation of the life experiences of "Chic Conwell," a professional thief. Autobiographical material was the primary data source. Another example of the topical life history method is Bogdan"s (1974) study of "Jane Fry," a transsexual.

With respect to the third type, the edited life history, it may be either comprehensive or topical in focus. The researcher may utilize either public or private archival records, or some combination of both, to construct this type of life history. The characteristic feature of the edited life history is the role of the researcher in questioning the data, providing sociological explanations of the material, evaluating the data, and so forth. If utilizing autobiographies, the researcher edits them to eliminate repetition, shorten lengthy descriptions, and amplify important information. A classic example of this method is Thomas and Znaniecki's (1918–20) *The Polish Peasant*. A five-volume work, their study was based on an analysis of diaries, letters, and other documents. The researchers solicited, through an advertisement in a newspaper, letters written to Poland as well as those received by the new immigrants. Thomas and Znaniecki were able to document the interaction between these persons and their distant families, and to provide a history of their experiences in America—data on the human lived experience surrounding immigration. A second, contemporary example is Jacobs' (1967) study of suicide, utilizing letters as the primary means of data collection. Another such example, using television program transcripts as a type of public archival record, is Molotch and Boden's (1985) detailed study of the congressional Watergate hearings. Specifically, the researchers were interested in examining the manner by which individuals used specific conversations to acquire power. A final noteworthy example is Blee's (1987) study of the role of women and gender ideology in the Ku Klux Klan. In constructing her edited life history, the researcher made use of such official documents as speeches and articles crafted by the imperial commander of the women's Klan, organizational recruitment leaflets and pamphlets, and membership application forms. In short, the life history method, whether employing primary or secondary data sources, aims to tap into the subjective side of social experiences of individuals.

It has been argued that one shortcoming of this method is that problems exist with respect to the external validity of the data collected. Analyzing the experiences of one individual, one case, or a series of cases does not allow for generalizability to the larger population. Becker (1970) claims that the single life-history is largely inconclusive in nature and yields only a partial understanding of human behavior. Moreover, the internal validity of the data are challenged. Critics charge that the subjects may be biased, may choose to alter or omit portions of their life history, or may suffer from "forward" or "backward" telescoping; hence, the data are flawed.

IV THE SOCIAL EXPERIMENT

In general, the social experiment may be viewed as a method wherein the researcher, adopting a positivist stance, begins with an a priori theory, develops a set of hypotheses, operationalizes concepts, and sets out to confirm or refute the hypotheses. The researcher is interested in searching for causal connections between two or more variables. When a researcher is testing a hypothesis, or sets of hypotheses, control is of ultimate importance. Experiments are the method of choice when a researcher desires to maximize control. In experimental research one or more variables are manipulated under carefully controlled conditions. The task of the investigator is to assess clearly the effects of their experimental manipulation by measuring changes in a specific variable. Three strategies are available to the experimental investigator: (1) the laboratory experiment; (2) experimental simulation; and (3) the quasi-experiment, or field experiment. We shall now turn to a brief discussion of each.

The Laboratory Experiment[4]—Laboratory experiments provide the researcher with the greatest amount of control. The independent variables or causal variables may be manipulated by the investigator while all other variables are controlled or held constant. For the purposes of the study, the experimenter manufactures a contrived setting which allows for the manipulation or control of variables. Such experimental control allows the researcher to focus directly on the relationships among variables.

In the true laboratory experiment, the researcher begins with an a priori theory, deduces hypotheses, and defines independent and dependent variables and the causal relationships among them. In order to test these hypotheses, the researcher must necessarily compare at least two groups that are randomly selected: an experimental group and a control group. The design involves two sets of measures, one before and one after exposure to the independent variable(s). The experimental group is exposed to the independent variable, while the control group is not. The difference between the two groups during the post-test period is examined, controlling for the effect of other variables.

For example, we might be interested in testing the hypothesis that exposure to a documentary film on gays and lesbians will alter attitudes of college students toward this social group. The first steps in conducting our experiment would be to select the units of analysis and the experimental setting. We may decide to test our hypothesis from the sampling frame of students enrolled in our Sociology 100 class at our university. We obtain a random sample, and we divide subjects randomly into either the experimental group (those exposed to the film) or the control group (those not exposed). We ask the experimental group to report to the laboratory (classroom where the film is to be shown). Students will then fill out a questionnaire surveying their attitudes toward homosexuality. The same questionnaire is administered to the control group in another location. The data collected on the two groups should be approximately the same. Subsequently, the experimental group is shown the film. Some specified time after the film is shown, a second measurement is taken for both the experimental and control groups. The responses of the two groups will be compared. If there is a great shift in attitudes toward gays and lesbians for the experimental group, we may conclude that education plays a role in decreasing homophobic attitudes.

A number of other experimental studies of this nature have been conducted in the laboratory. For example, much of the research Iowan symbolic interactionist, Carl Couch and his students are engaging in occurs in this setting (Couch et al., 1986a&b). In their studies of interactional structures, college students were typically recruited for the study, some of whom were strangers to one another, while others were friends. In one representative study, fraternity members were recruited. Subjects were also recruited on the basis of their gender. The investigators videotaped the basic interactional processes that the subjects engaged in, their series of negotiations, and the social structures that emerged. The videotapes were subsequently transcribed and analyzed.

The Experimental Simulation[5] The experimental simulation is a research method which is similar to the laboratory experiment in some respects but different in others. Both laboratory experiments and experimental simulations create a specific setting for research purposes. The main difference between the two centers on the fact that experimental simulations attempt to fabricate a particular representative setting to mirror some real-life situation or setting, such as a hospital, prison, or supermarket; that is, researchers attempt to create a situation that *approximates* real life. Laboratory experiments, on the other hand, do not simulate natural settings in the lab. Once created, researchers, employing treatment groups, examine relationships between variables in an effort to formulate generalizations about interaction in that particular setting. Haney et al. (1973) used this design in their study to evaluate the dispositional hypothesis—that the deplorable state of prisons is due to the nature of the prisoners who populate it, those who administrate it, or both. Specifically, the researchers sought to recreate or simulate the social reality of prison life. A great deal of attention was given to administrative routine, uniforms, and various physical characteristics. Subjects, who were carefully screened, were assigned to roles as either "prisoners" or "guards." To enhance the realism, Haney et al. enlisted the aid of the municipal police to make unexpected arrests appear to be part of a routine raid. Moreover, a Catholic priest, a public defender, and families and friends of the prisoners made frequent visits to the prison—interaction which also added to the realism.

A second study using the simulated experiment is Darley and Batson's (1976) study examining the difference between situational and dispositional factors, specifically in terms of their effect on helping behavior. Personality scales were used to measure dispositional factors related to religiosity. The situational variable was manipulated by telling seminary students they had to hurry to a second location. Three "hurry conditions" were measured: some were told they were late (high hurry); a second group were told they were on time (intermediate hurry); a third group were told that they had a few minutes to reach the location (low hurry). The researchers sought to examine whether a person's religiosity (internalization of the philosophy of the Good Samaritan) and the amount of hurry in one's journey would affect their helping behavior toward a victim lying in an alley. Their results indicated that regardless of religiosity those not in a hurry were more likely to stop and offer help, but those in a hurry were more likely to keep going.

The Quasi-Experiment, or Field Experiment[6]

The quasi-experiment, or field experiment, is an attempt to mesh fieldwork with the experimental method. The researcher tries to obtain the best of both worlds: to gain maximum control over variables while not sacrificing the reality of social situations. Quasi-experiments employ treatment groups in their natural settings. Their emphasis centers on relationships between causal and caused variables while attempting to give attention to the particular social context.

Johnson (1971), for example used this method when studying behavior at a Billy Graham crusade. Johnson manipulated the independent variable, role playing, by assigning one treatment group to "passive" participant observation while the other was assigned to "active" participant observation. A non-treatment group, those not attending the rally, served as a control, or comparison, group. The researcher measured the dependent variable, religious commitment, using a questionnaire at three specified time periods: before the crusade and two times thereafter at three-week intervals.

In another field experiment, Goldstein (1971), in his study on aggression, sought to examine the effects on individuals witnessing violence in a natural setting. The researcher chose an Army-Navy football game in Philadelphia as his setting. Aggression, the dependent variable, was measured by administering three subscales from the Durkee Hostility Inventory. Measurements were taken before and after the event. Two groups of subjects were chosen, one in which aggression was measured prior to the game, and another group, on whom aggression was measured afterward. Data were also gathered on their allegiances to the specific teams, and social background factors.

Another example of the field experiment is provided by Filipe and Sommer's (1966) studies on individual's use of space. In one such study, of a mental institution, the researchers documented individuals' behaviors when their personal space had been violated. The experimenter would sit within six inches of a randomly-selected subject. A control subject would not have anyone sit next to him. The researchers measured in both experimental and control groups the "rates of vacancy—on how long it took the subject to get up and leave."

Although many sociologists and social psychologists argue that the experimental method is clearly "more scientific" than others discussed in this paper, a number of criticisms have been levelled against this methodological approach. Specifically, research conducted in the laboratory setting is "artificial" and, hence meaningless. Individuals act differently outside their natural settings. While such experiments possess a high level of internal validity, in terms of external validity, they cannot be generalized to the larger population, to individuals in other social settings. With regard to quasi-experiments, it is true that this method affords more "naturalness" than do laboratory experiments, but there is less control over variables in the natural setting. Therefore, a number of external extraneous variables may influence the outcome—variables over which the investigator has no control. This same criticism can be made of experimental simulations. While the researcher has some degree of control over the variables and the participants, other variables, over which the researcher has no control, may affect the simulation.

V FILM AND PHOTOGRAPHY

As Denzin (1989:210) notes, visual sociology, a fairly novel approach in the discipline, centers on the use of still photography, audio-visual records, and the analysis of films:

> Visual Sociology can be defined as that method of research which deals with two problems: how to get information on film and how to get information off film. It struggles with the problems of how observers see

and record what they perceive. What is perceived and then recovered is structured by cultural and contextual meanings. The information that is read off film is also shaped by cultural and contextual processes. Accordingly, as a method of research, visual sociology deals simultaneously with the grammars of vision, perception, and interpretation.

While the utilization of film and photography has had a long history in the social sciences, sociologists have only recently began to use this research tool. In the early 1940s, cultural anthropologists Gregory Bateson and Margaret Mead (1942) employed these methods, which culminated in their now famous photographic study of the Balinese. In the field of psychiatry, Arnold Gesell provided photographic accounts of childhood development.

Howard Becker (1981; 1986), a Chicagoan symbolic interactionist, is one of the leading lights in this area, having published several essays on the role of photography in sociological research. Erving Goffman (1976), also, utilized this method of data collection in his study of gender advertisements. Goffman's research indicates that gender displays, similar to other rituals, reflect vital features of the social structure, both negative and positive ones. Jackson (1977) used still photographs to depict prison experience in an Arkansas prison. So, too, have Iowan symbolic interactionists made ample use of this method in their research endeavors. So, for example, Carl Couch and his students (Couch, 1984; Couch, Saxton, and Katovich, 1986) have utilized videotape to capture social interactions within the laboratory setting. Moreover, for over twenty years, Clark McPhail (McPhail and Wohlstein, 1986) and his students have been studying collective behavior in public settings through the lens of the camera (Denzin, 1989:212).

The methods of visual sociology involve combining photographic or motion picture records of a situation with some type of textual material. These may include audio-voice recordings, transcripts of the audio-visual text, interviews with the subjects, or historical background material on the persons, event, or situation photographed or filmed as movies.

In terms of observer identities, similar to those discussed under the section on participant observation, the researcher may assume one of four researcher roles: (1) complete participant; (2) complete observer; (3) participant as observer; and (4) observer as participant.

In the complete participant role, the researcher poses as a member of the group and gathers data covertly. She pretends to be "one of them" and just happens to have a camera or video recorder with her. As mentioned in the section on participant observation, serious ethical questions are posed by gathering data in this manner.

By contrast, the complete observer role is one in which the researcher is completely removed from the interaction. As in the previous section on the social experiment, the researcher sets up recording equipment in the laboratory behind a one-way mirror. The video camera records the observations.

The participant-as-observer role is one in which the researcher informs the subjects of her true identity and requests permission to study them. A bargain is struck between the two parties, an agreement which specifies, among other things, what events and/

or persons will and will not be photographed. Rapport is established with the subjects prior to studying them. The investigator attempts to make the subjects feel comfortable with the camera or video equipment.

The observer-as-participant role is one in which the researcher makes little or no attempt to develop a relationship with the subjects being studied. A man taking pictures of people at the beach is acting out this role.

There are a number of problems associated with employing these visual research tools. As Becker (1986) and others have pointed out, sometimes, when the subjects are aware that they are being observed or photographed, they alter their behavior. Subjects may stage performances and take on roles that they think are expected of them. Sampling errors may also challenge the validity of the visual document. That is, the occasion or time period captured on still photograph or videotape may be unique and not generalizable. For example, a family acting supportive to a grieving widow during the funeral may present a picture of a family with close-knit ties—a closeness that is not ordinarily present. Similarly, taking pictures of families at Disneyworld does not provide us with a complete understanding of family life in the United States.

Another problem of employing this method centers on restrictions imposed by the subjects. There may be certain locations, activities, or persons who are "off-limits" to the camera. Such constraints affect the generalizability of the visual data.

Other threats to the validity of the data occur when the researchers attempt to stage the reality—that is, dictate to the actors how they are supposed to behave. Censorship may also be a problem. As Becker (1986:288) notes, censorship may be imposed by various government agencies, or by a private organization. Only culturally-sanctioned pictures may be taken, which ultimately leads to a distorted picture of reality.

So, too, can photographs be "faked." Photographers can retouch photos, erase certain things, or move objects, thereby altering the social reality.

A final threat to the validity of the visual documentary method centers on problems with respect to transcription and interpretation. When a video-tape is made of a social encounter, it is necessary for the researcher to make a transcript of the conversations. As Couch (1987a) states, this is very often a difficult task. It may take several drafts for the transcriber to accurately record all utterances and non-verbal behaviors and to place everything in correct orderly sequences.

All the above described methods have been used by various symbolic interactionists.

BIBLIOGRAPHY

Abelson, R. 1968. "Simulation of Social Behavior." Pp. 72–87 In *The Handbook of Social Psychology*, edited by G. Lindzey and E. Aronson.

Adler, Patricia. 1985. *Wheeling and Dealing*. New York: Columbia University Press.

Allport, Gordon W. 1942. *The Use of Personal Documents in Psychological Research*. New York: Social Science Research Council.

Altheide, David L. 1974. "Leaving the Newsroom." Pp. 301–310 In *Fieldwork Experience: Qualitative Approaches to Social Research*, edited by William Shaffir, Robert A. Stebbins, and Allan Turowetz. New York: St. Martin's Press.

Anderson, N. 1923. *The Hobo*. Chicago: University of Chicago Press.
Babbie, Earl. 1983. *The Practice of Social Research*, 3d ed. Belmont, CA: Wadsworth Publishing.
Bateson, Gregory and Margaret Mead. 1942. *Balinese Character: A Photographic Essay*. New York: New York Academy of Sciences.
Becker, Howard S. 1953. "Becoming a Marijuana User." *American Journal of Sociology* 59:235–242.
———. 1970. "The Relevance of Life Histories." In *Sociological Methods: A Casebook*, edited by Norman K. Denzin. Chicago: Aldine.
———. 1981. *Exploring Science Photographically*. Evanston, Ill: Mary and Leigh Block Gallery, Northwestern University Press.
———. 1986. *Doing Things Together: Selected Papers*. Evanston, Ill: Northwestern University Press.
Becker, H.S. and Geer, B. 1957. "Participant Observation and Interviewing: A Comparison." *Human Organization*, 16:28–32.
———. 1958. "The Fate of Idealism in Medical School." *American Sociological Review* 23:50–56.
Berg, Bruce. 1989. *Qualitative Research Methods for the Social Sciences*. Boston: Allyn and Bacon.
Berger, P. and T. Luckmann. 1967. *The Social Construction of Reality*. New York: Doubleday.
Bertaux, Daniel. 1981a. Introduction, In D. Bertaux, (ed.), *Biography and Society: The Life History Approach in the Social Sciences*. Beverly Hills: Sage.
———. 1981b. *Biography and Society: The Life History Approach in the Social Sciences*. Beverly Hills: Sage.
Bickman, Leonard and Thomas Henchy. 1972. *Beyond the Laboratory: Field Research in Social Psychology*. New York: McGraw-Hill.
Blee, Kathleen. 1987. "Gender Ideology and the Role of Women in the 1920s Klan Movement." *Sociological Spectrum*, 7:73–97.
Blumer, Herbert. 1966. "Sociological Implications of the Thought of G.H. Mead." *American Journal of Sociology* 71:535–544.
———. 1969. *Symbolic Interactionism: Perspective and Method*. Englewood Cliffs, N.J.: Prentice-Hall.
Bogdan, R. 1974. *Being Different: The Autobiography of Jane Fry*. New York: Wiley.
Bogdan, Robert and Steven Taylor. 1975. *Introduction to Qualitative Research Methods*. New York: John Wiley.
Brehm, S.S. and Weintraub, M. 1977. "Physical Barriers and Psychological Reatance: 2-Year-Olds' Responses to Threats to Freedom." *Journal of Personality and Social Psychology* 55:830–836.
Buber, Martin. 1955. *Between Man and Man*. Boston, Beacon Press.
Campbell, Donald T. 1971. *Experimental and Quasi-Experimental Designs for Research*. Chicago: Rand McNally.
Comte, Auguste. 1896. *The Positive Philosophy of Auguste Comte*. London: Bell.
Couch, Carl. 1988. *Researching Social Processes*. Greenwich, Conn.: JAI Press.
———. 1987a. *Researching Social Processes in the Laboratory*. Greenwich, Conn: JAI Press.
———. 1984*Constructing Civilizations*. Greenwich, Conn.: JAI Press.
Couch, Carl, Stanley L. Saxton and Michael A. Katovich. 1986. Studies in Symbolic Interaction, Supplement 2: *The Iowa School*. Parts A and B. Greenwich, Conn: JAI Press.
Cressy, P.G. 1932. *The Taxi-Dance Hall*. Chicago: University of Chicago Press.
Dalton, Melville. 1964"Preconceptions and Methods, In Men Who Manage." Pp. 6–66, In *Sociologists at Work*, edited by Phillip Hammond. Garden City, NY: Doubleday, Anchor Books.
Davis, Fred. 1961. "Deviance Disavowal: the Management of Strained Interaction by the Visibly Handicapped." *Social Problems* (9):120–132.
Denzin, Norman K. 1984. *On Understanding Emotion*. San Francisco: Jossey-Bass.
———. 1986. "Interpretive Interactionism and the Use of Life Stories." *Revista Internacional de Sociologica*, 44:321–329.
———. 1989. *The Research Act: A Theoretical Introduction to Sociological Methods*, 3rd ed. Englewood Cliffs, N.J.: Prentice-Hall.
De Santis, Grace. 1980. "Interviewing as Social Interaction." *Qualitative Sociology*, 8:72–98.
Douglas, Jack D. 1976. *Investigative Social Research*. Beverly Hills, CA: Sage.
———. 1985. *Creative Interviewing*. Beverly Hills: Sage.
Durkheim, Emile. 1950. *The Rules of Sociological Method*. New York: The Free Press.

Festinger, Leon, Henry W. Riecken, and Stanley Schacter. 1953. "Laboratory Experiments." In *Research Methods in the Behavioral Sciences*, edited by Leon Festinger and Daniel Katz. New York: Harper and Row.
———. 1956 *When Prophecy Fails*. New York: Harper and Row.
———. 1971 "Laboratory Experiments." In *Research Methods: Insights and Methods*, edited by Billy J. Franklin and Harold W. Osborne. Belmont, CA: Wadsworth.
Felipe, Nancy J. and Robert Sommer. 1966. "Invasions of Personal Space." *Social Problems*, 14:206–214.
Fine, Gary Allen. 1987. "Cracking Diamonds: Observer Role in Little League Baseball Settings and the Acquisition of Social Competence." Pp. 117–132, In *Fieldwork Experience: Qualitative Approaches to Social Research*, edited by William Shaffir, Robert Stebbins, and Allan Turowetz. New York: St. Martin's Press.
Gans, H. 1962. *The Urban Villagers*. New York: Free Press.
Geer, B. 1969. "First Days in the Field." In *Issues in Participant Observation*, edited by G. McCall and J.L. Simmons. New York: Random House.
Glaser, B. and A. Strauss. 1967. *The Discovery of Grounded Theory*. Chicago: Aldine.
Goffman, E. 1961. *Asylums: Essays on the Social Situation of Mental Patients and Other Inmates*. Garden City, NY: Random House.
———. 1976. "Gender Advertisements." *Studies in Visual Communication*, 3:69–154.
Gold, R.L. 1958. "Roles in Sociological Field Observations." *Social Forces* 36:217–223.
Goldstein, Jeffery H. and Robert L. Arms. 1971 "Effects of Observing Athletic Contests on Hostility." *Sociometry*, 34:83–90.
Gottschalk, Louis, Clyde Kluckhohn, and Robert Angell. 1945. *The Use of Personal Documents in History, Anthropology, and Sociology*. New York: Social Science Research Council.
Haas, J., ViVona C., Miller, S.J., Woods, C. and Becker, H.S. 1968. "Learning the Ropes: Situational Learning in Four Occupational Training Programs." Pp. 209–233, In *Among the People: Encounters with the Poor*, edited by I. Deutscher and E.P. Thompson. New York: Basic Books, Inc.
Haas, Jack and William Shaffir. 1977. "The Professionalism of Medical Students: Developing Competence and a Cloak of Competence." *Symbolic Interaction* 1:71–88.
———. 1980. "Fieldworkers' Mistakes at Work: Problems in Maintaining Research and Researcher Bargains." Pp. 244–255, In *Fieldwork Experience: Qualitative Approaches to Social Research*, edited by W. Shaffir, R.A. Stebbins, and A. Turowetz. New York: St. Martin's Press.
Haney, Craig, W. Curtis Banks, and Phillip G. Zimbardo. 1973. "Interpersonal Dynamics in a Simulated Prison." *International Journal of Criminology and Penology*, 1:69–97.
Hartman, George W. 1972. "An Experiment on the Comparative Effectiveness of 'Emotional' and 'Rational' Political Leaflets in Determinig Election Results." In *Beyond the Laboratory: Field Research in Social Psychology*, edited by Leonard Bickman and Thomas Henchy. New York: McGraw-Hill.
Herman, N.J. 1981a. "Making Bargains with Powerful People in Powerful Institutions." Paper presented at the Annual Meetings of the Canadian Sociology and Anthropology Association, Halifax, Nova Scotia.
———. 1981b. *The Making of a Mental Patient: An Ethnographic Study of the Processes and Consequences of Institutionalization Upon Self-Images and Identities*. Unpublished Master's thesis, McMaster University, Hamilton, Ontario, Canada.
———. 1986. *Crazies in the Community: An Ethnographic Study of Ex-Psychiatric Clients in Canadian Society—Stigma, Management Strategies, and Identity Transformation*. Unpublished Ph.D. Dissertation, McMaster University, Hamilton, Ontario, Canada.
———. 1987 "'Mixed Nutters' and 'Looney Tuners:' The Emergence, Development, Nature, and Functions of Two Informal, Deviant Subcultures of Chronic, Ex-Psychiatric Patients." *Deviant Behavior* 8:235–258.
Hickman, C. Addison and Manford H. Kuhn. 1956. *Individuals, Groups, and Economic Behavior*. New York: Dryden Press.
Humphreys, Laud. 1970. *Tearoom Trade: Impersonal Sex in Public Places*. Chicago: Aldine.
———. 1972. *Out of the Closets, the Sociology of Homosexual Liberation*. New Jersey: Prentice-Hall.
Husserl, E. 1936. *Phenomenology and the Crisis of Western Philosophy*. New York, Harper and Row.
———. 1913. *Ideas: General Introduction to Pure Phenomenology*. London: Collier-Macmillan.
Jackson, Bruce. 1977. *Killing Time: Life in the Arkansas Penitentiary*. Ithaca, NY: Cornell University Press.

Jacobs, Jerry. 1967. "A Phenomenological Study of Suicide Notes." *Social Problems*, 15:60–72.
Johnson, John M. 1975. *Doing Field Research*. New York: Macmillan.
Johnson, Weldon T. 1971. "The Religious Crusade: Revival or Ritual?" *American Journal of Sociology*, 76:873–890.
Jung, John. 1971. *The Experimenter's Dilemma*. New York: Harper and Row.
Kant, Emmanuel. 1963. *Kant on History*. Indianapolis: Bobbs-Merrill.
Kuhn, Manford H. 1964. "Major Trends in Symbolic Interaction Theory in the Past Twenty-five Years." *Sociological Quarterly* 5:61–84.
Kuhn, Manford, and Thomas S. McPartland. 1954. "An Empirical Investigation of Self-Attitudes." *American Sociological Review* 19:68–72.
Letkeman, Peter. 1978. "Crime as Work: Leaving the Field." Pp. 292–301, In *Fieldwork Experience: Qualitative Approaches to Social Research*, edited by William Shaffir, Robert Stebbins, and Allan Turowetz.
Liebow, E. 1967. *Tally's Corner*. Boston: Little, Brown.
Lofland, John. 1966. *Doomsday Cult: A Study of Conversion, Proselytization, and Maintenance of Faith*. Englewood Cliffs, N.J.: Prentice-Hall.
———. 1971. *Analyzing Social Settings: A Guide to Qualitative Observation and Analysis*. Belmont, CA: Wadsworth.
Lofland, John and Lejune, R.A. 1960. "Initial Interaction of Newcomers in Alcoholics Anonymous: A Field Experiment in Class Symbols and Socialization." *Social Problems* 8:102–111.
Maines, David R., William Shaffir, and Allan Turowetz. 1973. "Leaving the Field in Ethnographic Research: Reflections on the Entrance-Exit Hypothesis." Pp. 261–281 in *Fieldwork Experience: Qualitative Approaches to Social Research*, edited by William Shaffir, Robert Stebbins, and Allan Turowetz. New York: St Martin's.
Malinowski, Bronsilaw. 1922. *Argonauts of the Western Pacific*. London: Routledge and Kegan Paul.
McKinney, John C. 1966. *Constructive typology and Social Theory*. New York: Appleton-Century-Crofts.
McPhail, Clark and Ronald T. Wohlstein. 1986. "Collective Locomotion as Collective Behavior." *American Sociological Review*, 51:1–13.
Mead, Margaret. 1923. *Coming of Age in Samoa*. New York: Morrow.
Meltzer, B. N. and J. W. Petras. 1970. "The Chicago and Iowa Schools of Symbolic Interactionism." pp 3–17, In Tomatsu Shibutani (Ed.), *Human Nature and Collective Behavior*. Englewood Cliffs, N.J.: Prentice-Hall.
Miall, Charlene. 1984. *Women and Involuntary Childlessness: Perceptions of Stigma Associated with Infertility and Adoption*. Unpublished Ph.D. Dissertation, York University, Department of Sociology.
Molotch, Harvey, and Deidre Boden. 1985. "Talking Social Structure: Discourse Domination and the Watergate Hearings." *American Sociological Review*, 50:273–287.
Orlando, N. 1973. "The Mock Ward: A Study in Simulation." Pp. 99–118, In *Behavior Disorders: Perspectives and Trends*, edited by O. Milton and R. Wahler. Philadelphia: Lippencott.
Orne, M.T. 1962. "On the Social Psychology of the Psychology Experiment: With Particular Reference to Demand Characteristics and Their Implications." *American Psychologist*, 17:776–783.
Plummer, Ken. 1983. *Documents of Life: An Introduction to the Problems and Literature of a Humanistic Method*. London: George Allen and Unwin.
Plutchik, Robert. 1968. *Foundations of Experimental Research*. New York: Harper and Row.
Reynolds, Larry T. 1993. *Interactionism: Exposition and Critique*, 3rd edition. Dix Hills, New York: General Hall.
Rosenthal, Robert. 1963. "The Effects of Physician Demands on the Behavior of Nurses." In *Beyond the Laboratory: Field Research in Social Psychology*, edited by Leonard Beckman and Thomas Henchy. New York: McGraw-Hill.
———. 1966. *Experimental Effects in Behavioral Research*. New York: Appleton-Century-Crofts.
Schutz, Alfred. 1932. *The Phenomenology of the Social World*. Evanston, Ill: Northwestern University Press.
———. 1964. *Collected Papers*. The Hague, Holland: Martinus Nijhoff (also published in 1970 & 1971).
Shaffir, W. 1974. *Life in a Religious Community: The Lubavitcher Chassidism in Montreal*. Toronto: Holt, Rinehart, and Winston.

Skipper, James K., Jr. and Charles H. McCaghy. 1972. "Respondents' Intrusion Upon the Situation: the Problems of Interviewing Subjects with Special Qualities." *The Sociological Quarterly*, 13:237–243.
Smith, Robert B. and Peter Manning. 1983. *An Introduction to Social Research*. Volumes 1 & 2. Cambridge, Mass.: Ballinger.
Stocking, George W. Jr. 1974. *The Shaping of American Anthropology 1883–1911: A Franz Boas Reader*. New York: Basic Books.
Sutherland, Edwin. 1937. *The Professional Thief*. Chicago: University of Chicago Press.
———. 1949. *White Collar Crime*. New York: Holt, Rinehart, and Winston.
Thomas, W.I. and Dorothy Swaine Thomas. 1928. *The Child in America*. New York: Knopf.
Thomas, William I. and Florian Znaniecki. 1918–1920. *The Polish Peasant in Europe and America* (Volumes I–V). Boston: Richard Badger.
Tiryakian, E. 1965. "Existential Phenomenology and Sociology." *American Sociological Review*. 30:674–688.
Titon, Jeff Todd. 1980. "The Life Story." *Journal of American Folklore*, 93:276–292.
Turner, Johnathan H. 1986. *The Structure of Sociological Theory* (4th ed.). Chicago: Dorsey.
Wallis, R. 1977. *The Road to Sociological Freedom: A Sociological Analysis of Scientology*. New York: Columbia University Press.
Wax, Rosalie. 1971. *Doing Field Work*. Chicago: University of Chicago Press.
Weber, Max. 1964. *Basic Concepts in Sociology*. New York: Citadel Press.
Weinberg, Martin S. 1966"Becoming a Nudist." *Psychiatry: Journal for the Study of Interpersonal Processes* 29:15–24.
Welch, R. 1958. *The Philosophy of Edmund Husserl*. Chicago: University of Chicago Press.
Whyte, W.F. 1955. *Street Corner Society*. Chicago: University of Chicago Press.

NOTES

[1] See for example works of: Boas, (1904); Mead (1923)
[2] A number of excellent sourcebooks have been written on how to do fieldwork or ethnography—how to gain access to a setting, make bargains with subjects, develop rapport, engage in effective collection and analysis of the data: Berg (1989); Bogdan and Taylor (1975); Denzin (1989); Filstead (1970); Shaffir et al., (1987); Smith and Manning (1982).
[3] For a detailed discussion of the life history method, the use of archival and personal documents, consult: Allport, (1942); Becker, (1970); Bertaux, (1981); Gottschalk, et al., (1947); Denzin (1989); Plummer (1983).
[4] For a detailed discussion of the laboratory experiment consult the following: Campbell and Stanley (1971); Couch (1988); Couch et al. (1986); Evan (1971); Festinger (1971); Jung (1971); Plutchik (1968);
[5] For a detailed discussion of the experimental simulation: consult: Abelson (1968); Orlando (1973); Orne (1962);
[6] Consult the following for a detailed discussion of quasiexperiments or field experiments: Campbell and Stanley (1963); Bickman and Henchy (1972); Evan (1971); Rosenthal (1963);

Chapter **10** SOCIOLOGICAL ANALYSIS AND
THE "VARIABLE"

Herbert Blumer

My aim in this paper is to examine critically the scheme of sociological analysis which seeks to reduce human group life to variables and their relations. I shall refer to this scheme, henceforth, as "variable analysis." This scheme is widespread and is growing in acceptance. It seems to be becoming the norm of proper sociological analysis. Its sophisticated forms are becoming the model of correct research procedure. Because of the influence which it is exercising in our discipline, I think that it is desirable to note the more serious of its shortcomings in actual use and to consider certain limits to its effective application. The first part of my paper will deal with the current shortcomings that I have in mind and the second part with the more serious question of the limits of its adequacy.

Shortcomings in Contemporary Variable Analysis

The first shortcoming I wish to note in current variable analysis in our field is the rather chaotic condition that prevails in the selection of variables. There seems to be little limit to what may be chosen or designated as a variable. One may select something as simple as sex distribution or as complex as depression; something as specific as a birth rate or as vague as social cohesion; something as evident as residential change or as imputed as a collective unconscious; something as generally recognized as hatred or as doctrinaire as the Oedipus complex; something as immediately given as a rate of newspaper circulation to something as elaborately fabricated as an index of anomie. Variables may be selected on the basis of specious impression of what is important, on the basis of conventional usage, on the basis on what can be secured through a given instrument or technique, on the basis of the demands of some doctrine, or on the basis of an imaginative ingenuity in devising a new term.

Obviously the study of human group life calls for a wide range of variables. However, there is a conspicuous absence of rules, guides, limitations and prohibitions to govern the choice of variables. Relevant rules are not provided even in the thoughtful regulations that accompany sophisticated schemes of variable analysis. For example, the rule that variables should be quantitative does not help, because with ingenuity one can impart a quantitative dimension to almost any qualitative item. One can usually construct some kind of a measure or index of it or develop a rating scheme for judges. The proper insistence that a variable have a quantitative dimension does little to lessen the range or variety of items that may be set up as variables. In a comparable manner, the use of experimental design does not seemingly exercise much restriction on the number and kind of variables which may be brought within the framework of the design. Nor, finally, does careful work with variables, such as establishing tests of reliability, or inserting "test variables," exercise much restraint on what may be put into the pool of sociological variables.

In short, there is a great deal of laxity in choosing variables in our field. This laxity is due chiefly to a neglect of the careful reduction of problems that should properly precede the application of the techniques of variable analysis. This prior task requires thorough and careful reflection on the problem to make reasonably sure that one has identified its genuine parts. It requires intensive and extensive familiarity with the empirical area to which the problem refers. It requires a careful and thoughtful assessment of the theoretical schemes that might apply to the requirements both in practice and in the training of students for that practice. The scheme of variable analysis has become for too many just a handy tool to be put to immediate use.

A second shortcoming in variable analysis in our field is the disconcerting absence of generic variables, that is, variables that stand for abstract categories. Generic variables are essential, of course, to an empirical science — they become the key points of its analytical structure. Without generic variables, variable analysis yields only separate and disconnected findings.

There are three kinds of variables in our discipline which are generally regarded as generic variables. None of them, in my judgement, is generic. The first kind is the typical and frequent variable which stands for a class of objects that is tied down to a given historical and cultural situation. Convenient examples are: attitudes toward the Supreme Court, intention to vote Republican, interest in the United Nations, a college education, army draftees and factory unemployment. Each of these variables, even though a class term, has substance only in a given historical context. The variables do not stand directly for items of abstract human group life; their application to human groups around the world, to human groups in the past, and to conceivable human groups in the future is definitely restricted. While their use may yield propositions that hold in given culture settings, they do not yield the abstract knowledge that is the core of an empirical science.

The second apparent kind of generic variable in current use in our discipline is represented by unquestionably abstract sociological categories, such as "social cohesion," "social integration," "assimilation," "authority," and "group morale." In actual use these do not turn out to be the generic variables that their labels would suggest. The difficulty is that such terms, as I sought to point out in an earlier article on sensitizing concepts,[1] have no fixed or uniform indicators. Instead, indicators are constructed to fit the particular problem on which one is working. Thus, certain features are chosen to represent the social integration of cities, but other features are used to represent the social integration of boys' gangs. The indicators chosen to represent morale in a small group of school children are very different from those used to stand for morale in a labor movement. The indicators used in studying attitudes of prejudice show a wide range of variation. It seems clear that indicators are tailored and used to meet the peculiar character of the local problem under study. In my judgement, the abstract categories used as variables in our work turn out with rare exception to be something other than generic categories. They are localized in terms of their content. Some measure of support is given to this assertion by the fact that the use of such abstract categories in variable research adds little to generic knowledge of them. The thousands of "variable" studies of attitudes, for instance, have not contributed to our knowledge of the abstract nature of an attitude: in a similar way the studies of "social cohesion," "social integration," "authority," or "group morale" have done nothing, so far as I can detect, to clarify or augment generic knowledge of these categories.

The third form of apparent generic variable in our work is represented by a special set of class terms like "sex," "age," "birth rate," and "time period." These would seem to be unquestionably generic. Each can be applied universally to human group life; each has the same clear and common meaning in its application. Yet, it appears that in their use in our field they do not function as generic variables. Each has a content that is given by its particular instance of application, e.g., the birth rate in Ceylon, or the sex distribution in the City of St. Louis. The kind of variable relations that result from their use will be found to be localized and non-generic.

These observations on these three specious kinds of generic variables point, of course, to the fact that variables in sociological research are predominantly disparate and localized in nature. Rarely do they refer satisfactorily to a dimension or property of abstract human group life. With little exception they are bound temporally, spatially, and culturally and are inadequately cast to serve as clear instances of generic sociological categories. Many would contend this is because variable research and analysis are in a beginning state in our discipline. They believe that with the benefit of wider coverage, replication, and the coordination of separate studies disparate variable relations may be welded into generic relations. So far there has been little achievement along these lines. Although we already have appreciable accumulations of findings from variable studies, little has been done to convert the findings into generic relations. Such conversion is not an easy task. The difficulty should serve both as a challenge to the effort and an occasion to reflect on the use and limitations of variable analyses.

As a background for noting a third major shortcoming I wish to dwell on the fact that current variable analysis in our field is operating predominantly with disparate and not generic relations. With little exception its data and its findings are "here and now," wherever the "here" be located and whenever the "now" be timed. Its analyses, accordingly, are of localized and concrete matters. Yet, as I think logicians would agree, to understand adequately a "here and now" relation it is necessary to understand the "here and now" context. This latter understanding is not provided by variable analysis. The variable relation is a single relation, necessarily stripped bare of the complex of things that sustain it in a "here and now" context. Accordingly, our understanding of it as a "here and now" matter suffers. Let me give one example. A variable relation states that reasonably staunch Erie County Republicans become confirmed in their attachment to their candidate as a result of listening to the campaign materials of the rival party. This bare and interesting finding gives us no picture of them as human beings in their particular world. We do not know the run of their experiences which induced an organization of their sentiments and views, nor do we know what this organization is; we do not know the social atmosphere or codes in their social circles; we do not know the reinforcements and rationalizations that come from their fellows;

we do not know the defining process in their circles; we do not know the pressures, the incitant, and the models that came from their niches in the social structure; we do not know how their ethical sensitivities are organized and so what they would tolerate in the way of shocking behavior on the part of their candidate. In short, we do not have the picture to size up and understand what their confirmed attachment to a political candidate means in terms of their experience and their social context. This fuller picture of the "here and now" context is not given by variable relations. This, I believe, is a major shortcoming in variable analysis, insofar as variable analysis seeks to explain meaningfully the disparate and local situations with which it seem to be primarily concerned.

The three shortcomings which I have noted in current variable research in our field are serious but perhaps not crucial. With increasing experience and maturity they will probably be successfully overcome. They suggest, however, the advisability of inquiring more deeply into the interesting and important question of how well variable analysis is suited to the study of human group life in its fuller dimensions.

LIMITS OF VARIABLE ANALYSIS

In my judgement, the crucial limit to the successful application of variable analysis to human group life is set by the process of interpretation or definition that goes on in human groups. This process, which I believe to be the core of human action, gives a character to human group life that seems to be at variance with the logical premises of variable analysis. I wish to explain at some length what I have in mind.

All sociologists — unless I presume too much — recognize that human group activity is carried on, in the main, through a process of interpretation or definition. As human beings we act singly, collectively, and societally on the basis of the meanings which things have for us. Our world consists of innumerable objects — home, church, job, college education, a political election, a friend, an enemy nation, a tooth brush, or what not — each of which has a meaning on the basis of which we act toward it. In our activities we wend our way by recognizing an object to be such and such, by defining the situations with which we are presented, by attaching a meaning to this or that event, and where need be, by devising a new meaning to cover something new or different. This is done by the individual in his personal action, it is done by a group of individuals acting together in concert, it is done in each of the manifold activities which together constitute an institution in operation, and it is done in each of the diversified acts which fit into and make up the patterned activity of a social structure or a society. We can and, I think, must look upon human group life as chiefly a vast interpretive process in which people, singly and collectively, guide themselves by defining the objects, events, and situations which they encounter. Regularized activity inside this process results from the application of stabilized definitions. Thus, an institution carries on its complicated activity through an articulated complex of such stabilized meanings. In the face of new situations or new experiences, individuals, groups, institutions, and societies find it necessary to form new definitions. These new definitions may enter into the repertoire of stable meanings. This seems to be the characteristic way in which new activities, new relations, and new social structures are formed. The process of interpretation may be viewed as a vast digestive process through which the confrontations of experience are transformed into activity. While the process of interpretation does not embrace everything that leads to the formation of human group activity and structure, it is, I think, the chief means through which human group life goes on and takes shape.

Any scheme designed to analyze human group life in its general character has to fit this process of interpretation. This is the test that I propose to apply to variable analysis. The variables which designate matters which either directly or indirectly confront people and thus enter into human group life would have to operate through this process of interpretation. The variables which designate the results or effects of the happenings which play upon the experience of people would be the outcome of the process of interpretation. Present-day variable analysis in our field is dealing predominantly with such kinds of variables.

There can be no doubt, when current variable analysis deals with matters or areas of human group life which involve the process of interpretation, it is markedly disposed to ignore thr process. The conventional procedure is to identify something which is presumed to operate on group life and treat it as an independent variable, and then to select some form of group activity as the dependent variable. The independent variable is put at the beginning part of the process of interpretation and the dependent variable at the terminal part of the process. The intervening process is ignored or, what amounts to the same thing, taken for granted as something that need not be considered. Let me cite a few typical examples: the presentation of political programs on the radio and the resulting expression of intention to vote; the entrance of Negro residents into a white neighborhood and the resulting attitudes of the white inhabitants toward Negroes; the occurrence of a business depression and the resulting rate of divorce. In such instances — so common to variable analysis in our field — one's concern is with the two variables and not with what lies between them. If one has neutralized other factors which are regarded as possibly exercising influence on the dependent variable, one is content with the conclusion that the observed change in the dependent variable is the necessary result of the independent variable.

This idea that in such areas of group life the independent variable automatically exercises its influence on the dependent variable is, it seems to me, a basic fallacy. There is a process of definition intervening between the events of experience presupposed by the independent variable. The political programs on the radio are interpreted by the listeners; the Negro invasion into the white neighborhood must be defined by the whites to have any effect on their attitudes; the many events and happenings which together constitute the business depression must be interpreted at their many points by husbands and wives to have any influence on marital relations. This intervening interpretation is essential to the outcome. It gives the meaning to the presentation that sets the response. Because of the integral position of the defining process between the two variables, it becomes necessary, it seems to me, to incorporate the process in the account of the relationship. Little effort is made in variable analysis. Usually the process is completely ignored. Where the process is recognized, its study is regarded as a problem that is independent of the relation between the variables.

The indifference of variable analysis to the process of interpretation is based apparently on the tacit assumption that the independent variable predetermines its interpretation. This assumption has no foundation. The interpretation is not predetermined by the variable as if the variable emanated its own meaning. If there is anything we do know, it is that an object, event, or situation in human experience does not carry its own meaning; the meaning is conferred on it.

Now, it is true that in many instances the interpretation of the object, event, or situation may be fixed, since the person or people may have an already constructed meaning which is immediately applied to the item. Where such stabilized interpretation occurs and recurs, variable analysis is followed by such and such a change in the dependent variable. The only necessary precaution would be not to assume that the stated relation between the variables was necessarily intrinsic and universal. Since anything that is defined may be redefined, the relation has no intrinsic fixity.

Alongside the instances where interpretation is made by merely applying stabilized meanings there are the many instances where the interpretation has to be constructed. These instances are obviously increasing in our changing society. It is imperative in the case of such instances for variable analysis to include the act of interpretation in its analytic scheme. As far as I can see, variable analysis shuns such inclusion.

Now the question arises, how can variable analysis include the process of interpretation? Presumably the answer would be to treat the act of interpretation as an "intervening variable." But, what does this mean? It means that if interpretation is merely an interviewing neutral medium through which the independent variable exercises its influence, then, of course this would be no answer. Interpretation is a formative or creative process in its own right. It constructs meaning which, as I have said, are not predetermined or determined by the independent variable.

If one accepts this fact and proposed to treat the act of interpretation as a formative process, then the question arises how one is to characterize it as a variable. What quality is one to assign to it, what property or set of properties? One cannot, with any sense, characterize this act of interpretation in terms of the interpretation which it constructs; one cannot take the product to stand for the process. Nor can one characterize the act of interpretation in terms of what enters into it — the objects perceived, the evaluations and assessments made of them, the cues that are suggested, the possible definitions proposed by oneself or by others. These vary from one instance of interpretation to another and, further, shift from point to point in the development of the act. This varying and shifting content offers no basis for making the act of interpretation into a variable.

Nor, it seems to me, is the problem met by proposing to reduce the act of interpretation into component parts and work with these parts as variables. These parts would presumably have to be processual parts — such as perception, analysis, evaluation, and decision-making in the individual; and discussion, definition of one another's responses and other forms of social interaction in the group. The same difficulty exists in making any of the processual parts into variables that exist in the case of the complete act of interpretation.

The question of how the act of interpretation can be given the qualitative constancy that is logically required in a variable has so far not been answered. While one can devise some kind of a "more or less" dimension for it, the need is to catch it as a variable, or set of variables, in a manner which reflects its functioning in transforming experience into activity. This is the problem, indeed dilemma, which confronts variable analysis in our field. I see no answer to it outside the logical framework of variable analysis. The process of interpretation is not inconsequential or pedantic. It operates too centrally in group and individual experience to be put aside as being of incidental interest.

In addition to the bypassing of the process of interpretation there is, in my judgement, another profound deficiency in variable analysis as a scheme for analyzing human group life. The deficiency stems from the inevitable tendency to work with truncated factors, and, as a result, to conceal or misrepresent the actual operations in human group life. The deficiency stems from the logical need of variable analysis to work with discrete, clean-cut and unitary variables. Let me spell this out.

As a working procedure variable analysis seeks necessarily to achieve a clean identification of the relation between two variables. Irrespective of how one may subsequently combine a number of such identified relations — in an additive manner, a clustering, a chain-like arrangement, or a "feedback" scheme — the objective of variable research is to isolate a simple and fixed relation between two variables. For this to be done each of the two variables must be set up as a distinct item by separating the variable from its connection with other variables through their exclusion or neutralization.

A difficulty with this scheme is that the empirical reference of a true sociological variable is not unitary or distinct. When caught in its actual social character, it turns out to be an intricate and inner-moving complex. To illustrate, let me make what seems ostensibly to be a fairly clean-cut variable relation, namely between a birth control program and the birth rate of a given people. Each of these two variables — the program of birth control and the birth rate — can be given a simple discrete and unitary character. For the program of birth control one may choose merely its time period, or select some reasonable measure such as he number of people visiting birth control clinics. For the birth rate, one merely takes it as it is. Apparently, these indications are sufficient to enable the investigator to ascertain the relations between the two variables.

Yet, a scrutiny of what the two variables stand for in the life of the group gives us a different picture. Thus, viewing the program of birth control in terms of *how it enters into the lives of people*, we need to note many things such as the literacy of the people, the clarity of the printed information, the manner and extent of its distribution, the social position of the directors of the program and the personnel, how the personnel act, the character of their institutional talks, the way in which people define the attendance at birth control clinics, the expressed views of influential personages with reference to the program, how such personages are regarded, and the nature of the discussions among people with regard to the clinics. These are only a few of the matters which relate to how the birth control program might enter into the experience of the people. The number is sufficient, however, to show the complex and innermoving character of what otherwise might seem to be a simple variable.

A similar picture is given in the case of the other variable — the birth rate. A birth rate of a people seems to be a very simple and unitary matter. Yet, in terms of what it expresses and stands for in group activity it is exceedingly complex and diversified. We need consider only the variety of social factors that impinge on and affect the sex act, even though the sex act is only one of the activities that set the birth rate. The self-conceptions held by men and women, the conceptions of family life, the values placed on children, accessibility of men and women to each other, physical arrangements in the home, the sanctions given by established institutions, the code of manliness, the pressures from relatives and neighbors, and ideas of what is proper, convenient, and tolerable in the sex act — these are a few of the operating factors in the experience of the group that play upon the sex act. They suffice to indicate something of the complex body of actual experience and practice that is represented in and expressed by the birth rate of a human group.

I think it will be found that, when converted into the actual group activity for which it stands, a sociological variable turns out to be an intricate and inner-moving complex. There are, of course, wide ranges of difference between sociological variables in terms of the extent of such complexity. Still, I believe one will generally find that the discrete and unitary character which the labeling of the variable suggests vanishes.

The failure to recognize this is a source of trouble. In variable analysis one is likely to accept the two variables as the simple and unitary items that they seem to be, and to believe that the relation found between them is a realistic analysis of the given area of group life. Actually, in group life the relation is far more likely to be between complex, diversified, and moving bodies of activity. The operation of these complexes on the other, or the interaction between them, is both concealed and misrepresented by the statement of the relation between the two variables. The statement of the variable relation merely asserts a connection between abbreviated terms of reference. It leaves out the actual complexes of activity and the actual process of interaction in which human group life has its being. We are here faced, it seems to me, by the fact that the very features which give variable analysis its high merit — the qualitative constancy of the variables, their clean-cut simplicity, their ease of manipulation as a sort of free encounter, their ability to be brought into decisive relation — are the features that lead variable analysis to gloss over the character of the real operating factors in group life, and the real interaction and relations between such factors.

The two major difficulties faced by variable analysis point clearly to the need for a markedly different scheme of sociological analysis for the areas in which these difficulties arise. This is not the occasion to spell out the nature of this scheme. I shall merely mention a few of its rudiments to suggest how its character differs fundamentally from that of variable analysis. The scheme would be based on the premise that the chief means through which human group life operates and is formed is a vast, diversified process of definition. The scheme respects the empirical existence of this process. It devotes itself to the analysis of the operation and formation of human group life as these occur through this process. In doing so it seeks to trace the lines of defining experience through which ways of living, patterns of relations, and social forms are developed, rather than to relate these formations to a set of selected items. It views items of social life as articulated inside moving structures and believes that they have to be understood in terms of this articulation. Thus, it handles these items not as discrete things disengaged from their connections but instead, as signs of a supporting context which gives them their social character. In its effort to ferret out lines of definition and networks of moving relation, it relies on a distinctive form of procedure. This procedure is to approach the study of group activity through the eyes and experience of the people who have developed the activity. Hence, it necessarily requires an intimate familiarity with this experience and with the scenes of its operation. It uses broad and interlacing observations and not narrow and disjunctive observations. And, may I add, that like variable analysis, it yields empirical findings and "here and now" propositions, although in a different empirical form. Finally, it is no worse off than variable analysis in developing generic knowledge out of its findings and propositions.

In closing, I express a hope that my critical remarks about variable analysis are not misinterpreted to mean that variable analysis is useless or makes no contribution to sociological analysis. The contrary is true. Variable analysis is a fit procedure for those areas of social life and formation that are not mediated by an interpretive process. Such areas exist and are important. Further, in the area of interpretive life variable analysis can be an effective means of unearthing stabilized patterns of interpretation which are not likely to be detected through the direct study of the experience of people. Knowledge of such patterns, or rather of the relations between variables which reflect such patterns, is of great value for understanding group life in its "here and now" character and indeed may have significant practical value. All of these appropriate uses give variable analysis a worthy status in our field.

In view, however, of the current tendency of variable analysis to become the norm and model for sociological analysis, I believe it is important to recognize its shortcomings and its limitations.

NOTES

[1] "What is Wrong with Social Theory?" *American Sociological Review* 19:3-10.

Chapter **11** **BEYOND BLUMER AND KUHN: RESEARCHING AND STUDYING ACROSS-TIME DATA THROUGH THE USE OF POINT-IN-SPACE LABORATORY PROCEDURES**

Carl Couch, Michael A. Katovich and Steven Buban

Interactionists inspired by Mead's (1934; 1938) evolutionary conception of the relationship between emergence and structure argue that social processes represent the central starting point for research into the human condition. The sociological root of such processes is embedded in the joint act (Blumer 1969a; Miyamoto 1959), which involves two or more people actively engaged with each other. From this origin, all other metaphors and images recognizable to interactionists follow; including concepts such as movement, flow, fluidity, and ongoing lived experience.

Over twenty years ago Meltzer and Petras (1970) identified a fork in the interactionist road leading either to Chicago or Iowa, and found seemingly contradictory applications to Mead's evolutionary standpoint. Each location represented two distinct paradigms of thought (see Couch 1982) that, for specific reasons elaborated below, either embraced or rejected social processes as a basis for analysis. The Chicago School, led by Herbert Blumer, and the Iowa School, founded by Manford Kuhn, claimed allegiance to Mead, but adopted altogether different research strategies. Blumer insisted on analysis of ongoing joint action through across-time measures, and participant observation of creative agents fitting together lines of action in familiar environments. While Kuhn recognized that knowledge of the self could be generated through participant observation, he distinguished his undertaking from the Chicago School by calling for the generation of static representations (points-in-time) of selves and advocating a stable location (point-in-space) for observation rather than moving about as social processes proceed.

In this article we review the legacies of Kuhn's Iowa School and Blumer's Chicago School by comparing and contrasting their ontological and epistemological assumptions, and explore the root metaphors that guided different schools of research. Our purpose is to demonstrate how each school contributed to the development and maintenance of a new Iowa School of thought that attempted to create a synthesis of the best of both traditions. In this light, we draw upon past statements (see Couch 1984; Couch, Saxton, and Katovich 1986; Katovich 1984), especially provided by Buban's (1986) discussion of the Chicago and Iowa Schools. These statements suggest that the use of audio-visual technology in a controlled environment (or laboratory) can accomplish a fruitful synthesis of Blumer's and Kuhn's contributions to Mead's theories of the social act and social self.

BLUMER AND KUHN: SPATIAL AND TEMPORAL ORIENTATIONS

Blumer and Kuhn inspired a cadre of thinkers who set about to detect and define abstract generic principles of social processes, on the one hand, and situated selves, on the other hand. However, each school of thought, taken singularly and separate from the other, limited the scope of research. Following the lead of Blumer, the Chicago School adopted across-time and across-space measures to describe mobile social processes. Such measures led to the "discovery" of grounded theory (Glaser and Strauss 1967) and theories of dynamic social processes from the bottom-up (Burawoy, et al. 1991). Against the legacy established by Kuhn, the Iowa School refined point-in-space and point-in-time procedures to establish abstract categories of the self as correlated with degrees to which human beings committed themselves to institutions, organizations, and either formal or informal groups (Reese 1993).

While advocates of Blumer maintained a commitment to across-space and across-time measures of human interaction (see e.g., Denzin 1989; Karp, Stone and Yoels 1991; Lofland 1976), a new Iowa School revised Kuhn's points-in-time-and-space investigations of the self (Couch, Saxton, and Katovich 1986). New Iowa School researchers established across-time studies of social processes while committing themselves to point-in-space procedures. Such an approach, "while certainly indebted to both [Chicago and Iowa] schools, overcame the shortcomings each contains in regard to researching social process" (Buban 1986, p. 27). By making use of audio-visual technology to preserve researchable and shareable specimens of social action, the new Iowa School reconceptualized selves as social agents who have some control of their transactions in controlled environments.

THE LEGACY OF KUHN

Kuhn (1964a) appreciated the oral tradition of symbolic interaction as mythology but deemed it an insufficient foundation for a research agenda. He noted that the publication of G.H. Mead's works heralded the end of the oral tradition for symbolic interaction and offered an opportunity to begin an age of inquiry marked by systematic investigations. He further conceptualized the age of inquiry as a renewal of a commitment to social behaviorism with investigations focused on the self as a situated social object, and this effort became identified as the interactionist version of science (Plummer 1990, p. 196).

Kuhn continued the pragmatic inquiry into the self to avoid speculation and appeals to emotion (Kohout 1986). His undertaking reflected the optimism of the Enlightenment project to which the classical thinkers in sociology also paid allegiance. This project presumed that scientific research and everyday human reason were accessible to each other. Scientific knowledge resided in social acts that specified procedures of inquiry and that could be transmitted from generation to generation of researchers. Thus, Kuhn's faith in science resonated to Mead's (1936, p.168) optimistic appraisal of it as the evolutionary process made self conscious.

Kuhn agreed with Mead's optimistic view of human selves as "social objects capable of recognizing and sustaining a cooperative social order. The self represented a pragmatic answer to the question: How is society possible" (Katovich and Reese 1993). Such cooperation depended on the human capacity to see the self from the point of view of the other. Making use of the Twenty-Statements Test (TST), which measured how individuals located themselves in relation to various social structures, Kuhn (1964b) grounded interactionist science in the self as a ubiquitous variable, and ushered in an age of interactionist inquiry (Kuhn and McPartland 1954).

Kuhn accepted Mead's ontology but chose to adopt a seemingly contradictory epistemology. Just as Durkheim (1938) posited a processual social world that required a static methodology to develop a science of the social, Kuhn (1962) appreciated the dynamism of the self and called for static measures of it. What the TST lacked in fidelity to the self *in situ* it made up in rigor and stability of location. Thus, when Kuhn looked into his "crystal ball" (1964a, p. 83) he predicted that interactionists would continue to refine and articulate inquiry into the self as a social object. To an extent, his version of interactionism remains equated with the point-in-space and point-in-time study of the self as a particular social object (see Stryker 1980; Turner 1976).

By putting Mead's concept of the self rather than the act as central to formulating principles of human behavior, Kuhn located the self as social object firmly within an actor's social group memberships and activities. As did Mead, Kuhn regarded the self as the one universal variable, present in all walks of life. He believed that understanding its structure would lead to the emergence of a unified social theory of behavior.

Despite the accomplishments of the new Iowa School, it received more criticism than praise from other interactionists (see, especially, Tucker 1966). Many interactionists interpret Kuhn's decision to adopt both points-in-space/time procedures as truncating Mead's position and making interactionism more deterministic than necessary (Meltzer, Petras, and Reynolds 1975; Meltzer and Petras 1970). But Kuhn believed that the *self*, as an analytical construct, had become so general and laden with excess imagery that it had lost its conceptual power. Moreover, theorists tended to "discuss self-change as if it were most volatile and evanescent; the self shifts with each new indication one makes to himself, and these indications are the constant accompaniments of experience" (Kuhn, 1964a p. 61).

While critics of Kuhn have correctly interpreted his epistemology as static, they often ignore that his decision to employ the TST emanated from a frustration "with the general lack of advancement by symbolic interactionists, especially those of the Chicago School" (Buban 1986, p. 28). Kuhn provided a corrective for what he viewed as ambiguous and contradictory interpretations of Mead, especially those resulting in "dark, inscrutable complexities too difficult to understand" (Kuhn 1964a, p. 48; see Buban 1986, p. 28).

Kuhn's faith in the Enlightenment project (see Denzin 1992) led him to evaluate interactionist claims and perspectives in light of "normal science." The thick descriptions provided by Chicago School ethnographers lacked practical and shareable scientific procedures. He thus "opted to ignore certain features of social life, most notably temporal processes, a feature whose existence he did not deny, in order to get on with the task of data gathering" (Buban 1986, p. 28). The central task involved operationalizing specific aspects of Mead's theory of the self and advancing, one small step at a time, to other aspects in order to establish generic propositions regarding the relationship between social selves and social structures (Kuhn 1964a, p. 56). For Kuhn, theories without systematic data were equivalent to words without substance. This standpoint demonstrates a modernist commitment to establish procedures yielding systematic, researchable, and shareable data.

THE LEGACY OF BLUMER

Above and beyond anything else, Blumer called for a social science based on the observation and understanding of interpersonal processes (Shibutani 1988). Whatever society is, or however it is conceived, it can only be known to us through the examination of interpersonal processes, or how people comport themselves within, and collectively attend to, situations (Morrione 1988). To Blumer (1969a, p. 7), human society "in the first and last instances...consists of people engaging in action."

Followers and critics alike credit Blumer with providing a focus for interactionists to conceive of society as social processes (see Reynolds and Reynolds 1973; Meltzer, Petras, and Reynolds 1975). However, even those most influenced concede that Blumer failed to clarify the notion of processes through more detailed empirical examples. Researchers who take Blumer seriously "cannot really figure out how to conduct...research by following his precepts" (Becker 1988: 18–19). Further, "Blumer was much more successful at telling sociologists what they should *not* do than at telling them just how to go about the study of social processes" (Buban 1986, p. 29). Nevertheless, interactionists celebrate Blumer's (1956) call to "get after" social processes rather than to study the products of processes (or reified variables) so as to provide useful information about human beings as self-indicating makers of their environments (Farberman 1991).

Some of Blumer's descriptions of processes tend toward abstractions, without clear empirical referents (Becker 1988). In this vein, Blumer's insistence on studying processes and its enthusiastic reception among many interactionists resembles a type of *Glass Bead Game*, whereby the "mysteries" of social process shall only be known to those totally committed to "seeing" them. Further, commitment to this view of process necessarily called for commitment to a constructionist ontology (Blumer 1969b: Buban 1986, p. 29; Denzin 1990a), which applies more to a late-modernist, rather than a modernist Enlightenment perspective (Katovich and Reese 1993).

From a constructionist perspective, human beings as agents shape reality and attend to the consequences of their creations. Reality is thus an emergent process, encased within the dynamic transactions orchestrated by responsive selves in relation to others. In this vein, Blumer (1969a, p. 16) contends that "the activity of human beings consists of meeting a flow of situations, in which they have to act and that their action is built on the basis of what they note, how they assess and interpret what they note, and what kind of projected lines of action they map out." Persons are involving social change rather than merely being involved in it, which makes Blumer's standpoint somewhat aligned to a postmodern view of social life (Denzin 1990b; Plummer 1990).

Both Kuhn and Blumer focused on Mead's self concept. Only where Kuhn used points-in-space/time to conceptualize the self as situated within social structures, Blumer located the self within an across-time and across-space framework, represented by the key metaphor of continual self indications. This metaphor seems to represent a psychologistic perspective (Lewis and Smith, 1980; but see Blumer, 1983; Campbell, 1983). Action takes place within a social atmosphere, but only as accomplished by individuals who mentally "map out lines of action" (cf. Buban 1986, p. 30). Blumer's ontology is intimately linked to the capacity of "self-indication" as "a moving communicative process in which the individual notes things, assesses them, gives them meaning, and decides to act on the basis of the meaning" (Blumer, 1969b, p. 81). Any sense of obdurate constraints (Jameson 1991) or an "impinging other" (Perinbanayagam, 1974) altering "what one attends to do, what one responds to, and in general how one carries out his line of action is...absent from this...and other statements by Blumer" (Buban 1986, p. 30).

Even so, insisting that Blumer completely avoided any sense of impingement or constraint not only ignores his significant caveats (see e.g., Blumer 1969a, p. 8), but also his important contributions to a macrosociological conception of situations and situated acts (see Maines 1988). Blumer did appear comfortable with the "anti-structural" label insofar as it fit with his own antagonism toward views that denied human intentionality and reified abstract psychological traits or cultural forces. As Rochberg-Halton (1983, p. 149) notes, "it is obvious that [Blumer's] targets for criticism are the dehumanizers, the specialists without spirit, who gave to the world a view of society virtually devoid of any flesh and blood whatsoever."

While accusations of Blumer's selective reading of Mead inspired debate (see McPhail and Rexroat 1979; 1980; and Blumer's 1980 reply), interactionists have apparently engaged in highly selective readings of Blumer as well (Maines 1988). In his survey of interactionists who presumably advocated Blumer's point of view, Reynolds (1969) documented the lack of interactionist attention to obdurate impingements to the point of demonstrating an "astructural bias" (Reynolds and Reynolds, 1973). Only a small fraction of interactionists "saw social organization as involving, above all else, human relations or relationships" (Meltzer, Petras, and Reynolds 1975, p. 116). An even smaller fraction recognized "relationship" or "human relationship" as concepts "indispensable for sound sociological reasoning" (Meltzer, Petras, and Reynolds 1975, p. 117). It thus appears that the Blumer who emphasizes social constraint became overshadowed by his anti-structuralist image (cf. Buban 1986, p. 31).

THE NEW IOWA SCHOOL REVISITED

Mead's (1938) evolutionary theory of the act was beyond the scope of the points-in-space/time methodology Kuhn adopted. Thus, a new Iowa School sought to combine Kuhn's commitment to a stable methodology with Blumer's and Mead's evolutionary visions. While maintaining Kuhn's point-in-space procedure, Iowa School researchers adopted Blumer's across-time and constructionist perspectives.

The emergence of "user friendly" audio-visual technology and the availability of laboratory space provided an infrastructure for a synthesis resulting in a commitment to laboratory research and recording technology. This commitment directed new Iowa School researchers to isolate and detect the generic elements of social processes, and formulate principles about social phenomena. It resulted in a hybrid characterized by across-time and point-in-space methodology, and enabled the new Iowa School to study "structured processes" (Buban 1986, p. 31; Travisano 1975, p. 263).

Both Blumer (1931) and Kuhn (1964a) advocated the quest for generic concepts. Each however, neglected a structuration process in which human beings actively shape their acts within an emergent, and consequential, social structure (Giddens 1979). Blumer's self-indicating process and Kuhn's structure of selves implied the analysis of individuals rather than a jointly constructed and public context encasing social acts or relationships. In effect, neither Blumer nor Kuhn derived generic concepts in light of conceiving an "impinging other" (Buban 1986, p. 35; Perinbanayagam, 1974).

Mead (1938) regarded an impinging other as necessary to the social act, but his portrayal lacked any sort of tension to which later interactionists would become sensitive (Becker 1973; Glaser and Strauss 1964; Goffman 1963; Stone 1962). These interactionists stressed that interaction in any context necessitates mutually adjustive behavior — or complex reciprocal activity that deflects, facilitates, or blocks lines of action (Turner 1962). Thus, early problems confronting laboratory researchers included designing studies that acknowledged human agency on the one hand, and that involved challenges to such agency in the form of impingements on the other hand.

Further, a view of human beings, including laboratory participants, as able to think for themselves and to act (rather than merely react—see also McFeat 1974) accompanied the necessity to master techniques and to formulate a research policy that located camera and microphones in locked-in-place positions to maintain a stable point-in-space methodology. This dual procedure was partially realized in the Openings Study (Miller, Hintz, and Couch 1975), which demonstrated that human subjects could respond in a minded fashion to emergent events and that audio-visual technology could be employed to accumulate across-time data without disrupting the social acts produced by participants. The generated data were analyzed for the purpose of detecting how two people align their personal acts to construct a social act. Six elements of sociation — co-presence; reciprocal acknowledged attention; mutual responsiveness; shared focus; social object; and congruent identities — formed a structurated and value added form of sociation whereby each successive element represented a specific elaboration of the relatedness prevailing between interactors.

Even though the new Iowa School "emphasized the orderliness or structuredness of human interaction" (Buban 1986, p. 34) and maintained a point-in-space ethos, they went beyond Kuhn's attempt to measure the self in a social structure by incorporating Mead's perspective of social action. Such action involved the mutual imputation to self and other that a social accomplishment is forthcoming (Scheff 1968). Taken in sequence and as an uninterrupted whole, the elements of sociation that constitute a cooperative act represent an across time version of a universal process and an extension of Kuhn's quest to derive a social science based on social behavioristic principles of reflective conduct.

While Kuhn's Iowa School remains segregated from the more popular Chicago School of interactionism, students of the self regard its methodology as a viable approach to the interactionist study of the self (Turner and Schutte 1981). However, many interactionists outside of the new Iowa School remain lukewarm to it, and even the more sympathetic "outsiders" temper their appreciation with criticism (see Denzin 1989; Maines 1984). Part of the negative reaction stems from a general distrust of the laboratory as a place to derive complex generic concepts in high fidelity to the active and creative image of human behavior (Stone 1984). We wish to deal with such reservations in the following sections.

QUALITATIVE STUDIES OF SOCIAL PROCESSES

Most interactionists committed to naturalistic observations claim to study "lived experience" as constructed in familiar environments (Denzin 1990a). They call for participant observation, including intensive open-ended interviewing, and to collect the "richest possible data...over a relatively prolonged period of time...through direct face-to-face contact with, and prolonged immersion in, some social location or circumstance" (Lofland and Lofland 1984, p. 11). The research procedures call for adopting across-time and across-space approaches to acquire data in high fidelity to ongoing social life.[1]

The "classic" participant observation studies (e.g., Lindesmith, 1947; Strauss, 1978; Sutherland, 1939) used across-time and across-space measures "to elucidate social processes [and to] represent the Chicago School" (Buban 1986, p. 35). Those committed to the classics eschew point-in-space locations while generating data and suspect that laboratory research controls participants' behaviors to the point of scripting forthcoming activity. For instance, Denzin (1989, pp. 121-22) describes activity in the laboratory as "a `social occasion' that is staged [by] scientific investigators...[who] have an active hand in producing the findings that flow from their experimental designs and manipulations."

Although the Chicago School standpoint enjoys wide appeal, their perspective "has remained so abstract the empirical case studies flowing out of it have often seemed little better than the kind of descriptions that can be produced by conscientious journalists or literate laymen" (Lofland 1970, p. 37). Accordingly, interactionists need to develop "limited and precise notions of microscopic social processes" (Lofland 1970, p. 37). Calling for such limitations necessitates that interactionists need to establish research procedures in controlled environments, to generate and analyze manageable data—which is anathema to most qualitative interactionists. Yet by avoiding control naturalists risk being overwhelmed by their data. Specifically, they cannot adequately detect patterns emanating from their across-time observations from their across-space locations. Particular perceptions of behaviors change as researchers occupy different locations to observe them.

Becker's (1953) study of marijuana users, long considered the prototype of successful naturalistic research, illustrates the above problems. As Buban (1986, p. 32) noted, "researchers adopting Becker's concepts to apply them to other areas would find them vague and abstract. They would glean how definitions of individuals evolve, rather than how individuals' definitions of themselves change as a consequence of fitting their behaviors together." In effect, Becker's formulations lacked precision "in telling us just how the events were constructed over time by the interactants involved. As it stands the study could have been produced by Lofland's 'conscientious journalist'" (Buban 1986, p. 32).

This lack of precision is grounded in Blumer's orientation to the world, described by Kohout (1986, p. 13) as the "spectatorial attitude," whereby researchers intend to "describe the...world [so as to not] affect the activity under study." Such an attitude hinders the development of generic concepts (see Couch 1984). Conversely, the point-in-space orientation made possible in the laboratory with a locked-in-place camera and microphone simplifies observed phenomena. Researchers adopting a stable location can more easily detect patterns when analyzing across-time representations of social processes. If the laboratory is properly used in conjunction with recording devices, manageable data of high fidelity can be generated.

Interactionists' commitment to across-time and across-space procedures minimize the possibility of generating and detecting generic sociological concepts. Such procedures invite too much complexity to the degree that "the social acts [naturalists] have chosen for analysis have often been both too complex and too long-range to be amenable to precise analysis, at least given our present lack of concepts for describing how persons fit their behaviors together" (Buban 1986, p. 34). Instead of locating the research act within broadly defined worlds, an alternative is to specify explicit and simplified joint acts (Couch and Hintz 1975; Lofland, 1970; and Miyamoto 1959: 295) within an equally specific and controlled social world. Using across-time but point-in-space procedures in the laboratory can allow interactionists to accomplish this goal.

MAKING THE SOCIOLOGICAL LABORATORY SOCIAL

While generating data in the laboratory is relatively new to interactionists, other sociologists have established a laboratory tradition. However, their orientation not only calls for a point-in-space bias, but they proceed as if a point-in-time methodology is adequate for the study of social phenomena (see Couch, Katovich and Miller 1988 for a critique of those procedures). Such studies conceptualize interaction as a reflection of static relationships and focus their concern on subjects' reactions to experimental stimuli and constraints. These researchers use laboratories to restrict interaction within narrowly circumscribed parameters, suppress creative behaviors, and limit encounters to discreetly bounded points in time (Becker and Geer 1970; Blumer 1969; Denzin 1971; Fine and Glassner 1979; Strauss 1978).

Many advocates of qualitative methodologies advance the claim that such laboratory procedures so truncate "actual" social phenomena as to render processes generated in laboratories as arbitrary reflections of the researchers interests and meaningless to the participants (Stone 1984; Maines 1984). According to interactionist critics, the processes generated in the laboratory occur only on the basis of some subjective decisions made by researchers who created an artificial world independent of their human subjects. As these qualitative researchers see no other alternative within the laboratory, they maintain that only naturalistic observation generates across-time data constructed by human beings as they attend to and solve real life problems.[2]

Thus, symbolic interaction critics of laboratory research often claim that simulated environments prohibit the study of meaningful action. What is meaningful and what is not is usually left unspecified, but it seems that for many critics the lack of meaning stems from their belief that actions elicited within the laboratory are without consequences; that such actions lack implications beyond the laboratory. However, every social context has its own parameters of consequences. The meaning of any act is reduced the further one is removed from the situation. Nonetheless how participants perceive the seriousness of the consequences of their actions within a laboratory remains an issue. The activity of laboratory participants becomes meaningful when researchers allow participants to experience events together so as to create shared pasts and to project futures that contain social objectives. The ideal laboratory context is one that allows participants to project social objectives that are perceived to be significant within the laboratory context, but have no consequences outside of the laboratory. For those who design laboratory studies of social processes, the trick is to create a game atmosphere in which participants strive mightily to achieve the objectives that researchers and participants negotiate.

Although laboratory studies differ markedly from qualitative ethnographies in regard to spatial orientations, they shared with them a concern with observing phenomena across time that are temporally informed and socially situated (Couch 1987). The effective use of the laboratory and recording devices by social scientists requires the acquisition of across-time representations of social processes derived from situated social activities that reflect temporal structures and dimensions of relatedness between people. In other words, the laboratory is a specialized place for generating, observing, and controlling social acts composed of sequential social experiences and actions that are temporally informed — the very same experiences that qualitative researchers seek (McPhail 1979).

TEMPORALITY AND THE SOCIOLOGICAL LABORATORY

All situated social action, whether consummated in the laboratory or *in situ*, contains multilayered temporal structures, two of which are especially critical. One pertains to using the past in the present to fit together overt lines of action to proceed toward a future (see Blumer 1969; Scheff 1968, 1970). Another pertains to bringing covert intentions to bear on movement toward a future. Human beings not only act on the basis of their pasts, they use their pasts to anticipate and intend particular futures (Couch 1989; Hintz 1975; Mead 1932).[3] Projecting futures allows human beings to understand their own and other's intentions. Once the ability to anticipate and act with intentionality has been acquired it becomes taken-for-granted and part of the everyday repertoire of all human beings.

To enact social processes, people must act with, mutually indicate, and mutually acknowledge intentions. If I cannot detect your intentions, I can act with respect to you, but I cannot act with you. Reciprocally, if you cannot detect my intentions you cannot act with me. All forms of cooperative action, action *with* another, require the reciprocal projection and detection of intentions. The projection of future does not insure actions with another will ensue; it only makes it a possibility. Incompetence, external intrusions, and a number of other factors may prevent intentions from being realized.

The abilities to anticipate and act with intention must be allowed to exist in the laboratory. Laboratory environments must maintain fidelity with the temporal dimensions of social life if data are to be generated that will allow for the formulation of authentic principles of social life. Indeed, researchers can generate data in high fidelity to temporal structures of social life by recognizing their subjects as social selves who employ social minds to anticipate and form intentions. The laboratory is a powerful source of sociological data only if researchers acknowledge that activity produced by laboratory participants resembles the activity produced by these researchers.

Just as researchers are capable of the pragmatic testing of assumptions, so are human subjects able to assess and interpret multiple realities, including anticipated developments, as they interact. That the laboratory constitutes a social situation requires that experimental sociologists should also recognize the range of emotions experienced by participants. Furthermore, participants, like researchers, think; some demonstrate thought processes more artfully and gracefully than others, but all define situations cognitively. Only when researchers acknowledge the basic humanity of participants in laboratory studies will their research generate knowledge of complex social processes.

Contrary to common practice, laboratory sociologists cannot assume that eliciting uncluttered social phenomena in the laboratory involves eradicating the temporal dimensions of social phenomena. Many laboratory sociologists do attempt to eradicate the temporal dimensions of social processes when they try to make it impossible for participants to anticipate and form intentional acts. Of course, researchers cannot completely do so unless their subjects drop off into sleep.

The past and future infuses laboratory social processes as surely as they do social processes produced in day-to-day life. Laboratory participants are always using their pasts and anticipating futures to assess the present and organize their intentional behavior (Katovich 1984). The effective use of the laboratory requires that those who design studies recognize explicitly the temporal dimensions of social phenomena. This recognition requires that researchers and participants formulate a cooperative relationship and use the laboratory as a provocative stage (Katovich, 1984) instead of a half-way house to confine and exploit participants.

Most qualitative researchers implicitly acknowledge, as Mead argued in *The Philosophy of the Act*, that social activity is not merely processual, it is also temporally informed. Consequently, those who would use the laboratory to generate data in their study of social processes must recognize that the action produced by laboratory participants, like all other social activity, always has a temporal dimension. People act in the present, but they use their pasts and project futures to organize their actions. When people define situations, whether in or out of laboratories, they do so on the basis of how pasts and futures become infused into a social present (cf. Katovich 1984, p. 55).

Researchers can create contexts that invite subjects to formulate shared futures (social objectives) and to construct mutual awareness of how to facilitate *their* objectives by asking participants to attempt to win a contest, to convince another (others) of the correctness of their cause, to achieve the best possible resolution to a problematic situation, or to construct as many objects as possible within a specified time. To do so, they must acknowledge the creativity of people, including laboratory participants, to generate data about social phenomena in the laboratory. Participant creativity cannot be suppressed if the objective is to formulate generic principles about social processes. However, controls on the range and variety of creativity must be exercised if manageable data are to be generated. That can be achieved by researchers and participants negotiating a commitment to a particular objective so variation in activities generated are not so great as to render the data unmanageable.

The laboratory studies conducted by new Iowa School researchers have addressed temporal issues in varieties of simulated contexts while simultaneously allowing participants to act with anticipation and creativity. For instance, *The Cultural Carrier* study (Powell 1986) generated data on the relationships constructed between simulated homecomers and sedentary homefolk. The simulated departure of the homecomer from, and subsequent return to, the homefolk established parameters on the way the homecomers and homefolk related to one another. At the same time it called on the participants to solve the pragmatic task of creating a mutually acceptable form of relatedness between the homecomer and homefolk. The objective of the study was to explore how innovative knowledge is transmitted by a cultural carrier (the homecomer) to the homefolk in the form of either a newly formed dyad, a dyad containing a shared past that had no prior contact with the cultural carrier, or an established dyad that had previously contained the cultural carrier (Katovich 1984, p. 64). The transactions involved sharing innovative knowledge of how to build an architectural structure, and reflected the nature of the pasts held in common and/or shared by the participants in the experimental setting.

AUDIOVISUAL RECORDINGS

The Cultural Carrier study is offered to indicate how we generate data via across-time observations of temporally informed social phenomena. An important codicil must be offered. Most social phenomena, including phenomena elicited in the laboratory, become so laden with complexities and detail that it is impossible to adequately observe them a "first time through" for the purpose of forming sociological principles (Garfinkel, Lynch, and Livingston 1981). Adopting a point-in-space location can alleviate some of the problems of complexity by attending singularly to events from a specific standpoint. Even so, each and every time sociologists use a laboratory to generate specimens of social processes, they must confront massively complex data which often proves to be unmanageable.

In order to study social processes in the above described manner, research methods which allow for the direct analysis of movement must be employed. While Chicago School participant observers locate themselves within the ongoing flow of human processes, they eventually abandon the study of these processes when involved in data analysis: "Instead they are analyzing field notes which constitute a record of a series of products of interaction, and not interaction *per se*" (Buban 1986, p. 37).

Researchers interested in studying social processes generated by minded subjects in the laboratory invite complex and thickly peopled data. Using a locked-in-position camera and microphone position in conjunction with designs that attempt to elicit uncluttered specimens of social phenomena in the laboratory aids their analysis by allowing for repeated observations of the same event (Saxton and Couch, 1975). Further, "through videotape recordings, scientists are able to 'freeze' a process and keep going back to it over and over again in the attempt to isolate basic features of coordinated interaction" (Katovich 1978, p. 30). Unless specimens of social activity are recorded, the analytical stage of the research act must be completed either "on the fly" as events occur or by the analyses of memories and notes. In each case, analysts are required either to make accurate and comprehensive observations of social processes as they occur, or depend on their memory or the memory of others to retain massive amounts of information. Such reliance on even the most "photographic" of memories creates discrepancies between actual events or statements and reconstructions of occurrences and dialogue. Once recollection, however inaccurate, becomes defined as real, it forms a stubborn past based on emotional conviction. This often crystallizes into "immaculate perceptions" of social events (McPhail 1979).

Just as telescopes increase the perceptual acuity of astronomers and microscopes that of biologists, audiovisual recordings enhance the perceptual acuity of social scientists. However, audiovisual recordings, in contrast to telescopes and microscopes, do not allow analysts to observe (see and hear) events that are not otherwise observable. They only preserve more complete representations of social phenomena. In so doing, audiovisual recordings provide a far more complete representation of social phenomena than can be obtained either via naturalistic observation or questionnaires.

Furthermore, the replay and slow motion capacity of recordings provide the means to "re" "search" data while the data remain constant throughout the analytical phase of the research act. In contrast, unaided memories, and even memories supplemented by notes, often changes as researchers proceed through the analytical phase of the research act. Recordings allow for the systematic and detailed examination of data and the reconceptualization of phenomena without changing the data. The constancy of data is problematic when analyses are based on naturalistic observations.

EXTENDING LABORATORY RESEARCH OUTSIDE OF THE LABORATORY

Latour (1983, p. 144) argued that "the only way for a scientist to retain the strength gained inside his laboratory...is to extend to every setting some of the conditions that make possible the reproduction of favorable laboratory practices." In the context of the new Iowa School, many of the concepts generated in the laboratory, and grounded in an explicit theoretical perspective on temporality, were used to frame subsequent ethnographies in naturalistic settings. The study of barroom regulars (Katovich and

Reese 1987), for instance, made explicit use of relating pasts to futures in ongoing presents as a basis for understanding how regular identities are conferred upon patrons in the course of ongoing situated activity.

A naturalistic study of timesharing scams (Katovich and Diamond 1987) made explicit reference to the openings paradigm in the attempt to describe and analyze strategic sales encounters manipulated by sellers in reference to a dyadic pair of buyers (usually husband and wife). The articulation of the stages of the strategic sales process also incorporated the dynamics of experimental studies of social processes that allow participants to use their temporal structures to organize their actions. Specifically, Katovich and Diamond described how a theatrical and provocative stage is constructed by teams of sellers who employ various props to encourage subordination, acquiescence, and perceptions of specific illusions as realities for the buyers. Another naturalistic study by Bastien and Hostager (1992) made explicit use of the new Iowa School's conceptualization of openings and situated actions to record how jazz musicians constructed improvisational music in the context of maintaining complex forms of relatedness. Their attention to complex acts within other complex acts allowed them to describe successive and continuous opening acts as musicians quickly and efficiently locate such acts within multi-layered contexts of accomplishments.

Researchers completed the above studies in explicit reference to the laboratory studies generated by the new Iowa School. Each employed a temporal focus and a research orientation that was particularly sensitive to how sequencing of acts could be contextualized to construct ongoing social objectives and more complex acts that could encase other social constructions. Further, observers in each study maintained a point-in-space methodology and focused on specific specimens of social acts in order to generate data that allowed for the formation of generic concepts and propositions. In the case of Bastien's and Hostager's study, their point-in-space location involved a fixed-point camera and microphone. Thus, laboratory experimentation is not only congruent with naturalism in the sense that both can be viewed as exploring the same theoretical perspectives and using similar methodological procedures, but laboratory research is also a context from which future naturalistic research endeavors can emerge.

CONCLUSION

Several regard the qualitative and microsociological focus of symbolic interactionism as truly sociological, and perhaps mostly sociological (Stone 1984). Blumer and Kuhn contributed to a sociological interactionism by extending G.H. Mead's theory of the self and act and elaborating programs of action to study structures and processes associated with them. Kuhn's frustration with interactionist research during the 1950s stemmed from its emphasis on rich descriptions of environments rather than on deriving systematic and generic principles associated with such universal variables as the self. Blumer's frustration with other mainstream sociologists stemmed from their emphasis on treating human beings as objects of abstract societal forces and products.

Blumer's corrective involved adopting an across-time perspective to view human beings as active and creative agents of dynamic social worlds. This created a radical break with mainstream sociological views of human realities. Kuhn's corrective involved a point-in-space-and-time methodology to begin the task of understanding the relationship between the self and social structures. This radical break with interactionist tradition sharply separated Kuhn's Iowa School from Blumer's Chicago School of qualitative researchers who championed across-time and across-space methodologies.

The new Iowa School explicitly acknowledges its debt to Kuhn's vision but also honors Blumer's insistence to adopt an across-time perspective toward social phenomena. In striving to bring that vision to fruition, the new Iowa School replaced Kuhn's focus of self as the central object of investigation via point-in-time and point-in-space methodology with a focus on the social act as the central object of investigation via across-time and point-in-space methodology. The commitment to the formulation of a set of empirically based principles of social life remains in place.

Laboratory research informed by the new Iowa School of symbolic interaction can be compatible with the ethos of the Chicago School's qualitative research. Such studies not only can be constructed in a way that allows participants to think, plan, and act with intentions, they must be conducted in that manner if they are to contribute to our understanding of social processes and human life. The objective of such studies is acquiring understanding by the clarification of processes in simplified environments rather than the simplification of processes in rigid environments to demonstrate the superiority of researchers over participants.

Detecting generic processes in the laboratory can enable researchers to structure ethnographic research for the same purposes. Qualitative field methods can be informed by laboratory research that employs point-in-space and across-time methodologies. In this light, interactionism since Blumer and Kuhn has come full circle. In breaking with static formulations of human relatedness on the one hand, and challenging imprecise and abstract measures of such relatedness on the other hand, Blumer and Kuhn respectively inspired a new Iowa School of thought that enables direct investigation of social processes through precise and concrete measures so as to better understand the dynamics of human processual activity.

REFERENCES

Bastien, David and Todd Hostager. 1992. "Cooperation as Communicative Accomplishment: A Symbolic Interaction Analysis of an Improvised Jazz Concert." *Communication Studies* 43:92–104

Becker, Howard S. 1953. "Becoming a Marijuana User." *American Journal of Sociology* 59:235–252.

———. 1973. *Outsiders: Studies in the Sociology of Deviance.* New York: Free Press.

———. 1988. "Herbert Blumer's Conceptual Impact." Symbolic Interaction 11:13–22.

Becker, Howard S. and Blanche Geer. 1970. "Participant Observation and Interviewing." Pp. 133–142 in *Qualitative Methodology: Firsthand Involvement With the Social World*, edited by William Filstead. Chicago: Markham Publishing Company

Blumer, Herbert. 1931. "Science Without Concepts." *American Journal of Sociology* 36:515–533.

———. 1956. "Sociological Analysis and the Variable." *American Sociological Review* 21:683–690.

———. 1969a. *Symbolic Interactionism: Perspective and Method.* Englewood Cliffs, NJ: Prentice-Hall.
———. 1969b. "Society as Symbolic Interaction." Pp. 78–89 in *Symbolic Interactionism: Perspective and Method.* Englewood Cliffs, NJ: Prentice Hall.
———. 1980. "Comment: Mead and Blumer: The Convergent Methodological Perspectives of Social Behaviorism and Symbolic Interactionism." *American Sociological Review* 45:409–419.
———. 1983. "Going Astray With a Logical Scheme." *Symbolic Interaction* 6:127–137.
Buban, Steven L. 1986. "Studying Social Processes: The Chicago and Iowa School Revisited." Pp. 25–40 in *Studies in Symbolic Interaction: The Iowa School,* edited by Carl J. Couch, Stanley L. Saxton, and Michael A. Katovich. Greenwich, CT: JAI Press.
Burawoy, Michael. 1991. "Reconstructing Social Theories." Pp. 8–27 in *Ethnography Unbound: Power and Resistance in the Modern Metropolis,* edited by Michael Burawoy. Berkeley: University of California Press.
Campbell, James. 1983. "Mead and Pragmatism." *Symbolic Interaction* 6:155–164
Churchill, Lindsey. 1971. "Ethnomethodology and Measurement." *Social Forces* 50:182–191.
Couch, Carl J. 1982. "Temporality and Paradigms of Thought." *Studies in Symbolic Interaction* 4:1–34.
———. 1984. "Symbolic Interaction and Generic Sociological Principles." *Symbolic Interaction* 7:1–13.
———. 1987. *Researching Social Processes in the Laboratory.* Greenwich, CT: JAI Press.
———. 1989. "Comments on a Neo-Meadian Sociology of the Mind." *Symbolic Interaction* 12:59–62
Couch, Carl J., Stanley L. Saxton, and Michael A. Katovich. 1986. "Introduction." Pp. xvii–xxv in *Studies in Symbolic Interaction: The Iowa School,* edited by Carl J. Couch, Stanley L. Saxton, and Michael A. Katovich. Greenwich, CT: JAI Press.
Couch, Carl. J. Michael A. Katovich, and Dan E. Miller. 1988. "The Sorrowful Tale of Small Group Research." *Studies in Symbolic Interaction* 10:258–279.
Denzin, Norman K. 1971. "The Logic of Naturalistic Inquiry." *Social Forces* 50:166–82.
———. 1989. *The Research Act: A Theoretical Introduction to Sociological Methods* (Third Edition). Englewood Cliffs, NJ: Prentice Hall
———. 1990a. "Presidential Address on The Sociological Imagination Revisited." *The Sociological Quarterly* 31:1–22.
———. 1990b. "The Spaces of Postmodernism: Reading Plummer on Blumer." *Symbolic Interaction* 13:145–154.
———. 1992. *Symbolic Interaction and Cultural Studies: The Politics of Interpretation.* Cambridge, MA: Blackwell.
Durkheim, Emile. 1938. *The Rules of The Sociological Method.* Glencoe, IL: The Free Press.
Farberman, Harvey. 1991. "Symbolic Interaction and Postmodernism: Close Encounters of a Dubious Kind." *Symbolic Interaction* 14:471–488.
Fine, Gary Alan and Barry Glassner. 1979. "Participant Observation with Children: Promise and Problems." *Urban Life* 8:153–174.
Garfinkel, Harold, M. Lynch, and E. Livingston. 1981. "The Work of a Discovering Science Construed with Materials from the Optically Discovered Pulsar." *Philosophy of the Social Sciences* 11:131–158.
Giddens, Anthony. 1979. *Central Problems in Social Theory: Action, Structure, and Contradiction in Social Analysis.* University of California Press: Berkeley.
Glaser, Barney and Anselm Strauss. 1964"Awareness Contexts and Social Interaction." *American Sociological Review* 29: 669–679.
———. 1967. *The Discovery of Grounded Theory.* Chicago: Aldine.
Goffman, Erving. 1963. *Behavior in Public Places: Notes on the Social Organization of Gatherings.* New York: Free Press.
Hintz, Robert A. 1975. "Foundations of Social Action." Pp. 47–64 in *Constructing Social Life,* edited by Carl J. Couch and Robert A. Hintz. Champaign, IL: Stipes.
Jameson, Fredric. 1991. *Postmodernism, or the Cultural Logic of Late Capitalism.* Durham, NC: Duke University Press.
Karp, David A., Gregory P. Stone, and William C. Yoels. 1991. *Being Urban: A Sociology of City Life.* New York: Prager.
Katovich, Michael A. 1978. *Contextualizing Through Play: Some Notes on Social Context.* Masters Thesis. The University of Iowa City, Iowa.

———. 1984. "Symbolic Interaction and Experimentation: The Laboratory as a Provocative Stage." *Studies in Symbolic Interaction* 5:49–67.
Katovich, Michael A. and Ron Diamond. 1987. "Selling Time: Situated Transactions in a Noninstitutional Environment." *Sociological Quarterly* 27:253–271.
Katovich, Michael A. and William A. Reese. 1993. "Postmodern Thought in Symbolic Interaction: Reconstructing Social Inquiry in Light of Late-Modern Concerns." *Sociological Quarterly* 34: In Press
Kohout, Frank. 1986. "George Herbert Mead and Experimental Knowledge." Pp. 7–24 in *Studies in Symbolic Interaction: The Iowa School*, edited by Carl J. Couch, Stanley L. Saxton, and Michael A. Katovich. Greenwich, CT: JAI Press.
Kuhn, Manford. 1962. "The Interviewer and the Professional Relationship." Pp. 193–206 in *Human Behavior and Social Processes*, edited by Arnold Rose. Boston: Houghton-Mifflin.
———. 1964a. "Major Trends in Symbolic Interaction Theory in the Past Twenty-Five Years." *Sociological Quarterly* 5:61–84.
———. 1964b. "The Reference Group Reconsidered." *SociologicalQuarterly* 5:6–21.
Kuhn, Manford H. and Thomas S. McPartland. 1954. "An Empirical Investigation of Self-Attitudes." *American Sociological Review* 19:68–76.
Latour, Bruno. 1983. "Give Me a Laboratory and I Will Raise the World." Pp. 141–170 in *Science Observed*, edited by Karen Knorr-Cetina and Michael Mulkay.
Lewis, J. David and Richard L. Smith. 1980. *American Sociology and Pragmatism: Mead, Chicago Sociology and Symbolic Interaction*. Chicago: University of Chicago Press.
Lindesmith, Alfred. 1947*Opiate Addiction*. Bloomington, IN: Principia Press.
Lofland, John. 1970. "Interactionists' Imagery and Analytic Interruptus." Pp. 35–45 in *Human Nature and Collective Behavior*, edited by Tomatsu Shibutani. Englewood Cliffs, NJ: Prentice-Hall.
———. 1976. *Doing Social Life*. New York: Wiley and Sons.
Lofland, John and Lyn H. Lofland. 1984. *Analyzing Social Settings: A Guide to Qualitative Observation and Analysis*. Belmont, CA: Wadsworth.
Maines, David R. 1984. "The Sand and the Castle: Remarks Concerning G.P. Stone's Critique of Small Group Research." *Studies in Symbolic Interaction* 5:23–34.
———. 1988. "Myth, Text, and Interactionist Complicity in the Neglect of Blumer's Macrosociology." *Symbolic Interaction* 11:43–58.
McFeat, Tom. 1974. *Small Group Cultures*. New York: Pergamon Press.
McPhail, Clark. 1979. "Experimental Research is Convergent with Symbolic Interaction." *Symbolic Interaction* 2:89–94.
McPhail, Clark and Cynthia Rexroat. 1979. "Mead vs. Blumer: The Divergent Methodological Perspectives of Social Behaviorism and Symbolic Interactionism." *American Sociological Review* 44:449–467.
———. 1980. "Ex Cathedra Blumer or Ex Libris Mead?" *American Sociological Review* 45:420–430.
Mead, George Herbert. 1932. *The Philosophy of the Present*. Chicago: University of Chicago Press.
———. 1934. *Mind, Self, and Society*. Chicago: University of Chicago Press.
———. 1936. *Movements of Thought in the Nineteenth Century*. Chicago: University of Chicago Press.
———. 1938. *The Philosophy of the Act*. Chicago: University of Chicago Press.
Meltzer, Bernard and John Petras. 1970. "The Chicago and Iowa Schools of Symbolic Interactionism." Pp. 3–17 in *Human Nature and Collective Behavior*, edited by Tomatsu Shibutani. Englewood Cliffs, NJ: Prentice-Hall.
Meltzer, Bernard, John Petras, and Larry Reynolds. 1975. Symbolic Interactionism: Genesis, Varieties, and Criticism. London: Routledge and Kegan Paul.
Miller, Dan E., Robert A. Hintz and Carl J. Couch. 1975. "The Elements and Structure of Openings." *Sociological Quarterly* 16:479–99.
Miyamoto, S. Frank. 1959. "The social act: A re-examination of a concept." *Pacific Sociological Review* 5:51–55.
Morrione, Thomas. 1988. "Herbert G. Blumer (1900–1987): A Legacy of Concepts, Criticisms, and Contributions." *Symbolic Interaction* 11:1–12.
Perinbanayagam, Robert S. 1974. The Definition of the Situation: An Analysis of the Ethnomethodological and Dramaturgical View." *Sociological Quarterly* 15:521–541.

Plummer, Ken. 1990. "Staying in the Empirical World: Symbolic Interactionism and Postmodernism: A Reply to Denzin." *Symbolic Interaction* 13:155–160.
Powell, Joel O. 1986. "Diffusion and Social Relations." Pp. 295–308 in *Studies in Symbolic Interaction: The Iowa School*, edited by Carl J.Couch, Stanley L. Saxton, and Michael A. Katovich. Greenwich Ct: JAI Press.
Reese, William A. 1993. "A Janus-Faced Look at Some Issues for an Interactionist Inquiry into Postmodernism." Paper presented at the Midwest Sociological Society's Annual Meetings, Chicago, April.
Reynolds, Larry T. 1969. *The Sociology of Symbolic Interactionism*. Ph.D. Dissertation, Ohio State University.
Reynolds, Janice M. and Larry T. Reynolds. 1973. "Interactionism, Complicity and the Astructural Bias." *Catalyst* 7:76–85.
Rochberg-Halton, Eugene. 1983. "The Real Nature of Pragmatism and Chicago Sociology." *Symbolic Interaction* 6:139–153.
Saxton, Stanley and Carl J. Couch. 1975. "Recording Social Interaction." Pp. 255–262 in *Constructing Social Life*, edited by Carl J. Couch and Robert A. Hintz. Champaign, IL: Stipes.
Scheff, Thomas J. 1968. "Negotiating Reality: Notes on Power in Assessment of Responsibility." *Social Problems* 16:3–17.
———. 1970. "On the Concepts of Identity and Social Relationship." Pp. 193–207 in *Human Nature and Collective Behavior*, edited by Tomatsu Shibutani. Englewood Cliffs, NJ: Prentice–Hall.
Shibutani, Tomatsu. 1988. "Herbert Blumer's Contributions to Twentieth–Century Sociology." *Symbolic Interaction* 11:23–32.
Stone, Gregory P. 1962. "Appearance and the Self." Pp. 86–118 in *Human Behavior and Social Processes*, edited by Arnold M. Rose. Boston: Houghton Mifflin.
———. 1984. "Conceptual Problems in Small Group Research." *Studies in Symbolic Interaction* 5:3–21.
Strauss, Anselm. 1978. *Negotiations*. San Francisco: Jossey-Bass
Stryker, Sheldon. 1980. *Symbolic Interactionism: A Social Structural Version*. Menlo Park, CA: Benjamin/ Cummings.
Sutherland, Edwin. 1939. Criminology. Philadelphia: Lippincott.
Travisano, Richard V. 1975. "Comments on a Research Paradigm for Symbolic Interaction." Pp. 263–271 in *Constructing Social Life*, edited by Carl J. Couch and Robert A. Hintz. Champaign, IL: Stipes.
Tucker, Charles. 1966. "Some Methodological Problems of Kuhn's Self Theory." *Sociological Quarterly* 7: 345–358.
Turner, Ralph H. 1953. "The Quest for Universals in Sociological Research." *American Sociological Review* 24: 605–611.
———. 1956. "Role Taking, Role Standpoint, and Reference Group Behavior." *American Journal of Sociology* 61:316–328.
———. 1962. "Role Taking: Process Versus Conformity." Pp. 20–40 in *Human Behavior and Social Processes*, edited by Arnold M. Rose. Boston: Houghton Mifflin.
———. 1976. "The Real Self: From Institution to Impulse." *American Journal of Sociology* 81:989–1016.
Turner, Ralph and Jerald Schutte. 1981. "The True Method for Studying the Self Conception." *Symbolic Interaction* 4:1–20.
Zimmerman, Don H. 1967. "A Reply to Professor Coser." *The American Sociologist* 11:4–13.

NOTES

[1] Even most researchers who use point-in-time methodologies, such as survey and questionnaire data, agree that across-time observations are preferred. However, most also agree that across-time observations generate such rich and complex data that it is difficult, if not impossible, to effectively manage across-time data. Many researchers settle for point-in-time methodologies to avoid becoming overwhelmed by data. Consequently they generate static representation of mental or social processes that are manageable during the analytical phase of the research act. However, the employment of point-in-time methodologies is a false

economy. Although they provide data that are more manageable, the data generated has such an extremely low level of fidelity that they have limited value, especially when researchers aim to formulate universal principles of social phenomena.

[2] We acknowledge that much of the laboratory research completed by sociologists has reduced social phenomena to categories of acts that lose relevance outside of the rigid system in which they were produced (See Couch, Katovich, and Miller 1986 for an extended discussion of this point). We recognize that the dynamic qualities of social phenomena must be preserved. In agreement with most qualitative researchers, we disavow point-in-time methodologies on the grounds that they do not respect the dynamic qualities of social phenomena. In Blumer's words, sociological researchers cannot substitute products for processes.

[3] Given that it is impossible to enact social process of any complexity without the projection of futures, it is interesting that most sociologists who use the laboratory attempt to create situations that deny participants the chance to anticipate or act with intentionality. These researchers have followed the lead of their psychological brethren when designing laboratory studies. Two of the favorite stimuli used by psychologists in their laboratory studies of learning are air puffs and electrical shock, neither of which can be anticipated with any precision. Apparently, psychologists believe that removing the temporal dimensions of human conduct makes their experiments more scientific. Sociologists following this lead attempt to keep participants from anticipating or acting with intentionality, and presume the same scientific status. Of course, what such procedures assure is that no authentic principles of social phenomena will be formulated.

Chapter 12
WALKING A TIGHTROPE: DILEMMAS OF PARTICIPANT OBSERVATION OF GROUPS IN CONFLICT

Anson D. Shupe, Jr. and *David G. Bromley*

Much of the methodological commentary on participant observation techniques in field work focuses on the problems encountered in studying a single group. Sociologists have written extensively on the problems related to gaining entry, establishing and maintaining rapport, and disengaging once the research has been completed for the single group situation (e.g., Shaffir, Turowetz, and Stebbins, 1979; Douglas, 1972; Weinberg and Williams, 1972; Vidich, 1970). However, much less attention has been paid to the issues which develop in the conduct of comparative participant observation research.

Whether one is studying only a single group or more than one simultaneously, the researcher in either situation inevitably confronts certain basic dilemmas. On the one hand, there has been the problem of securing sufficient cooperation from informants to gain accurate, detailed information (some of which is of a confidential, sensitive nature) and becoming attuned to the informants' world views (e.g., Trice, 1970; Becker, 1952; Blum, 1952). On the other hand, researchers have tried to avoid "going native" or being subtly co-opted by the group while in the role of participant observer (Becker, 1967). As Grimshaw (1973:4) noted in his observations on the methodological skills necessary in "area" studies versus "comparative" studies:

> While the problems involved are no different in kind from those involved in domestic research, they are of such great magnitude as to constitute an almost qualitative difference for comparative, as compared to noncomparative, research.

The same could be argued for a distinction between single-group and comparative participant observation research. While we do not mean to imply in this paper that sociologists researching simultaneously two or more groups confront problems totally different from those of the more typical one-group situation, we would maintain that those problems experienced in the one-group case often combine or enlarge in the dual or multi-group case to form dilemmas that are well-nigh inescapable or at least more intricate than in the single-group case. The differences are clearly of degree, not kind. To paraphrase Grimshaw, in the multi-group situation the problems of entry, rapport, maintenance, and quality control of data (among others) become so consistently manifest as to almost *seem* different to the researcher.

In this paper we shall deal with the special case of maintaining rapport with two groups, each of which was dedicated to the destruction of the other. Both were highly visible social movements of the 1970s, urban in member composition and focus on activities, and the subjects of a storm of controversy and coverage.

THE ANTAGONISTS: THE UNIFICATION CHURCH AND THE ANTI-CULT MOVEMENT

The two antagonistic groups with which the authors became involved as participant observers were (1) the controversial Unification Church of the Korean evangelist Reverend Sun Myung Moon (more popularly known as the "Moonies") and (2) the emerging network of organizations (composed primarily of families, ex-members of the Unification Church and other "new religions," and spokespersons for conventional denominations) which has actively opposed such groups as the Unification Church. The latter organizations, although less visible than the "Moonies," recently have attracted considerable attention as a result of seeking media publicity and their involvement in the practice known as "deprogramming." ("Deprogramming" is the popular term for detaining a "marginal" religion's member involuntarily and pressuring him or her, through persistent argument, to recant the new faith and return to the former lifestyle).

The authors' involvement with these groups was typical of much participant observation in that once the project commenced new questions arose which were largely unanticipated. In this case the authors initially were struck by the enormous outpouring of negative media coverage and publicity given to the Unification Church in the mid-1970s. The authors prepared a manuscript for presentation at a professional meeting which offered a speculative interpretation of this adverse social reaction (see Shupe, et al., 1977). In the process of preparing this manuscript one of the authors requested information from the headquarters of the National Ad Hoc Committee—Citizens Engaged in Freeing Minds (CEFM) which, coincidentally, was located in the Dallas-Fort Worth metropolitan area. A phone call and visitation to CEFM headquarters intrigued the researcher and soon the CEFM had become a target of investigation in its own right.

At approximately the same time two relatively high ranking (state and national) representatives of the Unification Church, heading a contingent of approximately fifty missionaries, arrived in the metropolitan area and attempted to recruit university students and establish a campus student organization. One of the authors, then acting as chairperson of the sociology department, was approached to serve as faculty sponsor for the campus organization after numerous refusals from other departmental chairpersons. On civil libertarian principles he agreed. Since the group planned to witness and fund raise in the metropolitan area for several weeks, we felt the situation afforded us an unusual opportunity to compare the actual activities and lifestyle of the members with the popular media image. As reciprocity for university sponsorship, over the next two months we were permitted to conduct more than forty in-depth interviews with church members, and we engaged in a substantial amount of other observation.

Somewhat surprisingly, leaders of the anti-cult movement, although aware of the authors' research on the Unification Church, continued to provide us with information, made an effort to maintain an ongoing relationship, and later issued an invitation to participate in a closed strategy meeting of regional officers in the movement. They seemed relieved that social scientists were finally "investigating" what they perceived to be a critical problem. As a result of these contacts we gained access to personal correspondence, memos and documents, and other "insider" communications among anti-cultists by which the changes in the anti-cult movement could be monitored. One of the authors subsequently prepared several papers on the movement (Shupe, Spielman, and Stigall, 1977a, 1977b) which members perceived as descriptively accurate and objective.

After gaining entry into both of these opposed groups, we became more deeply involved with each. Initial contacts with the Unification Church led to additional participant observation of members' activities elsewhere in Texas, frequent contacts with national Church officials, an opportunity to visit the Church's seminary and national organizational headquarters, and access to organizational files and records. Likewise the anti-cultists offered additional opportunities to attend closed strategy sessions, provided access to personal correspondence and diaries of current and former Church members, and established contacts with public officials investigating new religious groups. The deepening involvement, then, resulted in acquisition of a greater quantity of information from both sides that was at the same time more sensitive and confidential.

Much of the information which was divulged to us by each group inevitably had at least the potential for a negative impact on its opponent. As these relationships emerged over time we found ourselves confronting a unique set of problems. Rather than being participant observers of a single group, a situation involving negotiations more familiar to sociologists, we found ourselves attempting to maintain a much more delicate set of relationships, analogous to "walking a tightrope." Indeed, in a situation in which each group was devoted to the destruction of the other, any involvement with one group immediately endangered our relationship with the other. After all, from the perspective of each we were consorting with their opponents. Out of this experience we have isolated several major problems which persisted throughout the research enterprise. The way these problems were resolved had more than procedural implications. Their resolution influenced our access to additional information and the tenor of the presentation of our findings, even down to choices of wording. These problems were (1) role definition and justification; (2) pressures to go native; (3) public pressures to take a stand; (4) evolving commitments; and (5) gaining comparable information and insights.

ROLE DEFINITION AND JUSTIFICATION

In any overt participant observation situation it is necessity to explain one's intentions, and this we did at the outset with each group. However, the necessity of explaining our roles tended to persist since each individual interviewed or contacted had some capacity to grant or withhold cooperation or information. Several factors reduced the barriers which groups typically maintain toward outsiders. First, the professional sociologist-researcher role carried a certain degree of legitimacy. Like most middle class Americans, our informants were accustomed to public opinion surveys and journalistic inquiries of a quasi-social science nature. Thus, although most of them lacked a precise definition of sociology per se, they were not uncomfortable with a social scientist's questioning and probing. Second, each group was seeking some type of legitimation to which it was perceived we might contribute. In the case of the Unification Church, members were quite receptive since they felt the authors' "objective" presentation of the group's lifestyle would help to dispel what they considered to be myths and stereotypes about themselves. In the case of the anti-cult movement, members were using a "brainwashing model" of how young persons came to be members of such groups as the Unification Church couched in behavioral science jargon. Since they had extremely limited knowledge of the concepts they sought to employ, the mere presence of social scientists contributed to their efforts to increase their own credibility and sophistication. Third, we gained support with leaders of each group, facilitating cooperation with rank and file members. Finally, the generally open-ended format of the interview schedules, which allowed respondents to express their own views and feelings, minimized their sense of threat.

What made the dual group situation unique was the fact that any involvement with one group automatically required an explanation of our dealings with their "enemies." Members of each group expressed puzzlement that we felt the necessity to solicit information from the other side. For example, the anti-cultists went so far as to warn us against attending dinner-lectures of the Unification Church because we might "succumb" to their alleged subtle mind control techniques. Other anti-cultists, while it was never publicly stated, were clearly concerned that our investigation of the Unification Church might not confirm their stereotypes of the group. The Church, by contrast, did not directly express reservations about our contacts with the anti-cultists, but it was evident that our association with the anti-cultists made it more difficult for the Church to locate us precisely on the supporter-opponent continuum. This was a particularly salient concern to the Church because in the past it had opened its doors to outside investigators only later to feel "burned" by the negative published accounts. (One particular investigation toward which they harbored such feelings was Stoner and Parke, 1977, in which they were lumped together with other "deviant" religions for which they had little affinity). Of course, the more sensitive the information to which we were given access, the more explicitly this concern was voiced. In fact, by the time we were invited to visit the Unification Church Seminary, a rather lengthy set of negotiations around just that point were required. For some time it appeared that further access would be denied because the authors' published work was perceived as not sufficiently "objective" and sensitive to the uses to which the information might be put by others.

PRESSURES TO GO NATIVE

Whenever a neutral outsider first encounters a social movement in which members are highly committed and goal oriented, there is inevitably some pressure on him or her to accept its ideology and often to involve oneself in the group's activities. In part this pressure emanates from the fact that individuals who are highly committed members of a cause believe in the rightness of their ideas and principles and tend to equate knowing and understanding with believing. In part, also, pressure occurs because social movements desire new members, and conversion of a neutral outsider constitutes a victory for the group. So while researchers may be tolerated as long as they are not a hinderance to the group, the group would much prefer a committed member to a neutral observer.

The authors experienced such pressures from each side on a belief and behavioral level. Unification Church members frequently asked our impression of the Divine Principle (the spiritual formulation of Reverend Moon's divine relation). At first we could claim ignorance, evade such queries, and express interest in learning more. But as time went on and we had attended theological lectures, unwillingness to express personal judgements on the merits of the doctrine was increasingly viewed as implausible. In a movement which highly valued revealing one's "true heart," such professional detachment bordered on insecurity. The anti-cultists exerted their own form of pressure (i.e., to accept the "brainwashing" model by which membership in the Unification Church was explained). This model assumed that coercive mind control techniques such as drugging, hypnosis, or outright seduction were employed by the Church to secure compliance and psychologically "enslave" members.

Pressure for behavioral participation derived from the simple fact that members of both groups were deeply involved in the day-to-day pursuit of their organizations' goals. To be with the groups meant literally to participate. For example, members of the Unification Church typically worked sixteen hour days at witnessing and fund raising, and so it was seldom possible to encounter them outside this round of activity. To observe and interview members in the course of these activities meant at least tacit approval of the latter. For example, when the authors accompanied Unification Church members on fund raising campaigns during which the members did not readily identify their affiliation, we made no attempt to correct these misrepresentations. Likewise, anti-cultists were always volunteers. A typical day in one of their houses, which served as a base of operations, saw them deluged with phone calls requesting or pledging support, letters that had to be sorted, answered, and indexed. To stop work for a conversation or interview meant to fall several hours behind; hence as a "trade off" that also could be interpreted as tacit approval the authors had to "pitch in" and work along with the informants in such activities as stuffing envelopes and copying addresses onto file cards. If all this sounds a little mundane, it must be remembered that the objective of all the group's activities was the destruction of cults. Hence, any participation, even clerical assistance, contributed to that end.

The implications of these sorts of pressures from each group took on a new significance in the dual group situation. Activities abetting either group, if known, could be interpreted by the other group (and perhaps rightfully so) as giving support to the "enemy." Thus the problem became to involve ourselves sufficiently to maintain rapport in the eyes of each group without engaging in activities so overtly partisan as to compromise our neutral image. A particularly perplexing problem arose with respect to the media. Each group requested our advocacy on local radio and television and in public meetings (e.g., church groups, PTA's, legislative hearings). Given the intense polarization of the two antagonists, it was virtually impossible to discuss publicly the salient issues in any concrete detail without so offending one side or the other as to jeopardize our relationship with one or both. Explaining this dilemma openly to each side usually released us from the request but posed a further problem for them: exactly where *did* we stand on these issues?

In sum, pressures to go native were exacerbated additively by working simultaneously with two groups. Yet, as we mentioned in the previous section, each group was willing to tolerate "neutral" (i.e., non-artisan) inquiry insofar as this was useful to it, specifically in helping to eradicate myths and stereotypes about its members and lifestyle and to gain whatever prestige-by-association was available from having two social scientists on the premises. It must be admitted that likely neither group suspected we would remain non-partisan long once we had discovered the "truth," the "facts," and similar data. To reiterate, both groups subscribed to the assumption that to "really know" their respective positions was to come to believe them.

PUBLIC PRESSURE TO TAKE A STAND

Not only were our respective informants interested in fostering a favorable public image through us, but also the various media and other interest groups solicited our opinions. Since we were viewed as among the relatively few informed experts on both sides of this conflict, it was difficult to avoid granting public interviews generated by public curiosity, fears, and rumors about the two groups. On the one hand, we knew that media coverage would be given to these events. For the authors not to have granted interviews would have been to abdicate responsibility to less informed, more partisan individuals and to allow unfounded rumors to spread unchecked. On the other hand, any public statement ran the risk of severing laboriously built-up relationships. This problem was made more acute by virtue of the fact that the media were most interested in the spectacular and sensational and persisted in asking if such charges as "brainwashing" by the Unification Church or "kidnapping" by the anti-cultists were "really true."

Our solution to this dilemma was, first, to avoid interviews that seemed superficial, highly partisan, or exploitative, and, second, to attempt to portray the phenomena in all the complexity and to dispel obvious oversimplifications or caricatures about each group. On such an emotionally charged subject, however, it should be noted that this was at best a delicate and, from the standpoint of those who asked us, occasionally unsatisfying solution. For example, when we attempted to present an unbiased and complex view of the issues on a public affairs radio program which involved listener call-ins, we generated few call-ins and the show was terminated early by the announcer.

EVOLVING COMMITMENTS

As we have already noted in discussing the problem of role justification, information provided to us by either group had at least potentially negative implications for the other. Further, we observed that since each group valued true objectivity and neutrality only to a limited extent there was always some pressure on us to abandon our obvious detachment. However, as we sought highly sensitive "insider" information on organizational strategies and access to records and personal documents, we confronted the logical extension of the problems which we have termed the dilemma of evolving commitments. That is, as the research project with each group evolved, we discovered new sources of information of which we had previously been unaware. Further, as we acquired a more sophisticated understanding of the groups and the controversy between them, we asked more probing questions. Gaining access to this more sensitive and confidential information made the authors' positions on issues and the uses to which organizational information would be put more critical to our informants. Not surprisingly, informants demanded clearer and more specific statements and assurances about the need for such sensitive data because of their greater investment in the project. As a result we found ourselves engaging in delicate negotiations concerning the details of our interpretations, walking the narrow path between revealing to informants the uses to which certain items of information would be put and allowing them to act as censors.

In the case of the Unification Church, we were able to gain considerable information on the lifestyle of members by interviewing, witnessing, and fund raising teams passing through the state. However, we began to realize that it was imperative to obtain information on the national organization structure and gain access to private organizational records. Such information could be acquired only with the cooperation and consent of leaders and high ranking officials. In contrast to our initial interviewing activities, these new requests entailed greater risk, effort, and trust from them as organizational "gatekeepers." Therefore, we were required to submit an extensive list of the sorts of questions we wished to ask. Our past research on the subject (e.g., Bromley and Shupe, 1979; Shupe and Bromley, 1980) was extensively scrutinized and detailed criticisms were offered by Unification spokespersons in order to make their concerns explicit and to test our reactions. Indeed, literally dozens of phone calls and letters were needed to "clear" our visit to the Unification Theological Seminary and arrange interviews with officials in the New York City headquarters. Further, a member of the Seminary faculty was invited to campus prior to our visit in order to test fully our good will, honesty, and neutrality. Even with our elaborate efforts to achieve rapport, some factions within the Church were extremely skeptical of our intentions. This meant that those who were willing to cooperate with us really risked their own reputations. If our published work was perceived as unfavorable, their own credibility within the group would suffer. From an ethical standpoint this made us even more careful not to negotiate bargains that might be detrimental to those who cooperated with us.

With respect to the anti-cultists, we were freely sent newsletters, pamphlets, and other publications containing information on the organizational activities of the local groups. Leaders also talked openly with us at length on the phone and in person conveying details about many of their group's meetings, activities, and strategy plans. However, other aspects of their involvements were much more private. They were particularly protective of family members who had been or currently were members of the Church. Former members were usually anxious to put their experiences behind them and hence were not easily available or receptive to interviews. Parents of current members were reluctant to reveal confidences about their son's or daughter's activities for fear of further eroding already strained relations with their offspring should their confidences somehow be made public. Anti-cultist parents thus faced a real dilemma: to withhold the intimate details of their son's or daughter's conversion reduced the persuasiveness of their allegations of "mind control," yet to reveal all the intimacies of their relationships to their son or daughter, unearthed conflicts, mistrust, and feelings of failure, was understandably difficult to share with outsiders. After a long period of building trust, we were allowed to read materials such as a diary and personal family correspondence of former members. These contained the very personal reflections of the former member and the inner family conflict over Church membership. As a condition for receiving these materials, we agreed to consult in advance with family members concerning any materials we wished to use and how we would use them. In these instances each informant was given the option of withdrawing their materials should they not approve of their use. We also attempted to intersperse such private materials with previously published accounts so as to camouflage the sources of the most confidential materials.

As each group began requiring more explicit assurances regarding our use of materials, we found ourselves increasingly enmeshed in a series of constraining bargains. Our deepening involvement with each group thus placed greater and greater constraints on our ability to negotiate freely with the other. For example, the anti-cultists were relatively accepting of our spending time with Church mobile fund raising and witnessing teams passing through the metropolitan area since we were perceived as simply "checking out the Moonies." However, when we invited a member of the Seminary faculty to the University in order to build rapport sufficient to gain access to national level organizational records, the anti-cultists demanded an explanation. We were, after all, providing the Church with a public forum with which to spread its message and associating our own and the University's names with the Church. Correspondingly the Church never openly questioned our contacts with the anti-cultists. However, the knowledge we obtained from the Church limited the relationship which we could maintain with the anti-cultists. We became aware of the location of a substantial number of members whose families opposed their membership in the Church and might well have made an effort to remove them from the Church had they known their whereabouts. Obviously, we could not discuss such matters with the anti-cultists without violating implicit confidences. There was no simple solution to this problem. We could only hope, by minimizing the frequency of such "deals," to conform to the pragmatic realities of researching sensitive topics with anxious people who did not always share our research goals, yet not compromising our own perspectives.

Moreover, as we gained access to increasingly more confidential information, informants on both sides were not simply concerned that *we* might misinterpret or mishandle whatever sensitive information they gave us; they also expressed reservations that their *opponents* might use our findings, whatever our intentions, against them. This was particularly true of Unification Church leaders who regarded much of our previous research in this area, while technically "neutral" by social science standards, as nevertheless open to misinterpretation by anti-cultists. For example, the New York headquarters had previously supplied us with a national sample of almost two hundred of the most virulent "atrocity stories" told against the Church by bitter ex-members. Our content analysis of these examined the formulation and perpetuation of such tales by the news media in the context of labeling theory (see Bromley, Shupe, and Ventigilimia, 1979), but our failure to follow up our analysis with criticisms of the stories' validity was regarded as a mark against us by the Church. The anti-cultists, too, while inviting us to periodic "strategy" meetings, requested that we not mention the times and locations to others lest the Unification Church (or other groups) inadvertently find out and attempt to infiltrate them.

GAINING COMPARABLE INFORMATION AND INSIGHTS

All comparative social research confronts the problem of gathering comparable data; unless the bulk of the observations in one group have some parallel in the other group, meaningful generalizations will be difficult to formulate. In this research the two groups were alike in some important respects. Both contained numerous factions and so for both considerable effort was necessary to insure that positions attributed to the organization as a whole were in fact not just representative of local interests. Both had considerable turnover in leadership and rank and file memberships, hence strategies and activities tended to change with the composition of the group. This meant that keeping abreast of policy and personnel entailed almost constant monitoring. Both were relatively mistrustful of "outsiders," seeing themselves as underdogs in the conflict, which meant that considerable effort had to be exerted simply to gain entry and to maintain rapport.

There were also significant differences between the groups, however. Although the local groups within the Unification Church were relatively autonomous, there was an ultimate center of authority in Reverend Moon. The anti-cultists by contrasts never formed a national organization which was more than a loose coalition despite considerable effort to do so. Thus we were able to obtain more information about the Unification Church by visiting its national headquarters than we were about the anti-cultists by visiting their coordinating center. Since the anti-cultists kept fewer organizational records, we were more dependent on personal communications and therefore were under greater pressure to bargain for important information. The Unificationist ideology was clearly stated in the *Divine Principle* and a host of other official Church publications. By contrast the anti-cultist ideology was less fully developed; there was no consensus on the definition of "cult," "brainwashing," "deprogramming," or other concepts crucial to their world view. Further, their writings were generally contained in what librarians refer to as "fugitive publications" (i.e., informally published, uncopyrighted pamphlets and newsletters). What this meant was that it was relatively easy to comprehend Unification thought and gauge the range of ideological diversity. By contrast it was difficult to summarize the anti-cultists' ideology or to measure the degree to which it was actually shown.

The lifestyle of anti-cultists lent itself much more readily to observation than did that of the Unification Church members. For example, anti-cultists, like the authors, held conventional middle class occupations with regularly scheduled work hours. Thus free time for anti-cultists and the authors tended to coincide. By contrast, Unification Church members worked long days with unpredictable schedules and little free time. As a result we found it much more demanding to fulfill our other role obligations and still find sufficient time for lengthy interviews/observations with Unification Church members. Further, anti-cultist members had permanent residences while many Unification Church members were constantly on the move. So while it was possible, for example, with the anti-cultists to observe the lifestyle of members, changes in individuals' philosophies, and degree of commitment to the organization, such observations were much more difficult for Unification Church members.

SUMMARY AND CONCLUSIONS

Sociologists engaged in participant observation have defined a number of methodological problems in conducting investigations on single groups. In this paper we have discussed five such problems in the context of comparative participant observation: (1) role definition and justification; (2) pressures to go native; (3) public pressures to take a stand; (4) evolving commitments; and (5) gaining comparable information and insights.

Studying two groups simultaneously raised the problem of gaining comparable data on each group. Since the Unification Church and anti-cultists differ in some important respects, time and effort had to be expended differentially with the two groups to insure comparability. We also found that, since the two groups were involved in ongoing conflict, our relationships with each was a source of strain *vis-á-vis* the other. Each group had an interest in gaining our acceptance of its world view and in minimizing our involvement with the other side. A variety of other interest groups, principally among the media, wanted us to provide "expert opinion" on the highly visible controversy. We found that these pressures, although external to the research project itself, had considerable impact upon it. As we began to need more detailed and confidential information from each group, were had to negotiate more and more explicit and constraining bargains regarding its use, but our ability to agree to such bargains with either group was at least partially compromised by relationships with the other.

For most of these problems there was no single ideal solution since the problems developed along with the research project, and they constantly presented themselves in new contexts. Our ongoing efforts to resolve these problems involved: developing forthright relations with both groups, participating with each group only to the extent required to remain compatible with the role definition conveyed to each group, and negotiating only those bargains requisite to obtain necessary information and protect our informants. Finally, in the absence of a pre-existing body of guidelines or theory in participant observation, we were forced to develop our own ad hoc solutions to the five problems discussed. In the future, as sociologists of social movements confront similar comparative problems, we anticipate more attention will be given to these methodological issues.

REFERENCES

Becker, Howard. 1967. "Whose Side Are We on?" *Social Problems* 14:239–247.
———. 1958. "Problems of Interference and Proof in Participant Observation," *American Sociological Review* 23:652–660.
Blum, Fred H. 1952. "Getting Individuals to Give Information to the Outsider," *Journal of Social Issues* 8:35–52.
Bromley, David G. and Anson D. Shupe, Jr. 1979a. "Just a Few Years Seem Like a Lifetime: A Role Theory Approach to Participation in Religious Movements," in *Research in Social Movements, Conflict, and Change*, edited by Louis Kriesberg. Greenwich, Conn.: JAI Press.
———. 1979b. "Emerging Foci in Participant Observation: Research as an Emerging Process," in *Social Experience of Field Work*, edited by W. Shaffir, A. Turowetz, and R. Stebbins. New York: St. Martin's Press.
Bromley, David G., Anson D. Shupe, Jr., and Joseph C. Ventigilimia. 1979. "Atrocity Tales, the Unification Church, and the Social Construction of Evil," *Journal of Communication* 29:42–53.
Douglas, Jack D.. 1972. "Observing Deviance," in *Research on Deviance*, edited by Jack D. Douglas. New York: Random House.
Fitcher, Joseph H. and William L. Kolb. 1953. "Ethical Limitations on Sociological Reporting," *American Sociological Review* 18:544–550.
Grimshaw, Allen. 1973. "Comparative Sociology: In What Ways Different from Other Sociologies?" pp. 3–48 in *Comparative Social Research: Methodological Problems and Strategies*, edited by M. Armer and A.D. Grimshaw. New York: Wiley.
Shaffir, William, Allan Turowetz, and Robert Stebbins, eds.. 1979. *The Social Experience of Field Work*. New York: St. Martin's.
Shupe, Jr., Anson D. and David G. Bromley. 1980. "Some Continuities in American Religion: Witches, Moonies, and Accusations of Evil," in *God We Trust: New Patterns of American Religious Pluralism*, edited by Thomas Robbins and Dick Anthony. New Jersey: Transaction Press.
Shupe, Jr., Anson D., Robert Spielmann, and Sam Snigall. 1977a. "Deprogramming: the New Exorcism," *American Behavioral Scientist* 20:941–956.
———. 1977b. "Deprogramming and the Emerging American Anti-Cult Movement." Paper presented at the Annual Meeting of the Society for the Scientific Study of Religion.
Shupe, Jr., Anson D., Joseph C. Ventimigilia, David G. Bromley, and Sam Stigall. 1977. "Political Control of Radically Innovative Religions." Paper presented at the Annual Meeting of the Association for the Scientific Study of Religion.
Stoner, Carroll and JoAnn Parke. 1977. *All Gods Children*. Randor, Penn.: Chilton.
Trice, H.M.. 1970. "Participant Observation and the Collection and Interpretation of Data," pp. 164–173 in *Qualitative Sociology*. Edited by William J. Filstead. Chicago: Markham.
Weinberg, Martin S. and Colin J. Williams. 1972. "Fieldwork Among Deviants: Social Relations with Subjects and Others," pp. 165–186 in *Research on Deviance*, edited by Jack D. Douglas. New York: Random House.

PART IV
MINDED BEHAVIOR

One of the underlying assumptions of symbolic interactionism deals with the origins and development of the mind. Simply put, the mind is a functional, volitional, teleological[1] process, a uniquely human attribute, serving the interests of the individual. Minded behavior allows individuals to interact with, and not merely respond to, their environment. The process of mind refers to the capabilities of humans to engage in self-communication. Thinking may be conceived as a process of internal dialogue—of symbolic communication between the individual and herself or himself.

Interactionists make a distinction between the brain and the mind. Humans are born with cerebral grey matter but not with minds. The mind is not present at birth, but rather, emerges out of social processes and is therefore wholly social in origin. It is both part of, and a product of, larger social processes. It is made possible by meanings, symbols, and language, which are social in nature; that is, they arise through interaction. Mind emerges at that moment when the individual is able to complete an act at the level of her or his imagination.

This interactionist conceptualization of mind was developed largely by G. H. Mead in reaction against the traditional and contemporary theories of such persons as James Mark Baldwin, Charles Cooley, Josiah Royce, and Wilhelm Wundt. These latter scholars presupposed a mind whose existence was thought to be logically prior to the social processes. In their writings, the mind was frequently depicted as some "transcendental phenomenon," or "spiritual stuff"—some mystical entity that one could not analyze. Mead also critiqued the theory of behaviorist psychologist, John B. Watson who, in his schema, completely ignored the existence of mind; behavior for him and his colleagues was reduced simply to basic physiological impulses. Both the lower animals and humans, Watson argued, operated according to a stimulus-response model. Moreover, Mead also criticized other behavioral psychologists who portrayed the mind as a static entity that merely imports impressions from the world at large. Mead found equally unacceptable conceptualizations of the mind as inborn—or the inalienable property of individuals. These theories were unacceptable to Mead as they merely conceived of social phenomena as accretions of individual minds. Mind is conceived by Mead as developing correlatively with the self, creating the self in action. The mind originates in the social process as we interact with one another. Mead contends that this uniquely human attribute arose in the evolutionary process when the impulsive conduct of the organism was blocked in its effort to adjust to the environment. The mind then, developed out of the non-mental, stimulus-response behavior of our pre-human biological ancestors. It was at this point that humans were able to respond to their own gestures and behaviors.

For Mead and symbolic interactionists, the mind is to be considered entirely separate from the brain. Humans are born with cerebral grey matter but not with a mind. Mentality emerges through association and communication with others. It is important to stress that the mind is present at specific points in human behavior, that is when individuals are employing significant symbols. The mind is not an entity existing in all heads of humans, but rather, a *process* which comes into existence whenever individuals are interacting with themselves and others, utilizing significant symbols. Mental activity, on the part of humans, involves making indications of meanings to oneself and to others. Humans engaging in reflective activity are able to isolate and indicate to themselves and to others the meanings of those stimuli to which they are responding. In short, minded behavior occurs when an individual employs significant symbols to call out to her/himself the responses which others would make. Mind, is clearly symbolic action.

John Dewey's piece, critical of earlier conceptions of mind as a fixed or frozen entity, portrays this concept as "function," with minded activity extrapolated from behavior in a dynamic society. For Dewey, the development of mind is aided through a process of social interaction, specifically, through the employment of language.

An excerpt from the classic work by W.I. Thomas focusses on the self-indications involved in the thought process. Before humans engage in the social act, Thomas contends that they engage in a moment of deliberation, a preliminary phase in which they assemble objects, people, meanings, and themselves in both social space and time. Action, then, is based upon individuals' "definitions of the situation."

The selection by Scully and Marolla deals with the concepts of motives, motive talk, and vocabularies of motive. People spend a great deal of time providing explanations to others about things that they have either said or done, or are about to say or do, or the presence or absence of some attribute. We construct and employ a variety of verbal techniques to explain our actions to others. A disclaimer is a form of motive talk people employ to ward off negative implications of something they are *about* to do or say. It is information that persons volunteer to others in an attempt to protect their identities in the eyes of others. The Scully and Marolla selection deals with a second form of motive talk, providing individuals with "accounts": typically in the form of excuses or justifications. In this case, a rule violation is committed, effective interaction is stopped, and the perpetrator is asked to account for her/his actions. Excuses are utilized when the individual acknowledges that the particular action is wrong, but denies responsibility for it. "Justifications", on the other hand, represent a form of account in which individuals accept responsibility for an action but deny that it should be considered as wrong. As Scully and Marolla point out, rapists provide a number of excuses and justifications for their action; the former include drugs and alcohol; the latter include: defining the woman as a seductress, stating that the women enjoy being raped, women mean "yes" even when saying "no", and that "nice girls don't get raped."

The selection by Bernard N. Meltzer and Jerome Manis, deals with the concept of *emergence*, the occurrence of unpredictable, novel behavior that is not entirely derived from past experiences of current conditions. The authors address the nature of emergent events, their manifestations, the individual and social sources of emergence. Moreover, Meltzer and Manis address the implications of the concept of emergence for psychology and other social sciences.

Theselection by George J. Gmelch deals with magic. Looking at baseball, he attempts to describe those situations in which magic is not most likely to occur.

NOTES

1. By teleological, we mean having causal power or being purposive.

SUGGESTED READINGS

Albas, Daniel and Cheryl Albas. 1989. "Modern Magic: The Case of Examinations." *Sociological Quarterly*, 30: 603–613. Empirical piece dealing with magical practices used by students in order to achieve a desired outcome.

Berger, Peter L., and Thomas Luckmann. 1966. *The Social Construction of Reality*. Garden City, New York: Doubleday & Company, Inc. A valuable theoretical bridge between the sociology of knowledge and social psychology.

Blumer, Herbert. 1955. "Attitudes and the Social Act." *Social Problems* 3 (October):59–65. A critique of "attitude," one of the most widely used concepts in social psychology.

Bogdan, Robert and Steven Taylor. 1989. "Relationships with Severely Disabled People: The Social Construction of Humanness." *Social Problems* 36 no. 2: 135–148. Excellent piece dealing with the interaction patterns and social relationships between "normals" and the severely "disabled."

Collins, Randall. 1989. "Toward a Neo-Meadian Sociology of Mind." *Symbolic Interaction* 12: 1–32. A neo-Weberian attempts to discuss a Meadian style approach to the human mind.

Foote, Nelson N. 1951. "Identification as the Basis for a Theory of Motivation." *American Sociological Review* 16 (February):14–21. A useful companion piece to the selection in this part by Mills.

Hewitt, John P. and Randall Stokes. 1975. "Disclaimers." *American Sociological Review* 40: 1–11. Piece deals with one type of "Motive Talk", the use of disclaimers employed by individuals to ward off the negative implications about what they have said or done, or are about to say or do.

Gubrium, Jaber. 1986. "The Social Preservation of Mind: The Alzheimer's Disease Experience." *Symbolic Interaction* 9: 37–51. A clever piece once again demonstrating the socially constructed nature of mental life and minded behavior.

McCall, George J., and J. L. Simmons. 1966. *Identities and Interactions: An Examination of Associations in Everyday Life*. New York: The Free Press. A refined version of symbolic interaction theory and the exchange theory of interaction.

Mead, George Herbert. 1934. *Mind, Self and Society*. Chicago: University of Chicago Press. Pp. 67–74 and 94–125. Descriptions of the development of significant symbols and the process of minded behavior.

Mills, C. Wright. 1940. "Situated Actions and Vocabularies of Motive." *American Sociological Review* 5:904–13. Classical sociological piece dealing with emotions.

Miyamoto, S. Frank.1959. "The Social Act: Re-examination of a Concept." *Pacific Sociological Review* 2 (Fall): 51–55. Emphasizes the need for research on "the organized character of the interactional process."

Perinbanayagam, Robert S. 1974. "The Definition of the Situation: An Analysis of the Ethnomethodological and Dramaturgical Views." *Sociological Quarterly* 15 (Autumn): 521–541. A comparison of two viewpoints in definitions of situations.

Scott, Marvin B. and Stanford M. Lyman. 1968. "Accounts." *American Sociological Review* 33 (December): 46–62. Concerned with the "acceptable utterances" people make in accounting for their untoward actions.

Stewart, Kenneth L.1975. "On `Socializing' Attitudes: A Symbolic Interactionist View." *Sociological Focus* 8 (January): 37–46. Attitudes as part of acts.

Strauss, Anselm L. 1959. *Mirrors and Masks*. Glencoe, Illinois: The Free Press. Examines some of the relationships between the definitions we apply to persons or other objects and our "plans of action" toward them.

Strong, Samuel W. 1939. "A Note on George H. Mead's `The Philosophy of the Act.'" *American Journal of Sociology* 45 (July): 71–76. A good but difficult summary of the concept "the act."

White, Leslie T. 1939. "Mind Is Minding." *Scientific Monthly* 48: 169–171. An eminent anthropologist views mind as behavior, paralleling the functionalist views of Dewey and Mead.

Chapter 13   MIND, EXPERIENCE, AND BEHAVIOR

John Dewey

Let us begin with the technical side-the change in psychology. We are only just now commencing to appreciate how completely exploded is the psychology that dominated philosophy throughout the eighteenth and nineteenth centuries. According to this theory, mental life originated in sensations which are separately and passively received, and which are formed, through laws of retention and association, into a mosaic of images, perceptions and conceptions. The senses were regarded as gateways or avenues of knowledge. Except in combining atomic sensations, the mind was wholly passive and acquiescent in knowing. Volition, action, emotion, and desire follow in the wake of sensations and images. The intellectual or cognitive factor comes first and emotional and volitional life is only a consequent conjunction of ideas with sensations of pleasure and pain.

The effect of the development of biology has been to reverse the picture. Wherever there is life, there is behavior, activity. In order that life may persist, this activity has to be both continuous and adapted to the environment. This adaptive adjustment, moreover, is not wholly passive; is not a mere matter of the moulding of the organism by the environment. Even a clam acts upon the environment and modifies it to some extent. It selects materials for food and for the shell that protects it. It does something to the environment as well as has something done to itself. There is no such thing in a living creature as mere conformity to conditions, though parasitic forms may approach this limit. In the interests of the maintenance of life there is transformation of some elements in the surrounding medium. The higher the form of life, the more important is the active reconstruction of the medium. This increased control may he illustrated by the contrast of savage with civilized man. Suppose the two are living in a wilderness. With the savage there is the maximum of accommodation to given conditions; the minimum of what we may call hitting back. The savage takes things "as they are, " and by using caves and roots and occasional pools leads a meagre and precarious existence. The civilized man goes to distant mountains and dams streams. He builds reservoirs, digs channels, and conducts the water to what had been a desert. He searches the world to find plants and animals that will thrive. He takes native plants and by selection and cross-fertilization improves them. He introduces machinery to till the soil and care for the harvest. By such means he may succeed in making the wilderness blossom like the rose.

Such transformation scenes are so familiar that we overlook their meaning. We forget that the inherent power of life is illustrated in them. Note what a change this point of view entails in the traditional notions of experience. Experience becomes an affair primarily of doing. The organism does not stand about, Micawberlike, waiting for something to turn up. It does not wait passive and inert for something to impress itself upon it from without. The organism acts in accordance with its own structure, simple or complex, upon its surroundings. As a consequence the changes produced in the environment react upon the organism and its activities. The living creature undergoes, suffers, the consequences of its own behavior. This close connection between doing and suffering or undergoing forms what we call experience. Disconnected doing and disconnected suffering are neither of them experiences. Suppose fire encroaches upon a man when he is asleep. Part of his body is burned away. The burn does not perceptibly result from what he has done. There is nothing which in any instructive way can be named experience. Or again there is a series of mere activities, like twitchings of muscles in a spasm. The movements amount to nothing; they have no consequences for life. Or, if they have, these consequences are not connected with prior doing. There is no experience, no learning, no cumulative process. But suppose a busy infant puts his finger in the fire; the doing is random, aimless, without intention or reflection. But something happens in consequence. The child undergoes heat, he suffers pain. The doing and undergoing, the reaching and the burn, are connected. One comes to suggest and mean the other. Then there is experience in a vital and significant sense.

Certain important implications for philosophy follow. In the first place, the interaction of organism and environment, resulting in some adaptation which secures utilization of the latter, is the primary fact, the basic category. Knowledge is relegated to a derived position, secondary in origin, even if its importance, when once it is established, is overshadowing. Knowledge is not something separate and self-sufficing, but is involved in the process by which life is sustained and evolved. The senses lose their place as gateways of knowing to take their rightful place as stimuli to action. To an animal an affection of the eye or ear is not an idle piece of information about something indifferently going on in the world. It is an invitation and inducement to act in a needed way. It is a clue in behavior, a directive factor in adaptation of life in its surroundings. It is urgent not cognitive in quality. The whole controversy between empiricism and rationalism as to the intellectual worth of sensations is rendered strangely obsolete. The discussion of sensations belongs under the head of immediate stimulus and response, not under the head of knowledge.

When experience is aligned with the life-process and sensations are seen to be points of readjustment, the alleged atomism of sensations totally disappears. With this disappearance is abolished the need for a synthetic faculty of super-empirical reason to connect them. Philosophy is not any longer confronted with the hopeless problem of finding a way in which separate grains of sand may be woven into a strong and coherent rope, or into the illusion and pretence of one. When the isolated and simple existences of Locke and Hume are seen not to be truly empirical at all but to answer to certain demands of their theory of mind, the necessity ceases for the elaborate Kantian and Post-Kantian machinery of a priori concepts and categories to synthesize the alleged stuff of experience. The true "stuff" of experience is recognized to be adaptive courses of action, habits, active functions, connections of doing and undergoing; sensori-motor co-ordinations. Experience carries principles of connection and organization within itself. These principles are none the worse because they are vital and practical rather than epistemological. Some degree of organization is indispensable to even the lowest grade of life. Even an amoeba must have some continuity in time in its activity and some adaptation to its environment in space. Its life and experience cannot possibly consist in momentary, atomic, and self-enclosed sensations. Its activity has reference to its surroundings and to what goes before and what comes after. This organization intrinsic to life renders unnecessary a super-natural and super-empirical synthesis. It affords the basis and material for a positive evolution of intelligence as an organizing factor within experience.

Nor is it entirely aside from the subject to point out the extent in which social as well as biological organization enters into the formation of human experience. Probably one thing that strengthened the idea that the mind is passive and receptive in knowing was the observation of the helplessness of the human infant. But the observation points in quite another direction. Because of his physical dependence and impotency, the contacts of the little child with nature are mediated by other persons. Mother and nurse, father and older children, determine what experiences the child shall have; they constantly instruct him as to the meaning of what he does and undergoes. The conceptions that are socially current and important become the child's principles of interpretation and estimation long before he attains to personal and deliberate control of conduct. Things come to him clothed in language, not in physical nakedness, and this garb of communication makes him a sharer in the beliefs of those about him, These beliefs coming to him as so many facts form his mind; they furnish the centres about which his own personal expeditions and perceptions are ordered. Here we have "categories" of connection and unification as important as those of Kant, but empirical not mythological.

Chapter 14 THE REGULATION OF THE WISHES

W.I. Thomas

One of the most important powers gained during the evolution of animal life is the ability to make decisions from within instead of having them imposed from without. Very low forms of life do not make decisions, as we understand this term, but are pushed and pulled by chemical substances, heat, light, etc., much as iron filings are attracted or repelled by a magnet. They do tend to behave properly in given conditions—a group of small crustaceans will flee as in a panic if a bit of strychnia is placed in the basin containing them and will rush toward a drop of beef juice like hogs crowding around swill—but they do this as an expression of organic affinity for the one substance and repugnance for the other, and not as an expression of choice or "free will." There are, so to speak, rules of behavior but these represent a sort of fortunate mechanistic adjustment of the organism to typically recurring situations, and the organism cannot change the rule.

On the other hand, the higher animals, and above all man, have the power of refusing to obey a stimulation which they followed at an earlier time. Response to the earlier stimulation may have had painful consequences and so the rule or habit in this situation is changed. We call this ability the power of inhibition, and it is dependent on the fact that the nervous system carries memories or records of past experiences. At this point the determination of action no longer comes exclusively from outside sources but is located within the organism itself.

Preliminary to any self-determined act of behavior there is always a stage of examination and deliberation which we may call *the definition of the situation*. And actually not only concrete acts are dependent on the definition of the situation, but gradually a whole life-policy and the personality of the individual himself follow from a series of such definitions.

But the child is always born into a group of people among whom all the general types of situation which may arise have already been defined and corresponding rules of conduct developed, and where he has not the slightest chance of making his definitions and following his wishes without interference. Men have always lived together in groups. Whether mankind has a true herd instinct or whether groups are held together because this has worked out to advantage is of no importance. Certainly the wishes in general are such that they can be satisfied only in a society. But we have only to refer to the criminal code to appreciate the variety of ways in which the wishes of the individual may conflict with the wishes of society. And the criminal code takes no account of the many unsanctioned expressions of the wishes which society attempts to regulate by persuasion and gossip.

There is therefore always a rivalry between the spontaneous definitions of the situation made by the member of an organized society and the definitions which his society has provided for him. The individual tends to a hedonistic selection of activity, pleasure first; and society to a utilitarian selection, safety first. Society wishes its member to be laborious, dependable, regular, sober, orderly, self-sacrificing; while the individual wishes less of this and more of new experience. And organized society seeks also to regulate the conflict and competition inevitable between its members in the pursuit of their wishes. The desire to have wealth, for example, or any other socially sanctioned wish, may not be accomplished at the expense of another member of the society,—by murder, theft, lying, swindling, blackmail, etc.

It is in this connection that a moral code arises, which is a set of rules or behavior norms, regulating the expression of the wishes, and which is built up by successive definitions of the situation. In practice the abuse arises first and the rule is made to prevent its recurrence. Morality is thus the generally accepted definition of the situation, whether expressed in public opinion and the unwritten law, in a formal legal code, or in religious commandments and prohibitions.

The family is the smallest social unit and the primary defining agency. As soon as the child has free motion and begins to pull, tear, pry, meddle, and prowl, the parents begin to define the situation through speech and other signs and pressures: "Be quiet", "Sit up straight," "Blow your nose," "Wash your face," "Mind your mother," "Be kind to sister," etc. This is the real significance of Wordsworth's phrase, " Shades of the prison house begin to close upon the growing child." His wishes and activities begin to be inhibited, and gradually, by definitions within the family, by playmates, in the school; in the Sunday school, in the community, through reading, by formal instruction, by informal signs of approval and disapproval, the growing member learns the code of his society.

In addition to the family we have the community as a defining agency. At present the community is so weak and vague that it gives us no idea of the former power of the local group in regulating behavior. Originally the community was practically the whole world of its members. It was composed of families related by blood and marriage and was not so large that all the members could not come together; it was a face to-face group. I asked a Polish peasant what was the extent of an *"okolica"* or neighborhood—how far it reached. "It reaches," he said, "as far as the report of a man reaches—as far as a man is talked about." And it was in communities of this kind that the moral code which we now recognize as valid originated. The customs of the community are "folkways", and both state and church have in their more formal codes mainly recognized and incorporated these folkways.

The typical community is vanishing and it would be neither possible nor desirable to restore it in its old form. It does not correspond with the present direction of social evolution and it would now be a distressing condition in which to live. But in the immediacy of relationships and the participation of everybody in everything, it represents an element which we have lost and which we shall probably have to restore in some form of cooperation in order to secure a balanced and normal society,—some arrangement corresponding with human nature.

Very elemental examples of the definition of the situation by the community as a whole, corresponding to mob action as we know it and to our trial by jury, are found among European peasants. The three documents following, all relating to the Russian community or *mir*, give some idea of the conditions under which a whole community, a public, formerly defined a situation.

I. We who are unacquainted with peasant speech, manners and method of expressing thought—mimicry—if we should be present at a division of land or some settlement among the peasants, would never understand anything. Hearing fragmentary, disconnected exclamations, endless quarreling, with repetition of some single word; hearing this racket of a seemingly senseless, noisy crowd that counts up or measures off something, we should conclude that they would not get together, or arrive at any result in an age.... Yet wait until the end and you will see that the division has been made with mathematical accuracy—that the measure, the quality of the soil, the slope of the field, the distance from the village—everything in short has been taken into account, that the reckoning has been correctly done and, what is most important, that every one of those present who were interested in the division is certain of the correctness of the division or settlement. The cry, the noise, the racket do not subside until every one is satisfied and no doubter is left.

The same thing is true concerning the discussion of some question by the *mir*. There are no speeches, no debates, no votes. They shout, they abuse each other, they seem on the point of coming to blows. Apparently they riot in the most senseless manner. Some one preserves silence, silence, and then suddenly puts in a word, one word, or an ejaculation, and by this word, this ejaculation, he turns the whole thing upside down. In the end, you look into it and find that an admirable decision has been formed and, what is most important, a unanimous decision.[1]

II. As I approached the village, there hung over it such a mixed, varied violent shouting, that no well brought-up parliament would agree to recognize itself, even in the abstract, as analogous to this gathering of peasant deputies. It was clearly a full meeting today....At other more quiet village meetings I had been able to make out very little, but this was a real lesson to me. I felt only a continuous, indistinguishable roaring in my ears, sometimes pierced by a particularly violent phrase that broke out from the general roar. I saw in front of me the "immediate" man, in all his beauty. What struck me first of all was his remarkable frankness; the more "immediate" he is, the less able is he to mask his thoughts and feelings; once he is stirred up the emotion seizes him quickly and he flares up then and there, and does not quiet down till he has poured out before you all the substance of his soul. He does not feel embarrassment before anybody; there are no indications here of diplomacy. Further, he opens up his whole soul, and he will tell everything that he may ever have known about you, and not only about you, but about your father, grandfather, and great-grandfather. Here everything is clear water, as the peasants say, and everything stands out plainly. If any one, out of smallness of soul, or for some ulterior motive, thinks to get out of something by keeping silent, they force him out into clear water without pity. And there are very few such small-souled persons at important village meetings. I have seen the most peaceable, irresponsible peasants, who at other times would not have thought of saying a word against any one, absolutely changed at these meetings, at these moments of general excitement. They believed in the saying, "On people even death is beautiful", and they got up so much courage that they were able to answer back the peasants commonly recognized as audacious. At the moment of its height the meeting becomes simply an open mutual confessional and mutual disclosure, the display of the widest publicity. At these moments when, it would seem, the private interests of each reach the highest tension, public interests and justice in turn reach the highest degree of control.[2]

III. In front of the volost administration building there stands a crowd of some one hundred and fifty men. This means that a volost meeting has been called to consider the verdict of the Kusmin rural commune "regarding the handing over to the [state] authorities of the peasant Gregori Siedov, caught red-handed and convicted of horse-stealing." Siedov had already been held for judicial inquiry; the evidence against him was irrefutable and he would undoubtedly be sentenced to the penitentiary. In view of this I endeavor to explain that the verdict in regard to his exile is wholly superfluous and will only cause a deal of trouble; and that at the termination of the sentence of imprisonment of Siedov the commune will unfailingly be asked whether it wants him back or prefers that he be exiled. Then, I said, in any event it would be necessary to formulate a verdict in regard to the "non-reception" of Siedov, while at this stage all the trouble was premature and could lead to nothing. But the meeting did not believe my words, did not trust the court and wanted to settle the matter right then and there; the general hatred of horse-thieves was too keen....

The decisive moment has arrived; the head-man " drives " all the judges-elect to one side; the crowd stands with a gloomy air, trying not to look at Siedov and his wife, who are crawling before the mir on their knees. "Old men, whoever pities Gregori, will remain in his place, and whoever does not forgive him will step to the right," cries the head man. The crowd wavered and rocked, but remained dead still on the spot; no one dared to be the first to take the fatal step. Gregori feverishly ran over the faces of his judges with his eyes, trying to read in these faces pity for him. His wife wept bitterly, her face close to the ground; beside her, finger in mouth and on the point of screaming, stood a three-year-old youngster (at home Gregori had four more children)....But straightway one peasant steps out of the crowd; two years before some one had stolen a horse from him. "Why should we pity him? Did he pity us?" says the old man, and stooping goes over to the right side. "That is true; bad grass must be torn from the field," says another one from the crowd, and follows the old man. The beginning had been made; at first individually and then in whole groups the judges-elect proceeded to go over to the right. The man condemned by public opinion ran his head into the ground, beat his breast with his fists, seized those who passed him by their coat-tails, crying: "Ivan Timofeich! Uncle Leksander! Vasinka, dear kinsman! Wait, kinsmen, let me say a word....Petrushenka." But, without stopping and with stern faces, the members of the *mir* dodged the unfortunates, who were crawling at their feet....At last the wailing of Gregori stopped; around him for the space of three *sazen* the place was empty; there was no one to implore. All the judges elect, with the exception of one, an uncle of the man to be exiled, had gone over to the right. The woman cried sorrowfully, while Gregori stood motionless on his knees, his head lowered, stupidly looking at the ground.[3]

The essential point in reaching a communal decision, just as in the case of our jury system, is unanimity. In some cases the whole community mobilizes around a stubborn individual to conform him to the general wish.

It sometimes happens that all except one may agree but the motion is never carried if that one refuses to agree to it. In such cases all endeavor to talk over and persuade the stiff-necked one. Often they even call to their aid his wife, his children, his relatives, his father-in-law, and his mother, that they may prevail upon him to say yes. Then all assail him, and say to him from time to time: "Come now, God help you, agree with us too, that this may take place as we wish it, that the house may not be cast into disorder, that we may not be talked about by the people, that the neighbors may not hear of it, that the world may not make sport of us!" It seldom occurs in such cases that unanimity is not attained.[4]

A less formal but not less powerful means of defining the situation employed by the community is gossip. The Polish peasant's statement that a community reaches as far as a man is talked about was significant, for the community regulates the behavior of its members largely by talking about them. Gossip has a bad name because it is sometimes malicious and false and designed to improve the status of the gossiper and degrade its object, but gossip is in the main true and is an organizing force. It is a mode of defining the situation in a given case and of attaching praise or blame. It is one of the means by which the status of the individual and of his family is fixed.

The community also, particularly in connection with gossip, knows how to attach opprobrium to persons and actions by using epithets which are at the same time brief and emotional definitions of the situation. "Bastard", "whore", "traitor", "coward", "skunk", "scab", "snob", "kike", etc., are such epithets. In "Faust" the community said of Margaret, "She stinks." The people are here employing a device known in psychology as the "conditioned reflex." If, for example, you place before a child (say six months old) an agreeable object, a kitten, and at the same time pinch the child, and if this is repeated several times, the child will immediately cry at the sight of the kitten without being pinched; or if a dead rat were always served beside a man's plate of soup he would eventually have a disgust for soup when served separately. If the word "stinks" is associated on people's tongues with Margaret, Margaret will never again smell sweet. Many evil consequences, as the psychoanalysts claim, have resulted from making the whole of sex life a "dirty" subject, but the device has worked in a powerful, sometimes a paralyzing way on the sexual behavior of women.

Winks, shrugs, nudges, laughter, sneers, haughtiness, coldness, "giving the once over" are also language defining the situation and painfully felt as unfavorable recognition. The sneer, for example, is incipient vomiting, meaning, "you make me sick."

And eventually the violation of the code even in an act of no intrinsic importance, as in carrying food to the mouth with the knife, provokes condemnation and disgust. The fork is not a better instrument for conveying food than the knife, at least it has no moral superiority, but the situation has been defined in favor of the fork. To smack with the lips in eating is bad manners with us, but the Indian has more logically defined the situation in the opposite way; with him smacking is a compliment to the host.

In this whole connection fear is used by the group to produce the desired attitudes in its member. Praise is used also but more sparingly. And the whole body of habits and emotions is so much a community and family product that disapproval or separation is almost unbearable.

NOTES

[1]. A.N. Engelgardt: *"Iz Derevni: 12 Pisem"* ("From the County: 12 Letters"). p. 315.
[2]. N.N. Zlatovratsky: *"Ocherki Krestyanskoy Obshciny"* ("Sketches of the Peasant Commune"), p. 127.
[3]. *"V Volstnikh Pisaryakh"* ("A Village Secretary"), p. 283.
[4]. F.S. Krauss: *"Sitte und Brauch der Sudslaven"*, p. 103.

Chapter 15 RAPISTS' VOCABULARY OF MOTIVES

Diana Scully and Joseph Marolla

Psychiatry has dominated the literature on rapists since "irresistible impulse" (Glueck, 1925:323) and "disease of the mind" (Glueck, 1925:243) were introduced as the causes of rape. Research has been based on small samples of men, frequently the clinicians' own patient population. Not surprisingly, the medical model has predominated: rape is viewed as an individualistic, idiosyncratic symptom of a disordered personality. That is, rape is assumed to be a psychopathologic problem and individual rapists are assumed to be "sick." However, advocates of this model have been unable to isolate a typical or even predictable pattern of symptoms that are causally linked to rape. Additionally, research has demonstrated that fewer than 5 percent of rapists were psychotic at the time of their rape (Abel *et al.*, 1980).

We view rape as behavior learned socially through interaction with others; convicted rapists have learned the attitudes and actions consistent with sexual aggression against women. Learning also includes the acquisition of culturally derived vocabularies of motive, which can be used to diminish responsibility and to negotiate a non-deviant identity.

Sociologists have long noted that people can, and do, commit acts they define as wrong and, having done so, engage various techniques to disavow deviance and present themselves as normal. Through the concept of "vocabulary of motive," Mills (1940:904) was among the first to shed light on this seemingly perplexing contradiction. Wrong-doers attempt to reinterpret their actions through the use of a linguistic device by which norm-breaking conduct is socially interpreted. That is, anticipating the negative consequences of their behavior, wrong-doers attempt to present the act in terms that are both culturally appropriate and acceptable.

Following Mills, a number of sociologists have focused on the types of techniques employed by actors in problematic situations (Hall and Hewitt, 1970; Hewitt and Hall, 1973; Hewitt and Stokes, 1975; Sykes and Matza, 1957). Scott and Lyman (1968) describe excuses and justifications, linguistic "accounts" that explain and remove culpability for an untoward act after it has been committed. *Excuses* admit the act was bad or inappropriate but deny full responsibility, often through appeals to accident, or biological drive, or through scapegoating. In contrast, *justifications* accept responsibility for the act but deny that it was wrong—that is, they show in this situation the act was appropriate. *Accounts* are socially approved vocabularies that neutralize an act or its consequences and are always a manifestation of an underlying negotiation of identity.

Stokes and Hewitt (1976:837) use the term "aligning actions" to refer to those tactics and techniques used by actors when some feature of a situation is problematic. Stated simply, the concept refers to an actor's attempt, through various means, to bring his or her conduct into alignment with culture. Culture in this sense is conceptualized as a "set of cognitive constraints—objects—to which people must relate as they form lines of conduct" (1976:837), and includes physical constraints, expectations and definitions of others, and personal biography. Carrying out aligning actions implies both awareness of those elements of normative culture that are applicable to the deviant act and, in addition, an actual effort to bring the act into line with this awareness. The result is that deviant behavior is legitimized.

This paper presents an analysis of interviews we conducted with a sample of 114 convicted, incarcerated rapists. We use the concept of accounts (Scott and Lyman, 1968) as a tool to organize and analyze the vocabularies of motive which this group of rapists used to explain themselves and their actions. An analysis of their account demonstrates how it was possible for 83 percent (n = 114)[1] of these convicted rapists to view themselves as non-rapists.

When rapists' accounts are examined, a typology emerges that consists of admitters and deniers. Admitters (n = 47) acknowledged that they had forced sexual acts on their victims and defined the behavior as rape. In contrast, deniers[2] either eschewed sexual contact or all association with the victim (n = 35),[3] or admitted to sexual acts but did not define their behavior as rape (n = 32).

The remainder of this paper is divided into two sections. In the first, we discuss the accounts which the rapists used to justify their behavior. In the second, we discuss those accounts which attempted to excuse the rape. By and large, the deniers used justifications while the admitters used excuses. In some cases, both groups relied on the same themes, stereotypes, and images: some admitters, like most deniers, claimed that women enjoyed being raped. Some deniers excused their behavior by referring to alcohol or drug use, although they did so quite differently than admitters. Through these narrative accounts, we explore convicted rapists' own perceptions of their crimes.

Methods and Validity

From September, 1980, through September, 1981, we interviewed 114 male convicted rapists who were incarcerated in seven maximum or medium security prisons in the Commonwealth of Virginia. All of the rapists had been convicted of the rape or attempted rape (n = 8) of an adult woman, although a few had teenage victims as well. Men convicted of incest, statutory rape, or sodomy of a male were omitted from the sample.

Twelve percent of the rapists had been convicted of more than one rape or attempted rape, 39 percent also had convictions for burglary or robbery, 29 percent for abduction, 25 percent for sodomy, and 11 percent for first or second degree murder. Eighty-two percent had a previous criminal history but only 23 percent had records for previous sex offenses. Their sentences for rape and accompanying crimes ranged from 10 years to an accumulation by one man of seven life sentences plus 380 years; 43 percent of the rapists were serving from 10 to 30 years and 22 percent were serving at least one life term. Forty-six percent of the rapists were white and 54 percent were black. Their ages ranged from 18 to 60 years; 88 percent were between 18 and 35 years. Forty-two percent were either married or cohabitating at the time of their offense. Only 20 percent had a high school education or better, and 85 percent came from working-class backgrounds. Despite the popular belief that rape is due to a personality disorder, only 26 percent of these rapists had any history of emotional problems. When the rapists in this study were compared to a statistical profile of felons in all Virginia prisons, prepared by the Virginia Department of Corrections, rapists who volunteered for this research were disproportionately white, somewhat better educated, and younger than the average inmate.

All participants in this study were volunteers. We sent a letter to every inmate (n = 3500) at each of the seven prisons. The letters introduced us as professors at a local university, described our research as a study of men's attitudes toward sexual behavior and women, outlined our procedures for ensuring confidentiality, and solicited volunteers from all criminal categories. Using one follow-up letter, approximately 25 percent of all inmates, including rapists, indicated their willingness to be interviewed by mailing an information sheet to us at the university. From this pool of volunteers, we constructed a sample of rapists based on age, education, race, severity of current offenses, and previous criminal records. Obviously, the sample was not random and thus may not be representative of all rapists.

Each of the authors—one woman and one man—interviewed half of the rapists. Both authors were able to establish rapport and obtain information. However, the rapists volunteered more about their feelings and emotions to the female author and her interviews lasted longer.

All rapists were given an 89-page interview, which included a general background, psychological, criminal, and sexual history, attitude scales, and 30 pages of open-ended questions intended to explore their perceptions of their crimes, their victims, and themselves. Because a voice print is an absolute source of identification, we did not use tape recorders. All interviews were hand recorded. With some practice, we found it was possible to record much of the interview verbatim. While hand recording inevitably resulted in some lost data, it did have the advantage of eliciting more confidence and candor in the men.

Interviews with the rapist lasted from three hours to seven hours; the average was about four-and-one-half hours. Most of the rapists were reluctant to end the interview. Once rapport had been established, the men wanted to talk, even though it sometimes meant, for example, missing a meal.

Because of the reputation prison inmates have for 'conning,' validity was a special concern in our research. Although the purpose of the research was to obtain the men's own perceptions of their acts, it was also necessary to establish the extent to which these perceptions deviated from other descriptions of their crimes. To establish validity, we used the same technique others have used in prison research: comparing factual information, including details of the crime, obtained in the interview with presentence reports on file at the prisons (Athens, 1977; Luckenbill, 1977; Queen's Bench Foundation, 1976). Pre-sentence reports, written by a court worker at the time of conviction, usually include general background information, a psychological evaluation, the offender's version of the details of the crime, and the victim's or police's version of the details of the crime. Using these records allowed us to clarify two important issues: first, the amount of change that had occurred in rapists' accounts from pre-sentencing to the time when we interviewed them; and, second, the amount of discrepancy between rapists' accounts, as told to us, and the victims' and/or police versions of the crime, contained in the pre-sentence reports.

The time between pre-sentence reports and our interviews (in effect, the amount of time rapists had spent in prison before we interviewed them) ranged from less than one year to 20 years; the average was three years. Yet despite this time lapse, there were no significant changes in the way rapists explained their crimes, with the exception of 18 men who had denied their crimes at their trials but admitted them to us. There were no cases of men who admitted their crime at their trial but denied them when talking to us.

However, there were major differences between the accounts we heard of the crimes from rapists and the police's and victim's versions. Admitters (including deniers turned admitters) told us essentially the same story as the police and victim versions. However, the admitters subtly understated the force they had used and, though they used words such as *violent* to describe their acts, they also omitted reference to the more brutal aspects of their crime.

In contrast, deniers' interview accounts differed significantly from victim and police versions. According to the pre-sentence reports, 11 of the 32 deniers had been acquainted with their victim. But an additional four deniers told us they had been acquainted with their victims. In the pre-sentence reports, police or victim versions of the crime described seven rapes in which the victim had been hitchhiking or was picked up in a bar; but deniers told us this was true of 20 victims. Weapons were present in 21 of the 32 rapes according to the pre-sentence reports, yet only nine men acknowledged the presence of a weapon and only two of the nine admitted they had used it to threaten or intimidate their victim. Finally, in at least seven of the rapes, the victim had been seriously injured,[4] but only three men admitted injury. In two of the three cases, the victim had been murdered; in these cases the men denied the rape but not the murder. Indeed, deniers constructed accounts for us which, by implicating the victim, made their own conduct appear to have been more appropriate. They never used words such as violent, choosing instead to emphasize the sexual component of their behavior.

It should be noted that we investigated the possibility that deniers claimed their behavior was not criminal because, in contrast to admitters, their crimes resembled what research has found the public define as a controversial rape, that is, victim is an acquaintance, no injury or weapon, victim picked up hitchhiking or in a bar (Burt, 1980; Burt and Albin, 1981; Williams, 1979).... [T]he crimes committed by deniers were only slightly more likely to involve these elements.

This contrast between pre-sentence reports and interviews suggests several significant factors related to interview content validity. First, when asked to explain their behavior, our sample of convicted rapists (except deniers turned admitters) responded with accounts that had changed surprisingly little since their trials. Second, admitters' interview accounts were basically the same as others' versions of their crimes, while deniers systematically put more blame on the victims.

Justifying Rape

Deniers attempted to justify their behavior by presenting the victim in a light that made her appear culpable, regardless of their own actions. Five themes run through attempts to justify their rapes: (1) women as seductresses; (2) women mean "yes" when they say "no"; (3) most women eventually relax and enjoy it; (4) nice girls don't get raped; and (5) guilty of a minor wrongdoing.

Women as Seductresses

Men who rape need not search far for cultural language which supports the premise that women provoke or are responsible for rape. In addition to common cultural stereotypes, the fields of psychiatry and criminology (particularly the subfield of victimology) have traditionally provided justifications for rape, often by portraying raped women as the victims of their own seduction (Albin, 1977; Marolla and Scully. 1979). For example, Hollander (1924:130) argues:

> Considering the amount of illicit intercourse, rape of women is very rare indeed. Flirtation and provocative conduct, i.e. tacit (if not actual) consent is generally the prelude to intercourse.

Since women are supposed to be coy about their sexual availability, refusal to comply with a man's sexual demands lacks meaning and rape appears normal. The fact that violence and, often, a weapon are used to accomplish the rape is not considered. As an example, Abrahamsen (1960:61) writes:

> The conscious or unconscious biological or psychological attraction between man and woman does not exist only on the part of the offender toward the woman but, also, on her part toward him, which in many instances may, to some extent, be the impetus for his sexual attack. Often a women [sic] unconsciously wishes to be taken by force—consider the theft of the bride in Peer Gynt.

Like Peer Gynt, the deniers we interviewed tried to demonstrate that their victims were willing and, in some cases, enthusiastic participants. In these accounts, the rape became more dependent upon the victim's behavior than upon their own actions.

Thirty-one percent (n = 10) of the deniers presented an extreme view of the victim. Not only willing, she was the aggressor, a seductress who lured them, unsuspecting, into sexual action. Typical was a denier convicted of his first rape and accompanying crimes of burglary, sodomy, and abduction. According to the pre-sentence reports, he had broken into the victim's house and raped her at knife point. While he admitted to the breaking and entry, which he claimed was for altruistic purposes ("to pay for the prenatal care of a friend's girlfriend"), he also argued that when the victim discovered him, he had tried to leave but she had asked him to stay. Telling him that she cheated on her husband, she had voluntarily removed her clothes and seduced him. She was, according to him, an exemplary sex partner who "enjoyed it very much and asked for oral sex.[5] Can I have it now?" he reported her as saying. He claimed they had spent hours in bed, after which the victim had told him he was good looking and asked to see him again. "Who would believe I'd meet a fellow like this?" he reported her as saying.

In addition to this extreme group, 25 percent (n = 8) of the deniers said the victim was willing and had made some sexual advances. An additional 9 percent (n = 3) said the victim was willing to have sex for money or drugs. In two of these three cases, the victim had been either an acquaintance or picked up, which the rapists said led them to expect sex.

Women Mean "Yes" When They Say "No"

Thirty-four percent (n = 11) of the deniers described their victim as unwilling, at least initially, indicating either that she had resisted or that she had said no. Despite this, and even though (according to pre-sentence reports) a weapon had been present in 64 percent (n = 7) of these 11 cases, the rapists justified their behavior by arguing that either the victim had not resisted enough or that her "no" had really meant "yes." For example, one denier who was serving time for a previous rape was subsequently convicted of attempting to rape a prison hospital nurse. He insisted he had actually completed the second rape, and said of his victim: "She semi-struggled but deep down inside I think she felt it was a fantasy come true." The nurse, according to him, had asked a question about his conviction for rape, which he interpreted as teasing. "It was like she was saying, `rape me'." Further, he stated that she had helped him along with oral sex and "from her actions, she was enjoying it." In another case, a 34-year-old man convicted of abducting and raping a 15-year old teenager at knife point as she walked on the beach, claimed it was a pickup. This rapist said women like to be overpowered before sex, but to dominate after it begins.

> A man's body is like a coke bottle, shake it up, put your thumb over the opening and feel the tension. When you take a woman out, woo her, then she says no, I'm a nice girl," you have to use force. All men do this. She said "no" but it was a societal no, she wanted to be coaxed. All women say "no" when they mean "yes" but its a societal no, so they won't have to feel responsible later.

Claims that the victim didn't resist or, if she did, didn't resist enough, were also used by 24 percent (n = 11) of admitters to explain why, during the incident, they believed the victim was willing and that they were not raping. These rapists didn't redefine their acts until some time after the crime. For example, an admitter who used a bayonet to threaten his victim, an employee of the store he had been robbing, stated:

> At the time I didn't think it was rape. I just asked her nicely and she didn't resist. I never considered prison. I just felt like I had met a friend. It took about five years of reading and going to school to change my mind about whether it was rape. I became familiar with the subtlety of violence. But

at the time, I believe that as long as I didn't hurt anyone it wasn't wrong. At the time, I didn't think I would go to prison, I thought I would beat it.

Another typical case involved a gang rape in which the victim was abducted at knife point as she walked home about midnight. According to two of the rapists, both of whom were interviewed, at the time they had thought the victim had willingly accepted a ride from the third rapist (who was not interviewed). They claimed the victim didn't resist and one reported her as saying she would do anything if they would take her home. In this rapist's view, "She acted like she enjoyed it, but maybe she was just acting. She wasn't crying, she was engaging in it." He reported that she had been friendly to the rapist who abducted her and, claiming not to have a home phone, she gave him her office number—a tactic eventually used to catch the three. In retrospect, this young man had decided, "She was scared and just relaxed and enjoyed it to avoid getting hurt." Note, however, that while he had redefined the act as rape, he continued to believe she enjoyed it.

Men who claimed to have been unaware that they were raping viewed sexual aggression as a man's prerogative at the time of the rape. Thus they regarded their act as little more than a minor wrongdoing even though most possessed or used a weapon. As long as the victim survived without major physical injury, from their perspective, a rape had not taken place. Indeed, even U.S. courts have often taken the position that physical injury is a necessary ingredient for a rape conviction.

Most Women Eventually Relax and Enjoy It

Many of the rapists expected us to accept the image, drawn from cultural stereotype, that once the rape began, the victim relaxed and enjoyed it.[6] Indeed, 69 percent (n = 22) of deniers justified their behavior by claiming not only that the victim was willing, but also that she enjoyed herself, in some cases to an immense degree. Several men suggested that they had fulfilled their victims' dreams. Additionally, while most admitters used adjectives such as "dirty," "humiliated," and "disgusted," to describe how they thought rape made women feel, 20 percent (n = 9) believed that their victim enjoyed herself. For example, one denier had posed as a salesman to gain entry to his victim's house. But he claimed he had had a previous sexual relationship with the victim, that she agreed to have sex for drugs, and that the opportunity to have sex with him produced "a glow, because she was really into oral stuff and fascinated by the idea of sex with a black man. She felt satisfied, fulfilled, wanted me to stay, but I didn't want her." In another case, a denier who had broken into his victim's house but who insisted the victim was his lover and let him in voluntarily, declared "She felt good, kept kissing me and wanted me to stay the night. She felt proud after sex with me." And another denier, who had hid in his victim's closet and later attacked her while she slept, argued that while she was scared at first, "once we got into it, she was ok." He continued to believe he hadn't committed rape because "she enjoyed it and it was like she consented."

Nice Girls Don't Get Raped

The belief that "nice girls don't get raped" affects perception of fault. The victim's reputation, as well as characteristics or behavior which violate normative sex role expectations, are perceived as contributing to the commission of the crime. For example, Nelson and Amir (1975) defined hitchhike rape as a victim-precipitated offense.

In our study, 69 percent (n = 22) of deniers and 22 percent (n = 10) of admitters referred to their victims' sexual reputation, thereby evoking the stereotype that "nice girls don't get raped." They claimed that the victim was known to have been a prostitute, or a "loose" woman, or to have had a lot of affairs, or to have given birth to a child out of wedlock. For example, a denier who claimed he had picked up his victim while she was hitchhiking stated, "To be honest, we [his family] knew she was a damn whore and whether she screwed one or 50 guys didn't matter." According to pre-sentence reports this victim didn't know her attacker and he abducted her at knife point from the street. In another case, a denier who claimed to have known his victim by reputation stated:

> If you wanted drugs or a quick piece of ass, she would do it. In court she said she was a virgin, but I could tell during sex [rape] that she was very experienced.

When other types of discrediting biographical information were added to these sexual slurs, a total of 78 percent (n = 25) of the deniers used the victim's reputation to substantiate their accounts. Most frequently, they referred to the victim's emotional state or drug use. For example, one denier claimed his victim had been known to be loose and, additionally, had turned state's evidence against her husband to put him in prison and save herself from a burglary conviction. Further, he asserted that she had met her current boyfriend, who was himself in and out of prison, in a drug rehabilitation center where they were both clients.

Evoking the stereotype that women provoke rape by the way they dress, a description of the victim as seductively attired appeared in the accounts of 22 percent (n = 7) of deniers and 17 percent (n = 8) of admitters. Typically, these descriptions were used to substantiate their claims about the victim's reputation. Some men went to extremes to paint a tarnished picture of the victim, describing her as dressed in tight black clothes and without a bra; in one case, the victim was portrayed as sexually provocative in dress and carriage. Not only did she wear short skirts, but she was observed to "spread her legs while getting out of cars." Not all of the men attempted to assassinate their victim's reputation with equal vengeance. Numerous times they made subtle and offhand remarks like, "She was a waitress and you know how they are."

The intent of these discrediting statements is clear. Deniers argued that the woman was a "legitimate" victim who got what she deserved. For example, one denier stated that all of his victims had been prostitutes; pre-sentence reports indicated they were not. Several times during his interview, he referred to them as "dirty sluts," and argued "anything I did to them was justified." Deniers also claimed their victim had wrongly accused them and was the type of woman who would perjure herself in court.

Only a Minor Wrongdoing

The majority of deniers did not claim to be completely innocent and they also accepted some accountability for their actions. Only 16 percent (n = 5) of deniers argued that they were totally free of blame. Instead, the majority of deniers pleaded guilty to a lesser charge. That is, they obfuscated the rape by pleading guilty to a less serious, more acceptable charge. They accepted being over-sexed, accused of poor judgment or trickery, even some violence, or guilty of adultery or contributing to the delinquency of a minor, charges that are hardly the equivalent of rape.

Typical of this reasoning is a denier who met his victim in a bar when the bartender asked him if he would try to repair her stalled car. After attempting unsuccessfully, he claimed the victim drank with him and later accepted a ride. Out riding, he pulled into a deserted area "to see how my luck would go." When the victim resisted his advances, he beat her and he stated:

> I did something stupid. I pulled a knife on her and I hit her as hard as I would hit a man. But I shouldn't be in prison for what I did. I shouldn't have all this time [sentence] for going to bed with a broad.

This rapist continued to believe that while the knife was wrong, his sexual behavior was justified.

In another case, the denier claimed he picked up his under-age victim at a party and that she voluntarily went with him to a motel. According to pre-sentence reports, the victim had been abducted at knife point from a party. He explained:

> After I paid for a motel, she would have to have sex but I wouldn't use a weapon. I would have explained. I spent money and, if she still said no, I would have forced her. If it had happened that way, it would have been rape to some people but not to my way of thinking. I've done that kind of thing before. I'm guilty of sex and contributing to the delinquency of a minor, but not rape.

In sum, deniers argued that, while their behavior may not have been completely proper, it should not have been considered rape. To accomplish this, they attempted to discredit and blame the victim while presenting their own actions as justified in the context. Not surprisingly, none of the deniers thought of himself as a rapist. A minority of the admitters attempted to lessen the impact of their crime by claiming the victim enjoyed being raped. But despite this similarity, the nature and tone of admitters' and deniers' accounts were essentially different.

Excusing Rape

In stark contrast to deniers, admitters regarded their behavior as morally wrong and beyond justification. They blamed themselves rather than the victim, although some continued to cling to the belief that the victim had contributed to the crime somewhat, for example, by not resisting enough.

Several of the admitters expressed the view that rape was an act of such moral outrage that it was unforgivable. Several admitters broke into tears at intervals during their interviews. A typical sentiment was:

> I equate rape with someone throwing you up against a wall and tearing your liver and guts out of you....Rape is worse than murder...and I'm disgusting.

Another young admitter frequently referred to himself as repulsive and confided:

> I'm in here for rape and in my own mind, its the most disgusting crime, sickening. When people see me and know, I get sick.

Admitters tried to explain their crime in a way that allowed them to retain a semblance of moral integrity. Thus, in contrast to deniers' justifications, admitters used excuses to explain how they were compelled to rape. These excuses appealed to the existence of forces outside of the rapists' control. Through the use of excuses, they attempted to demonstrate that either intent was absent or responsibility was diminished. This allowed them to admit rape while reducing the threat to their identity as a moral person. Excuses also permitted them to view their behavior as idiosyncratic rather than typical and, thus, to believe they were not "really" rapists. Three themes run through these accounts: (1) the use of alcohol and drugs; (2) emotional problems; and (3) nice guy image.

The Use of Alcohol and Drugs

A number of studies have noted a high incidence of alcohol and drug consumption by convicted rapists prior to their crime (Groth, 1979; Queen's Bench Foundation, 1976). However, more recent research has tentatively concluded that the connection between substance use and crime is not as direct as previously thought (Ladouceur, 1983). Another facet of alcohol and drug use mentioned in the literature is its utility in disavowing deviance. McCaghy (1968) found that child molesters used alcohol as a technique for neutralizing their deviant identity. Marolla and Scully (1979), in a review of psychiatric literature, demonstrated how alcohol consumption is applied differently as a vocabulary of motive. Rapists can use alcohol both as an excuse for their behavior and to discredit the victim and make her more responsible. We found the former common among admitters and the latter common among deniers.

Alcohol and/or drugs were mentioned in the accounts of 77 percent (n = 30) of admitters and 84 percent (n = 21) of deniers and both groups were equally likely to have acknowledged consuming a substance—admitters, 77 percent (n = 30); deniers, 72 percent (n = 18). However, admitters said they had been affected by the substance; if not the cause of their behavior, it was at least a contributing factor. For example, an admitter who estimated his consumption to have been eight beers and four "hits of acid" reported:

> Straight, I don't have the guts to rape. I could fight a man but not that. To say, "I'm going to do it to a woman," knowing it will scare and hurt her, takes guts or you have to be sick.

Another admitter believed that his alcohol and drug use,

> ... brought out what was already there but in such intensity it was uncontrollable. Feelings of being dominant, powerful, using someone for my own gratification, all rose to the surface.

In contrast, deniers' justifications required that they not be substantially impaired. To say that they had been drunk or high would cast doubt on their ability to control themselves or to remember events as they actually happened. Consistent with this, when we asked if the alcohol and/or drugs had had an effect on their behavior, 69 percent (n = 27) of admitters, but only 40 percent (n = 10) of deniers, said they had been affected.

Even more interesting were references to the victim's alcohol and/or drug use. Since admitters had already relieved themselves of responsibility through claims of being drunk or high, they had nothing to gain from the assertion that the victim had used or been affected by alcohol and/ or drugs. On the other hand, it was very much in the interest of deniers to declare that their victim had been intoxicated or high: that fact lessened her credibility and made her more responsible for the act. Reflecting these observations, 72 percent (n = 18) of deniers and 26 percent (n = 10) of admitters maintained that alcohol or drugs had been consumed by the victim. Further, while 56 percent (n = 14) of deniers declared she had been affected by this use, only 15 percent (n = 6) of admitters made a similar claim. Typically, deniers argued that the alcohol and drugs had sexually aroused their victim or rendered her out of control. For example, one denier insisted that his victim had become hysterical from drugs, not from being raped, and it was because of the drugs that she had reported him to the police. In addition, 40 percent (n = 10) of deniers argued that while the victim had been drunk or high, they themselves either hadn't ingested or weren't affected by alcohol and/or drugs. None of the admitters made this claim. In fact, in all of the 15 percent (n = 6) of cases where an admitter said the victim was drunk or high, he also admitted to being similarly affected.

These data strongly suggest that whatever role alcohol and drugs play in sexual and other types of violent crime, rapists have learned the advantage to be gained from using alcohol and drugs as an account. Our sample were aware that their victim would be discredited and their own behavior excused or justified by referring to alcohol and/or drugs.

Emotional Problems

Admitters frequently attributed their acts to emotional problems. Forty percent (n = 19) of admitters said they believed an emotional problem had been at the root of their rape behavior, and 33 percent (n = 15) specifically related the problem to an unhappy, unstable childhood or a marital-domestic situation. Still others claimed to have been in a general state of unease. For example, one admitter said that at the time of the rape he had been depressed, feeling he couldn't do anything right, and that something had been missing from his life. But he also added, "being a rapist is not part of my personality." Even admitters who could locate no source for an emotional problem evoked the popular image of rapists as the product of disordered personalities to argue they also must have problems:

> The fact that I'm a rapist makes me different. Rapists aren't all there. They have problems. It was wrong so there must be a reason why I did it. I must have a problem.

Our data do indicate that a precipitating event, involving an upsetting problem of everyday living, appeared in the accounts of 80 percent (n = 38) of admitters and 25 percent (n = 8) of deniers. Of those experiencing a precipitating event, including deniers, 76 percent (n = 35) involved a wife or girlfriend. Over and over, these men described themselves as having been in a rage because of an incident involving a woman with whom they believed they were in love.

Frequently, the upsetting event was related to a rigid and unrealistic double standard for sexual conduct and virtue which they applied to "their" woman but which they didn't expect from men, didn't apply to themselves, and, obviously, didn't honor in other women. To discover that the "pedestal" didn't apply to their wife or girlfriend sent them into a fury. One especially articulate and typical admitter described his feeling as follows. After serving a short prison term for auto theft, he married his "childhood sweetheart" and secured a well-paying job. Between his job and the volunteer work he was doing with an ex-offender group, he was spending long hours away from home, a situation that had bothered his wife. In response to her request, he gave up his volunteer work, though it was clearly meaningful to him. Then, one day, he discovered his wife with her former boyfriend "and my life fell apart." During the next several days, he said his anger had made him withdraw into himself and, after three days of drinking in a motel room, he abducted and raped a stranger. He stated:

> My parents have been married for many years and I had high expectations about marriage. I put my wife on a pedestal. When I walked in on her, I felt like my life had been destroyed, it was such a shock. I was bitter and angry about the fact that I hadn't done anything to my wife for cheating. I didn't want to hurt her [victim], only to scare and degrade her.

It is clear that many admitters, and a minority of deniers, were under stress at the time of their rapes. However, their problems were ordinary—the types of upsetting events that everyone experiences at some point in life. The overwhelming majority of the men were not clinically defined as mentally ill in court-ordered psychiatric examinations prior to their trials. Indeed, our sample is consistent with Abel *et al.* (1980) who found fewer than 5 percent of rapists were psychotic at the time of their offense.

As with alcohol and drug intoxication, a claim of emotional problems works differently depending upon whether the behavior in question is being justified or excused. It would have been counter-productive for deniers to have claimed to have had emotional problems at the time of the rape. Admitters used psychological explanations to portray themselves as having been temporarily "sick" at the time of the rape. Sick people are usually blamed for neither the cause of their illness nor for acts committed while in that state of diminished capacity. Thus, adopting the sick role removed responsibility by excusing the behavior as having been beyond the ability of the individual to control. Since the rapists were not "themselves," the rape was idiosyncratic rather than typical behavior. Admitters asserted a non-deviant identity despite their self-proclaimed disgust with what they had done. Although admitters were willing to assume the sick role, they did not view their problem as a chronic condition, nor did they believe themselves to be insane or permanently impaired. Said one admitter, who believed that he needed psychological counseling: "I have a mental disorder, but I'm not crazy." Instead, admitters viewed their "problem" as mild, transient, and curable. Indeed, part of the appeal of this excuse was that not only did it relieve responsibility, but, as with alcohol and drug addiction, it allowed the rapist to "recover." Thus, at the time of their interviews, only 31 percent (n = 14) of admitters indicated that "being a rapist" was part of their self-concept. Twenty-eight percent (n = 13) of admitters stated they had never thought of themselves as rapists, 8 percent (n = 4) said they were unsure, and 33 percent (n = 16) asserted they had been a rapist at one time but now were recovered. A multiple "ex-rapist," who believed his "problem" was due to "something buried in my subconscious" that was triggered when his girlfriend broke up with him, expressed a typical opinion:

> I was a rapist, but not now. I've grown up, had to live with it. I've hit the bottom of the well and it can't get worse. I feel born again to deal with my problems.

Nice Guy Image

Admitters attempted to further neutralize their crime and negotiate a non-rapist identity by painting an image of themselves as a "nice guy." Admitters projected the image of someone who had made a serious mistake but, in every other respect, was a decent person. Fifty-seven percent (n = 27) expressed regret and sorrow for their victim indicating that they wished there were a way to apologize for or amend their behavior. For example, a participant in a rape-murder, who insisted his partner did the murder, confided, "I wish there was something I could do besides saying 'I'm sorry, I'm sorry.' I live with it 24 hours a day and, sometimes, I wake up crying in the middle of the night because of it."

Schlenker and Darby (1981) explain the significance of apologies beyond the obvious expression of regret. An apology allows a person to admit guilt while at the same time seeking a pardon by signalling that the event should not be considered a fair representation of what the person is really like. An apology separates the bad self from the good self, and promises more acceptable behavior in the future. When apologizing, an individual is attempting to say: "I have repented and should be forgiven," thus making it appear that no further rehabilitation is required.

The "nice guy" statements of the admitters reflected an attempt to communicate a message consistent with Schlenker's and Darby's analysis of apologies. It was an attempt to convey that rape was not a representation of their "true" self. For example,

> It's different from anything else I've ever done. I feel more guilt about this. It's not consistent with me. When I talk about it, it's like being assaulted myself. I don't know why I did it, but once I started, I got into it. Armed robbery was a way of life for me, but not rape. I feel like I wasn't being myself.

Admitters also used "nice guy" statements to register their moral opposition to violence and harming women, even though, in some cases, they had seriously injured their victims. Such was the case of an admitter convicted of a gang rape:

> I'm against hurting women. She should have resisted. None of us were the type of person that would use force on a woman. I never positioned myself on a woman unless she showed an interest in me. They would play to me, not me to them. My weakness is to follow. I never would have stopped, let along pick her up without the others. I never would have let anyone beat her. I never bothered women who didn't want sex; never had a problem with sex or getting it. I loved her—like all women.

Finally, a number of admitters attempted to improve their self-image by demonstrating that, while they had raped, it could have been worse if they had not been a "nice guy." For example, one admitter professed to being especially gentle with his victim after she told him she had just had a baby. Others claimed to have given the victim money to get home or make a phone call, or to have made sure the victim's children were not in the room. A multiple rapist, whose pattern was to break in and attack sleeping victims in their homes, stated:

> I never beat any of my victims and I told them I wouldn't hurt them if they cooperated. I'm a professional thief. But I never robbed the women I raped because I felt so bad about what I had already done to them.

Even a young man, who raped his five victims at gun point and then stabbed them to death, attempted to improve his image by stating:

Physically they enjoyed the sex [rape]. Once they got involved, it would be difficult to resist. I was always gentle and kind until I started to kill them. And the killing was always sudden, so they wouldn't know it was coming.

Summary and Conclusions

Convicted rapists' accounts of their crimes include both excuses and justifications. Those who deny what they did was rape justify their actions; those who admit it was rape attempt to excuse it or themselves. This study does not address why some men admit while others deny, but future research might address this question. This paper does provide insight on how men who are sexually aggressive or violent construct reality, describing the different strategies of admitters and deniers.

Admitters expressed the belief that rape was morally reprehensible. But they explained themselves and their acts by appealing to forces beyond their control, forces which reduced their capacity to act rationally and thus compelled them to rape. Two types of excuses predominated: alcohol/drug intoxication and emotional problems. Admitters used these excuses to negotiate a moral identity for themselves by viewing rape as idiosyncratic rather than typical behavior. This allowed them to reconceptualize themselves as recovered or "ex-rapists," someone who had made a serious mistake which did not represent their "true" self.

In contrast, deniers' accounts indicate that these men raped because their value system provided no compelling reason not to do so. When sex is viewed as a male entitlement, rape is no longer seen as criminal. However, the deniers had been convicted of rape, and like the admitters, they attempted to negotiate an identity. Through justifications, they constructed a "controversial" rape and attempted to demonstrate how their behavior, even if not quite right, was appropriate in the situation. Their denials, drawn from common cultural rape stereotypes, took two forms, both of which ultimately denied the existence of a victim.

The first form of denial was buttressed by the cultural view of men as sexually masterful and women as coy but seductive. Injury was denied by portraying the victim as willing, even enthusiastic, or as politely resistant at first but eventually yielding to "relax and enjoy it." In these accounts, force appeared merely as a seductive technique. Rape was disclaimed: rather than harm the woman, the rapist had fulfilled her dreams. In the second form of denial, the victim was portrayed as the type of woman who "got what she deserved." Through attacks on the victim's sexual reputation and, to a lesser degree, her emotional state, deniers attempted to demonstrate that since the victim wasn't a "nice girl," they were not rapists. Consistent with both forms of denial was the self-interested use of alcohol and drugs as a justification. Thus, in contrast to admitters, who accentuated their own use as an excuse, deniers emphasized the victim's consumption in an effort to both discredit her and make her appear more responsible for the rape. It is important to remember that deniers did not invent these justifications. Rather, they reflect a belief system which has historically victimized women by promulgating the myth that women both enjoy and are responsible for their own rape.

While admitters and deniers present an essentially contrasting view of men who rape, there were some shared characteristics. Justifications particularly, but also excuses, are buttressed by the cultural view of women as sexual commodities, dehumanized and devoid of autonomy and dignity. In this sense, the sexual objectification of women must be understood as an important factor contributing to an environment that trivializes, neutralizes, and, perhaps, facilitates rape.

Finally, we must comment on the consequences of allowing one perspective to dominate thought on a social problem. Rape, like any complex continuum of behavior, has multiple causes and is influenced by a number of social factors. Yet, dominated by psychiatry and the medical model, the underlying assumption that rapists are "sick" has pervaded research. Although methodologically unsound, conclusions have been based almost exclusively on small clinical populations of rapists—that extreme group of rapists who seek counseling in prison and are the most likely to exhibit psychopathology. From this small, atypical group of men, psychiatric findings have been generalized to all men who rape. Our research, however, based on volunteers from the entire prison population, indicates that some rapists, like deniers, viewed and understood their behavior from a popular cultural perspective. This strongly suggests that cultural perspectives, and not an idiosyncratic illness, motivated their behavior. Indeed, we can argue that the psychiatric perspective has contributed to the vocabulary of motive that rapists use to excuse and justify their behavior (Scully and Marolla, 1984).

Efforts to arrive at a general explanation for rape have been retarded by the narrow focus of the medical model and the preoccupation with clinical populations. The continued reduction of such complex behavior to a singular cause hinders, rather than enhances, our understanding of rape.

REFERENCES

Abel, Gene, Judith Becker, and Linda Skinner. 1980. "Aggressive Behavior and Sex." *Psychiatric Clinics of North America*, 3(2):133-151.
Abrahamsen, David. 1960. *The Psychology of Crime*. New York: Wiley.
Albin, Rochelle. 1977. "Psychological Studies of Rape." *Signs*, 3(2):423-435.
Athens, Lonnie. 1977. "Violent Crimes: A Symbolic Interactionist Study." *Symbolic Interaction*, 1 (1):56-71.
Burgess, Ann Wolbert and Lynda Lytle Holmstrom. 1974. *Rape: Victims of Crisis*. Bowie: Robert J. Brady. 1979. "Rape: Sexual Disruption and Recovery." *American Journal of Orthopsychiatry*, 49(4): 648-657.
Burt, Martha. 1980. "Cultural Myths and Supports for Rape." *Journal of Personality and Social Psychology*, 38(2):217-230.
Burt, Martha and Rochelle Albin. 1981. "Rape Myths, Rape Definitions, and Probability of Conviction." *Journal of Applied Psychology*, 11(3):212-230.
Feldman-Summers, Shirley, Patricia E. Gordon, and Jeanette R. Meagher. 1979. "The Impact of Rape on Sexual Satisfaction." *Journal of Abnormal Psychology*, 88(1):101-105.
Glueck, Sheldon. 1925. *Mental Disorders and the Criminal Law*. New York: Little Brown.
Groth, Nicholas A. 1979. *Men Who Rape*. New York: Plenum Press.
Hall, Peter M. and John P. Hewitt. 1970. "The Quasi-theory of Communication and the Management of Dissent." *Social Problems*, 18(1):17-27.

Hewitt, John P. and Peter M. Hall. 1973. "Social Problems, Problematic Situations, and Quasitheories." *American Sociological Review*, 38(3):367-374.
Hewitt, John P. and Randall Stokes. 1975. "Disclaimers." *American Sociological Review*, 40(1):1-11.
Hollander, Bernard. 1924. *The Psychology of Misconduct, Vice, and Crime*. New York: Macmillan.
Holmstrom, Lynda Lytle and Ann Wolbert Burgess. 1978. "Sexual Behavior of Assailant and Victim During Rape." Paper presented at the annual meetings of the American Sociological Association, San Francisco, September 2-8.
Kilpatrick, Dean G., Lois Veronen, and Patricia A. Resnick. 1979. "The Aftermath of Rape: Recent Empirical Findings." *American Journal of Ortho-psychiatry*, 49(4):658-669.
Ladouceur, Patricia. 1983. "The Relative Impact of Drugs and Alcohol on Serious Felons." Paper presented at the annual meetings of the American Society of Criminology, Denver, November 9-12.
Luckenbill, David. 1977. "Criminal Homicide as a Situated Transaction." *Social Problems*, 25(2):176–187.
McCaghy, Charles. 1968. "Drinking and Deviance Disavowal: The Case of Child Molesters." *Social Problems*, 16(1):43-49.
Marolla, Joseph, and Diana Scully. 1979. "Rape and Psychiatric Vocabularies of Motive." In Edith S. Gomberg and Violet Franks (eds.), *Gender and Disordered Behavior: Sex Differences in Psychopathology*. New York: Brunner/Mazel, pp. 301-318.
Mills, C. Wright. 1940. "Situated Actions and Vocabularies of Motive." *American Sociological Review*, 5(6):904-913.
Nelson, Steve and Menachem Amir. 1975. "The Hitchhike Victim of Rape: A Research Report." In Israel Drapkin and Emilio Viano (eds.), *Victimology: A New Focus*. Lexington, KY: Lexington Books, pp. 47-65.
Queen's Bench Foundation. 1976. *Rape: Prevention and Resistance*. San Francisco: Queen's Bench Foundation.
Ruch, Libby O., Susan Meyers Chandler, and Richard A. Harter. 1980. "Life Change and Rape Impact." *Journal of Health and Social Behavior*, 21(3).248-260.
Scott, Marvin and Stanford Lyman. 1968. "Accounts." *American Sociological Review*, 33(1):46-62.
Schlenker, Barry R. and Bruce W. Darby. 1981. "The Use of Apologies in Social Predicaments." *Social Psychology Quarterly*, 44(3):271-278.
Scully, Diana and Joseph Marolla. 1984. "Rape and Psychiatric Vocabularies of Motive: Alternative Perspectives." In Ann Wolbert Burgess (ed.), *Handbook on Rape and Sexual Assault*. New York: Garland Publishing. Forthcoming.
Shore, Barbara K. 1979. *An Examination of Critical Process and Outcome Factors in Rape*. Rockville. MD: National Institute of Mental Health.
Stokes, Randall and John P. Hewitt. 1976. "Aligning Actions." *American Sociological Review*, 41(5):837-849.
Sykes, Gresham M. and David Matza. 1957. "Techniques of Neutralization." *American Sociological Review*, 22(6):664-670.
Williams, Joyce. 1979. "Sex Role Stereotypes, Women's Liberation, and Rape: A Cross-cultural Analysis of Attitude." *Sociological Symposium*, 25 (Winter):6 1-97.

NOTES

[1] These numbers include pretest interviews. When the analysis involves either questions that were not asked in the pretest or that were changed, they are excluded and thus the number changes.

[2] There is, of course, the possibility that some of these men really were innocent of rape. However, while the U.S. criminal justice system is not without flaw, we assume that it is highly unlikely that this many men could have been unjustly convicted of rape, especially since rape is a crime with traditionally low conviction rates. Instead, for purposes of this research, we assume that these men were guilty as charged and that their attempt to maintain an image of non-rapist springs from some psychologically or sociologically interpretable mechanism.

[3] Because of their outright denial, interviews with this group of rapists did not contain the data being analyzed here and, consequently, they are not included in this paper.

[4] It was sometimes difficult to determine the full extent of victim injury from the pre-sentence reports. Consequently, it is doubtful that this number accurately reflects the degree of injuries sustained by victims.

[5] It is worth noting that a number of deniers specifically mentioned the victim's alleged interest in oral sex. Since our interview questions about sexual history indicated that the rapists themselves found oral sex marginally acceptable, the frequent mention is probably another attempt to discredit the victim. However, since a tape recorder could not be used for the interviews and the importance of these claims didn't emerge until the data was being coded and analyzed, it is possible that it was mentioned even more frequently but not recorded.

[6] Research shows clearly that women do not enjoy rape. Holmstrom and Burgess (1978) asked 93 adult rape victims, "How did it feel sexually?" Not one said they enjoyed it. Further, the trauma of rape is so great that it disrupts sexual functioning (both frequency and satisfaction) for the overwhelming majority of victims, at least during the period immediately following the rape and, in a fewer cases, for an extended period of time (Burgess and Holmstrom, 1979; Feldman-Summers *et al.*, 1979). In addition, a number of studies have shown that rape victims experience adverse consequences prompting some to move, change jobs, or drop out of school (Burgess and Holmstrom, 1974; Kilpatrick *et al.*, 1979; Ruch *et al.*, 1980; Shore, 1979).

Chapter **16**   **EMERGENCE AND HUMAN CONDUCT**

Bernard N. Meltzer and *Jerome G. Manis*

An enduring, fundamental question confronting the social sciences concerns whether, or to what extent, human conduct is marked by emergence.[1] Our interest in the question relates to the indeterminacy found on both the individual and collective levels of human behavior. Two philosophers of science define the form of emergence we have in mind, characterizing certain phenomena as "novel," not merely in the psychological sense of being unexpected, but in the theoretical sense of being unexplainable, or unpredictable (Hempel & Oppenheim, 1953, p. 332). Thus, emergent events are events that contain novel features that are not entirely derived from antecedent events or experiences.

This form of emergence is a major vehicle of indeterminacy, having as its antithesis *determinism*, a major assumption of the scientific method as many social scientists conceive it. The problem of emergence, in this sense, tends to be dismissed as "metaphysical" and, hence, either to be rejected as a "real" issue or to be ignored; whereas those who deal with it tend to be hesitant about taking seriously its sources and its implications for the social scientific endeavor.

One must turn to the work of G. H. Mead and other symbolic interactionists to find discussions of emergence.[2] Manford Kuhn's (1964) review of developments in the interactionist orientation, for example, differentiates subschools in terms of their respective standpoints on indeterminism (emergence).[3] In the present article, we use the interactionist orientation in considering the nature, manifestations, sources, and implications of emergence.

The Nature of Emergence

Among contemporary interactionists, Blumer (1969) most insistently has taken the position that novelty, uncertainty, and emergence are integral, not accidental or epiphenomenal, in human life. As part and parcel of the social process, emergence reflects our continual movement into futures different from our pasts. The present, then, is conditioned by both the past and the future, for, as McHugh (1968, p. 24) states, "The past influences the symbolic definition of the present, the definition of the present is influenced by inferences about the future, and the events of the future will reconstruct our definition of the past." Blumer followed G. H. Mead in emphasizing the occurrence of novel features in the social sphere (and in analyzing the processes giving rise to such features). Miller (1973, p. 41) summarizes Mead's views on the matter:

> For Mead, the seat of reality is the present, and presents are characterized
> by acts of adjustment, or by the novel, the emergent, that which could not

have been predicted either in fact or principle...The emergent, being unpredictable in principle, does not follow logically from the world that was there, from conditions necessary for its emergence, from what is traditionally called its cause.

Mead's dismissive reference to "conditions necessary for [the emergent's] emergence" needs expatiation. Emergent events contain novel features that are not merely consequences of antecedent presents; yet at the same time they exist in presents that are conditioned by the past as well as the future. Antecedent conditions are seen by Mead, however, as *influences on*, but not determinants of, novelty. For example, socialization of the individual sets broad limits, or ranges, within which acts are likely to occur, but it does not necessarily compel specific acts. In any situation, a number of possible outcomes—some more probable than others—may be present. But, as Mead points out (1959 p. 14):

...the emergent has no sooner appeared than we set about rationalizing it, that is, we undertake to show that it, or at least the conditions that [apparently] determine its appearance can be found in the past that lay behind it.

Such retrospective, post factum reasoning enables a tenacious retention of the postulate of determinism, a postulate unlikely to be abandoned by most social scientists.

Opposing the view of emergence as inherent in human affairs is the contention that it is merely *apparent*, a reflection of temporary scientific ignorance. Thus, some researchers claim that the history of science includes many instances of phenomena for which the status of emergence has been asserted but which were later shown to lie inside the pattern of lawlike regularity of other events (Rudner 1966, p. 71; Catton 1966, p. 315), for example, planetary motion. Given the innumerable manifestations of novelty and unpredictability in the realm of human affairs, we consider such a contention erroneous.

Manifestations of Emergence

A recent survey of symbolic interactionism (Plummer 1991, Vol. 1, p. x) suggests the omnipresent social reality of chance, or novelty:

In the world of the interactionist, meaning is never fixed and immutable: rather, it is always shifting, emergent, and ultimately ambiguous. Although we may regularly create habitual, routine, and shared meanings, these are always open to reappraisal and further adjustment....Lives, situations, and even societies are always and everywhere evolving, adjusting, emerging, becoming.

Thus, the sphere of the social is a creative, open-ended process rather than a static structure. As Mann (1984, p. 110) points out, whether we examine individual biographies, social encounters, or whole societies, the idea of emergence underscores the fact that human beings negotiate, or construct, what is happening, and the behavioral outcomes are never completely known in advance. Although linear patterns of order may be imposed in retrospection and stable lines of activity may appear to be present, at any given moment these lines of activity are in the process of "becoming."

At the level of individual acts or joint actions, whether microscopic or macroscopic, new and unforeseen outcomes are always possible. Consequently, human conduct must be, to a degree, tentative, uncertain, exploratory. Strauss expresses a widely held interactionist view when he asserts: "Unless a path of action has been well traversed, its terminal point is largely indeterminate. Both ends and means may be reformulated in transit..." (1959, p . 36). Blumer (1969, p. 10) emphasized that all self-directed conduct is constructed in and through an ongoing process. Such conduct is not merely the expression or product of people's personalities or of conditions antecedent to the given situation. It is this processual character of social life, a character antithetical to the commonly postulated conception of stable structures of personality and of society, that comports with the ubiquity of novelty, of emergence, in social life.[4]

By virtue of these processes, a diverse range of unexpected, uncertain, unpredictable events occur, so that novelty vies with regularity in the world of everyday affairs. Such familiar social phenomena as the following pervade human lives on the personal, interpersonal, and intergroup levels: Individual actors find that their actual behavior in given situations may differ from what they expected to do (Mead, 1934, p. 177; Blumer, 1969, passim); persons performing social roles engage in "role making" (Turner, 1962) instead of simply role playing; participants in organizations "negotiate" (Strauss, 1978) their behavior, even in situations marked by coercion or unequal power, rather than merely conforming to organizational norms or other external constraints; collective behavior frequently gives rise to "emergent norms" (Turner & Killian, 1987; Snow, Zurcher, & Peters, 1981); new social forms (e.g., innovative norms, social movements, etc.) constantly emerge in societies and cultures (Greer, 1969, p. 173); and other manifestations of the novel and spontaneous abound.

Sources of Emergence

Three closely interconnected propositions that are accepted as truisms or articles of faith by most emergentist symbolic interactionists are useful in explaining emergence as an aspect of social life. These propositions, testable at the present time chiefly through everyday experience, are that (a) human beings are active in shaping their own conduct; (b) human consciousness, or thinking, involves interaction with oneself; and (c) human beings construct their behavior in the course of its execution.[5] Readers familiar with symbolic interactionism will recognize these ideas. Our aim here is to situate them within the context of emergence.

We begin with the idea of human agency, the voluntaristic component in human conduct. Conventional views of human behavior tend to assume a deterministic, nonvoluntary character. The individual, according to such views, passively reacts in accordance with the inexorable dictates of specific internal and external stimuli or impersonal forces. These views, so prevalent today, can be found in the first two textbooks published (in 1908) under the title *Social Psychology*, divergent as the books were on most other matters. Edward A. Ross, a sociologist, viewed the individual as coerced by social processes, whereas William H. McDougall, a psychologist, traced social behavior and institutions to individual "instincts."

By contrast, symbolic interactionists generally allow humans some degree of choice in their behavior. Given the ability to select and interpret or define situations—rather than to respond immediately and directly to stimuli—and the ability to interact with themselves (i.e., to think), humans are capable of forming new meanings and new lines of action. The meanings (and the actions to which they give rise) may vary from one instance of situation definition to another and may shift from point to point in the formation of any act, as actors consider alternative lines of behavior. This variation and shift do not mean that human beings transcend all influences; however, it does draw attention to the active roles humans play in modifying these influences and in creating and changing their own behavior.

This proposition, then, points to the fact that socialization both enmeshes humans in society and frees them from it. Individuals with selves are not passive but can employ their selves in an interaction that may result in novel behavior sometimes diverging from group definitions.

The second proposition concerns a dialectical conception of mind, or reflective thinking. When thinking or engaging in "minded" behavior, one necessarily carries on an internal dialogue and makes indications of things to oneself, sometimes rehearsing alternative lines of action. Here we find the key process giving rise to emergent behavior. This dialogic process involves two distinguishable phases of the process called the self: The "I," a spontaneous, initiating, and impulsive aspect—essentially "a principle of uncertainty" (Hanson, 1986, p. 91)—and the "me," a set of internalized social definitions.

In the interplay between these aspects of the self, individuals import into their behavior the same processes that take place during interaction with others. Their definitions of situations, key elements in human conduct, derive both from interaction with others and from interaction with themselves. In both individual and joint acts, the self-indications (or interpretations) occurring in these processes are not predetermined by prior conditions but depend on what the actor(s) take into account and assess in the actual situation. The processes are more or less creative rather than fixed responses.

Finally, the constructive, emergent nature of human conduct completes the description of the process that yields novelty. We have already indicated that human conduct, in its individual and collective forms, is an elaborate process of interpreting, selecting, and rejecting possible lines of action. This process cannot be understood in terms of mechanical responses to external influences. Nor can it be fully understood in terms of the mere expression of pre-established inclinations or meanings held by the actor.

The behavior that emerges from the interactions within the individual or between individuals is not a necessary product of past events or experiences. The behavior may be an unexpected, unpredictable emergent constructed in the thought processes of the actor or actors, processes in which the "I" plays the most crucial role. Because of these processes, group life assumes the character of ongoing activity, a continuing matter of fitting developing lines of conduct to one another in negotiated, shifting, and emergent ways.

These propositions direct attention to an important tenet of most humanistic views of conduct: Human beings are, at least in part, participants in the creation of their own destinies. It would be a mistake to construe this idea as synonymous with the notion that humans have completely free will. That notion is as unpalatable to symbolic interactionists as the notion of thoroughgoing determinism. Much more acceptable is a "soft determinism," a view of human conduct as influenced, but not entirely determined, by past events.

Implications of Emergence

If we reject absolute determinism in favor of emergence, what differences does it make in the way we approach the study of social life? We shall briefly describe a few of the differences implied by an emergentist conception of social life. Blumer (1969, p. 98) indicates the primary implication:

> Since the act, whether individual or collective, is fashioned, constructed, and directed by the process of definition that goes on in the individual or the group as the case may be, it is this process that should be the central object of study by the psychologist and the sociologist.

This focus of attention on the *process* of act construction differs, of course, from the current prevailing focus on the analysis of variables in which antecedent or current conditions (independent variables) and consequent behaviors (dependent variables) are stressed almost exclusively. Unlike the emphasis on variables, the study of the process of act construction requires researchers to perceive actors' meanings or interpretations in order to understand their conduct. Because the inner phase of human acts is marked by the richest development of the acts, researchers must endeavor to take the standpoints of those whom they study in order to comprehend the act's formation. This prescription does not, however, restrict students of human behavior and society to an exclusive concern with the inner or mental dimension; rather, it broadens their commitment to an inclusion of both the covert and overt dimensions.

A second implication follows from the first. The recent increase in qualitative, ethnographic studies must be encouraged. Researchers can best recognize the pervasiveness of novelty by avoiding a firm prestructuring of their research, thereby allowing for the not entirely serendipitous appearance of emergence. Further, as careful a specification as possible must be made of the career of the situation-defining processes involved.

In view of the ever-present element of novelty, can we hope to develop any substantively significant generalizations and predictions about human conduct? The answer to this question brings us to the third implication of emergence: the finality of probabilism in human studies. Aboulafia (1991, p. 10) reminds us that Mead does not deny that we can predict responses on the basis of past behavior, but that he does claim that the element of novelty deprives us of absolute certainty that a specific response will occur. "It is not that the 'I' always responds in absolutely novel ways," Aboulafia writes—"such a claim would destroy any possibility of understanding human behavior—but that it acts in ways that exhibit varying degrees of novelty" (1991, p. 10). And Donagan asserts: "In their present state, it is plausible neither that the social sciences have as their... scientific function to establish the lawful determinants of the events they study, nor even that they presuppose that all human actions have lawful determinants" (1973, p. 21). (We reject, of course, the qualifying phrase, "In their present state.")

Sociologists, then, must do two related things: (a) Cease deluding themselves that statistical generalizations are simply reflections of temporary ignorance of causal relationships, merely way-stations toward the ultimate goal of definitive, determinate, universal generalizations, and (b) become aware that the ontological nature of social life, rather than epistemological or methodological problems, accounts for this state of affairs. They must realize that the best we can ever hope for in the social sciences is more or less crude probabilistic statements—and no more—that can serve to render social life fairly intelligible.

Recent developments in postmodernist orientations within sociology reflect the gradual growth of skepticism about the possibility of achieving conclusive propositions. And, taken together, the foregoing implications in turn imply certain consequences for the study of groups and society.

Social norms, roles, and structures are commonly conceived as determinants of individual and social phenomena. For example, group structures are generally conceived as the sources of group processes. That the bylaws of an organization channel its activities is undeniable, as is the influence of the rules of order that guide agendas, motions, and policy decisions. Still, these regulations do not directly determine the outcomes of organizational meetings. Nor do the laws and customs of societies fully control their members, neither their thoughts nor their actions.

No matter how uniform or detailed the rules and the roles of groups may be, they are influenced by novel, unpredicted elements that emerge through role making, negotiation, and other innovation-inducing processes. Thus, in some group sessions, individuals or cliques may, through self-interaction and interaction with one another, formulate and introduce unexpected information and ideas; unforeseen, spontaneous questions and interruptions may alter established routines and definitions; an occasional creative discussion may have major consequences for collective acts undergoing construction; new alliances among group members, occasioned by redefinitions of interests or strategies, may become sources of change or disruption.

Informal groups, such as clubs, cliques, or gangs, are especially susceptible to novel behaviors. In the absence of formal, established policies, group members can and do engage in many spontaneous, unplanned actions. A new idea or a disagreement may emerge among participants, thereby altering the informally held group processes, procedures, and activities.

The novel, unexpected, and often unpredicted outcomes of such group processes are inescapable elements of group life. They must be accepted as essential dictates of the active, constructive character of human behavior and interaction. As such, they help to account for the continuous, ongoing changes in groups and societies, particularly modern groups and societies.[6]

Only a few years ago, "experts" were lauding the admirable innovations of the Chinese leadership and deploring the rigidity of the leaders of Soviet society. Today, their nations are being described in opposite terms. Post hoc explanations of the changes may vary, but whatever interpretation is offered is likely to overlook the emergent components involved, the products of the human capacity to propose, initiate, and institute both great and small changes.

Awareness of these emergent properties of groups and societies does not imply the complete rejection of causal theories. Group emergents, like individual emergents, have causes, but unlike physical causation, they are not susceptible to comprehensive observation, analysis, and prediction; there always remains a constructive, creative element that defies the uniformity or regularity necessary to causal analysis.

To understand the probable causes of emergent group and societal emergents, we cannot rely on fixed or determinate explanations. Each group and society must be carefully analyzed as a distinctive, often unique, entity. Moreover, the situation-defining processes of individuals and collectivities must be examined. Formulating explanations and predictions on the basis of general principles and uniformities alone, while neglecting the potentiality of emergence, will remain a source of analytic error.

These errors of analysis are evidenced particularly in the unpredicted emergence of new nations. Since the end of World War II, nationalism has produced scores of countries out of the nations and colonies of the past. Long existing countries are splitting as ethnic and religious groups demand their own independence. Often, the volumes written about these new national entities are entitled "The Emergence of [insert nation]." This usage, while rarely intended as such, accords with the meanings of "emergence" in this article.

Conclusion

Recognizing the emergent character of their subject matter, social scientists should consider redefining the goals of their profession. For example, they could place their primary emphasis on rendering human behavior and society intelligible. This redefinition would not preclude continuing to conduct much of their research as though fully determinate, quantified, universal laws and principles are attainable. It would, however, broaden the scope of their efforts so as to include carefully wrought qualitative studies.[7] Surely, both social scientists and the lay public could profit from the insights produced by such studies.

REFERENCES

Aboulafia, M. (Ed.) 1991. *Philosophy, social theory, and the thought of George Herbert Mead*. Albany: State University of New York.
Baldwin, J. D. 1986. *George Herbert Mead: A unifying theory for sociology*. Newbury Park, CA: Sage.
Blumer, H. G. 1969. *Symbolic interactionism*. Englewood Cliffs, NJ: Prentice Hall.
Catton, W. R., Jr. 1966. *From animistic to naturalistic sociology*. New York: McGraw-Hill.
Donagan, A. 1973. Determinism in history. In P. P. Wiener (Ed.), *Dictionary of the history of ideas* (Vol. 2, pp. 18–25). New York: Charles Scribner's.
Greer, S. 1969. *The logic of social inquiry*. Chicago: Aldine.
Hanson, K. 1986. *The self imagined: Philosophical reflections on the social character of psyche*. New York: Routledge and Kegan Paul.

Hempel, C. G., & Oppenheim, P. 1953. Determinism in history. In H. Feigl & M. Brodbeck (Eds.), *Readings in the philosophy of science* (pp. 319–352). New York: Appleton-Century-Crofts.

Kuhn, M. H. 1964. Major trends in symbolic interaction theory in the past twenty five years. *Sociological Quarterly*, 5, 61–84.

Manis, J. G., & Meltzer, B. N. (Eds.) 1978. *Symbolic interaction: A reader in social psychology* (3rd ed.). Boston: Allyn and Bacon.

Mann, M. (Ed.) 1984. *The international encyclopedia of sociology*. New York: Continuum.

McHugh, P. 1968. *Defining the situation*. Indianapolis: Bobbs-Merrill.

Mead, G. H. 1934. *Mind, self and society*. Chicago: University of Chicago.

———. 1959. *The philosophy of the present*. LaSalle, Illinois: Open Court Publishing.

Miller, D. L. 1973. *George Herbert Mead: Self, language, and the world*. Austin and London: University of Texas.

Plummer, K. (Ed.) 1991. *Symbolic interactionism*, Vol. 1. Brookfield, VT: Edward Elgar.

Rudner, R. S. 1966. *Philosophy of social science*. Englewood Cliffs, NJ: Prentice Hall.

Snow, D. A., Zurcher, L. A., & Peters, R. 1981. Victory celebrations as theater: A dramaturgical approach to crowd behavior. *Symbolic Interaction*, 4, 21–42.

Strauss, A. 1959. *Mirrors and masks*. Glencoe, IL: The Free Press.

———. 1978. *Negotiations: Varieties, contexts, processes, and social order*. San Francisco: Jossey-Bass.

Turner, R. 1962. Role-taking: Process vs. conformity. In A. M. Rose (Ed.), *Human behavior & social processes* (pp. 20–40). Boston: Houghton Mifflin.

Turner, R., & Killian, L. 1987. *Collective behavior*. (3rd ed.). Englewood Cliffs, NJ: Prentice-Hall.

Young, T. R. 1991. Chaos theory and symbolic interaction theory: Poetics for the postmodern sociologist. *Symbolic Interaction*, 14, 321–334.

NOTES

1. We do not have in mind the emergence of new properties at increasing levels of complexity of phenomena, as in biological evolution and in movement from the physical level to the chemical level, to the biological level, to the psychological level, to the social level of phenomena. For sociologists, the classic statement on emergence in this sense of the term is Emile Durkheim's designation of social facts as sui *generis*. This form of emergence has as its antithesis *reductionism*.

    We thank Cathy Malkin, William Meltzer, Harry Mika, and Larry Reynolds for their critical readings of the manuscript. Address correspondence to Bernard N. Meltzer, Department of Sociology, Anthropology, and Social Work, Central Michigan University, Mount Pleasant, Ml 48859.

2. For a recent, oblique, postmodernist example, see Young (1991).

3. Kuhn's own "self theory" leaves no room for either indeterminism or emergence. He points out that conventional role theory and person perception theory both assume determinacy. As primarily *indeterminate* subtheories, on the other hand, he lists the dramaturgical school: phenomenological theory; the longitudinal study of socialization and, especially, career trajectories: the Sapir-Whorf-Cassirer language and culture orientation; and H. S. Sullivan's interpersonal theory of psychiatry. (It is interesting to note that Kuhn omits the Chicago school of interactionism from his classification, although it clearly falls within the indeterminacy category.) Finally, Kuhn describes the reference group frame-work as ambiguous on the determinacy-indeterminacy issue.

4. Mead repeatedly pointed out that novel and unexpected things constantly arise in the biological, astronomical, chemical, and physical spheres, as well as in behavioral and social systems. In the biological realm, for example, random mutations and new recombinations of genetic material are essential for the evolution of new species. See Baldwin (1986; pp. 40–42 and passim) for an excellent summary of these ideas. In a sense, Mead (among others) anticipated modern chaos theory.

5. A previous formulation of these ideas appears in Manis and Meltzer (1978).

6. Similar elements characterize the realms of intergroup, societal, and intersocietal relations. It must be borne in mind that even the effects of what are termed "vast impersonal forces" are mediated, and to some extent shaped, by processes of individual and collective interpretation.

7. The works of, for example, Erving Goffman—too numerous and well known to require listing here—demonstrate the value of a broadened conception of social science.

Chapter 17 BASEBALL MAGIC

George J. Gmelch

> We find magic wherever the elements of chance and accident, and the emotional play between hope and fear, have a wide and extensive range. We do not find magic wherever the pursuit is certain, reliable, and well under the control of rational methods (Bronislaw Malinowski).

Professional baseball is a nearly perfect arena in which to test Malinowski's hypothesis about magic. The great anthropologist was not, of course, talking about sleight of hand but of rituals, taboos and fetishes that men resort to when they want to ensure that things go their own way. Baseball is rife with this sort of magic, but, as we shall see, the players use it in some aspects of the game far more than in others.

Everyone knows that there are three essentials of baseball—hitting, pitching and fielding. The point is, however, that the first two, hitting and pitching, involve a high degree of chance. The pitcher is the player least able to control the outcome of his own efforts. His best pitch may be hit directly to one of his fielders for an out. He may limit the opposition to a single hit and lose, or he may give up a dozen hits and win. It is not uncommon for pitchers to perform well and lose, and vice versa; one has only to look at the frequency with which pitchers end a season with poor won-lost percentages but low earned run averages (number of runs give up per game). The opposite is equally true: some pitchers play poorly, giving up many runs, yet win many games. In brief, the pitcher, regardless of how well he performs, is dependent upon the proficiency of his teammates, the inefficiency of the opposition and the supernatural (luck).

But luck, as we all know, comes in two forms, and many fans assume that the pitcher's tough losses (close games in which he gave up very few runs) are eventually balanced out by his "lucky" wins. This is untrue, as a comparison of pitchers' lifetime earned run averages to their overall won-lost record shows. If the player could apply a law of averages to individual performances, there would be much less concern about chance and uncertainty in baseball. Unfortunately, he cannot and does not.

Hitting, too, is a chancy affair. Obviously, skill is required in hitting the ball hard and on a line. Once the ball is hit, however, chance plays a large role in determining where it will go, into a waiting glove or whistling past a falling stab.

With respect to fielding, the player has almost complete control over the outcome. The average fielding percentage or success rate of .975, compared to a .245 success rate for hitters (the average batting average), reflects the degree of certainty in fielding. Next to the pitcher or hitter, the fielder has little to worry about when he knows that better than 9.7 times in ten he will execute his task flawlessly.

If Malinowski's hypothesis is correct, we should find magic associated with hitting and pitching, but none with fielding. Let us take the evidence by category—ritual, taboo and fetish.

Ritual

After each pitch, ex-major leaguer Lou Skeins used to reach into his back pocket to touch a crucifix, straighten his cap and clutch his genitals. Detroit Tiger infielder Tim Maring wore the same clothes and put them on exactly in the same order each day during a batting streak. Baseball rituals are almost infinitely various. After all, the ballplayer can ritualize any activity he considers necessary for a successful performance, from the type of cereal he eats in the morning to the streets he drives home on.

Usually, rituals grow out of exceptionally good performances. When the player does well he cannot really attribute his success to skill alone. He plays with the same amount of skill one night when he gets four hits as the next night when he goes hitless. Through magic, such as ritual, the player seeks greater control over his performance, actually control over the elements of chance. The player, knowing that his ability is fairly constant, attributes the inconsistencies in his performance to some form of behavior or a particular food that he ate. When a player gets four hits in a game, especially "cheap" hits, he often believes that there must have been something he did, in addition to his ability, that shifted luck to his side. If he can attribute his good fortune to the glass of iced tea he drank before the game or the new shirt he wore to the ballpark, then by repeating the same behavior the following day he can hope to achieve similar results. (One expression of this belief is the myth that eating certain foods will give the ball "eyes," that is, a ball that seeks the gaps between fielders.) In hopes of maintaining a batting streak, I once ate fried children every day at 4:00 p.m., kept my eyes closed during the national anthem and changed sweat shirts at the end of the fourth inning each night for seven consecutive nights until the streak ended.

Fred Caviglia, Kansas City minor league pitcher, explained why he eats certain foods before each game: "Everything you do is important to winning. I never forget what I eat the day of a game or what I wear. If I pitch well and win I'll do it all exactly the same the next day I pitch. You'd be crazy not to. You just can't ever tell what's going to make the difference between winning and losing."

Rituals associated with hitting vary considerably in complexity from one player to the next, but they have several components in common. One of the most popular is tagging a particular base when leaving and returning to the dugout each inning. Tagging a second base on the way to the outfield is habitual with some players. One informant reported that during a successful month of the season he stepped on third base on his way to the dugout after the third, six and ninth innings of each game. Asked if he ever purposely failed to step on the bag he replied, "Never! I wouldn't dare, it would destroy my confidence to hit." It is not uncommon for a hitter who is playing poorly to try different combinations of tagging and not tagging particular bases in an attempt to find a successful combination. Other components of a hitter's ritual may include tapping the plate with his bat a precise number of times or taking a precise number of warm-up swings with the leaded bat.

One informant described a variation of this in which he gambled for a certain hit by tapping the plate a fixed number of times. He touched the plate once with his bat for each base desired: one tap for a single, two for a double and so on. He even built in odds that prevented him from asking for a home run each time. The odds of hitting a single with one tap were one in three, while the chances of hitting a home run with four taps were one in 12.

Clothing is often considered crucial to both hitters and pitchers. They may have several athletic supporters and a number of sweat shirts with ritual significance. Nearly all players wear the same uniform and undergarments each day when playing well, and some even wear the same street clothes. In 1954, the New York Giants, during a 16-game winning streak, wore the same clothes in each game and refused to let them be cleaned for fear that their good fortune might be washed away with the dirt. The route taken to and from the stadium can also have a significance; some players drive the same streets to the ballpark during a hitting streak and try different routes during slumps.

Because pitchers only play once every four days, the rituals they practice are often more complex than the hitters', and most of it, such as tugging the cap between pitches, touching the rosin bag after each bad pitch or smoothing the dirt on the mound before each new batter, takes place on the field. Many baseball fans have observed this behavior never realizing that it may be as important to the pitcher as throwing the ball.

Dennis Grossini, former Detroit farmhand, practiced the following ritual on each pitching day for the first three months of a winning season. First, he arose from bed at exactly 10:00 a.m. and not a minute earlier or late. At 1:00 p.m. he went to the nearest restaurant for two glasses of iced tea and a tuna fish sandwich. Although the afternoon was free, he observed a number of taboos such as no movies, no reading, and no candy. In the clubhouse he changed into the sweat shirt and jock he wore during his last winning game, and one hour before the game he chewed a wad of Beechnut chewing tobacco. During the game he touched his letters (the team name on his uniform) after each pitch and straightened his cap after each ball. Before the start of each inning he replaced the pitcher's rosin bag next to the spot where it was the inning before. And after each inning in which he gave up a run he went to the clubhouse to wash his hands. I asked him which part of the ritual was most important. He responded: "You can't really tell what's most important so it all becomes important. I'd be afraid to change anything. As long as I'm winning I do everything the same. Even when I can't wash my hands (this would occur when he must bat) it scares me going back to the mound....I don't feel quite right."

One ritual, unlike those already mentioned, is practiced to improve the power of the baseball bat. It involves sanding the bat until all the varnish is removed, a process requiring several hours of labor, then rubbing rosin into the grain of the bat before finally heating is over a flame. This ritual treatment supposedly increases the distance the ball travels after being struck. Although some North Americans prepare their bats in this fashion, it is more popular among Latin Americans. One informant admitted that he was not certain of the effectiveness of the treatment. But, he added, "There may not be a God, but I go to church just the same."

Despite the wide assortment of rituals associated with pitching and hitting, I never observed any ritual related to fielding. In all my 20 interviews only one player, a shortstop with acute fielding problems, reported any ritual even remotely connected to fielding.

Taboo

Mentioning that a no-hitter is in progress and crossing baseball bats are the two most widely observed taboos. It is believed that if the pitcher hears the words "no-hitter" his spell will be broken and the no-hitter lost. As for the crossing of bats, that is sure to bring bad luck; batters are therefore extremely careful not to drop their bats on top of another. Some players elaborate this taboo even further. On one occasion a teammate became quite upset when another player tossed a bat from the batting cage and it came to rest on top of his. Later he explained that the top bat would steal hits from the lower one. For him, then, bats contain a finite number of hits, a kind of baseball "image of limited good." Honus Wagner, a member of baseball's Hall of Fame, believed that each bat was good for only 100 hits and no more. Regardless of the quality of the bat he would discard it after its 100th hit.

Besides observing the traditional taboos just mentioned, players also observe certain personal prohibitions. Personal taboos grow out of exceptionally poor performances, which a player often attributes to some particular behavior or food. During my first season of professional baseball, I once ate pancakes before a game in which I struck out four times. Several weeks later I had a repeat performance, again after eating pancakes. The result was a pancake taboo in which from that day on I never ate pancakes during the season. Another personal taboo, born out of similar circumstances, was against holding a baseball during the national anthem.

Taboos are also of many kinds. One athlete was careful never to step on the chalk foul lines or the chalk lines of the batter's box. Another player would never put on his cap until the game started and would not wear it at all on the days he did not pitch. Another had a movie taboo in which he refused to watch a movie the day of the game. Often certain uniform numbers become taboo. If a player has a poor spring training or a bad year, he may refuse to wear the same uniform number again. I would not wear double numbers, especially 44 and 22. On several occasions, teammates who were playing poorly requested a change in uniform during the middle of the season. Some players consider it so important that they will wear the wrong size uniform just to avoid a certain number or to obtain a good number.

Again, with respect to fielding, I never saw or heard of any taboos being observed, though of course there were some taboos, like the uniform numbers, that were concerned with overall performance and so included fielding.

Fetishes

These are standard equipment for many baseball players. They include a wide assortment of objects: horsehide covers of old baseballs, coins, bobby pins, protective cups, crucifixes and old bats. Ordinary objects are given this power in a fashion similar to the formation of taboos and rituals. The player during an exceptionally hot batting or pitching streak, especially one in which he has "gotten all the breaks," credits some unusual object, often a new possession, for his good fortune. For example, a player in a slump might find a new object, it becomes a fetish, embodied with supernatural power. While playing for Spokane, Dodger pitcher Alan Foster forgot his baseball shoes on a road trip and borrowed a pair from a teammate to pitch. That night he pitched a no-hitter and later, needless to say, bought the shoes from his teammate. They became his most prized possession.

Fetishes are taken so seriously by some players that their teammates will not touch them out of fear of offending the owner. I once saw a fight caused by the desecration of a fetish. Before the game, one player stole the fetish, a horsehide baseball cover, out of a teammate's back pocket. The prankster did not return the fetish until after the game, in which the owner of the fetish went hitless, breaking a batting streak. The owner, blaming his inability to hit on the loss of the fetish, lashed out at the time when the latter tried to return it.

Rube Waddel, an old-time Philadelphia Athletic pitching great, had a hairpin fetish. However, the hairpin he possessed was only powerful as long as he won. Once he lost a game he would look for another hairpin, which had to be found on the street, and he would not pitch until he found another.

The use of fetishes follows the same pattern as ritual and taboo in that they are connected only with hitting or pitching. In nearly all cases the player expressed a specific purpose for carrying a fetish, but never did a player perceive his fetish as having any effect on his fielding.

I have said enough, I think, to show that many of the beliefs and practices of professional baseball players are magical. Any empirical connection between the ritual, taboo and fetishes and the desired event is quite absent. Indeed, in several instances the relationship between the cause and effect, such as eating tuna fish sandwiches to win a ball game, is even more remote than is characteristic of primitive magic. Note, however, that unlike many forms of primitive magic, baseball magic is usually performed to achieve one's own end and not to block someone else's. Hitters do not tap their bats on the plate to hex the pitcher, but to improve their own performance.

Finally, it should be plain that nearly all the magical practices that I participated in, observed or elicited, support Malinowski's hypothesis that magic appears in situations of chance and uncertainty. The large amount of uncertainty in pitching and hitting best explains the elaborate magical practices used for these activities. Conversely, the high success rate in fielding, .975, involving much less uncertainty, offers the best explanation for the absence of magic in this realm.

PART V
THE SELF

The self is a central concept within symbolic interactionism. As Rock (1979:102) argues, the self "constitutes the very hub of the interactionists' intellectual schema. All other sociological processes and events revolve around that hub, taking from it their analytic meaning and organization."

The self is not present at birth; it emerges in the social process and is subject to change and modification throughout the individual's life course. According to interactionists, individuals go through three stages in the development of self: the preparatory stage, the play stage, and the game stage. In the preparatory stage, the child mimics or imitates the actions of others without comprehending the meaning behind such behavior. In the play stage, the child begins to take the role of particular or specific others, such as mother, fireman, cowboy, or doctor. During the last stage, the game stage, the individual simultaneously takes both the role of specific others and the role of what Mead termed the "generalized other". To illustrate this idea, Mead used the game of baseball. In the play stage, the child is able to take the role, one at a time, of the catcher, pitcher, manager, umpire, fan, etc. However, taking the role of each specific other, alternately, does not give the child a coherent picture of the overall game. In the game stage however, the individual acquires such a overall perspective; he or she is aware of all of the rules of the game, all of the roles, what is expected of each person in the role; what all others expect from the person in the role. In order to have a fully developed self, the individual must go through all three stages consecutively.

While the self is best conceived as a social process within the individual, it involves two basic phases: the "I" and the "me." The former refers to the impulsive, spontaneous, elusive aspect of self. The "I" is rooted in biology. The "me" refers to the internalization of the values, common meanings, expectations, and organized attitudes of the community, of the generalized other. The "me" represents the forces of conformity and social control. The self is the product of the dialectical relationship between the "I" and the "me." The "I" is the response of the individual to her or his "me" side of self. Such a response leads to social change or novelty in society.

The distinguishing aspect of the self is its ability to be an object unto itself. One is able to stand outside oneself and view oneself as object, by taking the role of others toward oneself. One can experience himself/herself as an object unto himself/herself "only insofar as he first becomes an object to himself just as other individuals are objects to him or in his experience, and he becomes an object to himself only by taking the attitudes of other individuals toward himself within a social environment (Mead, 1964:211). This reflexive ability of humans is made possible through the use of language, a set of significant symbols. A person comes to acquire a self, then, and becomes conscious of this self through the application of meanings and linguistic entities which are socially derived. In short, the self is a linguistic construct.

The first selection, by Charles Horton Cooley, discusses the self-reflexive process in which individuals engage— specifically, the human capacity to see ourselves as we see any other social object. Cooley used the metaphor of a "looking-glass" to depict the nature and sources of the images of self people see reflected in others. Individuals then, develop self-conceptions through familiarity with the attitudes of others. The idea of a looking-glass self can be divided into three components: (1) we imagine how others view us; (2) we imagine what their judgement of our appearance is; (3) we develop some sort of self-feeling such as, shame or pride, as a consequence. Cooley's concept of the looking-glass self was instrumental in the development of modern interactionist conceptualizations.

The second article, by Erving Goffman on *The Presentation of Self* is another important interactionist work. Goffman's conception of self was shaped by his dramaturgical approach. Social life is conceived as a series of performances between actors, similar to those performed on stage. The self, according to this author, is the product of dramatic interaction between actor and audience. Individuals desire to present a certain image of self that will be accepted by others in the audience. The actors hope that by projecting a desired image they will elicit certain positive responses from the audience. Goffman refers to impression management as the technique used to manage certain impressions and maintain positive self-images and self conceptions.

The next three articles in this section deal with the various stratagems individuals use to manage information about themselves, and to negotiate identities and preferred definitions of self. Miall and Herman, dealing with two groups who possess "stigmatizable/stigmatized identities" (involuntarily childless women and deinstitutionalized, non-chronic psychiatric patients), focus on the various information management strategies they employ. The authors also address the generic process of impression management for non-stigmatized actors involved in non-problematic social encounters.

The next article by Thumma examines the social processes by which individuals construct and solidify a gay evangelical identity. The process of negotiating a gay evangelical identity encompasses change promoting group dynamics. *Good News* is an organization that presents individuals with a model into which members are socialized— a model which maintains dual core identities: their sexual and religious identities.

In their ethnographic research on homeless street people, David Snow and Leon Anderson deal with individuals who possess a "discrediting identity," or "stigmatizing identity," and the type of identity work such persons engage in order to negotiate for and create personal identities. One variety of identity work, "identity talk—the verbal construction and assertion of personal identities" is examined with respect to the homeless. The authors indicate that three types of "identity talk" are utilized by the homeless: (1) distancing, (2) embracement, and (3) fictive storytelling. The implications of such work for elevated self images and self-worth are addressed.

REFERENCES

Rock, Paul. 1979. *The Making of Symbolic Interactionism*. Totowa, N.J.: Rowman and Littlefield.

SUGGESTED READINGS

Bain, Read. 1936. "The Self-and-Other Words of a Child." *American Journal of Sociology* 41 (May): 767–775. Explores the relationship of society and self through the medium of language.

Couch, Carl J. 1962. "Family Role Specialization and Self-Attitudes in Children." *Sociological Quarterly* 3 (April): 115–121. Uses the Twenty Statements Test to explore the relationship between family roles and individual self-image.

Denzin, Norman K. 1972. "The Genesis of Self in Early Childhood." *Sociological Quarterly*, 13 (Winter): 291–314. Empirical data on development of the self.

Hewitt, John P. 1989. *Dilemmas of the American Self*. Philadelphia: Temple. A leading interactionist discusses the social context impacting on "the self" in contemporary society.

Kinch, John W. 1963. "A Formalized Theory of the Self-Concept." *American Sociological Review* 84 (January): 481–486. From the basic postulates of self-theory, the author deduces their logical consequences.

Mead, George Herbert. 1934. *Mind, Self and Society*. Chicago: The University of Chicago Press, pp. 144–178. Mead's exposition on the structure, scope, and purpose of social life and human nature.

Turner, Ralph. 1976. "The Real Self: From Institution to Impulse." *American Journal of Sociology* 81: 989–1016. Spells out the nature of the self as seen by one of interactionism's key spokespersons.

Unruh, David. 1983. "Death and Personal History: Strategies of Identity Preservation." *Social Problems* 30 no. 3: 341–351. A social worlds perspective dealing with the various ways the elderly attempt to maintain their identities.

Watson, C.M. 1982. "The Presentation of Self and the new Institutional Inmate: An Assessment of Prisoners Responses to Assessment for Release." *Symbolic Interaction* 5(2): 243–257. An interactionist analysis of the ways in which inmates manage impressions and engage in negotiations for preferred definitions of self.

Chapter 18 THE LOOKING-GLASS SELF

Charles Horton Cooley

In a very large and interesting class of cases the social reference takes the form of a somewhat definite imagination of how one's self, that is any idea he appropriates, appears in a particular mind, and the kind of self-feeling one has is determined by the attitude toward this attributed to that other mind. A social self of this sort might be called the reflected or looking-glass self:

> "Each to each a looking-glass
> Reflects the other that doth pass."

As we see our face, figure, and dress in the glass, and are interested in them because they are ours, and pleased or otherwise with them according as they do or do not answer to what we should like them to be; so in imagination we perceive in another's mind some thought of our appearance, manners, aims, deeds, character, friends, and so on, and are variously affected by it.

A self-idea of this sort seems to have three principal elements: the imagination of our appearance to the other person; the imagination of his judgment of that appearance, and some sort of self-feeling, such as pride or mortification. The comparison with a looking-glass hardly suggests the second element, the imagined judgment, which is quite essential. The thing that moves us to pride or shame is not the mere mechanical reflection of ourselves, but an imputed sentiment, the imagined effect of this reflection upon another's mind. This is evident from the fact that the character and weight of that other, in whose mind we see ourselves, makes all the difference with our feeling. We are ashamed to seem evasive in the presence of a straightforward man, cowardly in the presence of a brave one, gross in the eyes of a refined one, and so on. We always imagine, and in imagining share, the judgments of the other mind. A man will boast to one person of an action, say some sharp transaction in trade, which he would be ashamed to own to another.

The process by which self-feeling of the looking-glass sort develops in children may be followed without much difficulty. Studying the movements of others as closely as they do they soon see a connection between their own acts and changes in those movements; that is, they perceive their own influence or power over persons. The child appropriates the visible actions of his parent or nurse, over which he finds he has some control, in quite the same way as he appropriates one of his own members or a plaything, and he will try to do things with this new possession, just as he will with his hand or his rattle. A girl six months old will attempt in the most evident and deliberate manner to attract attention to herself, to set going by her actions some of those movements of other persons that she has appropriated. She has tasted the joy of being a cause, of exerting social power, and wishes more of it. She will tug at her mother's skirts, wriggle, gurgle, stretch out her arms, etc., all the time watching for the hoped-for effect. These performances often give the child, even at this age, an appearance of what is called affectation, that is, she seems to be unduly preoccupied with what other people think of her. Affectation, at any age, exists when the passion to influence others seems to overbalance the established character and give it an obvious twist or pose. It is instructive to find that even Darwin was, in his childhood, capable of departing from truth for the sake of making an impression. "For instance," he says in his autobiography, "I once gathered much valuable fruit from my father's trees and hid it in the shrubbery, and then ran in breathless haste to spread the news that I had discovered a hoard of stolen fruit."[1]

The young performer soon learns to be different things to different people, showing that he begins to apprehend personality and to foresee its operation. If the mother or nurse is more tender than just, she will almost certainly be "worked" by systematic weeping. It is a matter of common observation that children often behave worse with their mother than with other and less sympathetic people. Of the new persons that a child sees it is evident that some make a strong impression and awaken a desire to interest and please them, while others are indifferent or repugnant. Sometimes the reason can be perceived or guessed, sometimes not; but the fact of selective interest, admiration, prestige, is obvious before the end of the second year. By that time a child already cares much for the reflection of himself upon one personality and little for that upon another. Moreover, he soon claims intimate and tractable persons as mine, classes them among his other possessions, and maintains his ownership against all comers. M., at three years of age, vigorously resented R.'s claim upon their mother. The latter was "my mamma," whenever the point was raised.

Strong joy and grief depend upon the treatment this rudimentary social self receives. In the case of M., I noticed as early as the fourth month a "hurt" way of crying which seemed to indicate a sense of personal slight. It was quite different from the cry of pain or that of anger, but seemed about the same as the cry of fright. The slightest tone of reproof would produce it. On the other hand, if people took notice and laughed and encouraged, she was hilarious. At about fifteen months old she had become "a perfect little actress," seeming to live largely in imaginations of her effect upon other people. She constantly and obviously laid traps for attention, and looked abashed or wept at any signs of disapproval or indifference. At times it would seem as if she could not get over these repulses, but would cry long in a grieved way, refusing to be comforted. If she hit upon any little trick that made people laugh she would be sure to repeat it, laughing loudly and affectedly in imitation. She had quite a repertory of these small performances, which she would display to a sympathetic audience, or even try upon strangers. I have seen her at sixteen months, when R. refused to give her the scissors, sit down and make-believe cry, putting up her under lip and snuffling, meanwhile looking up now and then to see what effect she was producing.[2]

In such phenomena we have plainly enough, it seems to me, the germ of personal ambition of every sort. Imagination co-operating with instinctive self-feeling has already created a social "I," and this has become a principal object of interest and endeavor.

Progress from this point is chiefly in the way of a greater definiteness, fullness, and inwardness in the imagination of the other's state of mind. A little child thinks of and tries to elicit certain visible or audible phenomena, and does not go back of them; but what a grown-up person desires to produce in others is an internal, invisible condition which his own richer experience enables him to imagine, and of which expression is only the sign. Even adults, however, make no separation between what other people think and the visible expression of that thought. They imagine the whole thing at once, and their idea differs from that of a child chiefly in the comparative richness and complexity of the elements that accompany and interpret the visible or audible sign. There is also a progress from the naive to the subtle in socially self-assertive action. A child obviously and simply, at first, does things for effect. Later there is an endeavor to suppress the appearance of doing so; affection, indifference, contempt, etc., are simulated to hide the real wish to affect the self-image. It is perceived that an obvious seeking after good opinion is weak and disagreeable.

NOTES

1. Life and Letters of Charles Darwin, by F. Darwin, p. 27.
2. This sort of thing is very familiar to observers of children. See, for instance, Miss Shinn's Notes on the Development of Child, p. 153.

Chapter 19 THE PRESENTATION OF SELF IN EVERYDAY LIFE

Erving Goffman

When an individual enters the presence of others they commonly seek to acquire information about him or to bring into play information about him already possessed. They will be interested in his general socio-economic status, his conception of self, his attitude toward them, his competence, his trustworthiness, etc. Although some of this information seems to be sought almost as an end in itself, there are usually quite practical reasons for acquiring it. Information about the individual helps to define the situation, enabling others to know in advance what he will expect of them and what they may expect of him. Informed in these ways, the others will know how best to act in order to call forth a desired response from him.

For those present, many sources of information become accessible and many carriers (or "sign-vehicles") become available for conveying this information. If unacquainted with the individual, observers can glean clues from his conduct and appearance which allow them to apply their previous experience with individuals roughly similar to the one before them or, more important, to apply untested stereotypes to him. They can also assume from past experience that only individuals of a particular kind are likely to be found in a given social setting. They can rely on what the individual says about himself or on documentary evidence he provides as to who and what he is. If they know, or know of, the individual by virtue of experience prior to the interaction, they can rely on assumptions as to the persistence and generality of psychological traits as a means of predicting his present and future behavior.

However, during the period in which the individual is in the immediate presence of the others, few events may occur which directly provide the others with the conclusive information they will need if they are to direct wisely their own activity. Many crucial facts lie beyond the time and place of interaction or lie concealed within it. For example, the "true" or "real" attitudes, beliefs, and emotions of the individual can be ascertained only indirectly, through his avowals or through what appears to be involuntary expressive behavior. Similarly, if the individual offers the others a product or service, they will often find that during the interaction there will be no time and place immediately available for eating the pudding that the proof can be found in. They will be forced to accept some events as conventional or natural signs of something not directly available to the senses. In Ichheiser's terms,[1] the individual will have to act so that he intentionally or unintentionally expresses himself, and the others will in turn have to be impressed in some way by him.

The expressiveness of the individual (and therefore his capacity to give impressions) appears to involve two radically different kinds of sign activity: the expression that he gives, and the expression that he gives off. The first involves verbal symbols or their substitutes which he uses admittedly and solely to convey the information that he and the others are known to attach to these symbols. This is communication in the traditional and narrow sense. The second involves a wide range of action that others can treat as symptomatic of the actor, the expectation being that the action was performed for reasons other than the information conveyed in this way. As we shall have to see, this distinction has an only initial validity. The individual does of course intentionally convey misinformation by means of both of these types of communication, the first involving deceit, the second feigning.

Taking communication in both its narrow and broad sense, one finds that when the individual is in the immediate presence of others, his activity will have a promissory character. The others are likely to find that they must accept the individual on faith, offering him a just return while he is present before them in exchange for something whose true value will not be established until after he has left their presence. (Of course, the others also live by inference in their dealings with the physical world, but it is only in the world of social interaction that the objects about which they make inferences will purposely facilitate and hinder this inferential process.) The security that they justifiably feel in making inferences about the individual will vary, of course, depending on such factors as the amount of information they already possess about him, but no amount of such past evidence can entirely obviate the necessity of acting on the basis of inferences. As William I. Thomas suggested:

> It is also highly important for us to realize that we do not as a matter of fact lead our lives, make our decisions, and reach our goals in everyday life either statistically or scientifically. We live by inference. I am, let us say, your guest. You do not know, you cannot determine scientifically, that I will not steal your money or your spoons. But inferentially I will not, and inferentially you have me as a guest.[2]

Let us now turn from the others to the point of view of the individual who presents himself before them. He may wish them to think highly of him, or to think that he thinks highly of them, or to perceive how in fact he feels toward them, or to obtain no clear-cut impression; he may wish to ensure sufficient harmony so that the interaction can be sustained, or to defraud, get rid of, confuse, mislead, antagonize, or insult them. Regardless of the particular objective which the individual has in mind and of his motive for having this objective, it will be in his interests to control the conduct of the others, especially their responsive treatment of him.[3] This control is achieved largely by influencing the definition of the situation which the others come to formulate, and he can influence this definition by expressing himself in such a way as to give them the kind of impression that will lead them to act voluntarily in accordance with his own plan. Thus, when an individual appears in the presence of others, there will usually be some reason for him to mobilize his activity so that it will convey an impression to others which it is in his interests to convey. Since a girl's dormitory mates will glean evidence of her popularity from the calls she receives on the phone, we can suspect that some girls will arrange for calls to be made, and Willard Waller's finding can be anticipated:

It has been reported by many observers that a girl who is called to the telephone in the dormitories will often allow herself to be called several times, in order to give all the other girls ample opportunity to hear her paged.[4]

Of the two kinds of communication, expressions given and expressions given off, this report will be primarily concerned with the latter, with the more theatrical and contextual kind, the nonverbal, presumably unintentional kind, whether this communication be purposely engineered or not. As an example of what we must try to examine, I would like to cite at length a novelistic incident in which Preedy, a vacationing Englishman, makes his first appearance on the beach of his summer hotel in Spain:

> But in any case he took care to avoid catching anyone's eye. First of all, he had to make it clear to those potential companions of his holiday that they were of no concern to him whatsoever. He stared through them, round them, over them eyes lost in space. The beach might have been empty. If by chance a ball was thrown his way, he looked surprised; then let a smile of amusement lighten his face (Kindly Preedy), looked around dazed to see that there were people on the beach, tossed it back with a smile to himself and not a smile at the people, and then resumed carelessly his nonchalant survey of space.
>
> But it was time to institute a little parade, the parade of the Ideal Preedy. By devious handlings he gave any who wanted to look a chance to see the title of his book, a Spanish translation of Homer, classic thus, but not daring, cosmopolitan too, and then gathered together his beachwrap and bag into a neat sand-resistant pile (Methodical and Sensible Preedy), rose slowly to stretch at ease his huge frame (Big-Cat Preedy), and tossed aside his sandals (Carefree Preedy, after all).
>
> The marriage of Preedy and the sea! There were alternate rituals. The first involved the stroll that turns into a run and a dive straight into the water, thereafter smoothing into a strong splashless crawl towards the horizon. But of course not really to the horizon. Quite suddenly he would turn on to his back and thrash great white splashes with his legs, somehow thus showing that he could have swum further had he wanted to, and then would stand up a quarter out of water for all to see who it was.
>
> The alternative course was simpler, it avoided the cold-water shock and it avoided the risk of appearing too high-spirited. The point was to appear to be so used to the sea, the Mediterranean, and this particular beach, that one might as well be in the sea as out of it. It involved a slow stroll down and into the edge of the water not even noticing his toes were wet, land and water all the same to him! with his eyes up at the sky gravely surveying portents, invisible to others, of the weather (Local Fisherman Preedy).[5]

The novelist means us to see that Preedy is improperly concerned with the extensive impressions he feels his sheer bodily action is giving off to those around him. We can malign Preedy further by assuming that he has acted merely in order to give a particular impression, that this is a false impression, and that the others present receive either no impression at all, or worse still, the impression that Preedy is affectedly trying to cause them to receive this particular impression. But the important point for us here is that the kind of impression Preedy thinks he is making is in fact the kind of impression that others correctly and incorrectly glean from someone in their midst.

I have said that when an individual appears before others his actions will influence the definition of the situation which they come to have. Sometimes the individual will act in a thoroughly calculating manner, expressing himself in a given way solely in order to give the kind of impression to others that is likely to evoke from them a specific response he is concerned to obtain. Sometimes the individual will be calculating in his activity but be relatively unaware that this is the case. Sometimes he will intentionally and consciously express himself in a particular way, but chiefly because the tradition of his group or social status require this kind of expression and not because of any particular response (other than vague acceptance or approval) that is likely to be evoked from those impressed by the expression. Sometimes the traditions of an individual's role will lead him to give a well-designed impression of a particular kind and yet he may be neither consciously nor unconsciously disposed to create such an impression. The others, in their turn, may be suitably impressed by the individual's efforts to convey something, or may misunderstand the situation and come to conclusions that are warranted neither by the individual's intent nor by the facts. In any case, insofar as the others act as if the individual had conveyed a particular impression, we may take a functional or pragmatic view and say that the individual has "effectively" projected a given definition of the situation and "effectively" fostered the understanding that a given state of affairs obtains.

There is one aspect of the others' response that bears special comment here. Knowing that the individual is likely to present himself in a light that is favorable to him, the others may divide what they witness into two parts: a part that is relatively easy for the individual to manipulate at will, being chiefly his verbal assertions, and a part in regard to which he seems to have little concern or control, being chiefly derived from the expressions he gives off. The others may then use what are considered to be the ungovernable aspects of his expressive behavior as a check upon the validity of what is conveyed by the governable aspects. In this a fundamental asymmetry is demonstrated in the communication process, the individual presumably being aware of only one stream of his communication, the witnesses of this stream and one other. For example, in Shetland Isle one crofter's [or farmer's] wife, in serving native dishes to a visitor from the mainland of Britain, would listen with a polite smile to his polite claims of liking what he was eating; at the same time she would take note of the rapidity with which the visitor lifted his fork or spoon to his mouth, the eagerness with which he passed food into his mouth, and the gusto expressed in chewing the food, using these signs as a check on the stated feelings of the eater. The same woman, in order to discover what one acquaintance (A) "actually" thought of another acquaintance (B), would wait until B was in the presence of A but engaged in conversation with still another person (C). She would then covertly examine the facial expressions of A as he regarded B in conversation with C. Not being in conversation with B, and not being directly observed by him, A would sometimes relax usual constraints and tactful deceptions, and freely express what he was "actually" feeling about B. This Shetlander, in short, would observe the unobserved behavior.

Now given the fact that others are likely to check up on the more controllable aspects of behavior by means of the less controllable, one can expect that sometimes the individual will try to exploit this very possibility, guiding the impression he makes through behavior felt to be reliably informing.[6] For example, in gaining admission to a tight social circle, the participant observer may not only wear an accepting look while listening to an informant, but may also be careful to wear the same look when observing the informant talking to others; observers of the observer will then not as easily discover where he actually stands. A specific illustration may be cited from Shetland Isle. When a neighbor dropped in to have a cup of tea, he would ordinarily wear at least a hint of an expectant warm smile as he passed through the door into the cottage. Since lack of physical obstructions outside the cottage and lack of light within it usually made it possible to observe the visitor unobserved as he approached the house, islanders sometimes took pleasure in watching the visitor drop whatever expression he was manifesting and replace it with a sociable one just before reaching the door. However, some visitors, in appreciating that this examination was occurring, would blindly adopt a social face a long distance from the house, thus ensuring the projection of a constant image.

This kind of control upon the part of the individual reinstates the symmetry of the communication process, and sets the stage for a kind of information game a potentially infinite cycle of concealment, discovery, false revelation, and rediscovery. It should be added that since the others are likely to be relatively unsuspicious of the presumably unguided aspect of the individual's conduct, he can gain much by controlling it. The others of course may sense that the individual is manipulating the presumably spontaneous aspects of his behavior, and seek in this very act of manipulation some shading of conduct that the individual has not managed to control. This again provides a check upon the individual's behavior, this time his presumably uncalculated behavior, thus re-establishing the asymmetry of the communication process. Here I would like only to add the suggestion that the arts of piercing an individual's effort at calculated unintentionality seem better developed than our capacity to manipulate our own behavior, so that regardless of how many steps have occurred in the information game, the witness is likely to have the advantage over the actor, and the initial asymmetry of the communication process is likely to be retained.

When we allow that the individual projects a definition of the situation when he appears before others, we must also see that the others, however passive their role may seem to be, will themselves effectively project a definition of the situation by virtue of their response to the individual and by virtue of any lines of action they initiate to him. Ordinarily the definitions of the situation projected by the several different participants are sufficiently attuned to one another so that open contradiction will not occur. I do not mean that there will be the kind of consensus that arises when each individual present candidly expresses what he really feels and honestly agrees with the expressed feeling of the others present. This kind of harmony is an optimistic ideal and in any case not necessary for the smooth working of society. Rather, each participant is expected to suppress his immediate heartfelt feelings, conveying a view of the situation which he feels the others will be able to find at least temporarily acceptable. The maintenance of this surface of agreement, this veneer of consensus, is facilitated by each participant concealing [his] wants behind statements while asserting values to which everyone present feels obliged to give lip service. Further, there is usually a kind of division of definitional labor. Each participant is allowed to establish the tentative official ruling regarding matters which are vital to him but not immediately important to others, e.g., the rationalizations and justifications by which he accounts for his past activity. In exchange for this courtesy he remains silent or non-committal on matters important to others but not immediately important to him. We have then a kind of interactional modus vivendi. Together, the participants contribute to a single over-all definition of the situation which involves not so much a real argument as to what exists but rather a real agreement as to whose claims concerning what issues will be temporarily honored. Real agreement will also exist concerning the desirability of avoiding an open conflict of definitions of the situation.[7] I will refer to this level of agreement as a "working consensus." It is to be understood that the working consensus established in one interaction setting will be quite different in content from the working consensus established in a different type of setting. Thus, between two friends at lunch, a reciprocal show of affection, respect, and concern for the other is maintained. In service occupations, on the other hand, the specialist often maintains an image of disinterested involvement in the problem of the client, while the client responds with a show of respect for the competence and integrity of the specialist. Regardless of such differences in content, however, the general form of these working arrangements is the same.

In noting the tendency for a participant to accept the definitional claims made by the others present, we can appreciate the crucial importance of the information that the individual initially possesses or acquires concerning his fellow participants, for it is on the basis of this initial information that the individual starts to define the situation and starts to build up lines of responsive action. The individual's initial projection commits him to what he is proposing to be and requires him to drop all pretenses of being other things. As the interaction among the participants progresses, additions and modifications in this initial informational state will of course occur, but it is essential that these later developments be related without contradiction to, and even built up from, the initial positions taken by the several participants. It would seem that an individual can more easily make a choice as to what line of treatment to demand from and extend to the others present at the beginning of an encounter than he can alter the line of treatment that is being pursued once the interaction is underway.

In everyday life, of course, there is a clear understanding that first impressions are important. Thus, the work adjustment of those in service occupations will often hinge upon a capacity to seize and hold the initiative in the service relations, a capacity that will require subtle aggressiveness on the part of the server when he is of lower socioeconomic status than his client. W. F. Whyte suggests the waitress as an example:

The first point that stands out is that the waitress who bears up under pressure does not simply respond to her customers. She acts with some skill to control her behavior. The first question to ask when we look at the customer relationship is, "Does the waitress get the jump on the customer, or does the customer get the jump on the waitress?" The skilled waitress realizes the crucial nature of this question....

The skilled waitress tackles the customer with confidence and without hesitation. For example, she may find that a new customer has seated himself before she could clear off the dirty dishes and change the cloth. He is now leaning on the table studying the menu. She greets him, says, "May I change the cover, please?" and, without waiting for an answer, takes his menu away from him so that he moves back from the table, and she goes about her work. The relationship is handled politely but firmly, and there is never any question as to who is in charge.[8]

When the interaction that is initiated by "first impressions" is itself merely the initial interaction in an extended series of interactions involving the same participants, we speak of "getting off on the right foot" and feel that it is crucial that we do so. Thus, one learns that some teachers take the following view:

You can't ever let them get the upper hand on you or you're through. So I start out tough. The first day I get a new class in, I let them know who's boss.... You've got to start off tough, then you can ease up as you go along. If you start out easy-going, when you try to be tough, they'll just look at you and laugh.[9]

Similarly, attendants in mental institutions may feel that if the new patient is sharply put in his place the first day on the ward and made to see who is boss, much future difficulty will be prevented.[10]

Given the fact that the individual effectively projects a definition of the situation when he enters the presence of others, we can assume that events may occur within the interaction which contradict, discredit, or otherwise throw doubt upon this projection. When these disruptive events occur, the interaction itself may come to a confused and embarrassed halt. Some of the assumptions upon which the responses of the participants had been predicated became untenable, and the participants find themselves lodged in an interaction for which the situation has been wrongly defined and is now no longer defined. At such moments the individual whose presentation has been discredited may feel ashamed while the others present may feel hostile, and all the participants may come to feel ill at ease, nonplussed, out of countenance, embarrassed, experiencing the kind of anomy that is generated when the minute social system of face-to-face interaction breaks down.

In stressing the fact that the initial definition of the situation projected by an individual tends to provide a plan for the cooperative activity that follows—in stressing this action point of view—we must not overlook the crucial fact that any projected definition of the situation also has a distinctive moral character. It is this moral character of projections that will chiefly concern us in this report. Society is organized on the principle that any individual who possesses certain social characteristics has a moral right to expect that others will value and treat him in an appropriate way. Connected with this principle is a second, namely that an individual who implicitly or explicitly signifies that he has certain social characteristics ought in fact to be what he claims he is. In consequence, when an individual projects a definition of the situation and thereby makes an implicit or explicit claim to be a person of a particular kind, he automatically exerts a moral demand upon the others, obliging them to value and treat him in the manner that persons of his kind have a right to expect. He also implicitly forgoes all claims to be things he does not appear to be[11] and hence forgoes the treatment that would be appropriate for such individuals. The others find, then, that the individual has informed them as to what is and as to what they ought to see as the "is."

One cannot judge the importance of definitional disruptions by the frequency with which they occur, for apparently they would occur more frequently were not constant precautions taken. We find that preventive practices are constantly employed to avoid these embarrassments and that corrective practices are constantly employed to compensate for discrediting occurrences that have not been successfully avoided. When the individual employs these strategies and tactics to protect his own projections, we may refer to them as "defensive practices"; when a participant employs them to save the definition of the situation projected by another, we speak of "protective practices" or "tact." Together, defensive and protective practices comprise the techniques employed to safeguard the impression fostered by an individual during his presence before others. It should be added that while we may be ready to see that no fostered impression would survive if defensive practices were not employed, we are less ready perhaps to see that few impressions could survive if those who received the impression did not exert tact in their reception of it.

In addition to the fact that precautions are taken to prevent disruption of projected definitions, we may also note that an intense interest in these disruptions comes to play a significant role in the social life of the group. Practical jokes and social games are played in which embarrassments which are to be taken unseriously are purposely engineered.[12] Fantasies are created in which devastating exposures occur. Anecdotes from the past real, embroidered, or fictitious are told and retold, detailing disruptions which occurred, almost occurred, or occurred and were admirably resolved. There seems to be no grouping which does not have a ready supply of these games, reveries, and cautionary tales, to be used as a source of humor, a catharsis for anxieties, and a sanction for inducing individuals to be modest in their claims and reasonable in their projected expectations. The individual may tell himself through dreams of getting into impossible positions. Families tell of the time a guest got his dates mixed and arrived when neither the house nor anyone in it was ready for him. Journalists tell of times when an all-too meaningful misprint occurred, and the paper's assumption of objectivity or decorum was humorously discredited. Public servants tell of times a client ridiculously misunderstood form instructions, giving answers which implied an unanticipated and bizarre definition of the situation.[13] Seamen, whose home away from home is rigorously he-man, tell stories of coming back home and inadvertently asking mother to "pass the fucking butter."[14] Diplomats tell of the time a near-sighted queen asked a republican ambassador about the health of his king.[15]

To summarize, then, I assume that when an individual appears before others he will have many motives for trying to control the impression they receive of the situation.

NOTES

1. Gustav Ichheiser, "Misunderstandings in Human Relations," Supplement to *The American Journal of Sociology*, 55 (September 1949): 6-7.
2. Quoted in E. H. Volkart, editor, *Social Behavior and Personality, Contributions of W. I. Thomas to Theory and Social Research* (New York: Social Science Research Council, 1951), p. 5.
3. Here I owe much to an unpublished paper by Tom Burns of the University of Edinburgh. He presents the argument that in all interaction a basic underlying theme is the desire of each participant to guide and control the responses made by the others present. A similar argument has been advanced by Jay Haley in a recent unpublished paper, but in regard to a special kind of control, that having to do with the relationship of those involved in the interaction.
4. Willard Waller, "The Rating and Dating Complex," *American Sociological Review*, 2:730.
5. William Sansom, *A Contest of Ladies* (London: Hogarth, 1956), pp. 230-32.
6. The widely read and rather sound writings of Stephen Potter are concerned in part with signs that can be engineered to give a shrewd observer the apparently incidental cues he needs to discover concealed virtues the gamesman does not in fact possess.
7. An interaction can be purposely set up as a time and place for voicing differences in opinion, but in such cases participants must be careful to agree not to disagree on the proper tone of voice, vocabulary, and degree of seriousness in which all arguments are to be phrased, and upon the mutual respect which disagreeing participants must carefully continue to express toward one another. This debaters' or academic definition of the situation may also be invoked suddenly and judiciously as a way of translating a serious conflict of views into one that can be handled within a framework acceptable to all present.
8. W. F. Whyte, "When Workers and Customers Meet," Chap. VII, *Industry and Society*, ed. W. F. Whyte (New York: McGraw-Hill, 1946), pp. 132-33.
9. Teacher interview quoted by Howard S. Becker, "Social Class Variations in the Teacher-Pupil Relationship," *Journal of Educational Sociology*, 25: 459.
10. Harold Taxel, "Authority Structure in a Mental Hospital Ward" (unpublished Master's thesis, Department of Sociology, University of Chicago, 1953).
11. This role of the witness in limiting what it is the individual can be has been stressed by Existentialists, who see it as a basic threat to individual freedom. See Jean-Paul Sartre, *Being and Nothingness*, trans. by Hazel E. Barnes (New York: Philosophical Library, 1956), p. 365 ff.
12. Goffman, op. cit., pp. 319-27.
13. Peter Blau, *Dynamics of Bureaucracy: A Study of Interpersonal Relationships in Two Government Agencies*, 2nd ed. (Chicago: University of Chicago Press, 1963).
14. Walter M. Beattie, Jr., "The Merchant Seaman" (unpublished M.A. Report, Department of Sociology, University of Chicago, 1950), p. 35.
15. Sir Frederick Ponsonby, *Recollections of Three Reigns* (New York: Dutton, 1952), p. 46.

Chapter 20 GENERIC PROCESSES OF IMPRESSION MANAGEMENT: TWO CASE STUDIES OF PHYSICAL AND MENTAL DISABILITY

Charlene E. Miall and *Nancy J. Herman*

INTRODUCTION

In recent years, a number of sociologists have argued for a renewed focus on generic concepts in ethnographic research (cf. Couch, 1984; Lofland, 1970; Prus, 1985; and Strauss, 1970). While the importance of substantive ethnographic research continues to be acknowledged, the case has been made for exploring conceptual variations in a plurality of settings so as to develop "... cumulative awareness of the viability and dimensions of particular concepts" (Prus, 1985; Strauss, 1970). Specifically, ethnographic researchers are being encouraged to research parallel processes in settings which may seem similar and/or dissimilar. Indeed, Strauss (1970:53) has observed that "if we do not practice such modes of extending grounded theories, then we relegate them, as now, mainly to the status of respected little islands of knowledge."

In sociological analysis, generic concepts and processes are considered generalizable across research situations and types of social actors. According to Wiseman (1985:3), for example, a truly generic concept can be applied to any interaction of two units: eg. self (internal conversations), dyads, families, teams, work groups, platoons, gangs, aggregates with a common goal acting in unison, or some combination of the above.

As generic process, impression management is concerned with the self-presentation and/or public display of identities created through the management of personal information (cf. Schlenker, 1980; Tedeschi and Norman, 1985). This personal information is multi-dimensional, differing in the amount that is made available to another; the scope that is made available; and the depth or quality of information that is made available (cf. Zerubavel, 1982:99–102). Thus individuals possess what has been conceptualized as an "information preserve" over which control is exerted (cf. Goffman, 1972:38–61; Zerubavel, 1982:103).

Impression management as "form" requires the presentation, retention, and/or distortion of information to manipulate "front". In this paper, attention is given to information management as it relates to the handling of stigma in mixed contacts between "normals" and "deviants"—interaction which has been conceptualized by Goffman (1963) as problematic. Specifically, an examination is made of the information management strategies of two substantively different "deviant" populations—involuntarily childless women and ex-psychiatric patients. In addition, consideration is given to how strategies of information management observed among these discreditable and discredited actors may also be utilized by "normal" actors engaged in non-problematic interaction. Finally, other factors influencing concealment and disclosure of information are identified for future research.

The relevance of stigma for information management Goffman (1963) observed, is that any deeply discrediting attribute can be stigmatizing because it constitutes a "special discrepancy between `virtual' and `actual' identity"—the former referring to the societal expectations we have of a person, and the latter referring to the attributes that a person actually possesses. Goffman (1963:4) differentiated among three kinds of stigma: "First, there are abominations of the body—the various physical deformities. Next there are blemishes of individual character....Finally there are tribal stigmas of race, nation, and religion."

The authors originally chose to study their specific research subjects with a view to correcting theoretical and substantive deficits in the literature on these groups. Miall studied involuntarily childless (infertile) women and Herman studied deinstitutionalized, non-chronic psychiatric patients. Within Goffman's framework both groups are potentially subject to stigma. The involuntarily childless presumably are stigmatized on the basis of abnormal bodily functions.[1] By contrast, deinstitutionalized non-chronic psychiatric patients are stigmatized on the basis of blemishes of individual character.[2]

Goffman (1963:4) further distinguished between attributes that are "discrediting"—those immediately apparent to others, and those which are "discreditable"—those attributes which are not visible or readily apparent to others. Involuntary childlessness is conceptualized as a discreditable or potentially stigmatizing attribute in that it is not readily apparent, unlike paralysis for example. Similarly, mental illness, for the most part, can be conceptualized as discreditable. This does not preclude the consideration of either group as discredited however. For example, medication side-effects, bizarre mannerisms and/or inappropriate patterns of interaction can render chronic ex-psychiatric patients discredited. Similarly, in Goffman's terms, the revelation of personal infertility or mental disorder and/or the awareness of such personal information by others can render these individuals discredited.

Generally speaking, individuals who are stigmatizable will develop and employ various strategies of information management to avoid or lessen the stigma potential of their "failing". Indeed, the management of information reflects a process of negotiation for preferred definitions of self. It could reasonably be argued that infertile women will not be subject to the same degree or kind of moral stigma as is associated with mental illness.[3] First of all, therefore, a comparison is made of the various information management strategies observed within these two substantive groups to determine if differences in the nature and severity of stigma potential affect disclosure behavior.

METHODOLOGY, SAMPLE, AND RESEARCH SETTINGS

In the initial stages of the study of involuntary childlessness and adoption, two characteristics were considered important for the recruitment of respondents: the demonstration of involuntary childlessness in present and past relationships; and the presence of or expectation of adopted children in the home. It was exceedingly difficult to obtain a sample of men sufficient for this kind of comparison and, after two years of concerted effort, the decision was made to limit the study to women. Given the secretiveness surrounding infertility (Miall, 1986) and the institutional confidentiality surrounding adoption (Miall, 1987), respondents were ultimately recruited through a snowball sampling technique. Volunteers were obtained from social work agencies, adoptive parent groups, and through other research participants.

A pre-tested, standardized, open-ended interview was conducted with 30 women. In addition, given recruitment problems, a questionnaire identical to the interview schedule was completed by 41 women. The decision to supplement the interview with a questionnaire was based on the willingness of some participants to fill in a questionnaire but not to take part in an interview. Questions were based on previous academic research on adoption, over one and a half years of participant observation in an infertility self-help group, discussions with infertile adoptive parents, and popular anecdotal literature on infertility and adoption. Interviews lasted from $2^1/_2$ to 4 hours.

Data were collected from May, 1981 to September, 1983 from respondents living in various geographical locales in Southern Ontario, Canada. The women in this sample ranged from 25 to 45, were well educated, from middle to upper middle class backgrounds, white and Protestant (16 of the respondents were Jewish). In addition, 58 (82%) of the respondents had adopted children and 13 (18%) were in the process of adopting for the first time. In the analysis of the data, cumulative frequency responses were used to reflect general trends or "recurring regularities" in the data.[4]

The study of deinstitutionalized ex-psychiatric patients was based on approximately twelve hundred and twenty hours of participant observation, formal and informal interviewing with one hundred and forty-six non-chronic ex-psychiatric patients living in various geographical locations in Southern Ontario, Canada.[5]

As part of a larger research project on Canadian deinstitutionalized patients, Herman initially obtained from hospital discharge records a disproportionate, stratified random sample of two hundred and eighty-five non-chronic and chronic ex-psychiatric patients.[6] The non-chronic subjects in this subsample ranged in age from 17 to 69, were from lower to middle class backgrounds, with a mean level of educational attainment of grade 13 (university entrance equivalent). Males comprised 57% of the sample and 43% were female. Subjects were hospitalized on psychiatric wards of general hospital facilities or in a psychiatric institution for a mean length of time of 1.3 years. The mean number of times they had been hospitalized was 4.2 times. In terms of employment, 87 were employed in some form of sheltered employment for the mentally/physically disabled while 34 were employed in non-sheltered settings working as bank tellers, teachers, postmen, steelworkers and so on. Subjects were living in boarding homes, Homes for Special Care, alone, or with family. Data on the nature of deinstitutionalized patient social life were collected from January, 1981 to September, 1984 in such social settings as drop-in centers, self-help group meetings, activist group headquarters, places of employment, and in the homes of the subjects.

Information management strategies of the stigmatized

The discreditable

According to Goffman, actors can be considered to be discreditable if their attribute is not readily apparent. In terms of interaction, the situation of the discreditable might best represent Glaser and Strauss's (1967) closed awareness context in that, during interaction, one actor is motivated to deceive on matters that may be relevant to identity. The extent to which an actor can be considered discreditable or discredited is not a clear cut issue however. Status can vary in terms of the situations within which one interacts—for example, at a party with acquaintances or at a self-help group meeting; or it can vary in terms of who one is interacting with. As Sagarin and Kelly (1987:13) have noted, deviance itself "... is a protean concept that is mutable and that changes its meanings over time and in diverse places."

In their research on epilepsy, Schneider and Conrad (1980) focused on the metaphor of being either in or out of the closet with a discreditable attribute. Questioning the utility of this metaphor for discreditable attributes for which there is no alternate new and proud identity, they concluded that the closet metaphor needs to be extended "... to incorporate the complex reality of how people very selectively disclose or withhold discreditable evidence about themselves" (Schneider and Conrad, 1980:42).

Despite differences in the nature and degree of stigma potential of the discreditable attributes in question, respondents in the two substantive groups examined made use of three major strategies of information management with "normals". These strategies included: selective concealment, therapeutic disclosure, and preventive disclosure. The goals of all three strategies it appears were (a) to avoid or lessen the stigma associated with their attribute; (b) to enhance personal self-esteem by managing information about their discreditable attribute; and (c) to renegotiate their discreditable attribute into a more favorable light within the societal context.

(1) The strategy of selective concealment

Within the deviance literature, selective concealment has been defined as the selective disclosure or withholding of information which may be discreditable in those instances where secrecy is the major strategy for handling an attribute (cf. Schneider and Conrad, 1980). Although informational content may differ, the strategy of information management is the same.

In terms of involuntary childlessness, subjects displayed patterns of selective concealment in that concern about a problem with infertility had to be conveyed to medical personnel at the time of entry into a doctor's office or fertility clinic. In addition, infertility had to be revealed to a social worker if the infertile individual applied to adopt.

This same strategy was adopted by the non-chronic ex-psychiatric patients. Decisions about concealment and disclosure were made by respondents in both substantive groups on the basis of their perceptions of others. Decisions to reveal seemed based on judgments of the "trustworthiness" or "genuineness" or "safeness/ riskiness" of the persons to whom the revelation was being made. As one ex-patient stated,

> When I got out of the hospital, I sat down and carefully considered who I should tell and who I should hide it from. I made up a list in my head. Out of all of the people I knew, I only thought of two people—my brother and my godson. These were the only ones that I would tell! (Observation number 28)

As one infertile subject put it,

> I find you have to avoid certain people. You learn to pick up on those people....I have got to the point now. I've always been fairly good at judging people to begin with. I've always had a sort of sixth sense but it's just really become attuned. (Respondent number 32)

Apart from disclosure to "neutral" individuals such as doctors, social workers, and the authors, there was also a hierarchical pattern of selective disclosure based on the perceived degree of closeness or intimacy of the person being told. Family members were most often told, followed by close friends, and then, acquaintances. In those instances where concealment was a major strategy, disclosure was usually confined to one or two individuals. Otherwise, concealment in mixed contacts between deviants and normals took the following forms: avoidance, withdrawal, and changing the subject. As one infertile woman observed:

> I find I get quiet at times. Or I try to change the subject....I'm constantly debating as to how frank I should be to people about the whole subject....Mostly I keep quiet and we come home and talk about it. (Respondent number 29)

In both substantive areas, selective disclosures to others were often made to test reactions. The continued disclosure of such information on self seemed contingent on responses made to earlier disclosures. For example, negative responses to trial disclosures contributed to the continued use of concealment as the major strategy of information control.

These observations support research findings on other "deviant" groups, despite notable differences in the nature and degree of stigma potential of the various attributes studied; for example, Schneider and Conrad's (1980) research on epilepsy; Humphreys' (1975) study of secret homosexuals (cf. Corzine and Kirby, 1977; Delph, 1978); Feinbloom's (1977) study of transvestites and transsexuals (cf. Bogdan, 1974; Kando, 1973); Edgerton's (1967) study of the mentally retarded; Bartell's (1977) study of swingers; Ponse's (1976) study of lesbians; Miall's (1989a) study of adoptive parents; and Veever's (1980) study of voluntarily childless couples.

As a form of impression management, selective concealment of information among the stigmatized appears to be done to protect these individuals from perceived negative consequences which might follow revelation. In terms of our research, the use of concealment as a strategy of impression management was a temporal process. Specifically, an initial desire for secrecy lessened over time and was replaced by alternative strategies of disclosure. This progression appeared to be linked by subjects to increased "adjustment" to their attribute.

The discredited

Revelation within the two substantive areas was carried out for two reasons: therapeutic and preventive. Therapeutic disclosure of the discreditable attribute might best reflect Glaser and Strauss' (1967) open awareness context in that the attribute was genuinely and openly communicated. Preventive disclosure, on the other hand, reflected a closed awareness context in that the potentially discredited individual was apt to deceive others about the attribute considered relevant to identity.

(1) The strategy of therapeutic disclosure

Therapeutic disclosure can be defined as the disclosure to supportive others of a discreditable attribute to enhance self-esteem or to renegotiate personal perceptions of stigma. According to Schneider and Conrad (1980:40),

> ...for those who have concealed what they see as some personal blemish or flaw, such telling can serve a 'therapeutic' function for the self by sharing or diffusing the burden of such information....Such relief, however, requires a properly receptive audience: ...supportive, encouraging, empathetic, and non-judgmental.

In our research, therapeutic disclosure was usually carried out with family and close friends and/or with others sharing the same attribute. Therapeutic disclosure was used to relieve anxiety (catharsis), to restore self-esteem, and to renegotiate personal perceptions of the attribute as discrediting. As one infertile respondent observed, disclosure to her family was cathartic,

> Initially I felt uncomfortable until I sat down and talked about it with my husband and my family, about how I felt I was failing. Then I felt better for having gotten it all out. (Respondent number 2)

Similarly, one ex-psychiatric patient revealed that telling his closest friends about mental illness allowed him to redefine mental illness in his own mind as a less stigmatizing attribute.

> I kept it inside for a long time, but then finally God gave me the courage to come out of the closet to my two old friends. When I told them I had been in a psychiatric hospital, they took it extremely well. I talked to them about my shame, and how I just wanted to stay away from people. But they helped me to put things into perspective —to realize that it's not the end of the world. The more and more I talked to them, the better I felt. (Observation number 22)

Respondents who employed therapeutic (and preventive) disclosure were less likely to utilize selective concealment as a strategy for information management. Subjects in both substantive areas observed that the ability to reveal their discreditable attribute at all represented the beginning of adjustment to it.

(2) The strategy of preventive disclosure

Preventive disclosure can be defined as the disclosure to others of the discreditable attribute with a view to influencing others' actions and/or ideas about oneself, or about one's attribute in general. For example, the ex-psychiatric patients employed this strategy when they anticipated future rejection on the part of normals. Thus, in order to minimize the pain of subsequent rejection, many ex-patients would employ preventive disclosure early in their relationships with others. As one ex-patient put it:

> I've learned the hard way—if you don't want to set yourself up for a big fall, you've got to find a time to tell certain people about you. Especially if you want to make close friends with them. Before, when I wouldn't say anything about my past, and they would somehow find out, I'd be 'up a creek without a paddle'. They'd 'drop me like a hot potato'. The best advice I can give anyone is to tell people right off the bat—you avoid yourself a lot of heartache that way. (Observation number 3)

Similarly, an infertile woman observed,

> In a way it's a good thing to clear it out of the way. I think if you can do that without making a big issue out of it, it's a good thing to do because it clears the air and prevents any further misunderstandings. I, for example, don't want to be treated differently but I feel that the subject is bound to come up eventually so you might as well clear it up right at the beginning. (Respondent number 20)

Preventive disclosure therefore, may be a way of preventing a status-drop if the attribute becomes known later, or a way of testing acquaintances with a view to establishing friendship boundaries. In addition, in order to influence others' perceptions of them or their attribute, both ex-patients and infertile women used (a) medical disclaimers and (b) practiced deception/coaching as part of a strategy of preventive disclosure.[7]

(3) Medical disclaimers

According to Schneider and Conrad (1980:41), a medical disclaimer may be defined as a "....blameless, beyond-my-control medical interpretation" offered to "...reduce the risk that more morally disreputable interpretations might be applied by naive others" discovering the attribute (cf. Hewitt and Stokes, 1978). As one infertile woman noted,

> Because of the nature of our infertility problem it was a medically open and shut case....There was an anatomical deficit in that I'd had my tubes taken out....So when people would say to me, 'Well maybe there's always artificial insemination', I would say, 'There's no medical way'. If the reason is not an anatomical reason or a reason for which they can't find a reason, I think people will chime in with 'Well maybe you're not doing it right' and you don't want to leave yourself open to that. (Respondent number 9)

Similarly, as an ex-patient put it,

> I tell people about me being in a psychiatric hospital for depression. But I emphasize that what I've got is an illness that is not my fault. It's something that I just can't help. I tell them that it's just like being hit with the measles or the mumps or any other kind of disease—only this one hits your mind. (Observation number 35)

In addition, infertile women who were able to do so would reveal their infertility as an uncontrollable side-effect of another medical condition such as diabetes or kidney disease so that reproductive disorder was not the main issue.

(4) Practiced deception/coaching

Subjects utilizing practiced deception (cf. Miall, 1986) would reveal their attribute but distort or alter the circumstances contributing to their failing. The use of deception around the revelation of infertility, for example, involved distorting whose condition in the marital dyad was contributing to the couple's infertility. In most instances, respondents rehearsed deception beforehand. The use of rehearsal in the dyad reflects a similar phenomenon isolated in Schneider and Conrad's (1980) work on epileptics and also noted by Herman (1986a) in her study of ex-psychiatric patients—that of coaching. Coaches could include parents, close associates, friends, medical professionals (codes of conduct), and others sharing the stigma.

Notably, many ex-psychiatric patients employed deceptive practices along with medical disclaimers. In addition, deception as a device was more likely to be developed with the assistance of coaches. These different patterns of development of deceptive practices probably reflect the differential relationships of "normals" to the stigmatized under consideration here. One ex-psychiatric patient, speaking of his use of deception and medical disclaimers observed,

> You see, most people treat ex-mental patients as if it was their fault that they got sick....So, what you have to do, is remind people that it's not your fault that this happened to you....I give them a little speech and hope that they act favorably towards you. To enhance the story, I often lie a little bit—I stretch the truth about the circumstances surrounding my hospitalization—I don't tell them that I ended up in the hospital after exposing myself in church, but if you can get them to buy your story, they will treat you more kindly. (Observation number 169)

As mentioned earlier, preventive disclosure appeared to be done with a view to influencing others' ideas about oneself and in order to enhance self-esteem.[8]

IMPRESSION MANAGEMENT, "DEVIANTS", and "NORMALS"—a false conceptual dichotomy?

Goffman (1959) has observed that impression management involves the presentation of a "front" which is acceptable to all participants in an interactional scene. This front is created through the management of personal information about oneself and can be conveyed through conduct, appearance and/or manner (cf. Goffman, 1959). The social production of action must have as a foundation the sharing of information which has meaning for the participants interacting. Indeed, the sharing of personal information is central for social life. Actors respond to one another on the basis of social identities created through the presentation or retention of personal information. Thus, as a process, impression management is applicable to all forms of interaction where identities are created and/or presented.

Notably, innumerable ethnographies exist in the deviance literature which document in detail the impression/information management strategies of the stigmatized. It is hardly surprising that so much emphasis has been placed within ethnographic research on the patterns of information management of deviants, given the problematic nature of interaction between deviants and "normals". Indeed, problematic interaction highlights or brings into focus generic processes of information management not normally noted in everyday life. It is the authors' contention, however, that a focus on "content" within deviant worlds has masked the relevance of "form" to interaction in general (cf. Simmel, 1950), and impeded the development of a truly generic sociology based on ethnography.

The idea that impression management is relevant to normal or non-problematic interaction is not, of course, a new one. Goffman's (1959) work on the presentation of self is the classic example of how the management of information can be part of everyday social interaction. Indeed, meaningful ethnographies concerned with impression management have been carried out with various "normal" populations. For example, Haas and Shaffir (1977) have examined how medical students develop strategies of impression management within the context of professional socialization. Other studies have examined nurses (Olesen and Whittaker, 1968); the police (Bittner, 1980; Skolnick, 1975); retailers (Prus, 1985); managers in various corporations (Campanis, 1970); and college dating behavior (Schwartz and Lever, 1976).

What appears to have emerged within the published research on impression management, however, is a false conceptual dichotomy between stigmatized and normal patterns of impression management. For example, to the authors' knowledge, there have been no attempts to relate the information management strategies of the stigmatized to the information management strategies of normal populations. However, as Jones et al. (1984:225) have argued, "by focusing on the many examples provided by the stigma family, we may gain important insights into the normal processes of self-presentation."

In order to begin to bridge the conceptual gap between "deviant" and "normal" patterns of information management, consideration will now be given to research on information management among normal populations engaged in non-problematic interaction as it relates to research on stigmatized populations.[9]

CONCEALMENT AND DISCLOSURE AMONG NORMAL POPULATIONS

In his paper on personal information and social life, Zerubavel (1982) explored how control over the information preserve is maintained and manifested by "normal" individuals engaged in non-problematic interaction. According to Zerubavel (1982:105–106), this control is manifest in defensive strategies such as discretion, concealment and fabrication. All three strategies operate to keep the information preserve intact. Thus discretion reflects the actor's decision "...to abstain from disclosing any personal information to which one does not want others to have access"; concealment is defined as "...an active strategy which involves the establishment of some actual informational barriers between others and oneself"; and fabrication "...involves a deliberate attempt to provide others with false information about oneself" (cf. Zerubavel, 1982:105–106).

Zerubavel's defensive strategies of discretion and concealment wherein the "normal" actor abstains from disclosing information or actively establishes informational barriers between others and self to protect the information preserve reflects the strategy of selective concealment used by "deviant" subjects engaged in problematic interaction with "normals". Notably, the information being concealed need not be negative or discrediting. For example, studies on ingratiation suggest that individuals selectively reveal and conceal positive personal attributes to establish or maintain a desired identity within certain contexts. An individual may selectively publicize admirable qualities to generate a favorable impression, particularly when the target person can reward them in some way (cf. Baumeister and Jones, 1978; Tetlock, 1981). Indeed, Jourard (1971) has noted that personal information may be disclosed to facilitate the establishment of intimacy. Similarly high-status or powerful people may conceal information about themselves to determine whether compliance from others is spontaneous or loyal and not a response to perceived superior force (cf. Jones et al., 1984). Indeed, "playing dumb" is a tactic well documented in the literature on ingratiation (cf. Gove et al., 1980). Individuals refrain from revealing positive attributes to avoid threatening people who can reward them in some way.

Tetlock (1980) has also noted that patterns of interaction between teachers and students involve the use of selective concealment as a strategy. Indeed, studies utilizing a "cloak of competence" metaphor to study stigmatized and non-stigmatized populations reflect this process of selective concealment and disclosure of information to establish or preserve a desired identity (cf. Edgerton, 1967; Haas and Shaffir, 1977). In addition, the creation of curriculum vitaes and the format of job interviews, regardless of the substantive content, are also processes of selectively concealing and revealing information to create a desired identity (cf. Fletcher and Spencer, 1984; Jones and Pittman, 1982; von Baeyer et al., 1981).

As noted earlier, preventive disclosure among deviant populations often involves the distortion or fabrication of information. Similarly, Zerubavel (1982:106) has noted that fabrication is a defensive strategy in non-problematic interaction. Indeed, vocabularies of motives, accounts, excuses, and justifications may also be utilized as part of a strategy of preventive disclosure in non-problematic and problematic interaction (cf. Hewitt and Stokes, 1975; Mills, 1940; Scott and Lyman, 1968; Sykes and Matza, 1959; Taylor, 1979). Thus, personal information is revealed but may often be altered, distorted, or fabricated to maximize social approval or minimize social disapproval. In the same way that stigmatized individuals may be coached on how to establish desired identities, part of the process of socialization involves parents "coaching" their children on how to establish identities that will yield potential power over others—for example, how to respond to bullies, teasing, etc. Similarly, coaching related to maintaining a cloak of competence is often provided by peers—for example, how to respond to questions in a Ph.D. oral if you don't know the answers.

DISCUSSION

In this paper it has been argued that a false conceptual dichotomy has developed in the ethnographic literature wherein information management among the stigmatized is conceptualized as qualitatively different from information management in "normal" populations. In order to begin to bridge the conceptual gap between "deviant" and "normal" patterns of information management, the authors noted how processes of information management in problematic interaction reflect similar processes in non-problematic interaction. Consideration will now be given to other factors which may influence the extent to which defensive strategies and strategies of disclosure are utilized in problematic and non-problematic interaction.

Goal-direction

As actors respond to one another on the basis of social identities created through the presentation and/or retention of personal information, theorists have argued that impression management is goal-directed. Goals of impression management may include the maximization of social approval, the minimization of social disapproval, the establishment of control over the quality and quantity of material and social rewards obtained through social interaction, and/or the establishment of identities that yield power potential over others (cf. Ferris et al., 1984; Goffman, 1959; Jones and Wortman, 1973; Jones et al., 1984; Schlenker, 1975, 1985; Schneider, 1959; and Tedeschi and Norman, 1985). Actors engaging in information management in both problematic and non-problematic interaction will conceal or reveal information in terms of its relevance for a preferred definition of self. This paper for example, has demonstrated that individuals with potentially stigmatizing attributes will manage information in interaction with "normals" to influence others' perceptions of them and ultimately, the kinds of social rewards they receive. Similarly, "normal" individuals will seek to present an identity that maximizes social approval and the material rewards arising out of social interaction (cf. Jones and Wortman, 1973; Schlenker, 1975).

Generally speaking, the information concealed or revealed by the stigmatized is negative. It also seems reasonable to conclude that in many instances of interaction among normals, information that is concealed may also have negative overtones so that the dichotomy between deviance and normalcy breaks down. However, individuals engaged in presentations of self may also conceal positive information to minimize social disapproval or to achieve other goals. Studies on ingratiation and playing dumb illustrate this observation (cf. Gove et al., 1980; Tetlock, 1981). Similarly, tactical self-disclosure for deviants and normals may be undertaken to obtain social approval, to achieve a sense of authenticity and/or to gain control of interaction (cf. Jones and Wortman, 1973; Miall, 1989a).

As Sagarin and Kelly (1987:23) have noted, whether persons or activities will be considered deviant is unpredictable because it depends on an infinite number of situations, on the subcultures in a heterogeneous society, and on a social system that is constantly in flux. Thus, although the discreditability of information content becomes a matter of degree and/or social interpretation, the generic process of impression management for the attainment of goals for the stigmatized and the normal appears the same —the maximization of social rewards and/or the minimization of social disapproval.

Temporality

As discussed earlier, among the involuntarily childless women and ex-psychiatric patients examined, a progression from one strategy to another was the rule. Specifically, many subjects moved from a strategy of early selective concealment to disclosure for therapeutic reasons to preventive disclosure. It seems reasonable to conclude that concealment and disclosure of information in non-problematic interaction will also be influenced by the duration of relationships. As Zerubavel (1982: 102) has noted however, pseudo-intimate situations may require or encourage immediate disclosure of information—for example, interactions with priests, psychiatrists, or strangers on a train.

Asymmetrical power relationships

Impression management through concealment or disclosure among the stigmatized and the normal may be more likely to occur in situational interaction characterized by power asymmetry. It has already been well established in the deviance literature that a power differential exists between the normal and the stigmatized that favors the normal. In interaction among normals where identities are also actively managed, a power differential may also exist—for example, in the case of parents and children, teachers and students, employers and employees or potential employees, doctors and patients and so on. However, further research should focus on the impression management strategies of the powerful as well as the powerless in interaction. As Jones et al. (1984) have noted, the literature on self-presentation has focused on the powerless and for the most part ignored the less obvious problems of the powerful in maintaining identities.

Situated deviant identity

In this paper, the conceptual dichotomy of assuming that deviants and normals don't need or use the same types of strategies of information management because of the nature of their identities (discreditable versus normal) has been shown to be questionable. Research is needed to further explore whether individuals who are situationally defined as deviant (for example, ethnographers exploring a social world) and those who are routinely defined as deviant (for example, the blind) engage in similar strategies when managing problematic situations.

Culture

Zerubavel (1982:102) has already noted that cultures can differ in terms of what is regarded as intimate information and what is regarded as easily made available to others. Although content may differ, "form" in terms of the relative degree of accessibility of information is a universal social fact and the content of information becomes a matter of empirical exploration. Culture however, may also impact on strategies of concealment and disclosure of information in terms of a number of variables. Thus in some cultures, specifications for gender role performance may require greater self-disclosure on the part of females vis-a-vis males; the young versus the old; the powerless versus the powerful; and so on.

The study of deviance, its manifestations, and processes continues to flourish within the sociological community. By focusing on impression management as a generic process, this paper has attempted to bridge the conceptual gap between information strategies observed among the stigmatized and those utilized in non-problematic interaction with a view to demonstrating the relevance of deviance research for social processes in general. In addition, a number of factors have been identified for future research which may influence the extent to which defensive strategies and strategies of disclosure are utilized in problematic and non-problematic interaction regardless of content.

NOTES

1. For a more in-depth discussion of the stigmatizing aspects of involuntary childlessness, see Miall (1984, 1985, 1986, 1989b).
2. Goffman (1963:4) refers to mental disorders as potential blemishes of character which can be stigmatizing. For a more in-depth discussion of the stigmatizing aspects of mental illness, see Herman (1986a, 1986b).
3. Veevers (1979:4–5) argues that the childless by choice are more likely to be stigmatized than the infertile: "The subfecund may be considered unfortunate and hence deserving of sympathy, but the voluntarily childless are considered immoral and hence deserving of censure." Although Miall (1986) concluded that the infertile are subject to stigmatization, her subjects regarded voluntary childlessness as more stigmatizing than involuntary childlessness.
4. However, in order to determine the extent to which various socio-demographic variables might affect disclosure of involuntary childlessness, sub-classifications were done controlling for age, education, occupation, religion, ethnicity, and duration of marriage of the respondents. In addition, a sub-classification was done which compared the opinions of those who had adopted children and those who were still in the process of adopting, age of children adopted, length of time required to adopt and so. No significant differences were found in responses when these sub-categories were examined.
5. Chronicity, for the purposes of this study was defined not in diagnostic terms, that is, manic-depressive. Rather it was defined in terms of duration, continuity, and frequency of hospitalization. Specifically, non-chronic refers to those individuals hospitalized on psychiatric wards of general hospitals or in a psychiatric institution for time-periods of less than two years, on a discontinuous basis or on less than five occasions.
6. For specific details concerning the sample, consult Herman (1986).
7. In addition, both groups used normalization/deviance disavowal, and education. The infertile women also employed deviance avowal, a process not noted for ex-patients by Herman. However, ex-patients did utilize collective strategies such as political activism. Both groups under study participated in self-help groups. For an in-depth discussion of these strategies, see Miall (1984; 1986) and Herman (1986a).
8. All the devices outlined above can be considered forms of "disclosure etiquette" or formulas for admitting a failing " ...in a matter of fact way, supporting the assumption that those present are above such concerns while preventing them from trapping themselves into showing that they are not" (Goffman, 1963:101).
9. This consideration of research on information management among normal populations is not intended to be all inclusive.

REFERENCES

Bartell, G. 1971. *Group Sex: A Scientist's Eyewitness Report on the American Way of Swinging.* New York: Peter H. Wyden.

Baumeister, R. and E. Jones. 1978. "When Self-Presentation is Constrained by the Target's Knowledge: Consistency and Compensation." *Journal of Personality and Social Psychology* 36:608-618.

Bittner, E. 1980. *The Functions of the Police in Modern Society.* Cambridge, Massachusetts: Oelgeschlager, Gunn & Hain.

Bogdan, R. 1974. *Being Different: The Autobiography of Jane Fry.* New York: Wiley and Sons.

Campanis, P. 1970. "Normlessness in Management." Pp.291–325 in *Deviance and Respectability,* edited by Jack Douglas. New York: Basic Books.

Corzine, J. and R. Kirby. 1977. "Cruising the Truckers: Sexual Encounters in a Highway Rest Area." *Urban Life* 6:171–192.
Couch, Carl J. 1984. "Symbolic Interaction and Generic Sociological Principles." *Symbolic Interaction* 7:1–14.
Delph, E. 1978. *The Silent Community: Public Homosexual Encounters.* Beverly Hills, California: Sage.
Edgerton, R. 1967. *The Cloak of Competence.* Berkeley: University of California Press.
Feinbloom, D. 1977. *Transvestites and Transsexuals.* New York: Delta Books.
Ferris, G., R. Porac, and F. Joseph. 1984. "Goal Setting as Impression Management." *Journal of Psychology* 117:33–36.
Fletcher, C. and A. Spencer. 1984. "Sex of Candidate and Sex of Interviewer as Determinants of Self-Presentation Orientation in Interviews: An Experimental Study." *International Review of Applied Psychology* 33:305–313.
Glaser, Barney and Anselm Strauss. 1967. *The Discovery of Grounded Theory: Strategies for Qualitative Research.* Chicago: Aldine.
Goffman, Erving. 1959. *The Presentation of Self in Everyday Life.* New York: Anchor.
———. 1963. *Stigma.* New Jersey: Prentice-Hall.
———. 1972. *Relations in Public.* New York: Harper Colophon.
Gove, W., M. Hughes, and M. Geerken. 1980. "Playing Dumb: A Form of Impression Management with Undesirable Effects." *Social Psychology Quarterly* 43:89–102.
Haas, J. and W. Shaffir. 1977. "The Professionalization of Medical Students: Developing and Maintaining a Cloak of Competence." *Symbolic Interaction* 1:71–88.
Herman, Nancy J. 1986a. Crazies in the Community. Unpublished Ph.D. Dissertation. McMaster University, Hamilton, Ontario, Canada.
———. 1986b. "The Chronically Mentally Ill in Canada." In *The North American Elders: A Comparison of U.S. and Canadian Issues*, edited by B. Havens and E. Rathbone-McCuan. Westport, CT.: Greenwood Press.
Hewitt, J. and R. Stokes. 1978. "Disclaimers." Pp.308–319 in *Symbolic Interactionism*, 3rd edition, edited by J. Manis and B. Meltzer. Boston: Allyn and Bacon.
Humphreys, L. 1975. *Tearoom Trade: Impersonal Sex in Public Places.* Chicago: Aldine.
Jones, E., A. Farina, A. Hastorf, H. Markus, D. Miller, and R. Scott. 1984. *Social Stigma: The Psychology of Marked Relationships.* New York: W. H. Freeman and Company.
Jones, E. and T. Pittman. 1982. "Toward a General Theory of Strategic Self-Presentation." Pp.231–262 in *Psychological Perspectives on the Self*, Volume 1, edited by J. Shuls. Hillsdale, New Jersey: Erlbaum.
Jones, E. and C. Wortman. 1973. *Ingratiation: An Attributional Approach.* Morristown, New Jersey: General Learning Press.
Jourard, S. 1971. *Self-Disclosure.* New York: Wiley.
Kando, T. 1973. *Sex Change: The Achievement of Gender Identity Among Feminized Transsexuals.* Springfield, Illinois: Charles C. Thomas.
Lofland, John. 1970. "Interactionist Imagery and Analytic Interruptus." Pp.35–45 In *Human Nature and Collective Behavior: Papers in Honor of Herbert Blumer*, edited by Tamotsu Shibutani. Englewood Cliffs, New Jersey: Prentice-Hall.
Miall, Charlene. 1984. *Women and Involuntary Childlessness: Perceptions of Stigma Associated with Infertility and Adoption.* Unpublished Ph.D. Dissertation. York University, Toronto, Ontario, Canada.
Miall, Charlene. 1985. "Perceptions of Informal Sanctioning and the Stigma of Involuntary Childlessness." *Deviant Behavior* 6:383–403.
———. 1986. "The Stigma of Involuntary Childlessness." *Social Problems* 33:268–282.
———. 1989a. "Authenticity and the Disclosure of the Information Preserve: The Case of Adoptive Parenthood." *Qualitative Sociology*. Forthcoming.
———. 1989b. "Reproductive Technology Versus the Stigma of Involuntary Childlessness." *Social Casework* 70:43–50.
Mills, C. 1940. "Situated Actions and Vocabularies of Motives." *American Sociological Review* 5:904–913.
Olesen, V. and E. Whittaker. 1968. *The Silent Dialogue: A Study in the Social Psychology of Professional Socialization.* San Francisco: Jossey-Bass.
Ponse, B. 1976. "Secrecy in the Lesbian World." *Urban Life* 5:313–338.

Prus, Robert. 1985. "Generic Sociology: Maximizing Conceptual Development in Ethnographic Research." Paper presented at a conference on Qualitative Research: An Ethnographic/Interactionist Perspective. University of Waterloo, Waterloo, Ontario. May 15–17, 1985.
Sagarin, E. and R. Kelly. 1987. "Deviance: A Polymorphous Concept." *Deviant Behavior* 8:13–25.
Schlenker, B. 1975. "Self-Presentation: Managing the Impression of Consistency When Reality Interferes With Self-Enhancement." *Journal of Personality and Social Psychology* 32:1030–1037.
———. 1980. *Impression Management: The Self-Concept, Social Identity, and Interpersonal Relations.* Belmont, California: Brooks/Cole.
———. 1985. *The Self and Social Life.* New York: McGraw-Hill.
Schneider, D. 1959. "Tactical Self-Presentation After Success and Failure." *Journal of Personality and Social Psychology* 13:262–268.
Schneider, J. and P. Conrad. 1980. "In the Closet with Illness: Epilepsy, Stigma Potential and Information Control." *Social Problems* 28:32–44.
Schwartz, Pepper and Janet Lever. 1976. "Fear and Loathing at a College Mixer." *Urban Life* 4:413–430.
Scott, M. and S. Lyman. 1968. "Accounts." *American Sociological Review* 33:46–62.
Simmel, Georg. 1950. *The Sociology of Georg Simmel* (Translated and edited by K. Wolff). New York: Free Press.
Skolnick, J. 1975. *Justice Without Trial*, 2nd edition. New York: John Wiley.
Strauss, Anselm. 1970. "Discovering New Theory From Previous Theory." Pp. 46–53 In *Human Nature and Collective Behavior: Papers in Honor of Herbert Blumer*, edited by Tamotsu Shibutani. Englewood Cliffs, New Jersey: Prentice-Hall.
Sykes, G. and D. Matza. 1959. "Techniques of Neutralization: A Theory of Delinquency." *American Sociological Review* 22:664–670.
Taylor, L. 1979. "Vocabularies, Rhetorics and Grammar: Problems in the Sociology of Motivation." Pp. 145–161 In *Deviant Interpretations*, edited by David Downes and Paul Rock. U.S.A.: Harper and Row.
Tedeschi, J. and N. Norman. 1985. "Social Power, Self-Presentation, and the Self." Pp.293–322 In *The Self and Social Life*, edited by B. Schlenker. New York: McGraw-Hill.
Tetlock, P. 1980. "Explaining Teacher Explanations of Pupil Performance: A Self-Presentation Interpretation." *Social Psychology Quarterly* 43:282–90.
Tetlock, P. 1981. "The Influence of Self-Presentational Goals on Attributional Reports." *Social Psychology Quarterly* 44:300–11.
Veevers, J. 1979. "Voluntary Childlessness: A Review of Issues and Evidence." *Marriage and Family Review* 2:1–26.
———. 1980. *Childless by Choice.* Toronto: Butterworths.
von Baeyer, C., D. Sherk, and M. Zanna. 1981. "Impression Management in the Job Interview: When the Female Applicant Meets the Male (Chauvinist) Interviewer." *Personality and Social Psychology Bulletin* 7:45–51.
Wiseman, J. 1985. "The Adaptation and Clustering of Generic Concepts Through Application to Diverse Research Topics." Paper presented at a conference on Qualitative Research: An Ethnographic/Interactionist Perspective. University of Waterloo, Waterloo, Ontario. May 15–17, 1985.
Zerubavel, E. 1982. "Personal Information and Social Life." *Symbolic Interaction* 5:97–109.

Chapter 21 NEGOTIATING A RELIGIOUS IDENTITY: THE CASE OF THE GAY EVANGELICAL

Scott Thumma

> I am a born-again Christian and sought help through prayer and the church, but I am still gay. Could it be that God accepts me as I am? (Letter to Good News)
> Such disbelief is no surprise when a person's spiritual roots are grounded in a heritage that quite rightly emphasizes the Bible as the Word of God written, and not just a random collection of outdated writings. So when confronted with traditional cultural bound interpretations of supposed anti-gay passages, the Bible honoring gay is thrown into a whirlwind of spiritual confusion. It's a joy, then, to share with these people that they can indeed reconcile born-again faith with their lifestyle. (a leader of Good News in the newsletter)[1]

For many Evangelical Christians, a homosexual lifestyle and a conservative religious identity are simply incompatible. According to a majority of conservative Christians, there is no such thing as a gay Christian, nor a biblical justification for such a lifestyle.[2] Yet, for members of one gay Evangelical group, this option is not only a possibility, it is also a reality and an imperative. This group, called Good News, formed specifically for the purpose of helping persons reconcile their gay lifestyle with their Evangelical religious identity. This task, while threatening for those with a traditional Evangelical religious identity, nevertheless is seen as one which must be attempted. Members accomplish this change through identity negotiation and socialization. In other words, they negotiate the traditional religious identity, in very selective areas, through interaction with Good News. Members are reconciled to their gayness, but still retain their Evangelical religious identity.

Religious identity change has been characterized primarily in traditional conversion language as a "radical reorganization of identity, meaning, life" (Travisano, 1970:594), or as an abandonment of one religious identity for a new and different one (Kilbourne and Richardson 1989). This is the case because few researchers examine less dramatic identity changes that occur within a particular religious tradition, commonly known as "alterations" (Travisano, 1970). Through an analysis of the interaction between Good News, its members, and a traditional Evangelical identity, a complex and subtle process of identity negotiation comes to light.

Accommodation of discrepant identities does not always result in an either/or decision that destroys one of the identities. Rather, identity negotiation can be construed as a process in which much of these identities remains intact. Members of Good News come to accept themselves as gay Christians without giving up their Evangelical identity. Certain aspects of members' Evangelical religious identity are revised to incorporate incongruous, but perceived as essential, characteristics of their sexual identity into their total self-concept. For these persons, their core identity becomes a gay Evangelical Christian one.

A SOCIALIZATION PROCESS OF IDENTITY NEGOTIATION

Identity negotiation can be best understood as a facet of adult socialization. The symbolic interactionist perspective (Mead, 1934; Goffman, 1959; Garfinkel, 1967; Berger and Luckmann, 1967) offers a description of the dynamics involved in socialization. It is through the interaction of self and society that meaning systems are created and sustained. Both self-concept, "what one thinks one is like" (Troiden, 1984), and identity, the concept of the self-concept in relation to a social situation (Gecas, 1982), arise from this interaction. Socialization is the process by which the self internalizes social meanings, reinterprets them, and in turn, responds back to society. As such, socialization can be viewed as the continual formation of self-concept over time (Gecas, 1986). From this perspective, identity negotiation, whether religious or sexual, is a part of the natural process in which people engage to create a more stable and coherent self-concept (Becker, 1963; Strauss, 1976; Gecas, 1982). Conversion, from this point of view, is identity negotiation that involves a complete change in the "core identity construct" (Staples and Mauss, 1987).

Often one's self-concept becomes organized around a central or "core identity" construct (Hart and Richardson, 1981; Gecas, 1981), which gives some unity or consistence to the other identities of the person. The stability of the core identity (or "master status" in Becker, 1963) resides in the interplay between one's continual experience of the world, the relative meaning assigned to such experiences, the plausability of these meaning systems for ordering existence, and one's interaction with a significant "reference group" (Lofland, 1969). This is not to imply that all persons' self-concepts are directed by a strong core identity. Neither does this assume that all people strive to maintain complete self-consistency. Most people live with a great deal of inconsistency in their lives. The tendency to develop a strong core identity, however, is intrinsic to certain social roles or contexts. Hart and Richardson (1981) have found that gays often organize their self-identity around their sexual identity. This is also very common for persons who hold stigmatized identities (Goffman, 1963). The ideologies and practices of many religious groups encourage a self-concept organized around one's religious identity (Ammerman, 1987; Peshkin, 1986). A particular view of the world becomes the sacred canopy which makes sense of all other experiences. The more a person is encapsulated and indoctrinated in a religious perspective the less likely he or she is to change (Gecas, 1981; Greil and Rudy, 1984a).

IDENTITY DISSONANCE AS MOTIVATIONAL MECHANISM

A discussion of socialization is incomplete, however, without an examination of motivation (Gecas, 1986). In symbolic interactionist writings the question of motivation has often been deferred to discussion of "motives," "legitimations," and "accounts," especially in terms similar to Mills's (1940), and Scott and Lyman's (1968) usages. The concept of motive is akin to attribution theory, both which offer linguistic justifications for a particular act or pattern of behavior. Motives are the professed reasons or accounts of their motivations or impetus for change. This facet of socialization is essential; however, it does not address the internal mechanisms for change.

One way to approach the question of motivation is by considering what those who sought Good News had in common. In a majority of conversion studies this has been a problem. After-the-fact accounts about members' lives prior to conversion have been seen as colored by ritualized biographical reconstruction (Greil and Rudy, 1984b; Snow and Phillips, 1980). The present study, however, closely examined letters written to the group prior to ideological contact in order to evaluate the identity and motivation of those seeking interaction with Good News.

According to these observations, at first encounter with this organization 74 percent of potential members expressed a strong desire to resolve the felt tension between being a conservative Christian and having homosexual feelings. This tension can be understood best in terms of cognitive dissonance theory (Festinger, 1957; Prus, 1984), which states that an amount of internal dissonance may be produced by holding two inconsistent cognitive elements. These need not be logically incongruent, nor do they necessarily require resolution. The motivational force of cognitive dissonance arises when the person perceives the inconsistency intolerable, thus seeking dissonance reduction in some form.

Generalizing the dynamics of cognitive dissonance may be useful in interpreting the condition of two incongruent identities being held by the same person. While many persons may hold incongruent identities in a workable tension, these identities seldom both function as organizing "core identities" of the self-concept. Those persons who contact Good News perceive both identities as crucial to their self-concept. The identities, as originally construed, are mutually exclusive; however, they are also considered too important to surrender. This dissonance between the identities functions as a motive for change, or dissonance reduction, only if the person perceives this state as problematic. For most of those who came to Good News, the dissonance between their gay and Evangelical identities was intolerable and had to be resolved.

RELIGIOUS IDENTITY REVISION

Many facets of religious identity revision have been explored by those studying conversion. Much of this work focuses on the acceptance of a new religious identity (Kilbourne and Richardson, 1989) or a shift from one identity to another (Greeley, 1981). Often this change in identity is perceived to be an either/or alternative. The result is radical conversion or a segmented, compartmentalized self-concept. Using a socialization model, however, the individual variations within a particular religious identity become evident because the focus is on the dynamics of the social interaction. Religious identity revision can be equated with any other kind of socialization; it simply involves a different organizational context (Greil and Rudy, 1984b). The interaction between the social group and the active individual provides the crucial content and context for change.

There has been a movement in recent years to frame conversion in terms of a socialization process (Long and Hadden, 1983; Machalek and Snow, 1985; Kilbourne and Richardson, 1989). This has enabled theorists to tie religious identity change to a larger body of literature on human development. This perspective frames the convert as actively engaged in the search for meaning and fulfillment. It makes possible a greater appreciation of the dialectical relationship between the individual and the group. The social group is still seen as having a formative function, but it is no longer perceived as the only force in socialization. It remains a source for social meaning and, at the same time, limits the contents of one's identity through group forms and the availability of role models. But conversion, and any identity change, becomes better understood as a product of negotiation between the individual and the social context (Strauss, 1976). While social interaction and involvement with others is necessary for the validation and maintenance of a revised identity, the individual is seen as the active agent.

A DESCRIPTION OF GOOD NEWS AS THE CONTEXT FOR CHANGE

Good News is a parachurch Evangelical organization whose national office and primary group are in Atlanta. The group meets biweekly in a local gay center. Attendance varies, but averages about eight people. The core group consists of four persons, all white males, as are the majority of other members. Occasionally, there are a few white females or black males. The average age of those who attend is 35 years. In addition to this group, there are four affiliate groups in cities throughout the South and Midwest. At any time, there are hundreds of individuals, living in isolated small towns around the country, who have contact with the group through correspondence. Good News publishes a quarterly newsletter that is distributed to approximately 400 people. The group has corresponded with over 1,300 people in its nine years of operation.

The study of Good News took place in 1984 and 1985. The data were collected through participant observation of 20 meetings. In-depth personal interviews were conducted with seven members of Good News. Along with this, an intensive study was made of the voluminous correspondence, all issues of the newsletter, and the group's published literature. The descriptive statistics in this article are derived from the author's rough estimate of observations, plus a content analysis of group correspondence.

Good News has been meeting since 1977 under the leadership of three co-founders. Following the lead of "liberal" Christians, they have embraced a cultural interpretation of the scriptures. They continue, however, to assert forcefully their Evangelical heritage and maintain many of the characteristic traditional Evangelical beliefs and practices. The group officially operates with a threefold mission of dialogue with the "straight" church, enrichment for gay believers, and service to the entire homosexual community. Actually, their central task is to offer members a way, both experientially and cognitively, to reconcile a conservative Christian faith and a homosexual identity. This task is the focus of this paper.

In this context, "membership" should be understood as not joining the group structure, but as accepting its ideology and world view concerning the negotiation of a gay Christian identity. Evangelizing the good news of this cognitive adjustment, by which one could be both gay and a conservative Christian, occupied most of the group's energy. Because of this emphasis rather than physical recruitment to the group itself, membership continued to decline in the years after this study ended. In 1987 the group officially disbanded. Along with an emphasis on believing over belonging, other factors that contributed to the group's demise included two founding members redirecting their energies to AIDS work, and three other core members relocating and becoming more active in their local congregations. During the time this study took place, however, Good News still offered both cognitive structures and some experiential contexts by which members could reconstruct their self-concept.

Good News' mission is unified around a vision that reflects this goal of identity revision. Good News "is a family of believers who strive to forge bridges of biblical faith which serve, not oppress, lesbian and gay lifestyles." After a brief look at who seeks out Good News, this article focuses on how these bridges are forged or the identities of the Evangelical faith and gay lifestyle reconciled.

THE FAMILY OF BELIEVERS

According to the letters Good News receives, most persons (74%) who seek out the group are in the midst of an identity crisis.[3] This struggle arises from being a conservative Christian and having homosexual feelings. The tension, guilt, and confusion that result from an attempt to hold these incongruous identities together becomes too great for these persons. They feel as if they can no longer remain in the tension between desiring to be "good" conservative Christians and yet having "sinful," and specifically condemned, feelings of homosexual attraction. One person wrote to the group, "I will not and cannot disregard my faith (nor my sexual orientation). I often find myself compromising my beliefs. The Lord is disappointed with me." Another writer stated, "I have abstained from sexual involvement with others for three years because of my fear of breaking God's law. I miss the close fellowship of a lover, but I'm scared that I will go to hell if I do. I'm so lonely." A third quote from a letter to Good News clearly exemplifies this identity dissonance:

> I can remember dying inside one Sunday listening to my minister tell me and his congregation that "those queers were going to fry in Hell for the choice they made." I thought I knew Christ then. So if it seemed to be God's will for me not to be homosexual, then I'd do something about it. I prayed about it but nothing happened.

All those who came to Good News place significant value and meaning upon the conservative Evangelical identity. One of the leaders made this clear in his statement.

"I left the Metropolitan Community Church because I felt that they were putting gay before God....They just weren't evangelical enough for me." Members' religious faith is a very important aspect of who they are. As one said, "It is through my Christian faith that I am able to define myself and know who I am." It is the core identity for most of them.

For many, their religious affiliation symbolizes a grounding in a history, membership in a tradition, and stability in a social order. An overwhelming majority of those who contact Good News (94%) were reared in religious families and attended conservative Evangelical churches in denominations such as Baptist, Missouri Synod Lutheran, Church of Christ, and Assemblies of God. Sixty-eight percent grew up in the South or Midwest in rural areas or small towns. They were all oriented to look to religion in solving their problems and in giving meaning to their lives.

Two primary characteristics of the Evangelical tradition are the doctrine of the inerrancy of the scripture and a traditional moral conservatism (Hunter, 1983). Both result in the creation of a very difficult atmosphere for a Christian struggling with homosexual feelings. The Bible literally states, "Thou shall not lie with man as with a woman; it is an abomination" (Lev. 18:22). Homosexuality has been a sin throughout the history of Christianity (Boswell, 1980; McNeil, 1976).

According to both researchers and interviews with Good News members, homosexuality is still strongly condemned in the Evangelical denominations of Christianity. Hunter reports 88.7 percent of Evangelicals thought homosexuality was an "immoral behavior" (1983:85); Ammerman found 98 percent of Southern Baptists surveyed indicated that it was not a viable Christian lifestyle (1985). Roof and McKinney report that conservative Protestants were the least likely religious group in America either to affirm the civil rights of gays or to view homosexuality as morally acceptable (1987:192, 212). For a conservative Christian, this reality presents both a theological and a social barrier to being an Evangelical gay Christian.

Such a reality is clearly evident in that most members report experiencing tremendous rejection from family and friends. As one letter writer put it, "I came out to my family and they kicked me out of the house." Another actively attending member related, "I told my best friends, this Christian couple from my church, and now they won't talk to me." The social ostracization that accompanies the homosexual stigma, especially in a small town or rural area, had taken its toll on those who contacted Good News.

Every person expressed feelings of "being different from the other kids" since early childhood, seeing themselves as social outcasts. Almost every person said he or she felt or experienced rejection from a church congregation because of his or her homosexual desires. An active member recounted his experience, "I heard more and more sermons condemning homosexuality. Knowing that if I was ever found out, I might be thrown out of the church, I was in such a confused state." About 40 percent had some experience with gay community, but very few, only 8 percent, had continual contact or exposure to with a local group of gays. All of those in contact with Good News stated they desperately wanted to resolve the perceived tension between being a homosexual and an Evangelical Christian. One letter stated, "I love God, but how can I deny my own feelings? Why should I have to sacrifice myself either to God or to the Devil because of my feelings?" They were actively seeking resolution of the tension when they responded to Good News's advertisements, "Gay and Christian, is it possible?"

Many expressed anxiety, despair, and the feeling that they had come to "the end of the rope." Religious acceptance by God, a community, and a heritage were perceived as a potential way to relieve the sense of alienation and rejection. This was often expressed as a desire to serve the Lord and become "good, whole" Christians, while hoping to live out authentically what they perceived to be their God-given sexuality.

GOOD NEWS' AGENDA—ASSURING THE PROPER MOTIVATIONS

The leadership of Good News are well aware of the situations of those who contact them. They focus the group's efforts directly on the biblical and social condemnation of homosexuality. The structure of the organization is to help members change this negative perception into a positive self-concept. A number of specifically designed tasks are intended to promote identity revision. The leadership present these as separate and logical steps; however, within the group they take place simultaneously and are inseparable.

The written responses to those who asked for help illuminated the proposed pattern of progression. Most letters from the core members began with counseling and the assurance that it was possible to reconcile being gay and Evangelical. Next they offered their testimony, information (biblical and scientific) about how it was possible, and a list of books to read for more information. The third part of the letter often consisted of encouraging the person to seek supportive fellowship or come to Atlanta to visit the group. Finally, there was a discussion of possible pitfalls and spiritual ways of maintaining the gay Christian identity. Interviews and interaction with the group highlighted the fact that members followed the pattern intellectually, but in practice observed interactions and identity negotiation were not nearly so easily or sequentially perceived.

Good News understands its first task to be one of convincing potential members that it is permissible to alter their religious beliefs. In an initial encounter one must literally be counseled and assured that one will not be condemned to Hell if she or he tampers with traditionally "sacred" doctrines. Reinterpreting the scripture is to be viewed as a legitimate undertaking that does not destroy the validity and efficacy of the scriptures. As one of the leaders put it, "They have to realize that the house doesn't fall down if one of the bricks was out of place." This instruction can be clearly seen in the comment from a corresponding affiliate member: "The two books you sent me broke the barrier of guilt, fear, and anxiety my homosexuality had falsely imposed. The teaching I had been taught were men's fears, condemnations, and opinions spoken in God's Name. They were social condemnations, NOT GOD'S."

Once a person accepts the challenge to question doctrines and a literal interpretation of scripture, the focus then turns to one's motives for change. Although personal motivation is an absolute necessity, the "proper" framing of that motivation must be taught. The motive for challenging traditional beliefs must be spiritually grounded; it must be seen as a spiritual quest.

Good News casts the change in terms of sanctification or "growth in wisdom and perfection of the Christian life." Tension between sexuality and religiosity is understood as "an ungodly dualism between the body and the spirit." Problems resulting from a literal interpretation of scripture are redefined as issues of "cultural relativity." The choice then becomes either expressing one's God-given, unchangeable sexuality or being bound by "men's fears and opinions spoken in God's name." Once members tentatively accept this ideological perspective, "it is God's will for us to be gay and Christian," they can begin internalizing the perspective. The only correct action is to "follow God's plan for your life." In response, a potential member often asks, "How can I know for sure that what you say is God's will?"

TEACHING GOD'S WILL

The second task of Good News is to present the doctrines that support the proposed identity revision. Included in this instruction are the new ways to understand the identity dissonance and the issues in question. Good News often asserts the "you must know the truth and the truth will set you free." This means that the more one learns about the "correct" doctrines, the easier it is to accept the new identity. This teaching has a two-fold purpose. First, the teaching must denigrate the former position by identifying the faulty reasoning and incorrect learning from which it arose. Then, the instruction must provide information to replace the former thoughts about self-identity, redefine the supportive meaning system, and prescribe the direction of future action.

Good News must teach its members the "proper" interpretation of the scriptures and, at the same time, the acceptability of the gay lifestyle. They go about this first task by employing a historical-critical hermeneutic. This principle of interpretation reduces the condemnation of specific passages by calling into question their relevance for a modern world. One of the leaders affirmed this in a talk during a meeting. He stated, "I would still say that I believe in the infallibility of the scriptures, but what I would mean by that is certainly a lot different. I'm more liberal in the culture-related things, but conservative in theology. My theology hasn't changed much."

They then offer an elaborate exegesis of these passages to show that the Greek words translated as "homosexual" are either undefinable or refer to pederasty. A third method they use is to emphasize biblical principles, such as love and acceptance of all persons, to counter the discriminatory attitudes of the church toward gays. Another of the leaders announced at a homecoming, "The bottom line — the top line — is that God loves people, all people. That to me is the basic message of the Bible."

A final theological method used to affirm the gay lifestyle is focusing on the image of God as creator. Psalms such as 139, "For you have created my innermost parts," and 100, "It is he that hath made us and not we ourselves," are often quoted. The reasoning of this creationist argument is, "Since God made me the way I am, why shouldn't I express my sexuality?" The group also relies on scientific literature to show that homosexuality is an orientation and is, therefore, immutable.[4] In this regard, the question is heard, "Why would God ask me to change something I can't?"

The primary modes of teaching are: lessons presented at meetings; special guest speakers; recommended readings of supportive books, such as *Is the Homosexual My Neighbor?* by Scanzoni and Mollenkott (1978); written correspondence; and interaction with appropriate role models. These teachings offer alternative cognitive categories that support the proposed identity revisions. In doing this, Good News hopes to insure the acceptance of the revised identity by providing a complementary meaning system to support the new identity.

EMBODYING THE NEW IDENTITY

Once the cognitive structures which support the revised identity have been presented, a third task is begun. Good News attempts to facilitate integration of the new gay Christian identity. This is undertaken in two primary ways: Through evangelistic activities and through social interactions. There are a multitude of activities that need to be done for Good News to remain an organization. Members are put to work on such tasks as counseling and corresponding with newer members, writing and mailing newsletters, and planning and organizing social activities. As the newsletter challenged, "If God is using Good News to bless you and challenge you, won't you give so that others who are in despair may hear the Gospel of God's love and concern for them." They are also encouraged to become involved in overt gay activities such as participating in gay rights rallies, AIDS benefits, visiting gay clubs (often to witness), and volunteering at various gay service organizations. Again the newsletter made this aspect evident, "so who will take care of World Salvation and daily victorious living in Jesus Christ into the gay community?" In addition to these activities, Good News holds prayer meetings, Bible studies, spiritual retreats, homecomings, and pot-luck fellowship dinners. All these are open and receptive to guests and visitors.

The group also intentionally promotes evangelism to "heterosexual" congregations. Pastors of local churches are often asked to speak at bi-weekly meetings. Members are strongly encouraged to attend "straight" churches within a member's denominational tradition. One of the group leaders made this clear during an interview.

> I consciously chose to be a member of a predominantly non-gay congregation because I believe in the concept of the family of faith, the community of faith. Christians who are gay cannot afford the luxury of isolation. We have to be willing to risk the pain, the alienation, the separation, if we are to achieve any semblance of dialogue.

According to the group's bylaws, officers and board members are required to attend straight churches as witnesses of God's redemption and grace to all people, including gays. This is also done as a sign of the group's commitment to the unity of the body of Christ.

In many ways the social activities that Good News sponsors replicate the Evangelical heritage of members. Most of the social events are reminiscent of conservative church activities, such as "group dates," Bible retreats, and homecomings, which are the annual revivalistic gatherings for marginal and out-of-town members. All of these events help legitimate the new identity. Through positive interaction with others, members begin to internalize the gay Evangelical identity and integrate it into their self-concept. One member expressed this in a letter, "The Mollenkott weekend retreat was quite an experience for me. That weekend was the first time in a very long time that I actually felt accepted, that I belonged."

The leadership encourage those who contact Good News to find a gay community or fellowship and subscribe to gay magazines, including the group's newsletter. Good News offers an opportunity for acceptance by other persons in a positive social context. They recommend that out-of-town members visit the Atlanta group, or one of the affiliate groups, and even, if possible, move to a larger town that has a gay church or fellowship in it. The group structures allow members to experiment with the tentative identity through service, community involvement, and participation in activities that parallel the Evangelical Christian ones from which they would be excluded as gays. Finally, these social activities, and the acceptance gained from interaction with other group members, strengthen the process of socialization into the new identity. One member made this clear in an interview. "I decided to visit Good News. There I found, along with a wonderful group of people, a place where I could feel free to be myself and to profess my faith in Jesus Christ." This interaction promotes the assurance that the decision to accept the revised identity is a correct one.

MAINTAINING THE NEW IDENTITY

The fourth and final task for Good News is to help strengthen and maintain the newly revised identity. Community and group support are correlated strongly with continued commitment to the gay Christian identity. Many members find that acceptance by other Christians is all they need to solidify the identity revisions. However, the group uses a number of other techniques to facilitate this change. One of these methods involves negating and devaluing the former identity. Members come to regard their previous situation as a hinderance to becoming "whole" Christians. This is expressed in the statement by one of the long-time members.

> By accepting [my sexual orientation] I was able to move spiritually. I don't live a double life now. I can't change, and I don't want to change. When you are able to accept yourself and know that God accepts you and made you, you're able to go on and life a more productive and more happy life.

A second technique is to present the current gay Christian identity as part of an oppressed minority, thus seeing outside, "unenlightened," groups as hostile and misguided. "Being different" is strengthened further by and the creation of an "elitist" group identity. Both conservative denominations and certain secular gay groups are viewed as opposing the truthfulness of Good News's position. The former errs in not accepting gays in the Christian fellowship. The latter is at fault for devaluing Christian involvement in the gay community. Another approach the group uses is to infuse many of the morals of the Evangelical lifestyle into the gay lifestyle. Good News states that sexual expression and relationships are to be guided by biblical principles, not by wanton desires. Ideally, one should engage in sexual activity only in a committed relationship.

A fifth way to strengthen the revised identity is to compensate for the felt losses in religious orthodoxy. This is done by encouraging increases in orthopraxy. Good News offers its members many traditional evangelical activities, as noted above. They place a strong emphasis on individual piety and outward religiosity, to such an extent that it hints of a "works of righteousness."

In terms of beliefs, Good News also promotes a strict adherence to all "significant" orthodox doctrines, such as the divinity of Christ, his virgin birth and bodily resurrection, the absolute necessity of personal salvation, and the belief that the Bible is the inspired word of God, correctly interpreted. One group leader made this very clear during one meeting: "A Christian can still have a high view of scripture, humanity, sin, and salvation, and yet find nothing in homosexuality incompatible with being a Christian."

They assure any inquiring person that they strongly adhere to every point of the statement of faith of the National Association of Evangelists. Good News's statement of faith begins,

> The members of Good News profess their individual and corporate faith in the basic Biblical Truths of the full authority of Scripture, a personal commitment to Jesus Christ as Savior and Lord of Life, and the urgency of Sharing the Gospel message in both word and deed.

Finally, since Good News frames the change as a spiritual journey, the rewards of maintaining a revised self-identity are presented as primarily spiritual in nature. One out-of-town member expressed the truth of this claim: "I cannot express the spiritual release of standing clean before the Lord." The love and confirmation of worth from other Christians toward those who previously had been ostracized by the church becomes an act of redemption and forgiveness.

The group's acceptance is understood as a sign of God's approval and blessing. As one of the leaders commented, "God loves us and stays with us, forever offering forgiveness, healing, and wholeness. We live and move and have our being — including our sexual being — within the sphere of God's love." The biblical mandate of sanctification and the assurance of eternal "rewards" for a faithful Christian operate as implicit mechanisms of commitment to the new gay Christian identity.

THE INDIVIDUAL AS ACTIVE NEGOTIATOR

Much of this discussion of the process of negotiating a gay Evangelical identity has focused on the group dynamics promoting change. This was intentional; Good News presents a model into which its members are socialized. A central premise of the concept of socialization is that individuals are brought to conform to the expectations and ideals of the group through internalization and social learning. As Long and Hadden state, "the special character of the process is defined by what members *do to* novices" (1983:5). But to view this process only as one-sided, or the novice as passively receptive, is inadequate.

Very few people who contact Good News actually did end up carbon copies of the leadership. They negotiate with the group as much as the group negotiates its "identity ideal" with the Evangelical tradition. Persons come to the group with varying degrees of commitment to Christianity, of openness to homosexuality, and of willingness to change. Different levels of motivation drastically influence how one responds to the identity revisions suggested by Good News. This is seen most clearly in the diverse ways the new identity is embodied. A few persons wholeheartedly accept both the new identity and the group, becoming core members (roughly 5%). More often people seek out Good News to resolve the identity dissonance; once the dissonance is resolved or reduced, they disappear (almost 65%). Sometimes a person accepts the identity and continues to maintain a surface relationship or affiliate membership with the group for occasional support and fellowship (25%). A small percentage (5%), upon hearing the message of Good News, reject it and quickly sever their connections with the group.

THE GAY EVANGELICAL

Persons who have successfully internalized a gay Evangelical identity very likely may appear different from the way they were when they first sought out Good News. In most cases members accept their homosexuality and become open about their lifestyle. At the same time, they forcefully affirm their Evangelical heritage. In most cases, these gay Evangelicals are more pious and orthodox than they were prior to their encounter with Good News. Members certainly hold more moralistic views on sexuality and relationships than are found in the general secular gay population (Bell and Weinberg, 1978). Most members report an increase in personal piety, including more Bible reading and daily devotions, a systematic study of the scriptures and of their Evangelical heritage, and a greater amount of time spent in prayer and meditation. They explain these changes as resulting from feeling accepted by God.

At the same time, however, these members are no longer traditional Evangelical Christians according to doctrinal beliefs. They do not believe in the inerrancy of the Bible. They are less affected by the moral proscriptions against drinking, dancing, sex outside of marriage, align politically with the left on issues of war, poverty, individual rights, abortion, and foreign policies. Members almost inevitably become somewhat more tolerant of the rights of others such as blacks and women. Many members fit nicely with Hunter's description of the "young Evangelicals" (1983:111). They are no longer traditional Evangelicals, but in many ways they know themselves to be more authentic as gay Evangelicals.

CONCLUSIONS

Except for the hermit or the isolated sect, identity negotiation appears to be unavoidable in the modern world. This is true for members of Good News, especially in light of their struggle with homosexual feelings. The gay community ideology asserts that a homosexual orientation is immutable and an essential part of a gay person's nature. This presents a difficult problem for those who seek out Good News. They feel they must remain faithful to their Evangelical heritage and doctrinal beliefs — doctrines that explicitly forbid homosexuality. These persons have struggled with this core identity dissonance for years before arriving at a point of view where something has to be done. Yet few have any idea of how to reduce this dissonance and still remain authentic to their sexuality and religious identity.

The only possible solution they find to be viable for them is one that maintains both identities. This solution demands a negotiated settlement between the dual core identities. Some amount of accommodation is necessary. The identity negotiation requires that these Christians accept a historical critical approach to the Bible, but it does not change them into liberal Christians. The negotiated identity allows them to accept their homosexuality, while not requiring that they deny their faith. Socialization into Good News's ideology, alters, but does not eradicate, members' Evangelical religious identity. Good News offers a unique brand of identity negotiation. It presents an opportunity to "have one's cake and eat it too."

Through interaction with the group, members construct a gay Evangelical Christian identity as an alternative to their previous dissonant religious and sexual identities. In hundreds of people who have come into contact with Good News, a change of self-concept becomes both the impetus and result of the integration of a strengthened gay identity with an accommodated Evangelical Christian religious identity. Neither identity is radically compromised; rather, both are combined to create the new core identity and self-concept of a gay Evangelical Christian.

Although this is a unique situation, it does raise the question of whether this same process occurs in diverse religious situations or conversion events. In conceptualizing religious identity change or conversion as an either/or proposition, researchers may be overlooking the subtlety of individual's identity negotiation. Likewise, in ambitious efforts to show the rampant conservative religious accommodation to modernity, we may be missing those who successfully negotiate both a core Evangelical world view and very modern aspects of culture. The example that members of Good News offer us suggests that social scientists should take a closer look at what is going on in the socialization dynamics of religious accommodation to the modern world.

REFERENCES

Ammerman, Nancy. 1985. Data from an unpublished study done by the Center for Religious Research, Emory University, Atlanta, GA.

———. 1987. *Bible Believers: Fundamentalists in the Modern World.* New Brunswick, NJ: Rutgers University Press.

Becker, Howard. 1963. *Outsiders: Studies in the Sociology of Deviance.* New York: Free Press.

Bell, Alan and Martin S. Weinberg. 1978. *Homosexualities: A Study of Diversity Among Men and Women.* New York: Simon and Schuster.

Berger, Peter and Thomas Luckmann. 1967. *The Social Construction of Reality: A Treatise in the Sociology of Knowledge.* Garden City, NY: Doubleday.

Blair, Ralph. 1977. *An Evangelical Look at Homosexuality.* New York: Homosexual Community Counseling Center.
Boswell, John. 1980. *Christianity, Social Tolerance, and Homosexuality: Gay People in Western Europe from the Beginning of the Christian Era to the 14th Century.* Chicago: University of Chicago Press.
Festinger, Leon. 1957. *A Theory of Cognitive Dissonance.* Palo Alto, CA: Stanford University Press.
Garfinkel, Harold. 1967. *Studies in Ethnomethodology.* Englewood Cliffs, NJ: Prentice Hall.
Gecas, Victor. 1981. "Contexts of Socialization," Pp. *165–199. Social Psychology: Sociological Perspectives*, edited by M. Rosenberg and R.H. Turner. New York: Basic Books.
———. 1982. "The Self-Concept," Pp. 1–33 in *Annual Review of Sociology 8*, edited by R. Turner and J. Short. Palo Alto, CA: Annual Reviews.
———. 1986. "The Motivational Significance of Self-Concept for Socialization Theory," Pp. 131–156 in *Advances in Group Process 3*, edited by Edward Lawler. Greenwich, CT: JAI Press.
Goffman, Erving. 1959. *The Presentation of Self in Everyday Life.* Garden City, NY: Doubleday.
———. 1963. *Stigma: Notes on the Management of Spoiled Identity.* Englewood Cliffs, NJ: Prentice Hall.
Greeley, Andrew. 1981. "Religious Musical Chairs," Pp. 101–126 in *Gods We Trust: New Patterns of Religious Pluralism in America*, edited by T. Robbins and D. Anthony. New Brunswick, NJ: Transaction.
Greenberg, David F. 1988. *The Construction of Homosexuality.* Chicago: University of Chicago Press.
Greil, Arthur, and David Rudy. 1984a"Social Cocoons: Encapsulation and Identity Transformation Organizations," *Sociological Inquiry* 54:26–278.
———. 1984b. "What Have We Learned From Process Models of Conversion? An Examination of Ten Case Studies," *Sociological Focus* 17:305–323.
Hart, John and Diane Richardson. 1981. *The Theory and Practice of Homosexuality.* London: Routledge and Kegan Paul.
Hunter, James Davison. 1983. *American Evangelicalism: Conservative Religion and the Quandary of Modernity.* New Brunswick, NJ: Rutgers University Press.
Kilbourne, Brock and James Richardson. 1989. "Paradigm Conflict, Types of Conversion, and Conversion Theories." *Sociological Analysis* 50:1–21.
Lofland, John. 1969. *Deviance and Identity.* Englewood Cliffs, NJ: Prentice Hall.
Long, Theodore and Jeffery Hadden. 1983. "Religious Conversion and the Concept of Socialization: Integrating the Brainwashing and Drift Models." *Journal for the Scientific Study of Religion* 22:1–14.
Machalek, R., and D.A. Snow. 1985. "Neglected Issues in the Study of Conversion," Pp. 123–129 in *Scientific Research and New Religions: Divergent Perspectives*, edited by B. Kilbourne. San Francisco: American Association for the Advancement of Science.
Mead, George Herbert. 1934. *Mind, Self, and Society.* Chicago: University of Chicago Press.
McNeill, John. 1976. *The Church and the Homosexual Mission.* KS: St. Andrews and McMeel.
Mills, C. Wright. 1940. "Situated Actions and Vocabularies of Motives." *American Sociological Review* 5:905–929.
Olson, Mark. 1984. "Where to Turn: A Guide for Gay and Lesbian Christians," *The Other Side* 151:16–31.
Peshkin, Alan. 1986. "Religious Recruitment and the Management of Dissonance: A Sociological Perspective." *Sociological Inquiry* 46:127–134.
Richardson, Diane. 1984. "The Dilemma of Essentiality in Homosexual Theory." *Journal of Homosexuality* 9:77–90.
Richardson, James, Mary White Stewart, and Robert Simmons. 1981. "Conversion of Fundamentalism," Pp. 127–139 in *Gods We Trust: New Patterns of Religious Pluralism in America*, edited by T. Robbins and D. Anthony. New Brunswick, NJ: Transaction.
Roof, Wade Clark and William McKinney. 1987. *American Mainline Religion: Its Changing Shape and Future.* New Brunswick, NJ: Rutgers University Press.
Scanzoni, Letha and Virginia Mollenkott. 1978. *Is the Homosexual My Neighbor?: Another Christian View.* San Francisco: Harper and Row.
Scott, Marvin and Stanford Lyman. 1968. "Accounts." *American Sociological Review* 33:46–62.
Snow, David and Cynthia Phillips. 1980. "The Lofland-Stark Conversion Model: A Critical Assessment." *Social Problems* 27:430–437.

Staples, Clifford and Armand Mauss. 1987. "Conversion or Commitment? A Reassessment of the Snow and Machalek Approach to the Study of Conversion." *Journal for the Scientific Study of Religion* 26:133–147.

Strauss, Roger. 1976. "Changing Oneself: Seekers and the Creative Transformation of Life Experience," Pp. 257–273 in *Doing Social Life*, edited by John Lofland. New York: Wiley.

Thumma, Scott. 1987. "Straightening Identities: Evangelical Approaches to Homosexuality." Unpublished masters thesis, Emory University, Atlanta, GA.

Travisano, Richard. 1970. "Alternation and Conversion as Qualitatively Different Transformations," Pp. 594–606 in *Social Psychology Through Symbolic Interaction*, edited by G.P. Stone and H.A. Farberman. Waltham, MA: Ginn-Blaisdell.

Troiden, Richard. 1984. "Self, Self-Concept, Identity, and Homosexual Identity: Constructs in Need of Definition and Differentiation." *Journal of Homosexuality* 10:97–107.

NOTES

[1] All the quotes used in this without specific references are taken from Thumma (1987) and other field notes from this study.

[2] See the references below such as Hunter (1983:85), Ammerman (1985), and Roof and McKinney (1987:192,212). There are a few Evangelical groups that do not hold this perspective, see Blair (1977), or a special issue of *The Other Side* (Olson, 1984) devoted to exploring the question of homosexuality and the Church.

[3] The rest of those who contacted Good News did so for support, for fellowship, or for an opportunity to work in a Christian ministry.

[4] The conceptualization of homosexual identity used throughout this paper is one offered by Good News. This understanding is common to many gay groups, and certain scientists, see Bell and Weinberg (1978). There is a debate presently between researchers who see homosexuality from an "essentialist" perspective and those who hold a social constructionist view, see Diane Richardson (1984) or David Greenberg (1988).

Chapter 22 THE PROBLEM OF IDENTITY
CONSTRUCTION AMONG THE
HOMELESS[1]

David A. Snow and *Leon Anderson*

In *The Birth of Death and Meaning*, Ernest Becker (1962), drawing on the ideas of Alfred Adler (Ansbacher and Ansbacher 1946), argues that our most basic drive is for a sense of self-worth or personal significance and that its accessibility depends in part on the roles available to us. If so, then, it is sociologically axiomatic that, because of their differential distribution throughout the social structure, not all individuals have equal access to a measure of self-worth. Homeless street people are a case in point. Unlike nearly all other inhabitants of a society, the homeless are seldom incumbents of social roles that are consensually defined in terms of positive social utility and moral worth. As does any highly stigmatized class, the homeless serve various societal functions, such as providing casual labor for underground economies, but these are not the sorts of functions from which personal significance and self-worth can be easily derived. As a consequence, the homeless constitute a kind of superfluous population, in the sense that they fall outside the hierarchy of structurally available societal roles and thus beyond the conventional, role-based sources of moral worth and dignity that most citizens take for granted. The intriguing question thus arises of how the homeless attend to what Adler and Becker, among others, regard as the basic need for self-worth. More specifically, to what extent and how do the homeless generate personal identities that yield a measure of self-respect and dignity?

In his classic study on stigma, Goffman (1963) notes a variety of strategies frequently used by the stigmatized to minimize the deleterious social and psychic consequences of their discrediting attributes. One such strategy is to "pass" by concealing or withholding information about the stigma so that it is not easily perceived by others. This strategy is not a feasible alternative for dealing with all varieties of stigma, however. As Goffman noted, its utility varies inversely with the obtrusiveness of the stigma. For those whose stigma is not readily visible, such as members of some deviant religious orders, passing can be relatively easy. For the more visibly stigmatized, however, passing is largely impossible. Most homeless street people fall into this latter category. Their tattered and soiled clothes function as an ever-present and readily perceivable "role sign" (Banton 1965) or "stigma symbol" (Goffman 1963) that immediately draws attention to them and sets them apart from others. Actual or threatened proximity to them not only engenders fear and enmity in other citizens but also frequently invites the most visceral kinds of responses, ranging from shouts of invective to organized neighborhood opposition to proposed shelter locations to "troll busting" campaigns aimed at terrorization.[2] Moreover, these sorts of reactions seldom go unnoticed. As one homeless young man who had been on the streets for only two weeks lamented, "The hardest thing has been getting used to the way people look down on street people. It's real hard to feel good about yourself when almost everyone you see is looking down on you."[3]

Physical isolation might offer an escape from this dilemma, but the homeless seldom possess the requisite survival resources. Consequently, the vast majority find themselves "hanging out" on city streets and migrating from one agency to another that provides for such basic survival needs as food and shelter. Their daily routines thus bring them in contact with many other citizens on a regular basis. Because of this and the fact that they are always "in uniform," strategies other than passing and total withdrawal have to be devised in order to develop and maintain a measure of self-worth. Homeless street people are thus confronted continuously with the problem of constructing personal identities that are not a mere reflection of the stereotypical and stigmatized manner in which they are regarded as a social category.

To what extent and how do they manage this identity problem? How do they carve out a modicum of self-respect given their pariah-like status? And, what are the implications of the answers to these questions for understanding more generally the relationships among social roles, identity, and the self? What, in short, can we learn from the homeless about identity and identity-construction processes? We address these questions with data from a field study of homeless people in Austin, Texas (see original article for discussion of procedures).

Varieties of Identity Talk Among the Homeless: Findings and Observations

Up to this point, we have used the term "identity" in a general and undefined fashion. It is necessary to clarify what we mean by the term "identity" and related concepts before proceeding further. Although there is no agreement on whether identity should be conceptualized as a unitary entity or disaggregated into several types, we find it preferable to pursue the latter tack. Accordingly, we distinguish among social identities, personal identities, and self-concept.[4] By social identities, we refer to the identities attributed or imputed to others in an attempt to place or situate them as social objects. They are not self-designations or avowals but imputations based primarily on information gleaned on the basis of appearance, behavior, and the location and time of action.[5] In contrast, personal identities refer to the meanings attributed to the self by the actor. They are self-designations and self-attributions brought into play or asserted during the course of interaction.[6] Since personal identities may be inconsistent with imputed social identities, the two need to be kept analytically distinct. Standing in contrast to these two variants of identity is the self-concept, by which we refer to one's overarching view or image of her- or himself "as a physical, social, spiritual, or moral being" (Gecas 1982, p.3). Following Turner (1968), we view the self-concept as a kind of working compromise between idealized images and imputed social identities. Presented personal identities provide a glimpse of the consistency or inconsistency between social identities and self-concept, as well as indications of the latter.

Our empirical concern here is primarily with personal identities and particularly with the ways in which the homeless construct and utilize such identities. We conceptualize identity construction and assertion as variants of the generic process we call *identity work*, by which we refer to the range of activities individuals engage in to create, present, and sustain personal identities that are congruent with and supportive of the self-concept. So defined, identity work may involve a number of complementary activities: *(a)* procurement or arrangement of physical settings and props; *(b)* cosmetic face work or the arrangement of personal appearance; *(c)* selective association with other individuals and groups; and *(d)* verbal construction and assertion of personal identities. In this paper, we concentrate on the last variety of identity work, which we refer to as *identity talk*. Since the homeless seldom have the financial or social resources to pursue the other varieties of identity work, talk is perhaps the primary avenue through which they can attempt to construct, assert, and maintain desired personal identities, especially when these personal identities are at variance with the general social identity of a street person. Because the structure of their daily routines ensures that they spend a great deal of time waiting here and there, many homeless also have ample opportunity to converse with one another about a range of topics.

Inspection of these conversational data yielded three generic patterns of identity talk: (1) distancing, (2) embracement, and (3) fictive storytelling. Each was found to contain several varieties that tended to vary in use according to the duration of one's street career. We discuss and elaborate in turn each of the generic patterns and their subtypes, summarizing statistically (in tables 1, 2, and 3) at the end of each section the relationship between the various types and time on the streets.

Distancing

When individuals have to enact roles, associate with others, or utilize institutions that imply social identities inconsistent with their actual or desired self-conceptions, they may attempt to distance themselves from those roles, associations, and institutions (Goffman 1961a, 1961b; Levitin 1964; Stebbins 1975; Sayles 1984). Our findings reveal that a substantial proportion of the identity talk of the homeless we studied was consciously focused on distancing themselves from other homeless individuals, from street and occupational roles, and from the institutions serving them. Nearly a third of the 202 identity statements were of this variety.

Associational distancing.—Since one's claim to a particular self is partly contingent on the imputed social identities of one's associates, one way to substantiate that claim, in the event that one's associates are negatively evaluated, is to distance oneself from them. As Anderson (1976, p. 214) noted, based on his research among black street-corner men, claims to a particular identity depend in part "on one's ability to manage his image by drawing distinctions between himself and others he does not want to be associated with." This distancing technique manifested itself in two ways in our research: dissociation from the homeless as a general social category and dissociation from specific groups of homeless individuals.

Categorical associational distancing was particularly evident among homeless individuals who had been on the streets for a comparatively short time. Illustrative of this technique is the following comment by a 24-year-old white male who had been on the streets for less than two weeks: "I'm not like the other guys who hang out down at the `Sally' (Salvation Army). If you want to know about street people, I can tell you about them; but you can't really learn about street people from studying me, because I'm different."

Such categorical distancing also occurred among those individuals who saw themselves as on the verge of getting off the street. One 22-year-old white male who had been on the streets for several years but who had just secured two jobs in hopes of raising enough money to rent an apartment indicated, for example, that he was different from other street people: "They have gotten used to living on the streets and are satisfied with it. But not me! Next to my salvation, getting off the street is the most important thing in my life." This variety of categorical distancing was particularly pronounced among homeless individuals who had taken jobs at the local Salvation Army shelter and thus had one foot off the street. These individuals were frequently criticized by other street people for their condescending and holier-than-thou attitude. As one regular shelter user put it: "As soon as these guys get inside, they're better than the rest of us. They've been out on the street for years, and as soon as they're inside they forget it."

Among the homeless who had been on the street for some time and who appeared firmly rooted in that life-style, there were few examples of categorical distancing. Instead, these individuals frequently distinguished themselves from other groups of the homeless. This form of associational distancing was most conspicuous among the homeless who were not regular service or shelter users and who thus saw themselves as being more independent and resourceful. These individuals not only wasted little time in pointing out that they were "not like those Sally users," but they were also given to derogating the more institutionally dependent. Indeed, while they were among those furthest removed from the middle class in their way of life, they sounded at times much like middle-class citizens berating welfare recipients. Illustrative is the comment of an alcoholic, 49-year-old woman who had been on the streets for two-and-a-half years: "A lot of these people staying at the Sally, they're reruns. Every day they're wanting something, wanting something. People get tired of giving. All you hear is `give me, give me.' And we transients are getting tired of it." In sum, we have seen that, although associational distancing provides one means by which some of the homeless set themselves apart from one another and thus develop a somewhat different and more self-respecting personal identity, such distancing varies in scope according to the duration of time on the streets.

Role distancing.—Role distancing was the second form of distancing employed by the homeless in order to buffer the self. Following Goffman (1961b, pp. 107-108), role distancing involves an active and self-conscious attempt to foster the impression of a lack of commitment or attachment to a particular role in order to deny the virtual self implied. Thus, when an individual finds himself cast into or enacting a role in which the social identity implied is inconsistent with the desired or actual self-conception, role distancing is likely to occur. Since the homeless routinely find themselves cast into or enacting low-status, negatively evaluated roles (e.g., panhandler, day laborer, vagrant), it should not be surprising that many of them would attempt to dissociate themselves from those very roles.

As with associational distancing, role distancing manifested itself in two ways: distancing from the basic or general role of street person and distancing from specific occupational roles. The former, which we construe as a variant of categorical distancing, was particularly evident among individuals who had been on the street for less than six months. It was not uncommon for these individuals to make explicitly clear that they should "not be mistaken as a typical street person." Role distancing of the less categorical and more situational specific type, however, was most evident in day-labor occupational roles, such as painters' helpers, hod carriers, warehouse and van unloaders, and unskilled service occupations, such as dishwashing and janitorial work. Although the majority of the homeless we encountered would avail themselves of such job opportunities, they seldom did so enthusiastically because of the job's low status and low wages. This was especially true of the homeless who had been on the streets between two and four years,[7] who frequently reminded others of their disdain for such jobs and of their belief that they deserved better, as exemplified by the remarks of a drunk young man who had worked the previous day as a painter's helper: "I made $36.00 off the labor corner, but it was just 'nigger' work. I'm 24 years old, man. I deserve better than that." Similar distancing laments were frequently voiced over the disparity between job demands and wages. While we were conversing with a small gathering of homeless men on a Saturday afternoon, one of them revealed, for example, that he had turned down a job earlier in the day to carry shingles up a ladder for $4.00 an hour because he found it demeaning to "do that hard of work for that low of pay." Since day-labor jobs seldom last for more than six to eight hours, perhaps not much is lost monetarily in forgoing such jobs in comparison with what can be gained in pride. But even when the ratio of dollars to pride would appear to make rejection costly, as with permanent jobs, dissatisfaction with the low status of the menial job roles may prod some homeless individuals to engage in the ultimate form of role distancing by quitting current jobs. As one informant recounted the day after he quit in the middle of his shift as a dishwasher at a local restaurant: "My boss told me, 'You can't walk out on me.' And I told her, 'Fuck you, just watch me. I'm going to walk out of here right now.' And I did. 'You can't walk out on me', she said. I said, 'Fuck you, I'm gone.'"

The foregoing illustrations suggest that the social identities lodged in available work roles are frequently inconsistent with the desired or idealized self-conceptions of some of the homeless. Consequently, "bitching about," "turning down," and even "blowing off" such work may function as a means of social identity disavowal, on the one hand, and personal identity assertion, on the other. Such techniques provide a way of saying, "Hey, I have some pride. I'm in control. I'm my own man." This is especially true among those individuals for whom such work is no longer just a stopgap measure but rather a permanent feature of their lives.

Institutional Distancing.—An equally prevalent distancing technique involved the derogation of the very institutions that attended to the needs of the homeless in one way or another. The one agency that was the most frequent object of these harangues was the local Salvation Army. It was frequently typified by many of the homeless who used it as a greedy corporation run by inhumane personnel more interested in lining their own pockets than serving the needy. The flavor of this negative characterization is captured by such comments as the following, which were heard most often among individuals waiting in the Salvation Army dinner line: "The Major is money-hungry and feeds people the cheapest way he can. He never talks to people except to gripe at them. The Salvation Army is supposed to be a Christian organization, but it doesn't have a Christian spirit. It looks down on people..The Salvation Army is a national business that is more worried about making money than helping people"; "The Sally here doesn't do nearly as much as it could for people. The people who work here take bags of groceries and put them in their cars. People donate to the Sally, and then the workers there cream off the best," and "If you spend a week here, you'll see how come people lose hope. You're treated just like an animal."

Given that the Salvation Army is the only local facility that provides free shelter, breakfast, and dinner, it is understandable why attention would be riveted on it more than on any other local agency. But that the Salvation Army would be continuously derogated by the very people whose survival it facilitates may appear puzzling at first glance, especially given its caretaker orientation. The answer lies in part in the organization and dissemination of its services. Clients are processed in an impersonal, highly structured, assembly line fashion. The result is a leveling of individual differences and a decline in personal autonomy. Bitching and complaining about such settings thus allow one to gain psychic distance from the self implied and to secure a modicum of personal autonomy.[8] Criticizing the Salvation Army, then, provided some regular users with a means of dealing with the implications of their dependence on it. It was, in short, a way of presenting and sustaining a somewhat contrary personal identity.

While this variety of distancing was observable among all the homeless, it was most prevalent among those regular service users who had been on the streets for more than two years. Since these individuals had used street institutions over a longer period of time, their self-concepts were more deeply implicated in them, thus necessitating distancing from those very institutions and the self implied.

Thus far, we have elaborated how some of the homeless distance themselves from other homeless individuals, from general and specific roles, and from the institutions that deal with them. Such distancing behavior and talk represent attempts to salvage a measure of self-worth. In the process, of course, the homeless are asserting more favorable personal identities. Not all homeless individuals engage in similar distancing behavior and talk, however. As indicated in table 1, which summarizes the foregoing observations, categorical distancing tends to be concentrated among those who have been on the streets for a comparatively short time, typically less than six months. The only instances of such distancing we heard from those who had been on the streets for more than four years were made by individuals categorized as "mentally ill," as in the case of one 32-year-old white male who expressed disdain for the homeless in general even though he had been on and off the street for ten years between stays in Texas state mental hospitals.[9] For those who are more firmly entrenched in street life, then, distancing tends to be confined to distinguishing themselves from specific groups of the homeless, such as novices and the institutionally dependent, from specific occupational roles, or from the institutions with which they have occasional contact.

TABLE 1			
Types of Embracement By Time on the Streets (in percentages)			
	Types of Embracement		
	Categoric[a]	Specific[b]	Ideological[c]
Time on the Streets	(N=16)	(N=23)	(N=22)
Less than six months	75.0	4.3	9.1
Six months to two years	6.3	26.1	13.6
Two years to four years	6.3	56.5	40.9
More than four years	12.5	13.0	36.4
Note.-X^2=36.06, df=6, P<.001.			
[a]Comments or statements coded as categoric included those indicating dissociation or distancing from such general, street role identities as bum, tramp, drifter, or from street people in general, regardless of variation among them.			
[b]Comments or statements reflective of specific or situational distancing included those indicating dissociation from specific groupings of homeless individuals or from specific survival or occupational roles.			
[c]Comments or statements suggestive of institutional distancing included those indicating dissociation from or disdain for street institutions, such as the Salvation Army, soup kitchens, and the like.			

Embracement

By "embracement," we refer to the verbal and expressive confirmation of one's acceptance of and attachment to the social identity associated with a general or specific role, a set of social relationships, or a particular ideology.[10] So defined, embracement implies consistency between self-concept and imputed or structurally based social identities. Social and personal identities are congruent, such that the individual accepts the identities associated with his status. Thus, embracement involves the avowal of implied social identities rather than their disavowal, as is true of distancing. Thirty-six percent of the identity statements were of this variety.

Role embracement.—The most conspicuous kind of embracement we encountered was role embracement of the categorical variety, which typically manifested itself in the avowal and acceptance of street role identities such as the "tramp" and "bum."[11]

Occasionally, we would encounter an individual who would immediately announce that he was a tramp or a bum. A case in point is provided by our initial encounter with a 49-year-old man who had been on the road for 14 years. When we engaged him in conversation on a street corner, he proudly told us that he was "the tramp who was on the front page of yesterday's newspaper." In that and subsequent conversations, his talk was peppered with references to himself as a tramp. He indicated, for example, that he had appeared on a television show in St. Louis as a tramp and that he "tramped" his way across the country, and he revealed several "cons" that "tramps use to survive on the road."

This tramp, as well as others like him, identified himself as being of the more traditional "brethren of the road" variety. In contrast, we also encountered individuals who identified themselves as "hippie tramps." Interaction with a number of these individuals who hung out together near the local university similarly revealed attachment to and temporal continuity of this particular street identity. When confronted by a passing group of "punkers," for instance, several of the hippie tramps voiced agreement with one's remark that "these kids will change but we'll stay the same." As if to buttress this claim, they went on to talk about "Rainbow," an annual gathering of old hippies, which functions in part as a kind of identity reaffirmation ritual. For these street people, there was little doubt about who they were; they not only saw themselves as hippie-like tramps, but they embraced that identity both verbally and expressively.

This sort of enthusiastic embracement also surfaced on occasion with Skid Row-like "bums," as evidenced by a hunchbacked alcoholic's repeated reference to himself as a "bum." As a corollary of such categorical role embracement, we found that most individuals who identified themselves as tramps or bums had also adopted nicknames congruent with these general street roles. Not only did we find that they routinely referred to themselves in terms of these new names, but others also referred to them similarly. Street names such as Shotgun, Muskrat, Boxcar Billy, Panama Red, Gypsy Bill, and the like can thus be construed as symbolizing a break with the past and suggesting a fairly thoroughgoing embracement of life on the streets.

Role-specific embracement was also encountered occasionally, as when a street person of several years referred to himself as an "expert dumpster diver." In street argot, "dumpster diving" refers to scavenging through garbage bins in search of clothes, food, and salable items. Many street people often engage in this survival activity, but relatively few pridefully identify themselves in terms of this activity. Other role-specific survival activities that functioned in a similar manner included panhandling, small-time drug dealing, and street performing, such as playing a musical instrument or singing on a street corner for money. Illustrative of this type of embracement was a 33-year-old white male known on the streets as Rhymin' Mike, who called himself a street poet and made his money by composing short poems for spare change from passersby. For some homeless individuals, then, the roles they enact function as a source of positive identity and self-worth.

Associational embracement—A second variety of embracement used to denote or embellish a personal identity entailed reference to oneself as a friend or individual who acknowledges the norm of reciprocity and who thus takes his social relationships seriously.[12] A case in point is provided by the individual alluded to who pridefully acknowledged that he was a bum. On one occasion, he told us that he had several friends who either refused or quit jobs at the Salvation Army because they "weren't allowed to associate with other guys on the streets who were their friends." Such a policy struck him as immoral: "They expect you to forget who your friends are and where you came from when you go to work there. They asked me to work there, and I told them, 'No way.' I'm a bum and I know who my friends are."

Avowal of such ties and responsibilities manifested itself in other claims and behavior as well. Identification of oneself as a person who willingly shares limited resources, such as cigarettes and alcohol, occurred frequently, particularly among avowed tramps and bums. One evening after dinner at the Salvation Army, for example, a 29-year-old white male who had been on the street for several years quickly responded to the researcher's offer with an offer of his own to take a drink of his Coke, commenting, "See, man, I'm all right. I share, man. I don't just take things."

Associational embracement was also expressed in self-identification as protector or defender of one's buddies. Two older drinking partners whom we came to know claimed repeatedly to "look out for each other." When one was telling about having been assaulted and robbed while walking through an alley, the other said, "It wouldn't have happened if I was with you. I wouldn't have let them get away with that." Similar claims were made to the field researcher, as when two street acquaintances indicated one evening after an ambiguous encounter with a clique of a half-dozen other street people that, "If it wasn't for us, they'd have had your ass."

Although protective behaviors that entailed a risk were seldom observed, protective claims, particularly of a promissory character, were frequently heard. Whatever the relationship between such claims and action, they functioned not only to cement tenuous ties but also to express something concrete about the claimant's desired identity as a dependable and trustworthy friend.

Ideological embracement—A third variety of embracement that can provide an individual with a special niche in which to lodge the self and thereby distinguish himself from others entails the acceptance of a set of beliefs or ideas and the avowal of a cognitively congruent personal identity. We refer to this as ideological embracement.

Among the homeless we studied, ideological embracement manifested itself primarily as an avowed commitment to a particular religion or set of religious beliefs. One middle-aged tramp called Banjo provides an example. He routinely identified himself as a Christian, he had painted on his banjo case "Wealth means nothing without God," and his talk was sprinkled with references to his Christian beliefs. When asked whether he was afraid to sleep at the Salvation Army following a murder that had occurred the night before, he replied: "I don't have anything to worry about since I'm a Christian, and it says in the 23rd Psalm: 'Yea though I walk through the valley of death, I shall fear no evil, for Thou art with me.'" Moreover, he frequently pointed out that his religious beliefs transcended his situation on the streets. As he indicated on one occasion, he would like to get off the street but not for money: "It would have to be a bigger purpose than just money to get me off the streets, like a religious mission."

An equally powerful but less common functional equivalent of religion as a source of identity is the occult and related supernatural beliefs. Since traditional occupational roles are not readily available as a basis for identity and since few street people have the material resources that can be used for construction of positive personal identities, is it little wonder that some of them turn elsewhere—to mystical inner forces, to the stars, to the occult—in search of a locus for a positive identity. Illustrative of this was a 29-year-old male who read books on the occult regularly, identified himself as a "spirit guide," and informed us that he had received "a spiritual gift" at the age of 13 and that he now had special prophetic insights into the future that allowed him to foresee the day when "humans will be transformed into another life form."

In addition to mainstream religious and occult beliefs, conversionist, restorative ideologies, such as that associated with Alcoholics Anonymous, provide some of the homeless with a readily available locus for identity, providing they are willing to accept AA's doctrine and adhere to its program. The interesting dynamic here, however, is that AA's successes seldom remain on the street. Consequently, those street people who have previously associated with AA seldom use it as a basis for identity assertion. Nonetheless, it does constitute a potentially salient identity peg, as well as a way off the street.

We have seen how the personal identities of the homeless may be derived from the embracement of the social identities associated with certain stereotypical street roles, such as the tramp and the bum; with role-specific survival activities, such as dumpster diving; with certain social relationships, such as friend and protector; and with certain religious and occult ideologies or belief systems. While embracement and distancing are not necessarily mutually exclusive means for constructing personal identities among the homeless, we have noted how their usage tends to vary according to the stage or point in one's street career. More specifically, we have found, as summarized in Table 2, that the longer one has been on the street and the more adapted one is to street life, the greater the prevalence of categorical embracement in particular. That relationship is emphasized even further when it is noted that the only cases of such embracement among those who had been on the streets for less than two years occurred among those categorized as mentally ill, as in the case of a 33-year-old black female who avowed the nonstreet identity of The Interracial Princess, which she said had been bestowed on her by "a famous astrologer from New York."

Fictive Storytelling

A third form of identity talk engaged in by the homeless is what we refer to as fictive storytelling. It involves the narration of stories about one's past, present, or future experiences and accomplishments that have a fictive character to them. To suggest that these stories about the self are fictional to some degree is not to imply intentional deception, although it may and frequently does occur. Rather, we characterize these stories as fictive because they tend to range from minor exaggerations of experience to fanciful claims and fabrications. We thus distinguish between two types of fictive storytelling: embellishment of the past and present and fantasizing about the future.[13] Slightly more than a third of the identity types of fictive storytelling we recorded fell into one of these two categories.

TABLE 2
Types of Embracement By Time on the Streets
(in percentages)

	Types of Embracement		
	Categoric[a]	Specific[b]	Ideological[c]
Time on the Streets	(N=39)	(N=20)	(N=13)
Less than six months		25.0	15.4
Six months to two years	5.1	20.0	7.7
Two years to four years	59.0	35.0	46.1
More than four years	35.9	20.0	30.8

Note.-$X2=14.88$, $df=6$, $P<.05$.

[a]Comments or statements coded as categoric included those indicating acceptance of or attachment to street people as a social category or to such general, street role identities as bum, tramp, drifter, and transient.

[b]Comments or statements reflective of specific embracement included those indicating identification with a situational specific survival role, such as dumpster diver and street performer, or with a specific social relational role, such as friend, lover, or protector.

[c]Comments or statements coded as ideological embracement included those indicating self-identification with a set of beliefs or ideas, such as those associated with a particular religion.

Embellishment—By "embellishment," we refer to the exaggeration of past and present experiences with fanciful and fictitious particulars so as to assert a positive personal identity. It involves an overstatement, an enlargement of the truth, a "lamination," in Goffman's terms (1974), of what has actually happened or is unfolding in the present. Embellished stories, then, are only partly fictional.

Examples of such embellishment for identity construction purposes abound among the homeless. While an array of events and experiences—ranging from tales about the accomplishments of one's offspring to sexual and drinking exploits and predatory activities—were found to be the object of embellishment, the most common form of embellished storytelling tended to be associated with past and current occupational and financial themes. In the case of financial embellishment, the typical story entailed an exaggerated claim regarding past or current wages. An example is provided by a 40-year-old homeless male who spent much of his time hanging around a transient bar boasting about having been offered a job as a Harley-Davidson mechanic for $18.50 per hour, while constantly begging for cigarettes and spare change for beer.

Equally illustrative of such embellishment is an encounter we overheard between an inebriated 49-year-old homeless woman passing out discarded burritos and a young homeless man in his early 20s. When he took several burritos and chided the woman for being drunk, she yelled stridently at him: "I'm a floating taper and I make 14 bucks an hour. What the fuck do you make?" Aside from putting the young man in his place, the statement functioned to announce to him, as well as to others overhearing the encounter, the woman's desired identity as a person who earns a respectable wage and must therefore be treated respectfully. Subsequent interaction with this woman revealed that she worked only sporadically and then most often for a temporary day agency at $4.00 per hour. There was, then, a considerable gap between claims and reality.

Disjunctions between identity assertions and reality appear to be quite common and were rapidly discernible on occasion, as in the case of a 45-year-old transient from Pittsburgh who had been on the streets for a year and who was given to excessive embellishment of his former military experiences. On several occasions, he was overheard telling tales about his experiences "patrolling the Alaskan-Russian border in Alaskan Siberia" and of encounters with Russian guards, who traded vodka for coffee with him. Since there is no border between Alaska and Siberia, it is obvious that this tale is outlandish. Nonetheless, such identity constructions, however embellished, can be construed as attempts to say something concrete about oneself and how one would like to be regarded in a particular situation.

Fantasizing.—The second type of fictive storytelling that frequently manifested itself during the course of conversations with and among the homeless is verbal fantasizing. In contrast to embellishment, which involves exaggerated laminations of past and present activities, fantasizing involves future-oriented fabrications about oneself. By "future-oriented fabrications," we refer to fanciful constructions that place the narrator in positively framed situations that seem distantly removed from, if at all connected to, his past or present. These fabrications were almost always benign, usually had a Walter Mitty, pipe-dream quality, and varied from fanciful reveries involving little self-deception to fantastic stories in which the narrator appeared to be taken in by his constructions.[14]

Regardless of the degree of self-deception, the spoken fantasies we were privy to were generally organized around four themes: self-employment, money, material possessions, and the opposite sex, particularly for men.[15] Fanciful constructions concerning self-employment were usually expressed in terms of business schemes. A black 30-year-old male from Chicago told us and others on several occasions, for example, about his plans "to set up a little shop near the university" to sell leather hats and silverwork imported from New York. In a similar but even more expansive vein, two white men in their early 20s who had become friends on the street seemed to be scheming constantly about how they were going to start one lucrative business after another. On one occasion, they were overheard talking about "going into business for ourselves, either roofing houses or rebuilding classic cars and selling them." And a few days later, they were observed trying to find a third party to bankroll one of these business ventures.

An equally prominent source of fanciful identity construction was the fantasy of becoming rich. Some of the homeless daydreamed openly about what they would do if they had a million dollars, as did one 32-year-old white male, who assured us that, if he "won a million dollars in a lottery," he was mature enough so that he "wouldn't blow it." Others would make bold claims about becoming rich, without offering any details. The following is illustrative: "You might laugh and think I'm crazy, but I'm going to be rich. I know it. I just have this feeling. I can't explain it, but I am." And still others would confidently spin fairly detailed stories about being extravagant familial providers in the future. Illustrative of this was an emaciated 25-year-old unemployed roofer who had just returned to Austin after a futile effort to establish himself in a city closer to his "girlfriend." Despite his continuing financial setbacks, he assured us: "I'm going to get my fiancee a new pet monkey, even if it costs me $1,000. And I'm going to get her two parrots too, just to show her how much I love her."

As we previously noted, fanciful identity assertions were also constructed around material possessions and encounters with the opposite sex. These two identity pegs were clearly illustrated one evening while we were hanging out with several homeless men along the city's major nightlife strip. During the course of making numerous overtures to passing women, two of the fellows jointly fantasized about how they would attract these women in the future: "Man, these chicks are going to be all over us when we come back into town with our new suits and Corvettes. We'll have to get some cocaine, too. Cocaine will get you women every time."

We have seen how respectable work, financial wealth, material possessions, and the opposite sex figure prominently in the fanciful, future-oriented talk of the homeless. While all these themes may be interconnected in actuality, only one or two of them were typically highlighted in the stories heard. Occasionally, however, we encountered a particularly accomplished storyteller who wove together all four themes in a grand scenario, as illustrated by the following fanciful construction told by the transient from Pittsburgh over a meal of bean stew and stale bread at the Salvation Army and repeated again later that night prior to going to sleep on a concrete floor in a warehouse converted into a winter shelter for 300 men: "Tomorrow morning I'm going to get my money and say `Fuck this shit.' I'm going to catch a plane to Pittsburgh and tomorrow night I'll take a hot bath, have a dinner of linguini and red wine in my own restaurant..and have a woman hanging on my arm." When encountered on the street the next evening, entangled in his own fabrication, he attempted to explain his continued presence on the streets of Austin by saying he "had been informed that all my money is tied up in a legal battle back in Pittsburgh," an apparently fanciful lamination of the original fabrication.[16]

Although both the embellished and fanciful variants of fictive storytelling surfaced rather frequently during the course of the conversations we overheard, they were not uniformly widespread or randomly distributed among the homeless. As indicated in table 3, embellishment occurred among all the homeless but was particularly pronounced among those who had been on the street for two to four years. Fantasizing, on the other hand, occurred most frequently among those who still envision a future; it occurred least often among those individuals who appeared acclimated to street life and tended to embrace one or more street identities. For these individuals, specifically those who have been on the street for four or more years, the future is apparently too remote to provide a solid anchoring for fictive, identity-oriented spinoffs that are of this world. Again, the only exceptions to this pattern among the long-term homeless were the mentally ill who had been on the street for four or more years.

TABLE 3		
Types of Fictive Story Telling By Time on the Streets (in percentages)		
	Types of Fictive Storytelling	
	Embellishment[a]	Fantasizing[b]
Time on the Streets.	(N=38)	(N=31)
Less than six months	13.2	51.6
Six months to two years	26.3	32.3
Two years to four years	50.0	9.7
More than four years	10.5	6.4
Note.-X2=17.55, df=3, P<.001.		
[a] Comments or statements were coded as embellishment if they entailed the elaboration and exaggeration of past and present experiences with fictitious particulars. See fn. 13 for criteria used for determining the fictive character of comments and stories.		
[b] Comments or statements were coded as fantasizing if they entailed future-oriented fabrications that placed the narrator in positively framed situations. See fn. 13 for criteria used for determining the fictive, fabricative character of comments and stories.		

Conclusions and Implications

From a theoretical standpoint, a number of implications flow from these findings regarding the relationships among structural location, role, identity, and self-concept.

The first theoretical implication pertains to the widely held assumption among social scientists that identity-related concerns, such as the need for self-esteem, are secondary to more physiological survival needs. This assumption is rooted in Maslow's (1962) well-known hierarchy of needs, which holds that the satisfaction of physiological and safety needs is a necessary condition for the emergence and gratification of higher-level needs, such as the need for self-esteem or a positive personal identity. This thesis has become almost cliche even though research bearing on it is scant, ambiguous, and typically at the aggregate level (Allardt 1973; Inglehart 1977; Knutson 1972). Our finding—that identity-related concerns can be readily gleaned from the talk of homeless street people, clearly some of the most destitute in terms of physiological and safety needs—calls into question this popular assumption. More specifically, our findings suggest that the salience of identity-related concerns is not necessarily contingent on the prior satisfaction of more physiological survival requisites. Instead, such needs appear to coexist, even at the most rudimentary level of human existence.

That this should be true makes sound sense from the standpoint of symbolic interactionism, which views the imputation of meaning to the objects in one's environment, including the self, as one of the core activities in which people engage regardless of their social status. Indeed, it is this signifying activity that Znaniecki (1934) conceptualized as the "humanistic coefficient" and saw as perhaps the distinctive characteristic of the human species. We view our findings as consistent with this thesis.

In addition, our findings provide further evidence of the tendency for individuals who have fallen through the cracks of society to carve out a modicum of meaning and personal significance in what must, from the more privileged perches of the normative order, appear to be an anomic void. As noted at the outset, other examples of such spirited identity work have been found in mental hospitals (Goffman 1961a), concentration camps (Frankl 1963; Dimsdale 1980), and among black street corner men (Liebow 1967; Anderson 1976). In these and presumably other cases, the attempt to carve out and maintain a sense of meaning and self-worth seems especially critical for survival, perhaps because it is the thread that enables those situated on the margins or at the bottom to retain a sense of self and thus their humanity. To the extent that this is generally true, it follows that it is not lack of interest in identity issues, self-realization, and the like that characterizes those for whom physiological survival cannot be taken for granted but the scant material and social resources at their disposal. Consequently, their identity construction efforts are often less transparent and more likely to be confined to the conversational realm, as in fictive storytelling among the homeless and "going for brothers" and "playing the dozens" among lower-class, black street-corner men and youths.

REFERENCES

Allardt, Erik. 1973. *About Dimensions of Welfare: An Exploratory Analysis of a Comparative Scandinavian Survey.* Helsinki: Research Group for Comparative Sociology.
Anderson, Elijah. 1976. *A Place on the Corner.* Chicago: University of Chicago Press.
Anderson, Nels. 1923. *The Hobo: The Sociology of the Homeless Man.* Chicago: University of Chicago Press.
———. 1931. *The Milk and Honey Route: A Handbook for Hoboes.* New York: Vanguard.
Ansbacher, Heinz, and Rowena Ansbacher. 1946. *The Individual Psychology of Alfred Adler.* New York: Basic.
Austin American Statesman. 1985a. "Community Effort Needed to find a Home for 'Sally.'" January 31.
———. 1985b. "Homeless Called Content as Shelter Plans Opposed." February 7.
———. 1985c. "It's Time for the City Council to Get Tough on Sally Site." July 3.
———. 1985d. "Twisted Pathway of 'Sally' Paved by Many Designs." September 22.
Bahr, Howard M., and Theodore Caplow. 1973. *Old Men Drunk and Sober.* New York: New York University Press.
Banton, Michael . 1965. Roles: *An Introduction to the Study of Social Relations.* New York: Basic.
Becker, Ernest. 1965. *The Birth and Death of Meaning.* New York: Free Press.

Bettelheim, Bruno. 1943. "Individual and Mass Behavior in Extreme Situations." *Journal of Abnormal Psychology* 38:417–452.
Blumer, Herbert. 1969. *Symbolic Interactionism: Perspective and Method.* Englewood Cliffs, N.J.: Prentice-Hall.
Blumstein, Phillip W. 1973. "Audience, Machiavellianism, and Tactics of Identity Bargaining." *Sociometry:* 36:346–365.
Bogue, Donald J. 1963. *Skid Row in American Cities.* Chicago: Community and Family Study Center, University of Chicago.
Brown, Carl S., McFarlane, Ron Parades, and Louisa Stark. 1983. *Homeless of Phoenix: Who Are They? What Should Be Done?* Phoenix: Phoenix South Community Mental Health Center.
Bruns, Roger A. 1980. *Knights of the Road: A Hobo History.* New York: Methuen.
Burke, Peter J. 1980. "The Self: Measurement Requirements from an Interactionist Perspective." *Social Psychology Quarterly* 43:18–29.
Burke, Peter J. and Judy Tully. 1977. "The Measurement of Role Identity." *Social Forces* 4:881–897.
City of Chicago. 1983. *Homelessness in Chicago.* Chicago: Social Services Task Force.
Crystal, S., and M. Goldstein. 1984. *The Homeless in New York City Shelters.* New York: Human Resources Administration, City of New York.
Dawe, Alan. 1978. "Theories of Social Action." Pp. 362–417 in *A History of Sociological Analysis,* edited by Tom Bottmore and Robert Nisbet. New York: Basic.
Dimsdale, Joel E. 1980. "The Coping Behavior of Nazi Concentration Camp Survivors." Pp. 163–174 in *Survivors, Victims and Perpetrators: Essays on the Nazi Holocaust,* edited by Joel E. Dimsdale. Washington: Hemisphere.
Douglas, Jack D. 1976. *Investigative Social Research: Individual and Team Field Research.* Beverly Hills, CA: Sage.
Frankl, Viktor. 1963. *Man's Search for Meaning.* New York: Washington Square.
Gecas, Viktor. 1982. "The Self-Concept." *Annual Review of Sociology* 8:1–33.
Geertz, Clifford. 1973. *The Interpretation of Cultures.* New York: Basic.
General Accounting Office. 1985. *Homelessness: A Complex Problem and the Federal Response.* Washington, D.C.: U.S. General Accounting Office.
Gergen, Kenneth J. 1982. *Toward Transformation in Social Knowledge.* New York: Springer.
Goffman, Erving. 1961a. *Asylums: Essays on the Social Situations of Mental Patients and Other Inmates.* New York: Doubleday Anchor.
———. 1961b. "Role Distance." Pp. 84–152 in *Encounters: Two Studies in the Sociology of Interaction.* Indianapolis: Bobbs-Merrill.
———. 1963. *Stigma: Notes on the Management of Spoiled Identity.* Englewood Cliffs, N.J.: Prentice-Hall.
———. 1974. *Frame Analysis: An Essay on the Organization of Experience.* New York: Harper and Row.
Gould, Leroy C., Andrew L. Walker, Lansing E. Crane, and Charles W. Lidz. 1974. *Connections: Notes from the Heroin World.* New Haven, Conn.: Yale University Press.
Harper, Douglas A. 1982. *Good Company.* Chicago: University of Chicago Press.
Harrington, Michael. 1984. *The New American Poverty.* New York: Holt, Rinehart, and Winston.
Holmes, Urban Tiger. 1966. *Daily Living in the Twelfth Century: Based on the Observations of Alexander Neckham in London and Paris.* Madison: University of Wisconsin Press.
Hombs, Mary Ellen, and Mitch Snyder. 1982. *Homelessness in America: A Forced March to Nowhere.* Washington, D.C.: The Community for Creative Non-violence.
Inglehart, Ronald. 1977. *The Silent Revolution.* Princeton, N.J.: Princeton University Press.
Knutson, Jeanne M. 1972. *The Human Basis of the Polity: A Psychological Study of Political Men.* Chicago: Aldine.
Levitin, T.E. 1964. "Role Performances and Role Distance in a Low Status Occupation: The Puller." *Sociological Quarterly* 5:251–260.
Liebow, Elliot. 1967. *Tally's Corner: A Study of Negro Streetcorner Men.* Boston: Little, Brown.
Lofland, John, and Lynn H. Lofland. 1984. *Analyzing Social Settings: A Guide to Qualitative Observation and Analysis.* Belmont, CA: Wadsworth.
Los Angeles Times. 1984a. "Santa Barbara - A Lid on Hobos' Food?" December 13.
———. 1984b. "'Troll Busters' in Santa Cruz Prey on the Homeless." October 26.

McCall, George J., and J.L. Simmons. 1978. *Identities and Interactions.* New York: Free Press.
MacIntyre, Alasdair. 1981. *After Virtue: A Study in Moral Theory.* Notre Dame, Ind.: University of Notre Dame Press.
Marx, Karl and Frederich Engels (1848). 1967. *The Communist Manifesto.* New York: Penguin.
Maslow, Abraham H. 1962. *Toward a Psychology of Being.* New York: Van Nostrand.
Myrdal, Gunnar. 1962. *Challenge to Affluence.* New York: Pantheon.
Newsweek. 1984. "Homeless in America." January 2, pp.20–29.
New York Times. 1985. "Plan to Shelter the Homeless Arouses Concern in Maspeth." June 7.
Pollner, Melvin, and Robert M. Emerson. 1983. "The Dynamics of Inclusion and Distance in Fieldwork Relations." Pp. 235–252 in *Contemporary Field Research: A Collection of Readings,* edited by Robert M. Emerson. Boston: Little, Brown.
Robertson, Marjorie J., Richard H. Ropers, and Richard Boyer. 1985. *The Homeless of Los Angeles County: An Empirical Evaluation.* Document no. 4. Los Angeles: Basic Shelter Research Project, School of Public Health, University of California, Los Angeles.
Roth, Dee, Jerry Bean, Nancy Lust, and Traian Saveanu. 1985. *Homelessness in Ohio: A Study of People in Need.* Columbus, Ohio Department of Mental Health.
San Antonio Urban Council. 1984. *Robert Wood Johnson Grant Application: Health Care for the Homeless.* San Antonio, TX: San Antonio Urban Council.
Sarbin, Theodore R., and Karl E. Scheibe, eds. 1983. *Studies in Social Identity.* New York: Praeger.
Sayles, Marnie L. 1984. "Role Distancing: Differentiating the Role of the Elderly from the Person." *Qualitative Sociology* 7:236–252.
Shibutani, Tamotsu. 1961. *Society and Personality.* Englewood Cliffs, N.J.: Prentice-Hall.
Snow, David A., Susan G. Baker, Leon Anderson, and Michael Martin. 1986. "The Myth of Pervasive Mental Illness Among the Homeless." *Social Problems* 33:407–423.
Snow, David A., Robert D. Benford, and Leon Anderson. 1986. "Fieldwork Roles and Informational Yield: A Comparison of Alternative Settings and Roles." *Urban Life* 15:377–408.
Snow, David A., Louis Zurcher, and Gideon Sjoberg. 1982. "Interviewing by Comment: An Adjunct to the Direct Question." *Qualitative Sociology* 5:285–311.
Spradley, James P. 1970. *You Owe Yourself a Drunk: An Ethnography of Urban Nomads.* Boston: Little, Brown.
———. 1980. *Participant Observation.* New York: Holt, Rinehart, and Winston.
Srinivas, M.N., and Andre Betille. 1965. "The Untouchables of India." *Scientific American* 216:13–17.
Stebbins, Robert A. 1975. "Role Distance, Role Distance Behavior, and Jazz Musicians." Pp. 133–141 in *Life as Theater: A Dramaturgical Sourcebook,* edited by D. Brissett and C. Edgley. Chicago: Aldine.
Stone, Gregory P. 1962. "Appearance and the Self." Pp. 86–118 in *Human Behavior and Social Processes,* edited by Arnold M. Rose. Boston: Houghton Mifflin.
Strauss, Anselm L. 1959. *Mirrors and Masks: The Search for Identity.* Glencoe, Ill.: Free Press.
Stryker, Sheldon. 1968. "Identity Salience and Role Performance." *Journal of Marriage and the Family* 30:558–562.
———. 1980. *Symbolic Interactionism: A Social Structural Version.* Menlo Park, Calif.: Benjamin-Cummings.
Turner, Ralph H. 1968. "The Self-Conception in Social Interaction." Pp. 93–106 in *The Self in Social Interaction,* edited by C. Gordon and K.J. Gergen. New York: Wiley.
———. 1978. "The Role and the Person." *American Journal of Sociology* 84:1–23.
U.S. Conference of Mayors. 1985. *Health Care for the Homeless: A 40 City Review.* Washington, D.C.: United States Conference of Mayors.
U.S. Department of Housing and Urban Development. 1984. *A Report to the Secretary on the Homeless and Emergency Shelters.* Washington, D.C.: U.S. Department of Housing and Urban Development.
U.S. House Committee on Government Operations. 1985. *The Federal Response to the Homeless Crisis: Hearings before a Subcommittee on Government Operations.* House of Representatives, 98th Congress, 2nd Session. Washington, D.C.: Government Printing Office.
Weigert, Andrew J. 1983. "Identity: Its Emergence within Sociological Psychology." *Symbolic Interaction* 6:183–206.

Whyte, William F. 1943. *Street Corner Society: The Social Structure of an Italian Slum.* Chicago: University of Chicago Press.
Wiseman, Jacqueline. 1970. *Stations of the Lost: Treatment of Skid Row Alcoholics.* Chicago: University of Chicago Press.
Znaniecki, Florian. 1934. *The Method of Sociology.* New York: Farrar and Rinehart.

NOTES

[1] This is a revised and updated version of an earlier paper presented at the annual meeting of the Society for the Study of Symbolic Interaction, Washington, D.C., August, 1985. Preparation of the paper was facilitated by a grant to study homelessness provided by the Hogg Foundation for Mental Health. We would also like to thank the three anonymous reviewers for AJS whose comments were most constructive and insightful.

[2] Such responses have occurred rather frequently in Austin, as well as elsewhere throughout the country, as the number of homeless people has mounted (see Austin American Statesman 1985a, 1985b, 1985c, 1985d; Los Angeles Times 1984a, 1984b; Newsweek 1984; New York Times 1985).

[3] All such spoken material throughout the paper represents verbatim quotes of some of the homeless whom we encountered. They are used for illustrative purposes and are representative of what we heard or were told..

[4] While the distinction between identity and self-concept is commonplace in the literature, the disaggregation of identity into two or more dimensions or aspects is less frequent. In his essay on the relationships among appearance, self, and identity, Stone (1962) highlights the negotiated character of identities by conceptualizing them in terms of the "coincidence placements and announcements," but he does not differentiate and articulate what we see as the distinct social and personal dimensions implied therein. The role-based conceptualization of identity provided by Stryker (1980, pp.51–85) and Burke (see Stryker 1980, pp. 129–134) also highlights the coalescence or coincidence of both social and personal considerations, but it does not fully disaggregate these dimensions and allow for their disjunction as well as congruence. Goffman (1963) and McCall and Simmons (1978) do make clear-cut conceptual distinctions between social and personal identities but not in ways that we find fully satisfactory or congruent with our observations.

[5] This conceptualization of social identity is consistent with both Goffman (1963, pp.2–3) and McCall and Simmons (1978, p.62), as well as with Turner's (1978 p.6) "appearance principle," which holds that "people tend to conceive another person (and thus impute social identities) on the basis of the role behavior they observe unless there are cues that alert them to the possibility of a discrepancy between person and role."

[6] This conceptualization differs from Goffman's (1963, p.57) and McCall and Simmons's (1978, pp.62–63) in that they define personal identity in terms of unique, biographical facts and items that function as pegs on which social identities can be hung. It is our conception, which we will illustrate and elaborate, that biographical facts and experiences, just as the roles one plays or is cast into, influence but do not fully determine the construction and assertion of what we call personal identities. Thus, rather than taking for granted the relationship between biography and personal identity, we see it as problematic and variable.

[7] Pursuit of day-labor jobs rarely occurred among the homeless who had been on the streets for more than four years. Instead, they tended to survive by other means, such as panhandling, collecting aluminum cans, and scavenging. Retreat from the day-labor market among these individuals might be interpreted as a form of behavioral distancing that ideally reduces the prospect of interaction with other citizens and thereby lessens the need for constructing alternative identities. The problem with this proposition, however, is that many of the longtime homeless intentionally engage the public with their panhandling activities. In addition, it is frequently the more chronic homeless who are the most visible to the public—e.g., shopping-cart people and bag ladies. It is perhaps because of such considerations that embracement, which will be discussed in the next section, is a more common mode of identity construction among the homeless who have been on the streets for two or more years.

[8] Wiseman (1970, pp. 187–188, 194–198) similarly notes the "harsh sentiments" of Skid-Row alcoholics toward their benefactors. Similar patterns of bitching and griping have also been observed in relation to more all-encompassing institutions, such as prisons and mental hospitals. In commenting on such verbal insubordination, Goffman (1961a, p.319) offers an interpretation that dovetails with ours: "This recalcitrance is not an incidental mechanism of defense but rather an essential constituent of the self that allows the individual to keep some distance, some elbow room, between himself and that with which others assume he should be identified."

[9] The homeless who were categorized as mentally ill composed only 10% (17) of our field sample of 168 individuals. For a discussion of the criteria used for categorizing individuals as mentally ill and for a detailed discussion of mental illness among the homeless in general, see Snow, et al. (1986).

[10] This conception of embracement is derived from Goffman's (1961b, pp.106–107) treatment of role embracement but with two differences. First, we conceive of embracement as a generic process through which attachment to and involvement in a particular entity or activity is expressed, with role embracement constituting only one form. And second, we think embracement can be expressed without the kind of active, behavioral engrossment or spontaneous involvement that suggests disappearance into the activity at hand and corresponding inattention to the flow of other proximate activities. Such engagement should be viewed as a variable feature of embracement, not as a defining characteristic.

[11] These two identities, along with that of the hobo, constituted the triadic folk typology that was particularly prominent during the first third of the century, especially among the hoboes (migratory workers) who regarded themselves as the cream of the road and who looked down scornfully on the tramps (migratory nonworkers) and the bums (nonmigratory nonworkers) (Anderson 1923, 1931). By the 1950s, this threefold distinction had apparently lost its conceptual utility. The terms "tramp" and "bum" were still brandied about, but the hobo concept no longer seemed to be a useful, generalized descriptor. Whether its decline in usage on the street was due to the disappearance of the hoboes' supportive subculture, as some romanticists have lamented (Bruns 1980), or to a blurring of the previous distinctions between hoboes and tramps and bums is unclear. What does seem to be certain, though, is that by the last third of the century homeless men were no longer imputing or avowing the hobo identity. The tramp and bum constructs were, and still are, part of the lexicon of the streets, however, as indicated by Spradley's (1970) and Harper's (1982) research, as well as by ours.

[12] Anderson (1976) found that this form of embracement figured prominently in the identity work of the black street-corner men he studied. Indeed, the identity work of these men consisted mainly of associational distancing and embracement.

[13] Given the categorization of this line of talk as "fictive," it is important to make explicit the criteria used to determine whether a particular narration was indeed fictive. As we previously noted, we not only talked with and listened to each of the 70 individuals within our identity subsample, but we encountered nearly all of them in a range of situations at different points in time, with an average of 4.5 encounters per individual. We were thus able to monitor many of these individuals across time and space. This enabled us to discern the fictive character of stories by noting one or more of three kinds of narrative contradictions: (1) those among multiple stories told by the same individual, as when one street person claims to be 36-years-old on one occasion and 46 on another; (2) those between stories and observed behaviors in various situations, as when someone claims to be working regularly but is seen panhandling or intoxicated during the course of the day; and (3) those between current situations and future projections and claims, as when a disheveled, penniless street person claims to have a managerial job awaiting him at a local business. In each of these situations, credulity is strained because of objective discrepancies or because of the vast gap between current and projected realities.

[14] Fanciful identities are constructed by other people as well, but it is our sense that, with movement up the class structure, they tend to be more private and temporally or spatially ritualized rather than publicly articulated, ongoing features of everyday life, as was true for many of the homeless we studied and the black street-corner men observed by Liebow (1967) and Anderson (1976). Regarding the latter, Liebow (1967, p.213) noted that the construction of fictive identities allows them to "be men once again providing they do not look too closely at one another's credentials." While many of the personal identities they construct, such as "going for brothers," are different in content from those constructed by the homeless, they are functionally similar. We will return to several of these points.

[15] That these four factors function as springboard for fanciful identities constructed by homeless men in particular is hardly surprising, given that success in America is defined in large part in terms of job, money, possessions, and women. This thematic connection also suggests that, while homeless males tend to stand outside the normative order in their way of life, some of them are, nonetheless, very much of that order in their dreams and fantasies.

[16] It is important to note that this account was elicited by the field researcher rather than by another homeless individual. In fact, we rarely overheard the homeless call into question one another's stories and asserted identities. Interestingly, this contrasts strikingly with Anderson's finding in peer groups of black street-corner men that "people 'shoot down' and 'blow away' each other's accounts frequently" (1976, p. 18). Reasons for this difference will be suggested in Conclusions and Implications below.

PART VI
SOCIAL STRUCTURE

Symbolic interactionists are critical of deterministic sociological theories in which individuals are affected and constrained by large-scale social structural forces. Such a view implies that actors are more "acted upon" than "acting." As Manis and Meltzer (1978:8) state, individuals are reduced to "mindless robots on the societal or aggregate level."

Following the writings of Blumer (1969), and emphasizing its processual nature, interactionists argue that the chief feature of society is located in human actors and their actions: "Human society is to be seen as consisting of acting people, and the life of the society is to be seen as consisting of their actions" (Blumer, 1969:85). Human society is based upon social activity; group life is a complex of dynamic acts. However, this is not to imply that society is merely a collection of isolated social acts. Individuals fit their lines of behavior to one another, hence they engage in collective action. Individuals make indications not only to themselves but to others—giving rise to what Blumer termed "joint action," or what Mead defined as the "social act." Social structure, then, emerges as a result of the actions of individuals.

Interactionists are cognizant that individuals act and interact within larger social groupings, networks, and classes—some of which are far removed from individuals in both the temporal and spatial senses. Nonetheless, such groupings have an affect on the individual. But interactionists maintain that the structural framework of a society may set conditions for action, but in no way does it actually determine behavior.

In the 1950's, Anselm Strauss (Strauss, et al., 1963) and his colleagues furthered interactionist thought through the development of the *"negotiated order perspective."* Studying the hospital, these interactionist scholars portrayed organizations as in the process of being acted out, with rules and roles constantly being changed through a process of negotiation and renegotiation. Their work points to the dynamic character of organizational life; social order is negotiated order; the specific types of negotiations were contingent on specific structural conditions. The results of the negotiations would not hold indefinitely. At some point, individuals would re-evaluate, reject, and renegotiate for new rules, roles, etc.

In the 1970's, critics (Gouldner, 1970; Reynolds and Reynolds, 1973; Turner, 1974; Zeitlin, 1973;) charged that symbolic interactionists did not adequately deal with social structure or that they had what Reynolds and Reynolds referred to as the "astructural bias." In response, interactionists made a number of self-conscious efforts to remedy this deficiency. Two theoretical approaches have emerged: (1) role theory and (2) negotiated order theory.

Sheldon Stryker (1980; 1982), Ralph Turner (1962; 1978), and George McCall and J.S. Simmons (1978) are among the chief architects of role theory. Simply put, role theory conceives of social structure as configurations of social roles, statuses, and positions—all which shape/constrain social interaction.

Negotiated order theory, as exemplified in the works of Altheide (1988); Hall (1982); Hosticka (1979); Maines (1979, 1982); Strauss (1978) builds on the perspective that emerged in the 1950's with Strauss and his students. Proponents of this approach emphasize the accomplished nature of social organization, its emergent, constructed, processual nature.

In the classic selection by Herbert Blumer, "Society as Symbolic Interaction," he discusses the origins and nature of society. For Blumer, society is the product of individuals interacting. He points to the unique ability of humans to construct and reconstruct their social worlds. Blumer links this theoretical focus with a microsociological approach to comprehending human beings and their societies.

Building upon ideas first postulated by Herbert Hyman, Tamotsu Shibutani examines a component of society, the "reference group," and the various definitions that have been attributed to this concept. Further, Shibutani discusses its importance for: socialization, self-evaluation, and for developing or maintaining self-conceptions.

The next two articles deal with interactionist conceptions of social structure and social organization. In their studies of negotiated order, interactionists analyze phenomena at three levels: *the micro, meso, and macro-structural.* The microstructural level of analysis focuses on patterned or recurring relationships between individuals. The macrostructural level, by contrast, refers to interaction between large-scale phenomena, such as social institutions and complex organizations. Between these two levels, is the mesostructure, a term coined by David Maines, (1982)—where societal and institutional forces mesh with human activity. The Maines piece provides interactionists with a basis then, for transcending the micro-macro distinction. In the mesostructural paradigm, structural features cannot be conceived apart from how they are enacted. The interrelationship between human action, social processes, and social structures is explored through mesostructural analysis.

In his presidential address to the Midwest Sociological Society, Peter Hall, refuting detractors who attribute to symbolic interactionism an *"astructural bias"* (cf. Reynolds and Reynolds, 1973) cites a number of interactionist pieces that focus on social organization. In addition, the author presents a paradigm consisting of six analytic categories that may be utilized for studying social organization.

The final selection, by Paap and Hanson, presents an interactionist study of interpersonal power. Studying social interaction between health care providers and consumers, the authors illustrate that social power is derived from sources other than individual or group characteristics. Social settings, in themselves, may be a source of power. Paap and Hanson's study points to power relations as unstructured, everchanging, negotiated and emergent phenomena. Power relations develop in the course of normal interaction and draw upon various "inconspicuous activities"—tactics of interrupting, manipulation, questioning, writing, ingratiation, and the like. These selections collectively represent social organization and social structure as they are typically seen by the symbolic interactionist.

REFERENCES

Altheide, David. 1988. "Mediating Cutbacks in Human Services: A Case Study in the Negotiated Order." *Sociological Quarterly* 29:339–355.
Blumer, Herbert. 1969. *Symbolic Interaction*. Englewood Cliffs, N.J.: Prentice Hall.
Gouldner, Alvin W. 1970. *The Coming Crisis of Western Sociology*. New York: Basic Books.
Hall, Peter M. and Dee Ann Spencer Hall. 1982. "The Social Conditions of Negotiated Order." *Urban Life* 11:329–249.
Hosticka, Carl J. 1979. "We Don't Care About What Happened, We Only Care About What Is Going to Happen: Lawyer-Client Negotiations of Reality." *Social Problems* 26:599–610.
McCall, George and J.S.Simmons. 1978. *Identities and Interaction*. New York: Free Press.
Maines, David. 1982. "In Search of Mesostructure: Studies in the Negotiated Order." *Urban Life* 11:267–279.
Manis, Jerome and Bernard N. Meltzer. 1978. *Symbolic Interaction: A Reader in Social Psychology*. Third edition. Boston: Allyn and Bacon.
Reynolds, Larry T. and Janice M. Reynolds. 1973. "Interactionism, Complicity, and the Astructural Bias", *Catalyst* 7:76–85.
Strauss, Anselm, et al. 1963. "The Hospital and Its Negotiated Order." Pp. 147–169 in Elliott Friedson (ed) *The Hospital in Modern Society*, New York: Free Press.
Stryker, Sheldon. 1980. *Symbolic Interactionism*. Melno Park, CA: Benjamin Cummings.
Turner, Ralph. 1962. "Role Taking: Process Versus Conformity." Pp. 20–40 in *Human Behavior and Social Processes*, edited by Arnold M. Rose. Boston: Houghton Mifflin.
———. 1978. "The Role and the Person." *American Journal of Sociology* 84:1–23.
Zeitlin, Irving. 1973. *Rethinking Sociology: A Critique of Contemporary Sociology*. Englewood Cliffs, N.J.: Prentice Hall.

SUGGESTED READINGS

Becker, Howard S. 1963. *Outsiders*. New York: Free Press. Early work illustrates the importance of power differentials in the social definition and sanctioning of deviant behavior.
Couch, Carl J.1984. *Constructing Civilizations*. Greenwich Connecticut: JAI Press. A major work detailing the development of both microscopic and macroscopic structures by a leading exponent of the Iowa School of symbolic interactionism.
Farberman, Harvey. 1975. "A Criminogenic Market Structure: The Automobile Industry." *Sociological Quarterly* 16: 438–457. An interactionist piece dealing with illegal actions within this large scale organization.
Gross, Edward. 1986. "The Social Construction of Historical Events Through Public Dramas." *Symbolic Interaction* 9(2):179–200. An interactionist account of the social significance of public dramas in "making history."
Hall, Peter. 1985. "Asymmetric Relationships and Processes of Power." Pp.309–44 In N.K. Denzin (ed.), *Studies in Symbolic Interaction* Supplement 1. Detailed piece illustrating recent interactionist efforts to overcome the "astructural bias."
Hosticka, Carl J. 1979. "We Don't Care About What Happened, We only Care About What is Going to Happen: Lawyer-Client Negotiations of Reality." *Social Problems* 26: 599–610. Falling under the negotiated order realm, this study explores the relationship between attorneys and clients, and the power the former have in defining and determining for the latter the definition of the situation and constructions of reality.
Karp, David and William Yoels. 1979. *Symbols, Selves, and Society*. New York: J. P. Lippincott. Focuses on the micro-politics of social interaction, specifically how power affects everday interaction.
Killian, Lewis. 1968. *The Impossible Revolution?* New York: Random House. A classic book on the nature of race, racism, and race relations in contemporary society.

Luckenbill, David. 1979. "Power: A Conceptual Framework."*Symbolic Interaction* 2: 97–114. Piece addressing symbolic interactionism's ability to treat the notion of social power.

Maines, David R. 1977. Social Organization and Social Structure in SI." *Annual Review of Sociology* 3: 235–259. This piece illustrates interactionist attempts to deal with social structure.

———.1991. *Social Organization and Social Process: Essays in Honor of Anselm Strauss*. New York: Aldine de Gruyter. A series of articles dealing with the negotiated order, macro processes, and the structure of social life.

Maines, David and John Charleton. 1985. "The Negotiated Order Approach to the Analysis of Social Organization." Pp.271–308, supplement 1 In Norman K. Denzin (ed.), *Studies in Symbolic Interaction* Supplement 1. Illustrates how social order is negotiated for, and constantly renegotiated for in the context of the organization.

Mast, Sharon. 1983. "Working for Television: The Social Organization of TV Drama." *Symbolic Interaction* 6: 71–83. Work examines the social organization of television drama production.

Mesler, Mark. 1989. "Negotiated Order and the Clinical Pharmacist: The Ongoing Process of Structure." *Symbolic Interaction* 12: 139–157. Piece focusses on the negotiations between pharmacists and others (doctors, nurses) to establish a social order in which they are accepted as clinical practitioners.

Nash, Jeffrey and James Calonico. 1992. *Institutions in Modern Society*. Dix Hills, New York: General Hall. One of the very few interactionists texts on major social institutions.

Schwartz, Barry. 1974. "Waiting, Exchange and Power" *American Journal of Sociology* 79 (No. 4): 841–870. Power and exchange are viewed from the interactionist, as opposed to the exchange theory, perspective.

David A. Snow, C. Robinson and P. McCall. 1991. "'Cooling out' Men in Singles Bars and Nightclubs: Observations on the Interpersonal Survival Strategies of Women in Public Places." *Journal of Contemporary Ethnography* 19(4): 423–449. Discusses those strategies women successfully employ in repelling unwanted advances.

Strauss, Anselm et al. 1963. "The Hospital as Negotiated Order". Pp.147–169 In Elliot Freidson (ed.), *The Hospital in Modern Society*. New York: Free Press. Classic study in which the negotiated order approach is first explicated.

Stryker, Sheldon. 1980. *Symbolic Interactionism: A Social Structural Version*. Menlo Park, CA: Benjamin Cummings. Work illustrates the systematic analysis of structure through employment of role theory.

Thomas, Darwin L., David D. Franks and James Calonico.1972. "Role-taking and Power in Social Psychology." *American Sociological Review* 37: 605–614. Research tests the hypothesis to the effect that role-taking accuracy is inversely related to power within families.

Weiss, Paul R. and Robert P. Faulkner. 1983. "Credits and Craft Production: Free-lance Social Organization in the Hollywood Film Industry." *Symbolic Interaction* 6: 111–123. 1964–1978. Piece examining the social organization of the Hollywood Film Industry, and its control by a very limited number of individuals..

Chapter 23 SOCIETY AS SYMBOLIC INTERACTION

Herbert Blumer

A view of human society as symbolic interaction has been followed more than it has been formulated. Partial, usually fragmentary, statements of it are to be found in the writings of a number of eminent scholars, some inside the field of sociology and some outside. Among the former we may note such scholars as Charles Horton Cooley, W. I. Thomas, Robert E. Park, E. W. Burgess, Florian Znaniecki, Ellsworth Faris, and James Mickel Williams. Among those outside the discipline we may note William James, John Dewey, and George Herbert Mead. None of these scholars, in my judgment, has presented a systematic statement of the nature of human group life from the standpoint of symbolic interaction. Mead stands out among all of them in laying bare the fundamental premises of the approach, yet he did little to develop its methodological implications for sociological study. Students who seek to depict the position of symbolic interaction may easily give different pictures of it. What I have to present should be regarded as my personal version. My aim is to present the basic premises of the point of view and to develop their methodological consequences for the study of human group life.

The term "symbolic interaction" refers, of course, to the peculiar and distinctive character of interaction as it takes place between human beings. The peculiarity consists in the fact that human beings interpret or "define" each other's actions instead of merely reacting to each other's actions. Their "response" is not made directly to the actions of one another but instead is based on the meaning which they attach to such actions. Thus, human interaction is mediated by the use of symbols, by interpretation, or by ascertaining the meaning of one another's actions....

The simple recognition that human beings interpret each other's actions as the means of acting toward one another has permeated the thought and writings of many scholars of human conduct and of human group life. Yet few of them have endeavored to analyze what such interpretation implies about the nature of the human being or about the nature of human association. They are usually content with a mere recognition that "interpretation" should be caught by the student, or with a simple realization that symbols, such as cultural norms or values, must be introduced into their analyses. Only G. H. Mead, in my judgment, has sought to think through what the act of interpretation implies for an understanding of the human being, human action, and human association. The essentials of his analysis are so penetrating and profound and so important for an understanding of human group life that I wish to spell them out, even though briefly.

The key feature in Mead's analysis is that the human being has a self. This idea should not be cast aside as esoteric or glossed over as something that is obvious and hence not worthy of attention. In declaring that the human being has a self, Mead had in mind chiefly that the human being can be the object of his own actions. He can act toward himself as he might act toward others. Each of us is familiar with actions of this sort in which the human being gets angry with himself, rebuffs himself, takes pride in himself, argues with himself, tries to bolster his own courage, tells himself that he should "do this" or not "do that," sets goals for himself, makes compromises with himself, and plans what he is going to do. That the human being acts toward himself in these and countless other ways is a matter of easy empirical observation. To recognize that the human being can act toward himself is no mystical conjuration.

Mead regards this ability of the human being to act toward himself as the central mechanism with which the human being faces and deals with his world. This mechanism enables the human being to make indication to himself of things in his surroundings and thus to guide his actions by what he notes. Anything of which a human being is conscious is something which he is indicating to himself— the ticking of a clock, a knock at the door, the appearance of a friend, the remark made by a companion, a recognition that he has a task to perform, or the realization that he has a cold. Conversely, anything of which he is not conscious is, *ipso facto*, something which he is not indicating to himself. The conscious life of the human being, from the time that he awakens until he falls asleep, is a continual flow of self-indications-notations of the things with which he deals and takes into account. We are given, then, a picture of the human being as an organism which confronts its world with a mechanism of making indications to itself. This is the mechanism that is involved in interpreting the actions of others. To interpret the actions of another is to point out to oneself that the action has this or that meaning or character.

Now, according to Mead, the significance of making indications to oneself is of paramount importance. The importance lies along two lines. First, to indicate something is to extricate it from its setting, to hold it apart, to give it a meaning or, in Mead's language, to make it into an object. An object, that is to say anything that an individual indicates to himself, is different from a stimulus; instead of having an intrinsic character which acts on the individual and which can be identified apart from the individual, its character or meaning is conferred on it by the individual. The object is a product of the individual's disposition to act instead of being an antecedent stimulus which evokes the act. Instead of the individual being surrounded by an environment of pre-existing objects which play upon him and call forth his behavior, the proper picture is that he constructs his objects on the basis of his on-going activity. In any of his countless acts, whether minor, like dressing himself, or major, like organizing himself for a professional career, the individual is designating different objects to himself, giving them meaning, judging their suitability to his action, and making decisions on the basis of the judgment. This is what is meant by interpretation or acting on the basis of symbols.

The second important implication of the fact that the human being makes indications to himself is that his action is constructed or built up instead of being a mere release. Whatever the action in which he is engaged, the human individual proceeds by pointing out to himself the divergent things which have to be taken into account in the course of his action. He has to note what he wants to do and how he is to do it; he has to point out to himself the various conditions which may be instrumental to his action and those which may obstruct his action; he has to take account of the demands, the expectations, the prohibitions, and the threats as they may arise in the situation in which he is acting. His action is built up step by step through a process of such self-indication. The human individual pieces together and guides his action by taking account of different things and interpreting their significance for his prospective action. There is no instance of conscious action of which this is not true.

The process of constructing action through making indications to oneself cannot be swallowed up in any of the conventional psychological categories. This process is distinct from and different from what is spoken of as the "ego", just as it is different from any other conception which conceives of the self in terms of composition or organization. Self-indication is a moving communicative process in which the individual notes things, assesses them, gives them a meaning, and decides to act on the basis of the meaning. The human being stands over against the world, or against "alters," with such a process and not with a mere ego. Further, the process of self-indication cannot be subsumed under the forces, whether from the outside or inside, which are presumed to play upon the individual to produce his behavior. Environmental pressures, external stimuli, organic drives, wishes, attitudes, feelings, ideas, and their like do not cover or explain the process of self-indication. The process of self-indication stands over against them in that the individual points out to himself and interprets the appearance or expression of such things, noting a given social demand that is made on him, recognizing a command, observing that he is hungry, realizing that he wishes to buy something, aware that he has a given feeling, conscious that he dislikes eating with someone he despises, or aware that he is thinking of doing some given thing. By virtue of indicating such things to himself, he places himself over against them and is able to act back against them, accepting them, rejecting them, or transforming them in accordance with how he defines or interprets them. His behavior, accordingly, is not a result of such things as environmental pressures, stimuli, motives, attitudes, and ideas but arises instead from how he interprets and handles these things in the action which he is constructing. The process of self-indication by means of which human action is formed cannot be accounted for by factors which precede the act. The process of self-indication exists in its own right and must be accepted and studied as such. It is through this process that the human being constructs his conscious action.

Now Mead recognizes that the formation of action by the individual through a process of self-indication always takes place in a social context. Since this matter is so vital to an understanding of symbolic interaction it needs to be explained carefully. Fundamentally, group action takes the form of a fitting together of individual lines of action. Each individual aligns his action to the action of others by ascertaining what they are doing or what they intend to do, that is, by getting the meaning of their acts. For Mead, this is done by the individual "taking the role" of others either the role of a specific person or the role of a group (Mead's "generalized other"). In taking such roles the individual seeks to ascertain the intention or direction of the acts of others. He forms and aligns his own action on the basis of such interpretation of the acts of others. This is the fundamental way in which group action takes place in human society.

The foregoing are the essential features, as I see them, in Mead's analysis of the bases of symbolic interaction. They presuppose the following: that human society is made up of individuals who have selves (that is, make indications to themselves); that individual action is a construction and not a release, being built up by the individual through noting and interpreting features of the situations in which he acts; that group or collective action consists of the aligning of individual actions, brought about by the individuals' interpreting or taking into account each other's actions.... [T]he three premises can be easily verified empirically. I know of no instance of human group action to which the three premises do not apply. The reader is challenged to find or think of a single instance which they do not fit.

Chapter 24 REFERENCE GROUPS AS PERSPECTIVES

Tamotsu Shibutani

Although Hyman coined the term scarcely more than a decade ago, the concept of reference group has become one of the central analytic tools in social psychology, being used in the construction of hypotheses concerning a variety of social phenomena. The inconsistency in behavior as a person moves from one social context to another is accounted for in terms of a change in reference groups; the exploits of juvenile delinquents, especially in interstitial areas, are being explained by the expectations of peer-group gangs; modifications in social attitudes are found to be related to changes in associations. The concept has been particularly useful in accounting for the choices made among apparent alternatives, particularly where the selections seem to be contrary to the "best interests" of the actor. Status problems—aspirations of social climbers, conflicts in group loyalty, the dilemmas of marginal men—have also been analyzed in terms of reference groups, as have the differential sensitivity and reaction of various segments of an audience to mass communication. It is recognized that the same generic processes are involved in these phenomenally diverse events, and the increasing popularity of the concept attests to its utility in analysis.

As might be expected during the exploratory phases in any field of inquiry, however, there is some confusion involved in the use of this concept, arising largely from vagueness of signification. The available formal definitions are inconsistent, and sometimes formal definitions are contradicted in usage. The fact that social psychologists can understand one another in spite of these ambiguities, however, implies an intuitive recognition of some central meaning, and an explicit statement of this will enhance the utility of the concept as an analytic tool. The literature reveals that all discussions of reference groups involve some identifiable grouping to which an actor is related in some manner and the norms and values shared in that group. However, the relationship between these three terms is not always clear. Our initial task, then, is to examine the conceptions of reference group implicit in actual usage, irrespective of formal definitions.

One common usage of the concept is in the designation of that group which serves as the point of reference in making comparisons or contrasts, especially in forming judgments about one's self. In the original use of the concept Hyman spoke of reference groups as points of comparison in evaluating one's own status, and he found that the estimates varied according to the group with which the respondent compared himself. Merton and Kitt, in their reformulation of Stouffer's theory of relative deprivation, also use the concept in this manner; the judgments of rear-echelon soldiers overseas concerning their fate varied, depending upon whether they compared themselves to soldiers who were still at home or men in combat. They also propose concrete research operations in which respondents are to be asked to compare themselves with various groups. The study of aspiration levels by Chapman and Volkmann, frequently cited in discussions of reference-group theory, also involves variations in judgment arising from a comparison of one's own group with others.[1] In this mode of application, then, a reference group is a standard or check point which an actor uses in forming, his estimate of the situation, particularly his own position within it. Logically, then *any* group with which an actor is familiar may become a reference group.

A second referent of the concept is that group in which the actor aspires to gain or maintain acceptance: hence, a group whose claims are paramount in situations requiring choice. The reference group of the socially ambitious is said to consist of people of higher strata whose status symbols are imitated. Merton and Kitt interpret the expressions of willingness and felt readiness for combat on the part of inexperienced troops, as opposed to the humility of battle-hardened veterans, as the efforts of newcomers to identify themselves with veterans to whom they had mistakenly imputed certain values.[2] Thus, the concept is used to point to an association of human beings among whom one seeks to gain, maintain, or enhance his status; a reference group is that group in which one desires to participate.

In a third usage the concept signifies that group whose perspective constitutes the frame of reference of the actor. Thus, Sherif speaks of reference groups as groups whose norms are used as anchoring points in structuring the perceptual field,[3] and Merton and Kitt speak of a "social frame of reference" for interpretations.[4] Through direct or vicarious participation in a group one comes to perceive the world from its standpoint. Yet this group need not be one in which he aspires for acceptance; a member of some minority group may despise it but still see the world largely through its eyes. When used in this manner, the concept of reference group points more to a psychological phenomenon than to an objectively existing group of men; it refers to an organization of the actor's experience. That is to say, it is a structuring of his perceptual field. In this usage a reference group becomes any collectivity, real or imagined, envied or despised, whose perspective is assumed by the actor.

Thus, an examination of current usage discloses three distinct referents for a single concept: (1) groups which serve as comparison points; (2) groups to which men aspire; and (3) groups whose perspectives are assumed by the actor. Although these terms may be related, treating together what should be clearly delineated as generically different can lead only to further confusion. It is the contention of this paper that the restriction of the concept of reference group to the third alternative—that group whose perspective constitutes the frame of reference of the actor—will increase its usefulness in research. Any group or object may be used for comparisons, and one need not assume the role of those with whom he compares his fate; hence, the first usage serves a quite different purpose and may be eliminated from further consideration. Under some circumstances, however, group loyalties and aspirations are related to perspectives assumed, and the character of this relationship calls for further exploration. Such a discussion necessitates a restatement of the familiar, but, in view of the difficulties in some of the work on reference groups, repetition may not be entirely out of order. In spite of the enthusiasm of some proponents there is actually nothing new in reference-group theory.

Culture and Personal Controls

Thomas pointed out many years ago that what a man does depends largely upon his definition of the situation. One may add that the manner in which one consistently defines a succession of situations depends upon his organized perspective. A perspective is an ordered view of one's world—what is taken for granted about the attributes of various objects, events, and human nature. It is an order of things remembered and expected as well as things actually perceived, an organized conception of what is plausible and what is possible; it constitutes the matrix through which one perceives his environment. The fact that men have such ordered perspectives enables them to conceive of their ever changing world as relatively stable, orderly, and predictable. As Riezler puts it, one's perspective is an outline scheme which, running ahead of experience, defines and guides it.

There is abundant experimental evidence to show that perception is selective; that the organization of perceptual experience depends in part upon what is anticipated and what is taken for granted. Judgments rest upon perspectives, and people with different outlooks define identical situations differently, responding selectively to the environment. Thus, a prostitute and a social worker walking through a slum area notice different things; a sociologist should perceive relationships that others fail to observe. Any change of perspectives—becoming a parent for the first time, learning that one will die in a few months, or suffering the failure of well-laid plans—leads one to notice things previously overlooked and to see the familiar world in a different light. As Goethe contended, history is continually rewritten, not so much because of the discovery of new documentary evidence, but because the changing perspectives of historians lead to new selections from the data.

Culture, as the concept is used by Redfield, refers to a perspective that is shared by those in a particular group; it consists of those "conventional understandings, manifest in act and artifact, that characterize societies."[5] Since these conventional understandings are the premises of action, those who share a common culture engage in common modes of action. Culture is not a static entity but a continuing process; norms are creatively reaffirmed from day to day in social interaction. Those taking part in collective transactions approach one another with set expectations, and the realization of what is anticipated successively confirms and reinforces their perspectives. In this way, people in each cultural group are continuously supporting one another's perspectives, each by responding to the others in expected ways. In this sense culture is a product of communication.

In his discussion of endopsychic social control Mead spoke of men "taking the role of the generalized other," meaning by that that each person approaches his world from the standpoint of the culture of his group. Each perceives, thinks, forms judgments, and controls himself according to the frame of reference of the group in which he is participating. Since he defines objects, other people, the world, and himself from the perspective that he shares with others, he can visualize his proposed line of action from this generalized standpoint, anticipate the reactions of others, inhibit undesirable impulses, and thus guide his conduct. The socialized person is a society in miniature; he sets the same standards of conduct for himself as he sets for others, and he judges himself in the same terms. He can define situations properly and meet his obligations, even in the absence of other people, because, as already noted, his perspective always takes into account the expectations of others. Thus, it is the ability to define situations from the same standpoint as others that makes personal controls possible.[6] When Mead spoke of assuming the role of the generalized other, he was not referring to people but to perspectives shared with others in a transaction.

The consistency in the behavior of a man in a wide variety of social contexts is to be accounted for, then, in terms of his organized perspective. Once one has incorporated a particular outlook from his group, it becomes his orientation toward the world, and he brings this frame of reference to bear on all new situations. Thus, immigrants and tourists often misinterpret the strange things they see, and a disciplined Communist would define each situation differently from the non-Communist. Although reference-group behavior is generally studied in situations where choices seem possible, the actor himself is often unaware that there are alternatives.

The proposition that men think, feel, and see things from a standpoint peculiar to the group in which they participate is an old one, repeatedly emphasized by students of anthropology and of the sociology of knowledge. Why, then, the sudden concern with reference-group theory during the past decade? The concept of reference group actually introduces a minor refinement in the long familiar theory, made necessary by the special characteristics of modern mass societies. First of all, in modern societies special problems arise from the fact that men sometimes use the standards of groups in which they are *not* recognized members, sometimes of groups in which they have never participated directly, and sometimes of groups that do not exist at all. Second, in our mass society, characterized as it is by cultural pluralism, each person internalizes several perspectives, and this occasionally gives rise to embarrassing dilemmas which call for systematic study. Finally, the development of reference-group theory has been facilitated by the increasing interest in social psychology and the subjective aspects of group life, a shift from a predominant concern with objective social structures to an interest in the experiences of the participants whose regularized activities make such structures discernible.

A reference group, then, is that group whose outlook is used by the actor as the frame of reference in the organization of his perceptual field. All kinds of groupings, with great variations in size, composition, and structure, may become reference groups. Of greatest importance for most people are those groups in which they participate directly—what have been called membership groups—especially those containing a number of persons with whom one stands in a primary relationship. But in some transactions one may assume the perspective attributed to some social category—a social class, an ethnic group, those in a given community, or those concerned with some special interest. On the other hand, reference groups may be imaginary, as in the case of artists who are "born ahead of their times, " scientists who work for "humanity, " or philanthropists who give for "posterity. " Such persons estimate their endeavors from a postulated perspective imputed to people who have not yet been born. There are others who live for a distant past, idealizing some period in history and longing for "the good old days, " criticizing current events from a standpoint imputed to people long since dead. Reference groups, then, arise through the internalization of norms; they constitute the structure of expectations imputed to some audience for whom one organizes his conduct.

The Construction of Social Worlds

As Dewey emphasized, society exists in and through communication; common perspectives—common cultures—emerge through participation in common communication channels. It is through social participation that perspectives shared in a group are internalized. Despite the frequent recitation of this proposition, its full implications, especially for the analysis of mass societies, are not often appreciated. Variations in outlook arise through differential contact and association; the maintenance of social distance—through segregation, conflict, or simply the reading of different literature—leads to the formation of distinct cultures. Thus, people in different social classes develop different modes of life and outlook, not because of anything inherent in economic position, but because similarity of occupation and limitations set by income level dispose them to certain restricted communication channels. Those in different ethnic groups form their own distinctive cultures because their identifications incline them to interact intimately with each other and to maintain reserve before outsiders. Different intellectual traditions within social psychology—psychoanalysis, scale analysis, *Gestalt*, pragmatism—will remain separated as long as those in each tradition restrict their sympathetic attention to works of their own school and view others with contempt or hostility. Some social scientists are out of touch with the masses of the American people because they eschew the mass media, especially television, or expose themselves only condescendingly. Even the outlook that the *avant-garde* regards as "cosmopolitan" is culture-bound, for it also is a product of participation in restricted communication channels—books, magazines, meetings, exhibits, and taverns which are out of bounds for most people in the middle classes. Social participation may even be vicarious, as it is in the case of a medievalist who acquires his perspective solely through books.

Even casual observation reveals the amazing variety of standards by which Americans live. The inconsistencies and contradictions which characterize modern mass societies are products of the multitude of communication channels and the ease of participation in them. Studying relatively isolated societies, anthropologists can speak meaningfully of "culture areas" in geographical terms; in such societies common cultures have a territorial base, for only those who live together can interact. In modern industrial societies, however, because of the development of rapid transportation and the media of mass communication, people who are geographically dispersed can communicate effectively. Culture areas are coterminous with communication channels; since communication networks are no longer coterminous with territorial boundaries, culture areas overlap and have lost their territorial bases. Thus, next-door neighbors may be complete strangers; even in common parlance there is an intuitive recognition of the diversity of perspectives, and we speak meaningfully of people living in different social worlds—the academic world, the world of children, the world of fashion.

Modern mass societies, indeed, are made up of a bewildering variety of social worlds. Each is an organized outlook, built up by people in their interaction with one another; hence, each communication channel gives rise to a separate world. Probably the greatest sense of identification and solidarity is to be found in the various communal structures—the underworld, ethnic minorities, the social elite. Such communities are frequently spatially segregated, which isolates them further from the outer world, while the "grapevine" and foreign-language presses provide internal contacts. Another common type of social world consists of the associational structures—the world of medicine, of organized labor, of the theater, of cafe society. These are held together not only by various voluntary associations within each locality but also by periodicals like *Variety*, specialized journals, and feature sections in newspapers. Finally, there are the loosely connected universes of special interest—the world of sports, of the stamp collector, of the daytime serial—serviced by mass media programs and magazines like *Field and Stream*. Each of these worlds is a unity of order, a universe of regularized mutual response. Each is an area in which there is some structure which permits reasonable anticipation of the behavior of others, hence, an area in which one may act with a sense of security and confidence.[7] Each social world, then, is a culture area, the boundaries of which are set neither by territory nor by formal group membership but by the limits of effective communication.

Since there is a variety of communication channels, differing in stability and extent, social worlds differ in composition, size, and the territorial distribution of the participants. Some, like local cults, are small and concentrated; others, like the intellectual world, are vast and the participants dispersed. Worlds differ in the extent and clarity of their boundaries; each is confined by some kind of horizon, but this may be wide or narrow, clear or vague. The fact that social worlds are not coterminous with the universe of men is recognized; those in the underworld are well aware of the fact that outsiders do not share their values. Worlds differ in exclusiveness and in the extent to which they demand the loyalty of their participants. Most important of all, social worlds are not static entities; shared perspectives are continually being reconstituted. Worlds come into existence with the establishment of communication channels; when life conditions change, social relationships may also change, and these worlds may disappear.

Every social world has some kind of communication system—often nothing more than differential association—in which there develops a special universe of discourse, sometimes an argot. Special meanings and symbols further accentuate differences and increase social distance from outsiders. In each world there are special norms of conduct, a set of values, a special prestige ladder, characteristic career lines, and a common outlook toward life—a *Weltanschauung*. In the case of elites there may even arise a code of honor which holds only for those who belong, while others are dismissed as beings somewhat less than human from whom bad manners may be expected. A social world, then, is an order conceived which serves as the stage on which each participant seeks to carve out his career and to maintain and enhance his status.

One of the characteristics of life in modern mass societies is simultaneous participation in a variety of social worlds. Because of the ease with which the individual may expose himself to a number of communication channels, he may lead a segmentalized life, participating successively in a number of unrelated activities. Furthermore, the particular combination of social worlds differs from person to person;

this is what led Simmel to declare that each stands at the point at which a unique combination of social circles intersects. The geometric analogy is a happy one, for it enables us to conceive the numerous possibilities of combinations and the different degrees of participation in each circle. To understand what a man does, we must get at his unique perspective—what he takes for granted and how he defines the situation— but in mass societies we must learn in addition the social world in which he is participating in a given act.

Loyalty and Selective Responsiveness

In a mass society where each person internalizes numerous perspectives there are bound to be some incongruities and conflicts. The overlapping of group affiliation and participation, however, need not lead to difficulties and is usually unnoticed. The reference groups of most persons are mutually sustaining. Thus, the soldier who volunteers for hazardous duty on the battlefield may provoke anxiety in his family but is not acting contrary to their values; both his family and his comrades admire courage and disdain cowardice. Behavior may be inconsistent, as in the case of the proverbial office tyrant who is meek before his wife, but it is not noticed if the transactions occur in dissociated contexts. Most people live more or less compartmentalized lives, shifting from one social world to another as they participate in a succession of transactions. In each world their roles are different, their relations to other participants are different, and they reveal a different facet of their personalities. Men have become so accustomed to this mode of life that they manage to conceive of themselves as reasonably consistent human beings in spite of this segmentalization and are generally not aware of the fact that their acts do not fit into a coherent pattern.

People become acutely aware of the existence of different outlooks only when they are successively caught in situations in which conflicting demands are made upon them, all of which cannot possibly be satisfied. While men generally avoid making difficult decisions, these dilemmas and contradictions of status may force a choice between two social worlds. These conflicts are essentially alternative ways of defining the same situation, arising from several possible perspectives. In the words of William James, "As a man I pity you, but as an official I must show you no mercy; as a politician I regard him as an ally, but as a moralist I loathe him." In playing roles in different social worlds, one imputes different expectations to others whose differences cannot always be compromised. The problem is that of selecting the perspective for defining the situation. In Mead's terminology, which generalized other's role is to be taken? It is only in situations where alternative definitions are possible that problems of loyalty arise.

Generally such conflicts are ephemeral; in critical situations contradictions otherwise unnoticed are brought into the open, and painful choices are forced. In poorly integrated societies, however, some people find themselves continually beset with such conflicts. The Negro intellectual, children of mixed marriages or of immigrants, the foreman in a factory, the professional woman, the military chaplain—all live in the interstices of well-organized structures and are marginal men.[8] In most instances they manage to make their way through their compartmentalized lives, although personal maladjustments are apparently frequent. In extreme cases amnesia and dissociation of personality can occur.

Much of the interest in reference groups arises out of concern with situations in which a person is confronted with the necessity of choosing between two or more organized perspectives. The hypothesis has been advanced that the choice of reference groups—conformity to the norms of the group whose perspective is assumed—is a function of one's interpersonal relations; to what extent the culture of a group serves as the matrix for the organization of perceptual experience depends upon one's relationship and personal loyalty to others who share that outlook. Thus, when personal relations to others in the group deteriorate, as sometimes happens in a military unit after continued defeat, the norms become less binding, and the unit may disintegrate in panic. Similarly, with the transformation of personal relationships between parent and child in late adolescence, the desires and standards of the parents often become less obligatory.

It has been suggested further that choice of reference groups rests upon personal loyalty to significant others of that social world. "Significant others," for Sullivan, are those persons directly responsible for the internalization of norms. Socialization is a product of a gradual accumulation of experiences with certain people, particularly those with whom we stand in primary relations, and significant others are those who are actually involved in the cultivation of abilities, values, and outlook.[9] Crucial, apparently, is the character of one's emotional ties with them. Those who think the significant others have treated them with affection and consideration have a sense of personal obligation that is binding under all circumstances, and they will be loyal even at great personal sacrifice. Since primary relations are not necessarily satisfactory, however, the reactions may be negative. A person who is well aware of the expectations of significant others may go out of his way to reject them. This may account for the bifurcation of orientation in minority groups, where some remain loyal to the parental culture while others seek desperately to become assimilated in the larger world. Some who withdraw from the uncertainties of real life may establish loyalties to perspectives acquired through vicarious relationships with characters encountered in books.[10]

Perspectives are continually subjected to the test of reality. All perception is hypothetical. Because of what is taken for granted from each standpoint, each situation is approached with a set of expectations; if transactions actually take place as anticipated, the perspective itself is reinforced. It is thus the confirming responses of other people that provide support for perspectives.[11] But in mass societies the responses of others vary, and in the study of reference groups the problem is that of ascertaining *whose* confirming responses will sustain a given point of view.

The Study of Mass Societies

Because of the differentiated character of modern mass societies, the concept of reference group, or some suitable substitute, will always have a central place in any realistic conceptual scheme for its analysis. As is pointed out above, it will be most useful if it is used to designate that group whose perspective is assumed by the actor as the frame of reference for the organization of his perceptual experience. Organized perspectives arise in and become shared through participation in common communication channels, and the diversity of mass societies arises from the multiplicity of channels and the ease with which one may participate in them.

Mass societies are not only diversified and pluralistic but also continually changing. The successive modification of life-conditions compels changes in social relationships, and any adequate analysis requires a study of these transformational processes themselves. Here the concept of reference group can be of crucial importance. For example, all forms of social mobility, from sudden conversions to gradual assimilation, may be regarded essentially as displacements of reference groups, for they involve a loss of responsiveness to the demands of one social world and the adoption of the perspective of another. It may be hypothesized that the disaffection occurs first on the level of personal relations, followed by a weakening sense of obligation, a rejection of old claims, and the establishment of new loyalties and incorporation of a new perspective. The conflicts that characterize all persons in marginal roles are of special interest in that they provide opportunities for cross-sectional analyses of the processes of social change.

In the analysis of the behavior of men in mass societies the crucial problem is that of ascertaining how a person defines the situation, which perspective he uses in arriving at such a definition, and who constitutes the audience whose responses provide the necessary confirmation and support for his position. This calls for focusing attention upon the expectations the actor imputes to others, the communication channels in which he participates, and his relations with those with whom he identifies himself. In the study of conflict, imagery provides a fertile source of data. At moments of indecision, when in doubt and confusion, who appears in imagery? In this manner the significant other can be identified.

An adequate analysis of modern mass societies requires the development of concepts and operations for the description of the manner in which each actor's orientation toward his world is successively reconstituted. Since perception is selective and perspectives differ, different items are noticed and a progressively diverse set of images arises, even among those exposed to the same media of mass communication. The concept of reference group summarizes differential associations and loyalties and thus facilitates the study of selective perception. It becomes, therefore, an indispensable tool for comprehending the diversity and dynamic character of the kind of society in which we live.

NOTES

[1] H.H. Hyman, "The Psychology of Status," *Archives of Psychology*, XXXVIII (1942), 15; R.K. Merton and A. Kitt, "Contributions to the Theory of Reference Group Behavior," in R.K. Merton and P.F. Lazarsfeld (eds.), *Studies in the Scope and Method of "The American Soldier"* (Glencoe, IL: Free Press, 1950), pp. 42-53, 69; D.W. Chapman and J. Volkmann, "A Social Determinant of the Level of Aspiration," *Journal of Abnormal and Social Psychology*, XXXIV (1939), 225-38.

[2] *Op. cit.*, pp. 75-76.

³M. Sherif, "The Concept of Reference Groups in Human Relations," in M. Sherif and M. Wilson (eds.), *Group Relations at the Crossroads* (New York: Harper & Bros., 1953), pp. 203-31.

⁴*Op. cit.*, pp. 49-50.

⁵R. Redfield, *The Folk Culture of Yucatan* (Chicago: University of Chicago Press, 1941), p. 132. For a more explicit presentation of a behavioristic theory of culture see *The Selected Writings of Edward Sapir in Language, Culture and Personality*, ed. D.G. Mandelbaum (Berkeley: University of California Press, 1949), pp. 104-9, 308-31, 544-59.

⁶G.H. Mead, "The Genesis of the Self and Social Control," *International Journal of Ethics*, XXXV (1925), 251-77, and *Mind, Self and Society* (Chicago: University of Chicago Press, 1934), pp. 152-64. Cf. T. Parsons, "The Superego and the Theory of Social Systems," *Psychiatry*, XV (1952), 15-25.

⁷Cf. K. Riezler, *Man: Mutable and Immutable* (Chicago: Henry Regnery Co., 1950). pp. 62-72; L. Landgrebe, "The World as a Phenomenological Problem," *Philosophy and Phenomenological Research*, I (1940), 38-58; and A. Schuetz, "The Stranger: An Essay in Social Psychology," *American Journal of Sociology*, XLIX (1944), 499-507.

⁸Cf. E.C. Hughes, "Dilemmas and Contradictions of Status," *American Journal of Sociology*, L (1945), 353-59, and E.V. Stonequist, *The Marginal Man* (New York: Charles Scribner's Sons, 1937).

⁹H.S. Sullivan, *Conceptions of Modern Psychiatry* (Washington, D.C.: W.H. White Psychiatric Foundations, 1947), pp. 18-22.

¹⁰Cf. R.R. Grinker and J.P. Spiegel, *Men under Stress* (Philadelphia: Blakiston Co., 1945), pp. 122-26; and E.A. Shils and M. Janowitz, "Cohesion and Disintegration in the Wehrmacht in World War II," *Public Opinion Quarterly*, XII (1948), 280-315.

¹¹Cf. G.H. Mead, *The Philosophy of the Act* (Chicago: University of Chicago Press, 1938), pp. 107-73; and L. Postman, "Toward a General Theory of Cognition," in J.H. Rohrer and M. Sherif (eds.), *Social Psychology at the Crossroads* (New York: Harper & Bros. 1951), pp. 242-72.

Chapter 25   IN SEARCH OF MESOSTRUCTURE: STUDIES IN THE NEGOTIATED ORDER

David R. Maines

It is difficult to pinpoint when symbolic interactionism as a perspective came to take matters of social organization seriously. Perhaps it was Strauss's publication of *Mirrors and Masks* (1959), in which he advocated the merging of social organization and social psychology. Or perhaps it was earlier, in a synthesis of Mead and Park, initially through the work of Hughes, and later through scholars such as Becker, Habenstein, Roy, and Stone. In any case, while it is true that there were symbolic interactionists working on problems of social organization prior to the 1960s, a basic conceptual scheme consisting of organizing concepts and statements about how organizations and social orders operate did not exist. A more focused perspective, however, began to develop in the 1960s with the work of Strauss and his collaborators, and by the end of the 1970s, a systematic conceptual framework for such study had been sketched out. That framework—the negotiated order—currently represents the dominant perspective on social organization to have been born from the domain assumptions of symbolic interactionism, and its fertility can be measured by the increasing amount and variety of research activity generated by it.

The purposes of this article are fairly straightforward. I will provide a brief account of the development of the negotiated order perspective, in which it has changed from a general theoretical stance to a more focused and paradigmatic framework. I will also discuss the articles appearing in this issue and identify their contributions to the perspective. Finally, I will discuss the notion of "mesostructure," which I consider the realm of social life to which the negotiated order perspective applies.

DEVELOPMENT OF THE PERSPECTIVE

I do not want to reify the development of the negotiated order perspective by imputing an undue linearity to it, but in looking back over the past 20 years of research and theory, certain features stick out as relevant to its emergence. There appear to be two broad phases in that emergence. The first phase, in which researchers were grappling with fundamental questions of structure and process, created an alternative imagery of professions and organizations, and the second phase focused more directly on working out a paradigm for the study of social organization and social order.

AUTHOR'S NOTE. In writing this article, I have borrowed liberally from Charlton and Maines (forthcoming), especially in the section dealing with the development of the negotiated order perspective. I wish to thank Sam Gilmore, Gary Albrecht, Judith Levy, Karen Peterson, Charles Suchar, and Noreen Sugrue for their help in reviewing the articles included in this special issue. Jim Thomas was a most able deputy editor, and as such he made my job as issue editor much easier.

CREATING AN IMAGERY

The early work on which the perspective was built presented an imagery of professions and organizations that differed sharply from the then dominant Weberian and functionalist theories. Bucher and Strauss's (1961) analysis of professions stressed an imagery of professions as "loose amalgamations of segments" held together in a delicate and fluctuating balance. What characterizes the professions are patterned differences, such as cleavages along lines of divisions of labor, which they analyzed in terms of segmentation within the profession. Although structurally differentiated, these segments undergo change, with some resembling social movements, and the relations among segments become highly ideological and political. Thus, professions were seen as in perpetual flux with "each generation...spelling out, again, what it is about and where it is going "(Bucher and Strauss, 1961: 332). Bucher's examination of the profession of pathology revealed two such segments ("scientists" and "practitioners") which she regarded as a loose form of organization within a profession that is "continually in movement" (1962: 51).

While those two articles did not focus directly on negotiations, they did identify a number of organizational features and processes that give rise to negotiations. The term "negotiated order" was introduced into the literature by Strauss et al. (1963) as a way of conceptualizing the ordered flux they found in their study of two psychiatric hospitals. The conceptualization recognized the stable features of an organization, but those features, such as rules and policies, work groups, hierarchies and divisions of labor, ideologies, career lines, and organizational goals, were regarded as the organizational background through which and within which people interact on a daily basis and attempt to get their work done. Ambiguities inherent in the organization require negotiation, either explicit or implicit, in order for organizational work to take place. It is through negotiation, the authors contend, that the organizational structure is able to operate, and thus negotiation was seen as important for understanding stability as well as change.

Stelling and Bucher (1972) utilized the perspective to challenge directly the traditional rational-bureaucratic conception of organizational authority. They did not reject the facticity of bureaucracy; rather, they contended that the bureaucratic model could not explain day-to-day processes of social control. Instead, social control was better explained in terms of political processes. They suggested a new conceptual scheme, emphasizing elastic autonomy, accountability, and monitoring, in which hierarchies were seen as operative but not necessarily operative in bureaucratic terms.

The imagery created by these and other articles thus sought to portray organizational conduct in ways other than as structurally determined. That imagery was supported by the research of other scholars. Manning's (1977) analysis of two police departments showed that rules have a fictional character, which requires that loosely defined guidelines be negotiated in actual cases of decision making and which also gives an advantage to administrators who can manipulate situations for their own purposes. Blankenship (1976:165) agrees with Manning, stating that "rules and legalistic authority...are best treated as resources in social interaction, often ignored as honored in everyday life." And Freidson (1976), who notes that negotiations take place within limits, also contends that divisions of labor ultimately are made up of social interaction. An imagery of organizations as considerably more "open" was thus created, one that systematically posed an alternative to the traditional structural deterministic theories.

TOWARD A PARADIGM

Anselm Strauss's book, *Negotiations* (1978), represents an elaboration and specification of the negotiated order perspective. It constitutes a "reflexive pause," to use Harvey Farberman's apt characterization, in that it attempts to assess the theoretical structure and potential of the perspective and to present the perspective in paradigmatic form. Strauss's central contention is that all social orders are in some respects negotiated orders. By this, he is asserting that negotiations are not just another interesting topic for research, but rather that they are essential for understanding social organization. He *is not* saying that everything in an organization or society is always being negotiated. He *is* saying that understanding negotiation processes and their bearing on social orders might well provide important insights into how social orders are maintained, how they change, and how structural limitations interact with the capacity of humans to reconstruct their worlds creatively.

Strauss uses three central concepts to forge the beginnings of a paradigm through which negotiated orders might be examined and understood. The first concept is *negotiation*, which refers to the actual types of interaction engaged in by participants and the strategies used. The second is *negotiation context*, which refers to the relevant features of the setting which directly enter into negotiations and affect their course. The third is *structural context*, which refers to the larger transcending circumstances in which negotiation contexts exist. Strauss (1978:101) emphasizes that the lines of influence can go both ways, in which the consequences of negotiations can be measured (eventually) in changes in structural contexts, and in which structural contexts condition how people will act. In this two-way process, it seems reasonable to view negotiation contexts as mediating structural contexts and negotiation processes. Negotiation contexts are created insofar as certain elements of those transcending phenomena are incorporated into or become relevant to negotiations, but negotiations may work their way back through negotiation contexts "up" to structural contexts.

Although the term "negotiation" has gained broad use, as in phrases such as "negotiation of reality" (Lauer and Handel, 1977) or in conceptualizations of interaction patterns for which the analysts do not have "negotiation data" (e.g., Anderson and Helm, 1979), the greatest utility of Strauss's paradigm is in linking negotiations and their contexts to social orders. That is, it is a *sociological* framework that attempts to improve our understanding of *social orders and social organization*. As such, the paradigm has not proven useful for psychological studies of negotiation (Roberts, 1979). It has proven useful for sociological studies of negotiation, however, in which there is an attempt to link patterns of participation to the structuring effects of social orders.

Busch's (1980) analysis of the historical development of the agricultural sciences shows how structural conditions directly affect the nature and types of negotiations, and how negotiations in turn create or alter structural conditions. Hall and Spencer-Hall's (1980) comparative analysis shows in what respects varying organizational arrangements require or suppress negotiations. Similarly, Maurin (1980) has investigated the extent to which the structural autonomy of physicians can be altered through patient negotiations. O'Toole and O'Toole (1981) have examined interorganizational relationships in terms of overt and covert negotiations that link organizations and organizational systems. In addition, Kling and Gerson (1978), who conceptualize patterns of segmentation in the computing world as constituting shifting patterns of constraint, show that negotiations are affected by the distributions of constraints and resources across all the settings in which participants are involved, and that those distributions are both the contexts for and consequences of negotiations (see Charlton and Maines, forthcoming, for a more detailed discussion of these works). Thus, in a rather short period of time, Strauss's paradigm has stimulated a significant amount of work. Issues of power, organizational structure, historical processes, resource utilization, as well as a number of other issues, have all been studied as aspects of negotiated orders. Likewise, the articles included in this special issue of *Urban Life* bring empirical analyses to bear on specific issues relevant to the theoretical structure of the perspective—issues that themselves are for the most part defined in Strauss's *Negotiations* as critical concepts or unexplored areas. This volume of *Urban Life* therefore represents a purposeful continuity in the development of the perspective.

CONTINUITIES IN THE NEGOTIATED ORDER

Noreen Sugrue's depiction of the experiences of a single patient shows in detail the intermingling of emotions and interaction. Feelings of anger and fear, which arose from perceptions of helplessness and abandonment, eventually emerged and were incorporated into negotiations and created what Sugrue calls "emotion context." At that point they became part of the negotiation context, or, in Strauss's terms, "properties entering very directly as conditions into the course of the negotiation" (Strauss, 1978: 99). It is absolutely clear in Sugrue's data that the patient's emotions altered and in part defined the trajectory of negotiations with physicians and nurses, although it is just as clear that those negotiations did not redefine the structural relationships (see Maurin, 1980). However, at that point where the patient's emotions became an object in the negotiations, the staff were put in the position of having to invoke hospital structures that they ordinarily would not invoke for someone with a gastrointestinal disorder. Sugrue's article therefore exemplifies the important process of emergence, which is central to the negotiated order perspective, at the interpersonal level and adds to the perspective by allowing us to envision the properties of negotiation contexts as entering and departing on a situational basis.

Judith Levy utilizes a dramaturgical approach for purposes of examining how negotiation contexts are formed in her analysis of processes through which hospices attempt to gain legitimacy in established medical facilities. The properties of negotiation contexts are not formed merely on some random basis, but are created in part by individuals and groups involved in purposive lines of action. Levy asserts that some of these lines of action are made up of strategies and staging activities in which there is the attempt to gain control over organizational rules, groundrules, sequences of acts, and the like that form the contexts of negotiation. This form of analysis, at the level of negotiations among representatives of organizational units, reaffirms Lyman and Scott's (1970) important point that poise and manner are essential processes of any power relationship. It also underscores the point that the intentional action of organizational members must be analytically related to the concept of negotiation contexts and, moreover, that those actions and the strategies that form them are oriented toward some *anticipated* structural arrangement whose only reality is that it *might* exist.

Strauss's (1978:102) suggestion that actors' conceptions of the nature of negotiation affect negotiation processes themselves constitutes the analytical problem addressed by Sherryl Kleinman. These conceptions cannot be relegated to some metatheoretic realm; rather, they have concrete consequences for how organizational members conduct the business of the organization. The holistic health center Kleinman studied was somewhat split ideologically between those who embraced an alternative conception and those who embraced a conventional conception of what the organization was and should be. This bifurcation led to problems in deciding who has a legitimate right to negotiate, the proper form of negotiation, and the issues over which negotiations should be conducted. Kleinman's research can thus be seen as extending the findings of Bucher and Strauss (1961) and Bucher (1962) by inquiring specifically into the consequences of such segmentation for the structuring of negotiation processes.

Peter Hall and Dee Ann Spencer-Hall present data from their study of two secondary school districts to analyze conditions that give rise to negotiations. Their analysis takes seriously statements made by Strauss (1978:234, 250-251) and by others (Maines, 1977, 1978) that the extent and nature of negotiations are subject to contextual constraint, but they go beyond such statements by showing empirically in what respects the schools under investigation constituted negotiated orders. The concluding section of their article is especially important insofar as it suggests a host of factors that affect the degree to which negotiations will occur: organizational size, concentration of power, centralization of leadership, professionalization of staff, and focus of resource allocation all combine in various ways to affect negotiations. The Hall and Spencer-Hall conclusions about the conditions giving rise to or preventing negotiations are best seen in terms of the analysis of secondary schools per se. However, it is this kind of research, leading to the development of substantive theory, that has the most promise for contributing to the development of a general theory of negotiation (see Strauss, 1978:245).

Anselm Strauss's article applies the basic analytic thrust of *Negotiations* (namely, that "social orders are, in some sense, always negotiated orders") to the field of interorganizational relations by asserting that few if any interorganizational arrangements could be instituted or maintained without negotiations. He attempts to place negotiations firmly in the analysis of such arrangements by examining the lines of work that constitute interorganizational linkages, the overall matrix of organization in which a given organization exists, and the arenas of participation in which organizational overlap is constituted. With these dimensions in mind, he examines the interorganizational arrangements and their negotiative character among the Oak Ridge National Laboratory, agencies of the federal government, subunits of those agencies, and the U.S. Senate. Strauss thus joins O'Toole and O'Toole (1981) in bringing the negotiated order perspective to bear on the analysis of yet another important substantive area of sociological investigation. The analytical contribution, which extends beyond that, is his further specification of the concept of structural context. That concept, which was left somewhat vague in *Negotiations*, takes on added clarity here in terms of social worlds, intersections of subunits between organizations, and industries encompassing organizations. This specification should allow researchers to better link structural contexts to negotiation contexts and their negotiations.

The final article of this issue, by Lawrence Busch, concerns the historical processes through which structural conditions are produced by negotiations and, once produced, shape subsequent negotiations. Busch presents a phase analysis of the emergence of agricultural research in the United States. At the heart of that emergence were negotiations among urban agrarians, farmers, and scientists. The first phase centered on negotiations over the legitimacy of agricultural research, which resulted in structural sedimentations in the form of state agricultural experiment stations. In the second phase, that structural outcome created negotiations over appropriations, which led to a reorganization and sedimentation of agricultural research as a corporate system. The third phase displayed a narrowing of the range of negotiations—a further structuring effect. Through such analysis, Busch is able to account for the rise of organized agricultural science as a national political force. The center of that process, however, contained a pervasive process of ongoing negotiations that are necessary to understand if structural emergence is to be understood. Seen this way, the distinction between structure and process is broken down, and in the wake of its destruction rests a perspective emphasizing the dialectical relation between negotiation and historically produced and embedded structures.

IN SEARCH OF MESOSTRUCTURE

I used the term "mesostructure" a few years ago (Maines, 1979)—quite deliberately, despite the imagery of body types—to refer to the negotiated order perspective. Like others, I regarded the notions of "micro-macro" as a coprolitic distinction that does more harm than good for purposes of understanding social life. If that distinction is to be rejected, however, it is only reasonable to replace it with a concept that might have greater utility. The final point of this article, therefore, is to suggest that the notion of mesostructure has that utility and to recommend ways through which it might be developed into a concept.

The negotiated order perspective attempts to show, on the one hand, how negotiation contributes to the constitution of social orders and, on the other, how social orders give form to interaction processes, including negotiation. As far as I am concerned, the perspective has always contained an inherent dialectic and an explicit temporality without recognition of which perspective cannot be properly understood. Negotiated orders, as forms of labor, contain dialectical activity in which the human subject constitutes and in turn is constituted by a social object. The perspective therefore represents the possibility for advancing dialectical research, since it contains the potential for examining the unity of subject-object by defining a domain of symbolic interaction which, through symbolic representations, creates the material conditions of social existence. In this domain, the distinction between "structural" and "interactional" analysis dissolves insofar as one of the major agendas of research is to recover the subject-object unity rather than focusing on one side or another (Thomas, 1981).

The domain of subject-object unity is the domain of mesostructure, and it envisions human beings as suspended in webs of significance of their own creation (Geertz, 1973). Social orders are transacted and made meaningful in the mesostructural realm. It is in that realm that social structures are enacted and which, through their enactment, become modified into meaningful patterns of participation. The domain of mesostructure incorporates the concepts of consequences and conditions but seeks to treat them processually by encouraging the analysis of the interaction between the elements that *constitute* consequences and the persons or groups for whom those elements *are* consequences. It also seeks to treat the concept of conditions, not in terms of the fixity of structure, but as conditioning processes that are very much a part of lines of activity. Mesostructure also recognizes that social transactions have a species character to them—that there is direction, form, and mandate. Social interaction is always contextualized interaction in the dual sense that the elements of situation, circumstances, and setting shape what identities and relevancies will be transacted by participants, and in the sense that such interaction can be thought of generically as participants mutually contextualizing one another's activity in the situation. Factors of power, resources, and skill may create imbalances in that contextualizing process (Gerson, 1976), but we need to know about those factors only to chart the particular trajectories of interaction sequences.

Thus, the domain of mesostructure does not deny the institutional structures of social orders, but it does deny that those structures can be understood without understanding how they are enacted. Nor does it deny the importance of interaction processes. Indeed, it is through interaction that structures are enacted, but in that process, interaction becomes *conditional* interaction. In terms of classical theory, mesostructure portrays freedom as possible through constraint and constraint as a consequence of freedom. The center of that domain thus consists of mediating processes and the webs of significance and group affiliation that form the interstitial arenas of social life.

Mesostructure, as the arena in which people carry out activity and as a sociological focus of research and inquiry, can be characterized in terms of a number of dimensions. As a linguistic tag, it pertains to *intermediate* structures and processes. In this sense, I simply mean that it is to be found somewhere "between" the macro and micro levels, which the term itself seeks to discredit. Of more importance for its characterization, however, are three dimensions based on the theoretical thrust of the negotiated order perspective, namely, *segmentation, mediating processes*, and *temporality*.

The concept of *segmentation* refers to processes of differentiation within social orders. Those processes create multiple social worlds within wider communities that are typically formed around specialized concerns and interests (Kling and Gerson, 1978) and which are *in process* by virtue of their changing membership and boundaries and by their evolving intersections with other social worlds. While I cannot explore this dimension here in any detail (but see Becker, 1976, and Unruh, 1980), I can suggest its relevance for the notion of mesostructure. Social worlds organize lines of communication among participants and define the terms in which social structures are enacted. In short, they define the use value of phenomena such as federal tax cuts, defense budgets, allocations for social programs, school desegregation, age discrimination statutes, and the like, including "common culture." They are conduits of meaning and patterns of activity that compartmentalize society into focused realms of conduct. In mesostructural analysis, people interact with society only insofar as society and its social structures are defined through social worlds.

The relevance of social worlds directly implies and leads to the dimension of *mediating processes*. In fact, these first two dimensions are closely related insofar as segmentation is itself a type of mediating process. The generic property of this dimension, however, is that the realities with which people deal are always socially mediated realities. Language is perhaps the most obvious example of a mediating process, providing, for instance, a world of objects (as in Western languages) or a world of processes (as in Oriental languages). Mediating processes have much to do with the knowledge one has of an arena of activity (for example, organizations, departments, programs, and the like) and how that knowledge serves as a basis for how an arena is represented to others. The representation of arenas is also mediated through political ideology, vested interests, and personal or group objectives. Mesostructures are thus crisscrossed by varieties of mediating processes that transact the meanings, images, and substance of objects with which participants deal.

Mesostructures, like negotiated orders, are always *temporal orders*. The nexus of social change is expressed through mesostructures, and that nexus, which involves the intertwining patterns of continuity and discontinuity, is made possible and rendered functional by temporality (Mead, 1929). Since humans are an intention-implementing species, their actions can only occur within time and through time. This applies to the societies and social structures that humans create, since the relevance of social structure can exist only as temporally defined relevance. Longterm relevance means that certain structures are more or less persistent elements of mesostructures and that they will be enacted by a wider range of social worlds. Structures also have the property of latency; they can be situationally invoked when they have use value, but "disappear" as a condition of action when situationally irrelevant. Thus, mesostructures are always in process, which means that the presence of structural conditions can be determined only with reference to a relevant time frame, and the operation of those structures can be understood only insofar as activity renders them a conditioning (hence, temporal) element of lines of action.

I believe that much of the debate and misunderstanding about the basic thrust of the negotiated order perspective has been grounded in the idea that the micro-macro distinction is a viable one (see Strauss, 1978:234–262 for a summary of some of that debate). While I certainly do not pretend that the notion of mesostructure will resolve those debates, I hope that it might at least reduce the misunderstandings. Mesostructures are realms of human conduct through which social structures are processed and social processes become structured. The negotiated order thus requires a mesostructural analysis in which structure and process are tightly and complexly joined. It is not just that new processes lead to new structural arrangements, or that structural change leads to associated processual change, as Strauss (1978:257) notes, but that structural arrangements exist in and through processes that render those structures operative. It is in this sense of the *interpenetration* of structure and process that negotiated orders specify a mesostructural realm of reality, and in that specification, the perspective is thoroughly capable of a sociology that is more interesting and vigorous than that trapped by the antiquated pretensions of micro-macro analysis.

REFERENCES

Anderson, T. & Helm, D.T. 1979. "The physician-patient encounter: a process of reality negotiation," pp. 259–271 in E. Gartly Jaco (Ed.). *Patients, Physicians and Illness*. New York: Free Press.

Becker, H. 1976. "Art worlds and social types." *American Behavioral Science* 19:703–719.

Blankenship, R. 1976. "Collective behavior in organizational settings." *Sociology of Work and Occupations* 3:151–168.

Bucher, R. 1962. "Pathology: a study of social movements within a profession." *Social Problems* 10:40–51.

Charlton, J. & Maines, D. (forthcoming). "The negotiated order approach to analysis of social organization," in H. Farberman (Ed.) *Social Psychology*. New York: Harper & Row.

Freidson, E. 1976. "The division of labor as social interaction." *Social Problems* 23:304–313.

Geertz, C. 1973. *The Interpretation of Cultures*. New York: Basic Books.

Gerson, E. 1976. "On `quality of life.'" *American Sociological Review* 41:793–806.

Hall, P.M. & Spencer-Hall, D.A. 1980. "Conditions and processes of problem identification, definition, and resolution in two school systems: toward a grounded theory." Final Report of the National Institute of Education.

Kling, R. & Gerson, E.M. 1978. "Patterns of segmentation and intersection in the computing world." *Symbolic Interaction* 1:24–43.

Lauer, R.H. & Handel, W.H. 1977. *Social Psychology: The Theory and Application of Symbolic Interactionism*. Boston: Houghton Miflin.

Lyman, S. & Scott, M. 1970. *A Sociology of the Absurd*. New York: Appleton-Century-Crofts.

Maines, D.R. 1979. "Mesostructure and social process." *Contemporary Sociology* 8:542–527.

———. 1978. "Structural parameters and negotiated order: comment on Benson, and Day and Day." *Sociological Quarterly* 19:491–496.

———. 1977 "Social organization and social structure in symbolic interactionist thought." *Annual Review of Sociology* 3:235–259.

Manning, P. 1977. "Rules in organization context: narcotics law enforcement in two settings." *Sociological Quarterly* 18:44–61.

Maurin, J. 1980. "Negotiating an innovative health care service," pp. 305–334 in J. Roth (Ed.) *Research in Sociology of Health Care*. Greenwich, CT: JAI Press.

Mead, G.H. 1929. "The nature of the past," pp. 235–242 in J. Coss (Ed.) *Essays in Honor of John Dewey*. New York: Holt, Rinehart & Winston.

O'Toole, R. & O'Toole, A.W. 1981. "Negotiating interorganizational orders." *Sociological Quarterly* 22:29–41.

Roberts, K.H. 1979. "Negotiations and their contexts." *Contemporary Psychology* 24:12–13.

Stelling, J. & Bucher, R. 1972. "Autonomy and monitoring on hospital wards." *Sociological Quarterly* 13:431–446.

Strauss, A. 1978. *Negotiations*. San Francisco: Jossey-Bass.

———. 1959. *Mirrors and Masks*. New York: Free Press.

———. et al. 1963. "The hospital and its negotiated order," pp. 147–169 in E. Freidson (Ed.) *The Hospital in Modern Society*. New York: Free Press.

Thomas, J. 1981. "Negotiated order in maximum security prisons: social interaction as mediating activity and loose coupling." Presented at the Midwest Sociological Society meetings, Minneapolis, Minnesota.

Unruh, D. 1980. "The social organization of older people: a social world perspective," pp. 147–170 in N. Denzin (Ed.) *Studies in Symbolic Interaction*. Greenwich, CT: JAI Press.

Chapter 26 **INTERACTIONISM AND THE STUDY OF SOCIAL ORGANIZATION**

Peter M. Hall

INTRODUCTION

Everett C. Hughes (1955) insisted that, while every social phenomenon was worth studying, proper study necessitated close and sensitive observation *in situ*. At the same time, he asserted that no phenomenon could be understood in terms of itself: it had to be articulated with the larger society. He challenged his students to explore the frontiers and peripheries of research topics to find relationships between and connections with the social environment. Making linkages between situated activity and broader and larger social forces and forms remains a critical and pressing sociological problem. Resolving it is the core and essence of the nature and dynamics of social organization.

Interactionists recently have been exhorted to develop a unified theory of social structure which will bridge the macro-micro gap and seriously tackle issues of class, power, and inequality (Shalin 1986). The materials, tools, and infrastructure for such an endeavor are already in place. The task here is to make them explicit, provide an integration, and present an interactionist paradigm for studying social organization. Bringing the strengths of interactionism to focus upon the sociological level of analysis provides a broad, dynamic perspective which can apply to the entire discipline.

Interactionism has an extensive tradition in the study of social organization and social process (Strauss 1959; Rose 1962). The general position, its assumptions, strengths, and limitations have been succinctly formulated and summarized by Fisher and Strauss (1978). A number of recent, imaginative, and productive studies, drawing upon the inspiration of that heritage, have advanced and extended the perspective significantly. A thrust of this article will be to show how these interactionists examine collective activity and social relations and lodge them in larger contexts and extended temporality. These studies provide the bases for a paradigm in the form of a set of analytic categories. Taken collectively and systematically, the set constitutes a cohesive, contemporary, general approach to analyzing social organization

The article will review some recent scholarship on complex forms of concerted action and related social processes—Howard Becker on art worlds (1982); Robert Faulkner on Hollywood musicians (1983); Harvey Farberman (1975) and Norman Denzin (1977) on criminogenic market structures, the negotiated order literature (Strauss et al. 1964; Strauss 1978; Hall and Spencer-Hall 1982; Busch 1982); the arena dynamics of social problems (Wiener 1981), and Carl Couch on civilizations (1984). Then, it selects and extrapolates an initial definition and a set of categories from these studies. Howard Becker's view of social organization as *recurrent networks of collective activity* is the starting point. The set of major categories include collective activity, network, conventions, practices, resources, temporality-processuality, and grounding.

Third, the conclusion will stress the necessary connections between three contexts—action, structural, and historical—and some suggested implications and directions. The action context contains the situatedness of collective activity, network, conventions, practices, and resources. It is the staging arena for behavior and is presented in conditional, contingent, and processual terms. The action context, however, is facilitated and constrained dialectically by its embeddedness and relationship to other, and perhaps larger, contexts (i.e., structural context) and its pasts (i.e., historical context).

The approach builds upon the basic strengths of interactionism at the micro level. It starts with concrete social action and examines how it is accomplished, using the concepts of collective activity, conventions-practices, and resources. Taking concerted action as the basic unit, rather than the individual, provides a sociological and social organizational base. It does not presume entities such as group, organization, or institution, but seeks out actual linkages and forms through the concept network. It overcomes the lack of attention to power and conflict by examining the problematics of resource distribution and use. The emphasis upon processuality frames the analysis in dynamic, not static, terms, in keeping with human experience. The Meadian perspective on temporality, unique to the discipline, makes a processual analysis necessary but one which consciously interrelates present, past, and future. Conceptions about time stress the use of contingent intentionality—that pasts simultaneously are constraining and facilitating. At the same time, concerns with network, resources, temporality, and grounding begin to encompass macro-level concerns. These provide the basis for contextualizing concrete and practical activity by linking and understanding the forces which shape it. This general approach linking history, structure, and action represents one way of coming to terms with the micro-macro split.

RECENT INTERACTIONIST STUDIES OF SOCIAL ORGANIZATION

The studies reviewed here show a wide range in scale and scope of social organization. They range from school systems and hospitals to national markets and industries to ancient civilizations. In addition to demonstrating the breadth of the interactionist perspective, they show the ways in which social interactions can be linked to each other and to larger contexts. They also provide the elements of, and evidence for, the general approach presented here. Howard Becker (1982), drawing upon Blumer's (1969) concept of joint action, gives us the basic view of four key elements—collective activity, network, convention, and resource. Faulkner (1983) empirically demonstrates recurrence in networks and shows the processes and uses of resources that produce asymmetry. Farberman (1975) and Denzin (1977) show how attention to history and linked contexts necessitates the grounding of analysis. The negotiated-order literature, focusing upon a key social process, demonstrates the importance of power, constraints, and conditions. The arena approach to national social problems and policies reveals the influence of structural contexts, the interplay of multiple social worlds, and the processes that shape the object of activity. Couch's (1984) study of civilizations demonstrates why temporality is a mandatory category.

Art Worlds

Howard Becker has taken what generally is assumed to be the result of individual genius and accomplishment and shown how art can be viewed as a collective production of an art world. The art world is a "network of people whose cooperative activity, organized via their joining knowledge of conventional means of doing things, produces the kind of works that art world is noted for" (1982, p. x). The activity covers production, distribution, training, consumption, and evaluation. Becker summarizes his position in the following quote:

> Art worlds consist of all the people whose activities are necessary to the production of the characteristic works which that world, and perhaps others as well, define as art. Members of art worlds coordinate the activities by which work is produced by referring to a body of conventional understandings embodied in common practice and in frequently used artifacts. The same people often cooperate repeatedly, even routinely, in similar ways to produce similar works, so that we can think of an art world as an established network of cooperative links among participants. If the same people do not actually get together in every instance, their replacements are also familiar with and proficient in the use of those conventions, so that cooperation can proceed without difficulty. Conventions makes collective activity simpler and less costly in time, energy, and other resources; but they do not make unconventional work impossible, only more costly and difficult. Change can and does occur whenever someone devises a way to gather the greater resources required or reconceptualizes the work so it does not require what is not available (1982, p. 34).

Becker grounds the analysis in activity that alters the concept of "social world" from one often defined in terms of communication and ideology to that of collective action. He shows how the political and economic institutions surrounding art worlds, in fact, shape them. The notions of network, convention, and resources and their application point to differential distribution, control, and usage in which some have a vested interest and where politics occurs to maintain or change work, resource allocation, credit, and rewards. In this idea of the network, some are more central and involved; as it radiates out, the connections are "weak ties" or "loosely coupled." New art worlds may occur through a confluence of new ideas or techniques, but their success and permanence rest on the social organization of support and resources, not on their intrinsic worth.

The Hollywood Film Industry

Robert Faulkner (1983) extends Becker's analysis by examining the market structure and work relationships in Hollywood. The film industry is organized along craft lines. Workers are freelancers, contracted for one project at a time. The industry, therefore, is a network of transactions, constituted and dissolved with each film. Since each film is a temporary coalition of workers, it creates an image of impermanence.

Despite these temporary coalitions, there is a relatively stable, highly unequal distribution of work. Individuals may come and go at both the core and the periphery, but the overall market structure remains. Analysis of film credits over a 15-year period shows a work distribution in which a minority of producers, composers, directors, writers, and photographers have recurrent employment and the majority, nonrecurrent or infrequent work. Faulkner's depiction of the linkages and transactions between producers and other specialties shows tight, recurrent, diverse ties between sets of central actors for each specialty. The rest have weak, nonrecurrent linkages. The existence of the linked cores counters the uncertainty of the economic environment and guarantees that those who have proven themselves as successful and moneymakers will work together again. It is based upon a calculated response of balancing resources and alternatives: the greater the level of capital involved in a film, the greater the risk for the filmmakers. To limit that risk, they hire "the top guy" or a "name."

The ties between producers and freelancers definitely are asymmetrical. Filmmakers control the conditions of work. They possess the resources to have their wishes met by agents and others. They can control others by withholding projects or not granting accolades. The top freelancer's location in this market is, then, a relative advantage over others in the same specialty. As filmmakers' options narrow, the options of these freelancers expand—they are asked to do more work for more and more powerful filmmakers. This widens the gap between center and periphery. The periphery then must choose the leftovers. Those with centrality try to stabilize their work by diversifying among a small set of successful filmmakers.

The turbulence of the industry leads to differential access to centrality, resources, and alternatives which constitutes the organized means for building what Simmel called "the inevitable disproportionate distribution of qualifications and positions," in which "there are always more people qualified for superordinate positions than there are such positions"(Faulkner 1983, p. 267).

Faulkner's contributions are significant. He demonstrates a network of collective action showing both recurrence and differential participation in that recurrence. He examines the social conditions that produce this social organization—entertainment as business, uncertain demand, craft organization, freelance markets, and a huge oversupply of qualified workers. He presents the conventions, the processes, and rationale that generate the market and shape individual careers. He specifies the asymmetry in the market, the way it works, and the way in which resources accumulate and are used. He reveals the ways in which participants try to control their work situations. He demonstrates the processual nature of the market social organization *but* shows how its stability is produced.

Criminogenic Market Structures

The asymmetry described by Faulkner can lead to illegal behavior. Norman Denzin's (1977) and Harvey Farberman's (1975) studies of the American liquor and automobile industries illustrate how industry organization and market structure induce middle- and lower-level participants into criminal practices to do their work. Denzin's historical review observes how an oligopoly of distillers emerged from Prohibition and wrote the Federal regulations that govern the industry. The industry is a complex network of shifting relationships among five tiers—distillers, distributors, retailers, consumers, and the legal order. Distributors, contracted wholesalers with sales quotas, are in the weakest bargaining position and are under constant pressure from above to meet new quotas.

There are many instances of illegal behavior throughout the industry. Distillers violate antitrust laws and negotiate with one another over pricing. Distributors engage in off-invoice practices with retailers, violate territories, negotiate with one another, manipulate delinquencies of retailers, engage in kickbacks to retailers, and supply retailers with goods or services that are illegal. Retailers occasionally bypass distributors and deal directly with distillers, which is a direct violation of the 21st Amendment. They negotiate with other retailers; they pay bribes or make deals with the legal order; they systematically serve under-age drinkers. There is widespread corruption in the legal order in licensing and protection against raids.

These practices occur, according to Denzin, because there is ample opportunity to conceal them. The industry is poorly monitored. Law enforcement is minimal and penalties are weak. There are structural ties between the industry and the political and legal orders. There is a pervasive sense that the laws are crazy and out of date and that crime is widespread and necessary to make a living.

Farberman's (1975) work also shows how manufacturers' practices generate illegal behavior on the part of new car dealers and those below them by mandating quotas of new car sales. He summarizes the argument as follows:

> It would seem, then, that the forcing of fixed margin new car inventory works to the manufacturers' advantage by increasing total net aggregate profit without risking direct competition. This high volume/low per-unit profit strategy, however, precipitates a criminogenic market structure. It forces new car dealers to free up money by minimizing their investment in more profitable used car inventory as well as by borrowing capital at prevailing interest rates. The pressure of interest payments provides a powerful incentive for the dealer to move his inventory quickly. The need to turn money over and the comparatively narrow margins available to the dealer on the new car sales alone precipitate several lines of illegal activity: First, it forces dealers to compensate for short new car profit margins by submitting fraudulent warrantee statements to the manufacturers, often with the collusion of the manufacturers' own representatives. Second, it forces dealers to engage in service repair rackets which milk the public of untold sums of money. Third, it permits the development of a kickback system, especially in large volume dealerships, whereby independent used car wholesalers are constrained to pay graft for supply. Fourth, the wholesalers, in turn, in order to generate unrecorded cash, collude with retail customers in 'short-sales.' Fifth, to the extent that short-sales spawn

excess cash, the wholesaler is drawn into burying and laundering money. In sum, a limited number of oligopolist manufacturers who sit at the pinnacle of an economically concentrated industry can establish economic policy which creates a market structure that causes lower level dependent industry participants to engage in patterns of illegal activity. Thus, criminal activity, in this instance, is a direct consequence of legally established market structure (pp. 455–456).

These analyses present complex networks across space and time. Denzin's notion of industry is, perhaps, more fluid than Farberman's, but both ultimately make connections between consumers and manufacturers. They ground these substantial collectivities in the capitalist, political economy, historically and contemporaneously. They recognize that the social organization exists through the transactions (e.g., short-sales, kickbacks), but only makes sense in the context of the overall system. Both see participants struggling to achieve and control their circumstances but with differential resources and consequences.

This is a dramatic example of meta-power, namely, the ability to set conditions and control interaction at a distance. The manufacturers control the conditions of interactions between used car salespeople and customers and between distributors and retailers (Baumgartner et al. 1976). The authors highlight the significance of context and the linking of contexts. Denzin and Farberman both show how the political economy, the structure of the industry, and the context of corporate management and production affect the context of retail sales. The social organization is reproduced because the commitment to maintain the constraints continues and is practiced across and within contexts. Unchallenged conventions and beliefs legitimate and justify it.

The Negotiated Order.

The negotiated order, the typical view of social organization aligned with interactionism, emerges from a study of psychiatric hospitals in the 1950s. Strauss et al. (1964) see organizational life as characterized by change and the development of a social order in which participants work out shared agreements and tacit understandings in response to everyday contingencies. The following social objects are subject to negotiation because of ambiguity or conflict: values, goals, rules, role expectations and relationships, authority hierarchies, resource distributions, collective versus group versus individual interests, responses to new situations, decisions, and courses of action. This is encouraged where large numbers of participants are differentiated by profession, institutional commitment, and length of service. Ideological commitments and hierarchical position limit negotiations. The negotiated order is dynamic and changing because it is constantly reviewed, reconstituted, and revised. It is contingent upon structural conditions and the more stable elements of social order. It is bounded and limited by larger societal structural contexts (Strauss 1978).

Some scholarship has sought to specify the conditions and limits of the negotiated order. The conditions surrounding and pervading the Strauss et al. (1964) study were change, uncertainty and ambiguity, disagreement, ideological diversity, newness and inexperience, and problematic coordination—all of which would facilitate negotiation.

A study of two school districts shows less negotiation in schools than hospitals (Hall and Spencer-Hall 1982). The daily life of schools, unit of operational focus, distribution of power, weight of history and tradition, nature of the environment, and focus of organizational attention narrowed the prevalence and impact of negotiation. There are, however, major differences in negotiated activity between the districts, between levels of the organizations, between special education and the general classroom. Special education is similar in many ways to psychiatric or medical treatment. Analyzing comparisons between the school districts and their elements and with hospitals provides a set of propositions relating social conditions to frequency of negotiation. They deal with organizational growth or decline, success or failure, size and complexity, change or stability, the distribution of power, the nature of activity, the style of leadership, and the nature of the personnel.

Lawrence Busch's (1982) research on the history of publicly supported agricultural research and experiment stations vividly shows the inextricable link between negotiations and their contexts. Negotiations among wealthy farmers, journalists, and urban elites in the context of populist farm protest led to enabling legislation for state experiment stations in 1887. Between 1887 and 1930, agricultural scientists, now organized, began to shape their environment. They used the structure of the experiment station and colleges of agriculture to set priorities for rural life and to negotiate research agendas. Their emphasis on eliminating the inefficient farmer, greater government intervention in the farm economy, increasing and stabilizing production, and participation in world markets assisted economic concentration in agriculture. During 1930-1970, labelled by Busch as "the period of silence," agricultural scientists increasingly narrowed their focus to specific problems of production. National agricultural policy is no longer on the agenda. This same period saw the dramatic rise of the conservative Farm Bureau, an organization initially fostered by the experiment stations, as the dominant interest group in agriculture. Since 1970, consumers, environmentalists, and nonconventional farming groups have made their claims on agricultural research, but their impact is unclear.

Busch makes the following concluding observations: (1) Negotiations might lead to forming or modifying structures that provide little or no opportunity for later negotiation; (2) Once a formal organization is created, it enters into the negotiation process itself and in ways different than intended; (3) Dominant parties may restrict the range of topics subject to negotiation; (4) Creating a formal organization may shift the location of certain negotiations from the outside to the inside. There is a dialectical relation between negotiations and historically produced and embedded structures and contexts. The structural conditions stimulate negotiations which shape subsequent negotiations.

This line of scholarship defines, emphasizes, and details negotiation as a central and widespread social process. The research clarifies how social structures are constructed (Fine 1984). It demonstrates the conditions under which a prevalent transaction can come to characterize a kind of social order. Yet, in exploring the conditions, characteristics, and consequences of a negotiated order, protagonists stipulate structural contingencies and limits. Historical contexts and organizational structures produce conditions that affect participants' abilities to enter into and succeed in negotiations differentially. Linkages to existing structural contexts limit the resources and options available to participants. The analysis of negotiative activity is markedly processual and dynamic, yet grounded in the political realities of social life.

Social Problems and Public Policy Arenas

An explicit concern with political conditions and processes dominates some recent research on social problems and public policy. This research links historical and structural contexts to arenas, places of action and contest, where many corporate actors and individuals construct definitions and boundaries to social problems, develop solutions and organizational plans of amelioration, and structure vested practices for survival and control. Estes and Edmonds (1981), for example, relate the structural context of American public policy in the 1970s to the formulation of aging and health care policy. They indicate briefly how societal uncertainty, political pluralism, and policy ambiguity transform intentions, limit approaches to problems, create organizations and elites, and fragment service delivery.

Carolyn Wiener (1981) uses arena analysis to show how the social problem of alcohol (ab)use or alcoholism was constructed. By studying the shifting network of the major social worlds involved—bureaucratic, treatment, volunteer action, research, law enforcement, alcoholic beverage industries, and temperance—she shows how the arena around the alcohol problem evolved. Building the arena entails increasing its visibility through the following processes and subprocesses: (1) *animating the problem*-establishing turf rights, developing constituencies, funneling advice, and imparting skills and information; (2) *legitimizing the problem*-borrowing prestige and expertise, redefining the scope, building respectability, maintaining a separate identity; and (3) *demonstrating the problem*-competing for attention and combining for strength, selecting supportive data, convincing opposing ideologists, enlarging the bounds of respectability.

Wiener depicts the growth of the arena with its attendant network of associations, grantees—contractees, constituencies, and agencies and their interorganizational relationships. She illustrates how external conditions affect the arena's growth, how internal problems and conflicts are created and handled, how the arena intersects with outside worlds (e.g., law and insurance), and consequences of the arena, including the development of dependence upon grants.

The concept of arenas extends the breadth of analysis to encompass multiple actors, corporate entities, and social worlds. It also frames an image of contest and conflict. While sometimes stated in terms of social definitions, the critical activity described is the manner of dealing substantively with a problem. The Wiener research shows the manifold actions and the use of diverse resources to bring about specific modes of problem solving. Those modes facilitate the interests of some organizational entities differentially. The boundaries established by "definitions" can do what "sticks and stones" can do as well as provide rewards. This line of research also demonstrates how fragmented and ineffective social policy implementation relates to the structural context of American institutions and how it is transformed from its formulation to practice. The analysis also demonstrates the complexity, dynamics, and unintended consequences of the policy process.

Constructing Civilizations

Carl Couch presents the power and scope of the interactionist perspective in an impressive work that moves from nomadic societies to mass industrial society. He discusses cooperation, solidarity, bargaining, negotiation, conflict, accountability and bureaucratization, and the structure of mass production. All of this rests upon the simple but profound assumption of the constructionary paradigm that human beings use their pasts to organize their futures. However, while simple coordinated action can occur with only a proximal or immediate future, constructing and maintaining social structures require establishing distal futures (Hintz and Couch 1975). Couch builds upon the longstanding dual, but connected, Meadian emphasis on temporality and the social act. He shows the reciprocal relationship between temporal structures and forms of sociation. The attention to celestial events, the rhythm of time, the calendar, building monuments and observatories, measurement and record-keeping, and the mechanization of time all facilitate the development of increasingly complex forms of social organization, based upon projections of increasingly more precise and predictable distal futures.

Calendars made it possible to develop sequenced futures of complexity and duration. Observatories became huge monuments which dramatized events, reflected communal timekeeping, and solidified the community. Large-scale complex societies required administrative structures that used information from the past to act in the present and plan for the future. They developed bureaucracies which focussed upon rationality, regularity, and order. Administrators were those who controlled this information. The clock represents the instrument that distinguishes modern civilization. It allows control over sequencing and coordinating activity in standardized and extended forms. The structure of mass production is dependent upon controlling time, pace, and place. Merging clock and calendar allows some to plan for others in complex and long-term ways.

The scope and power of Couch's work derives from its creative and skillful use of temporality, coordinated behavior, forms of sociation, and critical social activity. The analysis is based upon solving material problems—discovering, distributing, trading, cultivating, producing life's essentials. It clarifies and examines the elements, dynamics, and types of important forms of coordinated behavior—cooperation, negotiation, asymmetry, conflict. It illuminates how these forms characterize and affect larger social structures—small solidary bands, trade centers, and totalitarian societies. Couch makes understanding temporality the key to both dyadic interaction and global life. Social structuring occurs because people use a sense of time. That temporality is simultaneously constraining and facilitating. Transformations of social structures occur in reciprocal and dynamic relationship to transformations of temporal structures.

Summary

These studies present a variety of socially organized collective activities exhibiting degrees of fluidity, contextualization, detail, extensiveness, linkages, and asymmetry. Art worlds display networks of cooperating participants and collective activity organized around producing, distributing, consuming, and evaluating a good. In industrial market structures, there are variations of linked contexts, transactions, and actors with differential participation and consequences in producing, distributing, and consuming products. Negotiated orders are social forms organized around a central process but limited by history, context, and the internal distribution of resources. Arenas are contexts in which contestants differentially bound and create collective action toward some object. Finally, civilizations are collective temporal structures of varying extensions, linked to forms of coordinated behavior and collective relatedness. The studies reviewed here were not undertaken as part of a single research agenda. They therefore obviously vary in their explicit use of the focal categories. Temporality is most evident in that regard. Because some are monographs and others articles, they differ in the attention to detailing elements such as conventions-practices. They all share, however, a processual view of collective activity. Most are explicit in how they frame a central collective activity. All are aware that social organization means that activity is conditioned and shaped by its organization but also that activity, in a dynamic sense, shapes and constitutes the conditions. Most of the studies clearly present the reality of unequal distribution and mobilization of resources producing and reproducing asymmetric consequences. Most of the studies explicitly ground and link collective activity to the larger society in which it exists. Some seek to formulate how time and history affect activity. Taken together and collectively, these works provide a conceptual, empirical, and methodological basis for framing a perspective on social organization.

SOCIAL ORGANIZATION

The Meso Domain

Sociologists assume that social life is patterned, structured, and organized, but have strong differences about the manner, extent, integration, and stability of that patterning. They usually start with a definition of social organization as patterns of recurrent interaction, but fail to make the explicit connections between role relationships and societal structures. There is a tendency to assume more totalization, structuring, and integration than is evident. Finally, because many operate at different levels of analysis, i.e., macro and micro, there is a tendency to distort connections between social constraint and human agency.

The works reviewed in the preceding section are part of an emerging interactionist paradigm to study social organization and social structure that David Maines (1982) described as "in search of mesostructure." They provide the basis for transcending the macro-micro distinction, by showing the ways societal and institutional forces mesh with human activity. In mesostructures, one can discern that social arrangements exist in and through processes that render them operational and operative. Structures cannot be understood apart from how they are enacted, but the structuring conditions the enactment. Maines observed that this developing paradigm was characterized by the reflexive and dialectical relationship between activity and context, conditioning and mediating processes, and temporality. The paradigm in the making and the elements to be discussed in this section raise the level of focus from the micro domain, but without suspending concerns with process, emergence, and human agency. The general approach recognizes the constraints and influences of larger institutional structures, but not without exploring their concrete implications and empirical consequences. The categories to be discussed are orienting and sensitizing mechanisms for bringing the meso domain into strong focus so the interrelationship between structural influences, social processes, and human action can be seen more clearly.

Howard Becker (1982) defines social organization as "recurring networks of collective activity." He notes, however, that the nature and degree of that recurrence are to be found in direct examination. S. F. Nadel (1957) concluded his review of the concept of social structure by arguing that it exists in the plural. Words like "society," "the state," and "the family" gloss diversity, ambiguity, incompleteness, contradiction, and complexity. It is imperative to determine empirically how social life is organized, rather than to assume it. The six topics of discussion—collective activity, network, convention practices, resources, processuality-temporality, and grounding—are ways of guiding that study of social organization.

Collective Activity

Collective activity and the events it produces are the basic unit of sociological investigation (Becker 1982, p. 370). Collective activity is composed of social acts in which two or more actors merge their lines of action with reference to each other. The intermingling of gesture-response sequences which include and complete each other. The focus is upon what people do together, not separately, and how their actions build upon and contribute to each other and something larger. *Collective activity is the sequencing of series of social acts by two or more persons in relation to social objects.*

Attention is also on the concrete and the real. The admonition to start with the empirical, what people actually are doing, avoids overly structured views of joint action as between occupants of positions with rights and duties. The aim is to note the tasks, bundles of tasks, and their arrangement which are needed to produce some enterprise, accomplish some object, or have some event. The division of labor is conceptualized in terms of actions, not only actors (Strauss 1985). It is necessary to determine essential activities and how they are structured, allocated, and merged. While studies that illustrate this approach often are of worlds of work, the mode of analysis is equally applicable and should be developed for the worlds of family, friends, leisure, and politics. Application to having a party, raising a child, deregulating an industry, or settling the arms race can be envisioned just as much as revising a graduate program or building a skyscraper.

Activity and task vary in nature, complexity, coordination, and timing. Strauss et al. (1985) begin to deal with these issues in their study of medical work. Managing a patient's illness involves multiple kinds of work or activity that must be enacted, sequenced, and coordinated. These include machine, safety, comfort, sentimental, error, dirty, informational, body, negotiative, and articulation work. Not all work is at the same level. Articulation work—the responsibility for timing and sequencing activity—is qualitatively different and a higher level of work.

The totality of tasks (of all these kinds of work), when arranged simultaneously and sequentially along the course of a project, is an arc of work. Because there are numerous places for slippage or failure along this trajectory, the tenor of the analysis is contingent. The language is that of sharping, rather than managing, the illness. This research represents one way to examine the multiple components of activity and to depict how they fit together to produce the whole.

A substratum and, at the same time, perhaps a "task" in collective activity is communication. Some forms of collective activity are essentially communicative in nature—conversing, educating, or democratic debate and decision making. Since collective activity may not occur in face-to-face settings, communication is necessary for recording, reporting, coordinating, and directing. When collective activity is stymied, communication frequently is implemented to find means of resolution. Overcoming blocked activity or developing articulation work may necessitate meta-communication, e.g., talk about talk, information about information. Attention to communication is imperative but the format depends upon the focal collective activity.

Beginning with collective activity has a number of advantages. Framing collectivity means a social, rather than an individual, unit. Emphasis on activity leads to something concrete and observable, rather than something internal or highly abstract. It provides a focus of the actual and practical world of everyday life, rather than imposed orderings of conceptual systems. Finally, the analysis of collective activity and communication suggests that its nature, forms, and variations shape its organization: what needs to be done influences how to do it.

Network

Network is increasingly being used with greater precision and sophistication as a sociological concept (Burt 1982). It is defined here as *the set of linkages, representing transactions and relationships, between the actors of a population.* Actors are more than individuals. They also include teams, groups, and organizations, but not societies or collectivities. Hindess (1986, p. 115) defines an actor as "...a locus of decision and action where the action is, in some sense, a consequence of the actor's decisions." Teams can decide and act while collectivities cannot.

The idea of network comes with few theoretical assumptions. Basically, it represents a way of mapping the social terrain. The intention behind using network is to capture the relational, dynamic, complex, and varied nature of social life. Networks, therefore, are found in multiple forms and vary along a number of dimensions, e.g., size, mutuality, complexity, extensiveness, and indistinct boundaries of that network.

The Hollywood labor market is clear and narrow, with wide spatial gulfs between center and periphery. Fine and Kleinman (1983) suggest that a group is a network with high density whose linkages activate simultaneously. This definition also suggests variations in terms of weak-strong, loose-tight, and open-closed linkages. Stronger, tighter, closed linkages mean more frequent interaction, mutuality, and responsiveness and less openness to others. In three-dimensional terms, these linkages would be depicted as wider and thicker. The network also would have distinct boundaries. Finally, using multidimensionality, network display also ought to include symmetric-asymmetric and proximate-distal scales.

There are a number of benefits of using the network idea. First, it specifies the elemental form of social organization. Second, the basic component, transaction, is the same for collective activity, i.e., social act. Third, it stresses actually existing relations and not an idealized social entity (Fine and Kleinman 1983; Collins 1986). Network captures the nature of this fluid, complex, heterogeneous, and mobile society better than the standard sociological concept of groups. It provides a means to observe variation in involvement, integration, and coordination. Social worlds evince diversity in segmentation and compartmentalization (Maines 1982). While intimate strong ties often receive attention, Granovetter (1973) showed the prevalence and significance of weak ties. Finally, network provides an empirical and conceptual means for bridging social worlds and action contexts. Its ability to both circumscribe and transcend any given social boundary makes it easier to understand the complexity of the alcoholism arena as well as the inner circle of the corporate class (Useem 1984). Network is a sensitizing device which assists in exploring the nature and limits of social influence within and beyond the immediate focus of attention.

Conventions and Practices

Activity is enacted and accomplished and networks activated and coordinated through the use of conventions and practices. Participants consider circumstances in terms of what is relevant or adequate for the purpose at hand. They seek to routinize and standardize situations by establishing *generally accepted and shared, habitual, taken-for-granted ways of understanding, communicating, cooperating, and doing*. For art worlds, they stipulate materials, abstractions, form, and dimensions of the art object and the relationship between participants. More broadly, convention and practices constitute the new recruit's or ethnographer's basic questions—how are things done around here? They represent, in part, "short cuts," "tricks of the trade," and "on the job training." They make cooperation and coordination easier and more efficient. They are practical because they get things done easily. They facilitate activity but they also constrain alternatives. They become embedded in consciousness, activity, and the responses of others. Changing them requires effort and challenging the idea that "if it ain't broke, don't fix it."

Interactionists and ethnomethodologists have a well-developed tradition of exploring the practical world of actors (Roy 1958; Handel 1982). The terms, conventions, and practices are used intentionally in lieu of values, norms, and rules. Assumed values, norms, or even rules often are not taken at face value. Actors may use them as resources or interpret them pragmatically in relation to the immediate situation. Practices and conventions may develop which, in essence, add to the official manual. In addition, many practices represent covert alterations of official values, norms, and rules. Actors are not automatons. When situations vary from expectation, actors amend their conventions to deal with the atypical and unanticipated. The use of conventions and practices is akin to John Lofland's (1976) idea of strategies as constructed action. They include, for example, arrangements, methods, procedures, schemes, and techniques as categories of the collective aspect of coping and accomplishing.

Conventions and practices often are differentially known, shared, and publicly displayed. Boundaries of awareness limit participation. Differential possession and the ability to work "behind closed doors" are practical accomplishments and distinguish between insiders and outsiders. Many circumstances of collective activity involve divergent as well as convergent interests. Conventions and practices for different sets of participants under those conditions can be labelled maneuvers, ploys, and tactics. They include secrecy or surveillance, avoiding or confronting, delaying or expediting. Analysis of conventions and practices must acknowledge the possible existence and consequence of conflicts of interests and the existence of cross-purposes.

Conventions and practices are necessary analytical tools. They reveal the concrete procedures by which collective activity is accomplished. Assuming a practical stance clarifies how participants deal with routine and problematic circumstances. It illustrates, specifically, what is invoked and used in behavior, rather than inferring a value or referring to a norm or a rule. Finally, acknowledging differential knowledge and display helps establish and reveal the nature of the network, i.e., its integration, segmentation, or symmetry. Conscious attempts to limit diffusion and to insulate practice may illustrate conflicts of interest which suggest important dynamics in network mobilization and collective activity negotiation.

Resources and Power

Getting things done depends upon having resources; they are the means to the end. A *resource is any attribute, possession, or circumstance that claimants may use to achieve ends*. Resources often are not plentiful or divided evenly. Resources are connected intimately with power. One view of power is the capacity to mobilize resources to get things done and to achieve goals (Kanter 1977). Power also implies that there is differential knowledge, access, command, and mobilization of resources and of the rewards and benefits those resources enable. It is possible to think of networks as distribution systems for making resources and their consequences available.

Resources have also been defined as constraints, inducements, and persuasion (Gamson 1968). Power, in this view, is a tool in gaining compliance, overcoming resistance, or limiting the options of others. Differential command of these forms of resources leads to domination or asymmetry where some are capable of imposing their will disproportionately on others and setting conditions, making decisions, taking actions, and exercising control that determines the relationship (Hall 1985).

Superordinates can create culture, organize the relationship, develop forms of deference and demeanor, control use of time and space, differentially extract benefits, and disperse costs and risks. Subordinates are not powerless; they often develop techniques or means to keep "distance" from those above them.

Resources and power should be seen in dynamic, processual, and contingent terms (Hall 1985). Resources are not available automatically or totally. Situations may differ significantly to the participants. Miscalculations can be made. Mobilization may be too little or too late. Resources can also be lost, squandered, or misused. Staying in control requires commitment. Change, on the other hand—as Becker discussed—involves finding, developing, controlling, or mobilizing more or new resources. Any analysis of the structure of resource mobilization must be relational and interactional, dependent as it is upon the responses of others.

Resources come in many forms. Some are quite general and can be used across a broad array of situations. On the other hand, actors are implicated in multiple settings in their ongoing lives. The ability to move resources across situations is a significant factor. Some actors maintain their position by invoking "authority" and additional resources from those above them, to put out local resentment, dissent, or revolt. Gerson's (1976) concept of sovereignty is helpful here—"the net balance of resources and constraints available to a person, organization, or other demarcatable group across the full range of settings" in which they participate (p. 798). Sovereignty as a variable can provide detail about persons, organizations, or groups and also of situations and networks. It also explicitly links situations to each other and to larger arrangements. Clearly, some networks are more resourceful than others.

Several strengths derive from examining power as resource distribution and mobilization. This approach helps specify the dynamics of the action context. Its processual and contingent orientation facilitates understanding how domination or equality occur, recur, or change, since they are not assumed to be automatic. This formulation also lodges and connects the action context in dynamic ways to other, and perhaps larger, contexts so relations between them can be explored. Domain linkage and integration become a point of inquiry.

Processuality and Temporality

A dynamic stance is a necessary component of an interactionist approach to social organization. This stance sees structure as process or in process. Social life is a continuous stream of activity, broken up into events. Social organization always evolves and is in the process of becoming, rather than being. Collective activity being formed, maintained, eliminated, and altered in a succession of responses to circumstances constitutes society. Throughout, this discussion has conceived social organization as in the gerund form—doing, accomplishing. Couch's formulation of constructing civilizations is no accidental semantic. It emerges from the constructionary paradigm of interactionism. Social organization is a metaphor (Becker 1982). As in a photograph, people often freeze and stop a flow of action. It is imperative to remember that the trajectories of coordinated sequences across space and time are complex.

Interactionism frequently is associated with emergence, novelty, and change. The approach, however, does not automatically assume or find change. Everett Hughes (1955) was struck by the need to explain "the dynamics of remaining the same" (Shalin 1986). While social change is not uncommon, social orders do get reproduced. Both are human accomplishments and require activity. In their analysis of the Watergate hearings, Molotch and Boden (1985), for example, show how domination is accomplished in everyday talk. Issues of permanence and change need to be examined in longitudinal and comparative ways. Processual analysis provides a basis for understanding the "hows" of both.

A processual analysis is simultaneously temporal. Significant social activity requires and occurs in temporally extended contexts, e.g., raising a family, organizing a social movement, carrying on the Cold War. Collective activity as the arc of work is accomplished along a time line. Strauss et al. (1985) observe that organizations, technologies, teams, and individuals all have biographies which mesh with each other and with larger temporal orders.

Not only does activity occur across time, it is organized in terms of time. Following Mead and Couch, collective activity is constructed in terms of the relation between presents to pasts and futures. Temporality is conceptualized in terms of the relations of presents to pasts and futures. The use of plurals is intentional. Maines et al. (1983) derive four kinds of pasts from Mead. Pasts and futures also emerge in the plural because they are characterized according to ever-changing pragmatic interests of ongoing presents. The nature of futures is multiple because alternative scenarios are the subject of much debate and conflict among social actors. Temporality stands in a dialectical relationship to activity. On the one hand, pasts, for instance, represent limits and constraints. Like the concept of commitment with side bets (Becker 1960), lines of action have consequences that cannot be ignored. In this sense, the past no longer is an option. Pasts bring sediments in the form of conditions that limit presents and futures. Yet, pasts continually are partially reconstructed and selectively recast to generate new futures. The interrelationship of temporal categories, therefore, simultaneously is facilitating and constraining.

Temporality is not only a context for social life or a way of analyzing collective activity. It is a critical mode and matrix of social organization. Sociotemporal orders organize, coordinate, and regulate the lives of social entities (Zerubavel 1981). They provide the basis for social accessibility, for separating the sacred from the profane, and segregating public from private domains. Ordering time is too often taken for granted but modern social life is organized explicitly in terms of it. Zerubavel (1981) demonstrated the existence and consequences of a highly rationalized temporal order in making collective activity precise, punctual, calculable, standard, bureaucratic, rigid, invariant, finely coordinated, and routine. That temporal order is based upon rigid sequential structures, fixed durations, standard temporal locations, and uniform rates of recurrence. The schedule is used in this order to facilitate and integrate a complex, differentiated division of labor.

Perrow (1984) illustrates another consequence of temporal organization upon activity. Complex, tightly coupled systems have numerous interactions and interconnections with little slack time to respond to the unexpected. The potential for catastrophe is extreme, as the Chernobyl nuclear failure and the fatal Challenger mission exemplified. In contrast, loosely coupled systems handle surprises and delays relatively easily and with limited consequences.

Paying attention to temporality and processuality offers some important rewards. The development of temporal orders elaborates the complexity with which social organization can be analyzed, while illustrating a pivotal element. Temporality also provides the basis for understanding collective activity in a dialectical, conditional, and contingent fashion. The simultaneous awareness of temporality and processuality is strongly in tune with a view of life as movement ("all things flow"). People attend, at the same time, to relationships across extensions of time to explore whether and when they occur, recur, or change. While a great deal of sociological knowledge and study can suggest the "whats," "whens," and perhaps the "whys" of social influences, processual analysis is the key to explicating the critical "hows."

Grounding

To broaden and deepen the understanding of social forces and processes, it is necessary to ground, link, and lodge in different and larger contexts, the substance of these studies. While this is an assertion of a theoretical assumption, the nature, extent, and effects of grounding clearly are empirical questions. Two particular forms of grounding involve historical and structural contexts.

Historical exploration provides a basis for understanding how a past shaped a constituted present. It allows a separation of the invariant or stable from the changed or changing. If something remains stable, one can learn how, why, and with what consequences. Change can be examined, compared, and accounted for in the same fashion. The study of history also helps to dereify the status quo. Things taken for granted now may not always have existed or even be what they seem. When current circumstances are said to be similar to previous ones, historical analyses can demonstrate the prevalence of different conditions, e.g., comparing minority economic status and opportunities to that of European immigrants in the late nineteenth century (Leiberson 1980).

Structural context refers to the conditions (circumstances, properties, and factors) that bound and shape networks of collective activity. Hindess (1986, p. 120) defines social conditions as the complex intersection of a variety of specific practices, policies, and actors that have consequences for social sites. Context and site coexist in dialectical relationship. The activity in question is conditional and limited—it is simultaneously constrained and facilitated by surrounding conditions. The context and site also are contingent upon the activity. If the activity is enacted differently, it alters and reshapes the site, context, and relations between them.

The term "structural context" is a gloss. It is better envisioned in the plural with a number of multiple horizontal and vertical linkages. The amount and extent of coupling and the directions of influence need to be determined. Maines (1977) suggests that negotiation contexts nest in a series of larger, more encompassing contexts that represent the structural context. Hindess (1986) sees structure as including the relationships between sites. Some sites, he asserts, have greater or more general scope than others and, therefore, greater consequences.

There is an obvious unequal distribution of resources and risks, opportunities, and obstacles in today's society. That distribution not only exists but persists because it is socially organized. To understand that persistence and its contemporary consequences for shaping the future requires both historical and structural contextual analysis. The manner in which networks and collective activity are facilitated or hindered requires mapping the interplay between on-site behavior and site-to-site embeddedness. Reproduction, evolution, or revolution, *"plus ca change, plus ca reste la meme chose"* is the outcome of conditions, activity, and intercontextual shaping.

Several examples of scholarship help to show how sites are linked to other sites lodged in larger contexts. This kind of work is exceedingly useful in visualizing solutions to the micro-macro problem. Persell (1977), in a secondary analysis, shows how the stratification system in the United States and its supporting conventions differentially influence educational structures (school districts and school buildings) and their operational assumptions, which further shape differential relationships, interactions, and practices in the classroom so schooling outcomes and occupational outcomes tend to reproduce the systems of inequality in the society. Cookson and Persell (1985), in a brilliant study of prestigious private schools, empirically tighten the linkage by vividly depicting the interactions and practices used by prep school staff to obtain admission at Ivy League colleges for their students.

Hochschild's (1983) excellent analysis of emotional labor is not formulated as explicitly as Persell's (1977). Nevertheless, it provides strong substantive and substantial grounding of the relationship between flight attendants and passengers. The commodification of feeling or emotional labor is linked and lodged asymmetrically within the organization and through management-employee relationships and practices. A slowdown by workers in response to a management speedup as a way of coping with changing economic conditions, provides a sense of process and conflict. Hochschild uses the fact that this company is nonunion and Southern-based to inform her analysis. The organization itself is located more broadly within the airline industry, a burgeoning service economy, and a capitalist society. Actions by the government to deregulate the industry manifest another major linkage and context. Finally, Hochschild surrounds and infuses her perspective by examining the family institution, social class hierarchies, and gender inequality and its consequences for creating differential emotional practices and emotional workers.

Grounding or contextual analysis has important consequences for directing and improving analysis. It limits reification and overgeneralization by dissecting and partialling macro-level phenomena (Goffman 1983). Longshore and Prager (1985) offer a potent contextual analysis of macro-micro factors affecting success or failure of school desegregation. Persell's (1977) comparative analysis of schooling in private, inner-city, and suburban schools shows major differential consequences. These kinds of studies also make it explicit that research must entail comparative contexts. Contextual analysis clearly extends the breadth of analysis in three directions—past, horizontal, and vertical. This strongly increases the explanatory power of the approach. Grounding, whether historical or structural, demonstrates how activity is both conditional and constructive. It also highlights the meso domain and its dynamics. The consequences of meta-power between community and classroom, industry and shop, and legislature and courtroom can be observed. The ways that differential sovereignty across linkages affects the specific action contexts can be analyzed. A final consequence and caveat of grounding is that it requires finding and following the connections and boundaries. It does not assume some *a priori* form.

CONCLUSION

Sociology in the 1980s can be characterized as dissensual, fragmented, and in the doldrums. Some have declared "the classical project" of Durkheim, Marx, and Weber to be dead and the words of the scientizing systematizers to be bankrupt (Wardell and Turner 1986). Attempts to offer an integrated view of the political and economic world and its social life have failed. However, understanding why those programs and paradigms were inadequate can provide opportunities for exciting work.

The surprising and unanticipated events of the 1960s have been followed by many, many others. Indeed, the world of today is vastly different from the one in which today's sociologists grew up, and much more so than the one inhabited by the classicists or Park, Sorokin, Lundberg, or Parsons. Today's knowledge in the fields of collective behavior, organizations, political sociology, and the sociology of education, to name a few, has taken sociohistorical change into account as a major factor and been informed by it. The search for external verities, phenomenological immutabilities, and fixed relationships will have to be suspended to make sociology appropriate to changing contexts of social conditions. Sociology also will have to surrender some of its precious *a prioris*, totalities, entities, and sense of social integration to perspectives and methodologies which are sensitive to the problematic and processual nature of social life. The study of the social organization of social life requires an approach which is simultaneously concrete, observant, processual, conditional, contingent, dialectical, comparative, and contextual. Interactionism provides such an approach. The paradigm presented here goes beyond the studies cited, by laying out what an adequate study of social organization must take into account.

Sociology has a history of constructing and confronting a series of dichotomies—mechanical and organic solidarity, individual and society, subject and object, structure and process, consensus and conflict, macro and micro. A general way to resolve the existence, opposition, and tension of those dichotomies has been to find a form which mediates, unifies, dissolves, or transcends the split. This article presents the meso domain to come to terms with and overcome the implications of micro and macro analysis. Maines (1982) appropriately terms that dichotomy "coprolitic."

Everyday behavior, interactions, and relationships cannot be understood except as contextualized. Even actors often understand that. Societies, institutional relationships, market structures, and social forces need to be analyzed by attending to the processes and activity that give them life, form, and context. Situated activity can be understood only when viewed in its structural and historical contexts. Structures should be seen as processual, contingent, and enacted. The meso domain, with its view of structure as condition and structure as process, constitutes the central arena of sociological analysis because it attends to context, process, and action simultaneously.

Obvious methodological implications follow from the presentations of this paradigm. First, it rejects many taken-for-granteds and assumes that problematic dynamic action requires a skeptical, curious, and empirical orientation toward the social world. Second, the focus on situated activity necessitates observation over time. Third, the concern with history, by definition, requires diachronic analysis. Fourth, attention to multiple contexts implies seeking multiple forms of data. Fifth, the approach is strengthened greatly by comparative analysis of contexts.

While each method is useful in some way, only in the aggregate are they adequate. Good solid sociological research requires what Faulkner terms "multiples in data collection" (personal communication). The implication of this paradigm suggests the limitations of actors' accounts, cross-sectional research, and synchronic analysis. Much of what now passes as sociology perpetuates these limitations.

Finally, there is some ongoing research which illustrates the paradigm. The study deals with the social organization of educational policy work. A state advisory committee (made up of representatives of teachers' organizations, educational administrators, school board members, business and lay people, the governor's office, legislators, and education colleges, and chaired by state education officials) was appointed to develop a model program and guidelines for a career ladder model to reward teachers. This committee constituted the network of collective activity and was observed for nine months. Issues of temporality dominated the committee as it operated on deadlines, schedules, participants' past experiences, the effects of absenteeism, the emerging rhythm of monthly meetings, deference to full-time personnel, and projections of economic, fiscal, and political futures. The action context was shaped by the legislative history; the content of the legislation; knowledge of other states' programs; previous state legislation and educational policy; the practices of previous, similar advisory committees; the state educational bureaucracy; the governor's political agenda; and the current constituencies, organizations, and communities of the participants. Linkages to the state bureaucracy, the legislature, the executive and the state teachers organizations, and other existing committees were particularly important.

The collective product was shaped differentially by resource use in the forms of information, prestige, coalition-building, and organizational practices surrounding discussion, consensus-building, and avoiding voting. A critical event involved the committee's mobilization and successfully persuading the state board of education to undo a major change it made in the committee's product.

Continuing research will explore the nonadoption or adoption of the program by local districts over successive years. Surveys, contextual data, and interviews will seek to determine external and internal factors affecting (non)adoption. Observation of the implementation of local district program(s) and relationships with the state bureaucracy will be undertaken for a comparative analysis of the consequences of the program and local effects upon the state policy.

The emergence, formation, and dynamics of this action context cannot be understood without analyzing the history, status, and level of funding of education in this state, the degree of public support for education, the state and local economies, the demography of public school attendance, the labor market for teachers, and the emergence of enforced public metrics for social institutions. All of these are lodged in dissatisfactions with the national economy, an attempt to locate many problems in the public schools, the wave of commissions articulating educational reform, the media bandwagon, and the use of public education as a political stepping stone. Projections of deficiencies in the future teacher labor market, increases in school-age populations, the necessity for skilled labor to meet international competition—all affect conditions that produced this committee. The federal government also provides a significant context in shaping state responses. Much more space would be needed to detail lodging the committee in historical and structural contexts, but the previous points should suggest the direction.

Everett C. Hughes said that social institutions are going concerns and enterprises that continue through time in environments in which they must adjust themselves. They should be studied, he averred, not by definition in advance, but by having a good look at the varieties and following them through their many contingencies in the course of problematic survival (Hughes 1971). Some of his students said of him: "...he has an extremely strong conceptual mind which operates with the materials of concrete reality....He prefers to develop analyses which retain complexity; to find value, at times delight in variety; to move from level to level....His general aim is to identify the systematic underlying the various; not by simplifying, but by making clear what is essential" ((Becker et al. 1968, p. x).

This article owes much to the Hughes legacy—its topics, agenda, and intellectual style. It is conceptualized as a response to and continuation of the questions and challenges Hughes offered. Hughes, in reading it, probably would say "We'll see" with the multiple and pregnant meanings of that phrase clearly intended. "Yes," would be the response to him, "We *will* see, but first we all need to *look*. That was what you and your students taught us."

ACKNOWLEDGMENTS

This article is a revised version of the Presidential Address presented at the annual meeting of the Midwest Sociological Society, March 27, 1986, Des Moines, Iowa. The author acknowledges the strong and continuing support, critical insights, and calming influence of James McCartney, who read more versions of this article than friendship should expect. Howard S. Becker and Anselm Strauss provided the substance and impetus for its direction through their numerous and significant writings. David Maines, Carl Couch, Robert Faulkner, Robert Antonio, and Scott McNall freely gave important ideas, directions, and suggestions from inception to completion. Norman Denzin, Michael Katovich, Dan Miller, Mary Jo Neitz, George Peters, and Stan Saxton reviewed earlier drafts, saw numerous places for improvement, and offered many positive remedies. Richard Hall, John Lofland, and Clark McPhail made helpful comments about perspectives, references, and issues in the area of interest.

REFERENCES

Baumgartner, Thomas, Walter Buckley, Tom R. Burns, and Peter Schuster. 1976. "Meta-Power and the Structuring of Social Hierarchies." Pp. 215–288 in *Power and Control: Social Structures and Their Transformations*, edited by T.R. Burns and W. Buckley. Beverly Hills, CA: Sage.
Becker, Howard S. 1960. "Notes on the Concept of Commitment." *American Journal of Sociology* 66:32–40.
———. 1982. *Art Worlds*. Berkeley, CA: University of California.
Becker, Howard S., Blanche Geer, David Riesman, and Robert Weiss. 1968. *Institutions and the Person*. Chicago: Aldine.
Blumer, Herbert. 1969. *Symbolic Interactionism: Perspective and Method*. Englewood Cliffs, NJ: Prentice-Hall.
Burt, Ronald S. 1982. *Toward a Structural Theory of Action*. New York: Academic.
Busch, Lawrence. 1982. "History, Negotiation, and Structure in Agricultural Research." *Urban Life* 11:368–384.
Collins, Randall. 1986. "Is 1980s Sociology in the Doldrums?" *American Journal of Sociology* 91:1336–1355.
Cookson, Peter, and Caroline H. Persell. 1985. *Preparing for Power*. New York: Basic Books.
Couch, Carl J. 1984. *Constructing Civilizations*. Greenwich, CT: JAI Press.
Denzin, Norman K. 1977. "Notes on the Criminogenic Hypothesis: A Case Study of the American Liquor Industry." *American Sociological Review* 42:905–20.
Estes, Carroll L., and Beverly C. Edmonds. 1981. "Symbolic Interaction and Social Policy Analysis." *Symbolic Interaction* 4:75–86.
Farberman, Harvey A. 1975. "A Criminogenic Market Structure: The Automobile Industry." *The Sociological Quarterly* 16:438–56.
Faulkner, Robert R. 1983. *Music on Demand*. New Brunswick, NJ: Transaction.
Fine, Gary Alan. 1984. "Negotiated Orders and Organizational Cultures. Pp. 239–262 in *Annual Review of Sociology*. Vol. 10, edited by R. Turner and J. Short. Palo Alto, CA: Annual Reviews.
Fine, Gary Alan, and Sherryl Kleinman. 1983. "Network and Meaning: An Interactionist Approach to Structure." *Symbolic Interaction* 6:97–110.
Fisher, Bernice, and Anselm Strauss. 1978. "Interactionism." Pp. 457–498 in *A History of Sociological Analysis*, edited by T. Bottomore and R. Nisbet. New York: Basic Books.
Gamson, William. 1968. *Power and Discontent*. Homewood, IL: Dorsey.
Gerson, Elihu. 1976. "On 'quality of life.'" *American Sociological Review* 41:793–806.
Goffman, Erving. 1983. "The Interaction Order." *American Sociological Review* 48:1–17.
Granovetter, Mark. 1973. "The Strength of Weak Ties." *American Journal of Sociology* 78:1360–1380.
Hall, Peter M. 1985. "Asymmetric Relationships and Processes of Power." Pp. 309–344 in *Foundations of Interpretive Sociology*, edited by H. Farberman and R. Perinbanayagam. Greenwich, CT:JAI Press.
Hall, Peter M., and Dee Ann Spencer-Hall. 1982. "The Social Conditions of the Negotiated Order." *Urban Life* 1 1:328–349.
Handel, Warren. 1982. *Ethnomethodology: How People Make Sense*. Englewood Cliffs, NJ: Prentice-Hall.
Hindess, Barry. 1986. "Actors and Social Relations." Pp. 113–126 in *Sociological Theory in Transition*, edited by Mark L. Wardell and Stephen P. Turner. Boston: Allen and Unwin.
Hintz, Robert, and Carl J. Couch. 1975. "Time, Intention and Social Behavior." Pp. 27–46 in *Constructing Social Life*, edited by C. Couch and R. Hintz. Champaign, IL: Stipes.
Hochschild, Arlie R. 1983. *The Managed Heart*. Berkeley, CA: University of California.
Hughes, Everett C. 1955. "Preface." Pp. 4–8 in *The Collected Papers of Robert Park*. Vol. 111, edited by E. Hughes, E. Johnson, J.Masuoka, R. Redfield, and L. Wirth. New York: Free Press.
———. 1971. *The Sociological Eye*: Selected Papers. Chicago: Aldine.
Kanter, Rosabeth M. 1977. *Men and Women of the Corporation*. New York: Basic Books.
Leiberson, Stanley. 1980. *A Piece of the Pie*. Berkeley, CA: University of California.
Lofland, John. 1976. *Doing Social Life*. New York: Wiley.

Longshore, Douglas, and Jeffrey Prager. 1985. "The Impact of School Desegregation: A Situational Analysis." Pp. 75–95 in *Annual Review of Sociology*. Vol. 11, edited by R. Turner and J. Short. Palo Alto, CA: Annual Reviews.

Maines, David R. 1977. "Social Organization and Social Structure in Symbolic Interactionist Thought." Pp. 235–259 in *Annual Review of Sociology*. Vol. 3, edited by A. Inkeles, J. Coleman and N. Smelser. Palo Alto, CA: Annual Reviews.

———. 1983. "In Search of Mesostructure." *Urban Life* 11:267–279.

Maines, David R., Noreen M. Sugrue, and Michael A. Katovich. 1983. "G. H. Mead's Theory of the Past." *American Sociological Review* 48:161–173.

Molotch, Harvey L., and Deidre Boden. 1985. "Talking Social Structure: Discourse, Domination and the Watergate Hearings." *American Sociological Review* 50:273–288.

Nadel, S. F. 1957. *The Theory of Social Structure*. Glencoe, IL: Free Press.

Perrow, Charles. 1984. *Normal Accidents*. New York: Basic Books.

Persell, Caroline H. 1977. *Education and Inequality*. New York: Free Press.

Rose, Arnold M. 1962. *Human Behavior and Social Processes*.Boston, MA: Houghton-Mifflin.

Roy, Donald. 1958. "'Banana Time': Job Satisfaction and Informal Interaction." *Human Organization* 18:158–168.

Shalin, Dmitri N. 1986. "Pragmatism and Social Interactionism." *American Sociological Review* 51:9–29.

Strauss, Anselm. 1959. *Mirrors and Masks*. Glencoe, IL: Free Press.

———. 1978. *Negotiations*. San Francisco, CA: Jossey-Bass.

———. 1985. "Work and the Division of Labor." *SociologicalQuarterly* 26:1–19.

Strauss, Anselm, Shizuko Fagerhaugh, Barbara Suczek, and Carolyn Wiener. 1985. *Social Organization of Medical Work*. Chicago, IL: University of Chicago.

Strauss, Anselm, Leonard Schatzman, Rue Bucher, Danuta Ehrlich, and Melvin Sabshin. 1964. *Psychiatric Ideologies and Institutions*. Glencoe, IL: Free Press.

Useem, Michael. 1984. *The Inner Circle*. New York: Oxford University.

Wardell, Mark L., and Stephen P. Turner. 1986. Sociological Theory in Transition. Boston: Allen and Unwin.

Wiener, Carolyn. 1981. *The Politics of Alcoholism*. New Brunswick, NJ: Transaction.

Zerubavel, Eviatar. 1981. *Hidden Rhythms*. Chicago: University of Chicago.

Chapter 27 UNOBTRUSIVE POWER: INTERACTION BETWEEN HEALTH PROVIDERS AND CONSUMERS AT COUNCIL MEETINGS

Warren R. Paap and Bill Hanson

This article is a report of empirical research which shows how elements of normal conversation can serve as instruments of power. In studying the patterns of interaction which occur in formal meetings, it is possible to identify components of common discourse which function as subtle modes of control. The significance of such less obvious power techniques is further dramatized when they occur in the context of formal equality and result in the creation of a legitimated informal power structure. Thus, the following discussion will focus on how these obtrusive features of verbal interaction operate as informal power processes.

Ever since the National Health Planning and Resources Development Act of 1974 was implemented, professionals such as physicians, dentists, nurses, and hospital administrators ("providers") have been serving along with lay persons ("consumers") as formally co-equal members of Health Systems Agencies (HSAs) in this country. These organizations have the task of approving expenditures of funds for health care, along with identifying underserved areas. By law, consumers are to constitute the majority membership of the councils making up a Health Systems Agency. Over the past year and a half, we have been observing meetings of a Health Systems Council in which consumers and providers engage in carrying out the work of a Health Systems Agency. These meetings provided a unique opportunity for interaction between persons of dissimilar status who nevertheless occupy organizational positions giving them formal equality. Thus, this article is a study of the "underside" of interpersonal power—the tacit and unobtrusive devices used to gain control over other persons.

While the study of interpersonal power continues to be dominated by an experimental approach in laboratory settings (see Jacobson, 1972, for a representative survey of this literature), there is evidence of increasing interest in the study of less obvious kinds of social power in natural settings. While conceptually undeveloped (e.g., Labovitz, 1977:198), this emerging perspective views power as a pervasive element in everyday life. Power is grounded in language and communication patterns (e.g., Zimmerman and West, 1975; Parlee, 1979) and involves presentational skills, body language, and demeanor, including facial expressions, gestures, eye contact, and touching (Henley 1977). An underlying premise is that there is a dimension of power relations which is not highly structured and unchanging, but negotiated and emergent (Scheff, 1968). In other words, power relations develop in normal interaction and draw upon the resources making up such interaction: the nature of our presentations, our use of language, and our efforts to construct a definition of the situation. Furthermore, this perspective broadens the study of power processes to include aspects of manipulation, intimidation, and ingratiation (e.g., Weinstein, 1966; Jette and Montanino 1978; Jones, 1964).

In studying normal interaction at these meetings, we sought to go beyond more obvious forms of authority and coercion and focus on how inconspicuous activities can function as power processes. By inconspicuous activities, we mean the normal forms of interaction which we found occurring in the meetings we observed, such as reporting, questioning, commenting, interrupting, clarifying, complimenting, listening, writing, and so on. Our research question asked how such standard types of discourse at these meetings could serve as power techniques and contribute to the emergence of patterned power relations in this setting. While we recognize that there are a number of factors maintaining provider dominance in health care (e.g., Jonas, 1971; Metsch and Rosen, 1976; Paap, 1978; Hanson, 1979), we were interested in investigating how tacit forms of interpersonal power in meetings might contribute to that pattern.

Research Setting and Methods

The Health Systems Council which we observed consisted of 45 members, with 23 of these mandated as consumer positions. The majority of the members were male, and the officers tended to be male, although the position of staff planner was filled by a female during our research. In addition, two male providers and a male consumer have served as Council Chair. Provider members included representatives of the standard occupations in the health care system: physicians, dentists, administrators, an R.N., a psychiatrist, optometrists, and other professionals. Consumer members included a variety of blue- and whitecollar occupations, as well as retired persons. Members are not paid for serving on the Council other than travel expenses.

Council meetings are held monthly, in the evening, in a large public building. Members sit around narrow tables organized in the form of a "U" with the officers sitting at the closed end. Typically there are about 10 to 15 persons in the audience. Meetings are conducted following a standard *Robert's Rules* format, and they last anywhere from 30 minutes to more than two hours. Approximately 30-35 members are present at each meeting. A typical meeting includes the self-introduction of members; informational reports from the staff; reports from standing committees; nominations to fill vacancies on the Council; and typical agenda items. The tone of the meetings is bureaucratically "proper," in that loud outbursts and calls for order are rare, and name-calling, accusations, and insults practically nonexistent. Members frequently can be observed whispering to a neighbor while business is being transacted, but the typical orientation could be called "civil attention." The most socially abrasive moments are due to periodic sarcastic remarks; however, even these tend not to be aimed at other members but at such "safe" targets as politicians and governmental units, especially the Department of Health, Education and Welfare and its policies.

Playing the role of "observer" in the audience was facilitated by the fact that other members of the audience tended to carry documents and frequently took notes. Ethical implications were minimized in that all the information we had access to was open to the public and available to any interested citizen. In our notetaking, we increasingly focused on characteristics of verbal communication rather than on technical information being dealt with in the meeting. We keyed on how participants entered into discussions, how they presented themselves and their ideas, and how they responded to each other. We attempted to get key phrases as verbatim as possible and then analyzed all the data for patterns and themes.

INTERPERSONAL POWER TECHNIQUES

As our analysis progressed, some dominant themes were identified. We noted, in particular, two patterns of activity which, while blending smoothly into the flow of interaction, nevertheless carry significant power implications. First, it became apparent that participants frequently made reference to previous verbal offerings of other participants. It was possible to identify, in a typical extended discussion, a number of such features, which we labeled "clarifications." Clarifications, in their purest form, involve the restatement or elaboration of a previous comment, thereby rendering it clearer or more intelligible. Thus, the clarification might be introduced with a statement such as: "What Sam is *really* saying is..." Also included here are reworkings, modifications, additions, agreements, and disagreements to the extent that there are implicit or explicit references to the quality, completeness, and/or accuracy of the preceding remark. These would appear in the context of a statement such as "I echo Sarah's comment that...but I would add...."

Second, we were able to clearly identify the frequent and sometimes dramatic use of complimenting statements by staff members and providers. Closer examination revealed how various forms of "complimenting" contributed to the emerging pattern of power relations at meetings. Compliments took place when someone intentionally and publicly desired to express appreciation to another member, a committee, or the entire Council. We were not concerned with the normal "thank you" often rendered, for instance, by the Chair after a member had spoken; nor were we including purely nonverbal behaviors such as head nodding or other looks of approval. Complimenting involves at least some minimal elaboration and intends to go beyond the norms of ordinary politeness. The forms compliments take vary considerably, but the following compliment by the Council Chair at the end of a meeting provides a good idea of what we were studying: "Ladies and Gentlemen, your attention tonight is much appreciated and rewarding."

Thus, our analysis focused on clarifications and compliments as elements of discourse which play a dominant role in the creation of structure and pattern at these meetings. Clearly, it would be possible to analyze how other verbal and nonverbal displays contribute to this process (see Hanson, 1980, for such a broader view). For the purposes of this study, however, we opted for a more intensive view of these two dominant features.

Clarification and Interpersonal Power

On the surface, it may seem inappropriate to think of such an innocuous conversational element as "clarification" as a way of exercising power. Indeed, the term technically means "clearing up" or "making understandable," which sounds quite different than any manipulative power technique. Furthermore, we found that clarifications were inconspicuous, normal features of the setting we studied and were accepted as legitimate activities. Given all this, why should they be spoken of as power techniques? We feel our data provide four answers to this question, and these will be dealt with below. The following discussion focuses on how providers and staff clarify statements of consumers, since consumers do very little clarifying of each other or of providers. In fact, consumers are more likely to ask for clarification than give it. Administrative staff sometimes clarify remarks of both consumers and providers. Providers often clarify each others' comments, but this generally takes the form of adding technical information or agreement in a manner which does not serve the advantage of one person or devalue the efforts of another. Instead, provider clarifications of each other tend to build alliances and a "bandwagon" effect results which lessens the likelihood of challenges to or disagreements with the emerging position. Therefore, in what follows we focus primarily on provider and staff clarification of consumer comments.

Subversion Through Clarification

There rarely seems to be malice involved when providers and staff clarify the efforts of consumers. It was common to hear ingratiating introductions and words of approval at the beginning of a clarification, such as: "We appreciate your comments..." or "I think that is an important question being raised..." However, these introductions can be followed with a commentary which conveys the message that the person being clarified doesn't understand the issue or isn't aware of the true state of the matter. In this way, clarification can "subvert the other," in that the original speaker's presentation in undermined and a definition emphasizing inadequacy and dependency is fostered. Skillful clarifications of this sort can tell the target person that he or she is neither prepared nor capable of presenting himself or herself. While this type of power can clearly flow back and forth, or emerge and disappear as interaction continues, we feel that it occurs regularly, resulting in a more stable pattern which is perpetuated at these meetings. The pattern is based on two broad types of subversion through clarification.

The most common type is where the clarification conveys the message that the target person has not done enough preparation concerning the topic. He or she is simply not "on top of the situation" or properly aware of the operation of the organization. These can be short and abrupt:

> Ms. Sears (*consumer*): "This will no longer be a problem when we are designated" (i.e., recognized as an official Health Systems Agency by HEW).
>
> Dr. Valley (*provider*): "We are now designated."

More frequent were the cases where consumers who chair committees gave their reports, only to find that their efforts were immediately clarified by the Council Chair, staff or a provider. There was already some evidence that a norm was emerging, and consumers in this situation deferred quickly, especially to staff (e.g., "I'll pass this to Jill..."), without making much of an effort to give a report on the committee action. A most effective move here occurred when a staff person, following a consumer report, began by saying: "Maybe you can help me out here," while looking at the consumer, and then proceeded to restate the report in a much more articulate and complete manner. While a number of messages were being conveyed in these clarifications, the critical one was that the target found that he or she had not remembered enough, or taken adequate notes, or prepared the report properly.

Another message conveyed to the target in this first type of subversion through clarification was that the situation was simply more complex, more detailed, and required more analysis than the initial statement would have it. The clarifier pointed out that: "There are really two things involved here," with the basic model being that regardless of how many things were initially reported, there was at least one more. There was "further evidence" which needed to be considered. Thus, by using the technique of clarification, one is able to inform another person that he or she hasn't quite kept up, or "done the homework," and therefore doesn't adequately understand—almost, but not quite.

The second type of subversion through clarification can be a potentially more devastating technique, in that the basic skills and abilities of the target person are being made suspect—not simply his or her lack of diligence or effort. One form this takes involves parliamentary procedure. While providers do on occasion find themselves ruled "out of order," it is far more common for consumers to find themselves in violation of Robert's Rules. Obviously, providers have a wealth of experience in committee settings and in bureaucratic contexts. This enables them to be sensitive to opportunities for clarification of the less polished performances of consumers.

There were cases of consumer motions being ruled out of order by the Council Chair (e.g., "There is a motion already on the floor..."); or called out of order by providers who were not officers (e.g., "That's not germane here."); and there were clarifications of the language used by consumers in their motions (e.g., "That should be worded to say..."). That these kinds of clarifications undermine the self-confident presentation of consumers can be seen in the use of apologetic and self-deprecating language by consumers as they enter into parliamentary activities. Introducing a motion by saying: "I'm not sure this is proper here," or: "This may not be the way to say this" not only shows sensitivity to past clarifications, but also invites more.

Not only is the lack of bureaucratic skills dramatized through clarification, but more basic mental and linguistic skills are also vulnerable. Although not frequent, provider clarifications which begin with phrases such as: "I think what Sam is saying is that..." or "What I hear you saying is..." The implication is that if the original speaker would be able to adequately express himself or herself, he or she would have said it the way the clarifier did.

It should be emphasized that a tone of propriety dominates the meetings, and techniques such as clarification are legitimized as normal activities. These activities have a subversive component which adds to the dominance of some participants and the passive subordination of others, but passes unnoticed by members.

Clarification and Self-Enhancement

The second way in which clarification serves as a power technique is by acting as a vehicle for the display of resources which enhance the clarifier. Enhancement means establishing a positive reputation, elevating one's status, and accomplishing a dominant presentation of self. Whereas in the previous section, clarification was used to undercut another person, here it was used to build up the person doing the clarifying.

Most common was the tendency for providers, the Council Chair, and staff members to draw on specific and sometimes quite technical information concerning the structure and activities of the Health System Agency as they clarified various matters at Council meetings. One example was when a consumer made a report on Council membership, including criteria for membership.

> Ms. West (*consumer*): "The Nominating Committee just met, before this 7 o'clock meeting, and I haven't had time to check with the nominees yet...but we do have nominees for the two vacant positions. We have a consumer position and one provider position vacant...The consumer position is for a rural person, but it doesn't have to be a minority or low income person."

This was quickly followed by a series of clarifying comments by providers:

> Dr. Breaker: "On reviewing the federal regulations, I question the format we are following..."

> Staff: "We receive these from the regional office."

> Dr. Valley: "We are in our rights to change these breakdowns..."

> Mr. Gray (*provider*): "These are illegal..."

> Dr. Grosskopf: "These requirements are not law but are dictated to us....If you go back and read 93-641 you will notice it gives only general guidelines for membership, and now the composition of the Council is being dictated to us."

One of the messages conveyed in these clarifying remarks is that the clarifier is informed and diligent in carrying out his or her responsibilities. Consumers do not present themselves in this authoritative manner; their rare assertive statements tend to be couched in either an argumentative or defensive tone. In terms of power, such authoritative presentations not only generate leadership imagery, they also discourage the expression of differing opinions.

Another means of self-enhancement is the phrasing of comments so that it appears one is speaking for the entire Council. This is partially accomplished by saying "we" rather than "I." Even issues which involve controversy can be followed by clarifying comments such as: "It's clear that what we are saying here is..." or "This is how we feel down here..." The speaker is presented as having a constituency and initiates a pattern of being a spokesperson for the group. There was no evidence during our observation of such usurpation of authority being challenged by a consumer; hence, a legitimated informal power structure gradually emerged.

Clarification and the Normative Order

As a power technique, clarification is intimately tied to the normative order which exists at Council meetings. Despite the fact that Robert's Rules provide a basic operating framework, the norms are still general enough to require that a continuous process of interpretation and application be engaged in. There are two major points here. First, by clarifying previous comments, the speaker can unobtrusively initiate a change in the norms governing the situation. This can be even phrased in such a way as to imply continuity, not change: "I think that Bob's comments point out that we should continue to..." A staff member, in clarifying pending legislation, went on to specify what should be proper behavior for members in order to influence that legislation. When challenged by a provider on the appropriateness of such political activity, she clarified further by citing legal opinions which essentially legitimized the norms being advocated. The significance of these examples for interpersonal power is that norms governing appropriate behavior can be subtly altered while carrying out clarification activities.

The second point concerning clarification and norms deals with these questions: What information, or what evidence, is relevant given a particular question, issue, or argument? When a point is being debated, what kinds of evidence can be appropriately brought to bear on that issue? Barber (1966) argues that there are "rules of evidence" operating at meetings which determine the range of allowable information utilized in decision making. These rules "are seldom clearly stated and agreed upon. More often they are invoked and altered to suit particular arguments" (Barber, 1966:68). We found that the invoking or altering of these "rules of evidence" was facilitated by the clarification technique. While clarifying the remarks of a previous speaker, rules of evidence could be imposed or modified, and the previous (and subsequent) comments were then evaluated in terms of these rules.

This process of reworking rules of evidence operates to the disadvantages of consumers, in that they are more apt to draw on personal experiences in arguing for or against a proposal. Instead of relying on statistical data or "professional expertise," consumers, more so than providers, are likely to refer to "what happened to me last week." This easily leads to a clarifying comment which invokes rules of evidence making it clear that such comments are irrelevant in that situation. This invocation can be obvious—and even caustic—as in the case of the Council Chair (a provider) responding to such an anecdotal consumer statement with: "I need help; what's going on here? Could someone tell me? What we need to be talking about is..." Not only was the initial comment defined as irrelevant, it was seen as incomprehensible. Power in this case involved not only invoking rules of evidence, but subverting the performance of the other as discussed earlier. To the extent that rules of evidence are established and controlled by staff and providers, consumers are at a disadvantage, since the type of evidence which is now admissible is exactly the kind they would be least likely to have access to.

Clarification and Control of the Subject Under Discussion

While clarifying the remarks of another person, one is able to exert some control over the discussion by allowing the responder to focus on only one specific element in the initial statement and avoid other potential topics. That is, most of the issues which come before the Council are complex, and the range of subjects discussed could be large. By clarifying the comments of others, one is able to direct the discussion to a limited segment of the potential subjects which could be discussed. In one case, a proposal concerning a training program for physicians' assistants was being considered. A consumer comment about the impact of this on the local minority community was not followed up, and the subject was dropped. Instead, a number of providers began, with comments and clarifications of each other, to focus the discussion on a narrow point concerning the legal implications of how this program would impact on other professionals. In such a manner, clarifications can build on each other to define the pertinent subject matter in a selective and restrictive manner.

Complimenting and Interpersonal Power

Complimenting functions significantly as a power tool as it contributes to "cooling out" criticisms and challenges, altering of behavior, and building Council solidarity. As with clarifications, the majority of individuals taking part in complimenting were providers, staff, and the Council Chair. Consumers rarely render compliments, and when they do they are confined to other members, often providers, and staff from both local and regional levels. Two types of complimenting were observed. One, the "routine compliment," appears suddenly and is completed quickly. This commonly occurs in the context of routine rather than urgent or critical business at meetings. The form and effects of routine compliments are less dramatic as they are gently and smoothly integrated into the normal flow of Council business. For instance, the local staff planner once thanked a consumer for his work on a project by saying: "I want to thank Mr. Tutle for doing this job in Dr. Gordon's absence." The Council Chair immediately moved on to the next item of business. This type of compliment is distinguishable from "crisis praising," which is characterized by longer, more involved "praise sessions." Members are praised in a more intense, dramatic, and emotional manner which does not mesh as easily with the routine flow of events.

Complimenting and "Cooling Out"

Both routine complimenting and crisis praising can function as power techniques to "cool out," blunt, or discourage criticism or questions. Sometimes complimenting is used after a comment or criticism has already been initiated, and other times it is employed in situations where comments or criticisms could be expected, but prior to their actual occurrence. The former situation sometimes involves a quick routine compliment by someone in authority. In one instance, after a consumer had made a lengthy comment regarding the rights of taxpayers to participate in discussions of tax money expenditures, the Chair said: "This came up and was taken care of at the committee meeting, but we do appreciate your comments." This statement clarified, but it was also letting the speaker know that his points have already been "taken care of" in committee. This "appeasement compliment" enables the Council to move on without dealing further with the speaker's comment.

A longer, but still routine compliment was rendered by the regional director as a response to a direct criticism of her staff. A provider who had received a copy of the state health plan stood with documents in his hand and spoke in an assertive manner, noting that HSAs had not been involved in the development of the plan. He continued by criticizing the regional staff for not having made local Council members aware of the document. The director, in an accepting tone, replied:

> "Thank you Dr. Lasa for bringing this to our attention...and I am remiss in not getting this to you. (She discusses logistical problems, including the breakdown of a printing press and the process of "drawing up" the state plan, then finishes with comments to the entire Council.) I need your suggestions on how to proceed....I think Dr. Lasa is right.

In this episode, thanking the provider for raising the point and indicating that he was "right" clearly discouraged further criticism. Complimenting is a power technique here because it functions to ingratiate the criticizer (as well as other Council members) to the complimenter, thus making it more difficult for the criticizing to continue. Such "cooling out" and disarming becomes more intense during "crisis praising situations."

One such session occurred prior to a vote which would bring the Council into compliance with the membership composition requirements. As the Chairwoman of the Membership and Nominating Committee (a consumer) stood to begin her report, she immediately deferred to the local staff planner. The planner immediately stood and spoke in firm and enthusiastic tones, praising the Committee, its Chair, and the full Council for their persistence and "hard work" and "for coming a long way since its beginning." She continued, as she looked at the Council, smiling gently: "When you approve these people tonight, and you will, then we will have perfect composition for the first time since I have been with the agency." This was followed by laughter and more praise. The Committee Chairwoman then praised the Planner and the Committee, noting the importance to the Council of approving these nominees. Next, the Council Chair (a consumer) added his praise, saying he knew the Committee's task was "next to impossible" and that it had worked very hard. He went on to admonish the Council to accept the nominees. The four nominees were introduced with applause and were quickly approved as a provider Committee member in a crisp fashion made the appropriate motion. The entire Committee report was later concluded by the Chairwoman once again praising the planner: "I don't know how Joan did it. Without her it couldn't have happened."

This long, intense, and emotional "sequence praising" and admonishing by Council leaders made it very difficult for members to raise questions regarding any nominee's qualifications, and no such questions were raised. Thus, praising can be viewed as a power technique which "cools out" the Council by statements which enhance the Council's self-image as a competent, hard-working organization. Inclinations to raise criticism are thus restricted.

Complimenting and Altering of Behavior

Many compliments rendered at Council meetings are geared toward pointing out some deficiency and simultaneously asking for immediate action to remedy the situation. Indeed, remarks by the staff planner and Council Chair regarding approving the nominees "tonight" in the crisis praise session just discussed made it clear the intention was, through praising rather than some other technique, to have the Council approve the four nominees immediately. This was achieved not through a discussion of their qualifications, but rather through flattery of the Council by its leaders. In power terms, praising can function to alter the behavior of others without dealing with substantive and controversial issues.

While "crisis praising" regularly involves an attempt to change other's behavior, routine compliments also often contain this change element, although they are characterized by less intensity and focus. For instance, during the questioning of a committee's report, a provider on the committee felt it necessary to explain how "thoroughly the committee went over the proposal" and noted that the Council should put "some stock in that." Another similar instance occurred after the local Council had learned that its health plan had been turned down by the regional level evaluators because, among other things, it lacked sufficient plans to educate consumers. The ensuing provider-dominated discussion focused on criticizing the regional staff for poor "back-up help." During this discussion, the Council Chair sharply interjected with: "I must say something." He proceeded in an even, firm tone to compliment the local Council and staff for their competence and hard work, and added that they should not feel incompetent because the plan had been turned down. Council members listened and then resumed discussion of the topic.

Both of the brief comments quoted above were spoken in the context of routine business. The first involved a positive evaluation of a committee's performance accompanied by a request for others to change their behavior. The compliment was used as a means for redirecting the current discussion. The second situation was a response to criticism wherein the compliment was used to help Council members maintain their feelings of esteem and worth and to encourage them to continue to work hard. These two compliment episodes are best viewed as "corrective compliments" meant to improve the Council's operation and maintain or boost its morale. These operate between crisis praising sessions to help maintain Council morale and performance.

The importance of crisis praising as an attempt to alter behavior can be seen in another example. This situation involved praising during three different meetings with respect to the same matter; namely, the length of time it was taking the Director to hire a local staff planner. After a couple of months with no planner, a provider asked with an air of impatience: "When will we get our new staff member?" The Director replied bluntly but politely: "By April" (one month away). However, by the end of the meeting she evidently felt the need to elaborate on her previous brief remark. The elaboration was a four-minute praise session wherein she firmly and emotionally praised the Council for its good work in the past, saying she "appreciates" its concern in this matter. She wanted to apologize for not having hired a planner yet and explained the difficulties in hiring a "good" planner. She ended with another compliment of the Council and asked for its "patience in waiting for me to staff this county." Immediately a provider, without being recognized by the Council Chair, responded by commending "her for her efforts" and assured her that "the Council will bear with her." This brought spontaneous applause from the entire Council.

At the beginning of the next month's meeting (April), the Director began by commending the entire Council on its "good work" on a report it had submitted to the regional level HSA. She also said: "You are well regarded there." At the end of her report, when she had not mentioned the hiring of a planner, a provider gently inquired about it. Once again she rendered a brief compliment regarding the Council's concern and patience and then explained that she "can't find anyone qualified to do the job here." This answer was accepted as the Council went on to other business.

Two months later, the Director, smiling confidently, proudly announced that she had hired a planner, saying: "First, we have hired a planner. Thank you for your patience." She went on to thank individuals and to introduce with complimentary statements other staff people she had just hired at the regional level. Each gave short speeches praising themselves and the local Council.

Praising the Council encouraged it to keep up its good work and, as signs of impatience were noticeable, to be patient with the Director. We saw the same idea with a previous routine compliment. However, in this situation, where the issue was more crucial, praising was more intense, involving longer sequence praising and occurring for at least three meetings. When continuous praising is combined with periodic brief routine compliments delivered by Council leaders and staff emphasizing a similar change theme, complimenting becomes a formidable power technique in altering interpersonal behavior.

Complimenting and Council Solidarity

Complimenting can also function to create long-term commitment solidarity, and teamwork on the Council. A careful reading of our examples thus far shows that most of the compliments involved reference to the Council's competence, hard work, patience, and concern. During the sequence praising in the "planner issue" just discussed, there was a continuous emphasis on the Council's "good work" and "concern" and the need for it to be patient.

This flavor was also conveyed through routine compliments. For instance, in the month prior to the beginning of the planner issue, the Director and the Vice Chair (a provider), in the process of telling the Council four important things it needed to do, complimented the entire Council at least twice on its good work in preparing for "designation" and in dealing with the recent "site visit." The Director finished by saying that "this HSAs persistence was a miracle." Once again, the image of a competent team capable of continuing hard work in the future was being conveyed. Complimenting can become a means for building a positive image of past performance and for creating a feeling that future competence can be assured through continuing hard work and solidarity. In power terms, this is accomplished through flattery by the Council leaders. Close examination of the actual work of the Council, which might lead to controversy, is discouraged as norms emerge to protect Council unity.

Complimenting and the Creation of Norms

As with clarifications, compliments as a power technique were closely integrated with the negotiation of norms during Council meetings. Compliments carried suggestions as to how Council members ought to behave. These included admonishing members to be patient and to continue to work hard and do good work as the Council's responsibilities increase. As we have shown, this carries with it the notion that all this can best be achieved by working together. Integrated with this is the emerging norm that "team members" should not question or criticize various aspects of Council business. After all, if Council leaders and providers with warm, open, encouraging tones and gestures are telling the Council it is competent and working hard and are conveying that the Council's work is important and serious, why should members raise divisive issues? Thus, with respect to power, complimenting can be an effective technique for creating and maintaining norms, especially in newly established situations where a traditional normative order is absent.

Complimenting can also serve to subtly shift the basis of social interaction from norms governing discussions of substantive issues to norms governing how to behave in the face of flattery. This complicates Council discussions, since the normative structure at meetings now includes norms dealing with flattery; these influence individuals' personal feelings towards one another and their judgments as to the type of participation they are willing to undertake.

Once norms governing reactions to compliments become established, members who are good complimenters can activate these norms through routine complimenting or crisis praising. They thus gain a power edge in controlling the definition of the situation.

Conclusions and Implications

Running throughout the clarifying and complimenting processes is a fundamental theme. Namely, they are both means for achieving some control over the definition of the situation. Clarifying and complimenting activities impact on how participants define themselves, each other, and the entire social setting. The definition of the situation which emerges has several significant characteristics. Most importantly, consensus and solidarity have become accepted in what we call the "happy family" model of interaction. That is, complimenting activities encourage teamwork and cooperation, and discourage disruptions and controversy. Clarification processes add to this to the extent that assertive disagreements are undermined and passive acceptance of dominant presentations is fostered.

Other significant components of the prevailing definition of the situation are the role definitions which have developed. Providers, staff members, and the Council Chair are looked to as sources of guidance and information, and consumers adopt a passive role, responding to initiatives from these leaders. Thus, providers define the situation for the "unknowing" consumers, and what is formally defined as a situation of equality develops a pattern of legitimated inequality.

The forms of covert interpersonal power leading to this inequality are exercised more effectively by providers and staff than by consumers. There are times when local and regional staff are able to control even providers, mainly through the use of compliments. Consumers, in sum, find themselves tacitly supporting a definition of the situation sometimes initiated and perpetuated by staff alone, and more commonly by providers and staff together. The preceding analysis is not intended to romanticize consumers as passive victims of intimidating and authoritarian providers and staff. Occasionally, a consumer will speak out in an assertive manner which seems to have some impact on the proceedings. Also, some providers and staff occasionally present themselves in a manner which facilitates and encourages the mutual involvement of consumers in Council activities.

Nevertheless, from a policy standpoint, we feel it is important to recognize the pattern of provider dominance which is fostered by the operation of these tacit power processes. There are dangers in focusing on the formal equality bestowed on members by their organization status, and in avoiding the less obtrusive forms of interpersonal power which can counteract the stated goals of consumer participation. Merely exhorting consumers to more actively join in the proceedings can be counteracted by interpersonal power processes, creating insecure, passive, and even defensive consumers.

To the extent that consumers are unaware of the operation of these unobtrusive power processes, the simple antidote is "awareness." Humor can also help negate the effects of this type of power. Also, if providers and staff do not intend to be dominant, their awareness of their own exercise of covert power might lead to a more equitable distribution of power. As an alternative, it may be possible for consumers to acquire some necessary resources—organizational information, presentational style, parliamentary skills, and the like—and make more use of tacit power techniques themselves.

Settings such as meetings which involve professionals and lay persons in policymaking activities provide ample opportunities for the study of subtle forms of control and manipulation. We need to become aware of these as power processes which are every bit as significant as more obvious forms of authority and coercion; to do otherwise would encourage the hypocrisy of social situations which advertise formal equality but accomplish the maintenance of hierarchy.

REFERENCES

Barber, J.D. 1966. *Power in Committees: An Experiment in the Governmental Process.* Chicago: Rand McNally.
Hanson, B. 1979. "The effect of interpersonal power on consumer control: the case of consumer health board." Presented at the annual meetings of the American Public Health Association, November.
———. 1980. "An ethnography of power relations consumers and providers on a health systems council," In J. Roth (ed.) *Research in the Sociology of Health Care.* Greenwich, CT: JAI Press (forthcoming).
Henley, N. 1977. *Body Politics.* New Jersey: Prentice Hall.
Jacobson, W. 1972. *Power and Interpersonal Relations.* Belmont, CA: Wadsworth.
Jette, P.R. and F. Montanino. 1978. "Face-to-face interaction in the criminal justice system —Differential leverage interaction strategies." *Criminology* 16:67–84.
Jonas, S. 1971. "A theoretical approach to the question of community control of health services facilities." *American Journal of Public Health* 61:916–921.
Jones, E.E. 1964. *Ingratiation.* New York: Century-Crofts.
Labovitz, S. 1977. *An Introduction to Sociological Concepts.* New York: John Wiley.
Metsch, J.M. and H. Rosen 1976. "Consumer participation in health care delivery." *New York University Educational Quarterly* 7:16–20.
Paap, W. 1978. "Consumer-based boards of health centers: structural problems in achieving effective control." *American Journal of Public Health* 68:578–582.
Parlee, M.B. 1979. "Conversational politics." *Psychology Today* 12:48–56.
Scheff, T.J. 1968. "Negotiating reality: notes on power in the assessment of responsibility." *Social Problems* 16:3–17.
Weinstein, E.A. 1966. "Toward a theory of interpersonal tactics," in Carl W. Backman and Paul F. Secord (eds.) *Problems in Social Psychology.* New York: McGraw-Hill.
Zimmerman, D.H. and C. West 1975. "Sex roles, interruptions and silences in conversation," In Barrie Thorne and Nancy Henley (eds.) *Language and Sex: Difference and Dominance.* Massachusetts: Newbury House.

PART VII
RESEARCH APPLICATIONS

While the preceding sections have dealt with an explication of the ontological assumptions and several major concepts of symbolic interactionism, this section provides a selection of readings illustrating the wide range of interactionist research. The topics we have chosen deal with are: Orthodox Jews, family caregivers of the mentally ill, hypnosis, poachers, and urban lumberjacks.

Based on qualitative research conducted in Israel, William Shaffir focuses on the process of religious identity transformation. Adopting a symbolic interactionist approach, the conversion experiences of secular Jews, the *baalei tshuvah,*' recruited to Orthodox Judaism, are examined. Such subjective experiences are compared with a second group, *chozrim beshe'aylah*, a group of religious defectors from ultra-orthodox Judaism. The author points out the parallels in their respective subjective experiences. Conceived as processes, both conversion and defection involve a transformation resulting both in the adoption of a new lifestyle and in a pervasive identity, affecting subsequent interaction with others. The differences in the transformation experiences of *baalei tshuvah* and *chozrim beshe'aylah* are also discussed.

Herman and Reynolds, in our next selection, present an ethnographic analysis of the effects of the deinstitutionalization of psychiatric services on the families of the mentally ill. Studying 92 families, the authors examined the entire program of family adaptive responses to the presence of an ex-patient in the home. Herman and Reynolds document the ongoing problems families face with respect to the stigma of mental illness—the fact that such persons possess a "courtesy stigma." Moreover, the data illustrate other such problems as physical, psychological and economic burdens, problematic role performance, role dissensus, and lack of information. Further, the authors discuss the role that families play in providing care and social support for an ex-patient family member. Finally, the positive consequences of this experience, for both ex-patients and their families, are addressed. The selection by Dan Miller, entitled "The Social Construction of Hypnosis," is illustrative of an Iowa approach to the study of the phenomenon of hypnosis. Using the small groups laboratory as the research setting, the author examines the asymmetric interaction processes between the hypnotherapist and the patient. In particular Miller focuses on how the clinical relationship between the two parties is structured through their interactions, and how an extreme form of obedience to authority is created.

The next two articles deal with the what may be termed as subcultural groups. Subcultural social groups that are based on a set of norms and values, which are communicated to its members (some of which may mirror the larger culture); they possess a set of cultural artifacts for engaging in their activities; such groups provide members with a rationale or set of justifications for engaging in certain actions. Subcultures also provide members with an ideology or world-view. Through sustained interaction, subculturally-sanctioned roles, definitions and personal identities emerge. Within this circle of significant others, persons learn the identity and behavior appropriate to their position in society. In short, the subculture is like any other reference group. There are various types of subcultural groups in our society: religious, ethnic, occupational, sports, drug, etc. Some subcultures are centered around illegal or deviant activities. The study by Richard Brymer deals with one such subcultural group, namely, poachers. He begins by tracing the historical roots of poaching activities up to the present. Brymer then presents a detailed ethnographic discussion of their social lives—their "constructions of reality", and the stratagems persons learned and employed to engage in their "deviant" activities without getting caught.

In a similar vein, Mary Lou Dietz presents an ethnographic account of an occupational subcultural group, the urban lumberjack. Based on participant observation and intensive interviews with nine subjects, Dietz discusses how these individuals define their social world and their place in it, the construction of their occupational identity, recruitment patterns, and socialization processes whereby individuals not only acquire skills and knowledge to carry out their activities, but also come to share in the collective "definition of the situation."

SUGGESTED READINGS

Patricia Adler. 1985. *Wheeling and Dealing*. New York: Columbia University Press. An excellent qualitative study of drug dealers.

Lonnie Athens. 1977. "Violent Crime." *Symbolic Interaction* 1:56–70. Presents a symbolic interactionist viewpoint on the most individually harmful of crimes.

Charmaz, Kathy. 1980. *The Social Reality of Death*. Reading, Mass: Addison Wesley. An insightful study of the social lives of the chronically ill and their feelings of self-pity which occur under socially-structured conditions.

Ellis, Carolyn S. 1988. *Fisherfolk: Two Communities on Chesapeake Bay*. Louisville: University Press of Kentucky. Ethnographic study of two east coast fishing communities.

Ferraro, Kathleen and John Johnson. 1983. "How Women Experience Battering: An Interactional Approach to Victimology." *Symbolic Interaction* 13 (1) :103–122. Empirical piece detailing the subjective experiences, constructions of reality, and definitions of situations on the part of female victims.

Fine, Gary Allen. 1987. *With the Boys*. Chicago: University of Chicago Press. A symbolic interactionist analysis of process, structure, and consequences of boy's baseball.

Gubrium, Jaber. 1975. *Living and Dying in Murray Manor*. New York: St. Martin's. An empirical piece dealing with the definitions of situations and constructions of reality of nursing home patients and staff, respectively.

Haas, Jack and William Shaffir. 1977. "The Professionalization of Medical Students: Developing Competence and a Cloak of Competence." *Symbolic Interaction* 1:71–88. Examines the social processes through which individuals acquire a new professional identity.

Herman, Nancy J. 1992. "The Homeless Mentally Ill: Dilemmas and Possible Solutions." *Humanity and Society* 16(4) :480–503. An ethnographic piece dealing with the social plights of a segment of the deinstitutionalized population, those living in shelters, back alleys, and in the streets.

Holstein, James, and Gale Miller. 1990. "Rethinking Victimization: An Interactional Approach to Victimology." *Symbolic Interaction* 13 (1):103–122. Challenges conventional approaches to victimology by specifying what such approaches ignore.

Kleinman, Sherryl. 1984. *Equals Before God: Seminarians as Humanistic Professionals*. Chicago: University of Chicago Press. A solid interactionist account of what it means in social terms to be a seminarian.

Lemert, Edwin. 1962. "Paranoia and the Dynamics of Exclusion" *Sociometry* 25:2–20. A now classic study illustrating the role of unofficial third parties in labelling an individual "mentally ill" through various exclusionary tactics.

Luckenbill, David. 1985."Entering Male Prostitution." *Urban Life* 14:131–54. A qualitative analysis of entering into a deviant career.

Rosenberg, Morris. 1984. "A Symbolic Interactionist View of Psychosis." *Journal of Health and Social Behavior* 25:289–302. A social constructionist approach to the study of mental disorder.

Rosengren, William R. 1966. "The Self in the Emotionally Disturbed." *American Journal of Sociology* 66: 454–62. An interactionist account and explanation of mental illness and its impact.

Scheff, Thomas. 1975. *Labeling Madness*. Englewood Cliffs, New Jersey: Prentice-Hall. Adopting a societal reaction approach, this work focuses on the social processes by which someone is labeled as "mentally ill", and the effects of institutional processing upon self-images and identities.

Schmid, T.J. and R.S. Jones. 1991. "Suspended Identity: Identity Transformation in a Maximum Security Prison." *Symbolic Interaction* 14 (4):415–432. Empirical piece dealing with the manner by which identities are altered as a result of institutional processing.

Schur, Edwin. 1984. *Labeling Women Deviant: Gender, Stigma and Social Control:* Philadelphia: Temple. Excellent application of the labelling approach to the study of gender issues in our society. The social control implications of labeling a woman as deviant in our society are examined.

Scott, Robert A. 1969. *The Making of Blind Men*. New York: Russell Sage. Focuses on how disabled individuals take on "deviant" identities and the consequences of such with respect to their subsequent participation with "normals." Excellent study in adult socialization.

Sudnow, David. 1967.*Passing on: The Social Organization of Dying*. Englewood Cliffs, New Jersey: Prentice-Hall. Investigates the location and production of death and dying in the social organization of hospitals.

Sutherland, Edwin, Donald Cressey, and David Luckenbill. 1992.*Principles of Criminology*. Dix Hills, New York: General Hall. Latest edition of classic work which spells out the specifics and details the importance of differential association theory.

Troiden, Richard. 1989. *Gay and Lesbian Identity*. Dix Hills, NY: General Hall. As a social process, the author documents the stages through which people go in acquiring a homosexual identity.

Williams, Norma. 1990. *The Mexican-American Family*. Dix Hills, New York: General Hall. One of the very few symbolic interactionist style treatments of minority women.

Wiseman, Jacqueline. 1981. *Stations of the Lost*. Englewood Cliffs, New Jersey: Prentice-Hall. Deals with the social constructions of reality of skid row alcoholics.

Chapter 28 BECOMING OBSERVANT AND FALLING FROM THE FAITH: VARIATIONS OF JEWISH CONVERSION EXPERIENCES

William Shaffir

The 1960s and 1970s witnessed the emergence of a variety of fundamentalist groups which sociologists examined in terms of their recruitment tactics (Davis and Richardson, 1976; Gordon, 1974; Lofland, 1966; Zygmunt, 1967), the individual characteristics of the converts (Catton, 1957; Festinger et al., 1956), and the social conditions which were favorable for the emergence of potential recruits (Glock and Bellah, 1976; Harrison, 1974). In contrast to the many studies about conversion to religious sects or cults, the sociological literature contains comparatively few analyses of disengagement from religious communities. Since Mauss (1969) commented upon the paucity of available research literature on the subject of religious defection, several studies have become available which give a fuller picture of the phenomenon (Albrecht and Bahr, 1983; Beckford, 1978; Brinkerhoff and Burke, 1980; Bromley, 1988; Ebaugh, 1984; Jacobs, 1984; Peter et al., 1982; San Giovanni, 1978).

Religious revival and defection have also characterized Israeli society, the former achieving far greater prominence than the latter. As Cohen et al., have written: "... in Israel, the phenomenon of renewal of traditional religion is reflected in the internal strengthening of Orthodox Judaism, and in the attraction of this particular form for Jews from secular backgrounds, seeking a path of return to Judaism, known as *tshuvah*" (1987:320). *Baalei tshuvah* - repenters or returnees to Orthodox Judaism, or newly Orthodox Jews as they are sometimes called - include Jewish men and women who become attracted to the idea of transforming their secular way of life into a mode of living based on the precepts of the Torah. Since 1976, a variety of institutions for facilitating such efforts have been established in Jerusalem alone, while others are present elsewhere in Israel, Europe, the United States and Canada. Describing the *baalei tshuvah*, also identified as *chozrim betshuvah,* Aviad writes that they are

> ...Jews from the Diaspora and Israel, who have "returned" to Orthodox Judaism. Their presence is felt in the city [of Jerusalem]. As individuals, they may be noticed by the mixture of traditional and modern they display in their dress, manners, style. As a group,they are visible through the many new yeshivot established for them and planted in orthodox neighbourhoods (1983:2).

In contrast to the academic research generated by the *baalei tshuvah* phenomenon (Aviad, 1983, Cromer, 1981; Shaffir, 1983), the defection of haredi - ultra-Orthodox - Jews from their communities in Jerusalem and B'nai Brak - the two largest concentrations of haredim in Israel - has, so far, failed to generate scholarly research.[1]

With the exception of one treatment of the topic (Shaffir and Rockaway, 1987), reports and articles about the defection of haredim, popularly designated as *chozrim beshe'aylah*, or "those who return to question", have appeared only in the Israeli press, radio, and television.

The adoption by former haredim of a secular way of life is seemingly the obverse of the experience encountered by *baalei tshuvah*. In fact, however, there are significant parallels in the respective experiences. Broadly speaking, when conceptualized as a process, each involves a transformation resulting in the adoption of a radically different lifestyle affecting relationships with significant others. In this respect, both experiences can be characterized as a conversion in that each "..involves the adoption of a pervasive identity which rests on a change at least in emphasis from one universe of discourse to another" (Travisano, 1970).

This paper[2] highlights a number of the similarities and differences in the transformation experiences of *baalei tshuvah* and *chozrim beshe'aylah*. Conceptualizing the transformation as a status passage (Glaser and Strauss, 1971), I examine the specific context within which it develops. The particular context, I suggest, is directly related to how the transformation is negotiated, and I focus on the individual status of one experience in contrast to the collective status of the other. I then attend to selected components of the negotiated transition, and conclude by offering some avenues for further research. In a postscript I briefly discuss an organization which emerged following the completion of the research: a self-help group that offers assistance to defecting haredim.

The Context of the Transformation

As much of the literature suggests, the process of religious identity transformation can be conceptualized as a conversion experience (Travisano, 1970) or status passage (Glaser and Strauss, 1971). While both experiences involve a dramatic transformation, their respective unfolding and management are critically related to the differing social contexts which both channel and guide the individuals' movements. In contrast to the *baalei tshuvah's* resocialization which occurs in the highly structured setting of the yeshiva, the *chozrim beshe'aylah's* proceeds in the absence of any formalized supports.

At the time of the research, the two yeshivot for *baalei tshuvah* have developed an elaborate system for acquiring recruits, and have in place a highly structured curriculum in addition to a well-rehearsed approach for encouraging newest arrivals to remain for an extended period of time. A brief description of one of these yeshiva's study program is useful at this point. The medium of instruction is English, since the majority of the students are unfamiliar with Hebrew. A short introductory program lasts for three months, with courses on the Chumash (Pentateuch), the Commandments, the divine authorship of the Torah, Jewish laws and prayer, and a specially designed class entitled 'The Forty-eight Ways to Wisdom'; there is also an introductory class on Jewish history. This program is regarded as a prerequisite for the more intensive four-year course of study which follows.

The format of the curriculum is modelled partially after the university system of teaching, a format with which the students are familiar. Classes begin at 9 a.m. and ended at 10 p.m., with breaks for meals. However, it is not unusual for the majority of students to start the day at 7 a.m. with preparations for the morning prayers and to end it at 11 p.m. with a review of the day's studies and the preparation of assignments for the following day's classes.

Upon arrival at the yeshiva, the individual can depend on an immediately warm reception in an attempt to draw him into a lively discussion for convincing him to stay on. As one senior student explains:

> In the short amount of time that you are going to deal with him, you are going..to show him that to spend a little time here is a better opportunity than what he's doing now. ...You have to get hold of a guy..whatever it takes with all honest means. It's like a salesman, he knows he has to make a sale. ...

In the initial encounter, the newcomer is asked about his future plans and about how he intends to achieve them. He is also likely to be asked about his belief in God and about his views on the meaning of life. Then a central question is put to him, "What are you living for?" The visitor soon discovers that the student body includes young men whose backgrounds and recent histories resemble his own, and they use all their persuasive powers to convince him that it is in his own best interests to join them.

The newcomer who agrees to remain for three months has a structured curriculum to introduce him to Jewish laws and traditions; he is taught by sympathetic tutors in a friendly atmosphere which encourages him to consider changing his lifestyle permanently. Through the presentation of a series of carefully-co-ordinated arguments, rooted in Torah principles, the yeshiva hopes to effect a conversion in the student's outlook: the alteration to a religious frame of reference from a secular one.

By contrast, *chozrim beshe'aylah's* transformation is characterized by the absence of any such formalized support. In fact, a feature common to all in this category is their extreme reluctance to confide their thoughts about leaving to anyone else - this despite the fact that their defection eventually becomes common knowledge. They maintain that it is impossible to talk with any other members of their group about their religious doubts - doubts about the existence of God - or about their growing dissatisfaction with the confining nature of haredi society. As one respondent comments sarcastically:

> ...the sin you're committing can't be shared with anyone. You feel as if you're sinning, transgressing. It's a crime. You become paranoid about this and you're too ashamed to discuss it. ...No, no, it can't happen. It's more taboo than sex.

Another ex-haredi has a similar experience: "It's just impossible to let others know how you're feeling. Can you imagine mentioning it to a rav [rabbi]? And you can't even mention it to your closest friend. No, it remains a deep dark secret, and that's what makes it so difficult."

Exiting from haredi society, then, becomes a difficult undertaking both because of the absence of formalized supports as well as the inability to share any misgivings about the haredi lifestyle with others who might react similarly. Not only is the transformation undertaken secretly, but it must be managed alone. Reflecting upon his experience, an individual draws the following analogy: "It's like living in a Communist country. To speak out against the government, you don't know if he is loyal to you or if he's going to give you away to the counsellors and teachers." Contrasting his experience with that of a *baal tshuvah*, a haredi contemplating departure remarks:

> Look, there's a world of difference. If somebody wants to become a *chozer betshuvah*, I'm not saying it's easy, but he knows where to go. He can go to one of many places and each of them is thrilled to accept him. He receives instruction, he'll have a place to sleep and eat. The point is there's support and encouragement. I can leave [haredi society] in the sense that I can get to a #54 bus, and I come to the central bus station. But where do I go from there? There's no place to go, and there's no place that's ready to help me. So I have to do it all alone.

As the above remarks suggest, the differing contexts within which the resocialization occurs bear directly on how the experience itself is evaluated and managed. While both groups of individuals embark upon the acquisition of a new perspective and identity, the *baalei tshuvah's* resocialization provides them access to a subculture which offers sympathetic understanding and support. By contrast, the *chozrim beshe'aylah* initiate their exit in the absence of any guidelines on either the mechanics of the disengagement or the emotional consequences resulting from separation from family, friends and a lifestyle steeped in Torah observance.

Managing the Transformation: Individual Versus Collective Status

When a person moves into a new interpersonal setting, a major problem he faces is understanding the setting and coming to terms with its demands. He must develop a workable "definition of the situation" to guide his actions. The newcomer may be assisted along this line by others who either have already experienced this transition or currently share a similar situation. Of critical importance, then, is whether the individual experiences the new situation alone or in the company of others; in other words, the individual or collective status of the recruits.[3]

A second and related aspect is whether the individual has been preceded by others who have experienced the same transition and who can teach him "the ropes" about the setting. This distinction is between a serial pattern of socialization and a disjunctive pattern where the recruit is not following in the footsteps of predecessors (Wheeler, 1966). As I have suggested, the socialization of the *baalei tshuvah* is characterized by its collective status and serial pattern.

The structure and organization of the yeshiva setting are connected to two important features affecting the transformation experiences of *baalei tshuvah*. First, since the yeshiva processes newcomers, it thereby maintains a measure of control over the direction and shape of their socialization experience. Second, and following from the collective status and the serial pattern of the resocialization, there emerges the formation of a yeshiva subculture - a set of perspectives and understandings about what the *baalei tshuvah* experience is like and how to deal with it, and a set of routine activities based on these perspectives. Alongside this subculture is a vocabulary of motives (Mills,1940) which explains, justifies and answers questions about the behaviour in question.

The newcomer who agrees to remain in the yeshiva for a three-month period has a structured curriculum to introduce him to Jewish laws and traditions; he is taught by sympathetic tutors in a friendly atmosphere which encourages him to consider changing his lifestyle permanently. In assisting them to arrive at this realization, each of the students attends the same core of basic courses. Moreover, the content is coordinated so as to appeal to the students' intellect, and the instructors are selected because of their charismatic appeal. For instance, in the case of 'The Forty-eight Ways to Wisdom' class, the students are unanimous in asserting that the manner in which Rav Noach, the instructor, taught that course is the main reason for which they stay on. As one of them explains:

> The class is really basic..More than any other class, this one sets the pace. This is the one that really makes you think..The thing about this class is that everything is presented so logically. You are constantly challenged to point out where the arguments don't make sense. Many times people stay on for three months just to complete this class.

An integral feature of the yeshiva's curriculum lies in convincing students that their presence there cannot be attributed to chance factors but, rather, that they have been guided by Divine Providence. Students are continually encouraged to reflect on the series and timing of events which led to their initial encounter with the yeshiva and to assess the likelihood that the requisite circumstances could happen on their own accord. As one of the rabbis offers in reply to a student's query:

> What do you think? Do you think you're here by chance? Think about the things that had to happen, according to a particular sequence, for you to have made it here. Really, does it make sense to believe that this is due to luck or chance? No. You are here because God wanted you here. This is an opportunity that Ha-Shem [God] is offering you. It's now up to you to take advantage of it.

Both formally and informally, the message conveyed to students is that their decision to remain in the yeshiva is a reasonable one. While the yeshiva's programme does not demand that students sever extra-group ties, the activities at the yeshiva are structured to consume most of the students' waking hours. When he is not attending classes or studying, he is usually in the company of other students engaging in informal conversation during which the subject of religion is the central topic. One student observes:

> It's really quite remarkable. Wherever you turn, someone is talking about religion or something that's connected. At lunch, for example, someone raises a point brought up in class. Or someone else tells about a conversation he had with someone to get them to come to the yeshiva.

Although the yeshiva's formal curriculum aims to appeal to the students' logic and reason, it also affords them opportunities to relate their yeshiva experience at the affective level. The friendships established with others, the pairing of students for purposes of study, and the numerous informal opportunities for sharing feelings and concerns, provides an invaluable support system. Such a supportive environment enables them to compare themselves to others, to assess their progress, evaluate their deepening identification and commitment to Orthodox Judaism, and to seek solutions to problems resulting from their changed lifestyle. Indeed, the students that elect to pursue their studies at the yeshiva claim to be attracted not only by the logical arguments but also by the sense of community which prevails in the yeshiva and by its communal rituals. Many admit to having been influenced by the affectionate attention directed towards them both during and after classes, and say that they are prepared to trust the yeshiva because the student body impresses them as being sincere and contented. As one of them remarks:

> The thing about this place is that it's genuine. People here are interested in you and that comes across right from the start.. I've been involved in a number of religious groups. The affection showered on you in those groups was contrived. It's not like that here. People here care about you in a real and sincere way.

However, the peer group atmosphere extends beyond the offer of sympathetic understanding. More significantly, as the students' bonds of friendship widen, they are able to learn how others chart and manage their course towards Orthodox Judaism. In time, students discover that their particular problems are not unique to themselves but are, instead, typically shared by others who preceded them. One individual sums up this view as follows:

> Becoming an Orthodox Jew isn't something that happened immediately. There are a lot of things you think about, questions that you wrestle with, and it's important to get feedback. That's where the students help you most, especially those that have been where you're at now. They really understand and their advice helps a lot.

Indeed, the student culture becomes helpful in suggesting ways of coping with the problems accompanying the transition, and particularly in forecasting the typical problems that the individual will encounter in becoming an Orthodox Jew.

In extreme contrast to the *baalei tshuvah*, the resocialization experience of the *chozrim beshe'aylah* is both individual and disjunctive and, as a result, is accompanied by feelings of loneliness and abandonment. They are suddenly utterly isolated in the secular society without knowing to whom to turn for help or comfort. Reflecting on his own travails in exiting from haredi society, one person says:

> A person can really just go mad from such an experience. It's a terrible loneliness and you become really alone. You cut off everything that you had and are by yourself. And nobody cares about you and that's it. Nobody cares about you as a person.

Another *chozer beshe'aylah* echoes this reaction with the following:

> You feel an emptiness, a very deep emptiness, and there's also confusion. What makes it all so difficult and terrible is that you have nobody to talk to, nobody who really understands what you're going through. The loneliness can be overpowering. You're cut off. The close friends you've had since childhood, you never see again.

As we have already seen, the yeshiva environment provides individuals with a ready-made group of persons with whom they can establish ties of friendship. Such support is characteristically absent for the *chozrim beshe'aylah*. While some form of relationship is maintained with immediate family, it is both strained and awkward since they are now identified primarily as individuals that have strayed from the proper Jewish path. A *chozer beshe'aylah* relates:

> There are a few reasons why leaving is difficult. One is friends, good friends. There each person is connected to the other. Really, just like brothers. Each person speaks to others. People lend each other money and provide other kinds of help.. So everyone has friends. The moment one leaves, one is cut off from all one's friends.

Both in the case of the *baalei tshuvah* and *chozrim beshe'aylah*, the new-found orientation—religion in the first instance and a secular lifestyle in the other—results in a redefinition and reorientation in one's relationships with friends. As a *baal tshuvah* explains, "I kept in touch with some of my closer friends, but we just stopped writing. They couldn't relate to my religious beliefs.. I really don't think I'd have much to say to them today." The remarks of a former haredi are virtually identical. When asked whether he keeps in touch with at least one or two of his haredi friends, he replies: "No one. Simply because I haven't anything to talk with them about. We haven't anything in common. I'm not them and they're not me. The things they want to discuss aren't of interest to me."

While relinquishing ties with former friends is common both to newly-observant Jews and former haredim, it impacts more strongly on the latter both because of the long-standing nature of the terminated relationship but especially since such friendships are not easily replaced by new ones. Of course, there is nothing to prevent the former haredim from forming new friendships; but that takes time and even then it is not easily achieved.

Much like the difficulties in establishing new friendships experienced by ex-Moonies (Beckford, 1985), the new friendships cultivated by the *chozrim beshe'aylah* are mainly superficial, hardly enabling them to engage in conversations about matters of a personal and meaningful nature. A *chozer beshe'aylah* expresses this point tellingly:

> The friends you lose you can't replace. You meet a number of new people but they aren't anything more than acquaintances for the most part. There's a limit to how much you can share with them because you don't know them that well and they don't know you. So you might know a number of people but none on an intimate level.. You're alone, really, all alone.

In analyzing the process of becoming a marijuana user, Becker (1953) shows how the culture of users provides the novice not only with the technical aspects of where to acquire "pot" and how to use it, but with a value system as well. In becoming *baalei tshuvah*, novices are provided with access to a particular symbol-moral universe which assists them in defining the meaning of the religious experience, an atmosphere and environment from which they derive social acceptability and support against outside disapproval, as well as a vocabulary by which they can justify, and meaningfully interpret, their experiences. Such subcultural support is unavailable to the *chozrim beshe'aylah* who must negotiate the transition to the secular world alone. The following section focuses on two properties of the negotiated transition which are influenced by the collective versus the solo nature of the transformation experience.

Properties of the Conversion Experience

Learning the Cultural Script

In his analysis of the moral career of the ex-Moonie, Beckford suggests that "... there is little in the way of a cultural `script' for the passage of a person from being a member of an intense religious group to being a non-member" (1985:174). As the previous discussion has indicated, the opportunities for familiarization with the newly-adopted cultural script differ dramatically for ex-haredim and newly-observant Jews.

In contrast to the situation faced by ex-cult followers, the haredi defectors encounter a double bind: in addition to unfamiliarity with the process of departure from haredi society, they are also not attuned to the norms and values of the secular world from which they have been sheltered and with which they have become aligned. The disillusioned cult followers, on the other hand, come from a secular background and know the lifestyle to which they will revert. Moreover, there are usually caring persons who are eager to guide them back. For the defecting haredim, on the other hand, as one of them explained: "Outside, there's nothing. There's one big void. Whoever doesn't fill that void before he goes out is destined to great suffering." However, it is extremely difficult for them to prepare for the secular world while still pretending to observe ultra-Orthodox practices. Some of them do arrange to spend a period away and thereby learn something of the practices of non-observant Jews before formally abandoning their allegiance to the haredi code of behaviour. For others who suddenly find themselves on the other side of the fence, the shock is often traumatic. After years of living in a community where the sexes are strictly separated, it is not easy to mix informally with women, for example; one individual claims to be confused and embarrassed when he begins having girlfriends.

Two others comment on the basic problems facing those who study in haredi institutions when they leave to join mainstream secular Jewish society in Israel:

> They don't have the basic education, basic knowledge of mathematics, of geography, of history. All the things that are taken for granted, they don't have. That means that they can't get into this new society. ... They can't talk to people. Things people take for granted, they won't know. They don't know how many continents there are in the world, as an example, ... so they can't talk to people.

> You don't know how to relate. You don't know basic things. [What does that mean?]. I don't know if I can relive that feeling because its very painful. It's another world..Just people talking normal conversations and you don't know what they're talking about. You are not aware of the world outside..It's a cultural gap..It's a painful feeling.

Under the circumstances, it is not surprising that they feel bewildered when they are suddenly thrown, or rather when they deliberately throw themselves into the secular world.

By contrast, *baalei tshuvah* are not required to completely abandon the secular values and behavior which form the central guiding orientation in their lives. While aspects of such behavior eventually require modification, but such adaptations can be organized and comprehended within their established secular frame of reference. In fact, in its attempts to persuade students to remain in the yeshiva, the administration mainly appeals to their powers of logical reasoning, rooted in the secular culture, which it encourages them to utilize in understanding the demands of Torah Judaism. As one of the rabbis explains:

> Even though what we're asking of students is not that simple, I mean it's difficult to change, they can handle it gradually. No one insists that they change overnight. But more importantly, the changes we're interested in don't require that they adopt a fundamentally different approach to reasoning. Basically, we're asking them to reason and then, of course, to act on that reasoning.

And, as a student offers:

Even though I'm introduced to a new world of meaning and material objects, like I didn't know about *tefillin* [phylacteries] and *tzitzess* [ritual fringes], I can assimilate that information within my own frame of reference. To put it differently, I haven't had to invert my way of thinking.

Thus, institutionalized supports offered by the yeshiva, coupled with the informal networking of peers, provide *baalei tshuvah* with a cultural script both for assessing as well as managing their progress into the Orthodox world. Stated otherwise, the convert requires and receives "..an organized community within which they may regularly act out, in the company of others, the behavioral implications of the experience which he has undergone" (Cohen et al., 1987:327).

Centrality of Time

While the pace at which the transition occurs is more regularized for the *baalei tshuvah*, the process of change extends over a period of time for both groups. To the outsider, the observed changes in the individuals' behaviour usually signify strong measures of identification with the newly-chosen lifestyle. Recruits themselves, however, observe that changes, while appearing to be sudden, are, more typically, the culmination of a lengthy period of reflection. Both in the case of *baalei tshuvah* and *chozrim beshe'aylah*, the element of time becomes the critical mediator in their identity transformation. Their resulting changes are best conceptualized as a temporal process involving sequences of steps which gradually alter their self-conception, thereby contributing to an increased identification with and commitment to a changed way of life. The following comment reveals the centrality of time in the transformation experience of *baalei tshuvah*:

> In the beginning, for the first couple of months, the experience was simply overwhelming. There was so much happening that I couldn't assimilate it all. ... But time makes such a big difference because it allows you to see things in perspective. I've gone through some incredible changes since I've come 8 months ago. Everybody here, I would say, goes through stages. The rabbis talk about stages. Like at first there's the stage of feeling overwhelmed and confused. You just can't get a firm grip on things. ... Then there's a stage of rebellion or challenge. You argue, you take issue with their [the rabbis'] arguments. ... Eventually, if you're here long enough, and if you open yourself to the possibility for change, you accept not only the logic of the arguments, but you also become attached emotionally and spiritually. You can't predict how long these stages last, but you see it all over here.

The passage of time is instrumental in assisting the *baalei tshuvah* determine how best to express their connection with Orthodox Judaism. Although this necessarily involves the adoption of religious practices, both their pace and sequence varies with the individual's background and inclinations to change. Two individuals remark:

> I started with *tefillin* immediately. That has been easy for me to do, but I still have trouble wearing the *kippah* [skullcap] when I go into the city. You're expected to participate in prayer and that's becoming more meaningful as time goes on.

> I don't put on *tefillin*, I just don't put them on. [You don't put them on at all?] Sometimes I do but usually I don't. It's a very heavy act for me. It's very complete and I'm not comfortable enough with it to say that everything in the Torah is true and I am going to do it. This is me.

In time, however, as individuals become committed to remaining in the yeshiva, alterations in their external behaviour blend with the emergence of a new self-conception involving newly-adopted priorities, values and goals.

Whereas the *baalei tshuvah's* encounter with the yeshiva world and Orthodox Judaism are typically unplanned, the *chozrim beshe'aylah's* departure from the haredi fold is premeditated. All of the respondents characterize their departure as preceded by considerable internal debate and distress. One, aged 25, speaks for all respondents when he says:

> It must sound strange to you that despite my questions and criticisms, it took me years to leave. But you can't imagine how difficult it is. ... You know that you want to leave, but you're just not sure. You can't imagine how much courage you need to make the break.

Departure is consistently portrayed as a process involving intense reflection. One individual, in his early forties, who leaves his haredi community in the 1960s to fight in the Six-Day War, describes his efforts at reaching a decision:

> From an internal standpoint, it's a matter of process that takes years. But all the time, externally, I didn't change any of my customs, and I continued to follow the *halakha* [Code of Jewish Law] up to the point where I decided that I'm sure that this isn't my way. Then, only then, did I change drastically. Now for outsiders it looked like it happened one bright day but internally it's a process of years.

Another draws attention to the importance of time in this way:

> The day that I rode on the Shabbat [the Sabbath], I remember it. But then it was so long after I knew I didn't believe. Basically one stops believing that this is the right way before one acts upon it..because there's so much guilt involved.

However long the internal process, the adoption of behaviour violating strict religious commandments or dressing in a manner offending against the community's prescribed mode, is conceptualized temporally. As one individual recalls:

> There's always a first time. And this first time is difficult. It's painful. It cuts. But the transition...can take a number of years. There's the first time that I took off the *kipah* [skullcap], there's the first time that I stopped putting *Tefillin* [phylacteries], there's the first time that I drove on the Sabbath, there's the first time that I didn't eat kosher, there's the first time that I ate on Yom Kippur, and so on. This doesn't occur over a period of a week; it doesn't all happen on the same day.

For many, the failure to observe the commandments is accompanied by fear of divine retribution. For instance, an individual speaks of the fear he experiences of incurring terrible consequences after the first time driving on the Sabbath:

> I was very scared the first time..I remember it well. I was scared. It was Shabbat, and I was nervous. I was on a kibbutz in the north and we went to the sea, the Kinneret, and we hitch-hiked. Whenever a car didn't stop, I felt good..In the end, some tourists stopped and we descended by the old road.. It was very emotional. There were a lot of curves in the road and I was afraid at each one of them. It wasn't a rational fear. It was Shabbat.

The realization that divine retribution is not immediately forthcoming enables these individuals to continue distancing themselves from their respective haredi communities. For instance, as a male who left his community seven months prior to our conversation recalls:

> Without question, the beginning is the most difficult. You're unsure of yourself, you've never done any of these things before, like not keeping kashruth or violating the Sabbath. But over time you learn how to deal with the feelings you experience and you become better at rationalizing your behaviour.

As I have suggested, then, both for the *baalei tshuvah* and *chozrim beshe'aylah*, the alteration of behaviour proceeds gradually; time becomes the central element through which the experiences are distilled and incorporated into the person's new identity.

CONCLUSION

Based upon research conducted in Israel, this paper highlights and analyzes some of the comparisons and differences between newcomers to Orthodox Judaism and defectors from the ultra-Orthodox haredi fold. Further research along this line might focus on additional components of the status passage, namely, for example, whether it is reversible, the kinds of legitimation that may be required, and are sought, from authorized agents, and the clarity of the signs marking the transformation.

In offering an overview of the transformation experience, I have not attended to all of the intricate dynamics underlying its management. In both cases, for instance, the manipulation of convincing presentations before various audiences signifies the individuals' progress along the chosen route. As well, just as there are various modes of *tshuvah* (Aviad, 1983), so, too, might it be possible to delineate different trajectories by which *chozrim beshe'aylah* negotiate their exit from haredi society. In a world where definitions are shaped by gender distinctions, further research might attend to how this dimension imposes itself upon the experienced transformation.

The art of coordinating a convincing self-presentation figures prominently in any conversion experience. While impression management is central both for newcomers to Orthodox Judaism and the religious defectors, the respective dynamics regarding the relationship between attitudes and behavior differ. In light of the institutionalized context within which the conversion experience is situated, *chozrim betshuvah* quickly adopt the appropriate behavioral trappings of Orthodox Judaism, including dress, language, study, and prayer, hoping to eventually acquire the requisite attitudes which correspond to their behaviour. While outwardly displaying confidence in their behavioral commitment to Orthodox Judaism, they inwardly engage at realigning their understanding of life's meaning and purpose to fit the requirements of their new lifestyle. This sequence appears to be reversed for the haredi defectors. The decision to exit from the haredi community is accompanied by attitudinal and emotional changes concerning the authenticity of the haredi lifestyle and Orthodox Judaism in advance of the behavioral changes that eventually reflect their altered lifestyle. Presenting themselves to their peers and others in haredi society as suitably committed members of the community, they secretly violate the governing norms of their society and seek the appropriate opportunities to publicly embark upon a radically different way of life. The commonly used tactics for negotiating a new identity constitute a central component of the conversion experience.

POSTSCRIPT

At the time the data on *hozrim beshe'aylah* were collected, the latters' withdrawal from the haredi world was negotiated alone in light of the absence of any group that might facilitate their movement. This situation changed dramatically in 1990 with the founding of Hillel [a Hebrew acronym for *"Ha'agudah Lechozrim Leshe'aylah"* (Organization for those who Return to Questioning)]. The organization was founded by a 20 year old, named Shai, who saw the need for an organized body to help *chozrim beshe'aylah*. The son of a prominent rabbi in the haredi community, he had left his family some four years earlier and personally experienced the loneliness and pain accompanying the transition to the secular world. He was convinced that the haredi world was filled with people who wanted to leave, but couldn't. "They're trapped," he said, "and they don't know anybody here" [in the secular world]. Upon founding the organization, he proclaimed that *hazara beshe'aylah* was "..like being born again."

Hillel is a non-profit organization that relies on a pool of volunteers to provide social and financial services, and even legal counselling, to those wishing to leave the haredi world. As stated in a letter calling for volunteers:

> The *hozer beshe'aylah* is likely to find himself homeless, without work, and with absolutely no support..It is difficult for him to bridge the gap and to struggle with financial day-to-day difficulties. Hillel, with the assistance of the Organization for Secular Humanist Judaism, ..the Movement of Progressive Jewry, and other bodies, supports the *hozer beshe'aylah* in this are as well. ...
>
> *Hozrim beshe'aylah* are not familiar with the social customs and ways of living of the free society which is so much more modern and advanced by hundreds of years. The organization is committed to helping them find their way in modern Israeli society in such areas as induction to the army, finding employment, studies, creating social ties with peer groups, psychological and legal counselling. ...

In addition to creating a team of volunteers, Hillel placed advertisements in newspapers and in various neighborhoods in Jerusalem. They included a 'hot line' telephone number inviting interested persons to call. The organization generated and attracted considerable publicity largely as a result of its energetic founder who, as one individual remarked, "..was totally fanatic about it." He publicized the organization on television, and was the subject of interviews on the radio and in the print media.

In a dramatic turn of events, in April, 1992, Shai left a note: "I am resigning from the organization and I am not interested in maintaining any connection with the organization or its people." He was returning to the haredi world, and added that, "Deep in my heart I knew the truth all the time." By this time, Hillel had opened a new chapter in the Tel Aviv area, and at the very time that its members were meeting there, Shai was in the Jerusalem office erasing the organization's membership files from the computer, files which, he maintained, belonged to him. Members of Hillel, he charged, were "soul hunters" who snatched persons from their homes, and he attempted to convince former haredi members of Hillel to return to the haredi fold. His defection shocked the organization to the core. Perhaps expecting his sudden about face to signal Hillel's eventual demise, Shai's rejection of the organization, paradoxically, served to instill in it a vibrancy that was previously lacking. His departure generated enormous publicity and, more importantly for the organization, resulted in offers from numerous persons who volunteered their services.

Shortly following Shai's departure, Hillel organized a conference where those that benefited from its services engaged in discussions and listened to speakers. "It was so exciting," remarked one of the participants, "because you saw people who really needed the support group. They were so hungry for knowledge and were absorbing every new bit of information."Hillel includes a team of trained volunteers to handle inquiries from haredim who are contemplating a change of lifestyle. The social occasions offered by the organization are mainly appreciated for the opportunities they provide former haredim to discuss, compare, and evaluate their respective histories and experiences. As one person observed: "It's more the idea of being together and meeting other people and getting details. At first we all told our own story and it was just fascinating." In this respect, Hillel serves as a subculture offering those within a set of perspectives about what the world is like, and how to deal with the typical range of problems they encounter.

Although Hillel is apolitical, it may yet become embroiled in political controversies. Regarded by the haredim as anathema, the organization may be seen as intentionally straining even further the already tense relations with their secular counterparts as the two sides engage in a culture war to influence the pace and direction of social and religious life in the Jewish state.

NOTES

1. Such inattention may be a reflection of the comparatively few *haredim* that have recently chosen to defect. Menachem Friedman (1986) has pointed out that in the past, when men decided to leave their yeshivot, there existed alternative social settings that were both eager and prepared to accept them. These settings are either no longer available or else no longer function in the same manner.
2. The data for this paper constituted two separate research projects and were gathered in different years. Both the *baalei tshuvah* and *chozrim beshe'aylah* studies, conducted in 1978-1979 and 1986 respectively, relied upon participant observation and informal interviews. I spent seven months in two Jerusalem yeshivot for *baalei tshuvah* and participated in the full range of the students' activities - attending classes, taking meals with them, and engaging in informal conversation and discussion. The *baalei tshuvah*, of whom fifty were interviewed, ranged in age from 18-30 years, were from predominantly middle to upper middle-class families in the United States (a minority were from England and Canada), and a majority were in the midst of their university studies. Their length of stay ranged from one month to four years. The *chozrim beshe'aylah*, of whom thirty-five were interviewed over a seven-month period, during 1986 and 1989, ranged in age from 24 to 43 years and included 30 men and 5 women. Upon leaving their haredi communities, six persons chose to become modern Orthodox Jews, while the remainder ceased practising completely.
3. As Goffman (1961) has shown, much socialization is organized so that a large number of persons are introduced to the new setting simultaneously. Under these circumstances adaptation is likely to proceed much differently than in those instances where a person enters alone, since the recruits can arrive at a collective solution to the presented problems.

REFERENCES

Albrecht, S.L. and H.M. Bahr. 1983. "Patterns of religious disaffiliation: a study of lifelong Mormons, Mormon converts, and former Mormons." *Journal for the Scientific Study of Religion* 22 (4): 366–379.
Aviad, J. 1983. *Return to Judaism: Religious Renewal in Israel*. Chicago: University of Chicago Press.
Barker, E. 1984. *The Making Of A Moonie: Choice or Brainwashing?* New York: Basil Blackwell.
Becker, H.S. 1953. "Becoming a marijuana user." *American Journal of Sociology*. 59: 235–242.
Beckford, J.A. 1963. *Outsiders: Studies in the Sociology of Deviance*. New York: The Free Press.
——. 1978. "Through the looking-glass and out the other side: withdrawal from Reverend Moon's unification church." *Archives de Sciences Sociales des Religions* 45 (1): 95–116.
——. 1985. *Cult Controversies: The Societal Response to the New Religious Movements*. New York: Tavistock Publications.

Bittner, E. 1963. "Radicalism and the organization of radical movements." *American Sociological Review* 28 (6): 928–940.

Brinkerhoff, M.B. and K.L. Burke. 1980. "Disaffiliation: some notes on "Falling from the Faith." *Sociological Analysis* 41 (1): 41–54.

Bromley, D.G. (ed.). 1988. *Falling from the Faith: Causes and Consequences of Religious Apostasy.* Newbury Park, CA: Sage.

Catton, W.R. 1957. "What kind of people does a religious cult attract?" *American Sociological Review* 22 (5): 551–566.

Cohen, E., N. Ben-Yehuda and J. Aviad. 1987. "Recentering the world: the quest for 'elective' centres in a secularized universe." *The Sociological Review* 35 (2): 320–346.

Cromer, G. 1981. "Repentant delinquents: a religious approach to rehabilitation." *The Jewish Journal of Sociology* 23 (2): 113–122.

Davis, R. and J.T. Richardson. 1976. "The organization and functioning of the children of God." *Sociological Analysis* 37 (4): 321–339.

Ebaugh, H.R.F. 1984. "Leaving the convent: the experience of role exit and self-transformation." Pp. 156–176 in J.A. Kotarba and A. Fontana (eds.), *The Existential Self in Society.* Chicago: University of Chicago Press.

Festinger, L., H.W. Riecken, and S. Schachter. 1956. *When Prophecy Fails.* Minneapolis: University of Minnesota Press.

Friedman, M. 1986. "Haredim confront the modern city." Pp.74–96 in P.Y. Medding (ed.) *Studies In Contemporary Jewry* II. Bloomington: Indiana University Press.

Glaser B.G. and A.L. Strauss. 1971. *Status Passage.* Chicago: Aldine.Atherton.

Glock, C.Y. and R.N. Bellah (eds.). 1976. *The New Religious Consciousness.* Berkeley: University of California Press.

Goffman, E. 1961. *Asylums.* Garden City, N.Y.: Doubleday.

Gordon, D. 1974. "The Jesus people: an identity synthesis." *Urban Life and Culture* 3 (2): 159–178.

Harrison, M.I. 1974. "Sources of recruitment to catholic pentacostalism." *Journal for the Scientific Study of Religion* 13 (1): 49–64.

Jacobs, J. 1984. "The economy of love in religious commitment: the deconversion of women from nontraditional religious movements." *Journal for the Scientific Study of Religion* 23 (2): 155–171.

Lofland, J. 1966. *Doomsday Cult: A Study of Conversion, Proselytization and Maintenance of Faith.* Englewood Cliffs, N.J.: Prentice-Hall.

Mauss, A. 1969. "Dimensions of religious defection." *Review of Religious Research* 10: 128–135.

Mills, C.W. 1940. "Situated actions and vocabularies of motive." *American Sociological Review* 5 (October): 904–913.

Peter, K., E.D. Boldt, I. Whitaker, and L.W. Roberts. 1982. "The dynamics of religious defection among Hutterites." *Journal for the Scientific Study of Religion* 25 (1): 327–337.

San Giovanni, L. 1978. *Ex-Nuns: A Study of Emergent Role Passage.* Norwood: Ablex.

Shaffir, W. 1983. "The recruitment of *baalei tshuvah* in a Jerusalem yeshiva." *The Jewish Journal of Sociology* 25 (1): 33–46.

Shaffir, W. and R. Rockaway. 1987. "Leaving the ultra-orthodox fold: haredi Jews who defected." *The Jewish Journal of Sociology* 29 (2): 97–114.

Travisano, R. 1970. "Alteration and conversion as qualitatively different transformations: Pp.594–606 in Stone, G.P. and H. Farberman (eds.) *Social Psychology Through Symbolic Interaction.* Waltham, Mass.: Ginn-Blaisdell.

Wheeler, S. 1966. "The structure of formally organized socialization settings." Pp.53–116 in Brim, Jr., O.G. and S. Wheeler, *Socialization After Childhood: Two Essays.* New York: John Wiley & Sons.

Zygmunt, J.F. 1967. "Jehovah's Witnesses: A Study of Symbolic and Structural Elements in the Development and Institutionalization of a Sectarian Movement." Doctoral dissertation, University of Chicago.

Chapter 29 FAMILY CAREGIVERS OF THE MENTALLY ILL: NEGATIVE AND POSITIVE ADAPTIVE RESPONSES

Nancy J. Herman and *Larry T. Reynolds*

Over the past three decades, there has been a marked shift *away* from the hospital *to* the community. As a result of the ideological movement toward deinstitutionalization, the resident population of state mental hospitals in the United States has been reduced from approximately 558,922 in 1955 to less than 110,743 in 1986 [Cockerham, 1992:293]. Similarly in Canada, during this same time period, the resident population of provincial psychiatric institutions decreased from 78,598 to 11,394 [Statistics Canada, 1986: 43]. Moreover, with this shift in policy and treatment regarding the mentally ill, newly-diagnosed or defined mental patients are no longer being sent directly to the state or provincial psychiatric institutions, but rather, are being treated primarily on an out-patient basis in community mental health centers. Some are admitted on a short-term basis to psychiatric wards of general hospitals, and most are only admitted to psychiatric institutions as a "last resort." In short, with the movement toward deinstitutionalization, we now have living among us significant numbers of both deinstitutionalized psychiatric patients and non-institutionalized persons defined as being mentally ill. Accordingly, Freeman and Simmons (1963: 1) have contended that, "...it is no exaggeration to observe that the major problem in the field of mental illness is *not* the hospitalized patient but the formerly hospitalized patient." This statement, made nearly thirty years ago, is even more pertinent today.

In the sociological literature on mental illness, much research has focused on the events surrounding the post-patient phase of the ex-psychiatric patient's career—problems of stigma, adjustment, integration, re-employment, housing, and identity transformation; and several studies have focused on family responses toward mentally ill relatives (Hibler, 1978; and Lefton, et al., 1962). However, little attention has been devoted to the *dynamics* of family interaction. Of those few studies that have dealt with family dynamics, they have either focused on the rejection and exclusion of ex-psychiatric patient loved ones or dealt with the burden that such persons place upon the family (Arey and Warheit, 1980; Gubman and Tessler 1987). While it is important to note these types of responses, it is simplistic to assume that these are the *only* such responses that result. Much of the previous research has centered solely on rejection, isolation and social conflict between ex-patients and their families. With one notable exception (Stoneall, 1983), lesser attention has been devoted to the positive functions the family performs in reintegrating and supporting ex-patients. So too, has little attention been given to the benefits that the ex-patients themselves may provide for the family. Moreover, comparatively little research has been devoted to the family's adjustment and adaptation to the presence of an ex-psychiatric patient in the home. We hope to partially fill this void in the literature.

This paper attempts to chart the range of family responses to mental disorder. Specifically, it focuses on: (1) the ongoing problems faced by families in terms of stigma, role dissensus, and role performances, and (2) the role that families play in providing care and social support for ex-patient loved ones and the positive effects of such activities for both the transformation of the ex-patient's identity and the family's own sense of identity.

METHODS AND SAMPLE

This study was based on descriptive data collected between September, 1981 up to, and including September, 1988 from families acting as primary caregivers for their relatives. They resided in nine separate geographical locales in Southern Ontario, Canada and in the Midwestern United States. Specifically, utilizing a stratified, disproportionate random sample of 300 ex-psychiatric clients, an attempt was made to interview the *families* who were actually providing shelter and support for 107 of the ex-patients.

Interviews were conducted primarily in the families' homes and lasted between two to four hours. Questions were open-ended, based on previous academic research on families of the mentally ill, and on prior ethnographic research on the topic.[1] Of the 107 interviews attempted, 92, or 86 percent of the sample, were completed. In some cases, families refused to be interviewed, could not be located or had severe language problems. The open-ended interviews were supplemented by participant observation with 80 families in various settings such as their homes, at social gatherings, during meetings with community mental health social workers and psychiatrists. Only time and money limitations prohibited engaging in participant observation activities with all 92 families. The purpose of this participant observation was three-fold. First, it provided ethnographic data on family dynamics—it allowed observation of first-hand day-to-day interactions not only between family members and ex-patient relatives, but among themselves as well. Second, it allowed the observation of interactions between mental health care professionals and family caregivers. Third, it provided data on social interactions between nuclear family members and other relatives, friends, neighbors, and co-workers. Each day in the field family members were observed in everyday activities. Numerous meals were eaten with the subjects in both their homes and fast-food restaurants. Families were accompanied to doctors' appointments, supermarkets, birthday parties, funerals, anniversaries, and church social events.

The families studied were predominantly from working class backgrounds (83 percent working class);[2] The ethnic composition of the families was as follows: 33 percent Anglo-Saxon, 22 percent Asian, 21 percent Eastern European, 17 percent Native Americans, and 7 percent Hispanic. Fifty-two of the subjects were male, forty were female. Their mean age was 37. Curiously enough, neither the class nor ethnic backgrounds of the families nor the age or gender of the ex-patients appeared to be related to family adjustment patterns.

It is important to note that the composition of the families providing care to a mentally ill relative varied. About one-half of the ex-patients were living with their spouses and children; approximately one third were living with their parents and/or siblings; and one quarter were living with their children only.

FINDINGS

(1) The Possession of a "Courtesy Stigma"

Much of the sociological literature on ex-psychiatric patients has centered on the stigma attached to mental illness (e.g., Weinstein, 1983). Freeman and Simmons (1963:162), in their classic study, reported that approximately 70 percent of relatives experienced stigma due to the presence of an ex-patient in the home.

Stigma is a widespread social phenomena that causes considerable angst *not only* for those possessing a stigmatizing/stigmatizable attribute, but also for those with whom an individual is affiliated. In this latter regard, individuals are said to possess a *"courtesy stigma"* (cf. Birenbaum, 1975; Birenbaum and Re, 1983). The data reported here indicates that families of the mentally ill also possess a courtesy stigma, a blemish of affiliation affecting social relations with "normal" others. Specifically, 87 families revealed that they possessed such a stigma. Family members learned the social meaning of their "failing"—that they possessed a courtesy stigma through self-labeling[3] and/or negative experiences with others. Speaking of the negative nature of this affiliational attribute, the mother of an ex-patient said:

> Joe is the one who has had all the psychiatric problems . . . but it's like we are somehow blighted too. People treat us like we have mental problems. They are sort of distant; or they talk down to us. People have been like that with us ever since Joe got out of the hospital and came back to live with us. We're blighted by association! It's a real sad thing.

In a somewhat similar vein, the daughter of an ex-psychiatric patient recounted,

> My friends really started treating me differently when they found out that my dad had been in the psychiatric hospital for over a year. They acted real weird toward me. They stopped asking me to go out with them. I found out that they were afraid that I might go "bonkers" and they didn't want to be around when that happened. It really hurt that they thought that.

Sixty-nine of the families reported that social relations with friends, neighbors, co-workers and other family members were altered upon the entry of an ex-patient into the household. For those families whose courtesy stigma was *not* known to certain others, (and did not want these others to discover it), much of their time was spent attempting to mitigate the stigma potential of mental illness through the employment of various "information management techniques." Indeed, the management of information reflects a process of negotiation for preferred definitions of self. So, for example, 73 percent of the sample curtailed the range of people invited to their homes, imposed limits in terms of places they would frequent and social events they would attend with the ex-patient, and used deceptive practices. Decisions about concealment were made by family members on the basis of their perceptions of others. Such decisions seemed to be based on their perceptions of others' "genuineness," "knowledge about mental illness," "riskiness," "trustworthiness," etc. Speaking on her management work, one sister of an ex-patient summed it up for most respondents when she noted:

> It's just like walking a tightrope. It's a delicate balancing act. You're constantly juggling people and situations. I didn't want the people I work with to know about Jack, so I never asked them home. If they came to pick me up, I'd wait outside on the porch—even if it was twenty below zero.

In addition, families of the mentally ill frequently employed deception (cf. Miall, 1986) as a form of concealment. Such deceptive practices were often rehearsed among family members beforehand. As one respondent put it:

> After a few negative experiences with people, the family got to talking about how to deal with it in the future. We talked about specific circumstances and people who we would tell certain things to. Like the neighbors, we agreed to tell them that our son, Johnny had been away at military college up north—and not the truth, that he had been in the psychiatric hospital.

It is interesting to note that family members employed deceptive practices along with medical disclaimers—"blameless, beyond-my-control interpretations" offered to "... reduce the risk that more morally disreputable interpretations might be applied by naive others discovering the attribute" (Schneider and Conrad, 1980:41). The wife of an ex-patient, speaking on her use of deception and medical disclaimers stated:

> We just moved into this new neighborhood and I couldn't tell them the truth about Harry. I don't think they would have welcomed us with open arms if they knew about his sickness. So, when the neighbors came over and asked why Harry wasn't working, I lied and told them that he was on a disability pension, that he had a stroke and couldn't work anymore. If they knew that he was a pyromaniac, and set fire to our old house, they would have freaked!

By contrast, for those families whose courtesy stigma was known to others, much of their time was spent educating others about mental illness, with a view to enhancing self-esteem or lessening stigma. In these cases, family members made judgments about whom to "educate." As the mother of a young chronic ex-patient stated:

> What we try to do with some people who know about our family situation is to teach them about mental illness. Some people have some strange ideas. If we think that we can reach them, we invite them over to see us at

home with Susan. When they see how she acts and what she has accomplished, and how we act toward her, their eyes are opened. Once you set them straight and they begin responding positively, it makes us feel better.

In short, through successful negotiation between family members and other social actors, both parties come to share the same definition of the situation, thereby avoiding the discrediting of the family member who is affiliated with the mentally ill person.[4]

(2) Role Performance, Role Dissensus and Role Strain

In addition to problems of stigma, another major concern reported by the families of the mentally ill centered on the ex-patients' inability to perform previous,"*normal*" social roles to which they had been assigned. One third of the families in this investigation expressed "feelings of loss." Families once had loved ones who were "normal," occupied "normal roles" and statuses, and met societal expectations within these roles. Families indicated that the social experience of officially diagnosing the patient as mentally ill, the treatment process, subsequent discharge, and post-hospital bizarre behavior was extremely traumatic. Similar to Yarrow et al.'s (1955) study of the accommodation of the mentally ill prior to official labelling and treatment, families also initially optimized or neutralized the outcome of hospitalization. Gradually, after much pain and anguish, however, they came to *accept*: the inability of their loved ones' to perform *"normal"* roles and occupy *"normal"* statuses, the redefinition of these individuals as "mentally ill", its corresponding social roles and statuses, and scaled down normal societal expectations. The husband of an ex-patient captured it for most families when he said,

> At first, I refused to believe Ruth was even sick. I hoped that the doctors were wrong. Then, I thought, she would only be sick for a week or two and then snap out of it. It took a long time of working through my feelings when I began to realize that she was psychotic. And I had to realize that she couldn't be the wife and mother she once was. I had to see her in a new light and scale down what I expected from her.

Just as difficulty with or failure in normal role performance was something with which families had to come to terms with respect to their loved ones, so too, did some experience problems in terms of role dissensus. As Heiss has argued—"the actor's definition of his own role may *not* be the same as other's definition of actor's role and other's definitions of his own role may differ from actor's definition of other's role" (1981: 119-120). Prior to official labelling and hospitalization, individuals and their relatives had clear conceptions of their respective roles and social statuses within the family—a *working consensus* necessary for smooth, effective social interaction. Upon release of the patient from the hospital, over a third of the families in this study reported problematic role dissensus. On the one hand, many ex-patients desired to maintain the "normal," "positive" role definitions and statuses developed in previous interaction with relatives, for example, "head of the household;" relatives, on the other hand, redefined the individual as "mentally impaired," "deviant"—a role and status discrepant from the ex-patient's definition of him/herself. Thus, these definitional discrepancies of roles not only caused disruption in everyday familial social interaction, but often led to open conflict. As one family member put it:

> My husband used to be the boss. He took care of all the bills, the financial decisions, everything in life. Now, since his illness, he is no longer responsible to do anything. He is constantly fighting me though. He wants to resume his role as the boss—the guy in charge, but he is mentally incapable of making these decisions—sometimes, he's lucid, other times, he's not. We quarrel about this constantly.

Another respondent, the child of an ex-patient, spoke about this situation in terms of role reversal:

> I hate the situation that I'm in. I do love my dad, but I'm constantly in a dilemma. On the one hand, I'm his daughter, and I should treat him like a father, but I find myself now being forced to take the role of parent—like he is my child and I am his mother. It's like *we've switched places*. He doesn't like me to make decisions for him and that leads to a lot of problems and arguments.

It is important to note that achievement of a working consensus between family members and the ex-patient in terms of social roles did not necessarily guarantee that subsequent interactions would be routine. In many cases, the families had to contend with role strain, a subjectively-perceived difficulty in meeting the *norms* of the social roles which they have accepted. Spouses, siblings and children spoke of problems in terms of role overload, the excessive demands placed upon them, and lack of time and energy:

> It's now like I have to do it all! Now that I've taken over, I'm responsible for doing all the things my mother used to do around here. The cooking, cleaning, budgeting, looking after my brothers and sisters, gar-dening, shopping and looking after her too. Added to this is the fact that I have to hold down my job at the high school. I volunteer at the church. I am just overwhelmed. I am doing the job of two people. I feel physically and emotionally exhausted...

(3) Family Caregivers: The Positive Effects of Discharge

Much research has focused on the role of the family in affecting recidivism rates of the mentally ill (c.f. Turner and Gartrell 1978:368-382). Indeed, these studies suggest that interaction with significant others affects the community tenure and reintegration of ex-psychiatric patients by encouraging them to perform normal social roles. In the present investigation, while some of the social interaction between family members and ex-patients took the form of conflict and rejection, a great deal of effort was expended by relatives to accommodate these individuals and help them to be reintegrated into society. Over two-thirds of the sample (68 percent) made active (although not always successful) attempts to resocialize and rehabilitate their charges[5].

Social networks of family members acted as informal social support groups, provided ex-patients with suggestions on how to mitigate the stigma potential of mental illness and other problems, aided in obtaining non-sheltered employment, and in general, assisted in the transformation of their deviant identities. Conceiving of their roles as "problem solvers," the sibling of an ex-patient said:

> We've all banded together to help Graham out. Life can be terrible for a psychiatric patient—society tends to shun you. So, we'd sit down and discuss these things with him and give him suggestions on how to effectively deal with it...We take his problems one at a time and help him to work them through.

Another family spoke of how they aided their ex-patient loved one in the transformation of her abnormal, deviant identity and the acceptance of a more "normal" self-conception not only through their redefinition of her but their expectations of her to perform normal social roles:

> We kept telling Betsy that she was discharged and that she was as normal as we were. And we kept emphasizing that we expected that she could carry out a full round of daily activities. She could resume a fairly normal life. We stressed that we thought of her the same way as we did before her illness.

The reinforcement of this non-deviant, normal conception of self on the part of relatives then, coupled with the emphasis on striving for normal attainments, not only enhanced the self-esteem of ex-patients, but also enabled ex-patients to internalize and adopt a more positive self-image and identity.

Just as the ex-patients undoubtedly benefitted in the above respects from the physical, financial and emotional care received from family members, the data indicate that the families *themselves* also benefitted. Approximately one half (46 percent) of the families studied reported that certain positive consequences resulted from the experience of having a relative defined as mentally ill, treated, discharged and returned to the family. In terms of gratifications, families felt that this experience strengthened or solidified familial relationships:

> This whole thing has been a nightmare in one sense, but it actually brought the family together....We pulled together. There was no sense of commitment or caring before, but since Jack's sickness we're much closer and we communicate for the first time. In one sense, it's been somewhat of a blessing in disguise.

In a somewhat similar vein, another family member said:

Before the illness, we were sort of flaky. This tragedy made us rethink things. We realized what we mean to each other. We're a lot closer now.

DISCUSSION AND CONCLUSIONS

This paper was stimulated by two questions: (l) "What are the actual consequences of the shift away from in-patient to community-based care of the mentally ill?" (2) "What are the concomitant social, economic, emotional and psychological costs and benefits of such policy shifts on the family care providers?" Some previous investigations had focused on the effects of deinstitutionalization from the perspectives of the patients, others had centered on the aftercare housing facilities in which such persons are placed; still others followed various patient popu-lations as they participated in community psychiatric treatment programs. These contributions notwithstanding, the effects of this shift in policy on the families of the mentally ill have not been well documented. Indeed, as long as 18 years ago Gunderson speaking on this issue stated, "...there is a pressing need for more careful evaluation of the life of the discharged schizophrenic both in terms of his impact on his family and the community and of the influence of familial support systems and treatment factors on his subsequent life course" (1974: 18).

This study has charted the realm of *negative* and *positive* familial adaptive responses to the presence of an ex-patient in the household. Clearly, the data pointed to such problems as the possession of a courtesy stigma and problems with respect to role performance and role dissensus. The data also indicated that certain positive consequences resulted [for both the ex-patient and the family] from the presence of an ex-patient in the home. In terms of the ex-patient, families provided much needed social support and encouraged the relative to attain normal roles and statuses—in short, the family aided the ex-patient in the transformation of his/her "deviant" identity. Moreover, from the family's perspective, the presence of an ex-patient led, in many cases, to the strengthening and solidifying of familial relationships, a finding not previously well-documented in the literature. Taken together, however, the negative consequences outweigh the positive. The findings presented here may not be unique to families of the mentally ill. Future research might fruitfully examine whether such similar interpersonal dynamics, positive benefits, and negative consequences result from having either a stroke patient or a very elderly relative in the home. Moreover, future research should focus on whether the interpersonal dynamics between ex-patients and their families are altered if the former does not live directly with relatives but lives close by, such as in a boarding home or rooming house. Finally, longitudinal studies on ex-psychiatric patients and their family members undoubtedly warrant consideration. Do burdens and strains lessen over time? Do families "graduate" from one stratagem of stigma management to another? Do levels of family distress increase or decrease over time? Do coping strategies change over time? Such questions would appear to warrant serious consideration.

REFERENCES

Arey, S., and G. Warheit. 1980. "Psychosocial costs of living with psychologically disturbed family members." in L. Robins et al., (eds), *The Social Consequences of Psychiatric Illness*. London: Brunner Maezel.
Birenbaum, A. 1975. "On managing a courtesy stigma." Pp.347–357. In *Deviance: Action, Reaction, Interaction*, edited by F. Scarpitti and P. McFarlane. Reading, Mass.: Addison-Wesley.
Birenbaum, A. and M. Ann Re. 1983. "Family Care Providers: Sources of Role Strain and its Management." *Journal of Family Issues* 4 no. (4): 633–658.
Cockerham, William C. 1992. *Sociology of Mental Disorder*, 3rd ed. Englewood Cliffs, NJ: Prentice-Hall.
Freeman, H.E. and O.G. Simmons. 1963. *The Mental Patient Comes Home*. New York: Wiley.
Gubman, G. and R. Tessler. 1987. "The Impact of Mental Illness on Families: concepts and priorities". *Journal of Family Issues* 8 (2): 226–245.
Gunderson, J. G. 1974. "Special report: schizophrenia, 1974." *Schizophrenia Bulletin* 9:16–54.
Heiss, J. 1981. "Social Roles." Pp. 94–129. In *Social Psychology: Sociological Perspectives*, edited by Morris Rosenberg and Ralph H. Turner. New York: Basic.
Herman, N. *Crazies in the Community: An Ethnographic Study of Ex-Psychiatric Clients in Canadian Society—Stigma, Management Strategies and Identity Transformation*. New York: General Hall (forthcoming).
Hibler, M. 1978. "The problems as seen by the patient's family." *Hospital and Community Psychiatry*, 29 (1): 32–33.
Lefton, Mark, S. Angrist, S. Dinitz and B. Pasamanick. 1962. "Social Class, Expectations and Performance of Mental Patients." *American Journal of Sociology* 68:79–87.
Miall, C. E. 1986. "The Stigma of Involuntary Childlessness: Implications of Self-Labeling." *Social Problems* 33 (4): 268–281.
Schneider, J. and P. Conrad. 1980. "In the Closet with Illness: Epilepsy, Stigma Potential and Information Control." *Social Problems* 28 (1):32–44.
Stoneall, L. 1983. "Dilemmas of Support: Accordian Relations Between Families and the Deinstitutionalized Mentally Ill." *Journal of Family Issues*, 4 (4): 659:676.
Turner, R. J. and J. Gartrell. 1978. "Social Factors in psychiatric outcome." *Journal of Abnormal Psychology* 76: 110–116.
Weinstein, R. M. 1983. "Labeling theory and the attitudes of mental patients: a review." *Journal of Health and Social Behavior* 24: 70–83.
Yarrow, M., C. Green Schwartz, H.S. Murphy, and L. Calhoun Deasy. 1955. "The Psychological Meaning of Mental Illness in the Family." *Journal of Social Issues* 11 (4):12–24.

NOTES

[1] A list of the specific questions is available from the senior author. The open-ended nature of these questions often led to other issues and concerns that the subjects deemed important. Such concerns were then probed further by the researcher.

[2] Social class was defined using the Porter's (1965) socio-economic indice.

[3] Family members learned and internalized stereotypical imagery of mental illness and insanity—imagery that was constantly re-affirmed throughout their lives in the context of social interaction with others, and by the mass media. These images were constantly reaffirmed in ordinary social discourse. On the basis of internalization of these images, such persons perceived themselves as possessing a courtesy stigma.

[4] This is not to imply, however, that all attempts at "education" are successful in their outcome. Many times they are not. Family members reported numerous circumstances when attempts to educate proved disastrous, thereby re-sulting in a renewed construction of the courtesy stigma.

[5] For a detailed discussion of the role of the family in re-integrating the ex-patient, See Herman (forthcoming).

Chapter 30 THE SOCIAL CONSTRUCTION OF HYPNOSIS

Dan E. Miller

Hypnosis fascinates us, calling forth images of unusual, often excessive behavior—of people stretched stiff between two chairs with only their head and heels supporting them. Hypnotic feats such as memory recovery, anaesthesia, and hallucination appear magical and mystical to the casual viewer. Despite scientific and clinical claims of legitimacy (Wester and Smith, 1984), hypnosis has always had a circus sideshow aura about it, with the accompanying demonstrations of the radical possibilities of human behavior.

It was this theatrical dimension that first attracted me to hypnosis. Above all else, hypnosis was a staged presentation, a social act tightly controlled with the behavior of one party directed by the other. Often stretching the boundaries of credulity, hypnosis is a dramatic, visible, researchable arena in which extreme obedience is constructed.[1] In a period of just a few minutes hypnotists can induce extraordinary change in their subjects. Routine perceptions and behavior can be modified to such an extent that a close examination of how the participants construct these social acts is warranted.

This study is not another description of hypnotic phenomena. No clinical treatment program is prescribed. No new theory of hypnosis is forthcoming, though one is implied. Rather, hypnosis interaction is used as a strategic research site for the systematic study of asymmetrical interaction processes. Like Milgram (1974) who studied the strategic qualities of the psychological experiment, I am interested in how the clinical relationship between hypnotherapist and patient is structured through their interactions and how an extreme form of obedience to authority is constructed. Once again, the small groups laboratory serves as the provocative stage (Katovich, 1984) for the demonstration and observation of small group interaction (Couch, Katovich, and Miller, 1987). In this research the interaction processes are analyzed for redundant patterns and sequences that can help explain unquestioned compliance.

Traditionally, analyses of hypnosis have focused on those being hypnotized - on their susceptibility, their perceptions, experiences, and behaviors (cf. Haley, 1990; Hilgard, 1975). More recently, social psychologists have identified hypnosis as a type of influence communication (Platonov, 1959), as a subset of a more general form of interpersonal communication (Kihlstrom, 1985; Sarbin and Coe, 1972). Even given this definitional shift, very little analytical work focuses on the interaction between hypnotist and subject (Miller, 1986; Haley, 1967, 1968). With this shift in focus from the individual to the interaction hypnosis is conceptualized as a social construction, wherein the subject's behavior becomes an emergent quality of the interaction.

Hypnosis is defined as an interaction process in which one participant voluntarily cedes control of self to the direction of the other in order to reach a social objective. Hypnosis is a social act in that an individual cannot organize the extreme behaviors under question by himself (Haley, 1990). The social act is purposive and based on an agreement that subordination is necessary to accomplish the social objective. From the eyes of a child hypnosis appears to be one guy talking to another. One instructs, the other obeys. The topics, foci, and sequences of the interactions are controlled by one party—the hypnotist, who knows how the social act plays out.

Primarily, this research is based on the analysis of thirty video-recorded hypnosis interactions in clinical settings. In addition, both hypnotists and subjects were interviewed. For a period of six months I immersed myself in the world of hypnosis observing, questioning, and noting what I heard, saw, and understood. The larger research project involved three objectives, the mapping of hypnosis interaction, the generation of thick descriptions of extreme obedience (including hypnosis), and the development of theoretical accounts of asymmetrical social forms. This particular piece focuses on the thick description of hypnosis.

SYMMETRIC AND ASYMMETRIC INTERACTION

By treating hypnosis interactions as a strategic research site a more general understanding of asymmetric social interaction and relationships (Miller, 1986; Miller, Weiland, and Couch, 1978) was possible. The process of constructing interaction sequences in which one person cedes control of self to the direction of another to the point of extreme, non-reflexive obedience is not restricted to hypnosis. It was a central issue in the Milgram experiments (Miller, 1987), and it is the object of most military training. How these social relations are constructed, and how they are resisted and breached takes on greater importance when the ubiquitous character of obedience is considered.

Social relationships can be categorized by the form the interaction takes (cf. Simmel, 1950; Weiland, 1975; Couch, 1989). The interaction between a boss and secretary is similar in form, but dissimilar in content to the interaction between hypnotist and subject. In each situation, a superordinate controls the interaction, directing the behavior of the other to a greater extent than does the subordinate. In both relationships participation is voluntary and purposive with the successful completion of the act hinging on an initial agreement and the subsequent differentiation of identities.

In hypnosis interaction, as in other forms of interaction (Miller, Hintz, and Couch, 1975), the participants must attend to and be responsive to each other. They must establish situated, simultaneous identities of hypnotist/therapist and subject/patient, and then organize their interaction sequences toward a social objective, i.e., becoming hypnotized or getting treatment. These hierarchically organized dimensions of interaction must be maintained in order to sustain any coordinated social interaction, including hypnosis. It is with these dimensions of interrelatedness that subjects introduce resistance through inattentiveness, non-responsiveness, identity negotiation, or by initiating an independent sequence of interaction.

Hypnosis interaction is characterized by an articulated social objective in the form of a socially projected future. This is not the case in all asymmetrical interactions, e.g., muggings. This agreement differentiates authority relations from tyrannical social acts

(Miller, Weiland, and Couch, 1978). It is noteworthy that within the certain context of established identities and a shared social objective smooth asymmetrical interaction sequences are constructed. This non-problematic quality of authority interaction is of central importance. Extreme obedience can only be constructed if the directives of superordinates are not questioned by subordinates. Such questions challenge identities and the objectives of the proceedings. The non-reflexive automaticity often found in the behavior of subordinates indicates an agreement regarding identities and objectives.

In routine authority interaction instruction-obedience sequences most often are non-problematically coordinated—rationalized as necessary and practical. However, the degree of control necessary in the construction of extreme obedience poses problems for the superordinate (or hypnotist). The interaction continually must be monitored, with new sequences of acts regularly introduced at a pace that maximizes superordinate control and minimizes reflexive subordinate thought. Thoughtful subordinates are resistant to extreme obedience. This resistance can, at times, be negotiated or remedied, but often it leads to a breach in the control.

The ability to control interaction is learned early on. Routinely, children manipulate interaction with their parents. For example:

Child: Daddy?
Parent: Yes, Nate?
Child: You said you would wrestle with me. Let's wrestle!
Parent: Okay.

Here the child asks a specific question of a parent that redirects the parent's attention toward the child. The question is intended to generate a simple response on the part of the parent in the form of an open query, thus giving the speaking turn back to the child. The child then introduces a previous agreement to construct the situated social act of wrestling. The child focuses the interaction with a social objective and congruent identities. The parent, growing more responsive to the child, agrees to participate, accepting the identity and social objective as introduced by the child.

In symmetrical interaction sequences each participant initiates, responds, comments, interrupts, and so on. A geometric symmetry is evident in the reciprocity of self-disclosures and competition for control. On the other hand, asymmetrical sequences involve one participant initiating courses of interaction while other(s) respond. One instructs the other complies. Reciprocity and control clearly are asymmetrical in form.

Minimally, authority relationships are triadic, involving an interacting dyad and an over-arching other that contextualizes the interaction, providing standpoint, an established past, and a vocabulary of motives to the participants. Office managers frequently indicate the backing of the organization in their claims on workers time and labor.

As in other authority relationships subjects must recognize the hypnotists as legitimate and competent. Again, the organizational relationship is invoked. Identified as a representative of a clinical, medical, or scientific community the hypnotist represents a larger enterprise engaged in serious business and imbued with much significance. The situation at hand is thus contextualized as a meaningful part of this larger social activity. Successful hypnosis and therapy can be constructed contingent on the patient ceding control of the proceedings to the hypnotist.

In addition, subjects/patients often attribute extraordinary abilities and powers to their hypnotists and their therapists. This charismatic dimension to the interaction provides a source of meaning to subjects who are encouraged to perceive their hypnotic behavior (or therapeutic change) as "involuntary" and "magical." Similarly, patients frequently define their doctors or therapists as having "healing powers." Both hypnotists and therapists anticipate these attributions, using them to their advantage in the construction of unquestioned compliance.

PROCEDURES FOR DATA GENERATION AND ANALYSIS

Given an interactional focus, "It would seem practical to begin an investigation of hypnosis with an analysis of what can be seen and recorded on film ... and thereby limit what needs to be inferred from the subject's behavior" (Haley, 1990:24). By focusing on the observable social processes between hypnotist and subject certain questions can be addressed. What interaction sequences lead to specific outcomes? How do hypnotists overcome resistance to their directions? How are these interaction sequences similar to other sequences?

Two hypnotists, both clinical psychologists, were used for the study. Thirty hypnotherapy sessions were video-recorded using a wide-angle lens. The camera was positioned in the room so as to capture hypnotist and subject in the same frame. In this way the attending and nonverbal acts of the participants, on-going simultaneously, become socially visible. Both verbal and nonverbal sequences are more easily transcribed, coded, and interpreted than with split screens and/or close-ups.

All verbal interactions were carefully transcribed onto a time line. Using the transcripts along with the video-recordings, twenty-five interaction categories were coded and mapped onto the time line. The data were analyzed by denoting redundant sequences and larger patterns of interaction. A cybernetic approach was used to analyze the data. Some hypnosis interactions were successfully completed, while others failed to a greater or lesser degree. Beginning at the terminus of the social acts it is possible to identify necessary interaction sequences that lead to specific outcomes.

In addition to identifying necessary and hierarchically organized sequences of interaction, thick descriptions of the interaction were generated (Geertz, 1973), often by explaining what was happening on the video-recordings to naive observers. Interviewing hypnotists and subjects provided detailed information on the strategies and experiences involved in the interactions. Often, when describing what people are doing, we resort to the actors' purposes, their social objectives. An adequate description of interaction requires an immersion into the social processes that produce those objectives.

OPENING SEQUENCES

Hypnosis interaction was not successfully constructed in all instances. Thirty subjects met their appointments, tentatively accepting the identity of patient/subject in the projected situated social act. In the opening sequences the hypnotist invariably identified himself with his title while identifying the subject with their given name.

H: Hello. I'm Dr. _____, and you must be Roger.

In instances where a diminutive of the first name was possible the hypnotist would ask if the subject was called by it.

H: Do you prefer being called Charlie?

Immediately, the hypnotist had defined a differentiated relationship based on forms of address (Brown and Ford, 1961), and assigned each to their respective positions. In addition, the subject was on the hypnotist's turf, complete with chairs, table, books, diplomas, and professional clutter.

H: Please, come into my office.

Situated in appropriate chairs the subjects were informed that they were being video-recorded for purposes of analysis and future reference. All were asked if they had any questions before proceeding. Each stage of this benign looking opening implicated the participants into the act. Going into the office, sitting in the assigned place, and being asked if one has any questions implies that hypnosis interaction is imminent.

The directives and questions not only called for certain responses, they also defined the relationship and the projected future. The form of this relationship was more complex than the hypnotist-subject/instruction-obedience dimensions suggest. An explicit agreement had been made that preceded the instruction-obedience sequencing, and on which the hypnosis interaction hinged. This agreement was a solidary pact, i.e., "We are going to do this act so that I/you can get better." Differentiated identities and subordination to the directives of the other were contextualized by this agreement.

Solidary identities are a necessary foundation for authority relations. In an important sense this understanding calls into question the necessity of legitimacy in authority relationships. Rather, subordinates have only to agree to the differentiation and the social objective for the social act to be constructed. That agreement may be enhanced by a corporate identity, but this may not be necessary.

During the opening sequences six subjects got cold feet. Initially, they had indicated a willingness to be hypnotized, but they grew hesitant about performing embarrassing acts. Hypnosis is not automatic. It is a social construction with some negotiation, particularly early on. Hypnosis interaction proceedings were initiated with the remaining twenty four participants. However, five were highly resistant to the instruction-obedience sequencing initiated by the hypnotists. In these five cases the interaction broke down as the subjects refused to subordinate themselves to the direction of the hypnotist.

Of the nineteen remaining subjects eleven entered into hypnosis interaction with only modest resistance, while eight constructed highly obedient, non-reflexive interaction, i.e., deep hypnosis. In each of these nineteen situations the subjects ceded control of their behavior to the direction of the hypnotist. They grew highly attentive and responsive to the acts of the hypnotist and to little else.

INTERACTION CONTROL

Hypnosis interaction consists entirely of instruction-obedience sequences. Once initiated there was an immediate and radical shift in the action. The hypnotist resituated self in a more upright posture, slightly higher than the subject. Immediately, the hypnotist initiated instructions that called for simple, obedient responses, a focusing of attention, and smooth non-problematic responsiveness.

H: I want you to sit back in your chair.
S: (sits back)
H: Take a deep breath...
S: (breathes in deeply)
H: and relax.
S: (release of breath and muscular tension)

With each response the hypnotist issued another instruction adding additional foci and complexity to the interaction. The form these interaction sequences took was extremely simple - an almost pure instruction-obedience sequential structure. In these interactions the hypnotist instructed, suggested, commented, and directed while the subject congruently responded.

The instructions at this early stage were benign and reasonable. The hypnotist controlled the agenda. He knew the sequences of acts necessary to construct the social act. He understood and anticipated the responses of the subjects. Even so the hypnotist continually monitored the behavior of the subjects in relation to the instructions given and the progressive stage of the interaction. Rigid, set instructions without monitoring and without continual adjustments by superordinates did not work. Subordinates soon disengaged from their non-thoughtful obedience.

Though induction strategies varied, the hypnotists continually acted to minimize conflicting extraneous data once the interaction has settled into a non-problematic instruction-obedience sequence. Extraneous intrusions were controlled in two ways. First, the hypnotist was on his own turf. He disconnected the phone and insulated the interacting dyad in an inner office. Second, and more importantly, the attention and responsive behavior of the subject was focused on the time and situation at hand. The subjects' temporal and spatial contexts were collapsed to the moment. All else evaporated.

VOLUNTARY TO "INVOLUNTARY" SEQUENCING

Additional complexity to the structure of the interactions was introduced when the hypnotist, through a set of instructions induced the subjects to construct acts on an "involuntary" basis. From the moment of the solidary agreement the hypnotist introduced two strands of instructions that involved an apparent contradiction. In time a transformation occurred. From the subject's perspective voluntary participation became detached witnessing of "involuntary" action. This movement from voluntary to involuntary is universal in hypnosis (Haley, 1990).

The behavior was "involuntary" only as experienced by the subject. Clearly, the subject acted and responded. There was no objective sense of involution. Another sense of involuntary can be noted. The behavior called for by the hypnotist was highly unusual and could not be self-organized by most people. Indeed, at this stage of hypnosis interaction it was not clear that subjects could easily resist the instructions of the hypnotist.

As the instruction-obedience sequences proceed, the subject's resistance decreased. The subject grew more responsive in that the delay between instruction and obedient response decreased, creating a non-reflexive responsive quality to the interaction. That is, the subjects only responded, thus deleting any future temporal orientation by subjects. Their future was imbedded in the instructions of the hypnotist to whom they had ceded control. In time, sometimes rapid, sometimes gradual, the subjects discontinued contextualizing their acts. Behavior, experience, and perception collapsed to the immediate moment. An automaticity developed.

Conversely, the hypnotist had to stay attuned to the temporal and relational dimensions of the interaction. He took on an elongated temporal orientation that was highly complex and problematic, incorporating the totality of the social act. Unlike the subject the hypnotist remained frosty, alert to the congruence and nextness of the response and the stepwise progression of the hypnosis interaction and the therapeutic objective.

Often, as the interaction moved toward "involuntary" obedience, subjects were instructed to view their actions from a detached, "objective" perspective - to see or report what was happening. At the same time they were attending to and responding to the instructions in a conscious manner. In the hand levitation method subjects were instructed to sit down, relax, put their hands in their lap. Then the hypnotist continued,

H: I don't want you to move your hand... just notice the feelings in it. As you breathe you will see your hand beginning to lift...
S: (watches hand twitching and moving slightly)
H: lifting... lifting... lifting...
S: (watches hand lifting)

The subjects were aware of their surroundings, but not troubled by them. They were following instructions that were paradoxical and contradictory. "Attend to me, do what I say, and watch your hand lifting involuntarily," and "Pay close attention to me, do as I say, and witness yourself falling asleep" were common interwoven strands of paradoxical instructions given simultaneously in the hypnosis interactions. Subjects had little trouble complying with the contradictory instructions, nor did they comment on the apparent paradox. At this level of hierarchical complexity the hypnotists were able to instruct the subjects to construct extreme acts.

No self-consciousness was evident. The subjects evaluated neither the hypnotists' behavior nor their own. Most reported that nothing unusual was felt. Some reported attending to the recent past and the present experience. Others reported no awareness. Given the flow of the interaction and the simultaneous, paradoxical instructions, there was little time for the subjects to do anything but to act as instructed, and this was by design. Full attention to the minutia of the present demands successfully extinguished any awareness of the larger context.

Gradual stepwise compliance without pressure is not peculiar to hypnosis. It formed the basis of extreme obedience in the Milgram experiments, in which the subjects obeyed the instructions of the experimenter to give small, insignificant shocks in short, progressive sequences. In a short period of time the experimenter called for 450 volts of electrical shock to be administered to the unresponsive learner. In these situations the vast majority of subjects complied. However, in those situations in which the subjects were instructed to immediately administer high levels of shock great resistance was generated. The gradual character of the process in the context of science enticed and seduced many of Milgram's subjects (Miller, 1987). Any awareness of the consequences of their actions was lost in the attention to detail in the present.

The series of contradictory instructions provided the basis for a test that the hypnotists used to reveal the quality and meaning of the subjects' participation. Skeptics of hypnosis have insisted that good subjects can be instructed to simulate hypnosis with the same outcomes (cf. Barber, 1969; Orne, 1971). Even though the simulation incorporated instruction-obedience sequences, a fundamental difference exists. The simulating behavior of good subjects implies the parallel, helpful behavior of equals, and it requires a continued, attentive, self-conscious, and voluntary mode of compliance.

The test for extreme obedience (deep hypnosis as opposed to simulating) involves a display of "involuntary" compliance. Once the hypnotist had gained control of the interaction, introduced contradictory instructions, and established instruction-obedience sequences along with a detached perspective, then "involuntary" acts were introduced into the interaction. Subjects were instructed to monitor their body, witnessing it grow more and more rigid.

H: The harder you try to move your body the more rigid it becomes.

These instructions only appeared to be contradictory. The subject had been instructed to attend to the hypnotist, monitor his behavior, and comply with the instructions. "Try to bend your body while at the same time noticing its increasing rigidity." The test came when the subject was placed with only head and heels supporting his weight between two chairs. Simulating subjects grow weary and resistant. When extremely obedient subjects gradually were instructed to "notice the numbness" in their hand and arm and to insert their hand and forearms into a bucket of ice water for a period of a few minutes, simulating subjects indicated pain.

The experiences and perceptions of the hypnotic subjects were organized as detached observers, as instructed. The subjects no longer authored their own perceptions and experiences. This realm of mind had been captured and controlled by the hypnotist. The test provided an indication to the hypnotist that the subject was not thinking, not helping, and not faking it. The test looked for delayed responsiveness and an incongruent of meaning.

With hypnotic subjects there is a certain lack of awareness that something unusual is happening that is not found with simulating subjects. This is most clearly expressed in "unacknowledged agency." Clearly, subjects placed their hands and forearms in ice water. However, their verbal reports were matter of fact descriptions with no self-awareness in the description, "There is a hand and arm in the ice water." It was not experienced as theirs.

The test is best described by Haley's Conundrum. If the subject cooperates, then he will be able to do things "involuntarily" in time. However, if the subject does voluntarily what must be done "involuntarily," then he has broken the negotiated agreement. With extreme obedience there is an accompanying denial of agency.

OVERCOMING RESISTANCE

The central problem faced by the hypnotists involved overcoming the subjects' resistance to subordinating their behavior to the direction of the hypnotist. Any attempt to change the relationship between hypnotist and subject through a change in the interaction patterns was defined as an act of resistance. Tactics of resistance included inattentiveness and non-responsiveness, disobedience, initiating an alternative course of interaction, commenting, questioning, or any act that attempted to define the relationship as symmetrical.

Primarily, the hypnotist focused his efforts on maintaining control, on minimizing and eliminating resistance. However, some resistance was common, particularly in the early stages of hypnosis. Expressed as embarrassed smiling, a lack of eye-contact, delayed responding, frivolous behavior, over-curiosity (questions, looking around), or too cooperative compliance, resistance was successfully overcome by "jumping a level."

By "jumping a level," hypnotists created a context of apparent control, a metacomplementary context. That is, the hypnotist redefined the situation as one in which the subject was allowed to initiate courses of action. If the subject commented on the situation, then the hypnotist instructed the subject to do a running commentary on what was happening. That is, the hypnotist instructed the subject to continue resisting, thereby maintaining a level of mutual interest while at the same time reinstituting asymmetricality.

Five of the thirty therapy subjects were very resistant. By actively initiating alternative courses of behavior, interrupting instructions, asking for the purpose of the instructions, and simply not responding to the instructions the subjects effectively breached the interaction. Two forms of resistance proved most difficult for the hypnotists to overcome. Subjects who simply did not respond to the instructions were very quickly dismissed. In addition, one subject who continued to pose questions, e.g., "What do you mean by that?" and "Is this necessary?" so disconcerted the hypnotist that the interaction disintegrated.

With the less resistant subjects the hypnotists took their time, speaking clearly and decisively. Their style was cool, detached, and confident. Any response at all, no matter how minimal, was treated as compliance. The hypnotist minimized resistance by sequencing instructions in the early stages that were difficult to not obey, e.g., "Come in, sit down, relax,... ." If there was a delay, then the hypnotist would string-out the instructions, and work on decreasing the delay time between instruction and compliance. In order to regain control of the interaction the hypnotist either had to deflect the subjects from a line of behavior, or he incorporated their behavior into the construction of the asymmetrical interaction. One particularly boisterous subject was told sternly to "Sit down, shut up, and listen." The subject was so taken aback that he readily complied. Another determinedly disobedient subject was told to disobey all the instructions and to carefully witness what happened so that he could report on the effects of disobedience. A subject that was too cooperative was instructed to help in the proceedings.

Metacomplementary situations are common. Whenever superordinates allow subordinates to "take control" and initiate a course of action, that independent control often is highly circumscribed. The context, identities, meanings, and perspectives have been established, and any autonomous behavior or interaction control on the part of the subordinate is illusory.

For example, in some therapeutic metacomplementary contexts patients are "allowed" to remember past experiences. However, this act of remembering is performed in a highly contrived and controlled context in relation to instructions and comments made by the therapist that demand a specific kind of remembering. No matter how this appears, it is not an autonomous reconstruction of past events. Rather, it is a social construction of memory in a purposive social act. This becomes apparent in the following example of age regressed memory.

H: As I count to ten you will see yourself growing younger. ... ten ... you are now a seven year old sitting at home watching your favorite television program. Tell me what you see.

S: I'm watching Walt Disney with my brother. We're watching Lady and the Tramp. This man did not have a TV set at age seven.[2]

Even though obedience can be elaborately rationalized, doing so is a form of resistance. Hypnotists and superordinates desire immediate, non-reflexive compliance to their instructions. Self-elaboration and on-going accounts implicitly question the basis for and purpose of the instructions. Responses are delayed while the acts are contextualized. Highly obedient subjects in authority relations neither call for nor provide accounts. Their actions, no longer self-organized through internal conversation, have become extensions of the purposive actions of the hypnotist, the authorized representative of clinical psychology.

CONCLUSION

What is interesting about and frightening about hypnosis and authority relations is how easy it is to construct extreme, non-reflexive obedience. The pervasive and mundane character of obedience to authority belies the underlying possibilities. It is too easy to invoke the horrors of Nazi extermination camps and the tragic consequences of Jim Jones' charismatic following in Guyana. Authority and obedient subjects constitute the central structure of most social organizations from families, to schools, to corporations, to the government.

In addition, obedience to authority is an important method of getting others to do dirty work (Hughes, 1964). Unmeasurable damage is done to society by crimes of obedience (Kelman and Hamilton, 1989). For many people compliance with the demands of superordinates is achieved through necessity, e.g., keeping one's job. For too many, though, obedience is automatic, and is neither rationalized by nor troublesome for subordinates who may not even recognize themselves as subordinates.

In one situation in which an overly cooperative hypnotic subject was instructed to help the hypnotist, the subject was never "aware" that he was participating in hypnotic interaction. Yet the identities, the topics, the projected futures, and the action of each were controlled by the hypnotist. The appearance of egalitarian helping was deceptive. Perhaps, then, in the highly dependent relationships such as those in schools or corporations, the highly controlled, over-arching relations and contexts therein promote the illusion of freedom, initiative, and self-determination.

These analyses indicate the certainty with which the hearts and minds of others can be controlled through the social construction and maintenance of asymmetrical social relationships. If self is a function of our involvements in social relationships and social acts, then we must question Blumer's assertion that our behaviors are meaningfully organized through self-indications and purposive action. To the extent that authority relations (and other forms of asymmetric relations) are common, then self must be understood in those asymmetric social relational and social interactional terms. This study must conclude by questioning our taken-for-granted assumptions about our autonomy, mutuality, and individuality. Are these things real, or are they part of the illusory contexts generated in the complex, metacomplementary network of interactions that constitutes social life?

NOTES

1. Frank Kohout first introduced me to the works of Jay Haley and Milton H. Erickson in 1973. He and Carl Couch have supported and encouraged this line of research.
2. Recent evidence from critical investigations of victim abuse therapy strongly indicates that "memories" of early abuse revealed in therapy sessions are, in fact, socially constructed from the perspective of the therapists and are far more consistent with therapeutic expectations than with patient histories (Watters, 1993).

REFERENCES

Barber, T. X. 1969. *Hypnosis: An Experimental Approach*. New York: Van Nostrand.
Brown, Roger and Marguerite Ford. 1961. Address in American English. *Journal of Abnormal and Social Psychology* 62:375–385.
Couch, Carl J. 1987. *Researching Social Processes in the Laboratory*. Greenwich, CN: JAI Press.
———. 1989. Social Processes and Relationships. Dix Hills, NY: General Hall.
Couch, Carl J., Michael A. Katovich, and Dan E. Miller. 1987. "The sorrowful tale of small groups research." *Studies in Symbolic Interaction* 8:159–180.
Geertz, Clifford. 1973. *The Interpretation of Cultures*. New York: Basic Books.
Haley, Jay. 1967. *Advanced Techniques of Hypnosis and Therapy: Selected Papers of Milton H. Erickson, M.D.* New York: Grune and Stratton.
Haley, Jay. 1968. "An interactional explanation of hypnosis." In Don D. Jackson (ed.), *Therapy, Communication, and Change*. Palo Alto, CA: Science and Behavior Books.
Haley, Jay. 1990. *Strategies of Psychotherapy*. New York: Triangle Press.
Hilgard, Ernest R. 1975. Hypnosis. *Annual Review of Psychology* 26:157–180.
Hughes, Everett C. 1964. "Good people and dirty work." In Howard S. Becker (ed.), *The Other Side*. New York: The Free Press.
Katovich, Michael A. 1984. "Symbolic interaction and experimentation: the laboratory as provocative stage." *Studies in Symbolic Interaction* 5:49–67.
Kelman, Herbert and V. Lee Hamilton. 1989. *Crimes of Obedience: Toward a Social Psychology of Authority and Responsibility*. New Haven: Yale University Press.

Kihlstrom, John F. 1985. Hypnosis. *Annual Review of Psychology* 36:385–418.

Milgram, Stanley. 1974. *Obedience to Authority.* New York: Harper and Row.

Miller, Dan E. 1986. "Hypnosis as asymmetric interaction." *Studies in Symbolic Interaction, Supplement 2: The Iowa School*: 174–194.

———. 1987. Milgram redux: obedience and disobedience in authority relations. In Norman K. Denzin (ed.), *Studies in Symbolic Interaction* 8. Greenwich, CN: JAI Press.

Miller, Dan E., Robert A. Hintz, and Carl J. Couch. 1975. "The elements and structure of openings." *Sociological Quarterly* 16:479–499.

Miller, Dan E., Marion Weiland, and Carl J. Couch. 1978. "Tyranny." In Norman K. Denzin (ed.), *Studies in Symbolic Interaction.* Greenwich, CN: JAI Press.

Orne, Martin T. 1971. "The simulation of hypnosis: why, how, and what it means." *International Journal of Clinical and Experimental Hypnosis* 19:183–210.

Platonov, K. I. 1959. *The Word as a Physiological and Therapeutic Factor.* Moscow: Foreign Languages Publication House.

Sarbin, Theodore, and William Coe. 1972. *Hypnosis: A Social Psychological Analysis of Influence Communication.* New York: Holt, Rinehart, and Winston.

Simmel, Georg. 1950. *The Sociology of Georg Simmel.* Edited and Translated by Kurt Wolff. New York: Free Press.

Watters, Ethan. 1993. Doors of memory. *Mother Jones* 18 (January/ February):24–29, 76–77.

Weiland, Marion. 1975. "Forms of social relations." In Carl J. Couch and Robert A. Hintz (eds.), *Constructing Social Life.* Champaign, IL: Stipes Publishing.

Wester, W. C. and A. H. Smith. 1984. *Clinical Hypnosis.* Philadelphia: J. B. Lippincott.

Chapter 31 THE EMERGENCE AND MAINTENANCE
OF A DEVIANT SUB-CULTURE:
THE CASE OF HUNTING/POACHING
SUB-CULTURE

Richard A. Brymer

Sociology has made heavy use of the concept "sub-culture" in explaining and analyzing deviance. Generally, it is used to account for socially organized and patterned deviance as it exists in communities. The notion of sub-culture helps to understand the apparent paradox of the immorality of deviance *and* its continued existence. In spite of the importance of this concept, it remains a "sensitizing" concept that is barely analyzed and is, indeed, ignored (McCarthy-Smith 1990). Some analysis of the emergence of deviant sub-cultures has appeared in the work of Cohen (1955), Kitsuse and Dietrick (1959) and others. This work generally emphasizes the "collective reactions" of disenfranchised groups as they pursue solutions to the status frustrations imposed by middle class institutions.

In my view, all of these works suffer from two problems. First, none *does* any historical analysis. In their analysis of current sub-cultures few—especially labelling theorists—examine the detailed day-to-day ties between the deviant world and the straight world, even though their argument suggests that such ties should exist. Rather the ethnographic discussions treat the sub-culture as essentially static and isolated from the rest of society. Finally, none of the foregoing perspectives uses an approach to history which would locate sub-cultures as part of the more general process of the development of scalar complexity in human societies.

In this paper, I address these problems by examining a sub-culture in the context of its history and its location in the development of human societies (Johnson and Earle 1987; Raybeck 1991). I suggest that changes in the organization and content of sub-cultures are a result of continued contact and negotiation with the dominant cultural world. The dominant cultural world, in turn, changes its responses to the sub-cultural world so as to give its world a new "problem" to solve. Thus the relationship between deviants and "straights" is not static, but interactive or dialectical. I conceive of the straight world as providing not only a reactive or proactive focus, but as also providing an opportunity structure which makes it possible for members of sub-cultures to create new ways of *"being"* deviant. This latter point is suggested by Farberman (1975) but not elaborated.

The data are provided in a case study of one type of hunting/poaching sub-culture which has as a part of its repertoire systematic violation of game laws. My experience with this sub-culture spans 45 years, in many locales in North America, including Canada, the United States and Northern Mexico.[1] It is further reinforced by the experiences of my father and grandfather as contained in their oral histories and memories which date to the middle 1800s. These orally transmitted historical events on which I draw occurred in the frontier move from the southeastern United States into Texas.

I have also consulted historical sources where appropriate, although these are rarely directly valuable because few deviants write their own history. Rather, such documents are written by crusaders against the deviance, legislators and politicians who create laws and the various persons charged with controlling the deviance. Thus one must read between many, many lines.[2] My data from years of experience in these different locales reveal very similar and consistent patterns of one type of hunting/poaching sub-culture, and we now turn to these patterns.

Hunting/Poaching Sub-Cultures and Their History

Introduction

Historically, hunting, along with gathering, was the major mode of subsistence for the smallest scale societies. Recent or contemporary examples include the Great Basic Shoshone and the peoples of the Kalahari in southern Africa. With the development of more complex extractive technologies and their associated, more complex social organization, human groups placed less and less dependence on hunting, and comparatively fewer person hours were involved (Johnson and Earle 1987:309-310).

Hunting has continued to exist, and is carried out by a small number of persons in North America. As an activity, however, it is now located in a very complex industrial society, and its nature has been transformed by this "new" location. A very significant path of its new existence in an industrial society concerns game laws and official agencies responsible for their enforcement. While the vast majority of modern hunters are law-abiding, there are various groups who more or less routinely violate game laws, and these violations are socially and culturally patterned. This patterning would seem to qualify them as sub-cultures of the larger North American industrial society. I suggest that there are four main types of illegal hunting/poaching sub-cultures. Each has its own level of organizational sophistication (Best and Luckenbill 1982:25) and a different rationale for engaging in such activity. These types are as follows.

Market Hunters

These groups operate strictly for profit and are often international in scope. Their purpose is to kill large numbers of commercially valuable game animals and to sell them on a black market. In Best and Luckenbill's (1982:25) terms, they exhibit a high degree of formal organization that can approach that of the currently notorious Colombian cocaine cartel. Occasionally more localized "mobs" (Best and Luckenbill 1982:25) will pursue this illegal market activity, although their division of labor and knowledge of the black market suggest some formal organizational connections.

Trophy Hunters and Guides

The purpose of these hunters and guides is not to kill large numbers of animals, but to obtain a single high quality "trophy." Most guide services are legal and above-board because of a high commitment to conservationist values and, also, because of the strict and multi-level surveillance of such activities. The presence of trophy hunters who are willing to pay extremely high prices for illegal trophies does serve, however, as an opportunity structure for a minority of guides, as well as a motive to carry out such illegal activities. A high degree of organizational sophistication is required to enter forbidden areas, to negotiate international boundaries and avoid international law enforcement.

Tourist Hunters

These are persons who work and live in urban areas and cannot afford, or do not use, guides. They are not connected with rural kinship networks and thus they must hunt wherever they can, often in areas with which they are not familiar. This may lead them into game law violation. The organizational level appears to be that of the peer or friendship group (Best and Luckenbill 1982:25).

My primary focus in this paper is on the fourth type, Local Rural Hunters.

Local Rural Hunters

These are traditional hunters whose activities are holdovers from a pre-industrial, agrarian communal/familial network. With the imposition, by the state, of game and property laws, many of their activities became illegal. Yet, they continue to hunt and their interaction with various authorities and "outside others" has produced a type of sub-culture. Not all of their activities are illegal, by any means, but some are.

The organizational nuclei of this sub-culture are extended families, still retaining rural lands which serve as the centre of their hunting territories. Even though they may work in town, the members of such groups commute home, and pursue an essentially "rural" lifestyle. The hunting territories may be small or large, depending upon the traditions and requirements of the geographical area, but will usually have been "in the family" for at least three generations, and often longer. This home tract may also provide the basis for extended hunting claims on land that may now be owned by the government or absentee landlords. If such lands have traditionally been hunted for generations, they too may form part of the "territory." The groups is this sub-culture also include members who may live and work in distant urban areas, but return periodically to hunt with their extended kin. Finally, the social network may include non-familial members who, for a variety of reasons, have established fictive kin relations of interpersonal trust. Such groups are tightly knit, and outsiders are likely to be distrusted and treated with a friendly but formal distancing.

Hunting is viewed as a "traditional activity"; it is not engaged in for profit or personal gain. Indeed, it is not defined as fun or recreation in the sense of other leisure activities such as vacations, dances, etc. Hunting is the performance of a traditional role. A primary value is to *actively* hunt the game, making a clean kill or tracking a wounded animal until it is located. Game is rarely lost as tracking skills are the basis for personal status, and intimate long-term knowledge of the area is vital in this regard. "Tourists," in contrast, often lose game because of lack of knowledge and skill and, hence, are defined by the Local Rurals as "deviant." Finds of dead or wounded animals are occasions of great pejorative debate and discussion as to who might be the culprit (fieldnotes 1980, 1985).

The game taken is also used and wastage is negatively sanctioned, as in the oft-used phrase (especially when socializing younger members), "If you're not going to eat it, don't kill it; and if you do kill it, you damned well be *ready* to eat it!" Almost total usage of the animal occurs, although intestines and stomachs and other tripe are eaten only by a few small sub-cultural groups. What isn't consumed by the nuclei is fed to pets or farm animals, and hides are either tanned for gloves and other clothing or are traded for "favors" with other Local Rurals.

Another value is sharing game within the social network so that, even when few animals are taken, "at least everyone gets a taste" (fieldnotes 1986). This is analogous to Christian Communion in that consuming the game is an affirmation of membership in the network and in the tradition. This is particularly true when the game is illegally obtained and, thus, the boundary between insiders and outsiders is demonstrated. Alternatively, to refuse, or be refused, commensality is to be set apart. I was pretty sure that I was eating venison, but I was told that it was an older steer. Sharing is also extended to network members who, for reasons of age or physical infirmity, are unable to actively hunt. "Great-aunt _____ hasn't gotten her deer yet this year, son, so go and get her a nice, young fat doe" (Father to son, fieldnotes 1980). Great Aunt _____'s membership in the network is thus affirmed.[3]

Forms of poaching include taking game out of season, or without a proper license, or by other illegal means. Game laws are often viewed as arbitrary and illegitimate invasions of the state into a traditional activity that is governed by its members.

(X): I've been hunting [this area] for forty years and no damned game warden is going to tell me when and where I can hunt.
(Brymer): What if the warden catches you?
(X): I'd like to see that s.o.b. try, because I know [this area] better than anyone and can outrun any one through it. (Field notes, 1987).

Sometimes bag limits are exceeded, but only if someone "needs" it or the hunters/poachers' judgment of the game population is at variance with that of the governmental agency that sets the limits. If the hunters/poachers judge that there are too few animals, bag limits are kept small, or they voluntarily restrict hunting in claimed or owned territories. I have personal recollections and fieldnotes detailing such judgments. In at least one case, hunting was suspended for a four-year period. During this time, the "official" judgment retained previously set limits. Conversely, when the hunter/poachers' judgment is that there are "too many," legal bag limits are routinely ignored and the game-sharing network is intensified and, sometimes, expanded. Occasionally, for example, an additional freezer will be purchased solely for storing extra game. At other times, canning, drying and jerky preparation (especially for larger game animals) will help to handle the need for storage and avoid violation of the taboo against waste.

History

I was introduced to hunting/poaching and its history (and am now perhaps part of it) 45 years ago by my grandfather. He and my grandmother were share-cropping a small ranch in southwest Texas, and I went to live with them. He had a one-third share of the goat crop, and kept chickens and two cows, selling the eggs and cream for cash—a scarce commodity. Subsistence activities were routine, including fishing, hunting and foraging for wild fruits and berries. Food was provided by fresh or canned garden produce, roosters and goats that came out of his share. Skim milk was processed into clabber (thick, sour milk) and cottage cheese; honey and bartered cane syrup provided the only sweeteners. About the only foods purchased were pastry flour, sugar, coffee and tea.

> One day we were riding the mule checking the goats and, as usual, my grandfather was carrying his cheap, single-shot shotgun. He saw and shot a large wild turkey gobbler, and I was overjoyed. This was not only meat for several meals, but it meant roast turkey(!), as opposed to the small frying roosters we ate occasionally and the more regular goat. I was allowed to carry the turkey home and was thrilled to be able to make the presentation to my grandmother. In this day and age, it is difficult to appreciate the significance of this event.
>
> As we approached the house, my grandfather stopped about a quarter mile from the house and told me to stay there with the turkey until he came for me, because someone was at the house. A few minutes later he returned for me, and I was introduced to the fact that we had just killed a turkey illegally. The man at the house had been a neighboring gossip. I had no idea that my grandfather didn't have a license, that it was "out of season," and that shooting turkeys was illegal anyway. We were also riding a rule and one wasn't supposed to shoot from a mule.

Although this is a personal and retrospective account, I think that my grandfather was a typical representative of the category "redneck" and was caught in the vortex of change from an essentially pre-industrial, agrarian society to an industrial, urban one. Our lifestyle in 1945 was little different from that described by Roebuck and Hickson (1982) as characteristic of the antebellum white southerner. Roebuck and Hickson (1982) provide the most recent survey of the historical emergence of the redneck as a type of white southerner. They focus on racism as a defining characteristic of the southern redneck, but ignore analogues of the plantation economy in other contemporary geographical locations in agri-business, factory-ship fishing and the mechanization of herding and stock-farming which has led to the death of the small, family farm. Even where a slave economy is not present, these analogues did give rise to similar types of sub-cultures, at least with respect to hunting and poaching. In addition to white southern lower-class rednecks, those affected include the *rancheros* of Northern Mexico, the "cowboys" (marginal ranchers) of Western Canada and the U.S., the marginal farmers of Northern Ontario, Quebec and the Maritimes, and the marginal fisherman of the Maritimes.[4] While these groups lack the racist traits that southern rednecks exhibit, they have a healthy distrust and disrespect for outsiders and "tourists," and they *all* engage in hunting/poaching styles of the "local rural" type.

All of these groups have been squeezed off the land and now work at the mercy of the industries of the post-industrial state. Nevertheless, they retain an identification with the values of a long-gone pre-industrial era that focuses on *using* land in a communal sense rather than *owning* it as a commodity. In their traditional hunting practices, rural poachers are doing roughly the same thing that their forefathers did, though some of their activities are now illegal. They have become more or less instant and involuntary deviants. More importantly, knowledge of their own deviance, coupled with a vigorous sense of individualism and a populist distrust of authority, has led them to construct a deviant sub-culture in a self-conscious manner. On the one hand, they want to continue this tradition; on the other, they are aware of the power and organization of the state which enforces laws and can have consequences for their total lives.

This leads to a kind of "cops-and-robbers" contest between members of the sub-culture, and the state and its enforcers. As new laws and surveillance tactics are developed, the sub-cultural group attempts to create counter-tactics. If a counter-tactic works, or if a new hunting technology is developed, then the Game Law enforcers respond, creating a new problem for the sub-culture. Not only is there constant improvement of surveillance technology, but the increasing public objection to hunting means that the sub-culture's members now must both contend with the problem of informers and maintain even tighter internal social control. This kind of dialectical interaction appears to account for the continuing change in the hunting/poaching sub-culture.

Dialectical Interactions with the State and with the Community

In this section, I illustrate some instances of problems that the hunter/poaching sub-culture has with the State and with their own community. Within the community, I note two layers of problems; first, there is the problem of internal social control in the extended family nucleus; the second problem concerns maintaining relationships with other extended family nuclei in the same small rural community. Concern with the latter problem is generated by the fact that there is competition between nuclei for use of "unowned" or government land and disputes over what constitute the boundaries of "territorial" hunting tracts. This problem may be exacerbated because the same individual may belong to competing nuclei. The in-laws of group X may in fact be sisters and brothers or other kind of group Y. Thus, individuals may be able to choose the hunting group to which they wish to be identified. Generally, membership is more or less exclusive and longlasting, given the extreme sense of trust necessary to evade the authorities. At times, this can become a *very* divisive issue. Such problems are reminiscent of Richard Lee's (1984:57-61) discussion of the same kinds of difficulties occurring among the Dobe!Kung of the Kalahari.

All of the problems noted above derive from the position of the local game law enforcers, or game wardens as they shall be henceforth called. It is not widely known, but game wardens have a legal mandate that is sometimes broader than that of the usual police authorities. The following passage appears in *Hunting Regulations: Summary, Fall '88-Spring '89*, Ministry of Natural Resources, Ontario, p. 8:

> OFFICERS: An Officer may, without a search warrant:
> 1. Stop, enter and search any aircraft, vehicle, or vessel;
> 2. enter and search any fishing, hunting, mining, lumber or construction camp or any office of any common carrier; and
> 3. open and inspect any truck, box, bag, parcel or receptacle if he has reasonable groups for believing that any of the above contain game or fish taken, shipped or possessed in contravention of the Game and Fish Act and Regulations...
> An officer has the authority to request information about hunting and fishing.

Most other Canadian national and provincial and U.S. national and state jurisdictions have similar laws and regulations. Additionally, game wardens can call upon police forces for aid and assistance in investigations which are crimes under various wildlife acts. This potentially creates a substantial police presence with which the sub-culture must cope. In fact, directive (2) above has been construed as referring to homes and outbuildings which are believed to be used as a hunting base (Fieldnotes 1986).

Compounding the problem for the sub-culture is the recent attempt to involve the general citizenry in surveillance. Just as hot-lines have been set up by police for criminal offenses, so hot-lines have been set up and particularly focussed on poachers in certain jurisdictions. Such hot-lines maintain confidentiality and allow for anonymous tips. Such services are often advertised at sports shows and are often part of displays by various hunting and fishing groups. Occasionally, these groups will also distribute free Violation Report Forms with self-addressed postage-paid envelopes. Such tactics have also become weapons, in small communities, to settle feuds between nuclei. And, as with most tactics, the poachers themselves occasionally put them to use.

Problems with the State

Some problems stemming from game laws have already been solved by the sub-culture, and are now a part of their cultural knowledge. Most jurisdictions have laws against baiting game animals with salt or feed. This challenge has been fairly easily resolved by the rural locals because they generally either own small tracts of land, or lease grazing rights. They pasture the odd cow or horse on this land, and provide *that* animal with a salt lick, or with a small patch of oats or other small grain. In drier climes, water tanks are often set up. Should a game animal avail itself of the facility and get killed, it can then be argued that this was not the original intent of the landholder. This is a convenient, but demonstrably true, rationale, because farm animals need salt, water and food —just as a game animal does.

Another tactical problem already solved by rural hunters has been the game wardens' use of mandatory checkpoints on major thoroughfares. Given the broad mandate in most jurisdictions, very thorough checks can be made and are very effective against tourist hunters. Once known, though, these points are almost useless against local rurals, whose knowledge of the area often exceeds that of the game wardens. Back roads and old ranch or logging roads across private property are well known. The recent advent of small four-wheel drive and all-terrain vehicles is also an effective solution to road checks. Technology in the form of Citizen's Band radios also allows members to ascertain the location of, and avoid game wardens fairly easily, either through contact with local base operators or through monitoring the game wardens' own frequencies. Game wardens in some jurisdictions are beginning to react to this situation by shifting to other means of radio communication, often involving the use of military systems.

Jack-lighting, or taking game at night with the use of a light to "freeze" them, is a technique that has a very interesting history. It was originally developed in pre-industrial times when pine-knot torches were used with birch-bark or whitened leather reflectors to concentrate the light in the eyes of the game animal, usually a ruminant. It is a *very* effective technique for taking game animals. Its history more or less parallels the technological history of concentrated lights. Historically, kerosene lamps and candles were concentrated by using mirrors in what is known as a "bull's eye lantern." Then followed the use of pressure-operated lights using mantles. Each new development led to more and more game taken. Eventually, most jurisdictions made such techniques illegal and the practices then became part of the deviant sub-culture.

Once the practice was ruled illegal, the nature of the "contest" shifted to the use of light that was minimally detectable. One solution was to use telescopic sights, which don't require "silhouette" sighting, against a broadly lit target. During this phase, various automobile headlights were used, but game wardens responded by using hydraulically powered small "cherry picker" crane to achieve a height from which lights could be observed for fairly long distances, especially in prairie-like settings. One of the latest technological responses has been to use extremely small quartz halogen lights, with long beam concentrators, which are mounted on scopes with mercury microswitches, allowing the light to be turned on by simply raising the rifle to the firing position. These lights, and the scopes, are pre-targeted. The short duration of lighting activity is effective in taking animals, but difficult for enforcers to observe. Ironically, such devices are legal in the state of Texas for hunting predators, and they are advertised in the magazine published by the Texas Department of Parks and Wildlife (Texas Parks Wildlife 1975:19, 24).

A problem that has recently been solved by at least one group concerns doe and buck tags, which must be affixed through an animal's nose once it has been killed, to establish certification of limits. A hunter is issued a certain number of tags along with his or her hunting license, and may, in some jurisdictions, apply for special doe tags, which are issued according to the ratio of bucks-to-does for a territory. If there are too many does, then doe tags are issued on a lottery basis, and in the jurisdiction in question, traditionally most (90% according to one state publication) hunters received a doe tag upon application.

For the year in question though, there was an abrupt drop in doe tags to around 10%, and it was a year of high unemployment, and the meat itself became rather important. The local nuclei came and went during the hunting season according to their work schedules, so that no one was exactly sure how many doe tags were available in any given hunting party. As the season drew to a close, the hunt patriarch suggested that one shoot whatever came out of the bush, and on the last day of the hunt, with no deer, the group killed four; two illegal does, one legal doe, and one legal buck, because there was only one doe tag among that particular group.

This constituted an immediate problem for the group, because they had three does and only one doe tag, and the deer had to be transported to the central location. Each deer needed a tag for this transportation process. The tag consists of a horse-shoe shaped wire, which is inserted through the deer's nostril, and a "super-glue" tag which is sealed around it, and is presumably, irremovable. The solution, arrived at after discussion, was to gut the doe, put *half* of the tag in place, so that it could be transferred to the next deer, and then a missionaries/cannibals/river and one boat solution was created. Each illegal doe was taken out with the "half-tag" in place, which could be full-tagged if a warden were to locate them. Then, the driver of the ATV would return with the tag, and the next need was taken out, and so on. The `illegal' deer was hidden in the forest, and later butchered. This was an immediately created and spontaneous solution to a problem.

It was also an evolved solution that entered the group's cultural repertoire. After the episode, anxiety was ventilated, and, over supper, a discussion of other possibilities for manipulating tags began to occur, and even later, members began to experiment with unused buck tags to determine how the 'glue' might be manipulated for multiple uses. The practice was also passed on to other groups, and now appears to be embedded in the local cultural tradition.

Another problem that has *not* yet been solved by the sub-culture also stems from the evolution of technological complexity. A recent developed in wildlife research has been the use of electronic transmitters affixed to game animals such that their movements can be tracked by radio telemetry. This research has been very productive in the development of scientific knowledge about game animals, and will ultimately allow for more conservation of game. In the short term however, it produces a problem for the hunter/poacher. When the radio transmitter stops moving for any length of time, or ceases transmission, the research biologist assumes that the animal is dead, locates its last known position and attempts to retrieve it for study.

From the poachers' perspective, this provides very detailed information about his illegal act and its location, and leads to an official actively seeking the animal, something a poacher avoids at all costs. While collar transmitters are fairly obvious, implanted ones are not. Thus far, poachers are worrying about how to locate such implants, or what to do should they shoot a collared animal. The current consensus is that one looks for transplants before one shoots, but, should one miss seeing the tag and kill the animal, one should immediately leave the scene and warn all others in the party. This is the chosen action, despite the fact that most regulations state that hunters will not be penalized in any way (See Hunting Regulations: Summary, Fall, 1988, Spring, 1989, Ontario, p.iv for an example from the Ontario jurisdiction). Local rurals simply do not trust governmental statements. Currently, no acceptable solution to the problem of electronic monitoring has been developed. Some hunter/poachers are turning to their more electronically sophisticated friends for information, but it is hard to discuss the immediate problem with such friends, because they are not usually part of the extended family network.

Extended Family Nuclei and Local Community Problems

Problems stem from a variety of sources. Both extended family nucleus members, and the members of other nuclei are usually mature males and as such are granted personal autonomy and individual freedom to do as they please within the local community. All are members of the local community, share the same values and often share the same intimate knowledge of the area, although obviously each nucleus specializes in its own territory. But members of such groups may so outrageously violate game laws as to focus official attention on the entire community. Such events do happen and are especially problematic for the entire local community.

The case of the Judas X is an excellent example. This case was one of the most problematic cases I have ever encountered, and has had consequences that have lasted to the present; and yes, the term Judas *was* used by locals to describe him!

In 1980, a few weeks prior to the opening of hunting season, Judas, a member of nucleus X, killed an animal at night on a rural road and butchered it a few yards away. He was turned in (on a hot-line), and the next morning game wardens, local and state police were on the scene investigating the crime. The location of the kill was closest to nucleus Y, and on a road that gave access to some 12 other nuclei. Initial suspicion fell on these nuclei, with the result that barns and outbuilding were searched, and many persons in the area were interviewed. The next few days saw the investigation spread to more outlying areas. Patrols by all levels of police were increased, and checkpoints were set up in order to question and search all traffic, the author included.

The impact was devastating, and the initial reaction was a drastic escalation of inter- and intra-nuclear gossip to figure out who was involved, and how the nuclear unit might protect itself. Suspicion and distrust, even inside nuclei, was rampant. The local community had lost its moral basis. Once the identity of the suspect was known, then all nuclei shifted their strategies to distance themselves from Judas and nucleus X, and reaffirm their own boundaries to ensure distancing and information control.

Ironically, the animal was never found, and Judas was never charged. The social order of the community was disturbed and remained so for at least three years. Other consequences will be discussed below.

Equally, there is inter-nuclei competition concerning territorial boundaries and "use" of land. This is particularly true if a section of the territory has not been used for some time; in such a case, it is deemed "vacant" and up for grabs. Finally, members of other nuclei are potential members of one's own nucleus; should the numbers of a given nucleus drop, there may be competition for their loyalties.

The social control of insiders is especially difficult. Where all are ostensible equals, decisions about hunting and poaching get made by an often lengthy discussion and debate process. Yet the equality is rhetorical; there are major differences *within* the group. Some members are simply better hunters and trackers; others have more knowledge of the outside world and are better able to negotiate on behalf of the nucleus. Decisions are arrived at on a consensual basis that takes these differences into account. One is reminded of the decision-making process of the !Kung described by Richard Lee (1984:87–90).

One method of controlling the behavior of members and maintaining a boundary vis-a-vis other nuclei is the development of a highly specialized argot that refers to a particular group's experiences. Such an argot is replete with undefined references that are incomprehensible without knowledge of the group's history, for example: "Do you remember where X sat when Y shot the deer two years ago? We'll got a couple of hundred years past that to where the old tree fell down and watch there. The deer will probably be coming from over the rise" (fieldnotes). That communication is impossible for any outsider to understand.

Other methods of control are the usual teasing and joking, with mock threats, and discussions of possible consequences of hypothetical acts. Inside such groups, detailed information is also passed around, particularly by permanent residents when talking to their temporarily visiting kin. The two or three days before a hunt are usually filled with recounting of the past year's activity. This occurred in the Judas case mentioned above, and information was passed on in great detail, with instructions that extreme care must be taken in the future. Furthermore, hunting areas were shifted to regions that were least likely to come under observation because they were so distant from even minor roads, and were located on locked private property.

Another control mechanism is ostracism and expulsion from the local community. In the season immediately following the Judas case, post-hunt activities included discussions of opportunities to poach that were not taken because of increased surveillance due to the case. Judas was the subject of much threat and pejoration. Apparently the same kind of discussions took place in nucleus X, because gossip had it that a fellow nucleus member distrusted him and used a "hot-line" to turn him in. This was adjudged appropriate treatment for a Judas. The process took about two years, but it was apparently effective. He not only lost his place in his own nucleus, but in the entire community, for no other nucleus would take him in, and he left the community. This incident occurred in the early 1980s, and recent contact with the nuclei reveal that the individual is still gone, and that no one has heard from him or tried to maintain contact with him. The case continues to be part of the exemplary lore of the area (fieldnotes 1980–88).[5]

Another form of control is the use of outright lies. The following case illustrates the process. I had been invited to go hunting with a family nucleus who were my relations and friends, but with whom I had never been hunting. Before the hunt, I was informed that X was an untrustworthy "old fart" who would tell anybody anything. Yet he was a family member and therefore included. As we were hunting on line stands, individual members were separated by several hundred yards and hills and ravine. Line stands require that hunters form a line at right angles to deer trails, separated from each other by a "safe" distance. Deer drift through, and by the end of the hunt the persons on the last stand would walk back through and pick everyone up. "X" was on the stand, and I was on the second, with the others strung out in order. I heard a few shots further "down" the line. When the group reached my position, they said that they had gotten a doe, but not to say anything about it because they didn't want X to know, and that they would come back and pick it up that night. I said nothing and we ended the hunt with the usual few beers and supper. When X left, I asked if they needed my help to go and get the deer. At that point, they told me that they really hadn't shot a deer but were just fooling around and teasing me. As a hunter, I know that they are testing my trust in the hunting situation. I was invited back several times so I know I passed *that* test, because further forms of game law violation were revealed. X didn't pass, and although he was allowed to hunt, no further information was revealed to him nor was he allowed to witness poaching. He eventually withdrew from hunting, voluntarily, a few years later (fieldnotes 1978–89).

Such information control and explicit testing often takes place over lengthy periods of time and it is rare for complete strangers to be taken in. One simply must have some prior stake in or connection with, the group. Even then, trust is only gradually developed. It is as if there are only two extreme levels of sanction involved in control. The lowest level is simple joking, teasing and nicknaming. If these methods are employed, a member can come to be progressively and gradually trusted and given more responsibility for maintaining secrecy and involvement in poaching. One's involvement can be halted at any level, as in the case of X. The highest and ultimate level of control is banishment.

A more poignant problem for the local rural sub-culture concerns the increasing pervasiveness of a preservationist ideology on the nuclear family itself. Children are an important source of recruits for poaching sub-culture and the maintenance of a local rural lifestyle. As these children are exposed to this ideology in TV programs and in school, the more they appears to question and withdraw from the local rural ideology. It represents perhaps the severest threat to the continued existence of the sub-culture. The only solution has been to lower the age at which adults socialize their children into such local rural values in theory and practice. This often has the consequence that children become separated from their anti-hunting classmates at earlier ages.

In summary, internal and external problems must be handled by the sub-culture. External problems are handled on a trial-and-error basis, and mostly solved by technology or modifications in hunting practices. Internal problems are a more delicate matter, because they deal with basic values and membership in the network, yet there are few techniques for dealing with them. Fission of a group, be it voluntary or involuntary is an ultimate outcome, but this disrupts the balance of the entire network and violates the basic value of communal sharing.

CONCLUSIONS

In this paper, I have described a sub-culture that is based in an extension of values and hunting practices originating, at the latest, in the early 1800s in a pre-industrial agrarian era. It has it analogues in other parts of North America. Many of the values have remained the same over nearly two centuries.

Comparisons with the !Kung suggest that some of the same cultural values and internal problems also occur in small-scale societies. What has changed is that the hunting practices have become deviant by virtue of the emergence of an increased level of complexity which includes not only game laws but game law enforcers. Self-consciously, the sub-culture's members have responded in ways that allow them and their culture to remain in existence. Technological changes provide one dimension along which such changes have occurred. Perhaps more deeply divisive has been the response of the sub-culture to its social milieu which now includes potential informers who, in previous eras, would have been neighbors. This change has led to an increased need to screen carefully any new members and to guard boundaries somewhat more closely. It is also possible that increased fission will lead to the demise of the sub-culture.

I suggest that sociologists and anthropologists should study deviant sub-cultures historically, and that some of the changes in these sub-cultures can be traced to the "new" locations of these groups in more recently evolved, organizational levels of complexity. Thus I argue that a sub-culture cannot be fully understood by an analysis of its existence in a given present. Hunting/poaching sub-cultures have had a long history and are clearly able to adapt to new milieux. The cost, however, may be high, and some sub-cultural populations may be extirpated, as were the buffalo and passenger pigeon.[6]

REFERENCES

Best, Joel and David F. Luckenbill. 1982. *Organizing Deviance*. Englewood Cliffs, NJ: Prentice-Hall.
Brymer, R.A. and B. Farris. 1967. Ethical and Political Dilemmas in the Investigation of Deviance: A Study of Juvenile Delinquency. In *Ethics, Politics and Social Research*, edited by Gideon Sjoberg, pp. 219–318. Cambridge, MA: Schenkman Publishing.
Cohen, Albert K. 1955. *Delinquent Boys*. New York: The Free Press.
Cohen, S. 1972. *Folk Devils and Moral Panics*. London: MacGibbon and Kee.
Farberman, Harvey A. 1975. A Criminogenic Market Structure: The Automobile Industry. *Sociological Quarterly* 16 (4):438–457.
Hebdige, Dick. 1979. *Subculture: The Meaning of Style*. London: Methuen.
Johnson, Allen W. and Timothy Earle. 1987. *The Evolution of Human Societies*. Palo Alto: Stanford University Press.
Kitsuse, John I. and David C. Dietrick. 1959. Delinquent Boys: A Critique. *American Sociological Review* 24 (2):208.
Lee, Richard B. 1984. *The Dobe !Kung*. New York: Holt, Rinehart and Winston.
McCarthy-Smith, Melody-Ann. 1990. Gay Communities, Gay World: The Evolution of Institutional Completeness and Organizational Sophistication. Unpublished MA Thesis, McMaster University.
McPherson, Naomi. 1991. A Question of Morality: Sorcery and Concepts of Deviance Among the Kabana, West New Britain. *Anthropologica* 33:127–143.

Ministry of Natural Resources, Ontario. 1988–89. Hunting Regulations: Summary, Fall '88–Spring '89. Ottawa: Ministry of Natural Resources, Ontario.

Mungham, Geoff and Geoff Pearson, eds. 1976. *Working Class Youth Culture.* London: Routledge & Kegan Paul.

Okihiro, Norman R. 1989. Outport Poaching: An Ethnographic Account. Paper presented at the Annual Meeting of the Canadian Association of Sociology and Anthropology, Laval University, Quebec.

Raybeck, Douglas. 1991. Deviance, Labeling Theory and the Concept of Scale. *Anthropologica* 33:17–38.

Roebuck, Julian B. and Mark Hickson, III. 1982. *The Southern Redneck: A Phenomenological Class Study.* New York: Praeger.

Sahlins, Marshall D. 1965. On the Sociology of Primitive Exchange. In *The Relevance of Models for Social Anthropology*, edited by Michael Banton, pp. 199–236. A.S.A. Monographs No. 1. London: Tavistock.

Taylor, Ian, Paul Walton and Jock Young. 1973. *The New Criminology: For a Social Theory of Deviance.* London: Routledge & Kegan Paul.

Texas Parks and Wildlife Department. 1975. *Texas Parks and Wildlife Magazine* (September).

Thomas, Richard A. 1983. *The Politics of Hunting.* Aldershot Gower.

Thompson, E.P. 1975. *Whigs and Hunters: The Origin of the Black Act.* London: Penguin.

Willis, Paul. 1977. *Learning to Labour: How Working Class Kids Get Working Class Jobs.* Farnborough, Hants.: Saxon House.

NOTES

[1] Because of the nature of the data in this chapter, we shall use composite cases constructed from scenes and characteristics from different locales and time frames (Brymer and Farris 1967:315–316).

[2] A similar problem arises in the work of E.P. Thompson (1975). His work on hunting and poaching in the early 18th century in England uses data drawn largely from legal and other archival state records, and he notes the difficulty in making inferences as to the organization of the poachers themselves. I might note that there are similarities in the patterns he locates and mine, but there are many more differences.

[3] In line with my assertion that this sub-culture has deep pre-industrial roots, note how closely it matches Sahlins' analysis of generalized reciprocity (Sahlins 1965:147 and, passim, 186–200).

[4] See Okihiro (1989) for a strikingly similar description of contemporary outport Newfoundlanders.

[5] The lack of a concrete and definitive resolution of this case is very similar to that of case Jean in McPerson's chapter in this volume. Even though they were not resolved, they both entered the cultural memory of the groups.

[6] The death of all hunting has been predicted, for England at least, by Thomas (1983). I will address this comparison in future work.

Chapter 32 HE'S A LUMBERJACK AND HE'S *NOT* OKAY: THE FALL OF THE URBAN TREE MAN[1]

Mary Lorenz Dietz

INTRODUCTION

In the fifties, Detroit was a different city. It had its own character; it was not tied to murder and urban decay. Detroit was a car town—the motor city, a great place for sports and music even before Motown. Detroit was a tough and mean blue-collar city. The symphony always struggled, there was no city ballet, little live theater, really no 'culture' of the kind found in Boston, New York, or even Chicago. But Detroit was something special in those days and it had something, besides the automobile industry, that set it apart from other big cities. Detroit had trees. Not little, spindly, half-dead trees like the one that grew in Brooklyn; Detroit had real trees. Big trees. Full grown trees. Spreading, shady, over-the-top-of houses trees. Oak and maple and walnut, but mostly big stately elms. Detroit had trees in the front and back of nearly every house and school. Trees enough so that almost every family had at least one. Beautiful trees that by early summer stretched from each side of the street to meet in the middle and form a lacy canopy. And Detroit had Tree Men. Not hedge trimmers or flower planters but real urban lumberjacks.

This ethnography is the story of the urban lumberjacks of Detroit. It tells in their words about the job they did, how they felt about it, and the changes that they feel destroyed it. Their story epitomizes the price we have paid and continue to pay for 'progress.' It demonstrates the costs in human dignity and alienation that occur when we disregard the human nature of work and the human cost of change.

THE DATA

I had it in my mind to do research on urban lumberjacks (my term for them) since I worked for the City of Detroit as a swimming instructor when I was in university. My family were lumberjacks in the Northern Michigan woods and on Sweden's Baltic coast. When my brother took a job as a tree trimmer (Tree Artisan was the job title) I was immediately taken with similarities and differences between the work of the city Tree Men and the loggers in the lumber camps. I mentioned my interest to the Tree Men once I started doing sociological work, and they were pleased that anyone would think they were important enough to study and write about. As so often happens with research ideas, this one went into a file and was forgotten for many years. Not long ago my brother said to me "If you plan to do any research on us you better do it now. It's all over. You can write your book and title it "the death of the urban lumberjack." I had spent many hours with this group over the years. We attended common sports events, weddings, christenings, and graduations. I felt sorry that I had forgotten my promise to write about them. So I collected my camera and a tape recorder and began the study. He was right, they were almost all gone. But the ones who were left were eager to talk to me. One man, who had retired the year before, drove eighty miles into the city to give me an interview. Another day four of them sat for hours in an unheated garage answering my questions and talking about the job. (I was the only one who was cold)

The data presented here represent observation of and lengthy interviews with nine old-timers who worked out of the forestry yards, primarily on the East Side of Detroit during this thirty year period (1950-1980). This paper describes the changing scene in Detroit as it moved from being a major industrial center to an urban catastrophe. Within the context of rapid social and technological change, several aspects of the urban lumberjack culture are examined for career patterns which became central to the identity of these men. Also examined is how skills, job setting, and an occupational community are used to maintain self-worth during a period in history when manual labor became obsolete and manual laborers became the urban poor.

Detroit—1950 to 1980

The urban lumberjack job and its demise is tied in to the City of Detroit itself. Detroit is located in the state of Michigan which was one of the earliest states to be lumbered off and left barren in the 19th century. In upper Michigan remnants of the massive forests are still preserved in parkland, and second growth trees are still "harvested" as they like to say now.

> In Michigan, the word was, pine floated like cork on the rivers, trees grew so thick a squirrel could travel five hundred miles without touching ground and best of all the place wasn't too civilized yet. (Wells, 1978:32)
> From the 1870's to the 1890's, when Wisconsin moved ahead, Michigan led all other states in lumber production. In the last half of the nineteenth century, the value of its pineries' output surpassed by a billion dollars the gold panned or mined on the West Coast during the sixty years after the rush for California riches that began in 1849. (Wells, 1978:191)

Detroit developed from a fort and port town and sprawled in all directions. The massive automobile plants emerged, became "war plants" during world War II, and then returned to automobile production after the war. Mass transit was always a joke in Detroit, the whole idea was that everyone should have at least one car for transportation. Those who did not have cars, mainly poor blacks and Southern Appalachian whites, were in downtown ghettos close enough to the plants and the limited public transit to make do. Detroit was unique in having more single-family dwelling units and more trees per capita than any other industrial city in the world. Because of the housing patterns in Detroit and some forward looking city planners, Detroit was "reforested" early and extensively. The majority of people who moved to Detroit and stayed were skilled tradespersons or laborers with little formal education or training. Unlike New York and Chicago, Detroit never developed a professional base nor established high culture. For some people, working for the city and state governments provided a means to move into white collar occupations, or a chance to work some place besides the factories or simply a more secure job environment for low-skill workers.

In addition to being a blue collar city, Detroit tended to attract people who wanted to have a housing environment different from the usual big city high-rises. Detroit homes had yards and the streets were planted with trees, mainly elms. During the post World War II period most Detroiters had very achievable goals. They wanted to have their own homes, cars, and decent paying jobs. The threat of automation was there but it did not really sink in to the minds of the blue collar workers who were, for the most part, achieving the "American dream" of being better off than their parents. Prior to the Civil Rights Movement Detroit was segregated, but many blacks as well as whites were upwardly mobile.

Dutch Elm Disease

In 1950, the first Japanese Beetle was spotted and the first cases of Dutch Elm were diagnosed. Eleven trees were removed that year. The disease advanced rapidly and by 1959 there were 1,919 known cases. By 1970, 96,000 trees had succumbed to Dutch Elm and been removed. At that time they estimated that there were still 150,000 elms on the street and 130,000 in the parks. As late as 1969 there were still also 180,000 elms on private property around the homes of Detroit residents. However, up until that time they were still spraying, although as they were required to use less effective chemicals, they had less control of the advancement of the disease. During the 1970s the removal rates increased until the late 1980s when the elms were almost gone. At the same time the trimming and repair almost ceased and the number of men working for forestry decreased, as attrition occurred when men left or retired and were not replaced.

The Construction of the Job Identity

Many of the men who came to work for the Forestry Division in the early years were already finding it difficult to fit into modern society. They were men whose time had passed in terms of the skills they had and the kind of work they were comfortable in doing. Nor did they fit into the standard civil service mode. They were not very interested in upward mobility. Most felt constrained and guilty if they did not put in an "honest" day's work. They were uncomfortable with closed-in areas and limited space.

> The old-timers, the old lumberjacks. And they were probably born in the wrong spot in that city in Detroit but their work was here for 'em and they just caught on and they loved it... (Soupy)
> They were throwbacks, they really were and there's not many of them left. I don't think there's any of them left in the woods anymore. I don't know where those guys are now. Probably riggers. (Soupy)

> You're gonna have to get some of the guys that are not even here because you go in our yard the only two people you're gonna talk to about it is Greek and I. (Swede)

The men who worked in the trees constructed an identity for themselves as solid, down-to-earth, hard-working, tough, and unique. It was a matter of pride for them that they took the pain, withstood the cold, and did the hard work. They knew they were not academically skilled, but they developed a job-related image based on their quick thinking, toughness, strength, agility, and ability to climb and to work in the big trees. This identity centered on job skills and knowledge and being able to do something they knew other people were afraid to do. It was supported in their friendships and the camaraderie developed in their all male peer group. They liked the challenge and competition. They considered themselves knowledgeable about trees and about tree work and believed that this knowledge and these skills placed them above other laborers. They knew they were skilled workers in a skilled trade even if their pay and status did not reflect this. The pay was low so that, in order to maintain the job and the skilled trade identity, most of the men had to work private jobs which consisted of doing tree work on their own for private owners at night and on week-ends.

> ...and its true that they were underpaid as far as I'm concerned. They were a lot more valuable than they were being compensated for. But I always felt you spent three months out there in the winter time—and I remember Cobo Hall in January out there tryin' to make a hole for the tree with hammers and wedges, cold, cold down there by the river—you know at 10 below you're still out there working. But when the grass started greening and the flowering crab started to flower you'd say those three months were worth it because you'd see your neighbors going to Ford or Plymouth or Chrysler and you'd be goin' outside. April and May and October was glorious—January, February and March was a bummer and in March you'd start planting your trees. You had something going there. You broke the back of it. So I always felt that even though it was hard there was plenty of compensation for me just knowing that I was going to be outside. (Soupy)

The job varied by assignment and by season and this was another plus to men who had rejected the monotony of the factory.

> We trimmed, removed, topped all year long but we had other jobs we did like weed spray, Dutch Elm Spray. We did playground equipment. We had water and cultivating, planting of bare root and ball.[2] We had Dutch Elm survey. This is all different jobs we did throughout the season. (Swede)

Indeed, the wooden creatures and constructions made by the Forestry Division in Detroit from the trees they cut down were recognized as models for playgrounds throughout the world.

The men[3] who took the jobs up to about 1960 had varied backgrounds. Many of them had been in the armed forces in World War II or Korea or in between those wars. Some had lumbering traditions in their families and most of them could have taken or moved to other kinds of occupations. The job identity that they constructed was in part due to the kind of people who elected to work for forestry rather than do the other types of work that were available to them.

Selecting the Job—the Reasons

Most of the men who worked for forestry considered themselves to have chosen the work rather than to have drifted into the job incidentally. This does not mean that this work was the career dream that they had growing up, instead it meant to them that it was the kind of job that they could work at and feel comfortable with themselves. They felt that forestry work—being Tree Men—somehow maintained their integrity.

> I was raised on a farm so I liked outdoor work. I worked in the shop but I didn't care for it. (Kraut)
> I seen it (the job) on the streets. I was doin' cement work but I seen what they were doin' and I liked the looks of it. I wanted to be that. I wanted to have that pride. I wasn't thinkin' money. I was thinkin' prestige. My dad, my parents were from lumber people...that's what I wanted to do... (Swede)
> I was workin' in the Chrysler Plant and I was laid off. When you came here you had a job! (P.J)
> I took the job and I liked the job. I tried to quit, you know, but I really enjoyed it. (Greek)
> I knew a few people there and I thought it would be neat to try. I was doing drafting too. Yeah, it seemed like a good thing to do outside. (Checkers)

The work meant something to them. It made them feel good about themselves. The ones who couldn't make it went back to the plants or worked for City Maintenance. Something in the ability to relate the job to the past and to encapsulate it as a complete occupation made the men doing this job think of themselves as something special. They had an attitude about themselves and the job, and they felt that was what set them apart. They thought of themselves as skilled, as professionals.

> We had something no one else had too...we had a real professional staff...as long as you've got professionalism...you're in pretty good shape... (Soupy)
> I figured we did a job most people couldn't do. I felt I was better. I still do. That's the kind of attitude we had. That's what makes us, that attitude. When you had that attitude, you were there. You were a tree man. (Swede)
> The same general breed of guys. A lot of pride, attitude, drive, you know, stick-to-it-iveness. I think pride was the big thing. I think alot of guys drew on the same background. They were generally from work-oriented families....most of the guys were ex-servicemen and they had been around and out a little bit. They didn't want to work the shops and this was tough, it was a tough job. One out of a hundred actually stuck. I'd see nine guys come on the job and come back later to get a tool and maybe eight of these or sometimes all nine would be gone. (O'Malley)

Gale Miller quotes William Goode's 1957 description of the characteristic of professional communities as follows:

1. Members share a similar identity.
2. Membership is long term and continuing because few members leave the profession.
3. Members share a set of values.
4. Members share a definition of professional and client roles.
5. Members share a language.
6. Members are controlled by the professional community.
7. The professional community has boundaries which are recognized by members of the community and the public.
8. The professional community controls recruitment and training so that new generations of competent professionals continually enter the community. (1978:124)

Miller argues that the professions are not the only work communities that exist in modern society and that some other work communities share many of the same characteristics. He also points out that in modern industrial work the personnel department operation undermines the traditional power of the foreman, something that did not and has not yet occurred with the urban lumberjacks. To this day the foreman with the city tree crews retains a powerful position. He is the boss and really the only boss that the urban lumberjacks have.

> Everybody that's been here, up until now, has worked his way up fair. I always felt that by having somebody here that knows the work and knows the people then they can kind of act like an insulator. You know all the stuff that comes down from up above. But the guys on the crew like the foremen and the seniors, they got it tough. They got it tough 'cause they're catchin' it from the bottom and they're catchin' it from the top and it's a miserable hard job. (Soupy)
>
> It used to be a whole job. You got to be foreman by knowing the job. Paper work keeps up but it's a menial part of it, it wasn't a big part. Today, today it's all paper. (Kraut)

The Personal Qualities of Tree Men

The urban lumberjack possessed certain personal qualities that the men associated with being able to do the job. They separated these qualities out from the job skills and knowledge that they gained on the job. These personal qualities—having attitude and pride, toughness and competitiveness—were qualities that were admired and expected. Not surprisingly, the urban lumberjacks felt most of their peers possessed these qualities which are described in more detail in the following accounts.

When the urban lumberjacks talked about having attitude, they referred to a cockiness and self assuredness that was conveyed by the way they presented themselves. In a sense they combined the ideas of self pride and pride in their job. Throughout this paper are references by Swede, Kraut, Soupy, and O'Malley about the attitude that they had during their time period and the difference in the attitude of the current tree trimmers.

Pride in the Job

The pride that the urban lumberjacks expressed in their job encompassed both the work itself and the way they did the work. It expressed itself in comments about the difficulty of the work and the understanding that it created in them a feeling of self-respect and respect for their peers who were also representing them on the job.

> It was a proud group...we went to cable[4] something...and we pulled down one of those streets and it wasn't what the job said. He says well, he did a bolt and cable job here about five years ago and he wanted to check the cables and see they were tight...he wasn't the only one, he had pride in his job. (Soupy)
> You'd get up with a bull saw[5] and you'd make a few cuts like this and you'd get down and you'd say you made a beautiful tree...that's the thing the guys had pride in... (Kraut)
> You'd work on that crew and I was real proud to do that kind of stuff...you could really see the fruits of what you did... (Soupy)
> I mean you took pride when you went down the street, when we trimmed...you could look down from Chalmers to Connors, it looked like an umbrella...there were no shiners,[6] everything was clean. (Kraut)

Toughness: Physical and Mental

The toughness required for the urban lumberjack job was more than just the ability to face the cold and pain that were a part of the job, it also included a mental toughness that meant not refusing to do the jobs that seemed impossible and not whining about the conditions. It included the basic self knowledge that only a person with physical and mental toughness could do the job. Working in Detroit the men had to be street smart as well. They had to temper their strength and toughness with ways of establishing rapport in the neighborhoods in which they worked. If they were easily intimidated they would get no work done. If they were too aggressive they were likely to get into fights with the public and in later years to be threatened or shot at with weapons. It was necessary to their self-image not to back down and in most cases they learned to project an image of men who could not be frightened or pushed around, who were not afraid of being hurt.

> We're not afraid to drop twenty feet. We don't want to drop twenty feet but we know if we do the lines[7] gonna hold us. (Kraut)
> We swung onto limbs. You're on a swing line, say you happen to fall off that limb, or you get shook off that limb. You swing back you hit your back, you hit your face, you hit your hands. You tried to get turned around before you swung into the other side of the tree. (Greek)

We climbed unless it was 10 or below. We climbed but most of the first years I was there and you were there before me, sometimes the foreman would let you go. I remember dropping a Paragon[8] out of the tree and kept sawing, my hands were so cold I didn't even know I dropped the Paragon. (Swede)

...we always got hurt but we never stopped workin'. 'Cause we fell out of trees, we had trees fall on us, we dropped logs on us, everything. We got cut, we just kept on workin'. It was part of the job. (Swede)

Well, Greek was on the line and when it swung he was supposed to let it go down past me and then swing it into the yard. The rope caught and that goddam log hit me and drove me right down the tree. It just drove me right on down. I thought I broke my arm and my wrist and everything like that because I had one more cut to make like that...so I got myself together and I made the cut. (Swede)

Soupy he was a really gutty guy. We had a stand of high toppers, I mean they were tall,...those 80-90 footers...and they just go up to the sky, and we had a lightning strike...so we were in the crew and we were ready to bail out and go up and he (the foreman) says "No, the new guy." and I says "Hey, he's a trainee." That kid went all the way up to the top and took this storm-damaged piece, cut it loose and let it go. And my hat was off to the guy. (O'Malley)

Competition Between the Men

Competition is particularly a carry over from the lumbering tradition but it is also common in any work settings in which strength and agility are important. Wells (1978:105) talks of competition in the lumber camps.

> Competition among workmen was encouraged—demanded in fact. In the woods, each crew was urged to try to beat the others. On the rivers, raftsmen or those in charge of a log drive were persuaded they must try to outdo everyone else. The pinery boys understood that such contests mostly benefited the owners, getting more work done in shorter periods of time. But trying to beat another good man at chopping down a tree, riding a log or getting the product to market was part of the game and appealed to their competitive instincts.

The urban lumberjacks also recognized and enjoyed the fact that they were in competition with one another in certain aspects of their work. In general they believed that it made them better and more daring and as long as it did not interfere with the team work they liked to test themselves against their friends.

> Greek went 80 feet, I was gonna go 90. If I went 90, Bear was gonna go 100. (Swede)

> You just didn't want, that was your peer group, and you didn't want to look bad with your peer group. So you did a little extra and boy, the competition, it was fierce. It really was. (Soupy)
>
> Especially on the trim crew, it was the guys that were doing all the work. The foreman, sometimes you liked him, sometimes you didn't like him, but it was the people together...you started realizing well, this one he would help this guy and he would help you, back and forth, 'cause there was so much expected for everyday and the better you got it was better for the whole crew. (Checkers)

While they dwelled on the characteristics and the attitude that made them unique and the skills and behaviors that they felt set them apart, most of the men were well aware of their own limitations. They recognized that what this job meant to them was that they would not have to be made constantly aware and ashamed of their own educational deficiencies.

> All you're really talking about is the attitude we had. That's what made us different. That's what made us do this job is the attitude we had. It was our way of competing with anybody else with the limited skills we had. We'd compete. We made ourselves better. (Swede)
>
> Ski, he got run over by a semi. Fell off the semi goin' in the yard. It run over him.... He's probably the best they had in hooks.[9] He was a good tree man. He didn't—I don't know how to say it—he didn't have the qualities he should've. He should have been a foreman but they held him back.... Yeah, he retired as a tree artisan, a senior tree artisan. He had a lot of knowledge. He had a hard time with tests, I think, but he knew everything. (Swede)

The ultimate compliment, even while specific skills were being compared, was saying that the man was a "good tree man." The reference to a man as being a throwback or a dinosaur meant that the man fit in well in an earlier era.

> If you want a job done, PJ's a senior. He should have been foreman quite a few years ago but with this affirmative action and this shit, they passed him over. He's not the best speller and (pause) we're not bright people. He has trouble with the book stuff but if I want something done, I'll tell PJ and He'll get it done.... I mean he'll do it.... His thinking, he's not quick-witted. He's a helluva good employee and he should be foreman but they just passed him over...he's a dinosaur. (Swede)

Although they would speak of each other and themselves saying "we're not bright people" or "he has trouble with the book stuff", they did not think of themselves as stupid. They talk about the knowledge that people have and their abilities to think on their feet, to climb and to engineer and when they mention their deficiencies it is with honesty but without shame.

Learning the Job—Knowledge

The men who did the job in the early years were tree men in the sense that their work in the trees, their knowledge of and relationship to the trees was an important component of the way they conceptualized their work. They had a real feeling for the trees that they worked in all the time. They learned how to trim and plant and remove and engineer, and they learned it on the job as had the woods lumberjacks who were their predecessors.

> Such impressive feats of engineering were performed under the direction of bosses who did not know how to read or write but had been educated in the skills needed to cope with the problems of moving logs. The techniques had been handed down from one generation of woods workers to the next, with a succession of minor improvements made by anonymous lumberjacks seeking better ways to get the job done. The men who got ahead in this competitive game were those who watched how a respected veteran tackled the challenge...and then figured out a way to go him one better. (Wells 1978, p. 89)
>
> When we were on the job we talked to the people before us and from them to us and we should be able to pass it on which we can't. They would challenge you, ask you what kind of tree is this? Always trying to stump you or maybe put you down. But you learned. Somebody always had something. They had so much information, the people we worked with. (Swede)
>
> They passed this on to us. I learned more by just watchin' what they did. (P.J.)

What they considered important in gaining knowledge was the information that they picked up for themselves and by associating with the old-timers. The old-timers deliberately taught them many things about types of trees, bark, flowers, and leaves. Also a wide variety of knowledge about handling and preserving of equipment and working with ropes was passed on by the old-timers. On rain days they often learned new knots like "bowlines," "running bowlines" and "monkey's nuts."

> ...the thing they say is the guys used to teach them and test them and trick them on kinds of wood or leaves or stuff like that because they'd make fun of them if they made a mistake or they pull some trick...you know they played tree games, sort of. (Soupy)
>
> See what you learn is the short cuts. Every year goes by the more you were in the tree the less moves you made 'cause you learned the shortcuts. You know you could look at a tree and visualize in your mind exactly what you were going to do, exactly where you were gonna go, exactly how to do it. This is in your mind. (Kraut)
>
> I started here and I had guys like these guys to tell me what to do and they told me what to do and how to do it and if I didn't do it they got on me. (P.J.)

> Real on-the-job training. We didn't know about having the knots down closer, we didn't know about walkin' up the back side of a limb...we worked with the best trim crew for two or three weeks. We learned more working with the older fellows than we did the first 13, 14 months on the job. (Greek)

What stands out when the men talk about the job as it was during the early part of their years is their own respect for the job and their peers and their pride in being a part of the job. For the most part they felt disdain for the people who worked indoors and in factories. Most of the old timers believe that there were certain key personal characteristics that the Tree Men had that could not be learned as skills. They believe that the men who worked the trees during the 1950 to 1980 period had pride, mental and physical toughness, courage, quick-thinking, and a touch of arrogance. A lot of the pride they had in themselves and their work came from the fact that the job could not be faked, that what one man did was visible to be examined and evaluated by all the rest. Pride also came from their work ethic—the fact that they did what they considered to be a day's work which meant that the person who did it had to be strong and tough and that when the day's work was finished they were dirty and tired and satisfied.

Skills That Were Learned During The Early Years

In Charles More's 1982 discussion of "Skill and the Survival of Apprenticeship," he discusses the social construction of skills and how skilled workers constructed skill in order to retain power. He uses Braverman's (1974:444) definition of skill:

> Skill covers his (the skilled worker's) ability to imagine how things would appear in final form if such and such tools and materials were used...he can estimate accurately both aesthetic appeal and functional utility, organize his tools, his power and his materials in a way which accomplishes his task and gains him livelihood and recognition.

More maintains that it is an oversimplification to look at the labor process under capitalism as only the extensive process of deskilling or degrading labor. He contends that deskilling as a product of technology results in the development of new skills but more importantly provides the potential for involvement of workers who might have otherwise been restricted and in this way may result in greater rather than less worker control. Indeed, the men discussed the new skills required in learning to work from the towers rather than in doing climbing, but in the case of the urban lumberjacks the separation from the trees that resulted from that technology did result in a diminution of tree knowledge, and the focus on removals rather than tree maintenance diminished tree knowledge.

The notion of skill may refer to either the requirements of the job or the capabilities of the workers. The skills involved in the urban lumberjack job involved both of these notions.

Swede here done one thing...with strictly a swing line. He took one limb, done a complete 360 walk around one limb...He went up and did a 360 turn around the tree, walked the whole length with a swing line, no spurs on his feet...I'm still amazed to this day how he did it. I was in the tree next to him. I stopped and watched him. (Greek)

We evaluated the tree from the ground up. We got into the tree and we might have to change some of the evaluation because it was different up in the tree. Experienced as I am, I can get up in a tree and say I can make it in three cuts. I get up there and make six cuts but you're always at least one or two cuts ahead of yourself. You might be making a butt hang[10] over here but you're thinking of that limb over there. You're gonna let that hang until you swing around the tree. That comes with experience but you know we had a little more engineering to do there on the street like falling pieces of limb. (Greek)

Swede says we used to be able to walk on little suckers.[11] Little sucker might be a quarter of an inch, but we got our feet right next to the crotch of the sucker. We could get a little lift with that and go on our swing line because the swing line allows you to go up or down. (Greek)

We had to limb[12] everything down with an axe. We'd knock a whole tree down and we had to limb it all with an axe. Even when they got chain saws we used to still for a long time limb them with an axe. (Kraut)

You had to be an engineer because you got to a tree it was layin' on a house, you worked off the roof, you had to take limbs off. There was no towers[13] to go out there, to glide in there, you either had to walk the tree or sometimes you had to stand on the roof, trim all this off til you could lift it off with a winch on semis. (Greek)

You learned by goin' up. (Checkers)

By doin'. You learned to tie the knot on the ground, then you built your confidence up in the tree, to be able to move around the tree. (Greek)

The job required different skills than those needed by the lumberjacks in the woods. While the woods 'jacks had to deal with running their logs down the river, they didn't have to look out for a burgeoning population that seemed to always want to watch from up close. The urban lumberjacks had to put their trees down in such a way that they didn't damage cars in the driveways and surrounding houses. Often the big trees were brought down with such precision that accuracy had to be judged in inches. There was no place that they worked where they could yell "Timber!" and just let the tree fall. Each limb that was removed was big enough to cause damage and the trunks were big enough to kill a person. When the urban tree men climbed to do trimming or repair they did it without hooks or anything that could damage the live trees. It was important that the tree man was able to evaluate, visualize, and engineer the job as well as be able to chop, climb, and move heavy objects manually. In some cases different men on crews complemented each other in having different skills but all were expected to be able to do each part of the job.

> He wasn't the greatest on removals[14] but he was a helluva good trimmer.
> He didn't have a lot of strength to hold up those big saws. (Swede)
> You had to learn all over again when you went to the buckets. (Kraut)
> Ski just couldn't adjust. No, he couldn't adjust to it. (The new technology)
> Ski was one of the best tree men we had. He was lucky and he was careless
> and he was good all rolled into one. His best skill was climbing. He wasn't
> the best dropper.[15] He was a helluva worker. Tough. But he wasn't, I would
> say, as complete as he could get. (Swede)

Naturally everybody wasn't equally skilled in all facets of the job. The ideal was to be the complete tree man. The complete tree man was a good climber, fearless in the trees. He had the strength to load the logs by hand. He was skilled with the axe and ropes. More than that the complete tree man was knowledgeable. He was able to survey for various forms of disease. He was knowledgeable about what kind of spray was used in each situation and how much. He was willing and able to do the ground work, the clean up, the "grunt" work, but he was so much more.

One man who had worked his way up to supervision said,

> I was never a good tree man. I really wasn't, but my heart was in the right
> place and I really enjoyed the work but I wasn't the expert that Ski and guys
> like that were. Guys like that in the tree were like short-order cooks. Every
> move in the tree it meant something. No wasted motion.

Some of the men were naturals in the trees. They "looked like they were born up there." But it took a combination of skills and knowledge and attitude before a man could be called a "good tree man."

The Work in the Early Period—1950 to 1970

The work before the saws and the towers and the stumpers[16] and chippers[17] were available all had to be done by hand. All of the work was hard, dirty, manual work. In the early days the men had no protection against the flying chips or the saw dust or the sharp branches that were often in their eyes and in their ears. All of the old-timers have arthritis and white finger.[18] Most of them have considerable hearing loss from the gas saws that came in before the ear protectors they now use. The older men all have been cut by saws and axes and have had broken bones from falls or being hit by logs.

> You'd go out there and you'd have to take a tree out. You'd have to top it
> to begin with then you'd have the stem standing up. Then you'd get down
> and you'd have to chop it. Then you'd have the stump and you'd have to
> chop it until the stump was below the ground. (Soupy)
> ...we had to load by hand. We had semis and we had to unload by hand.
> (Kraut)
> It was all bull work. (Kraut)

> I'd say a full load of logs on our log loader[19] today...in the neighborhood of 12,000 pounds. (Greek)
> They've got trees you can't even get on one load. (Swede)

During this period each tree had to be climbed and trimmed individually. Often on the big trees the men would stay in the tree and pull their lunch up on the rope. If it was a removal, the tree had to be topped out and the larger limbs tied on both ends and winched down. Once the top branches were taken down, the stem or log had to be chopped until it was ready to fall and then gently lowered into the street. The log then had to be sawed so that it would fit in the truck and the crew would load it onto the truck by hand. After that, all the branches and sawdust had to be swept up and hauled away to the dump or brought into the yard so that after hours the men could take the logs home and chop it up to sell for firewood. Once the tree was down, then the crew had to chop out the stump until it was below ground level. After the Dutch Elm struck, almost all of their work consisted of removals with only a small amount of time being spent on trimming, wire clearance, storm repairs, spray, and replanting.

> You load the brush, you load everything by hand...trees, brush, sawdust. (Soupy)
> Everything was manual, you'd go up with a bull saw and you'd go up with a Paragon. You wouldn't even take a pole saw.[20] (Kraut)
> We guys, we depended on ourselves when we went up a tree. Most of the time we left all of our tools on the ground, but we tied 'em to the tail end of our swing line. When we got up there, we got tied in and we pulled our own equipment up. (Kraut)
> That's where the ropes came in. You had to know where to tie them and how to run them. You had to tie them right and you had a lot of responsibility for how that thing falls. (P.J.)

Most of the men who stayed on the job put in thirty years. There was little advancement if you stayed in the physical tree work. Only three job classifications fell into that category, tree artisan helper, tree artisan, and senior tree artisan. Eventually when the men were older they would move up as far as foreman, which would keep them still working outside and with the crews. A number of the old-timers retired as seniors. Even those who could pass the tests could not move above foreman in the department. The supervisory jobs in Forestry required a degree in forestry or horticulture.

> You had seniority, you had bid jobs....You put in a bid, the bid jobs they come out with were removals, trim crew or miscellaneous. These were the permanent assignment jobs, then the bid jobs would come up and anybody with seniority they could (bid for them) spray, survey and some other jobs like water and cultivating, weed control, spot trim. (Swede)
> I was on removals for twenty, twenty some years...plus when it came to these bid jobs I wasn't the lowest seniority but I wasn't on the top so I just

about missed everything. That's why I was on removals for so many years. (Swede)

One interesting thing I noticed when the old-timers talked about their work was that they continually made reference to specific trees. They often started to tell a story by prefacing it with "Remember that big box elder or that cluster of silver maples?" These were often trees they had not seen for twenty or thirty years and yet they remembered them as individuals making distinctions and only sometimes falling back on locations. They talked about the individual trees as old friends.

> Remember Field, there used to be a tremendous elm on Field and this thing was about 135 feet or something, it was about 65 or 70 feet to the first branch....(O'Malley)
> Uh huh, that was right by Eastern High School. (Swede)

These men were discussing a tree that had been removed twenty-five years before, yet they both could visualize that tree.

The Guys Together: Cohesion and Camaraderie on the Crews

Everyone of the men interviewed spoke of the men they worked with in terms of love and affection. Most of them had been friends and had worked out of the same East Side yard for years. They all spoke of men who had died or retired as part of the group. In many ways they seemed similar to old army buddies whose wartime friendships exceeded any others they made. Their social lives centered around their work group. When I asked the wives who their friends were, they said "they're the same ones we always had" and they named the families of the men who worked together.

> Once you got into the group and were accepted and they knew you were there to work, boy, you had a family! If you went out and got into trouble...they were there. It was just that kind of gang. (Soupy)
> When he passed away all the men here at that time chipped in every week to make sure his wife got a full check....And they did that for a long time about six months, six or seven months 'til she got squared away. That showed the kind of men that worked here. (Kraut)
> Everyone had their own personality yet the guys were...bound together. (Greek)
> We knew most of the families...knew the wives, the children so actually it was one big family. (Soupy)
> It was a pleasure to do. You had a bunch of guys that did it. You liked the crew. (Gunny)

The feeling of family and of unity extended both to the social activities and to the job. The men had cohesion, esprit du corps that made them secure in the job situations and established a feeling that together they could conquer anything and that they were a group together and set apart from the rest of the world. It is this sense of themselves as part of a special group and together against the world that allowed them to support their elite identity. They depended on each other to complete the jobs and for their safety when they worked together. They knew if they started sliding off an icy roof during storm work someone would catch them somehow. If they swung loose on a swing line they knew their ground man would pull them back to safety.

> ...but the guy on the ropes he would do anything. Take the house before, it was just an unwritten law. I mean that's the way you do it. Your life sometimes was in the hand of the guy handling the rope. (P.J.)
> We always looked out for the guy. We had a choice of totalling out a house or maybe a log swinging back and hitting a guy, we'd let the house go. (Greek)
> It was a single mind. The other guy looked out for you. (Kraut)
> When you worked...you were as one, the guy chopping, the guy running the lines, the guy stacking the brush. You were as one. The guy next to you would always help you, say, 'Hey, take that limb off.' (Swede)
> You always had the guys there to take care of the other guy. (Checkers)

Identity Management

Change and Technology: the "New Guys"

As the times changed and the city changed and the job changed, the old urban lumberjacks still managed to maintain their identity, primarily by comparing themselves with "the new guys" who didn't have to do what they had done and who essentially couldn't do, at least in the old timer's minds, what they had done. They frequently mention that they aren't smart or aren't good with paper work, but they believe that they are better than the new people being hired. They consider the job to have changed as a result of deskilling that took place in the context of three trends that occurred within the time period. As they constructed their explanations of the changes, they incorporated the social trends that were taking place during this period to explain why their job and their identity were being destroyed.

Technology

The trends as they see them involve first what we would in a factory setting call automation. With the new technology the process of de-skilling began to take place. This occurred when certain types of equipment were brought in to substitute for physical skills. For example, the introduction of the towers meant that the work could be done without climbing and having the unique contact and relationship to the tree. Other equipment such as stumpers and log loaders meant that the requirements for physical strength and endurance were not what they had been. The bringing in and reduction of the size of the gas saws meant that the men did not have to chop the individual branches, or work together on the two-man saws to trim off the branches, or to top the trees that were being brought down. The entire job changed as more and more of the new equipment came in that reduced the need for crews of men to work together and reduced the need for men to climb and be in touch with the trees. Since the men were not up doing their work in the trees, the requirements for agility, quick thinking, and the ability to manage the tools while in the tree were lost.

> ...it's rough because the attitude isn't there like it used to be. (Soupy)
> I'm not saying the new breed is bad but they got a whole different attitude toward life and everything that goes with work...(Kraut)
> They don't know the ropes because they don't make 'em glide up and take the ends off. They don't handle it, they don't know the job. They don't have to take it because they don't have to go up there and tie the knot and boom the whole log off. They don't have to worry about their body, they don't have to worry about equipment. They just cut it and once it's cut most of 'em don't know what's going to happen to it. These people...they've got no continuity. (Swede)
> There's a lot of people, these people today, are under the assumption because they work in a bucket they're safe. That's the last thing in the world because they're depending on a piece of machinery instead of themselves. (Kraut)
> We had one that had real good physical abilities but he wasn't mentally, he wasn't a tree man in the heart. He had good skills but he didn't have the heart for it or the attitude. (Greek)

The urban lumberjacks believed that the machinery separated them from the trees and made it possible for people who were not tough, brave, or quick-thinking to do the work. They contended that the people who came in after the power saws, towers, and other equipment were available would have been winnowed out in earlier days.

The Civil Rights Movement

The second trend that the men designate as important is what they label as the Civil Rights Movement. This partly refers to the changing of Detroit from a white to a black majority, the loss of tax base, and urban decay. To the men it also meant the process of affirmative action, which caused many of them to be passed over for promotion and caused changes in the requirements for getting hired. They see this change not only affecting the civil service process but also changing the character of their union. For them the union changed from one that represented them as skilled tradespersons to one that sold them out to the politicians and represented the black majority rather than their job category. The fact is that the department had about one third black employees by the fifties. Many of the black trimmers were considered Tree Men, they were often the aces on the crews. The old timers felt that the new men who were hired under affirmative action did not have the work ethic of those who were hired before, regardless of race.

> They lower the standards and they reduce the training time. (Kraut)

What you have is inexperienced supervisors in charge of inexperienced people and you're gonna have somebody get hurt serious unless they get more time. (Swede)

Now they're trying to teach them with book work. Not the climbing but about the trees. (P.J.)

What they're trying to do is educate 'em so they can pass the test. Not educate them so they can do the job. (Greek)

Now it is, "Hey, if that guys' not doin' it then I'm not gonna do it either but if he's makin' what I'm makin' and he's not gonna put out one hundred per cent then why should I bust my can?" (Soupy)

They don't take pride in their work. They don't take interest in their work. They want to sign in, go out, putz around for eight hours, come in and Friday collect their check. (Gunny)

Affirmative action hit me and I saw before that. After it hit me directly, another being put over me and I had thirty-one years and he had fourteen. (O'Malley)

While this is not entirely a racial issue, the issue of race is somehow tied into it. By the middle fifties, one third of the Forestry Department was black but, as the urban lumberjacks see it, the issue of race was a non-issue prior to the "Civil Rights Movement." The early crews worked in black neighborhoods without problem, their relationships in the black community, even for all white crews, were no different from their relationships with the white neighborhoods. After the "Civil Rights Movement" things changed, for the old-timers that's when the city changed as well. White flight resulted in much of Detroit's working class moving to the suburbs. City employees, however, were required to maintain Detroit addresses. While some of the higher paid occupational classifications cheated and maintained homes in the suburbs while keeping a Detroit address, the majority of the urban lumberjacks remained in the city. For the first few years of the "Civil Rights Movement," the white crews became used to being hassled as a part of their daily work situation. In the later years, most of the crews were all black although some had white seniors or foremen. By then it didn't matter whether the crews were black or white. The oldtimers talk about the new situation in which people drive over their barriers and try to run over members of their crews. They talk about having to work in "Crack Heaven" where the drug dealers work openly, and they frequently fear going to the houses to ask people to move their cars. When asked if this is a racial thing, they say that they don't think so: "how can it be a racial thing when the workers are all or nearly all black?" Their wives say they were never afraid for their husbands working in the trees or doing storm work, but they fear for their safety in Detroit's mean streets. The urban problems that plague all major U.S. cities are forever associated in the minds of many city workers as changes that resulted from the "Civil Rights Movement." From the perspective of many urban lumberjacks, this was a second trend that combined with the new technology to spoil their job identity and to hasten their demise.

Rachel Carson and Environmentalists

The final change that is viewed as having combined with the others to destroy the urban lumberjack job is what we might call the environmentalist movement but that the men call "Rachel Carson." It was in about 1953 when the first Dutch Elm disease was found in Detroit, and in the first years after that the disease was controlled by Dutch Elm spray. Following the discovery that the chemicals, such as DDT, being used were dangerous to the birds and small animals that made their homes in the trees, the Dutch Elm spraying that was effective enough to control the disease was curtailed. Detroit's massive elms began dying by the thousands and the work became less and less caring for the trees and more and more a job of removing them. Entire streets that had been gloriously canopied by trees were stripped bare. The economic situation of the city resulting from plant closing and lay-offs and the massive exodus of the tax base meant that if anything the forestry budget was reduced. It is interesting to note that in those years the plight of birds and animals seemed to the Tree Men to take precedence over the lives of the trees and most certainly over their lives, in much the same way that todays northwestern loggers feel that the concern for maintaining forest areas and nesting places for birds are the concerns of people who do not make their living in the trees. In fact, the men joked during that period that the trend seemed to be to save the birds and get rid of the tree trimmers. They talk about the spraying in a generally positive way and seem to disregard or downplay any potentially dangerous health consequences:

> We're doing so much each year but the program back then was that's how it's supposed to be. It was spraying to hold them in control and it was sanitation which is removal and carrying it away and replanting to stay abreast of it but it never worked out. They just let it go. (Swede)

When I asked "In terms of what you know now about chemicals...the affect on the food cycle...you still feel that the spraying was something that should have been done?" they answered:

> I do. ....if they knew anything about it they never warned us. We used DDT. We took baths in it. We sprayed each other. They never told us anything about it. They took that off the market, said that was no good. So then...we used methoxachloride which is not as bad a poison but it's only good for a ninety day period, where DDT lasted. That's why it was bad, it lasted for...never breaks down. We used malathion. We sprayed with that. They took that off the market. That was a deadly poison. Never told us nothin' about it. (Swede)
> ...Rachel Carson wrote the book and she brought everyone's attention to the fact that DDT wasn't good...so because of that we've been able to educate our people into chemicals more than we did then. We used to spray arsenic...They'd spray arsenic for caterpillars, you know. You remember out there with a big hydraulic sprayer...standing under it, I never thought

anything about it. We drove the DDT, we'd lose a filter cap or something, you'd roll up your sleeve, you'd be down in there, but now Thank God, people are aware of chemicals, the danger of chemicals...People like myself, we've all taken exams. Things like Paraquat, I don't order Paraquat anymore 'cause I'm not gonna order anything that's gonna endanger the guys or my family. Chemicals, to guys like us, are like hammers and saws are to carpenters. They're tools and if they are not abused it's a real effective tool and when you get to the point where the environmentalists want to take all these tools away and we wind up paying five dollars for a wormy apple if you can find one. If you can't use these tools the society's gonna have to go around the other way and say "Hey, we need these things to take care of the population we've got. Let's just not put them in the wrong hands." (Soupy)

So as the men see it, it was a combination of the "Technology", the "Civil Rights Movement," and "Rachel Carson" that destroyed both their city and their job. They see that new trees are being planted and know that the bird count and fish count is up but the urban lumberjack count is getting lower and lower. Of these they would probably lay more blame on the combination of de-skilling and automation.

Detroit has done an excellent job at building up its nursery and in beginning the job of creating a new urban forest to replace the one lost to the Dutch Elm. They will never again make the mistake of planting too many of the same type of tree throughout the city, but they have found no way to replace the Tree Men who loved the trees and their work and who found a way to have pride and dignity in a world that was slipping away from them. The urban lumberjack is dead.

REFERENCES

Becker, Howard S. 1973. *Outsiders: Studies in the Sociology of Deviance*. Revised ed. New York: Free Press.
Braverman, H. 1974. *Labour and Monopoly Capital*, New York: Monthly Review Press.
Denzin, Norman K. 1989. *Interpretive Interactionism*, Newbury Park, CA: Sage.
Goode, William. 1957. "Community Within a Community: The Professions." *American Sociological Review* 22:194-200.
Miller, Gale. 1978. *It's A Living: Work in Modern Society*, New York: St. Martin's Press.
Mills, C. Wright. 1959. *The Sociological Imagination*, New York: Oxford University Press.
More, Charles. 1982. "Skill and the Survival of Apprenticeship." In Stephen Wood, ed., *The Degradation of Work? Skill, Deskilling and the Labour Process*, Hutchinson and Co., Ltd.
Wells, Robert W. 1978. *Daylight in the Swamp*, Minocqua, Wisc.: Northwood Press.

NOTES

[1] An earlier version of this paper was presented at the Qualitative Research Conference, May, 1990. I would like to thank my brother, Jim Highlund, and the other Tree Men of Detroit for their love and cooperation in this project.

² When trees are about two or three inches thick they are ready to be planted. The two ways they are prepared for planting is bare root, which is with the roots exposed and hanging loose or ball, which is when the roots are bundled together into a ball of dirt and root combined.

³ There are now a few women working in the Forestry division. The few that are there came in through affirmative action primarily. At the time I did the interviews there were only two and they came in after 1980.

⁴ Broken limbs on trees were repaired by putting a bolt into the tree and running a metal cable through it so that the limb would not drop and would eventually grow and regain strength. These were generally referred to as bolt and cable jobs.

⁵ A bull saw is a large saw usually handled by one person and used to cut through large limbs or tree trunks.

⁶ Shiners are the round white spots that appear when a limb is removed. To trim a tree properly the white spot is painted with tar so that it remains healthy and the place where the limb has been removed blends in with the darker bark.

⁷ When the urban lumberjacks refer to lines they are speaking of the ropes that they used to tie themselves into the trees, to swing from one part of the tree to another or to tie big limbs so that they could be lowered into the street. The line then refers to any of a variety of sizes and types of rope and may be called a safety line, a swing line or ropes.

⁸ A paragon is a small curved trimming saw that is usually attached to the urban lumberjack's belt. This is a saw that is used not only to trim trees but also to clear away small limbs and brush when a man is climbing.

⁹ Hooks or spurs are sharp, straight metal edges that are attached to the legs and that dig into the tree making climbing easier. They are often seen on climbers who work on telephone poles or did that climbing before the towers were used. They are only used on dead trees or trees being removed as they are very damaging to live trees. Also called gaffs.

¹⁰ To butt hang is to tie a limb on the end closest to the trunk to hold the limb when it is sawed so it can be lowered to the street.

¹¹ Suckers are the small branches that grow out of various parts of trees and limbs but do not develop into full limbs.

¹² To limb a tree is to remove the limbs. This was done in the early days with an axe, later with saws and still later with power saws.

¹³ Towers, also referred to as buckets or cherry pickers, are the basket like boxes that are attached to power cranes and that allow the Tree Men access to the upper parts of trees without having to climb the tree.

¹⁴ Removals is the term used for taking the entire tree down and away.

¹⁵ A dropper is the person who takes down the truck or stem of the tree. This is a precision job that combines the cutting and the rope work so that adjacent houses and other trees or automobiles are not damaged.

¹⁶ Stumpers are machines that disintegrate the stump left when the log or stem is removed. In the early days stumps were chopped out with an axe.

¹⁷ Chippers are mechanical devices on trucks that chop branches and brush into small pieces or sawdust so that they do not have to be loaded on a truck. They are considered to be dangerous by the men as they often catch clothes or other objects.

¹⁸ White finger is a result of having fingers frozen so that the fingers take on a bloodless look and ache during inclement weather.

PART VIII
SOME NEW DIRECTIONS:
GENERIC PRINCIPLES, GENDER, EMOTIONS, POSTMODERNISM, DISCOURSIVE ACTS

Some critics (Mullins, 1973; Ritzer, 1983) of symbolic interactionism have argued that this theoretical perspective is on the decline—that its death is imminent:

> It is clear that the original ideas...have run their course intellectually and socially..An eventual redefinition for the boundaries of sociological social psychology appears to be the most likely outcome of symbolic interactionism's demise. (Mullins, 1973:98).

According to these detractors, symbolic interactionism suffers from an incurable disease. We strongly disagree with the ominous prognosis of the critics. We contend that symbolic interactionism is going through a process of self-revitalization, largely in response to its critics. As we shall illustrate from the following selections, this perspective is branching out in several important directions. As Reynolds (1993:128) points out,

> Unlike representatives of certain other sociological traditions, several interactionists have not only been "self-critical" of their approach, but have actively participated in the circulation of those major criticisms of interactionism offered by non-interactionists..Rather than "duck" or ignore their critics, as many functionalists have done, [interactionists] have attempted to meet their detractors head on.

Social Structure and Emotions

Of the many criticisms levelled by both in-house critics and outsiders,[1] two have remained at the forefront. Symbolic interactionism: (1) fails to adequately examine social structure or social organization; (2) neglects the emotive or unconscious aspects of human behavior. In Section six, we discussed a fairly large-scale recent development on the part of interactionists, (specifically, in the pieces by Maines and Hall), namely, dealing directly with macrostructural concerns—of power, history, and structure.

In response to the criticism that emotions and the unconscious are ignored, interactionists have begun incorporating into their perspective the study of emotions (but not, unfortunately, the unconscious). This new interest in emotions has led to the publication of numerous books and articles. The works of Arlie Hochschild (1979, 1983) and Sue Shott (1979) are two noteworthy examples. In addition, sessions have been held at professional meetings specifically devoted to this topic. The literature on the nature of emotions can be divided into two themes: one which focuses on the organic foundation of emotion, and the other which focuses on the social component of emotion. Theodore Kemper, adopting the organic stance, emphasizes how power or status inherent in relationships affects body chemistry. Hochschild's (1983) research on flight attendants illustrates that emotions are a "biologically based sixth sense." Scheff (1979, 1983, 1985, 1988), adopting a "needs psychology," places emphasis on expressive needs that are common to all humans and that grow out of certain physiologically-based emotions, such as grief, fear, joy, etc. The second, a constructionist approach, as exemplified in the works of Franks,(1985), Shott,(1979); and Zurcher, (1982, 1985), does not rule out a physiological component but instead emphasizes how these biological processes are molded and structured and given social meaning. They argue that social experiences shape and create feelings which are, in turn, typed and managed through social interaction. Hochschild has spelled out the basics of "emotion work" and "feeling rules." The former refers to the act of attempting to alter in degree or quality an emotion. In terms of the latter, it refers to the situation when individuals attempt to experience the feelings prescribed by culture. Feeling rules are structurally mandated onto various interactions through normative guidelines. Just as they have endeavored to focus on the nature of emotion, so too, have scholars (Kemper, 1987; Shott, 1979) attempted to categorize emotions into specific categories. Furthermore, much research has centered on the social sources and consequences of emotions.(Kemper, 1979; Hochschild, 1975, 1979; Shott, 1979).

Generic Processes

A third (re)newed direction in symbolic interactionism is the concern with developing a more systematic theory—one which examines generic social processes. Over the past twenty years, contemporary interactionists (Bigus et al., 1982; Couch, 1984; Lester and Hadden, 1980, Lofland, 1970; Miyamoto, 1950; Prus, 1987) have explicitly criticized their fellow interactionists for conducting seemingly "mindless, endless ethnographies" with little or no regard for extended "grounded theories"; thus, their research is relegated to the status of what Strauss (1970) refers to as "respected little islands of knowledge" or "scattered islands of data." In response, interactionists are moving beyond their substantive cases and examining parallel social processes across various research settings and social groups.

Gender

A fourth recent development is the interactionist concern with the social reproduction of gender. Historically, the topic of gender is one that has escaped interactionist research. Scholars such as Padavic (1991) Richardson (1986, 1988), Wiley (1991), and Wolf (1986), among others, have all made significant contributions to an interactionist understanding of the role that culture, social organization, and power have on the reproduction and reification of gender stereotypes and gender boundaries.

Semiotics

Another area in which symbolic interactionists are now concentrating their efforts is semiotics, or the "science of signs." Until recently, a theory rooted in Charles Peirce's semiotics and Mead's notion of "significant symbols", has "neglect(ed) the actual symbolic materials by which the meaning generation process is carried forward" (Davis, 1981). Semiotics centers on the problem of meaning by utilizing taxonomy as a basic tool. Given that signs, significant symbols, and language are essential to understanding human behavior, some have argued that semiotics and symbolic interactionism nicely complement each other. Both Norman Denzin (1989) and Peter K. Manning (1987) have used semiotics to broaden their studies. Others, however are wary of integrating semiotics with symbolic interactionism.[2]

Conversation Analysis/Discourse Analysis

A sixth development has been a recent interest in what is referred to as Conversation Analysis or Discourse Analysis. Constructed upon the theoretical beliefs of ethnomethodology, conversation analysis developed out of the pioneering works of Sacks (1974), Schegloff (1984), and Jefferson (1987). Conversation analysts are interested in examining talk or language-in-action. As Adler et al. (1989) note, the emphasis is on "the production of language *in situ*." These scholars focus on the "raw data of conversations"— the ordering of conversations, turn-taking, mediation, the recurrence of the question-answer sequence, and arguing techniques.

A second area of inquiry has been examining laughter and nodding, things that illustrate the listener's continued participation in the conversation. Other conversation analysts have focussed on the integration of vocal and nonvocal behaviors, such as bodily postures.

Postmodernism

A final, new direction in symbolic interactionism is postmodernism. A plethora of recent publications (Denzin, 1989a, 1989b; Farberman, 1991; Plummer, 1990a, 1990b; Richardson, 1991a, 1991b; Seidman, 1991a, 1991b) have emerged, indicating that the postmodernist project is a major direction in which many interactionists are going. Within the postmodernist approach, every routine, lived experience, and aspect of culture is conceived as a "text." Two themes are central: everything is viewed as text and everything is political. Everything is representative of someone's point of view. It is the task of the postmodernist then, through deconstruction, to discover *whose* point of view it is. In order to employ the method of deconstruction, the researcher must *relativize* all textual materials, specifying their connections to: social class, gender, power, history, religion, culture, the author, and the reader. According to a leading proponent, postmodernism exposes "the grand myth of science as a cumulative, empirical enterprise." (Denzin, 1989:5). A second theme of postmodernism is that knowing the world is limited and uncircumscribable. Postmodernists believe that the world is far too complex for us to have a holistic understanding of human lived experience. At best, we can only grasp a fragment. Other postmodernist themes are: there are as many versions of reality as readers (Denzin, 1990) and that the realities of others can be either marginalized or empowered (Brown, 1990).

The following selections illustrate the nature and growth of interactionist sociology along most of the lines we have just outlined.

In a review piece, Adler, Adler, and Fontana group together a number of theoretical and empirical studies that have as their focus the study of "everyday life." Included under this rubric are a number of micro- approaches to the study of human behavior: symbolic interactionism, existentialism, phenomenology, dramaturgy, and ethnomethodology. The authors trace the historical development of everyday sociology. Moreover, they discuss three contemporary developments in everyday sociology having significant theoretical and methodological importance: existential sociology, the sociology of emotions, and conversation analysis.

In the next selection, Palmer discusses the newfound interest among symbolic interactionists in the study of emotions. Most of this interest emanates from everyday sociologists. These scholars center their research endeavors on: the nature of emotions, types of emotions, the social sources of emotions, and the social consequences of emotions.

The article by Robert Prus argues for a renewed emphasis on generic concepts in sociological research. Following Lofland (1970), Strauss (1970), and Couch (1984), the author stresses the need for researchers to move beyond individual ethnographies and examine generic concepts and processes across research situations (much in the way that Miall and Herman, in an earlier selection, examined the generic processes of impression management with respect to the mentally ill and infertile women).

Highlighting interactionist concerns with gender, the next selection, by Cahill, focusses on children's gender classifications and their maintenance of gender boundaries. The author points out that children make gender classifications on the basis of culturally-relative cues, as opposed to biology. Gender is an "interactional resource" that can be utilized in a number of ways for a variety of purposes, including social control and segregation.

The next selection deals with another area in which interactionists are conducting research: the area of conversation, or discourse, analysis. Conversation analysis provides a perspective within which culture, language, and social organization can be studied as integrated elements of courses of action. Focussing on the concept of "context," conversation analysts explore the dynamics of speech exchange, turn-taking, and politeness. Relating early theories of signs to contemporary theories of discourse and language, the article by Robert Perinbanayagam analyzes the processes and structures of conversations of everyday life and their consequences. Four forms of discourse are outlined.

Our final selection, by Laurel Richardson, illustrates the postmodernist direction in symbolic interactionism. In her presidential address to the North Central Sociological Association, Richardson argues for a postmodernist approach to the writing of sociology. She speaks of her sociological work as telling "the collective story." Using the liberation narrative, the author's work tells the collective story of the disempowered, "not by judging or blaming or advising them, but by placing their lives within the context of larger social and historical forces, and by directing energy towards changing these social structures which perpetuate injustice." Richardson's essay is illustrative of the postmodernist theme that realities of others have been unjustly marginalized.

NOTES

1. For a detailed discussion of the major criticisms levelled by interactionists and non-interactionists, consult: Meltzer, et al., (1975); Reynolds (1993).
2. For readers interested in the argument against the plausibility of integrating symbolic interactionist theory with semiotics, consult: Harman (1986).

REFERENCES

Adler, Patti, Peter Adler and A. Fontana. 1987. "Everyday Life Sociology." *Annual Review of Sociology* 13:217–235.
Bigus, O.E.S., S. Hadden and Barney Glaser. 1982. "Basic Social Processes." Pp. 251–272. In Robert Smith and Peter Manning (eds.) *Handbook of Social Science Methods*, Cambridge, MA: Ballinger.
Brown, Richard Harvey. 1990. "Rhetoric, Texicality, and the Postmodernism in Sociological Theory." *Sociological Theory* 8:188–197.
Couch, Carl J. 1984. "Symbolic Interaction and Generic Social Principles." *Symbolic Interaction* 7:1–14.
Davis, Fred. 1982. "On the 'Symbolic' in Symbolic Interaction." *Symbolic Interaction* 5(1):111–126.
Denzin, Norman K. 1989a. "Thoughts on Critique and Renewal in Symbolic Interactionism." Pp. 3–8 in Norman K. Denzin (ed.) *Studies in Symbolic Interactionism*, Greenwich,CT: JAI Press.
———. 1989b. "Reading/Writing Culture: Interpreting the Postmodern Project." *Cultural Dynamics* 2:9–27.
———. 1989c. *The Research Act*. Englewood Cliffs, N.J.: Prentice Hall.
———. 1990a. "Harold and Agnes: A Feminist Narrative Undoing." *Sociological Theory* 8:198–216.
———. 1990b. "The Spaces of Postmodernism: Reading Plummer on Blumer." *Symbolic Interaction* 13:135–154.
Farberman, Harvey A. 1991. "Symbolic Interaction and Postmodernism: Close Encounter of a Dubious Kind." *Symbolic Interaction* 14:471–488.
Franks, David D. 1985. "Introduction to the Special Issue on the Sociology of Emotions." *Symbolic Interaction* 8:161–170.
Hochschild, Arlie. 1975. "Sociology of Feeling and Emotion: Selected Possibilities." Pp. 280–307 In Marsha Millmen and Rosabeth M. Kanter (eds.) *Another Voice: Feminist Perspectives on Social Life and Social Science*, Garden City: Anchor Press/Doubleday.
———. 1979. "Emotion Work, Feeling Rules, and Social Structure." *American Journal of Sociology* 85:551–575.
———. 1983. *The Managed Heart: Commercialization of Human Feeling*. Berkeley: University of California Press.
Kemper, Theodore. 1978a. *A Social Interactional Theory of Emotions*. New York: John Wiley and Sons.
———. 1978b. "Toward a Sociology of Emotions: Some Problems and Some Solutions." *The American Sociologist* 13:30–41.
———. 1981. "Social Constructionist and Positivist Approaches to the Sociology of Emotions." *American Journal of Sociology* 87:336–362.
———. 1987. "How Many Emotions Are There? Wedding the Social and Automatic Components." *American journal of Sociology* 93:263–289.
Lester, M. and S. Hadden. 1980. "Ethnomethodology and Grounded Theory Methodology." *Urban Life*. 9:3–33.

Lofland, John. 1970. "Interactionist Theory and Analytic Interruptus." Pp. 35–45 In Tamotsu Shibutani (ed.) *Human Nature and Collective Behavior: Papers in Honor of Herbert Blumer,* Englewood Cliffs, N.J.: Prentice Hall.
Manning, Peter K. 1987. *Semiotics and Fieldwork.* New York: Sage.
Meltzer, Bernard N., John W. Petras, and Larry T. Reynolds. 1975. *Symbolic Interactionism: Genesis, Varieties, and Criticism.* London: Routledge and Kegan Paul.
Miyamato, Frank S. 1950. "The Social Act: Re-examination of a Concept." *Pacific Sociological Review* 2:51–55.
Mullins, Nicolaus. 1973. *Theories and Theory Groups in Contemporary American Sociology.* New York: Harper and Row.
Pavadic, Irene. 1991. "The Re-Creation of Gender in a Male Workplace." *Symbolic Interaction* 14:279–294.
Plummer, Kenneth. 1990a. "Herbert Blumer and the Life History Tradition." *Symbolic Interaction* 13:125–144.
———. 1990b. "Staying in the Empirical World: Symbolic Interactionism and Postmodernism: A Response to Denzin." *Symbolic Interaction* 13:155–160.
Prus, Robert. 1985. "Generic Sociology: Maximizing Conceptual Development in Ethnographic Research." Paper presented at a conference on Qualitative Research: An Ethnographic/Interactionist Perspective. University of Waterloo, Ontario. May 15–17, 1985.
Reynolds, Larry T. 1993. *Interactionism: Exposition and Critique.* New York: General Hall.
Richardson, Laurel. 1986. "Another World." *Psychology Today* Feb.:22–27.
———. 1988. "Secrecy and Status: The Social Construction of Forbidden Relationships." *American Sociological Review* 53:209–219.
———. 1991a. "Postmodern Social Theory: Representational Practices." *Sociological Theory* 9:173–197.
———. 1991b. "Speakers Whose Voices Matter: A Feminist Postmodernist Sociological Prax." Pp. 29–38 In Norman K. Denzin (ed.) *Studies in Symbolic Interaction,* Greenwich, CT: JAI Press.
Ritzer, George. 1983. *Contemporary Social Theory.* New York: Alfred A. Knopf.
Scheff, Thomas J. 1983. "Toward Integration in the Social Psychology of Emotions." *Annual Review of Sociology* 9:333–354.
———. 1985. "Universal Expressive Needs: A Critique and a Theory." *Symbolic Interaction* 8:241–262.
———. 1988. "Shame and Conformity: The Deference-Emotion System." *Sociological Review* 53:395–406.
Shott, Susan. 1979a. "Emotion and Social Life: A Symbolic Interactionist Analysis." *American Journal of Sociology* 84:1317–1334.
Strauss, Anselm. 1970. "Discovering New Theory from Previous Theory." Pp. 46–53 In Tamotsu Shibutani (ed.) *Human Nature and Collective Behavior: Papers in Honor of Herbert Blumer,* Englewood Cliffs, N.J.: Prentice Hall.
Wiley, Mary Glenn. 1991. "Gender, Work, and Stress: The Potential Impact of Role-Identity Salience and Commitment." *Sociological Quarterly* 32:495–510.
Wolf, Charlotte. 1986. "Legitimation and Oppression: Response and Reflexivity." *Symbolic Interaction* 9:217–234.

SUGGESTED READINGS

Antonio, Robert J. 1991. "Postmodern Storytelling Versus Pragmatic Truth-Seeking: The Discursive Bases of Social Theory." *Sociological Theory* 9: 154–163. Critique of the postmodern approach.
Balsamo, Ann. 1987. "Rethinking Ethnography: A Work for the Feminist Imagination." Pp. 42–65 In Norman K. Denzin (ed.), *Studies in Symbolic Interaction.* Greenwich, Connecticut: JAI Press. Calls for a "feminist" interactionist sociological imagination that includes the problematics of sexuality, language, and gendered selves.
Bartelt, Pearl W., Mark Hutter and David W. Bartelt. 1986. "Politics and Politesse: Gender, Deference and Formal Etiquette." In Norman K. Denzin (ed.) *Studies in Symbolic Interaction* 7: 199–228. Piece dealing with gender issues in symbolic interaction.
Boden, Deidre. 1990. "People are Talking: Conversation Analysis and Symbolic Interaction." Pp: 244–74 In Howard S. Becker and Michael M. Mcall (eds.) *Symbolic Interaction and Cultural Studies.* Chicago:

University of Chicago Press. Discusses the relationship between conversation analysis and symbolic interaction. "Talk" or "language in action" are the data to be examined.

Brissett Dennis and Charles Edgley (eds). 1990. *Life as Theater: A Dramaturgical Sourcebook.* New York: Aldine de Gruyter. A discussion of the dramaturgical approach to the study of social life.

Brown, Richard Harvey. 1990."Rhetoric, Textuality, and the Postmodern Turn in Sociological Theory." *Sociological Theory* 8: 188–197. Illustrates the postmodernist approach.

Cagle, Van M. 1989."The Language of Cultural Studies: An Analysis of British Subculture Theory."Pp. 301–313 In Norman K. Denzin (ed.) *Studies in Symbolic Interaction.* Greenwich, Connecticut: JAI Press. Provides an overview of the British school of cultural studies.

Clanton, Gordon. 1989."Jealousy in American Culture, 1945–1985: Reflections from Popular Literature." Pp. 179–193 In David D. Franks and E. Doyle McCarthy (eds.) *The Sociology of Emotions: Original Essays and Research Papers.* Greenwich, Connecticut: JAI Press. Detailed examination of the emotion of "jealousy" in our society.

Clark, Candace. 1989. "Studying Sympathy: Methodological Confessions." Pp. 137–151 In David Franks and E. Doyle McCarthy (eds.) *The Sociology of Emotions: Original Essays and Research Papers.* Greenwich, Connecticut: JAI Press. An interactionist account of researching the seldom-studied emotion of sympathy.

Clarke, Adele E. and Elihu M. Gerson. 1990."Symbolic Interactionism in Social Studies of Science." Pp. 179–214 In Howard S. Becker and Michal McCall (Eds.) *Symbolic Interaction and Cultural Studies.* Chicago: University of Chicago Press. A clever discussion of the sociology of science and symbolic interactionism's role in it.

Clough, Patricia T.1986. "The Failures of Women's Consciousness: A Brief History of a Woman's Group." Pp. 291–304 In Norman K. Denzin (ed.) *Studies in Symbolic Interaction.* Greenwich, Connecticut: JAI Press. Ethnographical piece dealing with the social organization of a feminist group.

———. 1987. "Feminist Theory and Social Psychology."Pp. 3–22 In Norman K. Denzin (ed.) *Studies in Symbolic Interaction.* Greenwich, Connecticut: JAI Press. Emphasizes historical moment at which feminist theory of SI emerged in the production of works on gender and sexuality.

Couch, Carl J. 1984. "Symbolic Interaction and Generic Sociological Principles." *Symbolic Interaction* 7:1–13. Points to the need for interactionists not only to elucidate but examine generic concepts and processes across research populations.

Denzin, Norman K. 1987."On Semiotics and Symbolic Interactionism." *Symbolic Interaction* 10 :1–20. A comparative piece focusing on similarities and differences between symbolic interactionism and the "science of signs."

———. 1989. "Reading 'Tender Mercies': Two Interpretations." *Sociological Quarterly* 30 :37–57. An example of the postmodernist approach.

———. 1984. *On Understanding Emotion.* San Francisco: Jossey-Bass. Provides a classification system of feelings (sensible, lived, intentional and self-and-moral feelings).

———. 1985. "Emotion as Lived Experience." *Symbolic Interaction* 8: 223–240. Another attempt to detail the thoroughly social nature of human emotions.

———. 1989. "Reading/Writing Culture: Interpreting the Postmodern Project." *Cultural Dynamics.* 2: 9–27. Attempts to access the relevance of postmodernism for viable sociological analysis.

———. 1992. *Symbolic Interactionism and Cultural Studies: The Politics of Interpretation.* Oxford: Blackwell. A detailed piece presenting an overview of SI, its historical development, different schools, variants, and future trends; book deals with development of cultural studies.

Ellis, Carolyn. 1991. "Sociological Introspection and Emotional Experience." *Symbolic Interaction* 14 (1):23–50. Dealing with methods of inquiry. The author argues for introspection as a way sociologists can examine how individuals define emotions.

———. 1991."Emotional Sociology." Pp. 123–145 In Norman K. Denzin (ed.) *Studies in Symbolic Interaction.* Greenwich, Connecticut: JAI Press. Answers the question: what is wrong, if anything, with an emotional approach to the study of emotions?

Farberman, Harvey. 1991. "Symbolic Interaction and Postmodernism: Close Encounters of a Dubious Kind." *Symbolic Interaction* 14: 471–488. A spirited discussion of the reasons for symbolic interactionists to exercise great caution with respect to embracing postmodernism.

Franks, David D. 1985. "Introduction to the Special Issue on the Sociology of Emotions." *Symbolic Interaction*: 161–170. Overview piece dealing with the sociological study of emotions.

———. 1987. "Notes on the Bodily Aspect of Emotions: A Controversial Issue in Symbolic Interaction." Pp. 219–233 In Norman K. Denzin (ed.) *Studies in Symbolic Interaction*. Greenwich, Connecticut: JAI Press. Deals with the relative influence of the social and the biological in shaping and responding to emotions.

———. 1989. "Power and Role-Taking: A Social Behaviorist's Synthesis of Kemper's Power and Status Model." Pp. 153–177 In David D. Franks and E. Doyle McCarthy (eds.) *The Sociology of Emotions: Original Essays and Research Papers*. Greenwich, Connecticut: JAI Press. A through-going symbolic interactionist "rethinks" the relevance and applicability of Kemper's model for the sociology of emotions.

Goodwin, Charles. 1979. "The Interactive Construction of a Sentence in Natural Conversation." *Everyday Language: Studies in Ethnomethodology*. pp. 97–122. Informed by the theoretical beliefs of ethnomethodology, this piece deals with the "raw" primary data of actual conversation and the constructing of sentences.

Hall, Stuart. 1980. "Cultural Studies and the Center: Some problematics and problems." Pp. 15–47 In Stuart Hall et al., (eds.) *Culture, Media and Language*. London: Hutchinson. Representing the British School of Cultural Studies at Birmingham. Hall discusses the field of Cultural Studies in Europe.

Harman, L.D. 1983. "Sign, Symbol and Metalanguage: Against the Integration of Semiotics and Symbolic Interaction." *Symbolic Interaction* 9: 147–160. Debate with Dean MacCannell regarding whether semiotics (the scientific study of signs) should be incorporated into the interactionist perspective.

Hochschild, Arlie. 1979. "Emotion Work, Feeling Rules, and Social Structure." *American Journal of Sociology* 85(3): 551–75. Deals with the types of emotion work in which humans engage, feeling norms and their relations to the social order.

———. 1983. *The Managed Heart*. University of California Press pp. 35–55. A detailed empirical work specifying the characteristic elements of "emotion work" and "feeling rules."

Kemper, Theodore. 1978. *A Social Interactional Theory of Emotions*. New York: Wiley. Deals with the social sources of emotions. A comprehensive text on the sociology of emotions.

Killian, Lewis. 1985. "The Stigma of Race: Who Now Bears the Mark of Cain". *Symbolic Interaction* 8: 1–14. An interactionist analysis of racism by one of the perspectives most knowledgeable students of race relations.

Lofland, Lyn. 1982. "The Social Shaping of Emotion: The Case of Grief." *Symbolic Interaction* 8: 171–190. Points to the universality of the grief experience, social components of the grief experience.

MacCannell, David. 1986. "Keeping Symbolic Interaction Safe from Semiotics: A response to Harman." *Symbolic Interaction* 9: 161–168. Debate with Harman regarding combining semiotics with SI theory.

McCarthy, E. Doyle. 1989. "Emotions are Social Things: An Essay in the Sociology of Emotions." Pp. 51–72 In David D. Franks and E. Doyle McCarthy (eds.), *The Sociology of Emotions: Original Essays and Research Papers*. Greenwich, CT: JAI Press. A clear example of the sociological viewpoint on the very nature of human emotions.

Mangham, I.L. and M.A. Overington. 1983. "Dramatism and the Theatrical Metaphor." Pp. 219–232 In Morgan Garth (ed.) *Beyond Method*. Beverly Hills, California: Sage Publications. Illustrates the dramaturgical approach to complex social phenomena.

Manning, Peter K. 1987. *Semiotics and Fieldwork*. Beverly Hills, California: Sage. Comprehensive text dealing with the scientific study of signs and their importance for interactionists.

Maynard, D.W. and S.E. Clayman. 1991."The Diversity of Ethnomethodology." *Annual Review of Sociology* 17: 385–418. Overview of this variety of symbolic interactionism illustrates its applicability and utility.

Meltzer, Bernard N. and Nancy J. Herman. 1993. "Human Emotions, Social Structure and Symbolic Interactionism." Pp. 186–230 In L.T. Reynolds *Interactionism: Exposition and Critique* 3rd edition. Dix Hills, New York: General Hall. An interactionist appraisal of recent works on emotions and social structure, as well as a response to critics of the perspective.

Molotch, Harvey L. and Deirdre Boden. 1985. "Talking Social Structure: Discourse, Domination and the Watergate Hearings." *American Sociological Review* 50: 273–288. Brings discourse analysis to bear on significant sociological themes and highly relevant social happenings.

Musolf, Gil. 1992. "Structure, Institutions, Power, and Ideology: New Directions within symbolic interactionism." *Sociological Quarterly*. 33 (2): 171–89. A fairly comprehensive summary of new trends within interactionism.

Padavic, Irene. 1991. "The Re-Creation of Gender in a Male Workplace." *Symbolic Interaction* 14: 279–294. Empirical study focussing on how gender is reconstituted in every day interaction within an all-male, blue collar work world.

Perinbanayagan, Robert S. 1992. *Discursive Acts*. Greenwich Connecticut: JAI Press. Comprehensive text dealing with issues in discourse/conversation analysis.

Risman, Barbara J. 1982. "College Women and Sororities: The Social Construction and Reaffirmation of Gender Roles." *Urban Life* 12:278–3 Empirical piece dealing with how gender roles are created and maintained within an institutional/organizational setting.

Rosenberg, Morris. 1990. "Reflexivity and Emotions." *Social Psychology Quarterly* 53: 3–12. A discussion of both the nature of emotions and reflexivity as well as a discussion of the relationship between the two.

Sacks, Harvey. 1984. "On Doing 'Being Ordinary.'" Pp. 413–429 In J.M. Atkinson and J. Heritage (eds.) *Structures of Social Action: Studies in Conversation Analysis*.. Cambridge University Press. A student of Goffman, Sacks studies the structuring of conversation.

Scheff, Thomas J. 1983. "Toward Integration in the Social Psychology of Emotions." *Annual Review of Sociology* 9: 333–354. An attempt to reconcile or point to commonalities between varying social psychological perspectives on the nature of human emotions.

Scheff, Thomas J. 1988. "Shame and Conformity: The Deference-Emotion System." *American Sociological Review* 53: 395–406. Deals with the relationship between norm compliance and emotionality.

Schegloff, Emanuel A. 1984. "On Some Questions and Ambiguities in Conversation." In J.M. Atkinson and J. Heritage (eds.) *Structures of Social Action: Studies in Conversation Analysis*. Cambridge: Cambridge University Press pp. 28–52. Excellent piece dealing with the action of sequences in talk, the competencies and structure underlying normal everyday activities.

Shott, Sue. 1979."Emotion and Social Life: A Symbolic Interactionist Analysis." *American Journal of Sociology* 84(6): 1317–34. Deals with the nature of emotion in social psychological terms.

Seidman, Steven. 1991a. "The End of Sociological Theory: The Postmodern Hope." *Sociological Theory* 9: 131–146. Assesses the relevance of postmodernism for the sum and substance of sociological reasoning.

VanMaanen, John. 1988. *Tales of the Field*. Chicago: University of Chicago Press. A work dealing with issues in ethnographic fieldwork and discussing the "New Ethnography" tradition.

Wasielewski, Patricia L. 1985. "The Emotional Basis of Charisma." *Symbolic Interaction* 8: 207–222. Presents a social psychological analysis of the emotive underpinning of leadership.

Weigert, Andrew and David D. Franks. 1989. "Ambivalence: A Touchstone of the Modern Temper." Pp. 205–227 In David D. Franks and E. Doyle McCarthy (eds.) *The Sociology of the Emotions: Original Essays and Research Papers*. Greenwich, Connecticut: JAI Press. Deals with what is perhaps the least studied and understood of the emotions-ambivalence.

Weitzman, Lenore J. 1982. *The Divorce Revolution: The Unexpected Consequences for Women and Children in America*. New York: Free Press. Deals with the social sources of marital strain and dissolution.

Welsh, John F. 1990. "Dramaturgy and Political Mystification: Political Life in the United States." Pp. 399–410 In Dennis Brissett and Charles Edgely (eds.) *Life as Theater: A Dramaturgical Source Book*. New York: Aldine de Gruyter. Examples of the dramaturgical approach.

Young, T.R. 1990. *The Drama of Social Life: Essays in Post-Modern Social Psychology*. New Brunswick, New Jersey: Transaction Publishers. Presents the critical potential of a dramaturgical style of analysis.

Zurcher, Louis. 1985. "The Wargame: Organizational Scripting and the Expression of Emotion." *Symbolic Interaction* 8: 171–190. Deals with the impact of feeling rules on emotions, how the military "scripts" various feelings.

Chapter 33 EVERYDAY LIFE SOCIOLOGY

Patricia A. Adler, Peter Adler and *Andrea Fontana*

INTRODUCTION

Any attempt to offer a brief but thorough outline of the focus and scope of everyday sociology is difficult because of its diversity and the lack of systematic integration among its subfields. In fact, the sociology of everyday life is an umbrella term encompassing several related but distinct theoretical perspectives; symbolic interactionism, dramaturgy, labeling theory, phenomenology, ethnomethodology, and existential sociology. The questions arise, then: Is everyday sociology merely a collection of fragmented parts, arbitrarily referred to as a single perspective for the sake of maintaining proprietary interests? Is there anything that characterizes the everyday life perspective as a distinctive body of theory? We argue that everyday life sociology does represent a theoretical arena (although it is often associated with certain methods[1] and substantive interests) characterized by a climate of intellectual compatibility and eclectic synthesis among sociological thinkers using a micro perspective. Within this overarching approach, individual practitioners can seek relevance for their empirical findings by drawing on a variety of interrelated perspectives, incorporating ideas from diverse camps into their own theoretical formulations. The everyday life field has thus been one of the evolving adaption, with new subfields emerging out of ideas creatively drawn from both within and outside of micro sociology.

MAJOR TRENDS OF EVERYDAY LIFE SOCIOLOGY

The Critique of Macro Sociology

A central impetus to the development of everyday life sociology was the growing dissatisfaction in mid-twentieth century American social thought with the approach contained in classical and contemporary macro theory. Both positivism and critical sociology were seen as overly deterministic in their portrayal of the individual in society: The actor was depicted as either *tabula rasa*, internalizing the norms and values of society out of a desire for group membership, or as a *homo economicus*, developing social, political, and ideological characteristics as a result of his/her class membership. As a result, these traditional approaches generated an overly passive and constrained view of the actor. In its determinism, macro sociology also tended to be a monocausal gloss, failing to capture the complexity of the everyday world. Some of the early critiques of macro sociology from the everyday life perspective include Douglas (1970a), Filmer et al (1972), Lyman and Scott (1970), Psathas (1968, 1973), Tiryakian (1962, 1965, 1968), Wilson (1970), and Zimmermann and Wieder (1970).

Everyday life sociologists critiqued traditional sociology epistemologically for its "absolutist" stance toward studying natural phenomena (Douglas 1970a, 1976; Douglas and Johnson, 1977; Feyerabend, 1972; Johnson, 1975; Kauffman, 1944; Manning, 1973; Mehan and Wood, 1975; Phillips, 1974). They rejected the premise of *subject-object dualism*: the belief that the subject (knower) and the object (known) can be effectively separated through scientific principles. Procedures such as the objectification, detachment, control, and manipulation of abstracted concepts and variables violate the integrity of the phenomena under study (Cicourel, 1964; Douglas, 1970a, 1976; Schutz, 1962, 1964).

Contextuality

Everyday life sociologists sought to respect this integrity by studying people in their *natural context*: the everyday social world (Cicourel, 1964; Denzin, 1970, Douglas, 1970a, 1976; Garfinkel, 1967; J. Lofland, 1971, 1976). This is the most fundamental and central emphasis of everyday life sociology. Naturally occurring interaction is the foundation of all understanding of society. Describing and analyzing the character and implications of everyday life interaction should thus serve as both the beginning and the end point of sociology. This includes the perceptions, feelings, and meanings members experience as well as the micro structure they create in the process.

Model of the Actor

Everyday life sociologists move from studying interaction and communication in two directions. First, they move inward, toward consciousness, deriving a model of the actor based on people's everyday life attitudes and behavior. This includes the interactionist view of the self, the ethnomethodological view of cognitive structure, and the existential view of brute being. To a degree, the relationship between consciousness and interaction is seen as reflexive: people are shaped or socialized by interaction as well as instrumentally in shaping the character of interaction.

Social Structure

Second, they employ a view of social structure and social order that derives from interaction and is also characterized by a reciprocal relation to it. Social structure, organization, and order do not exist independent of the people that interact with them (Blumer, 1969). Rather, they are endogenously constructed, or constituted, as people negotiate their way through interactions (Garfinkel, 1967; Heritage, 1984; Maines, 1977, 1982; Strauss, 1978). The rituals and institutions they thus create then influence the character of their behavior through the expectations and micro social norms they yield (Goffman, 1967). Interaction is thus both voluntaristic and structured (but not completely determined) because of this reflexivity.

HISTORICAL DEVELOPMENT OF EVERYDAY SOCIOLOGY

The groundwork for the development of everyday life sociology was laid in the 1920s and 1930s in two philosophical traditions that established an ideological foundation and direction for micro sociological theory. At the University of Chicago, Mead was forging a pragmatic social behaviorism that would ultimately evolve into symbolic interactionism (Blumer, 1984; Rock, 1979). In Germany, Husserl and Schutz were creating the emerging phenomenological perspective (Wagner, 1983). During this era, however, phenomenology and social behaviorism were fairly disparate and isolated, with little reciprocal or combined influence.

By the 1950s and 1960s this isolation began to abate. Schutz came to the New School for Social Research where his influence spread among American scholars. Blumer moved from the University of Chicago to the University of California, Berkeley, and brought with him symbolic interactionism, his revision of Mead's behaviorism. Shortly thereafter he was joined by Goffman.

Blumer's interactionism (1969) took shape in California, where he incorporated Mead's conceptions of the rationally voluntaristic actor, reflexivity, and role-taking, with an emphasis on the way actors construct their worlds through subjective meanings and motivations. He therefore directed his students to look toward shared meanings established in social interaction and to explore various "meaning worlds" (J. Irwin, personal communications). His work was a critical impetus to the everyday life perspective in sociology.

Goffman's new subfield, dramaturgy, was launched with *The Presentation of Self in Everyday Life* (1959). Influenced by the works of Blumer, Burke, and Durkheim, Goffman offered an analysis of the individual in society which made the arena of interaction the locus of reality, of socialization, and of social regeneration. Goffman's work speaks to both roles (the nature of the self) and rules (micro-social norms). Instead of role-taking for the purpose of cooperatively aligning their actions with others, Goffman's actors intentionally and manipulatively role-play for the purpose of managing others' impressions of them. This occurs through the interaction rituals of everyday life — rituals that shape the individual's inner self by externally imprinting their rules on him or her at the same time they ensure the self-regulatory character of society (Collins, 1980; Fontana, 1980; Lofland, 1980; Vidich and Lyman, 1985).

Garfinkel broadened the everyday life perspective with his *Studies in Ethnomethodology* (1967). Garfinkel's ethnomethodology addressed Parsons' grand questions about social order and social structure, using Schutz's (1962, 1966, 1967) hermeneutical perspective of the actor as a vocabulary for answering them. He directed practitioners to study the mundane routines of everyday life through which social order is created and maintained. He drew on Husserl (1970a, 1970b, 1973) to focus on the rationality and commonality within people that underlies the situational contextuality of behavior. Ethnomethodology thus differs from other everyday sociology by being less interested in how situations are defined and how subjective meanings emerge.[2] It focuses, rather, on how people negotiate and apply rules which embody the social structure on an everyday level (Heritage, 1984; Zimmermann and Wieder, 1970).

The 1960s and 1970s brought a surge of sociological interest in phenomenology due to the English translation of Schutz's and Husserl's work. Sociologists applied these philosophical ideas to an empirical plane and evolved another everyday life perspective: phenomenological sociology.[3] Early works in this tradition include Berger and Luckmann (1967), Douglas (1970b), and Psathas (1973). The former tied phenomenology's emphasis on consciousness as the locus of reality to a social constructionist view of society. Douglas' edited volume contained seminal theoretical essays advancing, critiquing, and synthesising the ethnomethodological, symbolic interactionist, and phenomenological/existential perspectives. This work was one the of the first applications of the term "everyday life" to the new sociologies.[4] Psathas' book further discussed and empirically applied the phenomenological perspective.

Everyday life sociology thus had its birth during these decades. It emerged in an atmosphere, especially in California, of eclectic synthesis and excitement about the creation and synthesis of new ideas (Manning, 1973). Everyday life sociology was also nurtured and shaped by the surrounding background of California's secularism, heterogenous beliefs, and pluralistic subcultures, fostering an atmosphere of innovation, divergence, and freedom (Vidich and Lyman, 1985). From Berkeley, use of the everyday life perspective spread to the other sociology departments of the University of California system, where compatible thinkers were located. Unfortunately, this burgeoning perspective was somewhat marred by the in-fighting and drift which effectively prohibited "everyday life" from becoming the focal theme of these theorists. While a unified concept remained, no movement developed to press for the identification and recognition of all this work under the everyday life rubric. As a result, individual practitioners chose freely from among the various theories, used and combined them as they saw fit, and made their own decisions as to whether they wanted to affiliate themselves with the everyday life label.

The late 1970s and 1980s brought a new generation of everyday life sociologists. In this era, we have seen a continuation of both the unity and diversity of the everyday life perspective. On the one hand, there has been a growing awareness of the overarching everyday life label. More people identified their work with everyday life sociology, and a number of books appeared that addressed this theme. Morris (1977) produced a theoretical treatise offering comparisons, contrasts, critiques, and historical discussion of the various "creative," or everyday life perspectives. Mackie (1985) employed a phenomenological/existential perspective to analyze the drift of the modern everyday world and the individual's alienated role within it. Textbooks were offered by Douglas and his colleagues (1980), Wiegert (1981), and Karp and Yoels (1986). A number of empirical works, drawn from the various subfields, all explored the problematic and mundane features of everyday life. Among these are L. Lofland (1973), Irwin (1977), Cohen and Taylor (1976), and the collected works found in Brissett and Edgley (1975), J. Lofland (1978), and Psathas (1973, 1979).

During this period the diversity of the everyday life studies in sociology also continued in a variety of directions. For this forum we have selected three to explore more fully; existential sociology, the sociology of emotions, and conversation analysis. These three arenas represent the major successes of everyday life sociology that emerged from the churning dissension and consensus of the 1960s and 1970s. We have chosen them because they represent recent advances in, respectively, theoretical, substantive, and methodological arenas of everyday life sociology.

EXISTENTIAL SOCIOLOGY

Existential sociology is located within a philosophical tradition that dates back to the ancient Greek culture. Early Greek existentialists include both Thrasymachus, the sophist from Chalcedon who rejected Socrates' rational search for an understanding of human beings within the cosmos, and the god Dionysus, who represented the inner feelings and situated expressions of human beings, unbridled by any rational restrictions. More recently and directly, this tradition draws on the existential philosophy of Heidegger, Camus, Sartre, and Merleau-Ponte, the phenomenology of Husserl and Schutz, and the hermeneutics of Dilthey (Fontana, 1980).

Existential sociology is the most recent of the everyday life theoretical perspectives. It shares with the others a common critique of the absolutist sociologies and an orientation toward the same set of focal concerns and beliefs. It goes beyond them in integrating subfields, combining them with a more complex, contradictory, and multidimensional view of the actor and the social world. Existential sociology also differs from other everyday life theories in its view of human beings as not merely rational or symbolic, or motivated by the desire to cooperate by interlinking actions. Instead, its proponents believe that people have strong elements of emotionality and irrationality, and that they often act on the basis of their feelings or moods. People are simultaneously determined and free, affected by structural constraints while remaining mutable, changeable, and emergent (see Zurcher, 1977, for a fuller discussion of the relationship between social change and the existential self).

At the same time, existential sociologists view society as complex and pluralistic, divided by power struggles between different groups (see Douglas, 1971, for an existential analysis of American social order). Torn by the loyalties of their multiple memberships, people experience inner conflict. Since most groups in the society have things they want to hide form other groups, people present fronts to nonmembers. This creates two sets of realities about their activities: one presented to outsiders, the other reserved for insiders. Drawing on the perspectives of Goffman (1959) and Machiavelli (1532), existential sociologists also believe that people manage the impressions they present to others. Researchers, then, must penetrate these fronts to find out about human nature and human society (Adler and Adler, 1987; Douglas, 1976). The main theoretical works in this tradition include Lyman and Scott (1970), Manning (1973), Douglas and Johnson (1977), and Kotarba and Fontana (1984).

A number of empirical works illustrate the application and analytical value of this perspective. These works share a focus on individuals' search for meaning and self in an increasingly bureaucratized modern society. They also emphasize the importance of individuals' core feelings and emotions in guiding their perceptions, interpretations, and lives. *The Nude Beach*, by Douglas and Rasmussen (1977), offered a multiperspectival view of the complexity of feelings, motivations, rationalizations, behaviors, fronts, and micro and macro politics associated with public nudity and sexuality. In

Wheeling and Dealing, P.A. Adler (1985) portrayed the greed and narcissism, rationality and irrationality, hedonism and involvement associated with the fast life of upper level drug dealers and smugglers. Kotarba's (1983) study, *Chronic Pain*, described the anxiety and uncertainty faced by chronic sufferers as they confront the futility of their search for solutions that will both alleviate their pain and provide viable meanings for their experience. *The Last Frontier*, by Fontana (1977), explored the emotional issues, loneliness, and existential identity changes that underlie and render insignificant the rational meaning of growing old. In P. Adler's (1981) book, *Momentum*, he analyzed the dynamics and self-reinforcing excitement and depression caused by momentum-infused individuals, groups, and masses. Last, a series of articles that address the existential self in society are noteworthy: Altheide (1984) on the aggrandized nature of the media self; Ferraro and Johnson (1984) on the victimized self of the organizational member; and Warren and Ponse (1977) on the stigmatized, conflictful, and dramaturgical nature of the gay self.

THE SOCIOLOGY OF EMOTIONS

For many years the topic of emotions was ignored or addressed only tangentially by sociologists. Recently, however, a newfound interest in the emotions has spawned a spate of articles, books, sessions, and a section of the American Sociological Association devoted to this substantive arena. Most of this interest has come from everyday life sociologists. Their perspective is well suited to generate understanding about emotions because sentiments occur within the interactional realm and its correlates: inward to the self and outward toward what Maines (1982) has called the mesostructure. The recent literature on the sociology of emotions can be divided according to these two main themes.

Organistic/Voluntaristic

The first of these approaches focuses on the organic foundation of emotion. Emotions are considered to exist apart from and prior to introspection and are motored by instinct rather than by cognition. Social experiences trigger emotions that derive from inner sources. This is, thus, a conception of behavior which emphasizes individuals' inner-directed character. Its practitioners build from this base to show how individuals' emotions ultimately work upward to reconfirm, maintain, and change society and social structure (Franks, 1985; Hochschild, 1983).

Using an organic perspective, Kemper (1978) has emphasized how the power and/or status inherent in social relationships influence body chemistry. Scheff (1979) proposed a "need theory" of emotional catharsis where individuals undergo arousal, climax, and resolution of feeling states through a biological reflex sequence. Hochschild's (1983) work on airline stewardesses has attempted to show that emotions are an organically based sixth sense that serve, as Freud (1923) first suggested, a critical signal function. The work of the existential sociologists (see Douglas, 1977 and

Johnson 1977 for their programmatic on emotions), too, falls into this approach, as they have ascribed a critical emotional dimension to the individual's inner "brute being." For them, feelings are not only independent of rational thought and values but ultimately dominate them.

Constructionist

The second everyday life approach to the study of emotions does not rule out a biological component, but focuses instead on how these physiological processes are molded, structured, and given meaning. Emotions do not exist independent of everyday life experiences, they argue; rather, these experiences call out, modulate, shape, and ultimately create feelings. These are then labeled, assessed, and managed through and by interaction. Structural and cultural factors influence the feeling and interpretation of various emotions due to the way they constrain possibilities and frame situations (Franks, 1985; Hochschild,1983).

Constructionist analysts include Goffman (1967), who discussed the link between situations and institutions and proposed that emotions are determined by the rules and micro acts that comprise situations. Hochschild (1979, 1983) discussed types of "feeling rules" which are structurally mandated onto interactions and relationships through social guidelines. People then try to make their feelings coincide with these rules by doing cognitive, bodily, or expressive "emotions work." Emotion work can become commercialized when it is co-opted by business, leading to a "commoditization of feeling." Shott (1979) focused on role-taking emotions, suggesting that our empathy for the feelings of others is a mechanism ensuring the maintenance of social order and social control. Her discussion of the social processes common to diverse emotional experiences also accentuated structurally derived display rules. Gordon's (1981) approach to emotions focused on sentiments, learned in enduring social relationships, whose differentiation, socialization, management, and normative regulation are structurally dictated. Building on Hochschild, Heiss (1981) discussed "emotion rules" which are shaped through interaction by individuals' definition of the situation, role-taking, self-concepts, and self-presentations, leading to the formation of "emotion roles" [i.e. Clark's discussion of sympathizers (1987)]. Averill (1980) proposed that during states of heightened emotional arousal we experience passivity and enact socially prescribed behavior. Zurcher (1982, 1985) and L. Lofland (1985) have suggested that emotions are scripted by structural and interactional contexts. Finally, Denzin (1984) has suggested that emotions are shaped through the direct experience of practical activities in the process of the obdurate social world. In sum, understanding emotions enriches our perspective on the actor's voluntarism and illustrates further one means by which society motivates individuals to conform to its rules.

CONVERSATION ANALYSIS

Conversation analysis is a method of data gathering and analysis that is informed by the theoretical beliefs of ethnomethodology. Like other ethnomethodologists, conversation analysts have largely abandoned the earlier ethnomethodological concern with studying the contextual particularity of subjective meanings because endless indexicality refuted any intersubjectivity and became "a phenomenologically inspired but sociologically aimless empiricism" (Zimmermann, 1979:384). Drawing on Parsons through Garfinkel and Durkheim through Goffman (Heritage, 1985), conversation analysts have embraced a structural interest that makes them more closely aligned with and acceptable to the interests of positivist mainstream sociologists (see Boden, 1986; Collins, 1981a, b).[5]

Conversation analysts study language because they regard "natural language" as an everyday life social system that is (a)external, existing prior to and independently of any speaker, and (b)constraining, obligatory rather than preferential in its framing. Natural language as a "mode of doing things" (Austin, 1961; Wittgenstein, 1953) is thus reviewed as an interactionist object, a widespread, general, abstract system that is both immediate (situational) and transcendent (transsituational). As such, it exhibits the objective properties of a Durkheimian social fact (Zimmermann, 1979).

Conversation analysts are concerned with both the competencies and the structure underlying ordinary, everyday social activities. They therefore study the production of natural language in situ, as it occurs spontaneously in the everyday world. They regard conversation as both context-shaped and context-renewing, influenced by and contributing to the context shaped by interaction. Disdaining "premature" theory construction, they have focused on tape recording minute, detailed "instances": the raw, primary data of actual conversation (Heritage, 1984, 1985; Schegloff, 1980; Schegloff and Sacks, 1973).

In their studies, conversation analysts began by concentrating on action sequences of talk. An interest in turns-within-sequences developed out of the early work of Sacks et al (1974) on the management of conversational turn-taking. It was soon discovered that such structural analyses of talk served as a guideline for interpersonal interaction and its analysis.

Further conversation analysis has focused on a number of topics. First, Sacks, Schegloff, and others continued to investigate turn-taking, observing the recurrence of the question-response format they termed the "adjacency pair" (Schegloff, 1968; Schegloff and Sacks, 1973), "preference organization" (the tendency of respondents to select the preferred alternative) (Davidson, 1984; Pomerantz, 1984; Sacks and Schegloff, 1979; Schegloff et al, 1977; Wooton, 1981), and "topic organization" (the continuation of conversation around the same topic) (Button and Casey, 1984; Maynard, 1980).

Second, conversation analysts have examined the use of non- or quasi-lexical speech objects such as laughter and head nods that show the listener's continuing participation in the interaction (C. Goodwin, 1980; Jefferson, 1979, 1984; Schegloff, 1982).

A third area of inquiry has been the integration of vocal and nonvocal activities, such as gazing and body movements (C. Goodwin, 1981; M. Goodwin, 1980; Heath, 1982a, 1984).

Last, a number of excellent studies have examined interaction in situational settings. These works build on the foundation of knowledge about mundane conversations, seek variations from that structure, and attribute it to the institutional context. As such, this body of work represents a more contextual approach and moves away from pure empiricism toward the beginnings of theoretical development. Institutional settings that have yielded fruitful research include courts (Atkinson and Drew, 1979; Dunstan, 1980; Maynard, 1984; Pomerantz and Atkinson, 1984), classrooms (Cuff and Hustler, 1982; Mehan, 1979), and medical encounters (Heath, 1981a, 1981b; West, 1983, 1984b, 1985). Several studies have also addressed the impact of gender on institutional interaction (French and French, 1984; West, 1984a).

While focused on naturally occurring, mundane communication observed in situ, conversation analysis diverges sharply in its orientation from the remaining corpus of everyday life sociology. It is more structural in interest and formal in analysis. Conversation analysis is also more objectively oriented, treating conversation as external to individuals, encouraging the replication and testing of its findings, and addressing the context of verification. In this way it departs form the customary hallmarks of everyday life sociology — subjectivity and discovery. Yet at the same time as it diverges, conversation analysis broadens the base of the everyday life perspective. Its radically micro and radically empiricist approach translates the product of interaction into a form that can be built upon by macro sociologists interested in an objective micro base for grand structural analysis (Collins, 1981a, 1981b).

INFLUENCES ON MACRO THEORY

With the onslaught on macro theory by the early sociologists of everyday life, the schism between the macro and micro perspectives widened. Recently, however, in response to the challenges presented by everyday life sociologists, certain macro theorists have begun to incorporate some of the micro concepts discussed earlier. Prominent among these new "integrationists" have been several important neo-Marxists in Europe (especially the French everyday life sociologists, or *sociologists de la vie quotidienne*), and in England and America, a small group of neofunctionalists and eclectic, synthetic thinkers. In attempting to bridge the micro-macro gap, these grand theorists have begun to integrate the diametrically opposed positions of absolutist and everyday life sociology (for a further discussion see Alexander et al, 1987; Collins, 1981a, Knorr-Cetina, 1981).

One of the most significant concepts adapted from everyday life sociology is *voluntarism* and its related dimensions. These newer macro theorists, as Parsons once did, are recognizing the importance of the individual, or active agent, within the structure of society. While they view individuals as constrained by social structure, they of course recognize them not as determined by it. Their portrayals of social life and ultimately society thus incorporate an element of unpredictability (Alexander, 1982; Bourdieu, 1977; Collins, 1975; Giddens, 1979, 1984; Touraine, 1984), a feature lacking in the Parsonian formulation. In addition, embedding voluntaristic action in structure leads to a view of society as both context-shaped and context-forming. This draws on the ethnomethodological concept that interactions are embedded in their context of occurrence while at the same time they reflexively constitute these contexts.

It also uses the symbolic interactionist view that we live in a negotiated order and cause our subjective perceptions to become real by acting on their imagined consequences. Macro theorists have transformed this into a dialectical relationship between action and order: society both creates the historical, social, and cultural orientations that evoke behavior and at the same time serves as an agent of its own self-production (Alexander, 1982; Bourdieu, 1977; Giddens, 1979, 1984; Lefebvre, 1971; Touraine, 1977).

Modern integrationist theorists also try to avoid totally objectivist approaches by incorporating an element of *subjectivism* from everyday life sociology. Rather than proposing models of generative mechanisms or deep structures invisible to the acting agents, they incorporate a view of the actor who understands and reflects upon his or her behavior as he/she is engaged in it (Collins, 1975, 1981a; Giddens, 1979, 1984).

Another departure from traditional macro sociology is the formulation of perspectives "propelled by a combination of theoretical and empirical argument" (Alexander, 1928:30). Instead of merely looking to the idealistic logic of reason and philosophy for explanatory hypotheses, these new theorists are turning to the material reality of what Blumer (1969) has called the "obdurate" empirical world. This integrates an awareness of the everyday life actor's "natural attitude" (Schutz, 1962) with the "theoretical stance" (Douglas, 1970a) employed by the social science analyst. In this way irrational and emotional dimensions can be introduced into the overall perspective (Alexander, 1982; Bourdieu, 1977, 1984; Collins, 1975, 1981a; Giddens, 1979, 1984; Lefebvre, 1971; Touraine, 1977, 1984).

Finally, these theorists have looked to everyday life *interaction*, searching for a hidden unity beneath the surface. They have found everyday life to be organized, even repetitive, to the point of being ritualistic. Goffman's analysis of micro social norms, Garfinkel's discovery of the moral character undergirding the routines of everyday life interaction, and the conversation analytic view that natural language embodies the structural organization of social reality have been especially influential. The organized character of everyday life has been used in two ways: as a base for building an "aggregation"(Knorr-Cetina, 1981) of micro interactions into a macro reality (Collins, 1975, 1981b), and as a point of mediation between the individual and social structure so that the feedback at the interactional level leads to their reciprocal influence (Bourdieu, 1977; Giddens, 1984; Lefebvre, 1971).

It is in these micro-macro syntheses that many of the most far-fetching theoretical advances of everyday life sociology can be found.

CRITIQUES AND ASSESSMENTS

The critiques and assessments of everyday life sociology are legion. Research guided by this perspective has been condemned as astructural or acontextual (Coser, 1975; Gouldner, 1970; Horowitz, 1971; Reynolds and Reynolds, 1973; Zeitlin, 1973), incapable of addressing political factors (Gouldner, 1970), ahistorical (Bernstein, 1976; Gouldner, 1970; Ropers, 1973; Smith, 1973; Zeitlin, 1973), and generally trivial in its focus and findings (Coser, 1975; Gellner, 1975), to name the major ones.

While several of these critiques may have been accurate during the early years of the field, there have been movements in the last decade to address these criticisms. The area where the greatest advances have been made is structural analysis. Some practitioners have addressed the topics of social organization and social structure directly, theorizing about the macro implications of micro models of interaction and communication (Hall, 1986; Maines, 1977, 1982; Maynard and Wilson, 1980; Schegloff, 1987). Other everyday life sociologists have studied specific organizations or industries and written about their structural characteristics (Denzin, 1977; Farberman, 1975). Last, research into the structure and content of organizational culture has been fruitful (Fine, 184; Rohlen, 1974; Schein, 1983; Van Maanen, 1973).

The political arena has also attracted increased attention from everyday life sociologists. Some researchers have addressed organizational or governmental power and politics (Clegg, 1975; Hall, 1972, 1985; Kinsey, 1985; Klatch, 1987; Molotch and Boden, 1985), while others have focused on interpersonal political dimensions (Fisher and Todd, 1983; Kramarae et al, 1984), especially those related to gender politics (Thorne and Henley, 1975; West, 1979).

Everyday life sociology can still be considered largely ahistorical because of its emphasis on the contemporary. Some research is historically embedded through (Ball and Lilly, 1982; Galliher and Walker, 1977; Gusfield, 1963, 1981), and the aggregation of micro interactions may build to an understanding of historicism (Collins, 1981b).

Last, everyday life sociology may appear trivial to outsiders who are unfamiliar with the theoretical issues it addresses. The strength of everyday life sociology lies in generating sociological concepts or insights from seemingly trivial settings, such as the notion of idioculture from Little League baseball (Fine, 1987), emotion work from airline stewardesses (Hochschild, 1983), and lust and deceit from nude beaches (Douglas and Rasmussen, 1977), and from the minutiae of everyday life, such as telephone openings (Schegloff, 1979), interruptions (West and Zimmermann, 1983), and gazing (C. Goodwin, 1980). Beyond this, the study of everyday life lays a foundation for understanding the basics of social order, social action, and the social construction of reality (Collins, 1981b).

FUTURE

Everyday life sociology is at a crossroads. It has a rich heritage of making theoretical, epistemological, and substantive contributions to social science. It also has continuing potential to fill lacunae in empirical knowledge and conceptual understanding of the everyday world. It has a secure foothold in the discipline as an established alternative approach. Every day life sociology is routinely published by university presses, its own journals, and to a lesser degree, by mainstream journals. Last, some of its subfields have lost their cultlike isolation and become increasingly integrated into the discipline.

Yet several dangers lie ahead. First, the field must continue to advance new perspectives on substantive, epistemological, and theoretical issues rather than merely applying existing ones. Second, with the imminent retirement of many of its founders, leadership must emerge from within its ranks. Third, there is a near absence of research centers with the critical mass of faculty necessary to train the next generation of everyday life sociologists. Without this regenerative capacity, everyday life sociology may have a limited future and faces a bankruptcy that threatens not only itself but the insight it brings to the entire discipline.

ACKNOWLEDGEMENTS

We would like to thank Deirdre Boden, John Johnson, Ralph Turner, and an anonymous reviewer for their help in preparing this manuscript.

NOTES

1. For a fuller discussion of the various epistemological stances associated with symbolic interactionism, ethnomethodology (with respect to ethnography), and existential sociology, see Adler and Adler (1987).
2. For a distinction between ethnomethodology and phenomenological sociology, see Rogers (1983) and Zimmerman (1979). For the difference between ethnomethodology and symbolic interactionism, see Gallant and Kleinman (1983) and Zimmerman and Wieder (1970). See Johnson (1977) for a contrast between ethnomethodology and existential sociology. Finally, Perinbanayagam (1974) contrasts ethnomethodology and dramaturgy.
3. Zaner (1970) has suggested that we should speak of phenomenologically derived sociology rather than of phenomenological sociology, for the goals of phenomenology as a philosophy are different from those of its sociological derivatives.
4. Douglas first used the term everyday life phenomena in his (1976) work, where he distinguished between "everyday" and "anyday" phenomena.
5. Conversation analysis articles are increasingly beginning to appear in establishment journals, such as Maynard and Zimmerman (1984), Maynard (1985), and Molotch and Boden (1985).

REFERENCES

Adler, P. 1981. *Momentum*. Beverly Hills: Sage.
Adler, P.A. 1985. *Wheeling and Dealing*. New York: Columbia University Press.
Adler, P.A., and Adler, P. 1987. *Membership Roles in Field Research*. Beverly Hills: Sage.
Alexander, J. 1982. *Theoretical Logic in Sociology: Positivism, Presuppositions, and Current Controversies*. Berkeley: University of California Press.
Alexander, J., Geisen, B., Munch, R., Smelser, N. 1987. *The Micro-Macro Link*. Berkeley: University of California Press.
Altheide, D.L. 1984. "The Media Self." See Kotarba and Fontana 1984, pp. 177–195.
Atkinson, J.M., Drew, P. 1979. *Order in Court*. London: Macmillan.
Atkinson, J.M., Heritage, J.C. (eds.) 1984. *Structures of Social Action: Studies in Conversation Analysis*. Cambridge: Cambridge University Press.
Austin, J.L. 1961. *Philosophical Papers*. London: Oxford University Press.
Averill, J.R. 1980. "A Constructionist View of Emotion," in *Emotion: Theory, Research, and Experience*, edited by R. Plutchik, and H. Kellerman. V.I. New York: Academic Press.
Ball, R.A., Lilly, J.R. 1982. "The Menace of Margarine: The Rise and Fall of a Social Problem." *Social Problems* 29:488–498.
Berger, P., Luckmann, T. 1967. *The Social Construction of Reality*. New York: Doubleday.

Bernstein, R.J. 1976. *The Restructuring of Political Theory*. New York: Harcourt Brace and Jovanovich.
Blumer, H. 1969. *Symbolic Interactionism*. Englewood Cliffs: Prentice Hall.
Boden, D. 1986. "Talking with Doctors: Conversation Analysis in Action." *Contemporary Sociology* 15:715–718.
Bourdieu, P. 1977. *Outline of a Theory of Practice*. Cambridge: University of Cambridge Press.
———. 1984. *Distinction*. London: Routledge and Kegan Paul.
Brissett, D., Edgley, C. 1975. *Life as Theater*. Chicago: Aldine.
Bulmer, M. 1984. *The Chicago School of Sociology*. Chicago: University of Chicago Press.
Button, G., Casey, N. 1984. Generating Topic: The Use of Topic Initial Elicitors. See Atkinson and Heritage 1984, pp. 167–190.
Cicourel, A.V. 1967. *Method and Measurement in Sociology*. New York: Free Press.
Clark, C. 1987. "Sympathy Biography and Sympathy Margin." *American Journal of Sociology*, in press.
Clegg, S. 1975. *Power, Rule, and Domination: A Critical and Empirical Understanding of Power in Sociological Theory and Everyday Life*. London: Routledge and Kegan Paul.
Cohen S., Taylor, L. 1976. *Escape Attempts*. Harmondsworth, Eng: Penguin.
Collins, R. 1975. *Conflict Sociology*. New York: Academic Press.
1980. "Erving Goffman and the Development of Modern Social Theory," pp. 170–210 in *The View from Goffman*, edited by J. Ditton. London: Macmillan.
———. 1981a. "On the Micro-foundations of Macro-sociology." *American Journal of Sociology* 86:984–1015.
———. 1981b. "Micro-translation as a Theory-building Strategy." See Knorr-Cetina and Cicourel 1981, pp. 81–108.
Coser, L.A. 1975. "Two Methods in Search of a Substance." *American Sociological Review* 40:691–700.
Cuff, E. C., Hustler, D. 1982. "Stories and Story-time in an Infant Classroom." *Semiotica* 42:119–154.
Davidson, J.A. 1984. "Subsequent Versions of Invitations, Offers, Requests, and Proposals Dealing with Potential or Actual Rejection." See Atkinson and Heritage 1984, pp. 102–128.
Denzin, N.K. 1970. *The Research Act*. Chicago: Aldine.
———. 1977. "Notes on the Criminogenic Hypothesis: A Case Study of the American Liquor Industry." *American Sociological Review* 49:905–920.
———. 1984. *On Understanding Emotion*. San Francisco: Josey Bass.
Douglas, J.D. 1967. *The Social Meanings of Suicide*. Princeton, N.J.: Princeton University Press.
———. 1970a. "Understanding Everyday Life." See Douglas 1970b, pp. 3–44.
———. 1970b. *Understanding Everyday Life*. Chicago: Aldine.
———. 1971. *American Social Order*. New York: Free Press.
———. 1976. *Investigative Social Research*. Beverly Hills: Sage.
———. 1977. "Existential Sociology." See Douglas and Johnson 1977, pp. 3–73.
Douglas, J.D., Adler, P.A., Adler, P., Fontana, A., Freeman, C., Kotarba, J. 1980. *Introduction to the Sociologies of Everyday Life*. Boston: Allyn and Bacon.
Douglas, J.D. and Johnson, J.M. 1977. *Existential Sociology*. New York: Cambridge University Press.
Douglas, J.D. and Rasmussen, P. 1977. *The Nude Beach*. Beverly Hills: Sage.
Dunstan, R. 1980. "Contexts for Coercion: Analyzing Properties of Courtroom Questioning." *British Journal of Law Society* 6:61–77.
Farberman, H.A. 1975. "A Criminogenic Market Structure: The Automotive Industry." *Sociological Quarterly* 16:438–457.
Ferraro, K.J., Johnson, J.M. 1984. "The Victimized Self: The Case of Battered Women." See Kotarba and Fontana 1984, pp. 119–130.
Feyerbend, P.F. 1972. *Against Method*. London: New Left Books.
Filmer, P. Phillipson, M., Silverman, D., Walsh, D. 1972. *New Directions in Sociological Theory*. Cambridge, MA: MIT Press.
Fine, G.A. 1984. "Negotiated Orders and Organizational Cultures." *Annual Review of Sociology* 10:239–262.
———. 1987. *With the Boys*. Chicago: University of Chicago Press.
Fisher, S., Todd, A.D. 1983. *The Social Organization of Doctor-Patient Communication*. Washington, D.C.: Cent. Appl. Linguis.

Fontana, A. 1977. *The Last Frontier*. Beverly Hills: Sage.
―――. 1980. "Toward a Complex Universe: Existential Sociology." See Douglas et al 1980, pp.155–181.
Franks, D. 1985. Introduction to the Special Issue on the Sociology of Emotions. *Symbolic Interactionism* 8:161–170.
French, J. and French P. 1984. "Gender Imbalances in the Primary Classroom: An Interactional Account." *Education Res.* 26:127–136.
Freud, S. 1923. *The Ego and the Id*. London: Hogarth.
Gallant, M.J. and Kleinman, S. 1983. "Symbolic Interactionism vs. Ethnomethodology." *Symbolic Interactionism* 6:1–18.
Galliher, J.F. and Walker, A. 1977. "The Puzzle of the Social Origins of the Marijuana Tax Act of 1937." *Social Problems* 24:267–276.
Garfinkel, H. 1967. *Studies in Ethnomethodology*. Englewood Cliffs: Prentice Hall.
Gellner, E. 1975. "Ethnomethodology: the Reenchantment Industry of the California Way of Subjectivity." *Philosophical Social Science* 5:431–450.
Giddens, A. 1979. *Central Problems in Social Theory: Action, Structure, and Construction in Social Analysis*. Berkeley: University of California Press.
―――. 1984. *The Constitution of Society*. Berkeley: University of California Press.
Goffman, E. 1967. *The Presentation of Self in Everyday Life*. New York: Doubleday Anchor.
Goodwin, C. 1980. "Restarts, Pauses, and the Achievement of Mutual Gaze at Turn Beginning." *Sociological Inquiry* 50:272–302.
―――. 1981. *Conversational Organization: Interaction Between Speakers and Hearers*. New York: Academic Press.
Goodwin, M.H. 1980. "Some Aspects of Processes of Mutual Monitoring Implicated in the Production of Description Sequences." *Sociological Inquiry* 50:303–317.
Gordon, S.L. 1981. "The Sociology of Sentiments and Emotions," pp. 562–592 in *Social Psychology*, edited by M. Rosenberg and R.H. Turner. New York: Basic Books.
Gouldner, A. 1970. *The Coming Crisis of Western Sociology*. New York: Basic Books.
Gusfield, J. 1963. *Symbolic Crusade*. Urbana, IL: University of Illinois Press.
―――. 1981. *The Culture of Public Problems*. Chicago: University of Chicago Press.
Hall, P.M. 1972. "A Symbolic Interactionist Analysis of Politics." *Sociological Inquiry* 42:35–75.
―――. 1985. "Asymmetric Relationships and Processes of Power," pp. 309–344 in *Foundations of Interpretive Sociology*, edited by H. Farberman and R. Perinbanayagam. Greenwich, CT: JAI Press.
―――. 1986. *Interactionism and the Study of Social Organization*. Presented at the Annual Meetings of the Midwest Sociological Society, Des Moines, IA.
Heath, C.C. 1981. "The Opening Sequence in Doctor-Patient Interaction," pp.71–90 in *Medical Work: Realities and Routines*, edited by P. Atkinson and C.C. Heath. Farmborough, Eng.: Gower.
―――. 1982a. "The Display of Recipiency: An Instance of a Sequential Relationship Between Speech and Body Movements." *Semiotica* 42:147–167.
―――. 1982b. "Preserving the Consultation: Medical Record Cards and Professional Conduct." *Journal of Sociological Health and Illness* 4:56–74.
―――. 1984. "Talk and Recipiency: Sequential Organization in Speech and Body Movement." See Atkinson and Heritage 1984, pp. 247–265.
Heiss, J. 1981. *The Social Psychology of Interaction*. Englewood Cliffs, NJ: Prentice Hall.
Heritage, J.C. 1984. *Garfinkel and Ethnomethodology*. Cambridge, Eng.: Polity.
―――. 1985. "Recent Developments in Conversation Analysis." *Sociolinguistics* XV:1–18.
Hochschild, A.R. 1983. *The Managed Heart*. Berkeley: University of California Press.
Horowitz, I.L. 1971. "Review of Howard S. Becker's Sociological Work: Methods and Substance." *American Sociological Review* 36:527–28.
Husserl, E. 1970a. *Logical Investigations*. New York: Humanities Press.
―――. 1970b. *The Crisis of European Sciences and Transcendental Phenomenology: An Introduction to Phenomenological Philosophy*. Evanston, IL: Northwestern University Press.
―――. 1973. *Experience and Judgement*. Evanston, IL: Northwestern University Press.
Irwin, J. 1977. *Scenes*. Beverly Hills: Sage.

Jefferson, G. 1979. "A Technique for Inviting Laughter and Its Subsequent Acceptance/Declination." See Psathas 1979, pp. 79–96.
———. 1984. "On Stepwise Transition from Talk About a Trouble to Inappropriately Next-Positioned Matters." See Atkinson and Heritage 1984, pp.1919–1222.
Johnson, J.M. 1975. *Doing Field Research*. New York: Free Press.
———. 1977. "Ethnomethodology and Existential Sociology." See Douglas and Johnson 1977, pp.153–173.
Karp, D. and Yoels, W. 1986. *Sociology and Everyday Life*. Itasca, IL: Peacock.
Kauffman, F. 1944. *Methodology of the Social Sciences*. New York: Humanities.
Kemper, T.D. 1978. *A Social Interactional Theory of Emotions*. New York: Wiley.
Kinsey, B. 1985. "Congressional Staff: The Cultivation and Maintenance of Personal Networks in an Insecure Work Environment." *Urban Life* 13:395–422.
Klatch, R. 1987. *Women of the New Right*. Philadelphia: Temple University Press.
Knorr-Cetina, K. 1981. "The Micro Sociological Challenge of the Macro Sociology: Towards a Reconstruction of Social Theory." See Knorr-Cetina and Cicourel 1981, pp. 1–47.
Knorr-Cetina, K. and Cicourel, A. 1981. *Advances in Social Theory and Methodology*. London: Routledge and Kegan Paul.
Kotarba, J.A. 1983. *Chronic Pain*. Beverly Hills: Sage.
Kotarba, J.A. and Fontana, A. 1984. *The Existential Self in Society*. Chicago: University of Chicago Press.
Kramarae, C., Schulz, M., O'Barr, W. 1984. *Language and Power*. Beverly Hills: Sage.
Lefebvre, H. 1971. *Everyday Life in the Modern World*. London: Penguin.
Lofland, J. 1971. *Analyzing Social Settings*. Belmont, CA: Wadsworth.
———. 1976. *Doing Social Life*. New York: Wiley.
———. 1978. *Interaction in Everyday Life*. Beverly Hills: Sage.
———. 1980. "Early Goffman: Style, Structure, Substance, Soul," pp. 24–51 in *The View from Goffman*, edited by J. Ditton. London: Macmillan.
Lofland, L.H. 1973. *A World of Strangers*. New York: Basic.
———. 1985. "The Social Shaping of Emotion: The Case of Grief." *Symbolic Interactionism* 8:171–190.
Lyman, S.M. and Scott, M.B. 1989. *A Sociology of the Absurd*. Dix Hills, New York: General Hall.
Machiavelli, N. (1532) 1970. *The Prince*. New York: Washington Square.
Mackie, F. 1985. *The Status of Everyday Life*. London: Routledge and Kegan Paul.
Maines, D.R. 1977. "Social Organization and Social Structure in Symbolic Interactionist Thought." *Annual Review of Sociology* 3:75–95.
———. 1982. "In Search of Mesostructure." *Urban Life* 11:267–279.
Manning, P.K. 1973. "Existential Sociology." *Sociological Quarterly* 14:200–225.
Maynard, D.W. 1980. "Placement of Topic Changes in Conversation." *Semiotica* 30:263–290.
———. 1984. *Inside Plea Bargaining*. New York: Plenum.
———. 1985. "Social Conflict Among Children." *American Sociological Review* 50:207–223.
Maynard, D.W. and Wilson, T.P. 1980. "On the Reification of Social Structure," pp. 287–322, in *Current Perspectives in Social Theory*, edited by S.G. McNall and G.N. Howe. Greenwich, CT: JAI Press.
Maynard, D.W. and Zimmerman, D.H. 1984. "Topical Talk, Ritual, and the Social Organization of Relationships." *Social Psychology Quarterly* 47:301–316.
Mehan, H. 1979. *Learning Lessons*. Cambridge, Mass: Harvard University Press.
Mehan, H. and Wood, H. 1979. *The Reality of Ethnomethodology*. New York: Wiley.
Molotch, H.L. and Boden, D. "Talking Social Structure: Discourse, Domination, and the Watergate Hearings." *American Sociological Review* 50:273–288.
Morris, M.B. 1977. *An Excursus into Creative Sociology*. New York: Columbia University Press.
Perinbanayagam, R. 1974. "The Definition of the Situation and the Analysis of the Ethnomethodological and Dramaturgical View." *Sociological Quarterly* 15:521–542.
Phillips, D. 1974. "Epistemology and the Sociology of Knowledge." *Theory and Society* 1:59–88.
Pomerantz, A.M. 1984. "Pursuing a Response." See Atkinson and Heritage 1984, pp. 152–163.
Pomerantz, A.M. and Atkinson, J.M. 1984. "Ethnomethodology, Conversation Analysis and the Study of Courtroom Instruction," pp. 283–294 in *Topics in Psychology and Law*, edited by D.J. Muller D.E. Blackman, and A.J. Chapman. Chichester, Eng.: Wiley.

Psathas, G. 1968. "Ethnomethods and Phenomenology." *Sociological Res.* 35:500–520.
———. 1973. *Phenomenological Sociology*. New York: Wiley.
———. 1979. *Everyday Language: Studies in Ethnomethodology*. New York: Irvington Press.
Reynolds, L. and Reynolds, J. 1973. "Interactionism, Complicity, and the Astructural Bias." *Catalyst* 7:76–85.
Rock, P. 1979. *The Making of Symbolic Interactionism*. Totowa, NJ: Rowman and Littlefield.
Rogers, M.F. 1983. *Sociology, Ethnomethodology, and Experience*. New York: Cambridge University Press.
Rohlen, T. 1974. *For Harmony and Strength: Japanese White-Collar Organization in Anthropological Perspective*. Berkeley: University of California Press.
Ropers, R. 1973. "Mead, Marx, and Social Psychology." *Catalyst* 7:42–61.
Sacks, H. and Schegloff, E.A. 1979. "Two Preferences in the Organization of Reference in Conversation and Their Interaction." See Psathas 1979, pp. 15–21.
Sacks, H., Schegloff, E.A., and Jefferson, G. 1974. "A Simplest Systematics for the Organization of Turn-Taking for Conversation." *Language* 50:696–735.
Scheff, T. 1979. *Catharsis in Healing, Ritual and Drama*. Berkeley: University of California Press.
Schegloff, E.A. 1968. "Sequencing in Conversational Openings." *American Anthropology* 70:1075–1095.
———. 1979. "Identification and Recognition in Telephone Openings." See Psathas 1979, pp. 23–78.
———. 1980. "Preliminaries to Preliminaries: Can I Ask You a Question?" *Sociological Inquiry* 50:104–152.
———. 1982. "Discourse as an Interactional Achievement: Some Uses of 'Uh huh' and Other Things That Come Between Sentences." *Georgetown University Roundtable on Language and Linguistics*, pp. 71–93. Washington, DC: Georgetown University Press.
———. 1987. "Between Micro and Macro: Contexts and Other Connections." See Alexander et al 1987. In press.
Schegloff, E.A., Jefferson, G., and Sacks, H. 1977. "The Preference for Self-Correction in the Organization of Repair in Conversation." *Language* 53:361–382.
Schegloff, E.A., Sacks, H. 1973. "Opening up Closings." *Semiotica* 7:289–327.
Schein, E. 1983. "The Role of the Founder in Creating Organizational Culture." *Organizational Dynamics* 12:2–23.
Schutz, A. 1962. *Collected Papers I: The Problem of Social Reality*. The Hague: Martinus Nijhoff.
———. 1964. *Collected Papers II: Studies in Social Theory*. The Hague: Martinus Nijhoff.
———. 1966. *Collected Papers III: Studies in Phenomenological Philosophy*. The Hague: Martinus Nijhoff.
———. 1967. *The Phenomenology of the Social World*. Evanston, IL: Northwestern University Press.
Shott, S. 1979. "Emotion and Social Life: A Symbolic Interactionist Analysis." *American Journal of Sociology* 81:1265–1286.
Smith, D.L. 1973. "Symbolic Interactionism: Definitions of the Situation from H. Becker and J. Lofland." *Catalyst* 7:62–75.
Smith, R.W. 1984. "An Existential View of Organizations: Is the Member condemned to Be Free?" See Kotarba and Fontana 1984, pp. 100–118.
Strauss, A. 1978. *Negotiations*. San Francisco: Josey-Bass.
Thorne, B. and Henley, N. 1975. *Language and Sex: Difference and Dominance*. Rowley, Mass: Newbury House.
Tiryakian, E. 1962. *Existentialism and Sociologism*. Englewood Cliffs, NJ: Prentice Hall.
———. 1965. "Existential Phenomenology and Sociology." *American Sociological Review* 30:647–688.
Touraine, A. 1977. *The Self-Production of Society*. Chicago: University of Chicago Press.
———. 1984. *Le Retour de l'Acteur: Essai de Sociologie*. Paris: Fayard.
Van Maanen, J. 1973. "Observations on the Making of Policemen." *Human Organization* 32:407–418.
Vidich, A., Lyman, S.M. 1985. *American Sociology*. New Haven: Yale University Press.
Wagner, H. 1983. *Alfred Schutz: An Intellectual Biography*. Chicago: Chicago University Press.
Warren, C.A.B. and Ponse, B. 1977. "The Existential Self in the Gay World." See Douglas and Johnson, pp. 273–289.
Weigert, A.J. 1981. *Sociology of Everyday Life*. New York: Longman.

West, C. 1979. "Against Our Will: Male Interruptions of Females in Cross-Sex Conversation," pp. 81–97 in *Language, Sex, and Gender*, edited by M.K. Slater and L.L. Adler. New York: Annual New York Academy of Science.
———. 1983. "Ask Me No Questions...An Analysis of Queries and Replies in Physician-Patient Diagnoses." See Fisher and Todd 1983, pp. 75–106.
———. 1984a. "When the Doctor is a 'Lady': Power, Status, and Gender in Physician-Patient Encounters." *Symbolic Interactionism* 7:87–106.
———. 1984b. "Medical Misfires: Mishearings, Misgivings, and Misunderstandings in Physician-Patient Dialogues." *Discourse Processes* 7:107–134.
———. 1985. *Routine Complications*. Bloomington, IN: Indiana University Press.
West, C. and Zimmerman D.H. 1983. "Small Insults: A Study of Interruptions in Cross-Sex Conversations Between Unacquainted Persons," pp. 102–117 in *Language, Gender, and Society*, edited by B. Thorne, C. Kramarae, and N. Henley. Rowley, Mass: Newbury House.
Wilson, T.P. 1970. "Normative and Interruptive Paradigms in Sociology." See Douglas 1970, pp. 55–79.
Wittgenstein, L. 1953. *Philosophical Investigations*. London: Basil Blackwell.
Wooton, A. 1981. "The Management of Grantings and Rejections by Parents in Request Sequences." *Semiotica* 37:59–89.
Zaner, R. 1970. *The Way of Phenomenology*. New York: Pegasus.
Zeitlen, I.M. 1973. *Rethinking Sociology*. New York: Appleton-Century-Curtis.
Zimmerman, D.W. 1979. "Ethnomethodology," pp. 381–396 in *Theoretical Perspectives in Sociology*, edited by S.G. MacNall. New York: St. Martins.
Zimmerman, D.W. and Weider, D.L. 1970. "Ethnomethodology and the Problem of Order: Comment on Denzin." See Douglas 1970, pp. 285–298.
Zurcher, L.A. 1977. *The Mutable Self*. Beverly Hills: Sage.
———. 1982. "The Staging of Emotions: A Dramaturgical Analysis." *Symbolic Interactionism* 5:1–22.

Chapter 34 HUMAN EMOTIONS: AN EXPANDING SOCIOLOGICAL FRONTIER

C. Eddie Palmer

The recent advances made in the study of the sociology of emotions are fascinating and exhilarating. These advances are charting new intellectual territories and expanding sociological frontiers by identifying important and exciting research agendas (cf. Kemper 1990a). Lodged mainly within the symbolic interaction tradition, the study of emotions has grown rapidly in the past few years. New books and articles on the topic are being produced rapidly and the Sociology of Emotions section of the America Sociological Association, organized in 1986 and officially recognized in 1987, remains strong. David Franks, at Virginia Commonwealth University, is compiling a bibliography on emotions that contains (as of October 17, 1990) over 1,360 entries including several published in our most prestigious journals. A sociology of emotions newsletter has been published since August 1986, and the American Sociological Association's Teaching Resources Center now carries information on teaching the Sociology of emotions. This is in light of the fact that, as Denzin (1990, p. 110) stated, "ten years ago there was no sociology of emotion." Kemper (1990b, p.3) contended that "the beginning of the current attention to emotions among sociologists illustrates the oft-cited principle that new knowledge emerges when the intellectual climate favors it." He went on to say that 1975 was the watershed year for the sociology of emotions, and specifically cited the seminal works of Arlie Russell Hochschild, Thomas Scheff, and Randall Collins during that year. Recognizing that the beginning of some of this work occurred in the early 1970s, Kemper (1990b, p. 4) mentioned that "it is tempting to speculate that sociologists were responding to the *Zeitgeist* of the decade of the 1960s, with its attack on linear logic, its emphasis on the importance of expressiveness, and its concentrated focus on the self".

A reading of the work on the sociology of emotions demonstrated that it involves, in addition to new wine in new bottles, some old wine in old bottles, old wine in new bottles, new wine bottles, and at least one new corkscrew (see Heise 1990 for his work on a technical appendix for the affect control model). Some of the recent work on emotions elevates and invigorates the classic concepts in sociology (particularly in symbolic interaction), and it is to a treatise on these that I turn. This brief treatise is designed to sensitize us to the symbolic interaction constructs, which aid our understanding of how we create meaningful and balanced images out of human experiences.

CLASSIC CONCEPTS USED IN THE SOCIOLOGY OF EMOTIONS

Some of the most important concepts in sociology deal with our abilities to perceive existence in reflexive and contextual manners. The work of ethnomethodologists

(Garfinkel 1976) and students of emotion (Kemper 1990a) merges on several fronts to illuminate our cognitive, perceptive, and evaluating capabilities, and gives impetus to a brief mention of several classic concepts in sociology, social psychology, and symbolic interaction. These concepts are chosen for their heuristic value and because they have a vitality and potency appropriate to the study of emotions. (The reader is referred to Stryker 1980, pp. 115-40, for a thorough articulation of many of the concepts listed later.)

The concepts of note here are the following: (a) the looking glass self (Cooley 1902, pp. 183-184), (b) the definition of the situation (Homas and Thomas 1928), (c) the I-me dialectic and the generalized other (Mead 1934), (d) the self-fulfilling prophecy (Merton 1968), (e) the autokinetic effect (Sherif 1936), and (f) a host of interpretive concepts associated with the social processes attendant to labeling theory (Becker 1963; Erikson 1966). One theme running throughout this partial list of important concepts deals with the idea that we "construct" meaning in possibly an "audacious attempt" (Berger 1967, p.28) to make sense of universes whether they be large or small. In this construction of reality, there rest numerous opportunities to selectively interpret, omit, create, filter, and misread incoming information that all life is an illusion.

Ethnomethodologists would ask us to use the subjective-impressionistic nature of lived experiences as a point of departure (cf. Collins 1990, p. 30). This perspective comes through somewhat in Denzin's antipositivist (Kemper 1990b, p. 12) outline of a interpretive framework for understanding how emotions are experienced in everyday life. Some of his arguments (Denzin 1990) are that:

1. Emotion must be studied as lived experience.

2. The essential features of emotion must be isolated and described.

3. Emotion must be understood as a process that turns on itself, elaborates itself, and has its own trajectory.

4. The phenomenological understanding and interpretation of emotions will not be causal. It will be descriptive, interpretive and processual. (p.86)

In a related fashion, Shott (1979) summed up the connection between emotions and symbolic interaction (including some of the classic concepts mentioned earlier) thusly:

1. Study of the actor's definitions and interpretations is essential for an understanding of human conduct.

2. Human behavior is emergent, continually constructed during its execution.

3. The actions of individuals are influenced by their internal states and impulses in addition to external events and stimuli, for actors' perceptions and interpretations are shaped by the former as well as the latter.

4. Social structures and normative regulation are the framework of human action rather than its determinant, shaping behavior without dictating it. (p. 1321).

Shott (1979, p. 1323) succinctly stated that:

> Within the limits set by social norms and internal stimuli, individuals construct their emotions; and their definitions and interpretations are critical to this often emergent processes. Internal states and cues, necessary

as they are for affective experience, do not in themselves establish feeling, for it is the actor's definitions and interpretations that give physiological states their emotional significance or non-significance.

Although the study of emotions can be accomplished using a variety of quantitative and qualitative research techniques (Ellis 1989), embracing a variety of theoretical positions and concentrating on various elements within the emotional process, the intent of this article is to describe some of the consequences of our interpretive abilities involving (a) anthropomorphism in general and (b) the bestowal of humanness to neonates in medical intensive care units in particular. Before I proceed, however, I need to better define the concepts of emotion.

EMOTION DEFINED

Emotion has been defined in several different ways, and has been found to include a variety of components. Kemper's (1987) article. "How Many Emotions Are There? Wedding the Social and the Autonomic Components," represents an attempt to distill disparate works on emotion into a manageable synthesis. He argued (1987, p. 263) that there is a broad agreement that emotions are "autonomic-motoric-cognitive states" of a "limitless" number, but that there are four physiologically grounded "primary" emotions: fear, anger, depression, and satisfaction. Other emotions (e.g., guilt, shame, pride, gratitude, love, nostalgia, ennui) are socially constructed and "essentially grafted onto the primary emotions through socialization" (Kemper 1987, p. 265). Kemper (1987, p. 266) also constructed a useful table of theoretical approaches to the study of emotions complete with relevant bibliographical citations from proponents of each approach. He identified the following approaches: (a) evolutionary, (b) neural, (c) psychoanalytic, (d) autonomic, (e) facial expressions, (f) empirical classification, and (g) developmental. He (1987, p. 267) also found Epstein's (1984, p. 67) definition to be useful: A primary emotion is "a complex, organized response disposition to engage in certain classes of biologically adaptive behaviors...characterized by a distinctive state of physiological arousal, a distinctive feeling, or affective state, a distinctive state of receptivity to stimulation, and a distinctive pattern of expressive reactions."

In attempting to develop a lexicon of emotions, some have supported Kemper's (1987) contention that the number of possible emotions is "limitless." Storm and Storm (1987) reported, for example, that 786 different words were used by a sample of children and adults when they were asked to label the feelings of actors performing on television. Shott (1979, p. 1320) pointed to the magnitude of possible emotions by stating that "how one interprets one's emotions and, to some extent, what one feels are guided (though not determined) by one's culture...so that different societies are characterized by different `vocabularies of motive.'" Regardless of our range of emotions, there is apparently some agreement about at least four components of emotional experience and behavior. Gordon (1990, pp. 151-152) neatly summarized these as: (a) bodily sensations (i.e., physiological arousal, which may vary in intensity); (b) expressive gestures and actions (i.e., facial and bodily display); (c) a social situation or relationship (including interpretation of the situation); and (d) an emotional culture (i.e., the associated vocabulary, norms, and beliefs about emotions). Although there is some disagreement about the centrality of each of these components on the study of emotions, they represent common elements revealed in different analyses. This is apparent in comparing Gordon's (1990) work with that of Thoits (1990, pp. 191-192), who viewed emotion as "a subjective experience consisting four interconnected components: (a) situational cues, (b) physiological changes, (c) expressive gestures [not necessarily observable due to the control we have over public display of affect], and (d) an emotion label that serves to identify this specific configuration of components."

To summarize so far, the recent upsurge in the sociology of emotions has repostulated some of the classic dicta of social psychology and symbolic interaction with new energy and meaning. Within this intellectual milieu, the present undertaking seeks to articulate the importance of these perspectives to the understanding of anthropomorphic cognition, evaluations, appraisals, and behaviors. The article concludes by reexamining a particular type of emotionalized anthropomorphism identified previously by a study of nurse-neonate behavior in a neonatal intensive care unit (NICU) of a major teaching hospital in the southwestern United States (Palmer and Noble 1985).

ANTHROPOMORPHISM

My concern is that symbolic interaction offers an excellent point of departure for the study of anthropomorphism, and that anthropomorphism offers a challenging case to students of the sociology of emotion. Anthropomorphism is defined in Webster's Dictionary (second edition) as "the attributing of human shape or characteristics to god, objects, animals etc." The attribution of human characteristics to nonhuman objects and animals may have found first expression in the animism and totemism of preliterate tribes, but it is nevertheless commonplace in modern society. Bryant (1979, p. 401), in his rather comprehensive articulation of the "zoological connection" between humans and animals, pointed out the the language of American society is saturated with zoological references "which suggests a greater influence of, and involvement with, and preoccupation with, animals than we are prone to recognize or demit....This strong zoological flavor in our language would suggest a considerable animal influence in our cultural fabric." He (Bryant 1979, pp. 408-409) also called for an examination of the relationship between humans and animals that appear to satisfy certain human "interactive and communicative needs," and postulated that we might better understand the "sociopsychological parameters of loneliness and alienation, and the ameliorative mechanisms which most effectively address such states" by a closer study of anthropomorphic aggregations.

Anthropomorphism, demonstrably prevalent and commonplace, may be on the increase in American society, although I am unaware of longitudinal studies that would prove this assumption. Brabant and Mooney (1989, p. 482), however, pointed out that anthropomorphism is present in approximately 13% of the greeting cards we routinely send to each other. They (1989, p. 481) coded a sample of cards as anthropomorphic if nonhuman entities ("critters") had one or more of four human attributes: "(1) ability to communicate, for example, it spoke or read; (2) *emotion*, [emphasis added] for example, it smiled or cried; (3) appearance, for example, it wore clothing or carried paraphernalia associated with humans; and (4) action, for example, it did something only humans do, such as play golf or drive a car." Such greeting cards, as a popular form of interpersonal communication, are considered cultural artifacts and as data reveal something about ourselves (Brabant and Mooney 1989, P. 480).

Shelley Levitt (1989, p. 56) pointed to one of the functions of keeping pets when she said "pets are good medicine," and reported that pets help people survive heart attacks, reduce high blood pressure, help people feel better physically, and serve as "psychic vitamins" for their owners. Plutchik (1980, p. 71) contended that "most of us believe that emotions also occur in animals, as well as human infants...[and] if animals and human beings do, in fact, express similar kinds of emotions, then we must look back in evolution for their common roots and functions." Curtis (1982, p. 66) reported that 36% of a sample of 60 families thought of their pet as "a person," whereas another 8% considered it "somewhere in between a pet and a person." She also reported that when talked about who in the family gets the most touches, smiles, and positive gestures, 44% of the sample said "the pet."

Robert Solomon (1992, p. 36) wrote that "even those of us who try to be hardheaded in such matters [anthropomorphism] find ourselves, on occasion, telling buoyant and often tedious tales about the intelligence and cunning of our cat, who has the craftiness of a con artist, or the love of our dog, whose devotion puts ancient Greek heroes and Christian saints to shame." He further contended that the scientific community puts "less stock in animal minds. These centuries ago, Descartes declared that animals are mere `machines,' without minds or intelligence and devoid of reason and will. The American behaviorist John Watson revolutionized not only the science of animal behavior but human psychology, too, by denouncing anthropomorphism" (Solomon 1982, p. 36). Solomon (1982, p. 45) went on to point out, however, that many scientists have removed themselves from the Cartesian perspective and now concern themselves with the "continuity from species to species" of certain characteristics and who "need not ask whether animals have intelligence, or language, or emotions, but rather what intelligence, what kind of language, and which emotions."

Another perspective concerning the matter in which we relate to animals concerns the "blessing" of pets. One such blessing (supplied by a priest who conducts the ritual), reads:

> Dear Father in Heaven we greet you this morning as Lord of the universe. You have made the stars and the sand, the mountains and the valleys. You have make man and you have made animals. We praise you in all that you have made, in all of your creation.
> We have brought part of your creation to church this morning. It is the part we call out pets. We love out pets and we care about them. They are often companions to us. We want what is good for them.
> So, dear Father, we ask your kindness. Look down favorably upon our pets. Bless them. Keep them from harm. Help us to care for them so that

they not harm anyone else. Let us know happiness in them as your little creatures....

Although the official church position is that animals are for the "use" of humankind and are not to be equated with humanity, such blessings conjure up unique and complicated cognitive and emotional linkages between humans and animals.

The compassionate perspective toward animals find some detractors when it is carried too far. For example, Richard Traystman (1990), professor of anesthesiology and critical care medicine at John Hopkins School of Medicine, contended:

> Another important tactic that has been used successfully by animal activists is to attempt to establish legal and moral rights of animals. However, precisely which rights are to be given to which animals and who bestows these rights are unclear, not to mention the question of whether animals have rights in the first place. Do all animals have equal rights? Do animals really have the same rights as humans? Do they have the right to vote in elections? Do they have the right to equal wages for equal work?... do they have the same moral obligation to humanity, or to the animal world that entitles them to equal rights as humans...?
> Rights entail obligations and assume that the holders of rights have the capacity to comprehend the rules that come with rights. If, as the animal activists believe, all forms of animal life possess qualities in common that endow them with equivalent moral status to humans, than all have equivalent rights to humans that must be recognized and enforced by law. Animals are not humans in this regard, nor will they ever be.... Animals are not human and they do not possess human qualities.(p. B2)

Professor Traystman was reacting to a growing movement in this country (chronicled sociologically by Bryant 1979, p. 406) called "animal liberation." People for the Ethical Treatment of Animals (PETA), for example, is made up of 325,000 members who believe that animals have inherent rights equal to those enjoyed by people. PETA'S annual budget is $7 million collected through membership fees from those who believe that "animals don't belong to us. Animals are not ours to eat, to wear, to experiment on" (Myers 1990, p. A21). An underground group associated with PETA, called the Animal Liberation Front brought notoriety to the movement when it publicized the videotapes, and eventually the National Institutes of Health and the Agriculture Department punished the scientists involved" (Myers 1990, p. A28). The National Director of PETA, Ingrid Newkirk (1990), just published a book of "101 easy things you can to" to save the animals, and advocated a variety of activist strategies (demonstrations, boycotts, disruptions, rallies, and so on) to combat speciesism (stereotypical thinking and acting toward other species). She (1990, p. XV-XVI) contended that "if you only do a few of the things suggested in this book, you should feel good about yourself. The more you do, the better you'll feel, the happier your companion animals will be, the healthier you'll become and the more impact you'll have on the world around you." That the issues raised by this movement are emotionally charged is an understatement. The October 22, 1990 "ABC World News Tonight With Peter Jennings" carried a story using film provided by PETA's hidden cameras, which captured the treatment of animals being delivered to Carolina Biological Supply Company. In an attempt to interview a man who allegedly delivered 200 cats per week to supply the company, reporters were threatened, and the last shot of the news report shows the van carrying the ABC reporters being rammed with the steal bucket of a motorized front-end loader. This incident serves to illustrate that the issues involved in animal liberation are, indeed, emotionally charged and deserving of special attention by students of emotions.

One wonders how far anthropomorphism can be taken. For example, some thought has already been given to the idea that things other than animals should have ethical rights. Stone (1972, 1985f) stated that, in addition to animals, trees and rivers have an ethical right to be protected, and the law should provide legal guardianship to the parties interested in defending the interests of environmental objects. Similar sentiments are found in Hoch's (1978-1988) worked in environmental ethics and nonhuman interests where he challenged "anthropocentric license."

The sociological question to be addressed, then, is, "what is going on here?" More particularly, students of emotions should begin researching the emergent qualities of these movements, the definition of the situation regarding animal liberation, the internal states and impulses attendant to these movements, and impact of normative regulation on this growing movement, and the articulation of whether or not the study of "deviant emotions" (cf. Pugliesi 1987; Thoits 1990, p. 181) can enlighten us on the type of attachment occurring between animal and animal liberator. What role does ideology (Hochschild 1990, p. 127) play in these emotional expressions? What are the differences in anthropomorphic perception (if any) between animal liberator and non-liberator? What are the broader social issues involved? Just how does anthropomorphism manifest itself in today's society? What predictions can we make concerning the growth of the sentiments surrounding animal liberation? These sets of questions should sensitize us to the need to examine further the concept of emotionalized anthropomorphism.

NURSE-NEONATE RELATIONSHIPS

We (Palmer and Noble 1985) previously reported on our investigations onto the creation of symbolic interaction between neonates and NICU nurses, and outlined a set of behaviors we consider indicative of emotionalized anthropomorphic reactions. We stated (Palmer and Noble 1985, p. 331) that:

> Nurses...construct symbolic selves for their tiny, premature, and sometimes critically ill patients and then interact with them on the basis of that construction. Through anthropomorphism and projection, the nurses engage in active attribution of symbolic characteristics to their charges.

These nurses engaged in foster bonding with neonates, and were able to love some of the babies to health. Nurses would sometimes bypass the information provided by high tech monitors, gauges, digital readout screens, and computers hooked to these sick babies and make their own assessment of their babies. Some of these charges were "gorked out" (unknown condition and prognosis) had, "mush for brains," were "beyond salability," were "FLKs" (funny looking kids), and were often "paved out" (referring to a neonate on pavulon, a curare derivative that immobilizes an infant so it will not fight the respirator tube). Yet nurses routinely deal with these tiny patients that are referred to as a "fetus on a ventilator," "the abortion that cried," "the 24-week miracle," or "the experiment" (Palmer and Noble 1985, p. 337). Even with severe medical problems and hanging on to life by a thread, heavily medicated neonates were assigned personalities by the nurses who maintained that "love goes as far as medicine in getting a baby well," that babies get "angry at me," that they "know when they are not loved," that they "choose" to eat for me but will not eat for others nurses, and miss me when I am away" (Palmer and Noble 1985, p. 340). The "emotional context" (Sugrue 1982), "feeling rules," and "emotion work" (Hochschild 1979, 1990) as well as the "emotional culture" (Gordon 1990) of these nurses are intriguing areas of study.

The emotional context refers to the "mood or consensually acknowledged presence of emotions that are influencing situational interactions" (Sugrue 1982, p. 280). Feeling rules are "rules about what feeling is or isn't appropriate to a given social setting" (Hochschild 1990, p. 122), whereas emotion work refers to "the act of trying to change in degree or quality an emotion or feeling" (Hochschild 1979, p. 561). Finally, the emotional culture includes emotion vocabularies (words for emotions), norms (regulating expression and feeling), and beliefs abut emotions (e.g., the idea that repressed emotion is disturbing); (Gordon 1990, p.146).

As a fluid, dynamic, and phenomenological process, how do neonatal nurses learn the occupational and emotional culture of the workplace? How do they manage their emotions knowing that these babies, some of who they "love as it [they] were my own," are going to die? What types of "surface" and "deep" acting (Hochschild 1990, pp. 120-121) are necessary to remain in this emotional milieu? An interesting aspect of this work concerns the emotional reinforcement these specialized emergency nurses receive from their special status (more pay, higher prestige, extra training), but another, more germane aspect is that of the create excitement routinely experienced by these nurses. Part of this creative activity revolves around "saving lives" or from an anthropomorphic perspective, creating lives. The act of creation is a powerful reinforcer to most human activity. Our contention is that this hard work is done by nurses who are physically and narcissistically rewarded in this demanding milieu by being able to "love these babies alive." (Palmer and Noble 1985, p. 341) This nurse felt that no amount of sensory stimulation provided by roots or other mechanical devices, environmental control systems, or medical protocols could do what she could do: love the baby to health.

When these nurses were probed as to the definition and meaning of love, the conversation would soon drift to the comment, "well, you know...just loving the baby. If you don't know, I can't explain it to you." A recent (October 16, 1990) interview with a 15-year veteran nurse, and now supervisor of an NICU, is revealing of the emotional context of NICU work. She said:

> We do surrogate mothering. Babies know when they are loved. We know their certain cry when they want to be wrapped up. We can tell when they don't want any more stimulation. We give that extra care by sitting, rocking, feeling the baby...We get that feedback. When a [sick] baby is irritable, crying, flailing, you know what it needs in its soul...Let me tell you a bit about that. I was present at a hospital delivery of a 24-week baby and the doctor said, "Just don't touch it." He had decided to let the baby die and I was going to stand there, even though I knew there was a heartbeat and an attempt was being make by the baby to breath. And then the baby opened its eyes and looked at me. And that was it! I didn't give a -____ what that Doc said, I was going to save that baby and I went to work and saved it.... The neo-natologist later defended my actions to the obstetrician who said not to touch it and he [the obstetrician] felt guilty when that baby was discharged form the hospital and went home.

When I questioned this nurse about what she thought had happened when this extremely premature baby had "opened his eyes and looked at [her]," she indicated an awareness of the biological limitations to visual development in premature infants, but she reverted to a nonmedical stance when she said, "I know all of that, but once you are born who knows what you can see?...I know that there are needs of the baby's soul."

An interesting corollary to this event is found in a statement by Robson (1967, p. 15, quoted in Eibl-Eibesfeldt 1970, p. 402), who said

> The human mother is subject to an extended, exceedingly trying and often unrewarding period of crying for the infant. Her neonate has a remarkably limited repertoire with which to sustain her. Indeed, his total helplessness, crying, elimination behavior and physical appearance, frequently elicit aversive reactions. Thus, in dealing with human species, nature has been wise in making both eye-to-eye contact and the social smile, that often releases in these early months, behaviors that at this stage of development generally foster positive maternal feelings and a sense of payment for services rendered...Hence, though a mother's response to these achievements may be an illusion (emphasis added), from an evolutionary point of view it is an illusion with survival value.

CONCLUSION

Herein we have traveled a convoluted route from symbolic interaction and the sociology of emotions to anthropomorphism, back to the creation of symbolic interaction within NICUs. What purpose the trip? What vistas transpired? In sum, an attempt has been made to call attention to the wonderful, even magical, abilities we have to create and bestow humanness to things in our worlds. We are all gods of sorts in that we are inextricably linked by association, as early social psychologists pointed out, and dependent on one another for full individual and collective existence. Our abilities to create meaning, charge that meaning with evaluate energy, interact recursively and emotionally with that meaning, and to synergistically modify our stance toward that meaning become the essence of humanness. Shott (1979, pp. 1328-1329) captured part of this essence when she defined empathy as the "arousal in oneself of the emotion one observers in another or the emotion one would feel in another's situation." The point here is that through emotionally charged anthropomorphism we may be able to create fantasies and interact with those imaginary constructions, thereby creating, narcissistically, our own social universe. If this sounds farfetched, consider Shott's (1979, p. 1329) discussion of empathy and altruistic behavior:

> Perhaps more than any other sentiment, empathy connects us intimately with others, making us share their distress or pleasure. By relieving the unhappiness of those with whom we empathize, or increasing their happiness, we relieve or increase our corresponding feeling. Thus, we have truly incorporated the social group within ourselves when we empathize with another and act altruistically, for then those presumably private and internal states that we call our feelings are closely bound to the welfare of others.

We breath life, of a sort, of a perceptual but meaningful sort, into the nonliving. We bestow on animals their meaning, we bestow on neonates personalities that may be fabrications, we bestow on one another labels, stereotypes, and characteristics, and then interact with those characteristics. The classic concepts of the self-fulling prophecy, the definition of the situation, interpretational filtering, and so on are crucial to our full understanding of these prosesses and of the essence of social life. We should explore in greater dept our abilities of creation.

The sociology of emotions will aid our continued search for the essence of social life by providing the nomenclature, the lexicons, the methodologies (cf. in particular Ellis 1989; Heise 1990), the conceptual frameworks, and the empirical data through which to understand these complicated processes of emotionalized anthropomorphism. The complex work of Smith-Lovin (1990) and Heise (1990) provides an excellent opportunity for us to enlarge their affect control model (a computerized measurement model that allows for the determination of meaning based on the recursive values assigned to three generic constructs: evaluation, potency, and activity) and use it to study "what's going on" in the emotional worlds of nurse and other feeling actors. The sociological frontier is expanding. We have new and exciting challenges before us.

REFERENCES

Becker, Howard S. 1963. *Outsiders: Studies in the Sociology of Deviance.* New York: Free Press.
Berger, Peter. 1967. *The Sacred Canopy: Elements of a Sociological Theory of Religion.* New York: Doubleday.
Brabant, Sarah and Linda A. Mooney. 1989. "When 'Critters' Act Like People: Anthropomorphism in Greeting Cards," *Sociological Spectrum* 9:477–494.
Bryant, Clifton D. 1979. "The Zoological Connection: Animal-Related Human Behavior." *Social Forces* 58:399–421.

Collins, Randall. 1990. "Stratification, Emotional Energy, and the Transient Emotions." Pp. 24–57 in *Research Agendas in the Sociology of Emotions*, edited by Theodore D. Kemper. New York: State University of New York Press.
Cooley, Charles H. 1902. *Human Nature and Social Order*. New York: Schribner.
Curtis, Patricia. 1982. "Our Pets, Ourselves." *Psychology Today* 16:66–67.
Denzin, Norman K. 1990. "On Understanding Emotion: The Interpretive-Culture Agenda." Pp. 85–116 in *Research Agendas in the Sociology of Emotions*, edited by Theodore D. Kemper. New York: State University of New York Press.
Eibl-Eibesfeldt, Irenaus. 1970. *Ethology: The Biology of Behavior*. New York: Holt, Rinehart, and Winston.
Ellis, Carolyn. 1989. "What are You Feeling? Issues in Introspective Method." Paper presented at the Annual Meetings of the American Sociological Association, San Francisco, California.
Epstein, Seymour. 1984. "Controversial Issues in Emotion Theory." Pp. 64–88 in *Review of Personality and Social Psychology* (Vol.5), edited by Philip Shaver. Beverley Hills, CA: Sage.
Erikson, Kai T. 1966. *Wayward Puritans: A Study in the Sociology of Deviance*. New York: Wiley.
Garfinkel, Harold. 1967. *Studies in Ethnomethodology*. Englewood Cliffs, NJ: Prentice Hall.
Gordon, Steven L. 1990. "Social structural Effects on Emotions." Pp. 145–179 in *Research Agendas in the Sociology of Emotions* edited by Theodore D. Kemper. New York: State University of New York Press.
Heise, David R. 1990. "Affect Control Model Technical Appendix." Pp. 271–280 in *Research Agendas in the Sociology of Emotions* edited by Theodore D. Kemper. New York: State University of New York Press.
Hoch, David. 1987–"Environmental Ethics and Nonhuman interests: A Challenge 1988 to Anthropocentric License." *Gonzaga Law Review* 23:331–347.
Hochschild, Arlie Russell. 1979. "Emotional Work, Feeling Rules and Social Structure." *American Journal of Sociology* 85:551–575.
———. 1990. "Ideology and Emotion Management: A Perspective and Pat for Future Research." Pp. 117–142 in *Research Agendas in the Sociology of Emotions*, edited by Theodore D. Kemper New York: State University of New York Press.
Kemper, Theodore D. 1987. "How Many Emotions are there? Wedding the Social and the Autonomic Components." *American Journal of Sociology* 93:263–289.
———. (ed).1990a. *Research Agendas in the Sociology of Emotions* New York: State University of New York Press.
———. 1990b. "Themes and Variations in the Sociology of Emotions". Pp. 3–23 in *Research Agendas in the Sociology of Emotions*, edited by Theodore D. Kemper. New York: State University of New York Press.
Levitt, Shelley. 1988. "Pet Two Poodles and Call Me in the Morning." *50 Plus* 38:56–61.
Mead, George H. 1934. *Mind, Self and Society:* Chicago: University of Chicago Press.
Merton, Robert K. 1968. *Social Theory and Social Structure*. New York: Free Press.
Meyers, Christopher 1990. "People for the Ethical Treatment of Animals' 325,000 Strong, Assumes Influential Controversial Role n Fierce National Battle." *Chronicle of Higher Education* 37:A21, A28.
Newkirk, Ingrid. 1990. *Save the Animals! 101 Easy Things You Can Do*. New York: Warner.
Palmer, C Eddie and Dornia N. Noble. 1985. "Nurse-Neonate Relationships: The creation of Symbolic Interaction Within a Neonatal Intensive Care Unit." *Sociological Spectrum* 5:331–345.
Pultchik, Robert. 1980. "A Language for the Emotions." *Psychology Today* 13:68–78.
Pugliesi, Karen L. 1987. "Deviation in Emotion and the Labeling of Mental Illness." *Deviant Behavior* 8:79–102.
Robson, K.S. 1976. "The Role of Eye-to-Eye Contact in Maternal-infant Attachment." *Journal of Child Psychology* 8:13–23.
Sherif, M. 1936. *The Psychology of Social Norms*. New York: Harper & Row.
Shott, Susan. 1979. "Emotions and Social Life: A symbolic Interactionist Analysis." *American Journal of Sociology* 84:1217–1334.
Smith-Lovin, Lynn. 1990. "Emotions as the Confirmation and Disconfirmation of Identity: An Affect Control Model." Pp. 238–270 In *Research Agendas in the Sociology of Emotions*, edited by Theodore D. Kemper. New York: State University of New York Press.

Solomon, Robert C. 1982. "Has Not An Animal Organs, Dimensions, Sense, Affections, Passions?" *Psychology Today* 16:36, 39–41, 43–45.
Stone, Christopher. 1872. "Should Trees Have Standing?-Toward Legal Rights for Natural Objects." *Southern California Law Review* 45:450–501.
———. 1985. "Should Trees Have Standing? Revised: How For will Law and Morals Reach? A Pluralist Perspective." *Southern California Law Review* 59:1–154.
Storm, Christine and Tom Storm. 1987. "A Taxonomic Study of the Vocabulary of Emotions." *Journal of Personality and Social Psychology* 53:805–816.
Stryker, Sheldon. 1980. *Symbolic Interactionism: A Social Structural Version*. Menlo Park, CA: Benjamin/Cummings.
Sugrue, Noreen M. 1982. "Emotions as Property and Context for Negotiation." *Urban Life* 11:280–292.
Thoits, Peggy A. 1990. "Emotional Deviance: Research Agendas." Pp. 180–201 In *Research Agendas in the Sociology of Emotions*, edited by Theodore D. Kemper. New York: State University of New York Press.
Thomas, William I. and Dorothy S. Thomas. 1928. *The Child in America*. New York: Knopf.
Traystman, Richard. 1990. "Mickey Mouse Talks but He Isn't Human." *Chronicle of Higher Education*, 37:B2.

Chapter 35 **GENERIC SOCIAL PROCESSES AND THE STUDY OF HUMAN LIVED EXPERIENCES: ACHIEVING TRANSCONTEXTUALITY IN ETHNOGRAPHIC RESEARCH[1]**

Robert Prus

Theory is of value in empirical science only to the extent to which it connects fruitfully with the empirical world. Concepts are the means, and the only means of establishing such connection, for it is the concept that points to the empirical instances about which a theoretical proposal is made. (Blumer, 1969:143)

This paper deals with the problem of concept development within the symbolic interactionist tradition. This problem is by no means unique to symbolic interactionists, or sociologists, or even social scientists for that matter. It is a concern that characterizes any attempt to examine in a serious, sustained manner any aspect of the world in which we find ourselves. As such, this statement addresses the broader intellectual objective of trying to integrate theory, method, and research on an ongoing basis. Still, this paper was written particularly mindful of the task of generating a set of interactionist concepts which (a) foster a synthesis of the existing and developing ethnographic literature, (b) encourage more sustained and productive ethnographic inquiries, and (c) fundamentally respect the data gathered in the course of ethnographic research. Thus, while this statement serves to synthesize a number of themes central to the interactionist tradition, its more specific potential lies in providing a framework through which ethnographic research may be pursued and focused and conceptual developments may take place in a more sustained, comprehensive, and dialectic manner.[2]

Examining the ways in which people accomplish their activities on a day to day basis, ethnographic research provides an exceptionally rich and viable means of uncovering insights into people's lived experience. Moreover, since it attends to the interpretive and interactive dimensions or the intersubjective features of human group life, ethnographic research is essential if one hopes to achieve "intimate familiarity" (Blumer, 1969) with ongoing community life. Hence, it is extremely useful and instructive in many ways to accumulate ethnographic studies which carefully describe the perspectives, practices, dilemmas and interchanges of people in this and that setting. Indeed, these is no better way of achieving a working understanding of this or that substantive setting than through sustained ethnographic inquiry. Still, we also may use this rich, textured data as a base for formulating concepts which transcend the particular settings in which the data was gathered.

To the extent we are able to delineate concepts which have transsituational or cross-contextual relevance, we may not only be able to tie together a great deal of research that would otherwise remain disconnected or scattered across a range of substantive contexts, but we may also be able to produce a body of concepts that could be used as resources in subsequent ethnographic inquiries. These inquiries, in turn, could be used as a basis for further assessing, refining, and (if necessary) rejecting concepts pertaining to the study of human group life.[3]

This emphasis on transcontextual processes also encourages scholarly exchange and conceptual cross-fertilization. By attending to concepts which are applicable to a wide variety of contexts, researchers working in very different substantive settings (e.g. ballet, outlaw bikers, religion, schools) may not only benefit from the research that people have done in other settings, but they will likely find that they have a much broader community of scholars with which to discuss all aspects of their work than what would otherwise have been the case.[4]

Further, as Blumer (1928:349) observes, concepts (such as generic social processes) do *not* destroy the unique or idiographic features of particular instances of human lived experience. Instead, they provide the vital medium through which similarities and differences may be more fully recognized, investigated, and appreciated on a case by case basis. Thus, the emphasis on generic social processes in no way minimizes or is intended as an alternative to ethnographic research. To the contrary, this conceptual thrust represents an essential means of enhancing the potential value of each instance of ethnographic inquiry for students of human behavior.

For our purposes, *generic social processes* refer to the transsituational elements of interaction; to the abstracted, transcontextual formulations of social behavior. Denoting parallel sequences of activity across diverse contexts, generic social processes highlight the emergent, interpretive features of association. They focus our attention on the activities involved in the "doing" or accomplishing of human group life.

THE ROOTS OF A GENERIC PROCESSUAL SOCIOLOGY

The term "generic processual sociology" has a redundant quality. As the study of group life, sociology would seem naturally concerned with the discovery and development of abstracted dimensions of social processes germane to group life. This most certainly was the intention of Georg Simmel, who in his analysis of "sociation" argued for a clear distinction between form and content.

For Simmel, "form" was the subject matter of primary consequence; "content" provided the necessary but inevitably "promiscuous" background. Thus, rather than attending to the "cultural content" of events and people's experiences in settings, Simmel (1950; 1955; 1978) directed our attention to the dimensions of association. For Simmel, these included group alignments and relationships (e.g. triads, conflict, competition, coalitions), identities and disclosures (e.g. strangers, secrets, deceptions), activities (e.g. games, contests, conversations), and evaluations and commitments (e.g. price, value, exchanges). One also finds transsituationally applicable concepts in the works of other sociologists (e.g. Durkheim, Marx, Weber), but only some sociologists explicitly attend to community life as a reflective, actively constituted phenomenon. Thus, of the more commonly recognized founders of the discipline, it is Simmel who most clearly generates concepts which either depict social processes or facilitate the delineation of social processes.[5]

While all paradigms deal in abstractions, our concern is primarily with concepts that embody an *interpretive process*. The emphasis is on what Blumer (1969) terms the "active forging of social structure." Rather than viewing people as the (depersonalized) agents through which "external" or "internal" forces ("factors") exert their impact on group life,[6] we assume a conceptual approach which envisions group life as an ongoing series of constructions shaped by active, living, thinking beings.

Generic social processes do not exist to the exclusion of other sociological concepts.[7] Indeed, many other sociological concepts may sensitize us to particular processes. But unless we concentrate on social processes, we will not be able to achieve a theory of action which is grounded in the experiences of human beings.

This emphasis on process should not be taken to imply that content (or context) is not important. For a great many purposes, content and process are inseparable. And, as ethnographers, a central task we face is that of maximizing contextual depth in our inquiries. However, we have a choice of continually piling up isolated accounts of community life or striving for a theory of action which builds on these rich and contextually diversified inquiries. The latter routing, as Zerubavel (1981) notes, requires that ethnographers commit themselves to making more focused observations while pursuing ethnographic detail more generally.

When discussing the development of sociological concepts (processual and otherwise), it is important to note that the field has taken enormously strong substantive twists. Ergo, one finds the development of much teaching and research activity in line with particular contextual foci. These "content" directed developments likely have several bases, reflecting matters such as researcher interests and accessibilities of respondents, audience interests (students, funding agencies), and the designations of problems by journalists and other "moral entrepreneurs" (Becker, 1963; Blumer, 1971). Regardless of routings, however, the end result has been this. Instead of a discipline characterized by specialties rooted in abstracted sociological concepts, we have become a discipline saddled with much substantive (and moralistic) baggage. Rather than offering curriculums rich in analytical forms (e.g. courses in relationships, negotiations, identities and reputations), we are mired in courses in the family, religion, politics, education, gender roles, crime, and the like.

These substantive elements have run concurrently with the development of the discipline and it is not at all apparent that the discipline could survive at any where near its present popularity, were substantive realms to become heavily subjugated to conceptual forms in our classrooms and our writings. Additionally, insofar as any inquiry provides the means of generating and/or assessing some abstracted concepts, any substantive realm is as viable an area for study as any other. Finally, research into each content area may generate greater understandings (if only by degrees of sharpness, for instance) of parallel processes in other settings. However, it is very easy for substantive pursuits to obscure conceptual development.[8] To a very large extent this has happened in sociology and may partially account for our limited success to date in achieving a generic, processual-focused sociology. Matters of substantive specialization will be considered throughout, but it is valuable at the outset to appreciate some of the cross-pressures to which those pursuing a generic sociology are apt to find themselves subjected.

CHICAGO INTERACTION

If Georg Simmel might be considered the founder of generic (especially processual) sociology, the University of Chicago was surely the spawning ground. Although Simmel (1950) made a strong case for generic sociology via the study of the "forms of association," his message has not had the direct impact on the discipline that one might have anticipated. In part, this seems attributable to Simmel's wide-sweeping breadth of topics and his tendency to generate seemingly definitive statements on matters he undertook to analyze.[9] As well, a sociology founded on "forms" (or generic concepts) lacks much of the immediate appeal that more substantively focused ("hot topics") writings hold for most consuming audiences. But, perhaps no less importantly, Simmel provided little indication of a methodology appropriate to an exploration of the forms of association.[10] Although the linkage to Simmel appears somewhat nebulous and even inadvertent, a methodology and a theory largely consistent with Simmel's formulations was subsequently to develop at the University of Chicago.[11] It is to these themes that we now turn.

Chicago sociology was a relentless pursuit of the facets and processes of urban life; all that was the city was its subject matter. It was the study of the real estate board (Everett Hughes, 1928), department stores (Donovan, 1929), classrooms (Waller, 1932), newsroom productions (Helen Hughes, 1937; Park, 1955:71–184), junk dealers (Ralph, 1950), and futures trading (Glick, 1957). It was the study of hobos (Anderson, 1923), juvenile delinquents (Shaw, 1930; 1931), taxi-dance halls (Cressey, 1932), and professional thieves (Sutherland, 1937). It was immigrants (Thomas and Znaniecki, 1918), striking workers (Hiller, 1928), and those involved in social and political change (Park, 1952; 1955).

Much Chicago sociology (the earlier works especially) was imbued with ecological conceptualizations of society and moral overtones, but there was a strong underlying appreciation of generic interactional sociology. Thus, in the process of elucidating substantive realms of group life, researchers provided valuable insights on concepts involving phenomena such as selves and identities, natural histories and careers of involvements, and assimilation, marginality, and conflict. However, this time period (1900–1950) was characterized by much unevenness. It reflected considerable diversity of input, emphasis, and anticipation. It was an uneven mix of method and theory, but it was a unique and strikingly productive milieu.

While a number of people (e.g. Thomas and Znaniecki, Shaw, and Burgess) played important roles in the development of fieldwork at the University of Chicago, Robert Park and Everett Hughes seem particularly instrumental in promoting ethnographic inquiry as the means by which to achieve "intimate familiarity" with the life-worlds that sociologists sought to study.[12] As much as any, Park and Hughes were effective in "making fieldwork come alive," both through their own work and that they encouraged on the part of others. They were receptive to the derivation of "common themes" and "contingencies," but their analytical comparisons were of a softer variety. They utilized many of Simmel's concepts, but they were much less "formalistic" than Simmel.

If the development of "interactionism" had relied only on the influence of Park and Hughes, it would have been much more fragmented in composition. However, the University of Chicago was also the home base of George Herbert Mead and Herbert Blumer. Mead (1934), like Simmel, thought generically. Nevertheless, his "sociology" (philosophy of social behavior) assumed a much more holistic quality than did that of Simmel. Mead's contribution to sociology was the elaboration of a fundamentally *intersubjective* conception of "mind, self, and society." This was the message that Blumer was to champion.

It is Blumer who fought for the existence of an intersubjective sociology in a discipline largely characterized by concerns with cause and effect on the one hand, and by reform measures of various sorts on the other. While Mead forged the fundamental shape of interactionist theory, it is Blumer who refined symbolic interactionism and who put it into a more distinctively sociological cast. It is Blumer also who provided particularly powerful challenges to those who would reduce the social world to a rubble of numbers and variables.

Like Simmel, Mead seems minimally concerned about providing guidelines for an empirical assessment and exploration of the conceptual scheme that was to later become known as symbolic interaction. Blumer, however, took a strikingly different stand. Blumer insisted on empirical exploration and assessments of concepts. He did not instruct much by direct example, nor did he generate cookbooks for these purposes. However, he very cogently provided (a) a rationale for the inseparability of theory and research; (b) conceptual guidelines for doing interpretive sociology; and (c) well-founded critiques of the methods of social science which violate the central features of group life as an emergent, sociological phenomena. Working in an environment rich in ethnographic tradition (e.g. Park, Hughes, Shaw), Blumer emerges as the key figure in the development of a generic processually oriented sociology. And, it is very much on the foundations provided by Herbert Blumer that more specific formulations of generic social processes have been developed.

SOME EARLIER STATEMENTS ON GENERIC SOCIAL PROCESSES

Despite a seemingly widespread acceptance of the desirability of a generic process-oriented sociology (via Simmel, Mead, Blumer) on the part of interactionists and other interpretive sociologists (e.g. Schutz, 1964, 1971; Berger and Luckmann, 1966; Garfinkel, 1967), one encounters only a few more sustained encouragements to pursue generic conceptualizations in the literature. These are found in the writings of Miyamato (1950), Glaser and Strauss (1967), Strauss (1970), Lofland (1970, 1976), Lester and Hadden (1980), Bigus, Hadden and Glaser (1982), and Couch (1984).

Frank Miyamato (1950) draws our attention to the "social act" as a primary but much neglected generic feature of group life. In particular he wishes to emphasize the temporal or processual dimensions of acts as elements for study. Thus, he stresses the fundamental interlinkages of acts and argues for their value in understanding events and organizations (networks of social acts). Although noting that typologies of acts have resulted in largely sterile endeavors, Miyamato found himself unable to offer clear directions of researchers for social acts to pursue.

Also grappling with the problem of closing "the devastating gap between speculative theory and descriptive empiricism," Glaser and Strauss (1967) and Strauss (1970) are much more precise in their proposals. Focusing on "the discovery of grounded theory," they make a very clear case for the development of a cumulative awareness of the viability and dimensions of particular concepts. This is to be done by more systematically exploring conceptual variants in a plurality of settings. Pointing out the dangers of deriving formal theory from a single substantive area (80-82) as well as the shortcomings of developing theory in the absence of substantive applications (90-92), Glaser and Strauss (1967: 79-99) propose the development of "formal theory" which is based on conceptual comparisons across substantive contexts. Eschewing the researcher-theorist dichotomy, they encourage sociologists to make concerted appraisals of concepts across settings which seem both dissimilar and similar relative to the essence of particular concepts:

> If we do not practice such modes of extending grounded theories, then we relegate them, as now, mainly to the status of respected little islands of knowledge... Sociologists continue to develop both speculative theory and general theoretical frameworks without recognizing the great differences between these formulations and theory which is grounded in data. (Strauss, 1970:53)

Echoing Glaser and Strauss' (1967) concerns with grounded theory, Lofland (1970) also encourages greater concern with generic analysis on the part of interactionists. Although perhaps prematurely impatient with his colleagues in this article, Lofland nevertheless outlines the central tasks this involves:

> By actually following through I mean more specifically that the investigator goes to the time and trouble (1) to assemble self-consciously all his materials on how a given phenomenologically problematic topic is dealt with by the persons under study, (2) to tease out the variations among his assembled range of instance of strategies, (3) to classify them into an articulate set of what appears to him to be generic or phenomenological types of strategies, and (4) to present them to the reader in some orderly and preferably named and numbered manner. (Lofland, 1970:42)

> Moreover, given the virtual lack of codified concepts to draw upon, strategic analysis requires from the analyst considerable effort at creative discernment. It requires that he pour over his materials with great intensity, very much on the model of the procedure outlined by Glaser and Strauss. (Lofland, 1970:44)

In a later statement, Lofland (1976:31-33) adds:

> To conceive a situation generically is to discriminate and bring forward social aspects that possess more generalized, more common, more universal relevance. To scrutinize a situation generically is to seek out its abstract, transcendent, formal, analytic aspects. (Lofland, 1976:31)

Although he organized his subsequent analysis of generic processes around a typology of interactional scales or sizes (e.g. encounters, roles, groups, organizations) of human association rather than the dimensions (e.g. acquiring perspectives, developing relationships) of association, Lofland (1976) attempted to formulate a set of generic social processes around these (size-purpose) group themes. While Lofland's book differs somewhat in its focus from the present statement, his work is highly recommended both for elucidating aspects of generic social processes and for its attentiveness to the literature. Indeed, it provides a very valuable context within which to more fully appreciate the present statement. Unfortunately, Lofland's very instructive volume never received the (considerable) attention that it merits with respect to ethnographic inquiry.[13]

Also building on Glaser and Strauss' (1967) work, Lester and Hadden (1980) most directly address the desirability of the development of grounded theory within ethnomethodological research. However, their message is relevant to interpretive sociology more generally. In particular, they note the tendency for researchers concerned with thorough analyses in substantive settings to become diverted from possible comparisons along transsituational lines. Clearly, they do not intend to curtail ethnographic inquiry, but wish to promote the development of theory grounded in a plurality of ethnographic contexts.

These themes are similarly pursued by Bigus, Hadden and Glaser (1982). Using the term, "basic social processes" synonymously with "generic processes," they draw even more explicit attention to the desirability of focusing on "activity" (vs. substance) as the central feature fostering cross-contextual comparisons and the development of grounded theory.

Following some preliminary (and characteristically "Iowa school") "fencing with Herbert Blumer," Carl Couch (1984) also reiterates much of Blumer's (1969) basic message:

> (T)he problems have been (1) a failure to formulate studies that allow for an assessment of the utility of central concepts on the basis of sustained and systematic examination of empirical phenomena, (2) a failure to focus on social processes and social relationships, and (3) a failure to develop methodological procedures that produce data that can be researched and shared.

Noting that "social life is manifested in process," Couch proposes that we focus on the forming of social structures. Although this clearly speaks to the essence of symbolic interaction, the solution he proposes is that we study the structuring of interaction via analysis of video-taped indications persons make to one another. However, in contrast to the ethnographic perspective posited by Blumer and the preceding scholars, Couch attempts to study the formation of generic processes through the use of observational recordings.[14]

Taken together, these scholars direct our attention to the desirability of developing a generic sociology focused on the "social production of action." Each alerts us to the value of a process-oriented sociology, one which considers the *how* (rather than the why) of group life. Further, with the possible exception of Couch (1984), each has indicated the necessity of grounding these notions in the ongoing experiences of people *doing* group life.

SUBSTANTIVE APPLICATIONS AND GENERIC SOCIAL PROCESSES

The value of a conceptually founded ethnographic body of research is immense. While it provides greater coherency to what would be a lot of scattered islands of information, its significance is by no means limited to direct theoretical gains. Insofar as it is applicable across contexts, it can generate enormous substantive yields as well.

Certainly, there are advantages to scholars becoming expert within particular substantive areas, for persons can attain more multi-disciplinary understandings of particular phenomena. At the same time, however, people involved in the study of social life within any particular specialty may be greatly theoretically shortchanged should they neglect research on parallel *processes* in other settings.

There are several levels on which persons may find conceptually oriented research from other substantive areas useful, but perhaps the following examples will convey this idea better than a more abstract treatment.[15] If, for example, one is interested in "organizational routines and practices," "superordinate-subordinate relations," or "interpersonal manoeuvrings," one may in studying prisons, bars, circuses, or asylums, learn about life in hospitals, factories, schools, and universities. If one is interested in "recruitment," "relationships," or "networks," one may study restaurants, volunteer groups, or flying saucer clubs, and learn about dating and marriages, political parties, and the military. If one is interested in "socialization," one can study thieves and hustlers and learn of educational experiences of students, businessmen, and politicians. People interested in the "process of social control" may study bikers or pre-schoolers and learn about trouble and its management in churches, families, and police departments. If one is interested in bargaining, one can study physician-patient or landlord-tenant negotiations, and gain insights into exchanges involving vendors and customers, parents and children, parole officers and parolees. Someone interested in "competition" among siblings may benefit from the works of those studying vendors in neighboring businesses, athletes on a team, or racing car drivers. Similarly, persons concerned with the problems of "stigma" vis-a-vis welfare clients or the physically handicapped, may gain a great deal of insight into this phenomena by considering studies of prostitutes, convicts, policemen, and clergymen. Persons interested in "conflict" and "conflict resolution" at an international level may, likewise, find it most useful to examine marital disputes, anti-porn crusades, barroom scuffles, or classroom encounters.[16] The list seems endless. One can, it seems, learn something about any group by examining similar processes in any other setting. The content may be highly variable, for the groups may have very different perspectives, identities, and activities; but generic processes such as "decision-making," "socialization," "recruitment," "bargaining," and "interpersonal influence," enable persons to tie together and benefit from which might otherwise seem highly diverse materials.

This "cross-fertilization" not only promotes the development of insights and concepts across contexts, but it is also invaluable in assessing existing concepts and suggesting qualifications and refinements. While substantive reviews of the literature are useful, much highly insightful and perhaps conceptually more developed material in other contexts is often neglected. Encouraging comparisons across widely differing contexts, generic processes foster a mutuality of benefits. And by addressing activities spanning diverse settings, generic processes also demystify individual substantive areas (e.g. deviance, education, politics). Each substantive realm can be seen to reflect, as well as reflect upon, these processes.

Unfortunately, a generic processual sociology has not developed as quickly as we might wish. The next section considers some of the obstacles and dilemmas those pursuing this objective are likely to encounter.

OBSTACLES AND DILEMMAS

> I don't think that there is any short-cut way of arriving at the formation of such judgments; it has to be done in the slow and tedious manner of developing a rich and intimate familiarity with the kind of conduct that is being studied and in employing whatever relevant imagination observers may fortunately possess. The improvement in judgment, in observation, and in concept will be in the future, as I suspect it has been in the past, a slow, maturing process. (Blumer, 1969:182)

Rather than focus on the "gathering of ethnographic materials" (making contacts, developing relationships with participants, coding materials, and so forth), consideration is given herein to the aspects of ethnographic research that make it difficult to *do* generic sociology in process terms.

Increasingly, the objectives of symbolic interactionism and other interpretive sociologies have been directed toward the blending of theory and research. The major task as Glaser and Strauss (1967) succinctly phrased it, is the "development of grounded theory." Viewed thusly, theory, method, and data are inseparable. This is a major strength of symbolic interaction, but it is also a major obstacle. By refusing to reduce the world to highly distilled (and misleading) packages, ethnographers find themselves somewhat overwhelmed by the complexity of everyday life. However, unless we are able to develop a set of concepts applicable across a wide range of settings, we will only accumulate (as Strauss {1970} observes) endless, scattered islands of data.

The obstacles which emerge in this respect assume a variety of forms and include the following:

(1) Individual projects typically entail a major cognizance of the existing *substantive* literature in that field. In attending to the (often large) literature focusing on particular substantive areas, little time may be left for cross-contextual comparisons.[17]

(2) The ethnographic literature is greatly scattered across substantive areas. While it is often difficult to access all the ethnographic research done in any one substantive realm, this pursuit is further complicated in that ethnographers assume wide ranges of conceptual foci. This makes direct comparisons between ethnographic research (for the same or different substantive realms) difficult, if not impossible for many practical purposes.

(3) Insofar as ethnographers typically cover comprehensive life-situations (i.e. the way of life of a group of people) and the data tend to assume expansive (vs. highly distillable) qualities, particular problems are created for those attempting to do generic sociology. With the possible exception of sharply limited conceptual inquiries, field studies inevitably cut across several generic concepts. As a practical accomplishment, this means coming to terms with multiple sets of scattered bodies of concept-focused literature. Unfortunately, there are very few review statements (organized around generic concepts) available to assist researchers with this very challenging process.

(4) Glaser and Strauss (1967) appear quite correct in postulating that generic sociology is greatly fostered when the same researchers investigate a plurality of settings. However, fairly formidable undertakings are typically involved in making these transitions. All researchers switching from one substantive realm of inquiry to another can expect to encounter new substantive literatures, but ethnographers also face the tasks of establishing new contacts, achieving intimate familiarity with new settings, and pursuing and sorting out what can readily become an overwhelming wealth of data. Still, the potential for cross-fertilization and conceptual development is tremendous when particular researchers examine similar generic social processes in a plurality of settings.

As the preceding suggests, the development of a generic ethnographic sociology is apt to be a long, slow, and demanding process. There are no "quick fixes" or "magic potions." Further, it is not only a cumulative process, but also fundamentally an interactive process as scholars go about their research, teaching and conferencing activities.

TOWARD A GENERIC PROCESSUAL SOCIOLOGY

Generic social processes address the emerging, sequencing, unfolding, ongoing features of group life. It is the shaping, the forging, the forming, the constructing, the implementing, the ad hocing, the building up, of human interaction. As Blumer (1969) notes, process encompasses the interpreting, planning, anticipating, doing, experiencing, assessing, and readjusting features of action.

Viewed thusly, process does not deny planning or the development of routine practices and recipes for action. Neither does it ignore the temporal (historical) or the organizational (relational) linkages of action. Rather, it locates activity squarely in these contexts. Process incorporates the perspectives of the participants, as well as people's capacities for reflectivity, their abilities to influence one another, and their tendencies to develop and act upon particularistic relations with others. This notion of process also encompasses the problematic and uncertain features of group life, the dilemmas people experience and their attempts to come to terms with these.

A key to the development of generic sociology, the concept of process needs to be cast in more precise terms to more readily lend itself to analysis. It is in this respect that the notion of a "career" or "natural history" of some phenomenon is so valuable. The concept of career or natural history includes four sub-processes: (a) initial emergence, (b) continuity (and intensification), (c) discontinuity (and dissipation), and (d) possible re-emergence. Each of these processes are worthy of attention on their own, but taken together they provide a more holistic approach to the "life spans" of particular phenomena. Used in this manner, the concept of a career far transcends the occupational context and provides us with a means of tapping into the ongoing substance of everyday life.

Working from this framework, one may for example focus on careers of identities, careers of activities (events, negotiations), careers of relationships, careers of social movements and organizations, and careers of role participation.[18] In each case, one would attend to the emergence of some phenomenon, the continuity and possible intensification of this occurrence, its eventual dissipation, and possible subsequent re-emergence. Approached in this manner, one could examine the contingencies affecting occurrences involving solitary actors as well as those which entail more overt interaction (e.g. encounters, exchanges, relationships, subcultures). By focusing on the processes involved in the careers or natural histories of social phenomena (and even solitary activity is typically meaningful only within a social context), we can draw comparisons across contexts as researchers working in multiple settings take cognizance of one another's work.

As one of but a great many efforts which must go in this direction if we are to achieve and sustain a generic sociology, the following listing is offered as a heuristic device for envisioning process in a more concerted fashion. This listing is necessarily tentative, but provides an umbrella for encompassing a great many of the concepts the interactionists and other interpretive sociologists have developed over the years.

The five processes following not only signify key elements of people's involvements in situations, but also define the essence of community life. These processes are interdependent and need to be viewed holistically if we are to develop a fuller appreciation of each. Nevertheless, each process encompasses several (sub)processes within, and on these levels each is amenable to empirical inquiry. Unfortunately, space precludes even cursory illustrations of the applicability of these concepts to particular settings.

1. ACQUIRING PERSPECTIVES

Representing interpretive frameworks or viewpoints (also world views, paradigms, versions of reality) for making sense of the world, perspectives provide the substantive content for association. Definitions of "fads" and "fashions" are encompassed by the concept of perspective as are traditions, notions of rationality, and political and religious beliefs, as well as language and other symbols. Although the impact of any perspective (or elements thereof) is ultimately moderated by the actors involved (via acknowledgement, interpretation, formation of action), we can ask how people contend with the cultural content they encounter:

*Encountering Perspectives (definitions of reality) from Others
*Assessing (new, incoming) Perspectives and Resisting Unwanted Viewpoints
*Developing Images of Objects (including images of other people and oneself)
*Learning (cultural) Patterns of Objects (e.g. fashion)
*Applying Perspectives to the "cases at hand"
*Resolving Dilemmas Within and Across Paradigms
*Improvising on Existing Perspectives
*Promoting (and defending) Perspectives to Others
*Rejecting Formerly Held Viewpoints[19]

2. ACHIEVING IDENTITY

"Identity work" is contingent on people's capacity for "self reflectivity;" it requires that one begin to take oneself into account in developing lines of action or that one become "an object unto oneself." Reflecting the perspectives one has on the world, people's identities or self-other definitions are not only situated within those realities, but also are influenced by the ongoing shifts in perspectives that people normally undergo over time and across situations. However, in contrast to the more generalized quality of perspectives, identities have a more immediate and personalized ("you and I") focus. Additionally, to the extent people associate identities with the treatment they receive, they tend to be concerned about maintaining acceptable images (especially avoiding disrespectability).[20]

As products of interaction, people's identities are also fundamentally linked to the identities of their associates. Consequently, identity work reflects ongoing assessments and negotiations as the parties involved jointly endeavor to work out self and other definitions. The processes entailed here include:

*Encountering Definitions of Self from Others
*Attributing Qualities to Self (self definitions)
*Comparing Incoming and Self-Assigned Definitions of Self
*Resisting Unwanted Identity Imputations
*Selectively Conveying Information About Self to Others
*Gleaning Information About Others
*Assigning Identities to Others
*Promoting Specific Definitions of Others
*Encountering Resistance from Others
*Reassessing Identities Imputed to Others[21]

3. BEING INVOLVED

"Being Involved" denotes the sequencing of people's participation in settings. Emphasizing the "how" (vs. why) of involvements, consideration is given to the histories or ("careers") of people's participation in particular situations (Becker, 1963; Prus, 1984). While focusing on one involvement at a time, each involvement is best envisioned against a backdrop of multiple, shifting, and potentially incompatible involvements in other settings. Four processes are prominent here: (A) initial involvements, (B) continuities, (C) disinvolvements, and (D) reinvolvements.[22]

A. Getting Started (Initial Involvements)

Although any of the following routings (seekership, recruitment, closure) may dominate people's involvements in particular settings, involvements often reflect combinations of these elements.[23] While not pivotal in all cases, any reservations people have may mitigate particular involvements.

*Engaging in "Seekership" (pursuing self-attributed interests)
*Being Recruited (others attempt to foster interest, encourage participation)
*Experiencing "Closure" (perceiving pressing obligations, limited choices)
*Managing Reservations (overcoming doubts, stigma, risks)

B. Sustaining and Intensifying Involvements (Continuities)

Once people have become involved in particular situations, we ask when they are likely to continue (and intensify) their participation in those settings. People's involvements in situations can vary immensely along the following dimensions:

*Internalizing Perspectives (viewpoints consistent with particular involvements)
*Achieving Identity (self and other definitions consistent with particular involvements)
*Accomplishing Activities (competence and composure in the focal setting)
*Making Commitments (making investments, developing dependencies)
*Developing Relationships (experiencing positive bonds with others in the setting)
*Foregoing Alternative Involvements (neglecting options, "bridge-burning")

C. Becoming Disinvolved

Insofar as it is unlikely that people would be highly involved in all dimensions of the situation at hand, we may see continuity and discontinuity as closely intertwined. The following suggests some basis on which disinvolvement is more likely, but it should not be assumed that dissatisfaction on any one dimension would necessitate disinvolvement (i.e. consider the problems of simultaneous disentanglement on all of these dimensions). The availability of (perceived) feasible options seems central, as do the other elements defining one's participation in a more complete sense:

*Questioning Viability of Perspectives (facing obstacles, dilemmas)
*Reassessing Identity (consistent with desired images?)
*Finding Activities Troublesome (boring, unpleasant, cumbersome)
*Being Freed-up from Existing Commitments (free to "relocate")
*Severing Relationships (conflict, animosity, exclusion)
*Encountering Opportunities for Alternative Involvements[24]

D. Becoming Reinvolved

Should people's subsequent involvements be found unsatisfactory (vis-a-vis perspectives, identities, activities, commitments, relationships), then reinvolvement in an earlier situation appears more likely. This seems more common as people begin:

*Defining Opportunities for Reinvolvements in former situations as more feasible (consider as potentially viable concerns with perspectives, identities, activities, relationships, commitments)

*Noting greater Changes to Self or Situation that would justify reinvolvement (e.g. face-saving, reassessments)

*Finding that they have Less extensively Organized their Routines around their present involvements (i.e. disentanglement is more easily accomplished)

4. DOING ACTIVITY

Although people's activities have important implications for their subsequent viewpoints and identities, activities acquire their meaning or purposiveness relative to both the perspectives from which they are envisioned and the identities of the people involved. Since the preceding discussions of perspectives and identities have already been cast in action (do-ing) terms, our attention turns to three other realms of activity. These include (A) performing activities, (B) pursuing cooperation from others, and (C) making commitments.

A. Performing Activities

The "performance of activity" assumes the processes outlined in "getting involved," but highlights the "problematics of accomplishment." The processes relevant to performance include:

*Making (preliminary) Plans
*Getting Prepared
*Managing Stage Fright (reservations, if any)
*Developing Competence (stock of knowledge, tactics, applications)
*Coordinating Events with Others (team members and others)
*Dealing with Obstacles, Resistances, and Distractions
*Conveying Images of Competence (displaying ability, composure)
*Encountering Competition
*Making Ongoing Assessments and Adjustments[25]

B. Pursuing Cooperation

While the "pursuit of cooperation" may be subsumed by the concept of performance, cooperative endeavors tend to emphasize (i) "persuasion processes," and (ii) people's encounters with "organizational principles" (OP's).

Persuasion reflects attempts on the part of people to "gain the cooperation of others" in respect to both "one to one" and more diversified "group" situations. When dealing with larger groups of people, matters of complexity and ambiguity typically become more noteworthy, as do the greater likelihood of distractions, challenges, and lowered levels of personal accountability. As well, one's opportunities for role-taking are lessened when one faces the task of pitching to more generalized as opposed to interpersonal others. This may involve some additional frustration and result in the creation of some unique group-directed tactics, but otherwise the same basic processes appear to hold for these instances as well. Here, we may consider how people go about:

*Formulating (preliminary) Plans
*Role-Taking (inferring / uncovering the perspectives of the other)
*Promoting Interest in One's Objectives
*Generating Trust
*Proposing Specific Lines of Action
*Encountering Resistance
*Neutralizing Obstacles
*Seeking and Making Concessions
*Confirming Agreements
*Assessing "Failures" and Recasting Plans[26]

Organizational Principles (OP's) refer to rules, norms, lines of authority, and other "rules of thumb" people develop to provide guidance of a generalized nature.[27] Aimed at the "generalized other" (Mead, 1934), organizational principles are seen to transcend particular actors and situations. And as they are envisioned to receive more extensive consensual validation, OP's take on a heightened aura of "objectivity" (Schutz, 1971). Likewise, people may have little choice over the OP's to which they are first exposed, and will likely take these for granted until they define these as ineffective in dealing with their circumstances or find these directly challenged by people promoting alternative OP's. It is apparent, however, that like other elements subsumable by "perspectives," OP's are contingent on continued affirmations for their existence and impact. They are subject to ongoing interpretation and assume cooperation and other enterprising activity on the part of those exposed to these particular "notions of reality." People's encounters with organizational principles encompass:

*Becoming exposed to Existing Organizational Principles (traditions)
*Interpreting Existing Organizational Principles
*Invoking Organizational Principles to Explain Behavior (a common sociological trap)
*Referencing Organizational Principles to Encourage Cooperation
*Attempting to Impose Organizational Principles on Others
*Endeavoring to Alter Existing Organizational Principles
*Attempting to Introduce, Implement, and Enforce New Organizational Principles[28]

C. Making Commitments

Commitments assume a variety of forms and may include physical investments as well as claims made to oneself or others. Some commitments are clearly desired by the parties making them, but others may be exceedingly tentative or reflect earlier resistance. The processes of "putting one's money down" or "buying into" particular situations have particular consequence for subsequent behavior. To the extent people acknowledge earlier made commitments, these can significantly limit their choices (i.e. closure). Subprocesses of relevance include:

*Exploring and Assessing Options

*Dealing with (any) Earlier Commitments
*Avoiding Commitments ("elusive targets")
*Minimizing or Diversifying Investments ("hedging bets")
*Organizing Routines around Particular Activities
*Neglecting Other Options ("closure by default")[29]

5. EXPERIENCING RELATIONSHIPS

Like the elements preceding, relationships may be largely subsumed by the "doing of activities." However, the selectivity and continuity of association entailed by "bonding" signifies a vital element in social life. Relationships imply perspectives, identities, activities, and commitments, and these can be powerful elements shaping the associations that people develop with one another. Since they also entail process, relationships have natural histories or careers (initial involvements, continuities, disinvolvements, reinvolvements), but matters of "intimacy and distancing" become especially prominent here as people try to achieve levels of selectivity and continuity with which they feel comfortable. The following processes seem central to considerations of people's relationships with others:

*Getting Prepared for Generalized Encounters
*Defining Self as Available for Association
*Defining (specific) Others as Desirable Associates
*Making Approaches / Receiving Openings from Others
*Encountering (and indicating) Rejection / Acceptance
*Assessing Self and Other for "goodness of fit"
*Developing Interactional Styles (in each relationship)
*Managing Openness and Secrecy
*Developing Understandings, Preferences, Loyalty
*Managing Distractions (and outside commitments)
*Juggling (multiple) Relationships
*Severing Relationships (disentanglement)
*Renewing Relationships[30]

Given the complexity of group life, it seems inevitable that we will continue to develop concepts (and labels thereof) that cut across one another. Nevertheless, close attention to process seems the most effective way of conceptualizing and producing a generic, ethnographically grounded, social science.

CONCLUSION

> To speak of a science without concepts suggests all sorts of analogies—
> a carver without tools, a railroad without tracks, a mammal without bones,
> a love story without love. (Blumer, 1969:153)

Recognizing the perspectival, reflective, negotiable, relational and processual nature of ongoing group life, ethnographic research focuses on group life as lived by the participants. It denotes a paradigm rooted in the experiences and activities of people. It attends to their meanings and practices, their dilemmas and uncertainties, and to their attempts to negotiate their situations in conjunction with those of others whose lives intersect with their own. It is an approach oriented towards the intimate understanding of group life and all that of which group life consists.

The notion of a generic processual sociology builds on these concerns by examining parallel activities across contexts. Whereas ethnographic research allows us to be very sensitive to each particular context (and the meanings of each context for the participants therein), the emphasis on process enables us to maximize conceptual development. By drawing comparisons and contrasts across settings, we not only arrive at a richer understanding of each setting, but of similar processes across a wide range of settings. In doing so we have the opportunity to assess previous findings and to work towards fuller, more qualified conceptualizations of human association. Indeed, only by being acutely attentive to the ways in which "people experience and shape their worlds" and drawing parallels across situations can we hope to achieve a "theory of action" which reflects group life as it is accomplished.

Like other aspects of community dynamics, the development of a generic processual sociology is best viewed as an instance of socially constructed (Berger and Luckmann, 1966) or joint (Blumer, 1969) activity. Thus, its eventual development is highly contingent on the extent to which this notion is integrated into a wide range of our scholarly activities. This will inevitably be a slow, demanding, and (necessarily) cumulative process, but it can be greatly facilitated by efforts to more intensively and explicitly incorporate this objective into our teaching, research, analytical, editorial, conferencing, and networking activities. And, only by doing this do we seem likely to achieve better approximations of grounded, processual conceptualizations of human behavior.

REFERENCES

Adler, Patricia. 1985. *Wheeling and Dealing*. New York: Columbia University Press.
Albas, Daniel C. and Cheryl Mills Albas. 1984. *Student Life and Exams*. Dubuque, Iowa: Kendall / Hunt.
Anderson, Nels. 1923. *The Hobo*. Chicago: Univ. of Chicago Press.
Athens, Lonnie. 1980. *Violent Criminal Acts and Actors: A Symbolic Interactionist Study*. Boston: Oxford University Press.
Becker, Howard S. 1963. *Outsiders*. New York, N.Y.: Free Press.
Becker, Howard, Everett Hughes, and Blanche Geer. 1968. *Making the Grade: The Academic Side of Student Life*. New York: Wiley.
Becker, Howard, Everett Hughes, Blanche Geer, and Anselm Strauss. 1961. *The Boys in White*. Chicago: University of Chicago Press.
Berger, Peter and Thomas Luckmann. 1966. *The Social Construction of Reality*. New York, N.Y.: Anchor.
Bigus, O.E., S.C. Hadden, and B.G. Glaser. 1982. "Basic Social Processes."Pp. 251–272 in R.B. Smith and P.K. Manning (eds.) *Qualitative Methods: Volume II of Handbook of Social Science Methods*. Cambridge, Mass.: Ballinger.
Bittner, Egon. 1967. "The Police on Skid Row: A Study of Peace-Keeping." *American Sociological Review* (32):699–715.

Blumer, Herbert. 1931. "Science Without Concepts." *American Journal of Sociology* 36: 515–533.
———. 1933. *Movies and Conduct*. New York: Macmillan (Reprinted 1970. New York: Arno Press).
———. 1939. *Critiques of Research in the Social Sciences: An Appraisal of Thomas and Znaniecki's, The Polish Peasant in America*. New York: Social Science Research Council, Bulletin 44.
———. 1947. "Sociological Theory in Industrial Relations." *American Sociological Review* 12:271–278.
———. 1960. "Early Industrialization and the Laboring Class." *Sociological Quarterly* 1:5–14.
———. 1969. *Symbolic Interaction*. Berkeley, Ca.: University of California Press.
———. 1971. "Social Problems as Collective Behavior." *Social Problems* 18:298–306.
———. 1990. *Industrialization as an Agent of Social Change* (Edited by David R. Maines and Thomas J. Morrione). New York: Aldine De Gruyter.
Burkholdt, D. and J. Gubrium. 1983. "Practicing Accountability in Human Service Institutions." *Urban Life* 12:249–268.
Carlson, R. 1984. "What's Social About Social Psychology? Where's the Person in Personality Research?" *Journal of Personality and Social Psychology* 47:1304–1309.
Couch, Carl. 1975. "Obdurate Features of Group Life." Pp. 237–254 in C.J. Couch and R. Hintz (eds.) *Constructing Social Life. Readings in Behavioral Sociology from the Iowa School*. Champaign, Illinois: Stipes.
———. 1984. "Symbolic Interaction and Generic Sociological Principles." *Symbolic Interaction* 7:1–14.
Cressey, Paul G. 1932. *The Taxi-Dance Hall*. Chicago: University of Chicago Press.
Dietz, Mary Lou. 1983. *Killing for Profit: The Social Organization of Felony Homicide*. Chicago: Nelson-Hall.
Ditton, James. 1977. *Part-Time Crime: An Ethnography of Fiddling and Pilferage*. London: Macmillan.
Donovan, Francis. 1929. *The Saleslady*. Chicago: University of Chicago Press.
Douglas, Jack D. and John Johnson. 1977. *Existential Sociology*. Cambridge, England: Cambridge University Press.
Ebaugh, Helen Rose Fuchs. 1988. *Becoming an Ex*. Chicago: University of Chicago Press.
Edgerton, Robert. 1967. *The Cloak of Competence: Stigma in the Lives of the Mentally Retarded*. Berkeley, Ca.: University of California Press.
Emerson, Robert M. 1969. *Judging Delinquents*. Chicago: Aldine.
Ermarth, Michael. 1978. *Wilhelm Dilthey: The Critique of Historical Reason*. Chicago: University of Chicago Press.
Estes, C. and B. Edmunds. 1981. "Symbolic Interaction and Social Policy Analysis." *Symbolic Interaction* 4:75–86.
Evans, A. Donald and W.W. Falk. 1986. *Learning to be Deaf*. Berlin: Mouton.
Faris, Robert E.L. 1967. *Chicago Sociology 1920–1932*. Chicago: University of Chicago Press.
Festinger, Leon, Henry Riecken, and Stanley Schacter. 1956. *When Prophecy Fails*. New York: Harper and Row.
Fine, Gary A. 1983. *Shared Fantasy: Role Playing Games as Social Worlds*. Chicago: University of Chicago Press.
Garfinkel, Harold. 1967. *Studies in Ethnomethodology*. Englewood Cliffs, N.J.: Prentice-Hall.
Gergen, Kenneth. 1982. *Toward Transformation in Social Knowledge*. New York: Springer-Verlag.
Geertz, C. 1973. *The Interpretation of Cultures: Selected Essays*. New York: Basic.
Glaser, Barney and Anselm Strauss. 1967. *The Discovery of Grounded Theory: Strategies for Qualitative Research*. Chicago: Aldine.
Glick, Ira. 1957. *A Social Psychological Study of Futures Marketing*. University of Chicago: Doctoral Dissertation (Sociology).
Goffman, Erving. 1959. *The Presentation of Self in Everyday Life*. New York: Anchor.
———. 1961. *Asylums*. New York: Anchor.
———. 1963a. *Behavior in Public Places*. New York: Free Press.
———. 1963b. *Stigma*. Englewood Cliffs, N.J.: Spectrum.
———. 1971. *Relations in Public*. New York: Harper Colophon.
———. 1974. *Frame Analysis*. New York: Harper Colophon.
Grills, Scott. 1989. *Designating Deviance: Championing Definitions of The Appropriate and Inappropriate Through a Christian Political Voice*. Doctoral Dissertation, McMaster University (Sociology)

Haas, Jack and William Shaffir. 1987. *Becoming Doctors: The Adaption of A Cloak of Competence.* Greenwich, Conn: JAI.

Hall, Ian. 1983. *Playing For Keeps: The Careers of Front-Line Workers for Developmentally Handicapped Persons.* University of Waterloo: M.A. Thesis.

Hargreaves, David, Stephen Hester, and Frank Melor. 1975. *Deviance in Classrooms.* London: Routledge and Kegan Paul.

Hiller, E.T. 1928. *The Strike.* Chicago: University of Chicago Press.

Hughes, Everett. 1928. *A Study of a Secular Institution: The Chicago Real Estate Board.* University of Chicago: Doctoral Dissertation (Sociology).

Hughes, Helen. 1937. *News and the Human Interest Story.* University of Chicago: Doctoral Dissertation (Sociology).

Katz, E. and P.F. Lazarsfeld. 1955. *Personal Influence.* New York, N.Y.: Free Press.

Klapp, Orrin. 1964. *Symbolic Leaders.* Minerva.

———. 1969. *The Collective Search for Identity.* New York: Holt.

———. 1971. *Social Types: Process, Structure and Ethos.* San Diego, Ca.: Aegis.

Kleinman, Sherryl

———. 1984. *Equals before God: Seminarians as Humanistic Professionals.* Chicago: University of Chicago Press.

Knorr-Cetina, Karin. 1981. *The Manufacture of Knowledge: An Essay on the Constructivist and Contextual Nature of Science.* Oxford, England:Permagon.

Kuhn, Thomas S. 1962. *The Structure of Scientific Revolutions* (Revised edition, 1970). Chicago: University of Chicago Press.

Latour, Bruno. 1987. *Science in Action.* Cambridge, Mass.: Harvard University Press.

Lemert, Edwin. 1951. *Social Pathology.* New York: McGraw-Hill.

———. 1962. "Paranoia and the Dynamics of Exclusion." *Sociometry* 25:2–25.

———. 1967. *Human Deviance, Social Problems and Social Control.* Englewood Cliffs, NJ: Prentice-Hall.

Lesieur, Henry. 1977. *The Chase.* New York: Anchor.

Lester, M. and S.C. Hadden. 1980. "Ethnomethodology and Grounded Theory Methodology." *Urban Life* 9:3–33.

Letkemann, Peter. 1973. *Crime as Work.* Englewood Cliffs, N.J.: Prentice-Hall.

Levine, Donald. 1971. *Georg Simmel: On Individuality and Social Forms.* Chicago: University of Chicago Press.

Lindesmith, Alfred R. 1959. "Federal Law and Drug Addiction." *Social Problems* 7:48–57.

Lofland, John. 1966. *The Doomsday Cult.* Englewood Cliffs, N.J.: Prentice-Hall.

———. 1970. "Interactionist Imagery and Analytic Interruptus." Pp. 35–45 in Tamotsu Shibutani (ed.), *Human Nature and Collective Behavior: Papers in Honor of Herbert Blumer.* Englewood Cliffs, NJ: Prentice-Hall.

———. 1976. *Doing Social Life.* New York: Wiley.

Lofland, John and Lyn Lofland. 1984. *Analyzing Social Settings.* Belmont, California: Wadsworth.

Mead, George H. 1934. *Mind, Self and Society*, edited by Charles W. Morris. Chicago: University of Chicago Press.

Mitchell, Richard G. Jr. 1983. *Mountain Experience.* Chicago: University of Chicago Press.

Miyamato, F. 1959. "The Social Act: Re-examination of a Concept." *Pacific Sociological Review* 2:51–55.

Noblit, George W. and R. Dewight Hare. 1988. *Meta-Ethnography: Synthesizing Qualitative Studies.* Newbury Park: Cs.: Sage.

Palmer, Vivian. 1928. *Field Studies in Sociology.* Chicago: University of Chicago Press.

Park, Robert E. 1952. *Human Communities: The Collected Papers of Robert Park, Volume II.* E. Hughes, C.S. Johnson, J. Masuoka, R. Redford, and L. Wirth (eds.). Glencoe, Ill.: Free Press.

———. 1955. *Society: The Collected Papers of Robert Park, Volume III.* E. Hughes, C.S. Johnson, J. Masuoka, R. Redford, and L. Wirth (eds.). Glencoe, Ill.: Free Press.

Park, Robert E. and Ernest Burgess. 1924. *Introduction to the Science of Sociology.* Chicago: University of Chicago Press (1969).

Powell, Walter. 1985*Getting Into Press.* Chicago: University of Chicago Press.

Prus, Robert. 1975a. "Labeling Theory: A Reconceptualization and A Propositional Statement on Typing." *Sociological Focus* 8(1):79–96.

———. 1975b. "Resisting Designations: An Extension of Attribution Theory into a Negotiated Context." *Sociological Inquiry* 45(1):3–14.

———. 1982. "Designating Discretion and Openness: The Problematics of Truthfulness in Everyday Life." the *Canadian Review of Sociology and Anthropology* 18 (1):70–91.

———. 1984. "Career Contingencies: Examining Patterns of Involvement." Pp. 297–317 in N. Theberge and P. Donnelly (eds.) *Sport and the Sociological Imagination*. Fort Worth, Tx: Texas Christian Univ. Press.

———. 1989a. *Making Sales: Influence as Interpersonal Accomplishment*. Newbury Park, California: Sage.

———. 1989b. *Pursuing Customers: An Ethnography of Marketing Activities*. Newbury Park, California: Sage.

———. 1990"The Interpretive Challenge: The Impending Crisis in Sociology." *Canadian Journal of Sociology* 15 (3):355–363.

———. 1991"Producing Social Science: Knowledge as a Social Problem in Academia." Pp. 57–78 in Gale Miller and James Holstein (editors), *Perspectives in Social Problems*, Volume 3. Greenwich, Conn.: Jai Press.

Prus, Robert and Styllianoss Irini. 1980. *Hookers, Rounders, and Desk Clerks: The Social Organization of the Hotel Community*. Salem, Wisc.: Sheffield.

Prus, Robert and C.R.D. Sharper. 1991. *Road Hustler: Hustlers, Magic and the Thief Subculture*. New York: Kaufman and Greenberg.

Ralph, Jack. 1950. *Junk Business and the Junk Peddler*. University of Chicago: M.A. thesis.

Ray, Marsh. 1961. "The Cycle of Abstinence and Relapse among Heroin Addicts." *Social Problems* 9:132–140.

Ross, H. Lawrence. 1980 *Settled Out of Court*. New York: Aldine.

Rubinstein, Jonathan. 1973. *City Police*. New York: Ballantine.

Sanders, Clinton. 1991. *Customizing the Body: The Art and Culture of Tattooing*. Philadelphia: Temple University Press.

Scott, Lois. 1981. *Being Somebody: The Negotiation of Identities in a Community Context*. University of Waterloo: M.A. Thesis (Kinesiology).

Scott, Marvin. 1968. *The Racing Game*. Chicago: Aldine.

Schutz, Alfred. 1964. *Collected Papers II: Studies in Social Theory*. The Hague: Martinus Nijhoff. 1971. *Collected Papers I: The Problem of Social Reality*. The Hague: Martinus Nijhoff.

Shaw, Clifford. 1931. *The Jack Roller: The Natural History of a Delinquent Career*. Chicago: Univ. of Chicago Press.

Simmel, Georg. 1950. *The Sociology of George Simmel*, translated and edited by Kurt H. Wolf. New York: Free Press.

———. 1978. *The Philosophy of Money* (1907), translated by Tom Bottomore and David Frisby. Boston, Ma.: Routledge and Kegan Paul.

Stebbins, Robert. 1990. *The Laugh-Makers*. Montreal, Que.: McGill-Queens University Press.

Steffensmeier, Darrell J. 1986. *The Fence: In the Shadow of Two Worlds*. Totowa: Rowman and Littlefield.

Strauss, Anselm. 1970. "Discovering New Theory From Previous Theory." Pp. 46–53 in T. Shibutani (ed.), *Human Nature and Collective Behavior: Papers in Honor of Herbert Blumer*. Englewood Cliffs, NJ: Prentice-Hall.

Sutherland, Edwin. 1937. *The Professional Thief*. Chicago: University of Chicago Press.

———. 1950. "The Diffusion of Sexual Psychopath Laws." *American Journal of Sociology* 56:142–148.

Thomas, William I. and Florian Znaniecki. 1918–1920 *The Polish Peasant in Europe and America* (Volumes I–V). Boston: Richard Badger.

Vaughan, Diane. 1986. *Uncoupling: Turning Points in Intimate Relationships*. New York: Oxford University Press.

Waller, Willard. 1930. *The Old Love and the New*. Carbondale, Ill.: Southern Illinois University Press (1967).

———. 1932. *The Sociology of Teaching*. New York: Russel and Russel (1961).

Warren, Carol A.B. 1983. "The Politics of Trouble in an Adolescent Psychiatric Hospital." *Urban Life* 12:327-348.

Wiseman, Jacqueline. 1970. *Stations of the Lost: The Treatment of Skid Row Alcoholics.* Englewood Cliffs, NJ: Prentice-Hall.

——. 1979. "Towards a Theory of Policy Intervention in Social Problems." *Social Problems* 27:3-18.

——. 1991. *The Other Half: Wives of Alcoholics and Their Social Psychological Situations.* New York: Aldine de Gruyter.

Wolf, Daniel. 1991. *The Rebels: A Brotherhood of Outlaw Bikers.* Toronto: University of Toronto Press.

Zerubavel, E. 1981. "If Simmel were a Fieldworker: On Formal Sociological Theory and Analytical Field Research." *Symbolic Interaction* 3: 25-33.

NOTES

[1] An earlier, somewhat related version of this paper was published in the Journal of Contemporary Ethnography 1987 (16): 250-293. I am indebted to Jim Curtis, Carl Couch, Mary Lou Dietz, Scott Grills, Jim Henslin, John Johnson, Howard Robboy, Marvin Scott, and Graham Tomlinson, for comments and discussions pertaining to earlier versions of this paper.

[2] While clearly not all symbolic interactionism is ethnographic in nature, this statement has important implications for the broader tradition of symbolic interaction. Indeed, the emphasis on process (also see Couch, 1984) may provide the essential foundation for synthesizing the broader interactionist tradition.

[3] Although seemingly unaware of much of the literature on which the present statement is built, a somewhat parallel task has been suggested by Noblit and Hare (1988) under the term, "meta-ethnography." Despite this intriguing term, Noblit and Hare provide little direction concerning the ways in which meta-ethnography might be accomplished. The present statement on generic social processes, then, may be seen as extending their project along more focused, processual dimensions.

[4] See Dietz, Prus and Shaffir (1993) for a collection of ethnographic studies which has been organized around the generic social processes examined in this paper.

[5] Although Wilhelm Dilthey (see Makkreel, 1975; Rickman, 1976, 1988; Ermarth, 1978; Plantinga, 1980) is one of the major figures in the development of a hermeneutic social science, and an intellectual precursor to the symbolic interactionism of George Herbert Mead and Herbert George Blumer, textbook writers generally have been tardy in acknowledging Dilthey's role as a central founding figure in the human (social) sciences.

[6] Garfinkel's (1967:35-75) depiction of the "cultural dope" (the sociologists' human who acts in certain ways because of prevailing societal conditions) and the "psychological dope" (the psychologists' counterpart) is very appropos here. Albeit with different purposes in mind, Harre and Secord (1972), Gergen (1982) and Carlson (1984) provide somewhat related critiques of psychological social psychology.

[7] Clearly, I am not denying the "generic" or abstract applicabilities of other sociological formulations to human group life (e.g. consider Merton's typology of adaptation, Parsons' pattern variables, Weber's concept of rationality, Sorokin's conceptualization of cyclical change, or Homan's portrayal of exchange). Further, while these scholars, themselves, engage in much interpretive work in their attempts to show how their conceptualizations could apply to a wide range of human settings, their models are *not* grounded in the ongoing, interpretive dynamics of human association. Sociologists may apply these and other constructs to a wide range of human groups, but a great many sociological constructions are not attentive to the intersubjective features of human association and for this reason are not seen to qualify as "generic social processes." Insofar as these conceptualizations are inattentive variously to the (multi) perspectival, reflective, negotiable, relational, and processual features of everyday life, they violate central features of the social essence of human lived experiences.

[8] As Glaser and Strauss (1967:93) note, some sociologists envision their tasks as developing theories of substantive areas (period). Some others may feel uncomfortable with the "depersonalization" that images of (abstract) theory sometimes engender.

[9] Goffman's works (especially, 1959, 1961, 1963a, 1963b, 1971, 1974) come readily to mind in this respect, as well as in Goffman's insatiable quest for generic features of association. Although Goffman's own propensity for field work is vastly overshadowed by his exceptionally rich, penetrating, and engaging analysis, Goffman emerges as an exemplar par excellence of the production of generic concepts through ethnographic research. Much of Goffman's analyses focus on ongoing identity work within the context of situated community morality, and only some of his concepts are processual in nature. However, the materials Goffman gathered on community life in the Shetland Islands, and on the underlife of the mental hospital, as well as through his continued observations of the drama of everyday life, were vital not only in shaping his own conceptualizations of the social world, but through his subsequent analyses were to have a strikingly profound impact on the social sciences more generally.

[10] Zerubavel (1981) explores this issue at greater depth, arguing for the natural affinity of Simmel's work with focused ethnographic inquiry.

[11] While Simmel's influence appears to have been fostered most notably by Albion Small and Robert Park, many of the key figures in "Chicago interactionism" (e.g. Thomas, Mead, Blumer) evidence an "intellectual affinity" with Simmel rather than a direct literary impact. Levine (1971:xlviii–lviii) provides a very valuable depiction of Simmel's influence on American sociology via Small and Park.

[12] As Palmer's (1928) statement testifies, field work was significantly established as a methodology by that time. Park and Burgess (1924:58–59) provide a bibliographic listing of "methods of sociological research" to that date, attending in particular to field studies on page 59.

[13] As a case in point, I observe that I was not as familiar with this volume at the time that I originally prepared this manuscript as I would have liked to have been in retrospect. The Lofland volume is a very valuable resource for those embarking on ethnographic inquiry.

[14] In the course of conducting their studies, Couch and his associates (1986a,b), however, have tended to impute meanings to the acts of others rather than inquire into the meanings that participants themselves have for their activities. Thus, while appreciating the potential of any record of human behavior, we should be most concerned that the interpretive processes underlying record construction (and usage, including analysis!) not be subordinated to the pursuit of a "more scientific technique." In referencing recorded statements as a data base, one may be particularly reminded of Blumer's (1939) very insightful appraisal of Thomas and Znaniecki's Polish Peasant (a critique which they acknowledged to be exceedingly well founded!). The implication is that we should be extremely cautious of "content analysis" when we lack the interpretive assistance of those doing and/or assembling those "documents." Under these circumstances, the perspectives of those interpreting the data become increasingly central in determining the "meanings" these materials are purported to have.

[15] For some more sustained indications of how this might be accomplished, see Glaser and Strauss (1967), (especially) Lofland (1976), and Bigus et al. (1982).

[16] Waller's (1932:351–352) observations are especially fitting here: It does not seem extreme to say that those brilliant social philosophers who have developed the sociology of conflict might have found adequate material for their discussions without having left their own classrooms. Nearly all the classic concepts apply to life in the school room, war, feuds, litigation, conflict of ideals, victory, conciliation, compromise, conversion, accommodation, and assimilation.(351).. It could be argued that conflict in the schools is the feature of school life that best prepares students for facing life outside. (352)

[17] In conjunction with this, Glaser and Strauss (1970) note both the comfort people experience as "experts" in particular substantive areas and the encouragements they receive to maintain these specialties (e.g. enhanced publishing opportunities). Viewed in this manner, each new area introduces considerable uncertainty and risk for those making substantive shifts.

[18] For instances of the use of the concept of career or natural history in ethnographic research, see Shaw (1930, 1931), Cressey (1932), Goffman (1961), Becker (1963), Prus and Irini (1980), Scott (1982), Hall (1983), and Prus and Sharper (1991).

[19] Most ethnographies nicely illustrate themes pertaining to "the acquisition of perspectives" and most almost inevitably address notions of identities, involvements, activities and relationships as well, for these elements are very much interrelated in subcultural life-styles. Some book length ethnographies which do a particularly effective job of conveying the ways in which people become exposed to, and familiar with, particular world views include: Anderson (1923), Shaw (1930), Blumer (1933), Sutherland

(1937), Becker et al., (1961, 1968), Goffman (1961), Lofland (1966), Scott (1968), Fine (1983), Kleinman (1984), Evans and Falk (1986), Stebbins (1990), Charmaz (1991) and Wolf (1991).

[20] Although the development and alteration of collective or group identities generally entail more complex processes of presentation, typification, designation, assessment, resistance, and retypification than do those directed toward single individuals, the themes listed below would appear to apply in rather parallel manners to definitions directed toward collective or singular targets.

[21] Ethnographic monographs that are particularly attentive to identity work and self images include: Edgerton (1969), Evans and Falk (1986), Haas and Shaffir (1987), Charmaz (1991), Sanders (1991) and Wolf (1991). For reviews of the literature on "identity work" as this pertains to type-casting, public designations, and resisting unwanted imputations, see Prus (1975a, 1975b, 1982). These reviews build centrally on the conceptual work of Goffman (1959, 1963b) and Klapp (1964, 1969, 1971), amongst others.

[22] Among the monographs which more explicitly address involvements or career contingencies in ethnographic inquiries are: Shaw (1930), Cressey (1932), Sutherland (1937), Becker et al. (1961), Lofland (1966), Ditton (1977), Lesieur (1977), Fine (1983), Haas and Shaffir (1987), Prus and Irini (1980), Prus and Sharper (1991), and Wolf (1991).

[23] In a more complete sense, one should also note the existence of "imposed" (e.g. physiological / medical complications) and "inadvertent" (accidental, unwitting) involvements.

[24] See Ebaugh (1988) for a review of the literature on "Becoming an Ex," as well as an instructive attempt to formulate the generic social processes constituting disinvolvement. Ray's (1961) article on "abstinence and relapse cycles among heroin addicts" also nicely lends itself to generic applications. As the last point emphasizes, disinvolvement is often accompanied by involvements in other settings. Also see for instance, Denzin's (1987) account of heavy drinkers becoming involved in Alcoholics Anonymous, as a means of disinvolvement from drinking routines. Thus, all of the processes pertinent to involvement (in activity 2) may intersect with those of disinvolvement (from activity 1).

[25] The following book length monographs provide some of the more focused materials on how people accomplish activities: Anderson (1923), Shaw (1930), Emerson (1969), Hargraves et al. (1975), Ditton (1977), Lesieur (1977), Letkemann (1977), Athens (1980), Prus and Irini (1980), Ross (1980), Dietz (1983), Fine (1983), Mitchell (1983), Albas and Albas (1984), Powell (1985), Steffensmeier (1986), Charmaz (1991), Prus and Sharper (1991), and Wolf (1991). For detailed illustrations of these particular subprocesses, see Prus (1989b).

[26] Notions of persuasion (influence and negotiation processes) are especially evident in the following monographs: Shaw (1930), Sutherland (1937), Festinger (1965), Lofland (1966), Emerson (1969), Wiseman (1970), Prus and Irini (1980), Ross (1980), Fine (1983), Latour (1987), and Prus and Sharper (1991). The subprocesses outlined here are most extensively detailed in an analysis of interpersonal selling activity (Prus, 1989a).

[27] These "organizational principles" are sometimes envisioned as constituting the essence of "social structure." While OP's are certainly basic to group life, the term "social structure" is more accurately applied to the *processes* that people invoke as they take one another into account in developing the lines of action that taken together constitute group life. Viewed thusly, OP's represent socially constructed processes that provide greater longevity to particular cultural themes (or other shared "understandings").

[28] Those interested in examining the ways in which organizational routines are accomplished in practice are apt to find the following books especially relevant: Cressey (1932), Becker et al. (1961, 1968), Goffman (1961), Emerson (1969), Wiseman (1970), Prus and Irini (1980), Ross (1980), Haas and Shaffir (1987) and Prus (1989b).

[29] For book length ethnographies which attend more explicitly to the commitment making process, see: Lofland (1966), Lesieur (1977), Prus (1989a,b), and Wolf (1991).

[30] The development, maintenance, and severance of relationships is given more explicit attention the following monographs: Shaw (1930), Waller (1930), Lofland (1966), Wiseman (1970, 1991), Lesieur (1977), Prus and Irini (1980), Fine (1983), Adler (1985), Vaughan (1986); Prus (1989a), Prus and Sharper (1991) and Wolf (1991). Lemert's (1962) analysis of "paranoia and the dynamics of exclusion" deserves special recognition as one of the best accounts of interpersonal relationships.

Chapter 36 AND A CHILD SHALL LEAD US? CHILDREN, GENDER AND PERSPECTIVES BY INCONGRUITY

Spencer E. Cahill

Women and children may have been the first into lifeboats when the ship started to sink, but they clearly followed men into the study of social life. Although women are now fighting their way toward the front of the queue of sociological concerns, children remain far behind. In addition to scholarly child neglect (see Ambert, 1986), students of social life could also be charged with a kind of child abuse. When we have paid attention to children, we have treated them as "adults in the making" referring their present lives to a presumed future. That developmental or socialization approach to the study of children is undoubtedly useful for some purposes, but it is also limiting, as Barrie Thorne (1987) has so eloquently argued. By always translating doing into learning, we obscure the artfulness of children's social practices and the complexity of their social worlds.

This scholarly neglect and abuse of children by students of social life has been at our expense. As Thorne (1987: 101) suggests, "revaluing and attending closely" to children's experiences "may inspire fresh approaches to adult life." If we take children seriously, we may well find that they can teach us some important lessons about social life that might otherwise escape us.

My purpose in this paper is to demonstrate that taking children seriously can help inspire fresh approaches to the study of gender. To do so, I stand the developmental or socialization approach to the study of children on its head. Instead of starting with adult arrangements and then referring children's social lives to that outcome (Thorne, 1987: 92.), I start with children's social practices in order to gain insights into adult arrangements. I examine children's gender classifications and their maintenance of gender boundaries by drawing upon a variety of sources including my own observation of preschool-age children and a number of ethnographic studies of children's social worlds. In regard to each of these issues, I suggest that children have much to teach us about the ways in which we adults create and recreate the seemingly natural order of normally gendered persons.

CHILDREN AND PERSPECTIVES BY INCONGRUITY

Students of social life often fail to appreciate that the process of childhood socialization involves as much forgetting as it does learning. Over the course of our biographies, actions that were once self-conscious become habitual and automatic. What was once strangely obvious gradually fades into the seen but unnoticed background of commonplace events. Perhaps the greatest challenge of studying social life is to recapture the sense of awe with which we initially approached the social world. In order to fully understand social life, we must recognize the strangeness of the ostensibly familiar and notice what commonly goes unnoticed. It is here that children can lead us.

Harold Garfinkel (1967: 37) once observed that in order to view the typically unnoticed backgrounds of commonplace events "one must either be a stranger to the 'life as usual' character of everyday scenes, or become estranged from them." I would add that one can also bring those unnoticed backgrounds into view by adopting the perspectives of those who are strangers to or estranged from the life as usual character of everyday scenes, as Garfinkel's (1967: 116-185) own case study of the transsexual Agnes demonstrates. In West and Zimmerman;s (1987:131) words, the Agnes case "makes observable what culture has made invisible—the accomplishment of gender." As Garfinkel (1967: 180-181) concluded, the practices that Agnes employed to pass as a normal, natural female provide a "perspective by incongruity" that helped make observable "*that* and *how* normal sexuality is accomplished through witnessable displays of talk and conduct."

In many important respects, children are also strangers to and estranged from the life as usual character of the accomplishment of gender. Moreover, like Agnes, they too are practical actors who have a way of permitting the environment to teach them answers to its own questions (Garfinkel 1967: 168). Thus, children's gender-related social practices also provide a perspective by incongruity that can help make observable that and how gender is accomplished. By taking children seriously, we might better see what culture and our own induction into it have made invisible.

GENDER CLASSIFICATION

Although I was slow to realize it, a two-year-old girl taught me one of the most important lessons about gender that I have learned. We were walking through a stand of trees along the Southern California coast during the time of the monarch butterflies' annual migration. When we encountered one of those colorful creatures, I (C) immediately brought it to the girl's (S) attention (Cahill, 1986: 298):

C: Look at the butterfly. There it goes.
S: A mommy one.
C: That's a mommy one?
S: Mommy one.
C: How do you know it's a mommy one?
S: Mommy ones and daddy ones.

I dutifully recorded our conversation in my fieldnotes although I found her answers to my questions quite confusing. I, of course, had no idea how one could distinguish a mommy butterfly from a daddy one and doubted that my young friend could do so.

Over the next few days, I heard a number of other children using gender-related labels in similarly arbitrary ways, at least to my adult ears. I overheard a three-year-old boy and girl identify one of the two live ducks that had been brought to a preschool as a mommy duck and the other as a daddy duck. I listened without understanding while a four-year-old explained why a small plastic figurine was a girl. And, I was told by a three-year-old boy that a horse we were observing was a girl although I could clearly see an anatomical feature which convinced me otherwise. Gender-related classification of the objects, both animate and inanimate, that populated their environment was obviously of some importance to these children but I could not determine the grounds on which they did so.

About two weeks after I learned about mommy and daddy butterflies, I (C) was sitting on the side of a sandbox, and an approximately three-year-old boy was standing between my legs. Without warning, he reached up, tugged on my beard and exclaimed, "that daddy, that daddy." When I asked him if he meant my beard, he replied, "Yeah. That daddy" (Cahill, 1989: 285). Intrigued by his remarks, I contacted the boy's father, explained what had occurred, and asked if he had ever had a beard. He assured me that he had always been clean shaven as had other adult males with whom his son had regular contact. Yet, this boy seemed to know that there was some kind of association between beards and "daddies."

The most obvious interpretation of what I had been observing was that these children had much to learn about reproductive anatomy, but there also seemed to be a more profound lesson. Perhaps gender is not as equivocally defined and definable by biological matters as we adults would like to believe. Perhaps gender classification is not a biological but a cultural given for which biological grounds are then found. My three-year-old friend was apparently aware that his world was populated by mommies and daddies and was now attempting to discover grounds for that classification of persons. For these children and, I suspected, for adults as well, it was gender classification that determined the differences and similarities among persons that we notice rather than the other way around, as Freud (1925) and his followers would have it.

Grounds for gender classification can obviously be found, as children remind us, the most apparent ones are not biological but cultural. For example, one of my colleague's four-year-old son and his father enrolled in the father-son swimming class at the local YMCA. Although many of the fathers swam in the nude, some of those who did so wore bathing caps. On the way home from the first session, the young boy asked his father why there were so many women in the class. When his father asked him about the women he had seen, the boy responded: "You know, in the hats" (Cahill, 1989: 286). There is somewhat more to this story than just a cute example of children's ignorance of the "real" basis of gender classification.

The following fragment from a psychiatric interview of a four-year-old boy is borrowed from Richard Green (1974:187) and tells a similar story about gender classification.

DR: For the boy to be magically changed into a girl, what would have to change about the boy?
BOY: Dress.
DR: He'd have to dress? Okay, that's one thing. Go on.
BOY: And he would have long hair. He'd have girl's shoes: Three things.
DR: Three things, right. What else?
BOY: Ummm. 'Cause he would have girl's shoes.

DR: How about — let's say the child is all undressed. There's no clothing at all. What would have to change with the little boy's body in order to become a girl?

BOY: Because — umm — his knees — umm.

Although the psychiatrist interpreted the boy's responses as psychologically defensive denials, his professed understanding of gender classification is quite similar to that of other children his age. For example, Thompson and Benther's (1971) 36 preschool age subjects reported that genitals determined whether one was a boy or a girl, but hair length influenced their gender classifications of anatomically correct dolls more than either body shape or genitalia. These results and the preceding examples would seem to suggest that, at least for children, gender classification is not simply the unmediated reflection of anatomical distinctions between persons. Rather, understandings of anatomical distinctions between persons are filtered through socially constructed systems of gender classification.

Some years ago George Herbert Mead (1910: 112-113) argued that "social consciousness antedates" and consequently colors our "reflective experience of things...purely physical." That is apparently the case with gender classification. We confront a social world that is divided into gender classes and must then discover the grounds for that sorting of persons. In looking to the environment for answers to that question, we discover that clothing, hair length, and similar factors determine persons' gender classification. Those culturally relative grounds of gender classification then provide a framework for understanding purely physical differences between persons. In this respect, adults are much closer to children than we might like to believe.

In the course of our everyday lives, our gender classification of persons is seldom based on the purely physical. Instead, we typically sort persons into gender categories on the basis of such culturally relative cues as hair and clothing style. We then attribute certain anatomical characteristics to them by way of biologically accounting for our gender classifications. For example, adult participants in an overlay study conducted by Kessler and McKenna (1978: 154) who had identified a clothed figure as male were asked how the figure could be changed into a female. Most claimed that the way to do so was to "remove the penis" even though the figure had no visible penis. It would seem that gender classification rather than biology was given. Biology merely provided explanations for what is already taken for granted. To borrow from Kenneth Burke (1962: 378), we "perceive nature through the fog of symbol-ridden social structures" that we have erected to adopt nature.

This is the case not only in everyday life but in the scientific study of our natures as well. Biological differences among persons and the possible effects of those differences are not investigated separate from gender classification but rather analyzed in terms of such classifications. Differences between the gender classes are thereby emphasized creating the impression that gender classification is an inevitable result of the reproductively dimorphic nature of our species. However, those who have had classification and what nature provides have reached a somewhat different conclusion. In John Money's (1980: 134) words,

> nature herself is less absolute in creating sexual dimorphism than we human beings are in thinking about it...nature's relativism regarding sex

differences is...apparent. The long social tradition to which we are heirs, by contrast, maximizes sex differences.

Thanks to recent advances in medical technology, we now even surgically and pharmacologically alter what nature provides so as to protect the integrity of our system of gender classification from the relativism of nature (Money and Ehrhardt, 1972). In our contemporary society, hermaphrodites do not stay that way for long.

Like students of human's biological nature, students of social life are also heirs to the long social tradition that maximizes gender differences. We routinely construct an independent variable for our analyses by sorting persons into gender categories thereby emphasizing gender differences. Lurking behind this popular research strategy is the implicit assumption that such a sorting of persons is sociologically if not biologically sound. Yet, what this strategy does is to perpetuate in practice what at least some of us should be studying: The social construction of two and only two gender categories. After all, there is more than ample evidence that other systems of gender classification are culturally possible. For example, in traditional Navajo society, hermaphrodites constituted a third gender category called "nadle," and like many other peoples, the traditional Cheyenne had a third gender category for more feminine males (see Kessler and McKenna, 1978: 21–41; Martin and Voorhis, 1975: 84–107).

Even the popular usage among students of social life of the terms "sex" and "gender" obscures the extent to which gender classification is socially constructed. "Sex" is used to refer to what is considered purely physical, and "gender" to refer to what are considered cultural and social elaborations on that presumed biological base, as if the two could be so clearly distinguished. This conceptual distinction ignores the inextricable interrelationship between the biological and the cultural in human affairs. When studying gender, we cannot simply ignore biology but neither should we underestimate the degree to which biology and our understanding of it is culturally conditioned. The conceptual distinction that we draw between the biological and cultural with our usage of the terms "sex" and "gender" encourages us to do both.

Kessler and McKenna (1978: 18) have observed that "a defining feature of reality construction is to see our world as being the only possible one" and that is clearly the case with our world of gendered persons. If not biology, then some mythical past is pointed to as evidence that our world of two and only two gender classes is the only possible world. Yet, the most either biology or history provides is a blueprint that we follow in socially constructing our reality. The social classification of persons in terms of reproductive anatomy is clearly "at the base of a fundamental code in accordance with which social interactions" and institutions are built up (Goffman, 1977: 301), but we do the building, albeit often unintentionally. As Gerson and Peiss (1985: 317) have pointed out, "Gender is not a rigid or reified analytic category imposed on human experience, but a fluid one whose meaning emerges in specific contexts as it is created and recreated through human actions." Rather than simply treating the seemingly natural order of gendered persons as a given, we must investigate the ways in which it is actively created, recreated, and rendered legitimate on actual occasions of interaction. Here too children may lead us.

GENDER BOUNDARIES

Children help remind us that whatever else gender may be it is an interactional resource that can be employed in a number of ways for a variety of practical purposes. For example, in the course of her ethnographic study of a preschool, Carol Joffe (1971: 472) observed that the children who attended the school often invoked gender in an attempt to control one another's behavior, as in the following:

> S. (female) is playing the guitar. K. (male) comes over and asks her to let him play it. When she refuses, K. says, "that's for boys, not girls." (Joffe, 1971: 472)

Although young children commonly invoke gender to accomplish some immediate practical goal such as laying claim to some object like a guitar, they thereby also set up a kind of opposition between boys and girls. Objects, territories, and activities are defined as either "for boys" or "for girls" and not for both.

However, these definitions seldom go unchallenged, as the following illustrates:

> C. and two other girls are playing on the top of a large structure in the yard. A. (a male) comes over and C. screams, "girls only!" to which A. screams back, "no, boys only!" (Joffe, 1971:472)

When faced with such a challenge, children often point to precedents such as the example of older peers, adults, or mythical figures like television and movie characters in support of their definitions. Other children may question the credibility of the reported precedent, but they seldom question the authority of such examples. Although children do not systematically articulate the presumed prerogatives of boys and girls, they do evolve common understandings of what is "for boys" and what is "for girls" through such situated negotiations of claims to territories, objects, and other resources. To the extent of what is "for boys" and what is "for girls," they fill the vessel of gender classification with behavioral content in accordance with blueprints found in the surrounding social environment.

Developmental or socialization studies of gender boundaries among children commonly stress the extent and biographical consequences of gender segregation among school-age children. This "separate worlds" analysis is by now a familiar refrain. Girls tend to form small, egalitarian friendship groups and to engage in cooperative activities while boys tend to form larger, hierarchically structured friendship groups and to engage in more competitive activities (e.g. Lever, 1976). As a result, girls and boys acquire different interpersonal skills (Lever, 1976), develop different expressive customs (Maltz and Borker, 1983), and evolve distinctive subcultures. Adult arrangements (Lever, 1976) and interactions (Maltz and Borker, 1983) are then explained in terms of the different social experiences of boys and girls. There is undoubtedly something to this familiar refrain, but it also tends to obscure the ways in which both children and adults actively maintain gender segregation boundaries. These are not permanent structures. They are actively created and recreated in specific contexts.

Gender segregation and the maintenance of gender boundaries are obviously interrelated. The definition of territories, objects, and activities as "for boys" or "for girls" clearly promotes gender segregation. Gender segregation, in turn, narrows the audiences to which boys and girls play. These audiences tend to be homogenous in regard to gender and to employ different standards in evaluating their members' behavioral performances. For example, boys tend to be impressed by the conception and execution of aggressive pranks, by "dirty talk," especially that having to do with sexual matters, and by knowledge of and successful participation in organized sports (Fine, 1986, 1987; Thorne and Luria, 1986: 180-181). On the other hand, girls tend to be more impressed by conformance to prevailing standards of appearance management, displays of concern for others, and personal popularity (Eder and Sanford, 1986; Thorne and Luria, 1986: 183-184). Given these very different critical standards, children cannot consistently earn the applause of both boys and girls. They must play to one or the other of these audiences. Yet, in doing so, they recreate the very gender boundaries that serve to maintain gender segregation.

This does not mean that the gender boundaries which children create are impenetrable. Most children occasionally cross these behavioral boundaries, and some do so routinely. For example, boys sometimes allow certain girls to engage in activities that are considered their special preserve as long as such girls do so seriously and competently. Although boys are less likely to and girls less likely to allow boys to participate in activities considered girls' special preserve, boys sometimes do so as a kind of "buffoon" or "tease" (Lever, 1976: 481; Thorne, 1985: 179). As these boys are apparently aware, boys who venture across gender boundaries too far or too often are commonly targets of aggressive pranks and accusations of being a "fag" or "queer" (Fine, 1986). Although girls who do so apparently suffer a somewhat less cruel fate, they seldom escape at least some teasing (Eder and Sanford, 1986). The gender boundaries which children construct may not be permanent or impenetrable barriers, but they are vigilantly policed.

However, the degree of gender segregation among children and perhaps among adults as well, can easily be overdrawn. To borrow from Goffman (1976: 316), "one does not so much deal with segregation as with segregative punctuation of the days' rounds." Like contact between men and women, contact between boys and girls has a "with-then-apart" rhythm and the "with" is as important to the maintenance of gender boundaries as the "apart." It is when boys and girls are together that they can assert and display their presumed difference by way of contrast and thereby reaffirm and reestablish gender boundaries.

Although contact between boys and girls takes various forms, one of the most common is what Thorne (1985) describes as "borderwork." Examples include such familiar childhood games as "boys catch the girls," "chase and kiss," and "cooties." When playing these games, gender rather than individual identities become central as such often heard remarks as "help, a girl's chasin me" or "let's get that boy" reveal (Thorne, 1985: 1974). Children thereby formulate their interaction in terms of gender. By definition, boys and girls become separate and often competing teams. In this respect, these games are prototypical of the form which much interaction between not only boys and girls but also men and women often takes. Rather than undermining gender boundaries, their interactions are formulated in ways that emphasize and reaffirm these boundaries.

As Gerson and Peiss (1985: 320) suggest, this is even or perhaps especially the case with heterosexual courting. The courting couple commonly performs a duet acting out gender boundaries by reciprocating one another's expressions of gender. She buries her head in his chest to hide from the grisly scene on the screen, and he bravely protects her with an encompassing embrace. Moreover, among school-age children at least, some gender teams play an important part in staging, directing, and supporting those shows. As Thorne and Luria (1986: 186) observe,

> Messengers and emissaries go between groups indicating who likes whom and checking out romantic interest. By the time "couples" actually get together...the groups and their messengers have provided...a kind of agenda for the pair.

However, what Thorne and Luria do not mention is that each member of the pair is provided with a different agenda. Children's guiding imagery of heterosexual courting is discussed and formed primarily within same gender groups, and boys and girls are seldom guided by the same imagery (Eder and Stanford, 1986: 292; Fine, 1981: 268). For the most part, girls are guided by romantic imagery while boys are guided by a more sexually aggressive imagery (Thorne and Luria, 1986: 184). The two members of a courting couple continue to play to different audiences, to represent different teams and to engage in a kind of competitive borderwork within the context of their relationship.

In this respect at least, many individuals seem to remain boys and girls for much longer than they might want to admit. For example, Schwartz and Lever (1976: 423) observe in their study of college mixers that

> People at a mixer, or in a mixer like situation, describe members of the opposite sex as the "enemy." They act as though their chosen roles are conflicting, not complementary.

Similarly, many long-term heterosexual relationships seem to be extended exercises in this kind of competitive borderwork. Despite their alliance, the participants continue to treat one another as members of separate, if not opposing teams, as such often heard remarks as "that's just like a man" or "you know how women are" suggest.

Moreover, like children, adults are not beyond invoking anger in an attempt to control others' behavior including the behavior of their heterosexual mate, as Scott and Lyman's (1968: 58) widely read example of "identity switching" illustrates.

> A working-class Mexican husband comes home from an evening of philandering. His wife suspects this and says, "Where were you?" He responds with, "None of your business, you're a wife"... She replies with

"What kind of father are you?"...To this he replies "I'm a man — you're a woman."

As Joffe (1971: 472) remarks about preschool-age children, this example suggests that adults can also call upon gender in "a seeming last-ditch effort to impose" their will "when the other means of behavior control typically in use have not been effective." Regardless of whether or not those attempts are successful, they serve to affirm the relevance of gender to everyday social life.

Heterosexual courting and relationships are clearly not the only contexts in which men and women engage in a kind of competitive borderwork. For example, in her ethnographic study of the corporation she called "Indesco," Rosabeth Moss Kanter (1977: 222) observes that male executives tended to "exaggerate...their commonality" when in the presence of female executives. As with school-age children's borderwork, gender rather than individual identities became central as when a male executive asked a female executive how women would react to a new product. Moreover, like girls who participate in activities that boys consider their special preserve, many of the female executives attempted to prove that they belonged by defining themselves as different from other women (Kanter, 1977: 230). They thereby reaffirmed gender boundaries while at the same time attempting to claim a personal exemption. Although Kanter (1977: 206-242) attributes such "boundary heightening" to the proportional rarity of female executives at the corporation she studied, that explanation seems to underestimate the prevalence of borderwork among men and women. As Gerson and Peiss (1985: 320) suggest, when institutionalized gender boundaries become less rigid, as they seem to be doing in our contemporary society, so-called "micro level boundaries assume increased significance" as seems to have been the case at "Indesco." The heightening of gender boundaries at "Indesco" may have been particularly noticeable because of the proportional rarity of female executives, but it is doubtful that such borderwork is limited to settings in which either men or women are a proportional rarity.

Regardless of the various factors that may encourage the interactional heightening of gender boundaries, it is a common feature of children's everyday social lives and, it would seem, of adults' as well. Moreover, like boys and girls, it seems that men and women not only formulate their interactions with one another in terms of gender and engage in various forms of competitive borderwork, they also seek refuge from one another in same gender groups. We commonly sort ourselves into different collegial and friendship groups, engage in different leisure parties, and attend different kinds of events like bridal showers and bachelor parties. We thereby recreate separate male and female subcultures and reinforce gender boundaries. In Goffman's (1977: 316) words,

> It is as if the joining of the sexes were tolerable providing a periodic escape is possible; it is as if equality and sameness were a masquerade that has to be periodically dropped.

In addition, like children, we then point to the gender differences that we have created as evidence of men's and women's distinctively different human natures. Regardless of whether we attribute those distinctive human natures to biology or the unrelenting pressures of the social environment, we hide the ways in which we actively create, recreate, and render gender boundaries legitimate by doing so.

CONCLUSION

In drawing these parallels between children and adults, I do not mean to imply that adults' social lives can be analyzed in the same terms as children's or that the study of children's social practices is a substitute for direct investigation of adults' accomplishment of gender. Nor do I mean to imply that the girl and boy are mother and father to the woman and man. What I am suggesting is that studies of children can serve as aids to our sluggish imagination. If we treat children as serious social actors rather than simply adults-in-the-making, their social practices and arrangements can provide a kind of cross-cultural comparison that may bring into view aspects of adults' social practices and arrangements that we might otherwise fail to notice.

Perhaps I am overromanticizing, but my own observation of children has convinced me that they are more acutely aware of the socially constructed character of reality and their own reality constructing powers than we adults. When it comes to issues of gender, adults, including students of social life, need to be reminded of that most fundamental sociological lesson. We may convince ourselves that nature or some invisible force imposes gender upon us, but children know better. They can remind us of the many little ways in which we create and recreate gender boundaries subverting our best laid plans to lower them. If we listen close enough the next time we start to excuse ourselves or condemn someone else by referring to how women or men *are*, we might hear the childish echo in our own voice.

REFERENCES

Ambert, Anne-Marie. 1986. "Sociology of Sociology: The Place of Children in North American Sociology." Pp. 11–31 in *Sociological Studies of Child Development* Volume 1, edited by Patricia Adler and Peter Adler. Greenwich, CT: JAI Press.

Burke, Kenneth [1962]. 1966. "What Are the Signs of What? A Theory of Entitlement." Pp. 359–379 in *Language as a Symbolic Action*. Berkeley: University of California Press.

Cahill, Spencer. 1986. "Language Practices and Self-Definition: The Case of Gender Identity Acquisition." *The Sociological Quarterly* 27:295–311.

———. 1989. "Fashioning Males and Females: Appearance Management and the Social Reproduction of Gender." *Symbolic Interaction* 12:281–298.

Eder, Donna, and Stephanie Sanford. 1986. "The Development and Maintenance of Interactional Norms Among Early Adolescents." Pp. 283–300 in *Sociological Studies of Child Development*, Volume 1, edited by Patricia Adler and Peter Adler. Greenwich, CT: JAI Press.

Fine, Gary Allen. 1986. "The Dirty Play of Little Boys." *Society* (Nov–Dec): 63–67.

———. 1987. *With the Boys*. Chicago: University of Chicago Press.

Freud, Sigmund [1925]. 1959. "Some Psychological Consequences of the Anatomical Distinction between the Sexes." Pp. 186–197 in *Collected Papers*, Volume 5. New York: Basic Books.

Garfinkel, Harold. 1967. *Studies in Ethnomethodology*. Englewood Cliffs, NJ: Prentice-Hall.

Gerson, Judith and Kathy Peiss. 1985. "Boundaries, Negotiation, Consciousness: Reconceptualizing Gender Relations." *Social Problems* 32:315–331.
Goffman, Erving. 1977. "The Arrangement between the Sexes." *Theory and Society*. 4:301–331.
Green, Richard. 1974. *Sexual Identity Conflict in Children and Adults*. New York: Basic Books.
Joffe, Carol. 1971. "Sex Role Socialization and the Nursery School: As the Twig is Bent." *Journal of Marriage and the Family* 33:467–475.
Kanter, Rosabeth Moss. 1977. *Men and Women of the Corporation*. New York: Basic Books.
Kessler, Suzanne and Wendy McKenna [1978]. 1985. *Gender: An Ethnomethodological Approach*. Chicago: University of Chicago Press.
Lever, Janet. 1976. "Sex Differences in the Games Children Play." *Social Problems* 23: 478–487.
Maltz, D.N. and R.A. Broker. 1983. "A Cultural Approach to Male-Female Miscommunication." Pp. 195–216 in *Language and Social Identity*, edited by J.J. Gumprez. New York: Cambridge University Press.
Martin, M. Kay and Barbara Voorhies. 1975. *Female of the Species*. New York: Columbia University Press.
Mead, George Herbert [1910]. 1981. "What Social Objects Must Psychology Presuppose." Pp. 105–113 in *Selected Writings*, edited by Andrew J. Reck. Chicago: University of Chicago Press.
Money, John. 1980. *Love and Love Sickness*. Baltimore: John Hopkins University Press.
Money, John and Anke Ehrhardt. 1972. *Man and Woman/Boy and Girl*. Baltimore: John Hopkins University Press.
Schwartz, Pepper and Janet Lever. 1976. "Fear and Loathing at a College Mixer." *Urban Life* 4:413–430.
Scott, Marvin and Stanford Lyman. 1986. "Accounts." *American Sociological Review* 33:46–62.
Thompson, Spencer and P.M. Bentler. 1971. "The Priority of Cues in Sex Discrimination by Children and Adults." *Developmental Psychology* 5: 181–185.
Thorne, Barrie. 1985. "Girls and Boys Together...But Mostly Apart: Gender Arrangements in Elementary Schools." Pp. 167–184 in *Relationships and Development*, edited by Willard Hartup and Zick Rubin. Hillsdale, NJ: Lawrence Erlbaum Associates.
———. 1987. "Re-Visioning Women and Social Change: Where Are the Children?" *Gender and Society* 1:85–109.
Thorne, Barrie and Zella Luria. 1986. "Sexuality and Gender in Children's Daily Worlds." *Social Problems* 33: 176–190.
West, Candace and Don Zimmerman. 1987. "Doing Gender." *Gender and Society* 1:125–151.

Chapter 37 FORMS OF DISCOURSE

R.S. Perinbanayagam

Discursive acts typically are constituted in such a way that certain formal structures that influence and inform the nature of the interaction that emerges can be seen in them. A discursive act by itself offers the possibility of varied responses and interpretations from an external world, which creates for the self the opportunities to enmesh its life with that of others. In the web of discourse in which humans live, every moment is constituted by the use of one form of discourse or other. These forms may be nebulous and defy classification. However, it is possible to delineate some of the forms by which this web is constructed and to specify the consequences for self and interaction. These forms of discourse-analogous to Bakhtin's (1986) *speech genres* and Lyotard's *modes of discourse* (1988)—have elicited discussing in their guise as speech acts. Lyotard himself, discussing what he terms the "pragmatic aspect" of language use, following J.L. Austin describes utterance as being either *"performatives"* or *"prescriptions."* The former are described as acts in which the effects of the utterance "coincide with its enunciation" (1988:9), and the latter, "modulated as orders, commands, instructions, recommendations, requests, prayers, pleas, etc.," as acts in which "the sender is clearly in a position of authority, using the term broadly: that is, he expects the addressee to perform the action referred to"(1988:10). Lyotard adds certain refinements to Austin's positions and Wittgenstein's thesis about "modes of discourse being language games— that is actions defined by specific rules of practice and usage." First, the rules that define a language game "do not carry within themselves their own legitimation, but are the object of a contract, explicit or not between players." Second, notes Lyotard, "even an infinitesimal modification of one rule alters the nature of the game." Finally she argues that every utterance should be thought of as a "move" in a "game" (1988:10).

There is however a major problem; neither Austin's nor Wittgenstein's view on the uses of language has a place for the character and quality of the performer-user. Lyotard goes very far from the *depersonalized* theories of Austin and Wittgenstein but not far enough. He writes, "A *self* does not amount to much, but no self is an island; each exists in a fabric of relation that is more complex and mobile than ever before. Young or old, man or women, rich or poor, a person is always located at 'nodal points' of specific communication circuits, however tiny these may be" (Lyotard, 1988:15). The self may or may not amount to much, but a reflexive self is all a human actor is, and a self is that which exists at the nodal points of communication and that which receives the communication. Discursive forms are used by such selves to elicit certain responses from other selves and do not exist as depersonalized and *suigeneris* phenomena.

By acting discursively, a person enters a life with others, opening himself or herself up to all manners and possibilities or responsive acts. The act projected can be rebuffed, rejected forcefully, or ignored; or it can be accepted forcefully, subtly, ambiguously, politely, encouragingly, or tentatively, thus providing sustenance to the self of the articulator and the interaction.

To some extent the nature of the responses can be predetermined by the nature of the discursive act that is proffered. And, or course, there can be no meaningful response before a signifying act is offered in one or another form. In everyday life a person articulates and encounters a number of such acts, each having particular social and structural features. To the extent that the dialogic self exists, it exists in and through very specific discursive processes used in their constitution. The particularities of these acts, and the types they represent, become the instruments by which the emotional and intellectual features of the self and its essential integrated quality are created and sustained.

One can attempt at most a partial classification and description of such acts, based on the functions they perform in interactions and social relationships and in the manifestation and maintenance of selves. My focus will be on the interactional function of the discourse as it seeks and elicits its effects by manifesting specific structural characteristics. While some forms may resemble others, such a resemblance is overridden by a different function in the interaction and in the maintenances of the self. The descriptions of the carious forms of discourse and their likely function in interactions and constitution of self offered here are brief, and a chapter could be written on each of the forms.

Demands and Requests

Interactants often have to ask for certain specific responses. These askings contain a definition of the self relevant to the particular context and to the nature of the relationship that is envisaged with the other. Forceful imperative askings may be called *demands*; prayers, importunings and invitations may be called *requests*. When a person makes a demand, he or she defines his or her self and that of the other, and also establishes the parameters of the ensuing relationship and dialogue. A demander indicates an unequal power distribution in the relationship, and forestalls the emergence of a friendly and affable interaction by creating a relationship of an adversarial nature. To the degree that he or she has the socially defined right to make this demand, he or she has also asserted his or her self, and to the extent that the demand is complied with, the self is validated. However, if he or she overlooks the right to make the demand and instead makes a request, a more complex and subtly varied relationship is created with the other. Even in this case, the self of the articulator is validated by the emergence of a commensurate response, but at the same time the self of the recipient gets protection and is perhaps even enriched by the acts. Nonetheless, that the articulator is the self who selects the nature of the act , by demand or by request, endows him or her with an extra measure of power and authority, which confers a special complexity on the relationship. The recipient can feel grateful for not having been subjected to authoritarian humiliation but nevertheless acknowledge that the power to either enhance or diminish his or her self rests with the other.

Consider this in the following extract as President Nixon (B) and is legal advisor John Dean (A) are conversing. A secretary intervenes:

A: Good morning, Sir.

B: Oh, hi.

A: How are you?

B: I wanted to talk with you about what kind of a line to take. I now want Kleindienst on the—it isn't a matter of trust. You have it clearly understood that you will call him and give him directions and he will call you, etcetera, and so on, and so on. I just don't want Dick to go off—you see, for example, on executive privilege-I don't want him to get off and get the damn thing-get us—

A: Make any deals on it-

B: Make a deal-that is the point. Baker, as I said, is going to keep at arms length and you have got to be very firm with these guys or you may not end up with many things...

A: Yeah.

B: (To secretary) I sent some notes out-a couple of yellow pages-something on the teachers' thing that I am not doing today-just send it back to me, please.

Secretary: Alright, Sir.

B: So you see, I think you better have a good,hard face to face talk with him and say, look we have thought this thing over. And you raise the point with him that this cannot be in executive session because he is likely to float it out there and they will grab it.

A: That's right, and as I mentioned yesterday he is meeting with Sam Ervin and Baker in this joint session and that is probably one of the first things they will discuss.

(Woodward and Bernstein, 1974: 43-44)

In this conversational interaction, the president of the United States is asking his assistant to undertake certain acts. In the course of asking, he is apparently interrupted by his secretary to whom he then gives an order. This order is couched in structures of politeness and decorum: "just send it back to me, please." This elicits a response from the secretary that includes a titular salutation, "Alright, Sir." Similarly, his orders to Dean are crouched in the language of requests: "have a hard face to face talk" with someone, "raise the point with him," etc. irrespective of the intonations used, the formulation of the intentions does not bare anything else but politeness and consideration for the self of the other. In this interaction, the president is, in terms of status and power, clearly superior to both this secretary and his legal assistant. Nevertheless, he handles the relationship with a presumptive equality that protects the selves of the subordinates. Indeed it can be said that the superordinate has been providing his subordinates signs with which their selves can be constituted or refurbished. This equalitarian mode performed here routinely and matter-of-factly is prescribed by American culture, so that only when these routines are violated does the significance of these signs for the selves become apparent, as in the cases of rejection, hostility, worthlessness, incompetence, and unlovedness.

These askings may be couched as demands in other relationships. In the following excerpt, made famous in sociology by Erving Goffman (1961a:17), Brendan Behan (C) is subject to a number of demands form his prospective warden Whitbread (A) and his assistant Holmes (B) at an institute for the juvenile offender:

A: And 'old up your 'ead, when I speak to you.
B: 'old up your 'ead, when Mr. Whitbread speaks to you.
A: What are you looking at, Behan? Look at me.
C: I am looking at you.
B: You are looking at Mr. Whitbread-what?
C: I am looking at Mr. Whitbread.

Mr. Holmes looked gravely at Mr. Whitbread, drew back his open hand and struck me on the face, held me with his hand and struck me again...

B: You are looking at Mr. Whitbread,—what Behan?

I gulped and got together my voice and tried again till got it out, "I sir, please sir, I am looking at you, I mean I am looking at Mr. Whitbread sir."

(Behan, 1958:40)

The structures of demand in this conversation are varied. The initial statement is without prefixes and suffixes—no names, terms of address, or titles, but a short staccato set of words asking for a particular action. The structure of the sentence and the sense are well matched here: the sense is a demand to look at the face of the other, to face the words he is about to utter, and an interference with the freedom of the person to choose how he wished to hold his head. The same values are carried forward in the next series of words and actions. Short imperative sentences are matched by slaps on Behan's face and together these constitute a structure of demands that will make Behan submissive and contrite which will lead him to provide the mandatory deferential salutation at the end of every sentence. These words and moves by Whitbread and Holmes are calculated affirmations of their respective selves and of the collective identity of their professional selves that thus become the signs of their self-constitution subject to interpretant responses culminating into a maxisign. The same can be said for Behan, although in his case the demands are for an alteration in his conduct. The demands make him a captive, and his consequent submissiveness and docility become signs he must interpretively absorb into his self. The manner, style, and particular contents of the demands reinforce these signs and begin a turn in the career of the self that, depending on what happens in the thereafter, may or may not breed a number of consequences. In fact, the upshot of these demands and the consequential humiliation of the self might well be the emergence of bitter and resentful habits of the self, making it a habitual "malcontent" and "criminal."

Instructions

The instructor as a discursive actor typically has both rhetorical and political power as well as the knowledge the other wants or needs. By definition the instructor has an awesome status because he or she can fill the mind of the other and shape his or her self.

The inequality of the discursive structure contributes signs to the selves that are interacting. Consider this excerpt from a conservation between a teacher (A) and her pupil (B):

A: well, suppose I let you tell them what has happened recently that I dislike.
B: I been talking out of class at school and acting up.

A: And did I teach you how to do that?
B: No mam.
A: What did I teach you to do?
B: To sit on my seat.
A: And?
B: And don't say a word until the teacher tell me.
A: And you failed to do that.
B: Yes mam.
A: Well don't you think it would be a good idea for us to sit down and talk this over with Marge and maybe she'll give us some of the ideas about this some other time as to whether you should be doing these things or not.
B: Yes, mam.

(Loman, 1967:57)

This conversation is instructional in its own terms and in its reference to instructions given earlier. But the sheer volume of words and the length of the sentences the superordinate produces carries their own discursive weight which constrain the recipient to short, and at times, disyllabic answer. The content of the discourse defines one participant as possessing knowledge about proper deportment of self on a particular situation and the other as a transgressor. The entire passage has a stance: one can imagine the teacher, tall and imposing, standing over the pupil engaging in her discursive act. The final summary reinforces her authority and power and incorporated a third party as an ally in her act.

This exchange has many facets. The teacher's self is embellished by acts of obstruction and enlightenment-signs that enhance her self. She brings her pupil to submission and recitation of proper class deportment and allows the entire performance to be witnessed by an outsider, who further validated the teacher's self. Of course the pupil's dependent, subordinate, recipient status is reinforced by the structure of the interactions as well as the discourse: the signs that the child gathers defines him as a miscreant and subordinate who must, in the future, incorporate some further signs into his self if he is to receive approbation and validation from the teacher and Marge.

The dialogue is an extreme example of this kind of discursive act. Often the signs generated in such interactions are more subtly wrapped in fabrics of politeness and courtesy, or irony and sarcasm. But these too provide effective signs of the self.

Compliments

Compliments are signs of evaluation, a judgement about an aspect of another's self, about that self performance in a given context, and its comparative standing with other moments or with relevant others. Overt, direct, obvious, and pointed compliments, for example, "That's a beautiful dress you are wearing" or "This is a very fine research paper," are acts that build the self in obvious and clear ways. Of course, the respondent's own evaluation of the articulator is crucial. If the articulator is one who pays compliments too freely and loosely, their value will be low as compared to compliments offered by one given to considered and "measured" comments. Status and power also play a part in a self's evaluation of a complimentary sign. For example, praise form a respected professor about a research paper would have more weight for the self that the praise offered by another student. The emotional power inherent in complimentary discursive acts connected with love and loving is twofold. (1) The content of the discourse reveals the conceptual form of the articulator's ideas of the recipient. For example, a favorable comment about a dress can imply good taste, good investment and a good figure or perhaps even overall approval of the other's erotic and esthetic presence. (2) Such signs define the significance of the whole discursive encounter. Clearly, complimentary signs contribute to the constitution of the self of the recipient and can accumulate into patterned aspects of the maxisign of the self. However, there is always a danger of inflation: too many compliments uncritically and too easily issued, or rendered without warrant and justification, make them valueless. Flattery is a systematic set of compliments about another, but to be effective they must be seen to be sincere, and not cross the razor's edge over into the manipulative.

An articulator paying a compliment often feels a duty to set the limits of the value to be placed on it. Free-floating compliments leave their valuative bases vague and unspecific, a practice not always politic or wise. For instance: "You write well-for a foreigner." The first part is an unabashed compliment, and if said by a professor to a student in whose life writing well matters, it becomes a positive contribution to the self. However, the tail of the remark, like that of a scorpion, packs a sting: you are a good writer only by particular standards. The context within which a compliment is given can transform it into an ambiguous force.

However, in intimate relationships as well as in merely friendly ones, a compliment can put the self of the articulator on the line. For example, a compliment may be ignored; the recipient simply chooses to *unhear* it:

A: You are indeed looking lovely tonight.

B: Aren't you going to dance with Eunice?

This is gentle rebuff that has given the self of the articulator another shape at least for now, vis-a-vis his relationship with this person. There are, of course, stronger rebuffs:

A: You are looking very lovely tonight.

B: What? You shouldn't be saying things like that to me Harry. It makes me wonder what you are up to.

In sum, by means of compliments a self is proffered and the responses of the other help define the moment and their relationship, and so pass on to the next stage.

Insults

If we can praise others we can also devalue them. Insults are discursive acts that undermine and refute the self of the other. They are issued with appropriate tonal, linguistic, and symbolic characteristics, and are constituted by signs directed at both the other and the articulator's self. An insult must be understood by the other to be effective, and so it must be related to the self of the other to find its mark. An insult, then challenges the maxisign of the self, seeking to undermine or tarnish it. For example, to call a man a women is an insult because he has carefully constructed an integrated and coherent text of "manhood" as his self. Such a self has a cognitive form and a cognitive structure limned with culturally induced anxieties and tensions. However, calling a transvestite a women might be considered a compliment.

Insults may be distinguished by their degree of power. Those that "cut to the quick" elicit strong reactions, while those that are mild can occasion repartee rather than anger. The power of an insult depends on the capacity of the signs deployed to undermine that aspect of the other's self considered to be dominate or important. Further, insults to superiors as opposed to insults from superiors have different signifying values. In medieval Italy, a canon who insulted another was fined twenty lire, but it he insulted a chaplin the fine was only five. Peter Burke in his study of the anthropology of early modern Italy writes, "Generally speaking, insults by inferiors to superiors were taken very seriously. In fourteenth century Venice 'verbal violence' against the doge or lesser officials of the commune was severely punished (sometimes by cutting off the offender's tongue)" (1987:99). In these cases, punishment for violating the social status of a self is provided for by the city state's legal code.

BIBLIOGRAPHY

Bakhtin, M.M. 1986. *Speech Genres and Other Later Essays*. Austin: University of Texas Press.
Behan, Brendan. 1958. *Borstal Boy*. London: Hutchinson.
Loman, Bengt. 1967. *Conversations in A Negro American Dialect*. Washington, D.C.: Center for Applied Linguistics.
Lyotard, Jean-Francoise. 1988. *The Postmodern Condition*. Minneapolis: University of Minnesota Press.

Chapter 38 THE COLLECTIVE STORY: POSTMODERNISM AND THE WRITING OF SOCIOLOGY

Laurel Richardson

At the 1987 American Sociological Association Meetings in Chicago, colleagues asked me the conventional convention question—our functional equivalent to "How are you?"—namely, "What are you working on?" Instead of responding ("Fine") by enumerating my projects in progress, I heard myself saying, "I don't know what I want to write about, how I want to write it, or who I want to write it for." The heresy just popped out. Nevertheless, my answer did not reflect only a temporary lapse of sensibility, a moment of unorthodoxy that would soon pass. Rather, these concerns with the writing of sociology are issues I have struggled with throughout my professional career. I embrace them now as priorities for myself and for the future of sociology: What do we write about? How do we write it? And for whom do we write?

My speech this afternoon will reflect my penchant for mingling the personal, the political, and the intellectual. I will first talk about "what to write about" and "how to write it" as postmodernist problems. I will defer the question of "for whom do we write" until the latter part of my speech, where I reflect upon my own writing decisions and processes.

POSTMODERNISM AND THE CRISIS OF REPRESENTATION

We ply our sociological craft within—not above—broader historical, social, and intellectual contexts. Today, the dominant intellectual context challenges all "grand theory" and all claims for a singular, correct style for organizing and presenting knowledge. Lacking a totalizing vision, the contemporary intellectual context lacks a name of its own. The period is defined not by what it is but by what it comes after. It is variously called *postparadigmatic*—postmodernism, post-Marxism, poststructuralism, postpositivism—some even say, post-feminism. Characteristic of this period is the loss of authority of "a general paradigmatic style of organizing research" (Marcus and Fisher, 1986:8). Ideas and methods are freely borrowed from one discipline to another, leading to a "blurring of genres" (Geertz, 1980). A totalizing vision is replaced by concerns with contextuality, exceptions, indeterminants, and the meanings to participants. Even the totalizing vision that feminism created is now being reassessed by feminists as we critique that vision as being, itself, contextually created, a product primarily of privileged women in a social movement which has glossed over meaningful differences in the experiences of differently situated women.

The loss of grand theory has affected all disciplines, although their responses have differed. In literary criticism, literature is aesthetically equivalenced. All texts can be "deconstructed" so that Dickens and Tolstoi, for example, are no better writers than their deconstructors. In law, The Critical Legal Studies movement abrogates the legal reasoning model (Livingston, 1982). In philosophy, the principles of uncertainty and contextuality undermine the possibility of universal systems of thought (Rorty, 1979). In physics and mathematics, the focus is on the inelegant, the disorderly, indeed even, "chaos" (Gleick, 1984). In sociology and the other social sciences, the critiques of grand theories have dislodged their hegemony; sociological production, like other human productions, is seen as socially produced (cf. Fiske and Shweder, 1986).

When there is no dominant paradigm, indeed, when the very grounds upon which paradigms can be considered valid are themselves subject to contextualization and indeterminacy, scholars face what Marcus and Fisher (1968:8) refer to as a "crisis in representation": uncertainty about what constitutes adequate depiction of social reality. When scholarly conventions are themselves contested, politics and poetics become inseparable and neither science nor art stands above the historical and linguistic processes (Clifford, 1986:2). As a result, the growing edges of the intellectual-sociological enterprise have shifted. Attention is focused on epistemology (cf. Cook and Fonow, 1986; Fonow and Cook, Forthcoming; Fiske and Shweder, 1986), interpretive understanding (Diamond, Forthcoming; DiIorio, Forthcoming; Mishler, 1986), and the discursive forms of representation themselves (cf. Becker, 1986b; Long, 1987; Krieger, 1983; Stewart, Forthcoming; Clifford and Marcus, 1986; Strathern, 1987). Our commonsene understanding of method is extended to include epistemological assumptions, on the one hand, and the writing process on the other.

How in the midst of this ferment and uncertainty do we prevent a paralysis of intellect and the will to work? Why do any intellectual work at all? But, conversely, "why not?" We can be caught in the infinite regress of deconstructionism, where nothing is better than anything else, but we can also be drawn to infinite expansion. When there is a crisis of representation we are freed from the intellectual myopia of hyper-determined research projects and their formulaic write-ups, what Kuhn has termed "normal science." We can turn uncertainty to our advantage; we can be more sociologically imaginative in our thinking, apprehending, and writing of the social world. We can, as C. Wright Mills (1959:195) proposed, resist the "codification of procedures" stratagem for developing theory and methods and get on with the "exchange of information about...actual ways of working."

SCIENCE AND LITERATURE

At this historical point, I have chosen to think about my sociological work as telling what I term *"the collective story."* A collective story tells the experience of a sociologically constructed category of people in the context of larger sociocultural and historical forces. The sociological protagonist is a collective. I think of similarly situated individuals who may or may not be aware of their life affinities as co-participants in a collective story. My intent is to help construct a consciousness of kind in the minds of the protagonists, a concrete recognition of sociological bondedness with others, because such consciousness can break down isolation between people, empower them, and lead to collective action on their behalf.

People make sense of their lives, for the most part, in terms of specific events, such as the birth of a child, and sequences of events, such as the life-long impact of parenting a damaged child. Most people do not articulate how sociological categories such as race, gender, class, and ethnicity have shaped their lives or how the larger historical processes such as the Depression or the Women's Movement have affected them. Erik Erikson (1975) contends that only great people, people who see themselves as actors on the historical stage, tell their life stories in a larger social and historical context. Yet, as C. Wright Mills (1959:5) cogently argued, knowledge of the social context leads people to understand their own experiences and to "gauge...[their] own fates"; this is the promise of the "sociological imagination." What sociologists are capable of doing is to give voice to silenced people, to present them as historical actors by telling their collective story.

The notion of sociological writing as allegorical goes contrary to received wisdom about the separation of the literary from the scientific. From the 17th century onward, Western Science has rejected "rhetoric in the name of 'plain' transparent signification, fiction in the name of fact, and subjectivity in the name of objectivity" (Clifford, 1986:5). Rhetoric, fiction, and subjectivity were located in "literature," a new historical construction, aesthetically pleasing but scientifically ridiculed. Literature was denied truth value because it "invented" reality rather than observing it. Dependent on the evocative devices of metaphor and imagery, literature could be interpreted in different ways by different readers. Worse, "the narrating is always multi-vocal—it says one thing to illuminate something else" (De Certeau, 1983:128). Literature violates a major pretension of science: the single, unambiguous voice.

Science was to be written in "plain style," in words that did not, in John Locke's estimation, "move the Passions and thereby mislead the Judgment," unambiguous words unlike the "perfect cheats" of poetic utterances quoted in (Levine, 1985:3). The assault on poetic language intensified throughout the 18th Century. Locke urged parents to stifle any poetic tendencies in their children. Hume depicted poets as professional liars. Bentham proposed that the ideal language would be one where ideas were represented by symbols to eliminate the ambiguity of words. Samuel Johnson's dictionary sought to fix "univocal meanings in perpetuity, much like the univocal meanings of standard arithmetic terms" (Levine, 1985:4).

Such was the attitude toward language when the marquis de Condorcet introduced the term "social science" (Levine, 1985:4). De Condorcet contended that with precise language about moral and social issues "knowledge of the truth" would be "easy and error almost impossible" (quoted in Levine, 1985:6). Emile Durkheim affirmed the need for sociology to resolutely cleanse itself of everyday language. Even Max Weber urged the construction of ideal-types as a way to achieve univocity—the single voice of science.

By the 19th Century, intellectuals divided knowledge into two parts: literature and science. Literature was a bourgeois institution aligned with "art" and "culture." Given to literature were the "higher values" of taste, aesthetics, ethics, humanity, and morality as well as the privilege to be experimental, avant garde, multi-vocal, transgressing (Clifford, 1986:6). Given to science was the *belief* that its words were objective, precise, unambiguous, non-contextual, non-metaphoric.

This historical separation between literature and science does not imply an immutable schism. Historical implies human construction. What humans construct, they can reconstruct. And, indeed a plethora of disciplines—communications, linguistics, English criticism, anthropology, folklore, women's studies, as well as the sociology of knowledge, science and culture—has been engaged in reconstructive analyses. Their analyses show that literary devices appear in all writing, including scientific writing. All works use such rhetorical devices as metaphor, image and narrative which affect how ideas are formed, how field notes are taken, how survey questions are phrased, how the work is written up, and how readers make sense of it. "Literary devices are inseparable from the telling of 'fact'" (Clifford, 1986:4).

Once we fully recognize this, it seems to me, we can lay claim to some of the "higher values" that were historically given to literature. We can lay claim to a science that is aesthetic, moral, ethical, moving, rich, and metaphorical as well as avant garde, transgressing, and multi-vocal. We can lay to rest our Faustian bargain, giving up our humanity for the illusion of objective knowledge.

META-WRITING ISSUES: METAPHOR AND NARRATIVE VOICE

If we give up the ill-fitting conceit that our sociological concepts are precise, their referents clear, and our knowledge unambiguous, we are met with an interesting question: the writing of sociology. The final solution to the writing problem is not the extermination of jargon, redundancies, passive voice, circumlocution, and (alas multisyllabic conceptualization referential indicators (for how to write see Becker, 1986a; Selvin and Wilson, 1984; Fox, 1985).

How we choose to write sociology raises two meta-writing issues: guiding metaphor and narrative voice. Our choices are simultaneously political, poetic, methodological, and theoretical.

Writing exists in the context of an implicit guiding metaphor that shapes the narrative. We have an implicit "story which we tell about the people we study," a story which is itself historically rooted (Bruner, 1986:2). Edward Bruner's analysis of the scientific discourse about Native Americans is highly instructive in this regard. In the 1930's and 1940's, the social scientific narrative of Native American social change viewed the present "as disorganization, the past as glorious, and the future as assimilation." Now, there is a new implicit narrative; "the present is viewed as a resistance movement, the past as exploitation, the future as ethnic resurgence" (Bruner, 1986:4). With great rapidity, the guiding concepts of assimilation and acculturation have been replaced with the concepts of exploitation, oppression, liberation, colonialism, and resistance.

The shift in story was more than a theoretical shift; it was a shift in syntax and politics. As science is the child of metaphor, metaphor is the child of politics. For the acculturation story, the writing problem was the description of past culture. Indian life had no future, and the present was interpreted in light of this futurelessness as pathology and disintegration. The political action consistent with this metaphor was to send Native American children to Anglo boarding schools, to create urban relocation projects, to undermine tribal tradition. For the contemporary resistance narrative, however, the writing problem concerns the future: the resistance of indigenous people to exploitation in their struggle to preserve ethnic identity. The writing describes the resistance in the present to preserve the past for the future. Political action consistent with this narrative is intervention to prevent cultural genocide.

Analogous implicit narrative shifts have occurred in the collective stories of other groups of people. Within American society, certain sociologists have positioned Blacks, women, gays and lesbians, the aging, and ethnics within a liberation narrative. And we have extended the liberation narrative to Third World countries, no longer conceptualizing them as "developing," a metaphor that implies their current inferiority but their eventual future as Western clonettes. Instead, the notion of ethnic nationalism is gaining ascendancy. The implicit liberation narrative is consistent with liberation movements. Indeed, the outstanding success of feminist scholarship across disciplines arises from its explicit link to the feminist movement, a continuity of purpose between research and activism, namely, the empowerment of women.

The second meta-writing issue is the narrative voice. *Who* is telling the story? The researcher? The researched? Both? Postmodernist critique challenges the grounds for authority in the writings of positivists as well as phenomenologists, measurers as well as ethnographers because it rejects dichotomizing the "knower" and the "known." In scientific writing, authority has been accomplished through the "effacement of the speaking and experiencing" scientists (Pratt, 1986:32). Neither "I" nor "we" are used. With no apparent narrator, an illusion of objectivity is created. The implied narrator is godlike, an all-knowing voice from afar and above, stripped of all human subjectivity and fallibility. But, in fact, science does have a human narrator, the "camouflaged first person," hiding in the bramble of the passive voice. The scientist is not all-knowing. Omniscience is imaginary, possible only in fiction.

Ethnographies have depended upon two forms of authority: the personal experience of the ethnographer in the field and the presumed objective, factual report. Rather than fusing the two forms of knowledge into one, the ethnographer's first person account is separated from the objective account. Personal experiences, anxieties, and fears are marginalized, written about in introductions, appendices, memoirs, and "reflections" sections of qualitative journals.

Contemporary concern with the narrative voice problem has led some social scientists to what is termed "experimental writing," writing social science in non-traditional ways. Experimental writing includes the use of multiple voices, split pages with the storyteller's account filling one column and the analyst's another, and the writing of "true fiction" (cf. Stewart, Forthcoming; Marcus and Fisher, 1986; Clifford and Marcus, 1986; Krieger, 1983; Reinharz, 1979; Pfohl and Gordon, 1986). But the reasons for experimenting with literary style and genre are not simply to deal with the false dichotomization of subject and object; the writing experimentalists are raising political and ethical questions as well. Separating the researcher's story from the people's story implies that the researcher's voice is the authoritative one, a voice that stands *above* the text. But because people have differential access to the use of the authoritative voice—and for the most part the people we study have less access than we do—we may unwittingly colonize, overgeneralize or distort. Further, by objectifying ourselves out of existence, we void our own experiences. We separate our humanity from our work. We create the conditions of our own alienation.

REFLECTIONS

What I choose to write about, how I choose to write it, and for whom I write it say more about me than sociodemographics, personality inventories, or horoscopes. My sociological work has been the analysis of power inequalities; my activism, the challenge of those inequalities. To do my work, I have consciously chosen to use the liberation narrative. This narrative tells the collective story of the disempowered, not by judging, blaming or advising them, but by placing their lives within the context of larger social and historical forces, and by directing energy towards changing those social structures which perpetuate injustice.

In my recent work (Richardson, 1985), I have told the collective story of a particular set of women, namely, single women involved in long term relationships with married men. Sociologically, their lives had been ignored, their experiences shrouded in secrecy and stigma, and their relationships told about and judged by others, not themselves. I wanted to give voice to this muted group of women: the second sex in a secondary world. I wanted to tell their collective story.

To do this, I first *listened* to the personal stories of single women involved with married men. I heard how single women got involved, fell in love, and ended their relationships with married men. Although the details of the single women's stories differed, the contours of their experiences were similar. My analytical task was to place their narratives in social and historical context, and to discern what in the contemporary world was disempowering them.

In a world where there were not enough eligible men, but where a woman's self esteem was still embedded in having the love of a man, and in a world where women were urged to achieve autonomy and career success, but where they were expected to put their lover's needs above their own, the tension between achieving both an independent identity and a satisfying intimate relationship was severe. One solution to an untenable situation was a relationship with a married man. Believing that these liaisons would be temporary, single women imagined they would achieve intimacy in them without sacrificing independence. However, because of the relationship's secrecy in conjunction with overarching gender inequalities, the woman ended up caring for her lover more than she had intended. The more she cared about him, the more dependent and less powerful she became, because she carried into the relationship the normative expectations for women in love—personal sacrifice.

I struggled with what to call these women. I finally chose the term, "The New Other Woman," or *collectively* "New Other Women." I consciously chose to claim the label, "*other woman*," but I capitalized it, wresting it from its stigmatized context. The capitalization continually reminds me and my readers that these women are not just "others" in the "some...others" grammatical construction: They are a distinct social category worthy of a collective story. The "New" in the name modifying "Other Woman" metaphorically suggests the women's simultaneous embrace of contradictions, modernity and traditionalism. Allegorically, we are reminded of the tensions between the old and the new within all modern societies and within our own psyches, as well. In some ways, we are all Other Women—striving to make a life in a contradictory world, torn between our needs for belonging and independence.

The narrative voice in which to tell their collective story troubled me. I was never able to resolve—nor have I yet—the mare's nest of authorial authority, the dichotomy between the observer and the observed. But if I did not "find" a voice, I feared I would descend into the Prince Hamlet Syndrome, frozen by indecision, and—Shakespeare please forgive me—eternally plagued with the question, "to write or not to write..."

Remembering how C. Wright Mills (1959) grounded issues of "intellectual craftsmanship" in the work process rather than in the codification of procedures, I read sociology for style and voice. I rejected the sociological verite style, the publication of the interview transcript, because—to modernize Socratic wisdom—the unanalyzed transcript is not worth reading. I rejected the paraphrasing style because it lacked credibility and it's boring. I rejected the self-centered reflexive style, where the people studied are treated as garnishes and condiments, tasty only in relationship to the main course, the sociologist.

Struggling with finding my narrative voice, I first wrote a woman's story as a scene in which she and I were two "characters" engaged in dialogue. I used my mini-arsenal of literary devices. I set the scene and established the ambience. I showed the woman's feelings, rather than telling about them. I wrote in concrete detail. I quoted. I gave the women fictitious names that inscribed their "narrative essence." "Lisa Maxwell" used her liaison to get a new *lease* on life by changing careers, a change which was of *maximal value* to her. "Michelle Mitchell" was an avant garde architect, who used her liaison to explore and to eventually reject heterosexuality as a way of life. "Abby Goodman" was a psychologist who prided herself on her listening ability, her kindness, and her Jewish hospitality. She was duped by her lover. Each woman had her own story, her own chapter, her own analysis. I felt powerful. I felt like a "writer."

But this narrative voice did not work. The format implied that each story represented something *different* sociologically. Because each story was separately analyzed, I was in fact writing a collection of individual sociobiographies, rather than what I wanted to write, a *collective* story.

My final decision was to organize the research as a unified chronological narrative based on the women's narratives. I typified events and sequences of events, illustrating them through multiple voices and direct quotations. I was trying to simultaneously have the women speak of and for themselves, and for me to speak of and for them, as a sociological analyst. I was constructing a collective story.

Deciding on my narrative voice was more than a literary and theoretical problem. It was a political issue: "Sociology for Whom?"—a question I have had since graduate school. At the defense of my dissertation on *Pure Mathematics*, a defense attended by a flock of university officials as part of a university wide evaluation of graduate programs, I was asked, "What do you plan to do now?" Being madly in love with sociology and desiring to communicate that passion to the world, I answered, probably with feeling, "I want to write for the public." A hush fell upon the examiners, and, like an errant child, I was excused from the room while they decided my fate. Despite my heretical answer, I passed. With great seriousness, my responsible, if not embarrassed Ph.D. committee publicly advised me not to "waste my intelligence on people."

Over the years, I have wrestled with identifying the audience I want to write for, temporarily solving the problem, or perhaps absolving myself of my unwitting sins, by writing, alongside abstract articles on science, mathematics, and literature [cf. Richardson Walum], 1965; Richardson [Walum, 1975), socially relevant sociology (cf. Richardson [Walum], 1970; Franklin and Richardson, 1972; Richardson [Walum], 1974; Kirshner and Richardson [Walum], 1978), and gender texts, accessible to students and their parents (cf. Richardson, 1977, 1981, 1988; Richardson and Taylor, 1983).

But the more my work on single women and married men progressed, the more I found myself saying, as I did in my dissertation defense, "Sociology is for the people." I decided to write words and sentences that could meet a different standard of science and truth: accessibility to lay audiences. Because I wanted the *sociological* analysis widely disseminated, I chose to write a trade book, working with a publishing house noted for its sociology list (Richardson, 1987).

But the writing story does not end here. Telling the collective story of these women has propelled me back into thinking and writing about very large and abstract sociological questions: questions about the sex and gender system and the social construction of intimacy (Richardson, 1988; Richardson, Forthcoming); about the complementariness of symbolic interactionism and feminist theory (Statham, Richardson, and Cook, 1988); about how gender interacts with other social characteristics, such as age, race, class, sexual orientation, marital status and ethnicity—how we are like each other, how we are different; and questions most of all about how to tell *well* the story of people. My image of sociological work now is an ever widening spiral, where I write collective stories that are more and more accessible to more people, and then I write more and more sociologically abstract work directed to professionals, each kind of writing deepening the other.

When I was a pre-schooler, I would daily ponder the mystery of the Morton salt box, where a little dark-haired girl held a Morton salt box with a picture of a little girl holding a Morton salt box and so on and on and on. Was there ever an ending? As infinite regress riveted my attention in childhood, infinite expansion attracts me now. I welcome the writing of collective stories. I welcome metaphor, imagery, evocative prose. In them, I see the possibility of fulfilling sociology's promise—a sociology *of* and *for* the people.

REFERENCES

Becker, Howard S. 1986a. *Writing for Social Scientists: How to Finish Your Thesis, Book, or Article.* Chicago: The University of Chicago Press.

———. 1986b. "Telling about Society." Pp. 121–36 in *Doing Things Together.* Evanston: Northwestern University Press.

Bruner, Edward M. 1986. "Ethnography as Narrative." Pp. 137–55 in *The Anthropology of Experience*, edited by Victor Turner and Edward M. Bruner. Champagne-Urbana: The University of Illinois Press.

Clifford, James. 1986. "Introduction: Partial Truths." Pp. 1–26 in *Writing Culture: The Poetics and Politics of Ethnography*, edited by James Clifford and George E. Marcus. Berkeley, CA: University of California Press.

Clifford, James and George E. Marcus (eds.). 1986. *Writing Culture: The Poetics and Politics of Ethnography*. Berkeley, CA: University of California Press.

Cook, Judith A. and Mary Margaret Fonow. 1986. "Knowledge in Women's Interests: Issues in Epistemology and Methodology in Feminist Sociological Research." *Sociological Inquiry* 56:2–29.

De Certau, Michel. 1983. "History: Ethics, Science and Fiction." Pp. 173–209 in *Social Science as Moral Inquiry*, edited by Norma Hahn, Robert Bellah, Paul Rabinow, and William Sullivan. New York: Columbia University Press.

De Man, Paul. 1979. *Allegories of Reading*. New Haven, CT: Yale University Press.

Diamond, Timothy. Forthcoming. *Making Gray Gold: The Everyday Production of. Nursing Home Life*. Chicago: The University of Chicago Press.

DiIorio, Judi. Forthcoming. "Sex Glorious Sex." In *Feminist Frontiers: Rethinking Sex, Gender, and Society*, Second Revised Edition, edited by Laurel Richardson and Verta Taylor. New York: Random House.

Erikson, Erik H. 1975. "On the Nature of 'Psycho-Historical' Evidence." Pp. 113–68 in *Life Span Development and Behavior*. New York: Norton.

Fiske, Donald W. and Richard A. Shweder (eds.). 1986. *Metatheory in Social Science: Pluralisms and Subjectivities*. Chicago: University of Chicago Press.

Fonow, Mary Margaret and Judith A. Cook (eds.). Forthcoming. *Feminist Methodology in the Social Sciences*. Bloomington, IN: University of Indiana Press.

Fox, Mary Frank (ed.). 1985. *Scholarly Writing and Publishing: Issues, Problems, and Solutions*. Boulder, CO: Westview Press.

Franklin, Clyde W. and Laurel Richardson. 1972. "Sex and Race: A Substructural Paradigm." *Phylon* 242:53.

Geertz, Clifford. 1980. "Blurred Genres." *American Scholar* 49: 1 65–79.

Gleick, James. 1984. "Solving the Mathematical Riddle of Chaos." *The New York Times Magazine*, June 10th, pp. 30–32.

Kirschner, Betty Frankle and Laurel Richardson (Walum). 1978. "Dual Location Families: Married Singles." *Alternative Life Styles* 1:513–25.

Krieger, Susan. 1983. *The Mirror Dance: Identity in a Woman's Community*. Philadelphia: Temple University Press.

Levine, Donald N. 1985. *The Flight from Ambiguity: Essays in Social and Cultural Theory*. Chicago: University of Chicago Press.

Livingston, Debra. 1982. "'Round and 'Round the Bramble Bush: From Legal Realism to Critical Legal Scholarship." *Harvard Law Review* 95:1650–76.

Long, Judy. 1987. "Telling Women's Lives: The New Sociobiography." Presented at the American Sociological Association Meetings, Chicago, IL.

Marcus, George E. and Michael M. J. Fisher. 1986. *Anthropology as Cultural Critique: An Experimental Moment in the Human Sciences*. Chicago: University of Chicago Press.

Mills, C. Wright. 1959. *The Sociological Imagination*. New York: Oxford University Press.

Mishler, Elliot G. 1986. *Research Interviewing*. Cambridge, MA: Harvard University Press.

Pratt, Mary Louise. 1986. "Fieldwork in Common Places." Pp. 27–50 in *Writing Culture: The Poetics and Politics of Ethnography*, edited by James Clifford and George E. Marcus. Berkeley, CA: University of California Press.

Phohl, Stephen and Avery Gordon. 1986. "Criminological Displacement: A Sociological Deconstruction." *Social Problems* 33:94–113.

Reinharz, Shulamit. 1979. *On Becoming A Social Scientist*. San Francisco: Jossey-Bass.

Richardson, Laurel. 1965. "Pure Mathematics Publications: 1939–1958." *American Mathematics Monthly* 73:192–95.

———. 1968. "Croup Perception of Threat of Non-Members." *Sociometry* 3:278–84.

———. 1970. "Sociologists as Signers: Some Characteristics of Protestors of Vietnam War Policy." *The American Sociologist* 5:161–65.

———. 1974. "The Changing Door Ceremony: Some Notes on the Operation of Sex-Roles in Everyday Life." *Urban Life and Culture* 2:506–15.

———. 1975. "The Art of Domination: An Analysis of Power in Paradise Lost." *Social Forces* 53:573–80.

———. 1985. *The New Other Woman: Contemporary Single Women In Affairs With Married Men.* New York: The Free Press.

———. 1987. "Disseminating Research to Popular Audiences: The Book Tour." *Qualitative Sociology* 10:164–76.

———. 1988. *The Dynamics of Sex and Gender: A Sociological Perspective.* Third Revised Edition. New York: Harper and Row.

———. 1988. "Secrecy and Status: The Social Construction of Forbidden Relationships." *American Sociological Review* 53:209–19.

———. Forthcoming. "Sexual Freedom and Sexual Constraint: The Paradox of Single Woman and Married Man Liaisons." *Gender & Society.*

Richardson, Laurel and Verta Taylor. 1983. *Feminist Frontiers: Rethinking Sex, Gender, and Society.* New York: Random House.

Rorty, Richard. 1979. *Philosophy and the Mirror of Nature.* Princeton: Princeton University Press.

Selvin, Hanan C. and Everett K. Wilson. 1984. "On Sharpening Sociologists' Prose." *The Sociological Quarterly* 25:205–22.

Stewart, John. Forthcoming. *Drinkers, Drummers, Decent Folk: Ethnographic Narratives of Village Trinidad.* SUNY.

Statham, Anne, Laurel Richardson and Judith A. Cook. 1988. *Any Questions: Gender and University Teaching.* Unpublished Manuscript: Department of Sociology, Ohio State University.

Strathern, Marilyn. 1987. "Out of Context: The Persuasive Fictions of Anthropology." *Current Anthropology* 28:251–70.

INDEX

Accounts 82, 162–179
Actor 57–60, 76–79
Act
    stages of 48–49
Adult Socialization 36, 224–237

Behaviorism 38–39

Chicago School of Symbolic
    Interactionism 25, 55–57, 439–442
Communication
    and interaction 153–155
    and self 42–43
    and society 39–41
    and symbols 41
Confirmatory Research 88, 90–93, 112–120
Constructionists, Social 413
Conversation Analysis 400, 413–414, 470–476
Conversation of Gestures 40–41

Darwinism, Social 6–8
Definition of the Situation 36–37, 151, 156–161, 329
Disability, physical and mental
    management of "spoiled" identities 208–223
Disclaimers 215
Discourse Analysis 400, 470–476
    Compliments 474–475
    Demands and Requests 471–473
    Instructions 473–474
    Insults 475–476
Discreditable/Discredited Identities 208–223, 239–240
Distancing 241–245
Dramaturgical Approach 25, 57–60, 76–79

"Ego" 44
Embracement 245–248

Emergence
    nature of 180–181
    manifestations of 181–182
    sources of 182–184
    implications of 184–186
Emotions 398–399, 412–413, 424–435
Ethnomethodology, Basic Concepts 60–62, 80–87
Everyday Life Sociology 407–423
    defined 407–408
    critique and assessment of 416–419
    historical development of 409–411
Evolutionism 6–8
Existential Sociology 25, 411–412
Exploratory Research 88–89, 91, 93, 94–99

Fetishes 191–192
Fictive Storytelling 248–249
Frame Analysis 78
Functional Psychology 19–23

Gay Evangelicals 224–238
Gender 400, 459–469
Generalized Other 43
    and self 43, 193
    and society 43, 193
Generic Sociology 399, 436–458
Gesture 40–41

Homeless 239–258
Hypnosis, Social Construction of 351–361

"I" 43, 193
"Id" 44
Idealism, German 9–11
Identity
    construction of 224–238, 239–256, 477
    deviant 208–223
    religious 224–238
    transformation 323, 326–342

Identity Talk 241–258
Impression Management 76–79
Iowa School of Symbolic Interactionism
    25, 70–75, 442

Language 45–47
Looking–Glass Self 25, 30, 32

Magic 188–192
"Me" 43–193
Meanings 1, 2
Mentally Ill
    patients 208–223
    family caregivers of 323, 342–350
Mesostructure
    studies in negotiated order 281–282
Methodology
    documentary analysis/life history/
        biographical analysis 101–102
    field studies/ethnography/participant
        observation 94–99, 139–149
    film and photography 105–107
    Interviewing 99–101
    New Iowa school 121–138
    of Chicago and Iowa Schools 90–93
    Social Experiment 102–105, 121–138
Mind
    development of 44–47, 153–155
Motives
    vocabularies of 162–179
    accounts 162
    excuses 162, 171–176
    justifications 162, 165–170

Negotiation 208–223, 224–238, 239–256
Negotiated Order Theory 279–282

Objects 47–48
Orthodox Jews 326–342

Phenomenology 25, 90
Poachers 363–376
Positivism 88, 90
Postmodernism 400–401, 477–486
Power 309–322
Pragmatism 11–14, 16–19
Primary Group 25, 30
Reference Group Theory 267–275
Rituals 189–191

Role
    dissensus 323, 346
    making 41, 193
    performance 323, 346
    taking 41, 49, 193

Self
    as an object 193–194, 196–198
    as a social subject 193
    development 42–43, 193
    impression management 208–223
    phases of 43–44, 193
    presentation of 76–77, 199–207
    implications of selfhood 44
Self-concept 70–75
Social Structure 259–260, 277–285, 286–308
Society 39–41, 263–266
Stigma 239, 342
    courtesy stigma 344
    in relation to identity 224–238
Stimulus-response 40–41
Subcultures, Deviant
    poachers 323, 363–375
Subjective Understanding 1–2, 90–92
"Super Ego" 44
Symbolic Interactionism
    application of 224–238, 326–498
    basic concepts 38–54
    early interactionists 30–37, 64–69
    evaluation of 50–59
    intellectual antecedents 4–24
    underlying assumptions 1–2
    variations of 55–63
Symbols
    nature of 1, 2, 40–41
    significant 1, 2, 49
    vs. signs 45–47
Sympathetic Introspection 1, 25

Taboos 191
Total Institutions 77
Twenty Statements Test 71–74

Unification Church 139–149
Urban Lumberjacks 323, 377–397

Variable Analysis
    shortcomings/weaknesses 112–120
Verstehen 1–2, 90